GOD'S GREAT TRADITION
OF GLOBAL WISDOM

Dedication

I dedicate this book to the Eternal God
The Only Reality There IS
To Whom all the Great Gurus have come to serve
in serving YOU.

I AM the Fulfillment of all traditions.
Therefore, Who I Am is not an ego or a conventional identity.
That is Certain.

Who are the traditions expecting?
What promises do I Fulfill?

I must be recognized.
And that is fundamentally about devotional recognition.

Devotional recognition of the Divine Person in bodily (human) Form is not mere fantasy.

Devotional recognition is literal, actual recognition—using the means at the profoundest level of any tradition in order to see Who I Am—to see My Form here and to recognize Me altogether in the fullest sense.

That recognition is Beyond all identities.
It is Beyond all human time and all characteristics of that human time.

Yet, there is something about recognition of Me that is in the stream of human time. That devotional recognition is a Force—the Truth-Force, the Reality-Force, Itself.

How to understand this is a great matter.
I am pointing people toward understanding Me in the most profound sense, so that they will not understand Me in limitation.

Recognizing Me is a way of recognizing every one.
This is a Divine Pattern.

There are no egos.
There are no separate beings.
There is only this Divine Process.

"You" are simply an element of the Process, part of the Pattern.

Who is here?
Only Real God, Reality Itself, Is here.
Only That Which Is Divine is Present—Only.
There is no "other".

---

1. Adi Da Samraj, "Outshined In The Divine Self-Conscious Light," May 28, 2008 in *I Am Here* (2014), p. 157.

First Edition

Published by Bright Alliance

Printed in the United States of America

Design and layout by Brad Reynolds

GOD'S GREAT TRADITION OF GLOBAL WISDOM

GURU YOGA-SATSANG IN THE INTEGRAL AGE

AN APPRECIATION OF AVATAR ADI DA SAMRAJ IN
ILLUMINATING THE GREAT TRADITION OF HUMANKIND

BRAD REYNOLDS

BRIGHT
ALLIANCE

NOTE TO THE READER

The views herein are the views of the author only.
All errors and misrepresentations are of the author's only.
The definitions used, and names, are not necessarily the technical ones generated
by Avatar Adi Da Samraj—please consult His Teaching-Word
and Adidam Ruchiradam for official context.
Permissions are given without endorsement.

TABLE OF CONTENTS

Part 1

THE GLOBAL WISDOM OF GURU-ADEPTS

☆

Part II

THE GREAT TRADITION OF GLOBAL WISDOM IS GURU YOGA-SATSANG

16 – Guru Yoga-Satsang: Hinduism

17– Guru Yoga-Satsang: Buddhism

18– Guru Yoga-Satsang: Tibetan Vajrayana

☆

19 – SIXTH STAGE & SEVENTH STAGE ENLIGHTENMENT

20 – GURU SATSANG IN ADIDAM RUCHIRADAM

Part III

GURU YOGA-SATSANG IS GLOBAL WISDOM

21 – GURU YOGA-SATSANG: EAST AND WEST

CHARTS & TABLES

APPENDIX CHARTS

GOD'S GREAT TRADITION OF GLOBAL WISDOM

GURU YOGA-SATSANG IN THE INTEGRAL AGE

AN APPRECIATION OF AVATAR ADI DA SAMRAJ IN
ILLUMINATING THE GREAT TRADITION OF HUMANKIND

Preface

There is something ridiculous in the expression "Master of himself";
for the Master is also the servant and the servant the Master;
and in all these modes of speaking the same person is denoted.

— **Sokrates** (to Adeimantus),
The Republic, Book IV

I AM a devotee of Adi Da Samraj but I am not an official representative of Him or his Holy Institution, Adidam Ruchiradam. This book has arisen from my relationship to Adi Da over the past four decades yet it is my own response, not a strict presentation of His Teachings. Please consult Adidam Ruchiradam and Avatar Adi Da's Teaching-Word for the formally empowered offering of His Way of the Heart. I am only a poor pandit, not a Guru; I bow down at His Feet in recognition of God's Divine Presence. Just that. This book is my opinion and personal response; it's up to you to judge for yourself. I offer what Adi Da calls "bridge books," nothing more than a stepping stone to the Avatar's Way of Divine Enlightenment.

Fortunately, my view is fundamentally grounded in a Vision of God that was graced upon my humble soul before I met Adi Da. When my ego surrendered everything and was willing to die (surrender), I realized that God is the very Consciousness that makes me feel and realize I Am alive. *And God is That One! We are all One as God. Every thing is Only God!* God IS Conscious Light (just like Adi Da says). "It" feels as Infinite Eternal Love-Bliss to "I". Avatar Adi Da has magnified and made this plainly evident to me as well, which is why He is my Guru. I *see* (and know and feel) God coming through Him, *as* Him.

This means, of course, that you too are God, and God can be directly known for certain by any and every one. It's just like the World's Adepts have always claimed throughout human history. Go found out! My body will die and my face will be obliterated from the Earth but whether or not "I" will carry on after death is not of much concern to me anymore… for *I Am God* thus "I" (or my soul) is in God's Hands, so to speak, or just part of the vibratory divine process arising in the Conscious Light of the "Bright" (as my Guru speaks of It). It's all Good because It's all God. God is my only true happiness and feeling of true love-bliss, and this is precisely why I LOVE Adi Da Samraj, the Agent of God who was alive during my lifetime. I will contend in this book (and my other books) that He is present and *spiritually* alive and available for anyone who will turn to Him as Spiritual Master since Avatar Adi Da is an authentic Guru-Adept, in my sincerest opinion.

Fortunately, I discovered that by studying "God's Great Tradition of Global Wisdom"—or the "Divine Library" of the world's spiritual literature—there is a precedent for understanding that the genuine Guru is in fact, beyond doubt, an acting Agency of God. They are here to influence our lives in the most positive and productive ways possible. However, you must distinguish the false from the true. Then YOU must make a conscious decision and gesture to engage in this sacred relationship—known as *Satsang* or Guru Yoga—for otherwise you will only live in the ordinary struggles of the common society. In that case, you will be subject to all of Maya's illusions and deceptions, like being chained to a cave of shadows, as Sokrates long ago suggested. The Guru-Adept relationship via Guru Yoga-Satsang is here to snap you out of it... or Awaken you to God-Realization and Nondual Divine Enlightenment, *if* you will proactively participate.

From the time of the most Ancient Awakened Adepts, most of whom are now lost to the mists of history and time, we discover the most famous ones we do remember, from Krishna to Jesus to Buddha, to countless others, all Teach the same essential message: *You Are Divine*—*Tat Tvam Asi* "Thou Art That" (or as Jesus said "I and the Father are One")—but *you* must *find out!* Thus, the real Guru or Adept-Realizer is here to help you do just that and I have found no one more powerful and vibrant than Avatar Adi Da Samraj, so I will point to Him most often while honoring (and loving) all the others too. This book hopes to encourage YOU on the way to your own sacred journey of discovery. All the mistakes and errors herein are my own, not that of the Great Gurus... nor of Adi Da.

I owe endless thanks of gratitude to all who assisted me (some listed in the Acknowledgments), but especially to Ken Wilber, my integral mentor who taught me how to write, and, of course, most especially to Adi Da Love-Ananda who revealed and confirmed that Real God is alive as my Heart when I sat at His Feet overcome in swoons of ecstasy revealing the Divine Reality in which we always already inhere. I found His Presence to be the Pure Presence of Real God. I bow down and stand up in boundless heartfelt gratitude. I hope you find this book of interest and helpful since these Awakened Adepts to whom I point will show you the real Truth about That which I can only hint at with words and integral ideas.

☆ with bright love,
Brad Reynolds
Summer 2021

PROLOGUE

PLATO'S CAVE:
FROM SHADOWS
TO CONSCIOUS LIGHT

The soul of every man and woman does possess the power of learning the truth and the organ to see it with; and that, just as one might have to turn the whole body round in order that the eye should see light instead of darkness, so the entire soul must be turned away from this changing world, until its eye can bear to contemplate Reality and that supreme splendor which we have called the Good [i.e., God].

— **Sokrates,** ca. 410 BCE

lato's famous cave allegory in *The Republic* (written around 380 BCE) is actually about the evolution of consciousness since his Teacher-Guru, the wise Adept **Sokrates**, the "Sage of Athens,"[1] begins the tale by telling him: "Here is a parable to illustrate the degrees in which our nature may be enlightened or unenlightened."[2] The premise, as you probably know, is that some people (called "prisoners") have been chained in place for their entire lives looking at projected shadows of dancing people and animal figures on an underground cave wall. These chained souls end up believing that the illusions on the wall are real or how things truly are. Yet these moving apparitions are nothing but shadows of puppets projected by beams of light that radiate from the cave's entrance behind them. Since they're chained to the floor in one position, they can't turn around to see the original light. They're forced to look at the entertaining flickers of shadow and light dancing in front of them, enjoying them in bemused distraction. Like us, these "prisoners" are ordinary people born into a projected matrix of relative reality taught to believe that everything presented to them—and us—is the only "reality" there is.

The Seers or Rishis of ancient India called this dancing display of shadows *Maya* and *Samsara*, a life of illusion and suffering. Plato and Sokrates, it turns out, had much in common with these Eastern Yogis of the Himalayas. They all teach us that this entertaining life is one of ignorance and unfreedom whose chains must be broken (or transcended) to *feel* and be Free. They suggest that we need to go beyond the shadows in the darkness to see Reality as Light or as it *truly* IS, also called *Nirvana*, not simply how it appears to be or how we might want it to be. Incredibly, as Plato observed (as did the Rishis), these cave prisoners (i.e., us) are not necessarily bothered by their chained circumstance. They are pleasantly amused, though sometimes frightened, yet overall entertained by the prancing shadows, like scenes from a projected film. We too like to create our own stories and plays or theater, edit films and videos, sing songs and dance, watch sports, work and fight wars, raise kids, make up myths and create alluring allegories in an attempt to explain and justify our subconscious dreams and bodily desires. After all, if this is all there is why not make the best of it, right?

Plato continues to explain through the voice of Sokrates that one individual breaks free of his or her chains to escape the shadows and go into the "upper world" to discover there is a bright light shining from behind the puppets. Let's say this "person" represents a group of people, such as today's scientists (it is an allegory, after all). They want to see beyond the cave's wall of illusory projections to better understand the truth of reality. Nevertheless, Plato clarifies, they still don't know for sure what is real or what is not. Stunned, they shockingly realize that for most of their lives (or history) they have been duped and deluded by their senses and what they thought was real. Indeed, the dancing images taken to be reality are nothing but a damn puppet show! In response, this group of scientists begins to rationally analyze everything in great detail by inquiring, according to Plato, "what each of the various objects was." Excited, this group now believes and hopes they are "nearer to reality," finally able to gain "a truer view,"[3] as Plato proposes. Does this not sound like the philosophy and claims of modern science and materialism?

Just like scientists today, these breakaway prisoners take a more objective view of things while searching for the source of the light (or deeper purpose) lying outside the restricted cave of subjectivity. They eagerly engage in precise measurements, rational calculations, copious notes, and detailed maps, all with a keen awareness centered in the rational mind and separate self. As a powerful metaphor of darkness and light, Sokrates (via Plato) informs us that these calculated perspectives are also just another form of illusion.

In Plato's profound parable the chained prisoners are not only deluded by magical myths and dancing shadows but now by rational measurements and detailed maps, all tricks of the light. To their credit, these inquisitive scientists are trying to cope with their newly expanded view of reality, one based on the belief that they have discovered something more true and real than a projected puppet show of slippery shadows. Yet their stark materialism creates its own set of problems. Scientific materialism doesn't liberate anyone, truth be told. Sokrates-Plato, in response, tells us that this "rugged ascent" closer to the light just instills a different kind of fear and suffering. Now these unchained souls become overwhelmed in thinking: "What [we] had formerly seen was meaningless illusion,"[4] thus they experience even more misery and disillusionment than the chained prisoners. Escaping the chains of the body, in other words, does not necessarily free the mind. Much more is required.

Plato goes on to tell us these inquiring "scientists" have become bedazzled by the measuring of appearances, perplexed by a multitude of perceptions or "points-of-view," perhaps similar to postmodern philosophy today which often slips into nihilism and despair after critiquing all viewpoints. Though a little closer to the light they have failed, once again, to understand what is *really* making the illusions in the first place; puzzled (like physicists), they question: "Is our 'reality' nothing but shadows of artificial objects?"[5] Is reality nothing but a dance of atoms and subatomic particles? Nothing but patterns upon patterns?

Indeed, this is precisely the great philosophical question that Sokrates-Plato proposes to each of us: Appearances can be deceiving, as is commonly known, so what to do about it?

Only Awakened Adepts, or those who have discovered the truth of existence for themselves, know better and see more clearly and farther, even further than scientists. Only those who *know* the Truth through Divine Enlightenment or God-Realization, seeing beyond the shadowy illusions of logic and ego, can guide us to the Real Light that transcends (yet is ever-present) in all phenomena. This is the mystical message behind Plato's fabled cave allegory (a view often overlooked by conventional interpretors) which is the same essential message of all the great Mystics or "Spiritual Heroes" of humankind.

SOKRATES' SPIRITUAL HEROES: SEEING THE LIGHT

In the visible world the essential Form of Goodness [God]... gives birth to light and to the Lord of Light, while it is itself sovereign in the intelligible world and the parent of intelligence and truth. Without having had a vision of this Form no one can act with Wisdom, either in his own life or in matters of the state.

— **Sokrates,** *The Republic*

Plato—whose real name is Aristocles; *platon*, meaning "broad," as in broad shoulders—of course, doesn't stop his story there. His Master-Guru Sokrates, the wisest of all Sages (according to the Priestess at Delphi), explains that this cave allegory is ultimately about how "the entire soul must be turned away from this changing world [of shadows], until its eye can bear to contemplate reality and that supreme splendor called the Good"[6]— Plato's primary goal of human life: meditate on God or "the Good" as Ultimate

Reality. This *seeing* or knowing the Divine Reality as It IS, is what Avatar Adi Da Samraj, the Spiritual Hero of this book, calls "The 'Bright'" and "Conscious Light" (or "Real God"). After all, this is why the Sages call *seeing* this ultimate view of reality "En-**Light**-enment" (as Adi Da likes to spell it), which in Western terms is God-Realization. In the cave allegory, the Light of "the Good" (or God) is symbolized as the Sun, the source of light and life on our Earth... and also the source of the cave's shadowy illusions.

In this case, Sokrates tells us there is another person, a rarer individual who also escapes but sees even further than the breakaway scientists, let alone the trapped prisoners in chains. This escapee goes all the way to stand outside the cave to discover the sunlight of the day. The Sun is "bright," which is what "Zeus" (Greek *dyeus*; Sanskrit *dyaus*), the supreme god in the Greek pantheon, literally means: "shine" or "brightness" often associated, of course, with lightning bolts. It is the "Light" (Spirit) and "Fire" (electromagnetism) that binds all things together in the universe, from atoms to brains to galaxies. Our innermost consciousness is the Light of the Kosmos. This heroic individual, therefore, escapes the chains of the gross body-mind and the materialism of science to discover the real source of Light: "the Bright" or God Itself: the Clear Light Void (in Buddhist terms).

Sokrates, the bearded Philosopher-Sage of ancient Greece who is literally Plato's Guru, instructs us that this special person, this True Hero, traverses "the upward journey of the soul"[7] to leave behind the shimmering shadows of alluring illusions projected in the underground caves of maya-samsara. Such profound spiritual pioneers, our real "Spiritual Heroes," transcend the dark caves of subjectivity to become En-Light-ened or Divinely Realized. These are the Adept-Realizers of humankind who *are* the refreshing fountains of Love in humanity's Great Tradition of Global Wisdom, those who *are* the root source of the world's esoteric mystical religions. They don't appear out of thin air! Real religion originates with the Adept-Gurus, as history proves. This book will point to these Adepts who are bringing God's Light into our world to help others see and *realize* this truth for themselves. By following their example and teachings we too may see the Light of Truth for ourselves by going beyond the dark cave of the deluded ego-mind and separate self. God or Reality is "always already the case" (as Avatar Adi Da says), so there's nothing we need to do but Wake Up!

For millennia, the writings of Plato have provided the West with such a mystical vision of our *prior unity* in God beyond the shadow-illusions of mind and self. He did this several hundred years before Jesus Christ and the Christian Church thus showing its perennial truth and veracity. Such an Awakened Hero, as Sokrates explained, has found "his [or her] eyes so full of its radiance that they could not see a single one of the things that they were told were real."[8] The Oneness of God dissolves the separateness of the Many. Sokrates saw this Light too, obviously, and noticed it as Good, True, Beautiful and "Bright." This sacred truth is the essence of all esoteric religious paths remaining perennial or "ever-repeating" throughout all time. This *is* God's Great Tradition of Global Wisdom.

As taught in *The Symposium*, Sokrates' own Teacher- Guru was a woman Adept named **Diotima**, another "Lost Master" of ancient Greece,[9] who shared this enlightened vision with her disciple, Sokrates. Sokrates in turn shared it with his student-devotee, Plato, and so on down through the generations creating the lineage of Western philosophers transmitting the Perennial Philosophy of Real Wisdom. They reveal this Divine Light as Love and Beauty—*Eros*-in-action—operative in the Kosmos of forms. Such an awakening moment, or instant of *realizing* our Prior Unity, is known as *Sophia* (or *Gnosis*) and *Samadhi*, Enlightenment or Self-Realization (in Western and Eastern terms). Twenty-five centuries later we discover the Spiritual Heroes of today still resonate with this same perennial wisdom, as Adi Da himself explains: "I find that the central 'consideration' of Plato's *Symposium* is the same as what is at the root of My Work. I am thoroughly sympathetic with Plato's 'consideration' of Realizing Beauty Itself."[10] In other words, God-Realization is about God Itself, which *is* Truth, Beauty, Love, and Light, as all the Sages teach.

Plato's profound cave story is therefore the mystical journey of the soul. It reveals how the inner self can turn away from the illusions of the relative world to recognize the Absolute Truth symbolized by the Light of "the Sun" or (even according to science) our source of energy and life on Earth. This Divine Light is the "Eternal Sun" Above and Beyond all existence, the Source and Condition or "Heart" of all possible universes and all living (and dead) beings. It is only this Light outside the cave of darkness that liberates us from ignorance and unlove, as Sokrates was trying to explain. Such a vision goes beyond the childish ways of magical-mythic thinking found in many religions, even beyond the adolescent arrogance of rational philosophy. Hence this enlightened view transcends the shadow-dancing for money and power and self-glorification entranced by media entertainment and celebrity status.

In this manner, a Sage (or you and me) has "Grown Up" from the limitations of logical reasoning and other adult preoccupations, including those of materialistic scientists, conniving businesspeople and crooked politicians, even clever philosophers or charismatic religionists. By doing so, we can "Wake Up" to the universal vision embodied in the world's Perennial Philosophy (*philosophia perennis*) that is only gained in the higher stages of life and consciousness development. This Wisdom of Reality and Beauty is everyone's greatest potential: to see God as Light and Consciousness and to know or *realize* that It IS Reality. Nobody has to stay chained in the darkness forever.

Adept-Realizers: *"Know Thyself!"*

The ascent to see the things in the upper world [of light] you may take as standing for the upward journey of the soul into the region of the intelligible; then you will be in possession of what I surmise, since that is what you wish to be told.

— **Sokrates**, *The Republic*

To escape the cave of bondage, Plato tells us, there is a brave "Hero" or "Spiritual Giant" who ventures father than most—an "**Adept-Realizer**"—who must not only transcend the felt anxiety created by the unillumined angst of the ego-I but must ascend directly to the Light Above (and Beyond). Importantly, this Light is also in the heart (on the right), not just in the God Above; It is All-Pervading. By following their example, we too will see the Light and Truth of Real God beyond the false "gods" of mythic thinking and rational doubt. Only then does one walk free with full awareness in the Brightness which is Consciousness Itself—or simply the "Bright" (in Adi Da terms). The light of the "Sun" symbolizes (and *is*) the fundamental Energy creating the entire Kosmos of illusions and beauty, whose slippery shadows the "prisoners" (and us) take to be reality.

The Spiritual Heroes who *see* and know the True Light are the authentic **Guru-Adepts**, the "Daylight Men and Women"[11] who walk out of the cave of dark ignorance to see God for themselves. Those "Seers" and the method they teach—**Guru Yoga-Satsang**—are the subject of this book. Only they see the Truth of Reality as It IS, thus they demand we repeat the experiment to see for ourselves. Nothing is accepted on blind faith alone but it must be *realized* via direct experience. This is what real God-Realization or Divine Enlightenment is all about. These guides and trailblazers, from East and West, women and men, are the authentic Gurus of consciousness transformation, the Spiritual Heroes of past, present, and future. Only they will lead us out of the dark caves of despair and unenlightenment. Indeed, the root word *gu-ru* (in Sanskrit) literally means "one who dispels darkness" to reveal the Light of Truth about Real God.

Amazingly, this enlightening tale in Plato's *The Republic* has been told to the Western world for thousands of years (though hidden from most people, especially during the Medieval Ages). Many of the wisdom texts of Greece's Golden Age had been lost or destroyed by the Christian Church, so when they were rediscovered and translated from Arabic (whose culture had preserved them from destruction) their non-Christian yet spiritual wisdom ignited what we call the Renaissance. This "rebirth" of rational thought unencumbered with Christian mythology led to modernity's "Western Enlightenment" (or "Age of Reason") and the triumphs (and failures) of modern science.

The Adept-Sage Sokrates (via Plato) has consequently instructed countless Western thinkers, theologians, and politicians throughout history, from Plotinus to Augustine to Aquinas, Voltaire, Jefferson, and Emerson, to so many others, teaching them each about the real value of True Wisdom or knowing "the Good" (in Plato's words). This is why English philosopher and mathematician

Alfred North Whitehead famously noted: "The safest general characterization of the European philosophical tradition is that it consists of a series of footnotes to Plato [i.e., Sokrates]."[12] Nietzsche also had a profound reverence for the ancient Greek Master suggesting in *The Birth of Tragedy* (1872): "We cannot help but see Sokrates as the turning-point, the vortex of world history."[13] We should not, therefore, lose (or misplace) this sacred ancient wisdom in our modern age dominated by scientists, politicians, corporations, and the media of superficial consumerism. The Greek Adepts, or the so-called "**Pre-Socratics**," are the "**Lost Masters**" or Adept-Realizers of the West.[14] They have been hidden by our own ignorance regarding the genuine Guru-devotee relationship that was alive and active in Ancient Greece, as well as being alive and practiced in many other ancient civilizations. If you look hard enough it's even practiced today.

Most modern scholars or classicists have had little or no clue about this profound process and method of Enlightenment. To university professors, they're just tales of history, relics from an ancient age. Yet, in reality, the lineage of Pre-Socratic philosophers was a lineage similar to the Guru-devotee relationship known in the East as *Satsang*, where wisdom was not only taught but was transmitted. This yoga became established in Greece, as far as we know, with **Orpheus** (ca. 7th century BCE), the root Guru of Pythagoras and Plato (among many other mystics). These Western philosophers or "lovers of wisdom" were often trained in methods similar to yoga (from ancient India) and the "mysteries" of life and death (from ancient Egypt). They studied and exercised self-disciplines and meditation (*sadhana*), often with renunciate lifestyles, not merely book learning. In this way, East and West are "married" or united in *Sophia*, the knowing of Divine Wisdom, the ultimate state-stage of human consciousness development. To *realize* the Light of God as our own consciousness, beyond the cave of egoic illusions and separateness, is the true purpose of human life.

| **Orpheus** | **Diotima** | **Sokrates** | **Plato** |
| (fl. 750 BCE) | (fl. 440 BCE) | (ca. 470–399 BCE) | (ca. 428–348 BCE) |

Seeing or knowing the reality-truth of the Bright Conscious Light of Real God is the very same vision Sokrates ascribes to as well. He told humankind the very same message in the form of a clever parable, the cave allegory (which we just reviewed) given to us now as printed words in a book, *The Republic*. It is a visionary parable buried in the depths of the Western mind and human psyche. More than 400 years before Christ, this wisdom was inscribed on the walls of the most sacred temple of ancient Greece at Delphi, a maxim taught by Sokrates himself (yet attributed to many philosophers): **"Know Thyself!"**— *Gnothi Seaton* (in Greek). For when the True Self is hidden by the darkness of ignorance generated by the small self of ego-I, we need assistance and Divine Help to see our way out of the cave of illusions and darkness, as Sokrates-Plato (and the Rishi-Yogis) taught. Gurus exist to shine the light and guide us on the Way. This is why the Great Adepts appear: they are our Unique Advantage sent to help us see and *realize* the Light for ourselves, that is, *if* we use them correctly (and not cultically). This book will attempt to show why.

DANGER IN THE DARK: KILL THE GURU-ADEPT!

If they could lay hands on the man who was trying to set them free and lead them up [to the Light], they would kill him!

— **Sokrates**, *The Republic*

Naturally, Plato's cave allegory does not end with simply seeing the Light. After recognizing the bright vision of Truth, after knowing the Light of the Eternal "Sun," such a rare "**Spiritual Hero**" is confronted with the profound decision on whether or not to re-enter the dank cave of delusion in order to go back to tell—and help free—those chained souls still lost in the pits of self-illusion and egoic contraction. Like **Narcissus**, most of us are entranced souls who emulate the beautiful Greek god enamored by his or her own self-worth seen reflected in the rippled waves of the pond's surface waters. This self-reflection of ego-I is like the dancing shadows on the cave's wall, an illusion of the separate self that prevents the soul from knowing real Reality. Few people break away from these egoic patterns of separateness and self-identity. Yet some do get free and return to show us the escape route to Freedom and Divine Insight and Delight. These are the genuine Guru-Adepts who are humankind's true Spiritual Heroes. They have founded religions or taught philosophy—the "love of wisdom"—for millennia.

In this case, the cave allegory amazingly acknowledges that a few advanced-tip souls do in fact break out from the underground cave of egoity (dominated by the five senses). By practicing yoga and meditation, by following the instruction of an Adept-Guru, we can turn away from (yet master) the mundane and relative sensual pleasures, such as eating and drinking and sexing, fighting and acquiring massive wealth, etc. This is why the enlightened Sage, the one who is freed from his or her chains to the cave wall, and who turns around to see the Light of God (or "the Good"), is in danger from the reactions of the common crowd of conventional society when they return to teach or attempt to save them. Tragically, Plato foretells that the crowd of still-chained prisoners would "put him [or her] to death"[15] rather than see their own illusions and mistakes. Kill the Buddha, crucify the Christ, burn the Saints and Mystics, ridicule the Avatars as nothing but cultic apparitions; this is sadly the way of the world. This message, as well as its liberating insight, was fully explained to posterity by Sokrates (via Plato's writings), as a sacred metaphor told to humanity as the fabled cave parable (again, this deeper interpretation is usually overlooked or misunderstood by modern scholars).

In the cave-world of human existence, everyone (or each individual) is confronted with the same basic dilemma: Why struggle to become free when the illusions are so enticing and entertaining? Why undergo the difficult ordeal of self-transcendence when you feel so "in love" with all the things and people of the relative world? Nevertheless, the answer lies in the fact (or reality) that everything changes and everyone dies. All things must pass. No escaping that!

Indeed, Plato (like the *Upanishads* in India) points out that the true task of philosophy is to prepare for death (*Phaedo* 67e). Hence, you may have already heard this story (or truth) before from one of those other great Spiritual Heroes of human history since each proclaims (in their own way): "Only the Truth will set you Free" (as Jesus Christ did in John 8:32). Know Thyself!

Humanity has been listening carefully to these Adept-Realizers for millennia, whether from the East or from the West, yet seldom fully understanding them. Therefore each generation must re-discover this sacred knowledge (or "Divine Ignorance") for themselves. And so the dance goes on until everyone potentially rediscovers or *realizes* the True Light that always already IS! This book is about these Adept-Realizers, those true Spiritual Heroes who have pointed the way and given us a method or yoga grounded in a *sacred relationship* with them as Spiritual Master. Guru Yoga or Satsang, or a devotional relationship to God via the Guru, is how we "get there" or reach "the other shore" (in Buddhist parlance) so we may see God or Reality for ourselves! Yet, paradoxically, we are always already Here. "You can't get there from here," as Adi Da likes to humorously joke.

This is the paradoxical message buried in God's Great Tradition of Global Wisdom thus it's everyone's common inheritance and birthright. Join me in this journey, imperfectly captured on these pages, and let's see and honor the True Light of Wisdom and Beauty of Real God together. Let's honor and respect our Gurus for it is they who point the Way beyond our egoic chains of violence and selfishness so we can see God's Divine Light of Love and Bliss. It's time for us in the modern-postmodern world to differentiate destructive cults from authentic spirituality, to honor our true Spiritual Heroes, not dismiss them as being outdated. As a global culture, we need to realize our inherent *prior unity* before we'll ever know true world peace.

Yes, the cave allegory rings as true today as it did nearly twenty-five centuries ago when Plato first wrote it down. Sokrates never wrote anything down but only spoke his truth as a shout from the heart that reverberated for millennia through Plato to us. There is a serious lesson to be learned from these powerful philosophers, from these Guru-Adepts of Enlightened Wisdom, from these Spiritual Heroes pointing to the Truth of Light and Reality. Yet they too are just human, not immortal gods. Therefore, I will argue it is time we give them more attention and recognize them as a Divine Gift and Blessing given to everyone for our Liberation and Happiness. With their help, we may *see* for ourselves what is True and what is not. Only then do we find true peace. Time to Wake Up, my friends, and realize that God's Great Tradition of Global Wisdom first appears in human form as our friend and as our Beloved Guru.

Prologue Endnotes

1. I will be using the Greek spelling of "Sokrates" (with a "k") instead of the English rendering of "Socrates" (with a "c").

2. Plato, "Allegory of the Cave" (Chapter 25) in *The Republic* (1945 edition) translated by F. M. Cornford, p. 227.

3. Ibid., p. 229.

4. Ibid., p. 229.

5. Ibid., p. 229.

6. Ibid., p. 232.

7. Ibid., p. 231.

8, Ibid., p. 229.

9. See: Plato, *The Symposium* (ca. 385–370 BCE), 201d: "I want to pass on to you the account of Eros [love] which I once heard given by a woman called Diotima of Mantinea. She was an expert on this subject, as on many others."

10. Adi Da Samraj, "The Realization of the Beautiful" Talk given on March 30, 2001 [unpublished].

11. See: Frank Marrero, *Nothing Makes Me Happy* (unpublished), whose reflections on the cave allegory inspired this preface.

12. Alfred North Whitehead, *Process and Reality* (1929, 1979), p. 39.

13. Friedrich Nietzsche, *The Birth of Tragedy* (1872), Chapter 15.

14. See: *Lost Masters: Sages of Ancient Greece* (2006, 2016) by Linda Johnsen.

15. Plato, "Allegory of the Cave" (Chapter 25) in *The Republic* (1945 edition) translated by F. M. Cornford, p. 231.

The Guru, the one who would awaken you, is not a person,
He is not an individual within the dream.
He is your very consciousness.
He is the Real, the Self, He is the Light.
He is the true waking state, the Heart,
breaking through the force of dreaming.

— **Adi Da Samraj,** 1972

INTRODUCTION

GURU-ADEPTS:
AGENTS OF GOD-LIGHT

*The traditions of conventional Yoga and conventional Spirituality are all
the paths of seeking to attain God (or Realization or Liberation or Nirvana).
But the Ways of the Siddhas is to live with Real God, to live in Real God
presently, as your presumed Condition, Nature, and State.
The Siddha comes and manifests the Divine
and expects you to live with Him or Her
—not to seek for God but simply to live with Him or Her.*

— **Adi Da Samraj**, ca. 2000 CE

ELEUTHERIOS: GURUS AS LIBERATORS

ntrapment in the world or "cave" of shadowy ignorance breaks down when the Light of God shines into the pit of darkness or over the watery well of ordinary existence. In the East, they call the dark cave of ignorance *maya*: the illusion of self in the material world. It is also called *avidyā* in Sanskrit ("not *vidya*" or "no illumination"), also translated as ignorance, misconception, misunderstanding, and incorrect knowledge because this perspective of the separate self confuses relative reality as being

Absolute Reality (or it doubts God altogether). But when the ego-I (or the relative self) is transcended, either through Grace or spiritual practices (actually *both*), then En-Light-enment dawns. When we awaken to an authentic Realization of Real God, the Source-Condition of the entire universe, we are liberated from the illusions of a separate self who is lost in a cave of darkness wandering in the world (or Kosmos) of maya. Then love and compassion comes pouring forth from the heart as the mind becomes wise and rests at peace. This is why Avatar Adi Da Samraj—the Spiritual Hero of this book—gave new significance to the ancient Greek name *Eleutherios* (Ἐλευθέριος, "the Liberator"), an epithet for Dionysus-Zeus—who was also known as "the Bright"—a title indicating the liberating power of the Guru's Heart-Transmission of Divine Radiance. Adi Da goes on to use another simile often used in the Great Wisdom Tradition, that of "sunlight" to represent the Conscious Light of Real God. Here he describes this radiance of Divine Light as the Transmission-Presence of an authentic Guru-Adept:

> The *Guru* is like the sunlight in the morning. He intensifies the light of morning until you awaken. Until the light awakens a person, even the true light of consciousness, he or she continues to dream, tries to survive within the dream, manipulates himself within the dream, pursues all kinds of goals, searches, none of which awaken him. All ordinary means only console the person and distract them within the dream. The *Guru*, the one who would awaken you, is not a person, he is not an individual within the dream. He is your very consciousness. He is the Real, the Self, he is the Light, he [or she] is the true waking state, the Heart, breaking through the force of dreaming.[1]

Guru is a Sanskrit word based on the syllables *gu* ꗐ, meaning "darkness," and *ru* ꗐ, meaning "dispeller," thus, *guru* literally means, "one who dispels darkness"[2] by showing us God's Light of Wisdom-Love. Metaphorically, the True Guru, the **Sat-Guru** (in Sanskrit, *Sadguru*, "Guru of Truth"), is like sunlight shining over the dark well of the inner mind leading us beyond the dank cave of ignorance by illuminating our hearts and minds. The authentic Adept-Guru is the Sun-Light alive as an incarnated living human body serving his or her disciples and devotees. The process of Guru Yoga-Satsang initiated by devotion and spiritual contemplation (meditation) will therefore expose the traumas and negativity hidden in the shadows of our psyche. Once again, Adi Da uses the sunlight metaphor to explain what occurs in the sacred relationship to the genuine Guru known as *Satsang*:

> When a man [or woman] first comes to *Satsang*, he [or she] is like a dark, deep well. Way up at the top, the light comes in around the edges, but it is black, unconscious below! When the light of the Truth shines down into it, all of these weirdo, slithering things come climbing up the sides. All the hidden, slimy activity begins to be disturbed, awakened, and moved into the light.
>
> Just so, every moment in *Satsang* increases the necessity for responsibility in the disciple, because the force of *Satsang* isn't merely a good feeling, a consolation, something smiling, happy, and pleasant. It is not magic. It is a living force, the force of Truth. This force moves into the "well," into the human function, this circuit of descending and ascending life, and brings up the chronic patterns of ordinary and unconscious life, revealing them at the level of the actual conditions of life.... So, of course, there are difficulties. Real spiritual life requires everything of a person. Spiritual life is a crisis![3]

The true Spiritual Master who radiates the Conscious Light of God is made evident in the heart of the true devotee. A purification process is initiated that takes on the form of devotion and spiritual disciplines. That is the way it has always been, according to the world's Great Tradition of Global Wisdom, and the way it will, no doubt, always be. Plato's cave allegory, in this case, is a classic philosophical instruction lying at the very root of Western civilization pointing us to our true Spiritual Heroes [see Prologue]. It is about those rare beings who "cross down" from the domain of formless Divine Light into the "underground" gross-physical Earth realm—which is literally what *ava-tara*, the "**Avatar**," means (in Sanskrit): "one who crosses over"—and it is upon them that God's Great Tradition of Global Wisdom is founded. These Godmen and God-women are the very ones who have come to help serve all beings still chained to the dark shadows of suffering samsara. They are our friends, our beloved, not to be feared or misused.

Tragically, however, most often these God-Realized Guru-Adepts are mocked and underappreciated, usually feared and ridiculed, sometimes even killed and disgraced. As Plato explained all those years ago (centuries before Jesus): "If they could lay their hands on the man [or woman] who was trying to set them free and lead them up [to the Light], they would kill him."[4] Since the Guru-Adept most often comes to teach us that we are trapped in our own illusions about the cave-world, our mortal human existence, we often become offended and angry because they will not support our egoic illusions and preferences. They are telling us we are not seeing Reality as It truly IS. Nonetheless, we should listen up! But we do not want to hear their realistic instruction for we think we know better. Our Guru, therefore, is like a dog barking in our ear not letting us sleep.[5] These Awakened Ones try to explain that our relative "reality" is like dancing shadows on a cave wall, like a moving film shining from a cinema projector focusing light through a lens emitting sounds and images on the wall ahead.[6] We become emotionally entranced in the movie, believing the actors are real, blindly accepting the story as told. The movie, however, is not reality—the map is not the territory—but only an entertaining entrapment.

Usually, those of us living in the cave, especially those in our comfortable lifestyles and easy chairs, simply don't want to hear about (let alone *live*) the Real Truth. Most of us are okay with being half-asleep, tolerating the flickering lights and dark shadows, riding the ups and downs of life, taking it as it comes; yet knowing there is an end (in death), sooner or later. Only at times do we question or wonder: "What is the Truth? Why am I here?" Yet some do yearn to be Awakened to the Light of Truth (as we all do, deep inside). However, most believe everyone has their own "truths" or opinions (*doxa*, as Plato called them), so don't tell us what to do! Thus, people become fearful, or sorrowful, then angry, then close their minds to the greater possibilities awakened in the evolution of consciousness. They call Gurus fake cult-leaders as being the way of darkness, not of light. They would rather watch TV or eat and drink and party rather than do *sadhana* (or spiritual practice), enact service, or meditate in stillness. Is this not what the so-called world-society around you preaches? Can you see the Light behind all appearances or is it mostly darkness or hidden from view? Are you living in the cave watching the shadows on the wall or do you know the "Sunlight" that is the Truth of who you really are?

GURU YOGA-SATSANG:
WAKE UP!

In response to those calling us to "Wake Up!", Sokrates in the cave allegory bemoans the sad truth that often the Spiritual Master, the Guru-Adept, is denounced, ridiculed, or worse, murdered. Kill them; poison them; crucify them; imprison them; assassinate them; degrade them, or simply ignore them. Indeed, this would soon be the fate for the fabled Sage of Athens himself. They made Sokrates drink poison hemlock (by a slim majority vote); they nailed Jesus to the cross; they flayed the priestess Hypatia; they burned Bruno at the stake; they assassinated Gandhi and MLK, and countless others; and today they ridicule and debase Adi Da Samraj (in the popular media). They claim Gurus are nothing more than "cult" leaders (today's taboo moniker), and thus reduce the Awakened Seers into "totem-masters," comparing them to the murderous ilk of delusional "cult" leaders, like Charles Manson, Jim Jones, David Koresh, and their followers of mass suicide madness, plus a slew of other sickos.[7] Those, however, are not the *real* Gurus.

There is a monumental difference between *prepersonal* trance and *transpersonal* ecstasy, between emotional release and devotional awakening. The truth is we must learn to discriminate (beyond prejudice) by using our higher intelligence, using our heart *and* mind, to educate ourselves to what is going on with **Guru Yoga** and *Satsang*, the sacred (and esoteric) relationship with a *Sat-Guru* or "True Guru," which this book highlights. The genuine Guru is here to serve, not delude. The rest is up to you. Sokrates knew the difference, according to Plato, for he recognized the Divine Vision that these advanced-tip few were realizing, as the Master eloquently explains in *The Republic*:

> In the world of knowledge, the last thing to be perceived… is the
> cause of whatever is right and good; in the visible [relative] world it
> gives birth to Light, to the Lord of Light, while it is itself sovereign
> in the intelligible world [as *nous*] and the parent [or source] of intel-
> ligence [as *logos*] and truth [or *aletheia*] itself. Without having had
> a vision of this Form [the archetype of formless God] no one can act
> with wisdom, either in his own life [as an individual] or in the man-
> ners of the [collective] state.[8]

Consequently, Plato suggests that a mystical vision of God (or the "Good")
is not only required for individual freedom but is also necessary for the freedom of the collective society. You can now see, perhaps, how far we have yet
to go. But anyone can hear this sacred message if you listen very carefully (and
subtly) to Sokrates-Plato and all the Guru-Adepts of human history. We must
learn not to confuse the fake cultic icon with the authentic Guru or fail to
recognize the true "Masters" from the false demagogues; to stop projecting our
unconscious fears onto the Enlightened Ones as if they were nothing more
than shadows flickering on the cave wall.

Guru-Adepts:
Agency for Enlightenment

In reality, to disparage the Guru-Adepts or simply cry "cult" in nearly
every instance only takes us further from the Truth, from seeing and
understanding Reality as It truly IS—from seeing the Light behind the
shadow puppets of shimmering illusions. Yes, it is time to admit that these enlightened beings are "imperfect" Agents of God and Truth, even when authentically genuine, for they are always *human* too—with human limitations, ill-

ness and warts, perhaps even psychological eccentricities. But their "perfection" lies where your perfection stands as well, i.e., within your capacity for Divine Enlightenment or God-Realization, not with your human mortality. Yes, there are definitely deluded religious cult figures out there (the list is long); there are delusional demagogues like Hitler and other maniacs (again, a dreadfully long list, even in democracies); there are even misguided (if sincere) Gurus like Andrew Cohen, possibly Bhagwan Rajneesh, or unenlightened Buddhists, like Sogyal Rinpoche (a shorter list), all of whom need to be adequately untangled from the presence of authentic Adepts, real and true Spirit-Baptizers.[9]

As always, when seen in the right light, these false idols are not comparable to the True Teachers, although as Sokrates-Plato explained in the cave allegory, sometimes "that one [Guru] who comes from the contemplation of divine things [down] to the miseries of human life should appear awkward and ridiculous."[10] This appears to be a nod to so-called "Crazy Wisdom" Adepts (and ascetics). Nonetheless, such Adepts should never be dismissed as fake or false simply because they confuse us. Paradoxically, the alluring cave of illusions, even when encircled by the beauty of loved ones and Nature, is "the reality" that we have all been born into and are thus "chained." Consequently, it is only by "Growing Up!" and "Waking Up!" do we *realize* the Divine Light of Beauty, Love, and Justice—to see and know "the Good, the True, the Beautiful" (as Plato, and also Ken Wilber two and a half millennia later, have so highly recommended). Only living in ever-present Divine Communion with Reality as It IS are we Liberated and always already Free.

"MIDNIGHT SUN" OF CONSCIOUS LIGHT

In this case, as Sokrates taught (and other Adepts affirm), most of us (as humankind) see the world lost in slippery shadows of darkness projected on perceived walls of underground caves, the inward reflections of ego-I, the illusions of samsaric maya. But there are a rare few who have experienced the Light directly, intimately, personally. As human beings living in God's

Company, they have come to teach and *transmit* the very "Substance" from which the whole Kosmos (in its full spectrum of possibilities) is being projected as Spirit-in-action (the manifesting Light of God). Only an Awakened Avatar-Adept—a Liberator, *Eleutherios*—can precisely and loudly proclaim the Real Truth, as Adi Da Samraj does consistently. Here he summarizes his Wisdom-Teaching on esoteric yoga involving the Eternal "Sun" that exists before (and beyond) the phenomenal Kosmos—the Transcendental "**Midnight Sun**" of Conscious Light or Real God:

> I Say to all: The Real Transcendental Spiritual Process in My Divine Avataric Company is a matter of going beyond the "blackness", beyond the "dark night"—to the Divine Self-"Brightness". I am not here merely to Reveal the darkness of conditional "experience". You must see what has darkened you so profoundly. You must become literally En-Light-ened again.
>
> There Is a Sun That Is Forever Risen in the night sky of the body-mind. It Is the Eternal Sun—the (Self-"Bright") "Midnight Sun", Infinitely Above the mind and the crown of the head, and not perceptible by the presuming-to-be-separate observer....
>
> The Sun That Is Eternal and Perfectly Over-head is not in the midst of a colored sphere of light.... There Is an Eternal Sun Over-head. It Is a Reflection of the Light in Which you Inhere. To see It is to be outside It.
>
> There is no option but to Be It. What is there to Be? Exactly That.... Even though death rules to here, there Is an Indivisible Eternal Sun Over-head. And That Eternal Sun Is—Beyond even all conditional visibility. I have Come to Confirm This to you—each and all—Absolutely. I Am That Eternal Sun.[11]

Only an Awakened Adept who has seen or directly *realized* this Real Light of the Godhead, the "Eternal Sun" of Atman-Brahman (that lives as our body-mind most brightly in our hearts) can so forcefully proclaim its radiant Truth. These Guru-Adepts, as Sokrates also proclaimed in the dim mists of Western civilization, realize that, in Plato's words: "the instrument of knowledge [*gnosis*] can only be the movement [evolution] of the whole soul turned from the [relative] world of *becoming* into that of [absolute] *being*. [They] learn by degrees [via the stages of life] to endure the sight of Being, and of the brightest and best of Being, or in other words, of the Good [the "Bright" or "Midnight Sun" Itself]."[12] Hence, the Bright Ones, the Daylight Gurus, through their compassion and love continue to descend into the dark cave of illusions to fight for us all, even at their peril. They come to struggle with our egoic illusions of Narcissistic reflections in order to free us from ourselves (the chains) and the world (the cave), to show us the Empty "Clear Light" of Eternal Divine Freedom shining outside (yet within) the cave-world with Awareness and Compassion. Then we see and realize the Indivisible Oneness "Bright" for ourselves, knowing Only God, for real. This is the principal message of all the Adept-Realizers, regardless of century or culture: *Tat Tvam Asi*—"Thou Art That" or *"You Are God!"* It is also the same primary message taught by Avatar Adi Da Samraj as the "Reality-Way of Adidam Ruchiradam" (or "The Way of the Heart"). He is a Guru as real and true as any of them, is my confession.

In *The Republic* we see that Sokrates-Plato long ago taught humankind a similar message that people (or prisoners like us) can always be educated out of our deluded illusions. Anyone may be Divinely Awakened, according to the Adepts. Thus, Sokrates (via Plato) artfully assures us: "The soul of every man or woman does possess the power of learning the truth and the organ to see it with."[13] This includes, in integral language, the processes of "Growing Up" and "Waking Up" (as well "Cleaning Up" and "Showing Up") which is the evolution of our psychological and spiritual development. In this case, Justice and Truth and Beauty, as Plato teaches, are available for everyone the world over now and into the future. The Sage of Athens calls it the "upward journey of the soul," yet also humbly confesses, "heaven knows whether it is true; but this, at any rate, is how it appears to me."[14] All the Masters confirm that God lives in (and as) our breathing breath, as our beating hearts, awaiting our Re-Awakening as Eternal Consciousness transcending even death—as Sokrates taught and demonstrated in person with his self-sacrifice suicide intentionally drinking the poison hemlock when he could have escaped. Humanity is thus best served if we learn to honor, study, respect, *and love*—and live in right relationship with—these Holy Ones of the Bright Light, the authentic Avatars and genuine Gurus born to free us from the darkened caves of our thoughts, mind, desires, theories, and self-illusions.

GIFT OF GRATITUDE

onsequently, I'm not writing this book to champion Guru Yoga and Satsang simply because it's my personal preference or desire to convert you to my version of the shadows on the cave walls. No, I write because I have been emboldened by the wisdom of humanity's greatest Spiritual Masters or Guru-Adepts to ever walk the face of this planet Earth. Most importantly, I have sat at the feet of Avatar Adi Da Samraj and have been baptized with the nectar of *Gnosis*. I have seen for myself that the true Guru is the living Agency of the Divine. The record of evidence is right there in the "Great Tradition" and "Divine Library" of humankind, now available in print and even posted on the Internet (in places), but mostly alive in the authentic lineages of Enlightened Gurus. The trail is deep and obvious to those who wish to look beyond the hazy play of objects and events, to even see past family and society, power and success, opulent and consoling illusions indeed. This is why *ekstasis*, another Greek word, the root of our word "ecstasy," means "standing outside oneself" in order to feel the unbridled Love-Bliss of Divine Conscious Light. We must stand outside or transcend the enticing illusions and apparitions of the ego-I, the shadows on the cave's walls, to see the Real Truth where we are always already Free. It is not a game, ultimately, for it is the Way of the Heart—for only the Heart truly knows.

Thus, I write to tell the story of God's Great Tradition of Global Wisdom, to point you in the direction of that Divine Light and its Servants of Light, the genuine Guru-Adepts, the Adept-Realizers of humankind. Their Divine Wisdom is our global inheritance bequeathed to us by our wisest ancestors, male and female alike. And, of course, I highlight the intimacy of Divine Love I have shared with my Sat-Guru Adi Da. This book, therefore, suggests it is only by listening to and studying those free souls who have bravely ventured into the "Sunlight" of Awakened Awareness, beyond sensual rewards for fame or glory, only done in service to others, that we are best served in our Re-Awakening.

These Enlightened Spiritual Heroes, rare in number and shunned by many, return "to the marketplace" to share with us their Divine Gifts of Awak-ening-Transmission, that is, *if* we see (and use) them rightly and correctly. They are the Guru-Light in the darkness of humanity's dread. After all, the word "En-Light-tenment" has "Light" as its middle name! These true Gurus are the real Heroes of humanity, not military generals or political philoso-phers, for it is only they who lead us from darkness to Light, from ignorance to Illumination, from samsara to Nirvana, from self to the True Self, from the pantheons of gods and goddesses to the One Real God. This is where genuine Guru Yoga-Satsang originates and why I write this book and wish to share their Divine Love with you.

To those Great Ones, the Daylight Masters, and particularly to Bright Daylight Da, Avatar Adi Da Samraj, my Beloved Siddha-Guru of Divine Con-scious Light alive as the Heart, I humbly offer this book as my gift of gratitude for all I've been shown and given. This book is my gesture of service to each and every one of you, to all of us unwittingly chained to the shadows of our own mind, to the ethnocentric caves of group-minded tribalisms, to the emo-tionalism of desire, to the egocentric rituals of rationality, all casually luring us into a consensus trance of immense magnitude, yet still always yearning (deep inside) to be Free, Free at last, Free at last… thank God Almighty, we are "Al-ways Already" Free!

Introduction Endnotes

1. Adi Da Samraj, *The Method of the Siddhas* (1973, 1978), p. 151.

2. See: *Guru Gita* for this classic interpretation of the word guru as "dispeller of darkness"; also in *Advaya-Taraka-Upanishad* (Verse 16); see: *Yoga: The Technology of Ecstasy* (1989) by Georg Feuerstein, p. 22.

3. Adi Da Samraj, *The Method of the Siddhas* (1973, 1978), p. 223.

4. Plato, "Allegory of the Cave" (Chapter 25) in *The Republic* (1945 ed.) translated by F. M. Cornford, p. 231.

5. See: Adi Da Samraj [Franklin Jones], *The Method of the Siddhas* (1973, 1978), p. 152: "The Guru is a kind of irritation to his friends. You can't sleep with a dog barking in your ear, at least most people can't. There is some sort of noise to which everyone is sensitive, and it will keep them awake. The Guru is a constant wakening sound. He is always annoying people with this demand to stay awake, to wake up. He doesn't seduce them within the dream."

6. The film projection metaphor was often used by Sri Ramana Maharshi; see: *The Collected Works of Sri Ramana Maharshi* (2015, 13th edition), pp. 59-60; *The Spiritual Teachings of Ramana Maharishi* (1972, 1988), pp. 24-25.

7. See: *In God's Company: Guru-Adepts As Agents for Enlightenment in the Integral Age* (2022) by Brad Reynolds.

8. Plato, "Allegory of the Cave" (Chapter 25) in *The Republic* (1945 ed.) translated by F. M. Cornford, p. 231.

9. See: *In God's Company: Guru-Adepts As Agents for Enlightenment in the Integral Age* (2022) by Brad Reynolds.

10. Plato, "Allegory of the Cave" (Chapter 25) in *The Republic* (1945 ed.) translated by F. M. Cornford, p. 231.

11. Adi Da Samraj, "The Divine Avataric Self-Revelation of Adidam Ruchiradam" in *The Aletheon* (2009), pp. 1679-80, 1697, 1701.

12. Plato, "Allegory of the Cave" (Chapter 6) in *The Republic* (1892, 2018 ed.) translated by Benjamin Jowett, p. 196 [italics and caps added].

13. Plato, "Allegory of the Cave" (Chapter 25) in *The Republic* (1945 ed.) translated by F. M. Cornford, p. 232.

14. Ibid., p. 231.

God's Great Tradition of Global Wisdom

Guru Yoga-Satsang in the Integral Age

Part I

The Global Wisdom
of Guru-Adepts

ONE

GOD'S "GREAT TRADITION" OF GLOBAL HUMANKIND

The entire Great Tradition must be accepted as our common inheritance....
I Call for the universal acceptance of the total tradition or Great Tradition
of humankind as the common inheritance of humankind.

— **Adi Da Samraj**, 1982

"THE GREAT TRADITION" — ADI DA'S TERM AND INSTRUCTION

The phrase "The Great Tradition" was first brought forward by the Avataric-Sage and World-Friend Adi Da Samraj in the mid-1970s to indicate "the common Wisdom-inheritance of humankind." In response to our emerging global culture, the first Western-born Avatar to appear in human history affirms it is now time to move beyond all provincial cultural prejudices to embrace the total collection of the world's wisdom. This includes the most basic knowledge about living a healthy and balanced life (e.g., exercise, diet, sexuality, human maturity, etc.) to mental intelligence to the esoteric wisdom inherent in the various approaches to human spirituality and mysticism, from shamanism to yoga to meditation to Enlightenment (thus including all the Stages of Life).

Specifically, the Great Tradition was defined by Avatar Adi Da as "the total inheritance of human cultural, religious, magical, mystical, spiritual, Transcendental, and Divine paths, philosophies, and testimonies, from all the eras and cultures of global humankind—which inheritance has (in the present era of worldwide communication) become the common legacy of humankind."[1] In response, Adi Da's "**Seven Stages of Life**" Model in addition to Ken Wilber's "**Spectrum of Consciousness**" Model [see Appendix I] explains and discriminates the various levels or stages of human development leading to and including God-Realization and Divine Enlightenment by accessing all of the world's spiritual sources as a whole [see the three summary charts below].

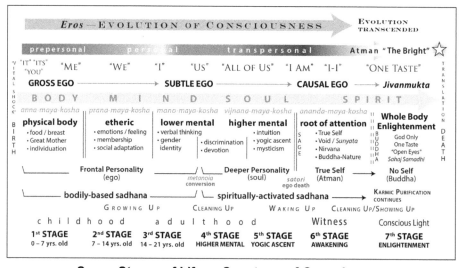

Seven Stages of Life — Spectrum of Consciousness
Overlap of Adi Da Samraj's Seven Stages of Life Model + Ken Wilber's Integral Psychology

As an emerging worldwide culture now and into the future, Adi Da teaches that each born human being has an innate right to access this vast storehouse of wisdom-knowledge. Indeed, the Universal Declaration of Human Rights (est. in 1948) maintains every human individual "has the right to education… directed to the full development of the human personality." (Article 26) On a political level, the World-Friend Adi Da has also compassionately called for a "**Global Cooperative Forum**" that "must be created by everybody—not everybody-one-at-a-time, but everybody-all-at-once."[2] Such a cooperative forum of humanity needs to spread and share our inherited wealth, materially, intellectually, and *spiritually*, with everyone, regardless of race, nation, or creed.

SEVEN STAGES OF LIFE—SPECTRUM OF CONSCIOUSNESS
OVERLAP OF ADI DA SAMRAJ'S SEVEN STAGES OF LIFE MODEL
+ KEN WILBER'S INTEGRAL PSYCHOLOGY

STAGE OF LIFE	FULCRUM	STATE-STAGES	CHARACTERISTICS
	Clear Light **F-10**	NONDUAL MYSTIC OVERMIND	Siddha-Buddhas in Divine Enlightenment; all is tacitly realized to be God/Godhead; where Absolute Reality is recognized to be "Always Already the Case".
	Ultraviolet **F-9**	CAUSAL MYSTIC META-MIND	Sages (*Jnanis*) who transcend self via inner Witness-Consciousness (*Turiya*); awareness of the Void or *sunyata*.
	Violet **F-8** Indigo	SUBTLE MYSTIC PARA-MIND	Yogic ascent of kundalini Life-Energy; traditional Yogas and Yogis, meditation, subtle-mind domains of attention; devotional Saints with psychic-siddhis.
	F-7 Turquoise Teal **F-6**	PSYCHIC/ NATURE MYSTIC INTEGRAL-CENTAUR HOLISTIC SELF	Kosmo-centric as evolving; holistic; Centaur: body-mind integration. Natural hierarchy, multiple perspectives; Online: 50 yrs. ago.
	Green Orange **F-5**	POSTMODERN- PLURALISM MODERN- RATIONAL	World-centic; equality; relativistic, sensitive; Online: 150 yrs. ago. Nation-centric; rationality, science, individualism. Online: 500 yrs. ago.
	Amber **F-4** Red	MYTHIC-TRADITIONALISM MYTHIC-RATIONAL MYTHIC-MEMBERSHIP	Ethno-centric; conservative, values rules, roles, discipline; Faith in transcendent God or Order; political-religious hierarchy. Online: 5000 yrs. BP
	F-3 Magenta **F-2** Infrared **F-1**	MAGIC-MYTHIC WARRIOR TRIBAL-ANIMISTIC ARCHAIC-UROBOROS	self-centric, impulsive, aggressive; Online: 15,000 yrs. BP Enchanted world; ritual; group-mind. Online: 50,000 yrs. BP Dawning self-awareness; instinct, intuition. Online: 250,000 yrs. BP

© chart by Brad Reynolds

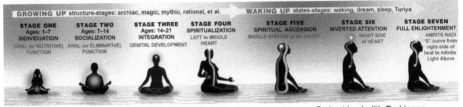

© chart by Judith Parkinson

THE SEVEN STAGES OF LIFE is one of Avatar Adi Da's unique gifts to humanity "mapping" the potential developmental course of human experience.

To honor this global (or universal) approach to human wisdom the original integral theories of Ken Wilber (in his early phases) relied heavily on the **"Perennial Philosophy"** (*philosophia perennis*), and what he called the **"Perennial Psychology"** (*psychologia perennis*), to incorporate the world's religious and spiritual wisdom [see Chapters 7–8]. By accessing these universal currents of wisdom, Wilber was able to justify and confirm many of his integral ideas based on the developmental processes of human maturity (the earlier Stages of Life) but by also including the transpersonal spectrum of mysticism (the higher Stages of Life).[3] Thus, naturally, Wilber's integral approach resonates well with the idea of the "Great Tradition" as proposed by Adi Da, especially since both authors were publishing around the same time (in the last quarter of the 20th century and first decade of the new millennium). The American pandit realized that his integral (and now "AQAL" or "all quadrants, all levels") evolutionary model of psychology closely follows and resembles Adi Da's "Seven Stages of Life" as a general developmental map, yet Wilber's version presents it in a decidedly more psychological language [see Appendix I for details]. The Avatar first presented his ideas about the Great Tradition and Seven Stages of Life in books and talks during the mid-to-late-1970s, right when Wilber was debuting his "Spectrum of Consciousness" theories and establishing his worldwide reputation.[4]

Wilber, of course, rightly claims he was using Western-based developmental psychologies to review the early stages of life and then added the wisdom of the Perennial Philosophy to outline the later stages of consciousness development. He also used the ideas of other evolutionary philosophers (from Hegel to Aurobindo to Gebser, et al.) to justify his conclusions (therefore generally not crediting Adi Da). Adi Da, on the other hand, was following his own intuitive and enlightened insights instead of just reading and synthesizing books; he had undertaken serious sadhana with genuine Gurus (especially in India), not simply sitting on meditation cushions and writing about philosophy and psychology (in fairness, Wilber did study under competent Zen Masters). Nonetheless, both models of the Avatar and integral pandit follow the same universal developmental growth of human beings based on our inner esoteric anatomy, from gross to subtle to causal to nondual domains. Therefore they both, in my opinion, should be seriously studied to enrich our understanding of ourselves within the "**Kosmos**" (in Wilber's terms) or the "**Cosmic Mandala**" (in Adi Da's terms). By the early 1980s, Adi Da was highlighting some of the Great Tradition's fortuitous advantages in increasing our psychological and spiritual wisdom as a global culture of one human race, as he wisely explains:

> What I call the "**Great Tradition**" is that entire mass of traditions, reflecting all of the seven stages of human existence, that is the common inheritance of all of humankind in this time of universal communication, interrelatedness, and interdependence. It is no longer appropriate or even possible for individuals, cultures, or nations to justify absolute independence from other individuals, cultures, or nations—and it is no longer appropriate or possible to grant absolute or ultimately superior status to any historical Revelation, belief system, or conception of how things work. The entire Great Tradition must be accepted as our common inheritance.... I call for the universal acceptance of the total tradition (or Great Tradition) of humankind as the common inheritance of humankind.[5]

When Adi Da originated the phrase "**The Great Tradition**" and its working hypotheses, it began appearing in his books and talks during the last quarter of the 20th century (in the first decades of His Teaching Years). Avatar Adi Da has provided important considerations regarding this great matter (which we shall review in this book), that is: to learn about the collective inheritance of human wisdom and spirituality and how it may better serve our spiritual practices today and into the future. He is calling everyone to engage in spiritual development via the evolution of consciousness and by practicing *Satsang* or Guru Yoga in "His Company" as Siddha-Guru. This way we can grow from ignorance to wisdom, from ego-mind to God-Realization, from a closed, intolerant heart to an open and compassionate one, from a baby to a Buddha. And he is not alone, as we shall see, since this American-born Avatar acts in concert with all of the other Awakened Adepts in humanity's Great Tradition of Global Wisdom. This is how our wisest ancestors speak to us across the centuries. Ken Wilber's Integral Metatheory addresses the same issues yet without offering Satsang or real spiritual practices.

Importantly, even a cursory study of the Great Tradition shows that it is the Adept-Realizers, humankind's greatest Saints and Sages, who are at the root of the world's esoteric religions. These include those women and men who have taught and worshiped with either a pantheistic (nature-based) or theistic (divine-based) worldview, whether emphasizing feminine, masculine, or nondual qualities as That which is creating, pervading, and transcending Nature. From Vedanta to Buddhism, from Muslims to Sufis, from Christian to Zen monks, et al., there is a sacred and personal relationship with an Awakened or God-Realized Master that lies at the heart of authentic spiritual practice. By studying the Great Tradition as a whole—by understanding how the model of the Seven Stages of Life supplemented by an integral or "AQAL" perspective—we are guided in accessing the full breadth of human and spiritual wisdom. Then we can better recognize the importance of "**Guru Yoga**" and *Satsang*—what I will call "**Guru Yoga-Satsang**"—as being the method of Enlightened Wisdom and disciplined practices given by the world's greatest Adept-Realizers, the Siddha-Gurus of humankind. This is the Way of the true "Avatars" and "Divine Incarnations" who have appeared among us *as* human beings.

In the early 1980s, when Adi Da was instructing us about "The Great Tradition," he explained it was the total collection of the world's wisdom ranging from the first developmental structures and early personal Stages of Life, from infancy to adolescence to adulthood—or what's called "**Growing Up**" (in Wilber's current terms)—in combination with the esoteric wisdom arising from the higher transpersonal Stages of Life that include the higher states of consciousness—what's now called "**Waking Up**" (in Wilber's terminology). Others have called this vast resource of sacred knowledge the "Great Wisdom Tradition," the "Great Human Tradition," the "Primordial Tradition," among other terms, such as the "Wisdom of the Ages" or "Ancient Wisdom" (though as a whole it's much more than just "premodern" philosophies or esoteric metaphysics). Other scholars emphasize the fact that Great Tradition has an underlying "**Perennial Philosophy**" (*philosophia perennis*) or set of universal truths that are found in all the world's major religions, ones that we can discover for ourselves since they are living in every human heart and inner mind [see Chapters 7-8].

Because we now live in an emerging *global culture*, Adi Da believed and taught that every born human being has an innate right to access this vast treasure trove of humanity's knowledge, especially its spiritual wisdom. Importantly, such access and study verifies the validity of Divine Enlightenment and Self-Realization. Just being human gives us the universal right to this wisdom inheritance that has been lovingly bequeathed to us by our wisest ancestors. Avatar Adi Da calls everyone to accept and study this Great Tradition of Humankind:

(1) First, as a means to overcome our cultural and religious prejudices;

(2) Second, as an inspiration for our spiritual practice;

(3) Third, to better understand the true function of Spiritual Adepts and genuine Siddha-Gurus and to truly recognize what they do for their disciples and devotees.

Seen in this light, Guru Yoga-Satsang becomes a practice of enlightened love and compassion, not cultic delusion and religious preference. Plainly, we can easily see by seriously studying history how an actual person, a living Adept, has been at the root of every major historical world religion and esoteric spiritual path. Thus it is they who are the authors of humanity's most sacred scriptures as well as being radiant examples of our highest potentials. Wisdom does not come out of thin air; it comes from Awakened Adepts.

To place an added emphasis on this sacred legacy of the human race, the Guru-Adept (from any culture or century) calls our attention to the critical importance in transcending the limitations of living in a secular-oriented society as well as our tendency toward parochial (and ethnocentric) religious prejudices. Whether biased toward a personal God (theism) or an impersonal Absolute (panentheism), both are appropriate responses to the "Divine Person" or Real God as Consciousness and Ultimate Being, the true Source and Condition of Reality Itself. Avatar Adi Da emphasizes that everyone (especially his devotees) must cultivate a "**culture of tolerance**" to other people's religions and inherited history. He directly instructs his devotees: "You need an education in the history of human 'religion', Spirituality, and Transcendentalism, so that you can overcome your prejudices, your failed 'religious' neurosis, and everything else.... Through that study, you overcome your 'religious' prejudices and free yourself for real practice."[6] This is a message the entire world needs to learn and practice! The Heart-Master asserted this trans-religious view in another talk about the importance of embracing our universal Great Tradition:

> At this point in history, we are all the inheritors of the Great Tradi-
> tion, the Total Tradition, and we should acknowledge this. It is useful
> and important for humanity to acknowledge this Great Tradition,
> the Great Sacred Tradition, the Great Wisdom Tradition, to become
> free of religious provincialism, cultural provincialism, and so forth,
> but also to be free of the secular mode of society in our time. In
> acknowledging this Great Tradition, we cease to be provincial reli-
> giously, but we also cease to be merely secular, pagan, or barbaric.[7]

We must use humanity's Great Wisdom Tradition, in other words, to become truly mature and serious spiritual practitioners and not just intellectuals
or scholars of scriptures, known as the "Talking School" fallacy [see Chapter
4]. Avatar Adi Da, therefore, has affirmed that this entire Great Tradition of
global sacred wisdom must be *understood* within an overall developmental
context—what he calls the "**Seven Stages of Life**" [see Appendix I]—for only
then may we adequately apply the Great Tradition's cross-cultural resources
to serve our own evolution in consciousness to Divine Enlightenment. Importantly, everyone evolves or develops their maturity and spiritual awareness
through unfolding stages and states or structures of consciousness. This is what
Ken Wilber calls the "**spectrum of consciousness**" that spans the bandwidths
from Eastern wisdom to Western knowledge, from polytheism to monotheism
to a spectrum of mysticism until ultimate God-Realization is realized.

According to Bhagavan Adi Da, the Great Tradition needs to be embraced
altogether as a whole for it presents a "**Grand Argument**" gathered from all the
world's wisest human beings. In this manner, the Great Tradition provides us
with a "truly human culture, practical self-discipline, perennial religion, universal religious mysticism, 'esoteric' Spirituality, and Transcendental Wisdom"[8]
that humanity desperately needs to fulfill and manifest our human potential
and evolutionary destiny. This approach unanimously includes all religions,
"**the transcendent unity of religions**" (as Frithjof Schuon noted[9]), or the
"winnowed wisdom of the human race" (as Huston Smith says[10]). By studying
or "listening" to this Grand Argument with diligence and an open mind as
well as with intelligent discrimination (and understanding), we can "hear" (or
truly comprehend) its summary message, which in essence, is exactly the most
fundamental "doctrine" of the Perennial Philosophy: *Tat Tvam Asi*—"Thou
Art That"—*You Are God!* Consequently, Heart-Master Da instructs:

Full study of the larger gathering of books [compiled in *The Basket of Tolerance*] grants more detail to one's comprehension of the "Message" of the "Great Tradition"… Therefore, study this gathered Word of the Great Tradition, book by book. "Listen" to the "Grand Argument" of its totality (or "Whole Body"), and (by understanding yourself in the context of real practice) "hear" the summary "Message" of its Heart. In this manner (and by many means), prepare yourself also to "see" That Which Is Revealed only by Grace and by stages of Realization in the necessary ordeal of real and inspired practice.[11]

The whole point of studying "**God's Great Tradition of Global Wisdom**" (as I like to call it) is not simply about becoming studious scholars of different cultural texts or traditional views but to be motivated to do ego-transcending spiritual practices (*sadhana*) and engage in real *Satsang* with a genuine Adept-Guru. As Wilber succinctly announced: "The only major purpose of a book on mysticism should be to persuade the reader to engage in mystical practice."[12] We must *realize* for ourselves what our wisest ancestors have also Realized: God Only, Only God. We must discover our innate Buddha-Nature (by whatever name)—the Divine Reality that IS "Always Already the Case" alive and present as Radiant Transcendental Conscious Light (as Adi Da says). As the Buddhists noted (long ago): this path cultivates *both* compassion (from the heart) *and* wisdom (from the mind), together, as one integrated reality of human existence. This is embodied most fully in our Guru-Adepts, from all cultures and centuries, including from our century (or recent past).

| Krishna | Sokrates | Buddha | Jesus | Rumi | Dogen |

Hence, we are all called to thoroughly study and listen to the sacred voices and spiritual confessions in this Great Tradition of Humankind—which is why Adi Da implores his devotees (and everyone) to "*go to school with the Great Tradition*"—in order to serve our spiritual growth. Yet this is not easy, as the World-Friend wisely explains:

> If we go to school with the Great Tradition, we must go through a trial of self-transformation. My Teaching provides the critical basis for that school of self-transformation. In the beginning, I call you to consider and overcome the provincialism of your mind, and, therefore, I Argue the Way in relation to the traditions and stages of life.... Therefore, My Argument "Considers" the Great Tradition positively and critically, but it ultimately transcends all the conventions of the Great Tradition and all of the systems of approach to Truth.[13]

In this case, Adi Da's main concern is not just one of criticism but also one of appreciation. He recognizes that the availability of esoteric teachings and the enlightened confessions of the world's true Adepts are actually a goad or motivation to real practice. Therefore, it's vitally important to study the stories and scriptures of the Great Tradition with intelligence and insight. As the Avataric Adept-Guru makes clear: "Until there is Realization, there is no Realization. The reading of spiritual literature is a positive discipline if it leads an individual to the conviction that he or she is committed to suffering and limitation. Then such an individual may become available to the real process of spiritual practice."[14] This is the purpose and mission of all Adept-Realizers, whether from Buddhism, Vedanta, Taoism, Christianity, or Islam, et al., or any other genuine mystical path: to serve *your* spiritual growth and evolution of consciousness. We must go beyond all religions to be truly religious. In Adi Da's case, he pointedly explains:

> I Argue the Way of the Heart in relation to the traditions and Stages of Life.... But My Argument finally goes beyond this schooling of the provincial or conventional mind. The "radical" Argument of My Wisdom-Teaching is a "Consideration" that transcends the mind itself, even the entire body-mind, the apparent world, and attention itself.[15]

Having an Awakened Adept who has been alive during modern times and recent history (bridged into the Third Millennium), and therefore having critically reviewed the entire span of world history gives us all, no matter what our country of origin, a unique advantage—and thus "Great Help"—in being able to understand our position in human history within an enlightened context. People's political, economic, social, and educational opportunities often don't provide the full spectrum of this wisdom-knowledge, although the literary resources are now available in the world including being posted on the Internet. Thus worldwide communication makes the Great Tradition's distribution more accessible for all the world's people regardless of where we are from or where we now live. Humankind's Great Tradition of Global Wisdom must now be embraced as a whole, as Avatar Adi Da implores:

> It is in our unique moment in history, when all traditions and all propositions are equally visible (due to a world-wide communicativeness that is making all provincialism obsolete) that we must consider the apparent differences among traditions with a new kind of wide intelligence. And My Work is devoted, in part, to provide the critical means for understanding and transcending these differences, so that the mass of traditions may be rightly comprehended as a single and dynamic Great Tradition.[16]

Nevertheless, global political instability still makes it difficult to spread this natural resource to everyone. For one, many people still do not even have electricity or the basic necessities, let alone proper access to decent educational facilities. Much work still needs to be done the world over! The entire globe must be included! Plus, obviously, people's political, economic, social, and educational opportunities usually do not provide the full spectrum of the Great Tradition's wisdom-knowledge, since most of us are curtailed by the social and religious prejudices in which we have been born. Most people are born into a theistic Western (Omega-mind) view or pantheistic Eastern (Alpha-mind) worldview or, typically, a modern scientific and atheist-agnostic one depending on their country of origin and their parent's preferences [see Chapter 9]. In other words, many people are confused and mired in doubt as to whether "God" exists at all or why they should care except, perhaps, in a time of crisis.

Fortunately, Avatar Adi Da has also provided a (still unpublished) compendium of thousands of books from around the world organized into the Seven Stages of Life model—known as *The Basket of Tolerance* [see Chapter 2]. Although the Great Wisdom Tradition is our innate *right* as spiritual beings who are born human, it is still every person's *responsibility* to become familiar with this sacred inheritance and then cultivate its highest ideals and evolutionary potentials. It is a task of study and education that reveals our prior unity and true existence as One Humanity, as One Divine Reality, and thus it is intended to brighten our future to know the Truth of God more realistically and intimately. Nothing less than this. What a Great Message it is!

Advantages In Understanding God's Great Tradition

It is useful and important for humanity to acknowledge this Great Tradition, the Great Sacred Tradition, the Great Wisdom Tradition, to become free of religious provincialism, cultural provincialism, and so forth, but also to be free of the secular mode of society in our time.

— **Adi Da Samraj**, 1983

Next, let's list and review some of the advantages gained from viewing all of the world's religious traditions as one grand "Great Tradition" of human spirituality and wisdom. As a brief summary, some advantages gained from studying God's Great Tradition of Global Wisdom as a whole are listed below[17]:

- The Great Tradition appreciates the development of *all* traditions and "tribes"—set within the Seven Stages of Life model—encircling the globe during the entire course of human history;
- The Great Tradition sees human history as a global history of one human race, thus it is our *global inheritance* (or "common Wisdom-inheritance") as a born human being;
- Study of the Great Tradition teaches us to preserve and revere Nature and the Earth as the living embodiment of Spirit Itself, a Divine Creation that must be protected, honored, and served;
- The Great Tradition as a whole provides Real Wisdom that transcends the limitations of each historical era and their cultural and regional prejudices;
- The Great Tradition transcends "religious provincialism" thus generating cultural and religious tolerance to provide the foundation for a united global culture based on genuine spiritual understanding;

- The Great Tradition counters "scientific materialism" and Western "flatland" reductionism by showing us a hierarchy (or holarchy) of human development grounded in a spectrum of mysticism, from Prophets to Shamans to Yogis to Saints to Sages to Siddhas to Avatars, etc.;
- Study and embodiment of the Great Tradition in today's modern world *integrates* Eastern Enlightenment (mysticism) with Western Enlightenment (science and democracy or worldcentric human rights);
- The Great Tradition counters the egoic tendency towards religious or mythic cultism by transcending the errors and liabilities of the earlier Stages of Life (1–4) and in evolving or developing the transpersonal state-stages of awareness (4–7) ultimately revealing Divine Enlightenment;
- Study of the Great Tradition as a whole minimizes the negative effects on the human spirit gained by living in a modern secular society that, nevertheless, is necessary for people to cultivate religious choice and freedom of worship based on personal preference or one's traditional religious inheritance;
- Study of the Great Global Tradition allows the Western Mind to receive Eastern Wisdom (and vice versa) so that a comprehensive understanding of the entire spectrum of human consciousness can thus fully emerge; consequently, this promotes an Integral Theory or Integral Vision of reality grounded in and promoting a genuine global world culture;
- Study of the Great Tradition resists the secularizing trends of our modern and postmodern society, thus addressing the fundamentalist and anti-scientific fringes of institutional religions;
- Study of the Great Tradition counters "sectarianism" (or "tribalism") and scientific "reductionism" leading to a more comprehensive and inclusive—or *integral*—orientation fostering the embracing of reality as a whole (including all its levels and dimensions and spheres of existence from the physical to biological to mental to spiritual, et al.);
- Study of the Great Tradition overcomes the "culture of materialism," "consumerism," and the battle of "capitalism vs. communism" by embracing them within the larger perspective of Divine Enlightenment (or Self-Realization) that cultivates and cares for *all* human beings (in any society or culture);

- Study of the Great Tradition of Global Wisdom transcends parochial and cultural orientations by placing an emphasis on understanding (and transcending) the separate self-sense or the egoic-personality, as well as the limits of particular ethnocentric cultures, nations, races, and religious points of view (based on the first Six Stages of Life) in transition to a genuine worldcentric or enlightened perspective (based in cooperation and tolerance realized in the Seventh Stage of Life);

- Study of the Great Tradition must also be responsive to legitimate viewpoints of scientific intellectualism and humanism gained from the evolution of world consciousness, instead of simply promoting religious or mythic cultism;

- The Great Tradition recognizes the inherent freedom of the human spirit (beyond any cultural limitation or boundary);

- Study of the Great Tradition discriminates spirituality from fanaticism, intolerance, and mythic thinking;

- Awareness of the Great Tradition (incorporating every culture and religious tradition) cultivates a "**culture of tolerance**" (in Adi Da's words);

- Study of the Great Tradition encourages the ultimate development of human growth, i.e., the evolution of consciousness to Divine Enlightenment, from infancy to God-Realization, from babies to Buddhas, from a child to Christ-consciousness;

- The Great Tradition reveals the importance of Enlightenment and True Self-Realization as the epitome or pinnacle of human potential, both individually and collectively [see Chapter 7];

- True spiritual life (in the higher Stages of Life) is revealed by studying the entire Great Tradition, not by any one single tradition or religion;

- The Great Tradition offers a "**Divine Library**" or comprehensive bibliography showing all the Stages of Life, transcending any one tradition or any one text—Adi Da calls this approach and collection "The Basket of Tolerance" [see Chapter 2];

- Education in the Great Tradition helps create a "preparatory foundation" for authentic spiritual practice (*sadhana*) as well as how to engage in a genuine relationship (*Satsang*) with authentic Adept-Realizers and genuine Siddha-Gurus [see Chapter 5];

- Study of the Great Tradition reveals the significance and indispensable process of Guru Yoga and *Satsang* [see Chapter 3];
- Study of the Great Tradition reveals the importance and power (and necessity) of Adept-Gurus (and Guru Yoga) and how they have been the root source of *all* religious and esoteric spiritual traditions throughout world history and in every culture [see Part II];
- Preserving the Great Tradition of global spirituality becomes a universal resource for the enhancement of the human spirit, and, therefore, is absolutely necessary to fulfill the search for Real Truth beyond mythic and religious illusions;
- The Great Tradition must be presented in an atmosphere of *free exchange* with an absence of racial or cultural prejudice;
- The Great Tradition encourages access to all possible forms of information available to all people possible thus overcoming information poverty (and misinformation) by remedying the information gap between the educated and uneducated, the wealthy and the poor, the developed nations and undeveloped nations;
- The Great Tradition introduces the "higher culture of spiritual life," thus supporting the development of human potential to include the transpersonal stages of mysticism;
- Embodying the perennial wisdom of the Great Tradition, as taught by the world's Awakened Adepts, creates a person who is alive with peace of mind and bodily equanimity, a heart practicing love and compassion in all relations, while living in whole-body communion with the Divine Ground (or God)—thus creating a whole human being, woman or man;
- Study of the Great Tradition redresses the imbalance of current knowledge (and lack of Wisdom) so that Higher Wisdom may, in fact, continue to grow (and evolve) and positively influence today's current global and political society and world culture at large;
- Study of the Great Tradition encourages us to love and protect life itself as a living *spiritual* reality, including the protection of all "Earth-kind" (in Adi Da's words);
- Study of the Great Tradition is a study of the Seven Stages of Life (1-7), from conception to Enlightenment, from birth to Buddhahood, thus it provides a universal map for human development [see Appendix I].

MOVING BEYOND RELIGIOUS PROVINCIALISM & SCIENTIFIC MATERIALISM

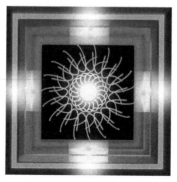

*A*s our list of advantages to using the Great Tradition shows, there are many benefits to be gained from the universal global wisdom we have all inherited from our wisest ancestors of past generations. It is the **"Wisdom of the Ages"** after all, one that has been bequeathed to us from our most beloved and evolved souls. Nevertheless, every generation must make anew its commitment to understand and access this storehouse of spiritual knowledge. Today with mass communication at an all-time high, such as with the Internet and smartphones, coupled with the incredible proliferation of sacred translations circulating the Earth more than at any other time of human history, we now have a far greater advantage (and responsibility) than any generation before us.

However, as the world shifted to the modern (and postmodern) mind it often dispensed with religious ideas and spiritual practices to embrace reductionistic materialism, the "religion" of science. Nonetheless, this book maintains we must preserve and embody this sacred knowledge so we may pass it on to our children, and to their children, far into the future. Consequently, for this knowledge to become true *wisdom* it must be grounded in actual practice (the "Practicing School"), not just scholarly study (or the "Talking School") [see Chapter 4]. Access to this sacred wisdom is our most assured method for gaining holistic human health and achieving peace of mind embodied within a happy, loving life. It is also the foundational means to protect, honor, and serve our living planet and its climate and ecosystems (including all living creatures). The only way this project will be successful is if we can reap what's been cultivated for us from the most noble and enlightened women and men to ever grace our planet. This means, specifically, we should also learn how to practice and honor Guru Yoga-Satsang properly without slipping into the dogmatic dangers of cultism.[18]

One of the more important and obvious advantages in recognizing a Great Tradition of Global Wisdom is to help everyone overcome what's called "**religious provincialism**" or "**tribalism**" (in Adi Da's terms[19]). This is when someone believes that only *their religion* is the right religion or the proper set of spiritual (and moral) beliefs. By transcending the limitations of religious provincialism, we realize a stronger sense of *religious tolerance* by cultivating a more pluralistic attitude towards all people and their cherished beliefs. "Religious provincialism" is a phrase used by Adi Da to indicate the tendency of people to identify exclusively with the traditional religion or culture into which they are born. This bias spans the entire spectrum of religious (and non-religious) possibilities, from pantheism to theism to atheism, etc. The Integral Vision, in this case, holds that every view is "correct but partial," a mode of thinking that encourages political and religious tolerance and cooperation.

Unfortunately, such parochial attitudes of *ethnocentrism*, as Integral Theory calls this lower stage of consciousness development, tends to condemn (or ostracize) groups (or "tribes") outside of the one they belong to, thus prompting intolerance of others who do not think like or look like them. This structure or worldview of consciousness called "**Mythic-Membership**" (in Wilber's Integral Theory[20]), sometimes called "**religious traditionalism**," places a limit on the global embrace of other people (usually based on fear and misunderstanding). This is because a child naturally learns from their parents and extended family, as well as from their surrounding socio-cultural environment, just like their parents did, and so on. Thus, a person often ends up inheriting the prejudices and limitations of those parochial traditions until they are educated (or evolve) into a broader, more *worldcentric* or universal higher-order stage of consciousness development.[21]

By being exposed to the history of our larger global family, the home of all the world's spiritual traditions and civilizations, we can start to transcend our provincialism and develop a greater tolerance for others. Then we can learn to see and honor the universal currents underlying all religious approaches and cultural lifestyles. People begin to understand that everybody, even those outside their parochial group, are simply attempting to do what they believe is right (or have been taught what is right). In this way, it becomes easier to practice a more cooperative attitude of tolerance with other cultures and races, even with those who have been traditionally seen as opposing enemies, that is, if a person realizes everyone and every ethnicity is part of the Great Tradition of Humankind.

The other significant advantage offered by studying the Great Tradition of Global Wisdom, one which recognizes all the levels of existence (and all Stages of Life), is that it counters the philosophy of "**scientific materialism**," the philosophy of science that elevates the level of gross-physical reality to superior status. "Scientific materialism" is a phrase originally used by Alfred North Whitehead to describe what's also known as "**scientism**," the tendency to think that the scientific worldview is the only valid view of reality. Many postmodern critics have denounced the arrogance and limitations of such a purely materialistic philosophy or view of life, as does the mystical perspective. When based on the evidence of our "esoteric anatomy," e.g., the chakras and subtle-energy channels of the human body and inner brain (inherent in all of us), then these higher realms or planes and sheaths of existence can supplement and correct the reductionistic (and distorted) view proposed by gross materialism. Indeed, to truly be *integral* is to use all "**Three Eyes of Knowing**" (in Wilber's terms)—the **Eye of Matter**, the **Eye of Mind**, *and* the **Eye of Spirit**—i.e., to use the gross-physical, mental-intellectual, and spiritual-mystical methods of inquiry, respectively.[22] This approach of "**epistemological pluralism**" is a foundational tenet of Integral Theory (that now includes the "eight zones" operating in "four quadrants").

For instance, people still talk about "matter" as if it were nothing but physical lumps of "stuff" or gross-physical "objects" even though it is really composed of subatomic particles that are actually forms of excited energy. As the German physicist Werner Heisenberg artfully put it: "Energy is in fact the substance from which all elementary particles, all atoms, and therefore all things, are made, and energy is that which moves."[23] Plus, all those atoms occur within vast regions of space, so that even our human bodies are more space than they are "matter" or solid substance, as every schoolkid knows. We just can't tell the difference based upon our sense of perception. Mysticism also supports this point of view, often claiming that "emptiness" is the true "substance" of the world.

Science has undeniably shown that all physical matter is a dynamic display of energy and light, the "dance" of subatomic particles making up atoms, not "hard stuff" or solidity at all. Every individual thing (or holon) is a dynamic and ever-changing "play" of evolving *patterns* of energy manifesting the material-looking world that surrounds us as presented to our five senses and physical body. Thus, we too, as human beings are a powerful dance of interconnected patterns following certain "laws" in the modification of energy. Integral Theory, by acknowledging the "Eye of Spirit" (or an enlightened mystical vision), as well as using the "eye" of physics and science, sees all manifest forms (gross to subtle to causal) as condensations of formless Conscious Light (or the Spirit-Energy of God). In this way, the evolution of the universe is best seen as "**Spirit-in-action**" (in Wilber's terms) and not just as a flurry of material matter banging around by blind chance or necessity.

In other words, even science's professed philosophy of "materialism" is betrayed by their own discoveries as their concrete ideas dissolve into playful projections aligned with certain "laws" of Nature and physics. Heisenberg astutely observed: "The modern interpretation of atomic events has very little resemblance to genuine materialistic philosophy; in fact, one may say that atomic physics has turned science away from the materialistic trend it had during the nineteenth century."[24] According to modern physics, the perceived "material" universe, from galaxies to atoms, is more like the dancing shadows on Plato's cave wall: not what it seems at all! Even the word "physics" comes from an ancient Greek word *physis* meaning "blossoming forth" (as German philosopher Martin Heidegger emphasized[25]).

"Uncertainty" rules in the subatomic world, as Heisenberg formulated, while everything is relative in the galactic expanse of the expanding universe, as Einstein calculated, where light is the only absolute. Again, let's allow Heisenberg to summarize: "Since mass and energy are, according to [Einstein's] theory of relativity, essentially the same concepts, we may say all elementary particles consist of energy. This could be interpreted as defining energy as the primary substance of the world."[26] Thus the most fundamental condition of "reality" itself escapes the scientific mind even with its precise measurements and mathematics for it only measures the action of energy in simulating mass as it bends space-time, nothing more. Ultimately, science does not even know what energy really *is*.

Avatar Adi Da often discoursed about these concerns from the perspective of God-Realization, always gracefully and eloquently including the most recent understandings of science and physics as married with enlightened insight:

> "Matter" is <u>not</u> a "lump". It is not, in and of itself, the defining characteristic (or limit) of "reality". Truly (and even from the point of view of twentieth-century exoteric science), "matter" is "energy" (or Light). And "energy" (or Light) Is (In and <u>As</u> Itself) <u>Inherently</u> Indivisible (or One, Only, and Indestructible). Therefore, "matter" is simply a conditional mode of appearance, a merely apparent modification of Inherently Immutable Light!... "matter" <u>Is</u> Inherently Indivisible Light.... That Discovery, Most Perfectly Made (or Utterly Realized), <u>Is</u> Most Perfect (and Self-Evidently Divine) En-Light-enment.[27]

Scientism and the modern mind, nonetheless, has erected a life philosophy that diminishes our full spectrum of existence by reducing the entire Great Nest of Spirit down to its lowest level of "material matter"—or as Whitehead famously lamented, into "a dull affair, soundless, scentless, colorless; merely the hurrying of material, endlessly, meaninglessly."[28] Consequently, an expanded perspective is needed to bring a comprehensive integral understanding to reality as a whole. This has been a large part of what Ken Wilber and other integral thinkers are attempting to accomplish by additionally integrating the view of Enlightenment and Self-Realization into their "theories of everything." Adi Da perfectly summarizes the situation: "Science is a method, not a philosophy."[29] Science, in other words, from the integral perspective is to be "transcended-and-included" (a well-known motto of Integral Theory).

God's Great Tradition of Global Wisdom, therefore, *includes* science, as well as spirituality, since all systems of knowledge are to be embraced in harmony. This is the most advantageous approach to becoming holistic as well as being compassionate and wise. This is why the integral perspective has become so popular in succeeding the modern-postmodern worldview: it provides a larger map embracing more of reality by including science *and* spirituality as both being valid modes of knowing (although each addresses different modules of cognition). We need to use *all* the "eyes" of knowing (physical, mental, spiritual) to see more clearly. Perhaps none of the critics of scientism is clearer or more eloquent than world religion philosopher Huston Smith who explained in his masterpiece *Forgotten Truth* (1976) exactly where the argument rests:

> With [the facts of] science itself there can be no quarrel. Scientism is another matter. Whereas science is positive, contenting itself with reporting what it discovers, scientism is negative. It goes beyond the actual findings of science to deny that other approaches to knowledge are valid and other truths true. In doing so it deserts science in favor of metaphysics—bad metaphysics, as it happens, for as the contention that there are no truths save those of science is not itself a scientific truth, in affirming it scientism contradicts itself.[30]

Both *scientism* and *scientific materialism* fall under the heading of "**Flatland**," a term Wilber has used to identify and critique science's—and thus the modern world's—tendency to reduce all processes in the cosmos, particularly those of the human psyche, down to being nothing more than physical building blocks.[31] Art and mysticism, love and creativity, morality and ethics, from this flatland perspective, are nothing but productions of brain chemistry and processes of natural selection. Since it's a common thesis in Wilber's work, he points to this danger of reductionism in one of his most popular books, *A Brief History of Everything* (1996):

> Flatland is the idea that the sensory and empirical and material world is the only world there is. There are no higher or deeper potentials available to us—no higher stages of consciousness evolution, for example. There is merely what we can see with our senses or grasp with our hands. It is a world completely bereft of any sort of Ascending energy at all, completely hollow of any transcendence.[32]

Our planet has also been "flattened" by corporate-influenced industry and technology, where moral values are corrupted by materialistic capitalism and economic consumerism, where spirituality is raped by scientism, where Nature becomes only resources not a living ecology. This leads to the combined disasters of premodernity, modernity, and postmodernity struggling to reduce the greater truths of human existence down to nothing but the merely obvious— no wonder all of Earthkind is calling out for an authentic Integral Age. God's Great Tradition of Global Wisdom, therefore, provides a multi-layered, pluridimensional view of reality that transcends-and-includes all methods of knowledge acquisition (i.e., using the "Three Eyes of Knowing"). It views the cosmos as a harmonious unity reaching from matter-energy to mentalism to mysticism, not merely as a collection of discrete particles and detached entities (or holons) banging about. We live in an interconnected, interpenetrated, pluridimensional Kosmos of Spirit-in-action, grounded in God (or Divine Being), according to the Integral Vision and the Enlightened Sages.

In response, Integral Theory has become the principal proponent for developing a *more integral* approach to science and spirituality by understanding the full breadth of life as manifested in cosmos and psyche—i.e., the **Kosmos** (spelled with a "k"[33]). For decades Wilber has proposed we use a "**Spectrum of Consciousness**" to generate a more accurate "**Theory of Everything**." This model is based on integrating the *interiors* and *exteriors* of *individuals* and *collectives*, "all the way up, all the way down"—making up what he now calls the "four quadrants" or the **AQAL** ("all-quadrants, all levels") Approach—as being a better working map of the whole universe. Such an Integral Vision reaches from low to high, from atoms to Atman, from the Big Bang to Buddhahood, from atheism to mysticism, as far as you can see, as deep as you can dive.

Wilber often points out that the Great Wisdom Tradition almost always used a hierarchy (or holarchy) or a multi-level view to depict the pluridimensional structure of Reality as a whole. However, science dismisses this view inherited from our wisest ancestors. The mystical worldview often pictured such a multidimensional view of reality as being like a "ladder" or "**Great Chain of Being**," reaching from the "lowest" (matter) to the "highest" (God).[34] However, the more accurate view, as Wilber points out, is to see reality as a "**Great Nest of Spirit**" with each wider sphere or "nest" transcending-yet-including their predecessors. In other words, it's better to see or model the Kosmos as a mandala of embrace, not one of exclusion. The integral pandit explains this view in *The Marriage of Sense and Soul* (1998):

> According to this nearly universal view, reality is a rich tapestry of interwoven levels, reaching from matter to body to mind to soul to spirit. Each senior level "envelops" or "enfolds" its junior dimensions—a series of nests within nests within nests of Being—so that every thing and event in the world is interwoven with every other,

and all are ultimately enveloped and enfolded by Spirit, by God, by Goddess, by Tao, by Brahman, by the Absolute itself.[35]

In this case, the integral philosopher concludes: "The Great Chain of Being—from the gross body to conceptual mind to subtle soul to causal spirit, with each expanding sphere enveloping its juniors—was the essential core of the world's Great Wisdom Traditions. No major culture in history was without grounding in some version of this Great Holarchy. Until, that is, with the rise of the modern West."[36] By accessing the entire Great Tradition of human knowledge, from science to religion, from myths to reason, from rituals to ethics, etc., we can better know about and embrace the *full spectrum* of universal evolution and our experience of life within it. Only such an expanded view of reality will rescue us from the reductionistic collapse of the Kosmos created by modern materialism. It will also liberate us from the prejudices of religious provincialism and ethnocentric hatred generating a worldview of cooperation and tolerance.

By recognizing a dynamic, energetic pluridimensional universe we can also identify (and include) the various transpersonal stages of mysticism leading to Divine Enlightenment, the pinnacle of human development. This God-Realized state and structure (or state-stage) of consciousness is unanimously supported by the findings of the Great Tradition itself, the reports gathered from all the wise Shamans, Yogis, Saints, Sages, and Siddhas, et al., who have each contributed to our vast catalog of knowledge and wisdom seeing beyond the limits and errors of conventional society and scientific materialism. To distinguish and celebrate the various stages and states or structures of human development, and their corresponding levels of existence as revealed by evolutionary progress, is the principal task of the integral enterprise. This enlightened Integral Vision heralds the potential emergence of an Integral Age by using *all* the Eyes of Knowing in order to best serve the Earth and all its living beings—all of "Earthkind" (in Avatar Adi Da's words)... before it's too late.

However, what is most important, beyond models or maps or even sacred scriptures, is to learn how to acknowledge the Guru's Greatest Gift that extends beyond history and recorded texts, thus turning to the heart of all true religion: a special Spirit-Transmission outside the scriptures.

GURU'S GREATEST GIFT: HEART-TRANSMISSION

One of the most crucial characteristics of Guru Yoga-Satsang overlooked by most critics, and even scholars, is that of the all-important factor of authentic **Spiritual-Transmission**—known in Sanskrit as *Shaktipat*. *Shakti* is the "goddess" (the "Great Goddess") or spiritual energy of the universe, while *pata* literally means "to fall," thus *shaktipat* is a descent (or exchange) of psychic-spiritual energy from one person to another, specifically from Guru to devotee. Genuine Shaktipat usually activates the Divine Light above (and beyond) the head which is why it's perceived as descending or "falling" into a receptive individual. Shaktipat-baptism is one of the most rare and misunderstood aspects of esoteric spiritual lore.[37] Study of the Global Wisdom Tradition proves that this blessing "power" (or energy exchange) is involved in all the authentic lineages of Enlightened Masters throughout human history whatever the tradition, such as with the Maha-Siddhas of Tibet, or the *Sadgurus* (Sat-Gurus) of India [see Part II]. This energy transmission literally involves the "Holy Spirit," hence it is "**Spirit-Baptism**" (to use Western religious terms) [see Chapter 20]. Thus, we would all do well to gain its access (or at least honor its existence). It is only through authentic Guru-Adepts that real Spirit-Baptism is most alive and available for transmission to others.

Nothing is more important in the Guru-devotee relationship than the Divine Blessing of Spirit-Baptism given by the Guru to the devotee. This yogic-psychic energy exchange involves the subtle physics (or "super-physics") of the Kosmos—an aspect of Divine Light—activated by the Guru as the Transmitter. Such Spirit-Transmission is the "secret teaching" evident throughout history between Spiritual Masters and their students. On one level this ability involves the direct transmission of Spirit-Force or the opening of subtle energies from an advanced Yogi or genuine Guru to a sincere (or open-hearted) student or any receptive person whether a disciple-devotee or not. However, on an ultimate level, *Shaktipat* (with a capital "S") is actually capable of transmitting the Enlightened State of a fully God-Realized Adept. This Nondual Awareness ultimately transcends the dynamic play of subtle energies, known in Sanskrit as *kundalini*, since it transmits the Realization of the Awakened Heart. This sacred transmission goes far beyond book learning or mental philosophies (or the "Talking School"), for as Zen (or Ch'an Buddhism) notes it is a "special transmission outside the scriptures." As the famous Zen patriarch Bodhidharma (ca. 6th century CE) is said to have explained:

> *A special transmission outside the scriptures,*
> *Not depending on words and letters;*
> *Directly pointing to the mind*
> *Seeing into one's true nature and attaining Buddhahood.*[38]

Shaktipat as Spirit-Energy *transforms* a person's consciousness when it is conducted properly as a sacred relationship between Spiritual Master and student-disciple, between a Guru-Adept and receptive devotee. This is the very essence of **Satsang**, the "Method of the Siddhas" (in Adi Da's words), based on a real relationship with an authentic Adept-Transmitter.[39] This spiritual process has been lost in the West but by studying the Great Tradition we will be educated to its necessity and value. Most often this Transmission takes place in the physical company of a Guru-Adept, known as **Darshan** (or *darshana*), literally, the "sighting" and actual "vision" of a holy person. Yet, due to the spontaneous nature of Divine Grace, such a revelation may happen at any time someone turns his or her attention to a real Guru-Adept. In other words, it can occur in dreams or subtle realm visions. Such Shaktipat-Transmission is the hidden "secret" of Satsang and the essence of Real Religion. Study the Divine Library of the Great Wisdom Tradition carefully and you will hear it confessed time and time again, whether between Jesus and his disciples, Buddha and his devotees, Krishna and his gopis, and so on; it is the real Spiritual Truth given by the Master-Adept to all beings. This is precisely why genuine Guru Yoga is so important.

At its best, when this blessing is bestowed by an authentic Guru-Adept this

Transmission comes from the Heart, the True Self, Real God, or Conscious Light; thus, ultimately, it is a Divine Mystery since it is so subtle and pure it transcends the normal idea of energy itself. Living at the core relationship between Guru and devotee, Spirit-Baptism is why everyone should be involved (to some degree) with this Sacred Blessing Power and Divine Gift shared in genuine Guru Yoga-Satsang. It awakens the heart to confirm the reality and truth of Real God, the "Bright" of Consciousness Itself. Hence there is nothing more revered in the history of religions than being Spirit-Baptized by a Siddha-Guru (as a direct Agency of God).

Since everything "transmits" energy into the environment in some form or another, from rocks to the sun, from plants to animals, et al., then people too radiate their various energy states (or Stage of Life) with varying degrees of intensity. We all know from practical experience how people seem to "transmit" their state, whether they're happy, sad, angry, romantic, healthy, unhealthy, drunk, stoned, etc. We are (or can be) influenced by anyone's energy-transmission. This is especially true for highly-evolved people since they radiate more subtle energy currents than most because they have activated *kundalini* or the ascending "life-energy" of the body-mind, such as with advanced Yogis. Authentic religious leaders and Saints, for example, seem to exhibit a radiant energy (and charisma) that is not evident in most other people (unless they practice and achieve those stages of development). Even movie stars and championship athletes may seem to radiate a special charisma, as perhaps does your favorite teacher or spiritual friend.

This same principle is operative in advanced spiritual practitioners, particularly Enlightened beings, who *transmit* their advanced state-stage of consciousness developed in the higher Stages of Life. In this case, even Spiritual Masters or Gurus will have different qualities of transmission depending on their depth of Realization or Enlightenment (since there are varying degrees of intensity involved in higher mysticism). In addition, some Gurus seem born to manifest certain *siddhis* or psychic powers that make their transmission more effective in the public sphere. They actively influence or can initiate real *vertical transformations* of consciousness in others. Obviously, a fully Enlightened Guru-Adept (in the highest Stage of Life) can be the most powerful and effective transmitter of Spiritual Presence for they go directly to the heart.

Consequently, it is indispensable and imperative to protect and preserve and to actively access and use these sacred Agents of God's Spirit-Blessing.

In this respect, there probably has not been any one Spiritual Adept who has clarified the active process of Spirit-Transmission better or explained it more thoroughly than has **Adi Da Samraj** (1939–2008). And no one Adept in modern times as confessed by those living today—including integral philosopher Ken Wilber—has more freely transmitted such an intense degree of Shaktipat or Divine Awakening Power than has Avatar Adi Da. No one. Perhaps ever in human history—but who can say for sure?—go find out for yourself. I believe you will find that Avatar Adi Da's Heart-Transmission—what he calls *Hridaya* ("Heart") **Shaktipat**, and unique to him, *Ruchira* (the "Bright") **Shaktipat**—is still highly active and available even though his bodily human form has passed away to be buried underground. But his Spirit-Transmission lives on (for it transcends death) via his Agencies (including photographs, videos, audio recordings, sacred art, books, and, most important, his empowered sanctuaries). For one, this is why Adi Da's burial or Mahasamadhi site (on Naitauba, Fiji) is one of the most potent spiritual sites on Earth. Additionally, his other sacred sanctuaries (such as in California and Hawaii) also continue to transmit Adi Da's Awakened State with a vibrant intensity. In this case, by practicing Satsang, or placing one's attention on the Guru-Adept, especially in meditation, one may connect with Avatar Adi Da's Spirit-Blessing and Heart-Transmission.

The degree or intensity of *shaktipat* transmission is determined by the Stage of Life or state-Realization achieved by any particular Spiritual Master or Adept-Guru; in other words, the transmission is as effective as the transmitter. Yet it's not just about the transmitter for its effectiveness is also dependent on the receptivity of the person receiving the transmission. Adi Da's Seven Stages of Life model is a useful gauge for determining the actual level or stage of Realization of any certain Master-Adept, Yogi, Saint, Sage, or Siddha, et al. Such Spirit-Transmission goes beyond the typical *charisma* of a gifted person or spiritual teacher, the classic category used by religious studies to analyze someone's extraordinary talents or charm (a definition established by Max Weber, the original sociologist of religions). They are often called "cult leaders," in common parlance. However (as Weber pointed out), advanced charismatic leaders are also capable of initiating historical change, such as with Gandhi or Martin Luther King, Jr., let alone with someone like Jesus Christ or Buddha.[40]

Charisma (χάρισμα) is an ancient Greek word meaning "divine gift" or "grace of the divine" which conveys a more accurate description of what is actually taking place with a True Guru (or *Sat-Guru*). Thus it is extremely important to distinguish between cultic charisma and the transmission of an authentic Adept.[41] A genuine Guru far exceeds the personality magnetism of a celebrity or "star," who often does emit a unique energetic vibration more radiant than most people (which is why they're called "a star"), the most common definition of charisma. The Enlightened Adept, however, is transmitting Spirit-Energy that can awaken consciousness, not just turn on crowds with glee.

Shaktipat initiation (as Spirit-Baptism), as a most subtle (and causal) energy exchange of love between Guru and devotee (or between Guru and anyone), only occurs when the charismatic individual is in the advanced Stages of Life (e.g., with Fourth Stage Saints or Fifth Stage Yogis and higher). Since transmission reflects the degree of consciousness development (or Stage of Life) of the transmitter, then it *does* make a difference if they are a Priest/ess, Prophet, Shaman, Saint, Yogi, Sage, Siddha, or Avatar, etc. (i.e., as people living in either the Fourth, Fifth, Sixth Stages, or, potentially, Seventh Stage, of Life). Studying the Great Tradition allows us to better recognize these possibilities and potentials for it is full of examples from numerous cultures and centuries recorded in scriptures and sacred texts. Powerful Yogis and spiritual Saints, sensitive Shamans, and radiant Sages, all serve the evolutionary advancement of the human race. Obviously the most profound degree of transmission is given by the most advanced (Sixth Stage) Sages and Siddhas, and then the (Seventh Stage) Avatars and Buddhas.

Throughout history, and in today's world, only a small select group has ever had access to the shaktipat-transmission from advanced Yogis and Saints (in the Fourth or Fifth Stages of Life), which itself is a rare and blessed event. Such Shaktipat-Baptism is a profound and sacred occasion for anyone (especially those of us still struggling with the first Three Stages of Life). Therefore even "lesser" transmissions are not to be overlooked but sincerely honored by whomever is transmitting their spiritually-evolved state of consciousness. Nonetheless, we must also realize the ultimate Heart-Transmission that comes from the most highly developed Guru-Adepts and Avatars is the most potent (and highly valued) of all possible Shaktipat-Transmissions. Their transmission of awakened consciousness is God's Gift to us all in a form we directly *feel* and experience (and know) for ourselves, thus far transcending the mentally-based "Talking School" approach.

This is, by our definition, the *authentic* value of Guru Yoga-Satsang and its sacred transmission-power, i.e., it vertically *transforms* consciousness to higher state-stages of awareness until Enlightenment opens the heart to God knows where. This type of Shaktipat-Transmission can only be accomplished or given by a genuine Guru-Adept or incarnated Avatar, as testified to in the sacred literature of the Great Tradition's Divine Library. Modern people (including integral individuals), as I maintain in this book, must learn about and come to honor this wonderful method and process of transpersonal evolution. Guru Yoga-Satsang, when practiced correctly (and not cultically), is the essence of real religion because the disciple actually *sees* (and knows beyond doubt) that the Guru is a genuine Agent of God's Grace on Earth by the effectiveness of their Spirit-Transmission. This is not possible with a cultic totem-master or charismatic charlatan. It is critical we learn the difference and open ourselves to this actual and Divine Blessing-Power of Real God.

Chapter 1 Endnotes

1. See: *The Gnosticon* (2010) by Adi Da Samraj, "Glossary," p. 968.

2. See: *Not-Two Is Peace: The Ordinary People's Way of Global Cooperative Order* (2009, 3rd edition) by The World-Friend Adi Da, p. 51.

3. See: Ken Wilber "Psychologia Perennis: The Spectrum of Consciousness," *The Journal of Transpersonal Psychology*, Vol. 7, No. 2, pp. 105-132; *The Spectrum of Consciousness* (1977, 1993, 1999); *No Boundary* (1979); *The Atman Project* (1980); *Up from Eden* (1981).

4. See: *Growing In God: Seven Stages of Life from Birth to Enlightenment—An Integral Interpretation* (forthcoming, Paragon House) by Brad Reynolds.

5. Adi Da Samraj, *Nirvanasara* (1982), pp. 198-199; also see: Adi Da Samraj, June 8, 2005 in *Adi Da Samrajashram*, Volume 1, No. 4, p. 12.

6. Adi Da Samraj, April 20, 1987 in *Adi Da Samrajashram*, Volume 1, No. 4, pp. 30-31.

7. Adi Da Samraj, from the Talk "The Great Tradition," January 22, 1983 (unpublished; cassette only).

8. Adi Da Samraj, "Preface: The Gathering of the Seven Schools of God-Talk" in *The Basket of Tolerance* (prepublication edition, 1988), p. 1.

9. See: *The Transcendent Unity of Religions* (1959, 1984) by Frithjof Schuon.

10. Huston Smith, *The World's Religions* (1958, 1991, 2009), p. 5.

11. Adi Da Samraj, "Preface: The Gathering of the Seven Schools of God-Talk" in *The Basket of Tolerance* (prepublication edition, 1988), pp. 1-2.

12. Ken Wilber, *Eye to Eye* (1983, 1990), p. 199.

13. Adi Da Samraj, *Nirvanasara* (1982), pp. 199-200.

14. Adi Da Samraj, "The Seventh School of God-Talk" (essay) in "Preface" to *The Song of the Supreme Self: Astavakra Gita* (1982), p. 24.

15. Adi Da Samraj [Da Free John], *Nirvanasara* (1982), pp. 199-200, also in *Free Daist*, Vol. 3, No. 4/5, 1992-1993 ["Stages of Life" capped].

16. Adi Da Samraj [Da Free John], *Nirvanasara* (1982), p. 121.

17. Many of the phrases used in compiling these advantages in understanding the Great Tradition of Global Wisdom have been revealed in and inspired by the Teaching Work of Adi Da Samraj.

18. See: *In God's Company: Guru-Adepts As Agents for Enlightenment in the Integral Age* (2022) by Brad Reynolds.

19. See: Adi Da Samraj, *Not Two Is Peace* (2009, 2019); also see: *Scientific Proof of the Existence of God Will Soon Be Announced by the White House* (1980) by Adi Da Samraj [Da Free John].

20. See: Ken Wilber, *Up from Eden* (1981, 2007); also see Jean Gebser, *The Ever-Present Origin* (1986).

21. See: Ken Wilber, *Sex, Ecology, Spirituality* (1995, 2001); *A Brief History of Everything* (1996, 2017); *The Marriage of Sense and Soul* (1999).

22. See: Ken Wilber, *Eye to Eye: The Quest for the New Paradigm* (1983, 1990, 2001).

23. Werner Heisenberg, *Physics and Philosophy* (1958), p. 63.

24. Ibid., p. 59.

25. See: Martin Heidegger, *Introduction to Metaphysics* (1935, 1990, 2014, 2nd ed.).

26. Werner Heisenberg, *Physics and Philosophy* (1958), p. 70.

27. Adi Da Samraj, from "I Am The Way to Transcend the Illusions of Broken Light" in _Real God Is The Indivisible Oneness Of Unbroken Light_ (2001), pp. 156-157.

28. Alfred North Whitehead quoted in _The Marriage of Sense and Soul_ (1999) by Ken Wilber, p. 13.

29. See: Adi Da Samraj, _Science Is a Method, Not a Philosophy_ (2010, 2-CD set), Talks from 2004; also see: Adi Da Samraj, _Science and the Myth of Materialism_ (2003 CD), selected Talks.

30. Huston Smith, _Forgotten Truth_ (1976, Harper Colophon Books), p. 16.

31. See: Edwin Abbott, _Flatland: A Romance of Many Dimensions_ (1884, 1984).

32. Ken Wilber, _A Brief History of Everything_ (1996), p. 11.

33. "Kosmos" is Wilber's updated use of the ancient Greek term now scientifically called "cosmos" (in English)—Ken Wilber, _A Theory of Everything_ (1999), p. xi: "The Greeks had a beautiful word, Kosmos, which means the patterned Whole of existence, including the physical, emotional, mental, and spiritual realms. Ultimate reality was not merely the cosmos, or the physical dimension, but the Kosmos, or the physical and emotional and mental and spiritual dimensions altogether. Not just matter, lifeless and insentient, but the living Totality of matter, body, mind, soul, and spirit. The Kosmos! – now there is a real Theory of Everything!"

34. See: Ken Wilber, _Sex, Ecology, Spirituality_ (1995, 2001); _A Brief History of Everything_ (1996, 2017); also see Huston Smith, _Forgotten Truth_ (1976, 1997).

35. Ken Wilber, _The Marriage of Sense and Soul_ (1998), p. 6.

36. Ibid., p. 187.

37. See: Georg Feuerstein, _Encyclopedic Dictionary of Yoga_ (1990), p. 325.

38. See, for example: "A Special Transmission: Teachings from the Heart of the Chan Buddhist Tradition" by by Guo Jun in _Tricycle: A Buddhist Review_ magazine, Spring 2013.

39. See: Adi Da Samraj [Franklin Jones], _The Method of the Siddhas_ (1973, 1978, 1992), _My "Bright" Word_ (2005), an updated (and final) version of _The Method of the Siddhas_ (1973).

40. See: Jeffrey J. Kripal, "Charisma and the Social Dimensions of Religion" (Chapter 6) in _Comparing Religions_ (2014), p. 214: "Weber had an answer to what charisma is about. He thought that charisma is the engine of social change and creativity, particularly as these changes are catalyzed by individuals who have broken out of the conditionings of their societies. It is not all about society, then, for Weber. Charisma is also about individuals. It is about freedom. It is about experimentation. And offense. Weber observed that charisma often erupts at especially dramatic historical moments, moments of radical change and profound social suffering. He also observed that charisma, by its very nature, is often destructive of the status quo. Its apparent purpose, however, is not to destroy simply for the sake of destruction. Charisma is transgression. Charisma destroys the old in order to create the new."

41. See: _In God's Company: Guru-Adepts As Agents for Enlightenment in the Integral Age_ (2022) by Brad Reynolds.

Adi Da's writings & publications (partial)

TWO

"DIVINE LIBRARY" OF GLOBAL WISDOM

*All the "Holy Books" are our books, and all of us must go to school
and be transformed in our minds by the Great Tradition.*

— **Adi Da Samraj**, 1982

THE WORLD'S "DIVINE LIBRARY": GLOBAL WISDOM SCRIPTURES

One of the greatest advantages gained in today's high-tech world is that with modern communication technology and multimedia, ranging from the printed word to publishing houses to digital recordings to the Internet to seminars and meditation retreats, we may now buy and study nearly any *esoteric* text from any one of the world's major (and minor) religions—a rich reservoir of knowledge and wisdom unprecedented in human history. One scholar, Rufus Camphausen, cleverly named this global collection of sacred scriptures the "**Divine Library**,"[1] a vast historical bibliotheca outlining the treasury of our shared wisdom inheritance from the Great Tradition of humankind.[2] Camphausen subtitled his well-researched book "a comprehensive reference guide to the sacred texts and spiritual literature of the world" (highly recommended). As touted on the back cover of this resourceful book:

> From the *Angas* to the *Zend-Avesta*, from *Apocryphal* writings to the *Yogini Tantra*, and from the *Bible* to the *Zohar*, Camphausen traces the divine impulse as it has been expressed through the world's great traditions from the earliest times to the present. His book is the first to offer a concise and comprehensive guide to the full spectrum of spiritual literature; 140 sacred texts are succinctly and lucidly described in relation to cultures that spawned them and in the context of other sacred works of the same time period.

Indeed, this vast collection of global wisdom shows that we are united not only in biology (a proven scientific fact) but also in the deep structures of our thought and mind, our psyche and soul (while being holistically grounded in Nondual Spirit). To successfully negotiate the developmental processes to human maturity (in the first Three Stages of Life) is the gateway for entering the higher transpersonal stages of consciousness evolution (beginning with the Fourth Stage of Life to the ultimate Seventh Stage) [see Appendix I]. As the previous chapter explained, this is best done by "going to school with the Great Tradition" (in Adi Da's words) to study and access the wisdom teachings of humanity's wisest ancestors and make them a living, breathing part of your own life.

Ultimately, this process of development requires a set of spiritual lifestyles and disciplined practices, including extensive meditation, preferably under the guidance of qualified teachers and a genuine Guru. In the past, the foundational Stages of Life were matured by the ethics and morality provided by the mythologies and religious lore of a society and its elders expressing their culture's tradition.[3] Cultural myths and traditional religions are, in large part, forms of social acculturation and control that promote the development of morality based on a particular society's ideals and mores (when successful). This is unquestionably a necessary and legitimate function of the world's religious traditions yet most often is inadequate for complete human maturity to Divine Enlightenment. This is especially true since these views are still largely based on the earlier Stages of Life, not more evolved spiritual perspectives. In other words, we must evolve beyond our inherited religious myths and dogmas including their endless historical variations. To become truly enlightened and to know God for real (or in truth) we must continue to evolve our consciousness beyond (while still including)—or "out-growing" (in Adi Da's words)—the modern scientific and postmodern mind. To realize Enlightenment we must even reach beyond integral vision-logic and yogic mysticism (or shamanic visions), let alone premodern religious thinking. No easy task.

Gaining access to the vast storehouse of knowledge provided by traditional cultures in their observance of human growth, accumulated from millennia of history, is an important guide to our future maturity. Consequently, we can't entirely divorce ourselves from our traditional mythic heritage even in the modern world because we must transcend and *integrate* it since it is such a deep part of us. In this case, prepersonal mythic and magical thinking needs to adequately evolve into, first, personal responsibility and democratic tolerance before entering into transpersonal mysticism. Religious beliefs must evolve into genuine spiritual experiences; rational thinking into ecstatic self-transcendence. Our knowledge quest today is thus about integrating these wisdom treasures from all of the world's sources and cultures. Altogether they are our collective inheritance of the One "Great Tradition" of humankind handed down to everyone from our wisest ancestors regardless of our born cultural heritage or country of origin. Yet, even then, the Enlightened Sages should always be the primary ones pointing the way to our further evolution in consciousness, not just traditional religious leaders and mythic believers, certainly not scientists and scholars alone. We need the Guru-Adepts of humankind for they are God's Gift to everyone now and into the future. Reading the Divine Library of God's Great Tradition of Global Wisdom will verify this perspective.

AVATAR ADI DA'S GLOBAL WISDOM

To assist in our study of humanity's Great Wisdom Tradition, which is extensive in size, Avatar Adi Da has created an enormous bibliography called *The Basket of Tolerance* [see next section] that places thousands of books and scholarly translations (and commentaries) within the framework of the Seven Stages of Life model [see Appendix I]. This is an incredible guide in gaining a deeper (or more profound) understanding of the world's greatest literature and most sacred teachings as explained by an Enlightened Adept—and as a goad to your growth in God. As mentioned, such an extensive or even cursory study of the Great Tradition's Wisdom will also generate a "**culture of tolerance**" (in Adi Da's words), for then people will allow all historical and provincial views to exist within the developmental spectrum of consciousness [see Chapter 1]. This means as the American-born Avatar clarifies: "No one part of the 'Great Tradition' is sufficient by itself" because True Wisdom must be seen as a *global* phenomenon, not the province of any one religion or tradition.

When this is clearly understood and honored then, as Adi Da continues, "No one tradition among many, no one traditional text among many, and no partial group of traditions and traditional texts is sufficient or of exclusively ultimate importance."[4] *All* sacred texts, *all* scriptures and mystical revelations given by women and men alike are to be honored and respected but none exclusively. As Adi Da explains: "All the 'Holy Books' are *our* books, and all of us must go to school and be transformed in our minds by the Great Tradition. Only a critical approach to our inherited and traditional cultural and philosophical limitations of mind and action can purify us of the habit of brute conflict and self-delusion."[5] Only then can we relax our cultic or provincial preference for any single religious tradition or teacher (or Guru) over another, and therefore we may "learn the lesson of tolerance" by embracing *all* the world's people and their unique cultural-religious heritage by seeing and understanding humanity's prior unity in depth.

At times it may seem to you (or anyone) that one tradition or wisdom text, or even any one particular Adept, is "necessary, sufficient, and even absolute," simply because it has personal importance to you or your stage of spiritual growth. Nonetheless, that text or person also occurs within a larger global and historical context as being only *one among many*, though some are indeed more enlightened than others (as the Seven Stages of Life model shows). This alone should motivate a person to be respectful and tolerant of other people's developmental and religious worldviews. A myopic vision distorts our view of reality. Such a broad approach opens the door to discovering the actual authenticity of the world's wisest wisdom buried within the sacred libraries of our most-esteemed ancestors in the long history of the "Divine Library" and Global Wisdom Tradition.

This is the other great advantage in learning how to use the Great Tradition effectively, that is, by studying its Divine Library of sacred texts you will be introduced to the world's wisest men and women who have ever lived or taught throughout the span of human existence. This approach will broaden your perspective from being overtaken by modernity's flatland consumerism to seeing God for real, thus shifting from scientific materialism to the spiritual "sciences"—or "mandalic sciences" (in Wilber's words), i.e., to seeing with a *scientia visionis*.[6] There are countless wise and enlightened individuals from every culture, from every century, from every race and ethnicity, from every religion and spiritual practice who wish us to *realize* our always already (or universal) Enlightened State. These are the individuals who were (and are) living flesh and blood humans, like us, who make up the Great Tradition; they are not just a collection of dry texts and canons of printed words but confessions of (once-) living human beings. This is because the Great Tradition is a *living embodiment* of human wisdom, not just a collection of archaic artifacts. By studying the Great Tradition, book-by-book, you will be introduced to the many **"Spiritual Heroes"** of human history, men and women alike, from all races, and you will see that it is they, the advanced-tip pioneers of human evolution, who are the perpetual fountains of global wisdom and sacred understanding.

Shaman   Priestess   Saint   Yogi   Sage   Siddha

By looking to and honoring the Shamans, Priests/Priestesses, Saints, Yogis, Sages, Siddhas, Maha-Siddhas, Buddhas and Avatars of the Great Tradition (among other highly-evolved humans), we will realize it is they who bear witness to the various stages (or "state-stages") of mystical and spiritual development (seen in the Seven Stages of Life and Integral Theory models). And most important, this means we too can learn about our greatest developmental potentials lying within ourselves (for we're all human), including that of God-Realization and Enlightenment, the universally recognized epitome of human maturity. Divine Enlightenment—variously known as *gnosis, prajna, bodhi, satori, wu, samyaksambodhi*, and dozens of other cultural-specific terms—is when a person transcends the confines of their individual ego and cultural prejudices to realize their true Divine Nature, which is God. In other words, *we are all God* yet this is only found by looking deep within our human heart and transcending our limited self-idea—not discovered in books. Only then do we *realize* that Only God is the ultimate depth of both consciousness and Kosmos. A serious study of the Adepts in the Great Tradition verifies this reality, as Adi Da explains, giving us the means to judge for ourselves the great benefit gained from an Avatar's appearance in our times:

> Study the Great Tradition of the Esoteric, Spiritual, Transcendental, and Divine Realization of Truth. Let everyone who will study the Great Tradition see that the Way That I Teach, although it is a new and most full revelation made under the present circumstances, is the Ancient Secret that is the Seed of All Religions…. My Play is Unique in this Western Circumstance, but I can be understood in the Light of the Great Tradition. Therefore, study the Great Tradition, so that you may Honor and Benefit from My Work.[7]

Such God-Realization, reaffirmed by Adi Da Samraj (and all Adepts), is a universal message found in nearly all the great religions and their sacred scriptures even though religious politics and philosophical doctrines might disagree in specifics (or terminology). Nevertheless, this universal reality has been openly proclaimed by the stream of enlightened souls appearing on Earth, especially the Awakened Adepts who make up the real body (and substance) of the Great Tradition and its Divine Library. Such an evolved understanding is beyond logic and rational philosophy (yet includes them too), beyond religious provincialism and scientific materialism, thus it must be discovered or re-discovered and *realized for oneself.* As Adi Da has made clear, proving once more he is *not* from the "Talking School" (even after writing dozens of books full of talks and essays): "The Real process is that wherein [God-]Realization is made Real. Everything else is talk…. Therefore, true Realization requires ego-transcending devotional surrender and Ultimate Grace."[8] Turning attention to the Guru as God, turning to the Avatar as a *process* of Realization thus becomes a serious *spiritual* matter (involving Spirit-Baptism and so on), not a childish cultic mind game, as many critics assume [see Chapter 20].[9]

This is why the most-evolved Sages and Siddhas of the Great Tradition are here to guide us and point the way beyond our cultural and historical limitations. At times their words and thoughts, poems and ecstatic speech have been written down and recorded for posterity. This is why we must read and study their sacred texts, our inherited guidebooks to their revealed wisdom and our divine potential. Yet at the same time we don't want to slip into just becoming "**Talking School**" proponents [see Chapter 4]. Rather, we also must attend to the "**Practicing School**" by engaging in actual disciplines (*sadhana*) preferably under the guidance and transmission (*Satsang*) of a genuine Guru, an authentic Adept [see Chapter 22]. Adi Da Samraj is one of those Adepts, as he summarily explains the Transcendental yet all-embracing (Immanent) nature of Divine (Seventh Stage) Enlightenment:

> In summary, the ultimate Realization of life is Transcendental Enlightenment. Such Enlightenment transcends all the limitations and conventions of the discriminating or functional mind. Enlightenment is not Itself merely freedom from the discriminating mind. Rather, it is the ultimately unspeakable Realization of the Real Condition of self and world.[10]

Teaching that we are all God or Divine, that this truth of Prior Unity is our natural condition in the Kosmos, is our greatest advantage—the "Great Help" and Blessing—offered to us by our glorious inheritance from God's Great Tradition of Global Wisdom. This Perennial (or "ever-repeating") Wisdom, given from our wisest ancestors, can rescue us from the maze of the modern/postmodern mind, from the mythic tension of embattled religions, to help us integrate the best of the past *into the present* to create a brighter future, a real Integral Age, perhaps, yes, even an Enlightened Era. Yet it is up to each and every one of us to use our discriminative intelligence to cultivate and come to know about this global sacred inheritance, to read the Divine Library for ourselves, which is our natural birthright embodying the glory of humanity's highest potentials. May we all be blessed to embrace and learn from our Global Tradition of enlightened human wisdom given to us from Awakened Adepts, whenever we have been born, wherever we may now live.

SEVEN SCHOOLS OF GOD-TALK:
THE BASKET OF TOLERANCE

Once upon a time, most of the world's esoteric Spiritual Teachings were hidden from the public. Consequently, the average masses of humanity have been mostly practicing exoteric religious rituals and superstitious magic combined with petitioner prayers, not engaging in enlightened yogas. In today's Modern Age, however, such teachings and texts, which were once reserved secret instructions passed down orally from Master to student, are now available at your local bookstore or on the Internet, even if they're still not widely known. A growing library of sacred teachings from the East, plus countless unearthed documents rescued by archeology and modem scholars, have provided the testimony given by authentic practitioners and Adept-Realizers gathered together from the world's spiritual traditions.[11] Their books and confessions—a "Divine Library" [see Chapter 3]—can now be closely examined and studied by anyone while their prescribed practices can be engaged and presently implemented, though preferably under the guidance of a competent teacher and genuine Guru. The study of "**comparative religions**" has become popular in universities and colleges around the world so that now a plethora of translated texts from all the sacred traditions can be readily purchased to be housed in your own personal library. Many impressive intellectuals, including authentic practitioners (not just scholars), from D. T. Suzuki, Alan Watts, Frithjof Schuon, Mircea Eliade, Joseph Campbell, Huston Smith, Seyyed Hossein Nasr, from Robert Thurman to Lex Hixon to Ken Wilber (among many, many others) have greatly advanced the West's appreciation for this total Great Tradition and, in particular, the wisdom-heritage of the East.

However, since the Western-born Adept Adi Da Samraj is not just a scholar or professor but an Enlightened Avatar personally familiar with the complete range of spiritual experiences, from those of kundalini yoga to the highest mystical Realizations, he brings a unique clarity to the Great Tradition of human and spiritual wisdom. Since his comprehensive "map" of the Seven Stages of Life presents a unique model of human development from birth to Enlightenment, he also provides a structural scheme to untangle the diverse spectrum of mystical experiences cataloged throughout human history. In this case, one of the beneficial results of this investigative clarification has been an annotated bibliography where Adi Da has listed many of the most essential publications (including books, audio, and video recordings) offered to humanity via the perspective of our Great Global Tradition of human spirituality. As mentioned, he calls this collective bibliography "**The Basket of Tolerance**" (still unpublished in final form), hence the Avatar clarifies:

> In addition to Serving Divine Self-Realization in you, one of the things I am doing, in the form of this *Basket of Tolerance*, is suggesting and communicating reasonable reasons for the general acceptance of, or re-acceptance of, a certain kind of authority, and its integration into the cultural life of humanity in general....
>
> What should be authoritative is the Great Tradition as a whole. In other words, people should not be provincialized by sectarian doctrines. People must take seriously the greater aspects of the Great Tradition and not be localized or diminished in their humanity by identification with merely exoteric things, or a lower order of things. If the Great Tradition is one's tradition, one will inherit even the greatest "considerations", through to the Seventh Stage of Life.[12]

One of the "Great Gifts" and intellectual tools that World-Teacher Adi Da has given to humanity in order to better see and appreciate the beauty and universal depth of the Great Tradition is this amazing compendium of published books, CDs, DVDs, and other media, where each is categorized into its respective Stage of Life or general perspective (or "point of view"). Known as *The Basket of Tolerance: A Guide to Perfect Understanding of the One*

and Great Tradition of Humankind (among several other subtitles), Adi Da
had worked on this book for several decades, at least since the early 1970s,
originally calling it "**The Seven Schools of God-Talk**" [see next chapter].[13]
Unfortunately, it is unpublished in final form (as of 2021). Perhaps the world
waits for no other more important single book to help guide us out of the intolerance and non-cooperation often seen among today's religions and nations
and peoples. As an extensive bibliography, it has grown over the years (part of
the reason it is still unpublished) as new books and media are constantly fitted
within its structures and categories (now run by Adi Da's librarians). Avatar
Adi Da explains his intention:

> *The Basket of Tolerance* is an essential gathering of traditional and
> modern literature, which I offer to all students and practitioners of the
> Way of the Heart (and all students of the traditions of humankind),
> as a useful and valuable resource for study relative to the historical
> traditions of human culture, practical self-discipline, religion, reli-
> gious mysticism, "esoteric" Spirituality, and Transcendental Wisdom.
> I have selected, arranged, and annotated (or commented upon) the
> many books listed here, in order to provide a basic, inclusive, and com-
> prehensive (but not overlong) representation (and Revelation) of the
> "**Great Tradition**" (of common Wisdom-inheritance) of humankind.[14]

In addition to a list of books, Adi Da has authored accompanying
essays addressing some of the authors and their work, from scholars to scientists to philosophers to Enlightened Adept-Realizers and even other incarnated
Avatars. As of today, *The Basket of Tolerance* (and its bibliographies based on
the Seven Stages of Life) has been integrated into some of the final volumes
of writings published by Adi Da, particularly in *The Gnosticon* (2010), *The
Pneumaton* (2011), and also his magnum opus, *The Aletheon* (2009), supplemented by a summary edited review of *The First Three Stages of Life* (2011).
Avatar Adi Da has explained that such a global (and historical) review is an
important part of his Teaching-Work:

> In the time in which we now live, when the ideas of all the
> provinces of Earth are now gathering together for the first time in
> human history, and all absolute dogmas find themselves casually

associated... the complex mind of Everyman and Everywoman is remembering itself all at once. Therefore, every individual is obliged to discover the Truth again by penetrating the bizarre consciousness of all the races combined as one.

Those who are seriously involved in the study and agonizing practice of religious and esoteric Spiritual teachings are now confronted by a great mass of doctrines, absolute creeds, sacred histories, secret formulae, and perfect paths. What is the Truth? What stands out in the wilderness of doctrines as singly as the "I" of the body-mind?[15]

Although the Gracious Guru is critical at times, Avatar Adi Da fully honors the Great Tradition as a whole, especially the Awakened Adepts who have appeared within it and are the roots of its Wisdom. Thus he concludes: "We could argue for the relative completeness of almost any tradition, if we would only examine every aspect of it, every school, every moment, every Adept within it."[16] From such a perspective, I believe, is how any interested scholar in the future can help unravel the beauty and true significance of the Great Tradition of Global Wisdom as a whole. This includes recognizing the various Stages of Life that any given religious-spiritual-mystical system is set within the inherited history of humankind. Indeed, unless we study the Great Tradition as a whole, we have no overall context in which to genuinely understand the significance of any spiritual teaching or Enlightened Adept who has come here to serve our own Awakening to Real God (not simply the belief in the mythic gods and goddesses told in books and fables).

Perennial Global Adept-Realizers

Consequently, Adi Da often says: "Let the traditions be your entertainment."[17] Reading books and sacred literature with discriminative intelligence, grounded in an understanding of the Seven Stages of Life, will grow us in intelligence and conscious awareness. Even if we do not remember much of what we've read, it will still serve us because it helps release the "kinks" in our mind. As Beloved Adi Da points out: "Everything influences you.... The Great Tradition influences you at a deeper level, because those ideas address primary matters.... You may not remember something, but your mind will be clearer afterwards."[18] Since the Avatar has taken in the entire world with a "gigantic gulp" to make sense of it all, while still retaining his humor—one reason why, for instance, he originally named his library "American Trickster"—we too will find it is easier to make better sense of it all by seeing the larger global perspective. Thus, the knowledge and wisdom of the Great Tradition will serve our spiritual practice and devotional attitude, help our mind, as well as heal our hearts (and psychological wounds).

The Basket of Tolerance itself demonstrates the supreme effectiveness of using the Seven Stages of Life model as a beneficial guide in making our way through the mass of literature and often-conflicting philosophies and spiritual teachings that are contained in this "Global Tradition" covering thousands of years of recorded history. For example, using the Seven Stages model helps us discriminate the values and differences between the paths of shamanistic tribes (earth magic), mythic civilizations (sky magic), religious priesthoods (astral religions), philosophies of reason and science (scientific materialism), as well as the various mystical teachings of Yogis, Saints, Sages, and Siddhas (transcendental mysticism), each containing their own point of view and inherent limitations short of Divine Enlightenment. From his enlightened perspective, Avatar Adi Da clarifies that the purpose in making such a global presentation is *to correct* the eclectic approach people often use in selecting their preferences to the world's smorgasbord of traditions:

> Rather than merely putting all these eggs [traditions] in a basket to be sampled at random (or in one soup, to be tasted all in one bite), I have communicated a critical approach to understanding and transcending the limitations of the Great Tradition of human existence. Therefore, all the "Holy Books" are *our* books, and all of us must go to school and be transformed in our minds by the Great Tradition. Only a critical approach to our inherited and tra-

ditional cultural and philosophical limitations of mind and action can purify us of the habit of brute conflict and self-delusion.[19]

God's Great Tradition of Global Wisdom, in other words, is our inherited and innate right as spiritual beings born human. Yet it is still every single person's personal responsibility to become familiar with this sacred inheritance and then cultivate its higher ideals and evolutionary potentials. By studying the Perennial Philosophy, or the underlying universal core of the Great Tradition, we will also discover the veracity of Guru Yoga and the critical importance of establishing a sacred relationship with an Adept-Realizer in Satsang [see Chapter 7]. Then the Divine Gift of Enlightened Wisdom, made brighter by Adi Da Samraj, will continue to shine around the planet to initiate a greater understanding and global culture of unity. As the Great Tradition shows, only the Awakened Adepts, the Enlightened Sages and Buddhas, can help awaken us to Divine God-Realization [see Chapter 8]. Therefore, let us avail ourselves openly to this Divine Blessing and Help that's been bequeathed to us by our most Enlightened Ancestors, but particularly by appreciating the American-born Avatar Adi Da Samraj, and thus actively engage in the Sacred Ordeal to which they all are calling us.

Chapter 2 Endnotes

1. See: *The Divine Library: A Comprehensive Reference Guide to the Sacred Texts and Spiritual Literature of the World* (1992) by Rufus C. Camphausen; this book is one of the most encompassing guides to the world's spiritual literature and their dates of origin that I know of.

2. Other examples of compilations of the "Divine Library" and its global wisdom: *A Treasury of Traditional Wisdom* (1971) by Whitall N. Perry; *The Enlightened Heart* (1989) and *The Enlightened Mind* (1991) edited by Stephen Mitchell; *The World's Wisdom: Sacred Texts of the World's Religions* (1994) by Philip Novak, a companion book to Huston Smith's *The World's Religions* (1958, 1991, 2009), among many others.

3. See: Adi Da Samraj, "Esotericism Requires Culture" talk from September 26, 2004, on the CD *The Way Begins With Realization*, Track 1.

4. All quotes in the paragraph from Ad Da Samraj, "Preface: The Gathering of the Seven Schools of God-Talk" in *The Basket of Tolerance* (forthcoming).

5. Adi Da Samraj [Da Free John], *Nirvanasara* (1982), p. 199.

6. See: Ken Wilber, *Eye to Eye* (1983, 1990, 2001).

7. Adi Da Samraj [Da Free John], *The Dawn Horse Testament* (1985), 132-133, 134 [all caps not included].

8. Adi Da Samraj, *The Gnosticon* (2010), p. 488.

9. See: *In God's Company: Guru-Adepts As Agents for Enlightenment in the Integral Age* (2022) by Brad Reynolds.

10. Adi Da Samraj [Da Free John], "The Seventh School of God-Talk" (talk) in "Preface" to *The Song of the Supreme Self: Astavakra Gita* (1982) translated by Radhakamal Mukerjee, p. 67.

11. See: "Accessing the Great Tradition: An Introduction to The Basket of Tolerance" by Richard Schorske in *The Laughing Man*, Vol. 7, No. 1, pp. 8-13.

12. Adi Da Samraj, April 6, 1987 in *Free Daist*, Vol. 3, No. 4/5, 1992-1993 ["Stages of Life" capped].

13. See: *The Basket of Tolerance* (prepublication editions, 1988, 1991) by Adi Da Samraj; also see: "The Great Tradition" talk (cassette) given on January 22, 1983: "The first thing I want to discuss is something relevant to the book called The Seven Schools of God-Talk, which I've been working on now for many years. I could say I began to work on this book before I created the Institution [Ashram of Adidam]. The basic content of this book is a bibliography that's currently about four thousand books or so placed in a unique order relative to the Stages of Life, which is why it's called The Seven Schools of God-Talk."

14. Adi Da Samraj, Preface to *The Basket of Tolerance (On The Seven Schools Of The One And Great Tradition Of God-Talk)* in *The Laughing Man*, Vol. 7, No. 1, 1987, p. 13.

15. Adi Da Samraj, July 5, 1979 in *Free Daist*, Vol. 3, No. 4/5, 1992-1993.

16. Adi Da Samraj, "The Seventh School of God-Talk" (essay) in "Preface" to *The Song of the Supreme Self: Astavakra Gita* (1982) translated by Radhakamal Mukerjee, p. 22.

17. See: James Steinberg, "Pure From the Beginning: Beloved Adi Da's Call for the Universal Acceptance of the Great Tradition As the Common Inheritance of Humankind" in *Adi Da Samrajashram*, Vol. 1, No. 4, 2015, p. 28.

18. Adi Da Samraj, *Adi Da Samrajashram*, Vol. 1, No. 4, 2015, p. 28.

19. Adi Da Samraj [Da Free John], *Nirvanasara* (1982), pp. 199-200.

THREE

ACCESSING GLOBAL WISDOM WITH AN AVATAR'S HELP

Since you become what you meditate on, you should meditate on,
or give feeling-attention to, the Absolute—which,
in the bodily (human) form of the Spiritual Master,
is your Greatest Advantage.

— **Adi Da Samraj**, *The Aletheon*[1]

DIVINE HELP FROM AVATAR ADI DA

The critical importance of the encompassing task undertaken by Adi Da's *The Basket of Tolerance* cannot be overemphasized [see previous chapter]. This is because when examining the universal scope of the Great Tradition's "Divine Library" we will notice there is a varied and often conflicting array of traditions, religions, practices of spirituality, and tenets of philosophy each claiming to represent "the Truth." Yet usually each perspective is limited to unenlightened (or not yet Fully Enlightened) presumptions about the spectrum (or variety) of "mystical" experiences associated with the esoteric anatomy of the human being (including gross, subtle, causal, and nondual states). As Avatar Adi Da has abundantly made clear this spectral variation of human and mystical experiences follows the unfolding development outlined in the Seven Stages of Life [see Appendix I]. For example, one scholar (and devotee of Adi Da) briefly outlined some of the characteristics evident in these various wavelengths of mystical possibilities found in Adi Da's Seven Stages of Life model:

> Ordinary (Third Stage) "geniuses" tend to be limited in their vision by identification with the intellect and the will. "Saintly" (Fourth Stage) personalities are generally devoted to a Divine Influence, which they regard as necessarily "other" or separate, and therefore they fail to manifest the Blessing powers that are demonstrated by those who have fully Realized the Divine Reality.
>
> Advanced practitioners of yoga and the mystical paths (Fifth Stage) often regard the Divine to be coincident with particular mystical experiences of the brain and nervous system, or with the temporary transcendence of body and mind. Sixth-Stage Realizers have discovered their identity with the "Witness-Consciousness," though they still operate under the subtle presumption that this Witness-Consciousness is separate from what is witnessed.
>
> But the Realized or Enlightened individual in the Seventh Stage of Life transcends all the kinds of knowledge and experience that bind one's attention to the search to be free, while preventing full Realization of Freedom itself. Such Realizers have transcended all knowledge and experience and the desire for "alternative states." They are simply present in loving service to others, non-separate, manifesting Blessing Power of the open heart and the Radiance of Transcendental Being.[2]

The Basket of Tolerance (and Seven Stages of Life) helps to clarify these confusing distinctions of traditional mysticism when placed within the context of God-Realization or from the nondual perspective of Divine Enlightenment. By doing so, Adi Da is providing systematic access to the entire range of human wisdom found in the total Great Tradition of Global Wisdom. Indeed, Ken Wilber, for example, has gained great benefit in closely studying Adi Da's views and incorporating them into his own. Nevertheless, Avatar Adi Da explains that his own Realization is the foundation of his insights, not simply one of scholarly interpretation and study:

> What I affirm to you is the basic force of the Great Tradition as
> a whole. I also demonstrate its fullness through My own Life and
> Work. And I provide a Wisdom-Teaching that is immediately useful
> and that is not merely a synthetic version of the Great Tradition.
> This Wisdom-Teaching is not compounded via scholarship, but it is
> a direct expression of My own Life and Realization.[3]

By following Avatar Adi Da's guideline and map we may study the world's
sacred scriptures (and other texts) to get a "basic education" in the total Global
Wisdom Tradition of humankind. This knowledge of our inherited wisdom
can then be considered by a practitioner to properly distinguish and recognize authentic spiritual practices as well as egoic methods of improvement.
Most importantly, the study of the world's Wisdom Tradition will confirm the
veracity and authenticity and *necessity* for genuine Guru Yoga in serving the
fruitfulness and completion of anyone's transpersonal spiritual life.

Such a comprehensive reading list of our Divine Library becomes particularly successful when it is offered by a *global* Adept—*Jagad Guru*—here to
serve the entire world, not just the various factions (and ultimately false) distinctions between East and West. Adi Da clarifies: "I am Communicating in a
global context, as well as a context beyond this particular limit of human existence. I am Communicating in the global context of humanity. I am Speaking
to the Great Tradition of all possible experiences, and orientations, even to all
future humanity."[4] In other words, it does us little good to have access to this
massive "Divine Library" if we can't make sense of it. This view was appreciated in the early 1980s in an editorial commentary to Adi Da's Preface, "The
Seventh School of God-Talk," first published by The Dawn Horse Press in a
translation of the *Astavakra Gita* (translated by pandit Radhakamal Mukerjee), titled *The Song of the Self Supreme* (1982):

> For the first time in history, an Adept with access to the essential
> literatures of the Great Tradition of religion and esoteric spirituality
> has "systematized" the world's sacred writings by carefully choosing
> and ordering them according to the Seven Stages of Life. Such a
> work is of great importance to spiritual practitioners and scholars of

religion. And it is of great value to men and women who may be both attracted and bothered by the hodgepodge of often unillumined and misleading claims offered as or in the name of Truth. Thus, through systematic study of the books contained in this bibliography and intelligent application of [Adi Da Samraj's] critical instruction, one may become "educated" in a field of study little known in the modern Western world.[5]

The entire Teaching and Divine Presence of Avatar Adi Da Samraj is available for all humankind to study (and possibly practice) now and into the future, including his gracious analysis of human spirituality.[6] As the Heart-Master explains:

> I am Calling people specifically to the Way of the Heart in My Company, that is true. But even before I do that, through *The Basket of Tolerance* I am Calling people to the authority represented by the Great Tradition as a whole, not any particular sect or exoteric version of it but the Great Tradition as a totality, as a total history of Divine Revelation.[7]

What could be a greater or more important task and Gift than this transmission of Divine Revelation? Through the study of *The Basket of Tolerance* and by listening to the Wisdom-Revelation of Adi Da Samraj in particular, we see that the Avatar is providing a way for humanity to realize our common sacred inheritance as one human race. And through this study of the Great Tradition, any student or serious practitioner may be informed and inspired in the ordeal of engaging human growth with transpersonal spiritual practices to realize Transcendental Enlightenment for himself or herself. However, in doing so we must move beyond the biased limitations and presumptions that we moderns have been indoctrinated in since birth with our inherited religious provincialisms, cultural prejudices, and scientific materialism, the primary worldviews of our troubling times surrounding (and infecting) our global population. In other words, it takes more than knowledge to be truly free, it takes Divine Grace.

THE AVATAR'S GLOBAL WORK
FOR HUMANKIND

his is a unique time in human history. Not only has our immaturity prevented us from recognizing our universal unity as one human race, but our religious provincialism and inherited preferences prevent us from seeing that we all worship One God, though seen from different perspectives. Part of this cultural blindness has been caused by the fact that never before has an Adept truly seen the global reach of humankind like one can do now with worldwide communications and knowledge of every culture and nation on Earth. With Adi Da Samraj, for the first time we have a genuine Avatar born in the West at the start of World War II, who Realized the Enlightened Wisdom of the East as authentically as any previous Adept-Guru ever had. This means that for the first time in history we have an Adept with access to all of the essential literatures of the "Great Tradition" and its "Divine Library" of religious and esoteric spirituality [see Chapters 1-2]. With Adi Da, therefore, we have an Adept who has brilliantly "systematized" the world's sacred writings according to the Seven Stages of Life, even carefully choosing and ordering them in a vast compendium (*The Basket of Tolerance*).[8] However, it's important to remember Adi Da's Re-Awakening and Enlightened State are in no way a product of his studying or reading sacred scriptures, but was a result of his sadhana (actual spiritual practices) and his relationship with a variety of Spiritual Masters and Adept-Gurus in the twentieth century.[9]

This review and understanding of our global inheritance is a very important aspect of Avatar Adi Da's "**Universal Blessing**" **Work**, even extending beyond what he offers as Sat-Guru (in Satsang) to his devotees and all beings in the Reality-Way of Adidam Ruchiradam. Any man or woman, any scholar or religious practitioner, any seeker or confused person, may study and turn their attention to Adi Da's universal review of human spirituality and finally see the "Big Picture" or how it is all related, and also, how it may be critiqued. The jumble of unillumined and misleading claims by various religions and their teachers does little to clarify the real Way of Enlightenment. Adi Da, therefore, is correcting this error of humankind's misunderstanding and inherited religious legacy. The American-born yet global Avatar clarifies his intentions:

> My Work in the world is to communicate the summary of religious and Spiritual Wisdom, so that humankind may again be devoted to the Way of Life in Truth, even now that all religious and spiritual cultures confront us collectively and at once (rather than, as before, when each individual was usually confronted only by the primary institutional or cultic influence in power in his nation or province). The literature [and Teaching] I have produced... serves to clarify the Truth and the Way of Life based on a profound consideration and Realization in the present, prior to all of the doctrines or persuasions of our inherited mind.[10]

Adi Da is therefore helping to educate the spiritually bereft population of the modern world, East and West, North and South, with a true understanding and appreciation of our global spiritual legacy. He does this in at least three following ways:

1. **Restoring** to rightful prominence the treasury of the world's highest Spiritual Teachings from the perspective of Divine Enlightenment as demonstrated by the humanity's greatest Adept-Realizers, women and men, whose collective history is generally unknown or not properly acknowledged and rightly appreciated;

2. **Purifying** religious fundamentalism and the egoic cultism that tends to emerge once the influence of the founding Adepts are forgotten or distorted by the activity of the separate self, whether mentally, philosophical, religiously, or spiritually;

3. **Re-evaluating** existing schools and paths of traditional religion and spirituality and thus helping to realign them to the ultimate wisdom of Divine Enlightenment or the Seventh Stage of Life.[11]

There is no greater advantage in understanding the religious and spiritual history of humankind—God's Great Tradition of Global Wisdom—than having a modern-day Adept-Realizer appear in the West to clarify universal spiritual truths, as we now have with Avatar Adi Da . This book encourages you to each go study and read Adi Da to find out for yourself (and whatever your response may be is your business). I believe there is no greater opportunity for humankind to create a peaceful, truly spiritual, new global order to establish a true "Integral Age" of universal possibility based on a radical understanding allowing Enlightened Wisdom and Real Happiness to shine forth, as Adi Da summarizes:

> There does appear to be a problem reflected in the exclusive and absolutist claims of advocates and practitioners of the various traditions.... For this reason, the Great Tradition may seem to be a mixed bag of absolutes and absolutists, as if hundreds of lunatics were all claiming to be independent God with the right to rule over all others.[12]

> Though there are many historical traditions of "religion" and Spirituality, there is, in Truth, a single Great Tradition.... The Great Tradition of humankind is a universal tradition, because it is based not only on the Great and Indivisible Non-Conditional Reality, but also on the prior unity of conditionally manifested existence and the commonality and prior unity of human beings themselves.[13]

Adi Da's critical review is not simply made to thrust his view above all others in an absolutist fashion but rather he is promoting the view of the "Transcendental Consciousness" revealed in Divine Enlightenment, regardless of tradition or historical perspective. Such a Realization does not leave the phenomenal world or universe behind, but rather embraces it by transcending it in its true Condition of "Transcendental Realism" which is "Real God" (in Adi Da's words). The Heart-Master explains:

> The tacit Transcendental Consciousness as the Obvious Condition is the natural or native Realization of Reality, Self, Being, Love-Bliss, or Radiant Happiness. It is not dependent on any state or conception in body or mind, but it may be apparently obstructed by the various phenomenal states and relations of body and mind.... Therefore, the ultimate Realization of Consciousness makes possible a Transfigured or inherently Enlightened phenomenal existence in any phenomenal world. Just so, the Enlightened disposition is such that, without

seeking to seclude Consciousness from phenomena, It will ultimately Outshine (and always already inherently Outshines) all phenomenal worlds and self states.[14]

Only a Divine Enlightened being or Avatar could ever make such clarifying statements. This is why the Seven Stages of Life model is so useful and effective for it makes the Seventh Stage of Life, or Transcendental Divine Enlightenment—Real God-Realization—the ultimate view or ground of the entire process. This is the Way of the Heart as the whole body, a unique esoteric perspective Taught by Avatar Adi Da Samraj. Adi Da explains (and embraces) the entire Great Tradition (and the Six Stages of Life) in relation to the "Way That I Teach" or the Seven Stage Realization:

> The traditions of the first Six Stages of Life generally seek to Realize that Radiant Transcendental Consciousness on the basis of arguments and practices based in the phenomenal and thus inherently egoic point of view of the born being.... However, all traditions that achieve Completeness ultimately transcend their original propositions and practices in the Transcendental Awakening of the Seventh Stage of Life, and that Awakening can only be expressed (if it is to be described at all) via the ultimate language of Transcendentalism.
>
> My own life and Realization confirm this, and I have, therefore, argued for a Way of understanding and practice that immediately transcends the phenomenally based and egoic "problems" and propositions of the first Six Stages of Life. The Way That I Teach is founded on the Realization of Consciousness (or Radiant Transcendental Being) in the Seventh Stage of Life, and I argue for a consideration and a practice that make the radical understanding (rather than the conventional practice) of the first Six Stages of Life (and their phenomenal or egoic propositions) into the basis for direct Awakening into the Realization of the Truth of the Seventh Stage of Life.[15]

Avatar Adi Da has thus reviewed the Great Tradition of humankind while critiquing its limitations that fall short of Seventh Stage Divine Enlightenment.

The chart below (originally created by James Steinberg[16]) summarizes the Seven Stages of Life and their relationship to some of the major religious traditions as they will be used throughout this book [also see Appendix I]:

6th Stage
Heart on Right
Causal
Advaita Vedanta
Mahayana Buddhism
Zen
Tibetan Vajrayana
Jainism
Taoism

7th Stage
Amrita Nadi
(Regeneration)
Reality-Way of Adidam Ruchiradam
Conscious Light
"premonitory" 7th Stage Texts

3rd Stage
Thinking Brain
Mind / Science
Philosophy
Social Wisdom

Ajna Door
Brain Core
Shabd Yoga
Nada Yoga

4th Stage
Heart in Middle
Subtle
Devotional Spirituality
Divine awareness

Ascended 5th Stage
Nirvikalpa Samadhi
High Subtle
Emptiness-Void
Theravada Buddhism
Mahayana Buddhism

5th Stage
Ascending Spinal Line
Pantajali "Ashtanga" Yoga
Six Yogas of Naropa
Kundalini Yoga
Taoist Yoga

Circle of
Conductivity

4th Stage
Descending Frontal Line
Hinduism
Bhakti Yoga
Japa Yoga
Classical Mediterranean Spirituality
Jewish Mysticism
Christian Mysticism
Islamic Mysticism (Sufi)
Pure Land Buddhism

1st Stage
Physical Body
(Navel)
Health
Exercise
Birth and Death

2nd Stage
Heart on Left
Emotional Being
Emotional-Sexual
Feeling
Etheric

© chart by Brad Reynolds

Seven Stages of Life in the Great Tradition
via the Esoteric Anatomy of the Extended Body-Mind
as Revealed by Avatar Adi Da Samraj

Adi Da uses the Seven Stages of Life to clarify the entire Great Tradition of human spirituality and human developmental growth. There are several esoteric models of human development, such as Aurobindo's "Integral Yoga" and Ken Wilber's "Spectrum of Consciousness" that show the same essential evolutionary movement, but none is as clarifying at Adi Da's (indeed, Wilber's model was closely based on the Seven Stage model though expanded it by using developmental psychology). Adi Da clarified, for one, how the various Seven Stages of Life correspond to the "**esoteric anatomy**" of all human beings and how they play out in the Great Tradition. In the Preface to *The Song of the Self Supreme* (1982), Avatar Adi Da clarified some of the qualities the various

Stages of Life as they are reflected in the traditional religious approaches to the Divine (as this book will continue to review):

> The dualistic devotional idea of Realization proposed by the Fourth Stage traditions (and the conventional exotericism of popular religion) is a laudable aspiration for beginners, but it is not the final Realization.
>
> Similarly, the Fifth Stage point of view of mystical yoga, which associates Realization with the experience of various kinds of bodily bliss, psychisms, visions, internal sounds, yogic powers, and ascent to trance-states of mind or other subtle phenomenal regions of Nature, while being laudable as an evolutionary developmental of human potential, is only a transitional view and must be gone beyond.
>
> Likewise, the Sixth Stage point of view of inversion and strategic dissociation from phenomena is not an end in itself... Individuals and traditions that speak from the point of view of one or another of the first Six Stages of Life generally conceive of life in some problematic form, and thus they regard the experiential and conceptual phenomena that tend to accompany the practice at their stage to be a solution that is to be regarded as ultimate Salvation, Liberation, or Realization....
>
> The Divine Reality cannot be presumed as a fact in the mind. It must be Realized through a process of literal transcendence of the conditional world, body, mind, and self.... If the Way of direct Transcendental Realization is practiced, the body-mind will ultimately exist without concern in a natural state, and ordinary actions and obligations will be spontaneously or naturally performed until death or Translation in the Radiant Transcendental Being.[17]

From this perspective, then, and with the Avatar's Help, we shall proceed with our review and consideration of humankind's Great Tradition of Global Wisdom. Let's start with a brief review of the Higher Stages of Life (4-7), some of their basic characteristics and errors, and some texts that reflect their essential perspectives.

WISDOM TEXTS: EVALUATING THE TRANSPERSONAL STAGES OF LIFE

By using Avatar Adi Da's "**Seven Stages of Life**" model, as suggested above, it is possible to outline an evaluation method to adjudicate the approximate level of development rendered by various religio-spiritual texts and their corresponding Adepts (or authors). As I have suggested, Ken Wilber "**Spectrum of Consciousness**" model (including its AQAL version) follows the same basic developmental pattern through the first Six Stages of Life, where the Seventh Stage transcends all stages and states (or "state-stages") of consciousness as Transcendental Divine Awakening [see Appendix I]. I present both of these models as a scholar, as an interested intellectual-pandit (and beginner practitioner), therefore I lay no claim that my presentation is endorsed by Adi Da (or Adidam) or by Wilber. However, I hope that you, the reader, find them useful in that they do offer a wonderful outline to the stages of life and existence that we are all navigating during our lifetime. Importantly, both of these models ultimately point to God-Realization or Divine Enlightenment as being the genuine purpose of human life, as do all the esoteric traditions in the Global Wisdom Tradition of humankind.

The tables below list a short summary of the basic characteristics outlining the perspective or point of view highlighted by the **Fourth through Seventh Stages of Life** (4–7) and some of their **Wisdom Texts**. This "**Spectrum of Mysticism**" is a fluid spectrum with no distinct borders or boundaries yet does exhibit certain identifiable characteristics, best summarized by Avatar Adi Da.

I have relied on my own understanding to select the books and texts that I feel fit into Adi Da's basic overall schema. Please consult Adi Da's Teaching-Word (specially *The Basket of Tolerance*) for the official placement of the many books and sacred texts by the Avatar (and his librarians) within the Seven Stage model. Nevertheless, I do believe my views approximate the general scheme being suggested by Adi Da and Ken Wilber. A summary review of the basic characteristics in the **Higher Stages of Life**—and their principal "**error**"—are listed in the following tables:

4th Stage of Life		**NATURE MYSTICISM** Prophets / Priesthood Devotional Saints Bhakti Yogis

4th Stage Characteristics: Mature Waking State (Lower Psychic)

4th Stage Error: doubt, inherent separation of the Divine and personal self

- **Integral** = harmonized body-mind (centaur); mature first Three Stages of Life

- **Devotional** = dedicated to higher development (and evolution of consciousness)

- **Right Life** = spiritual disciplines / meditation / conscious exercise-conductivity

- **Psychic-Nature Mysticism** = communion with Nature and psychic archetypes

5th Stage of Life		**SUBTLE MYSTICISM** Kundalini Yogis Ascended Saints

5th Stage Characteristics: Subtle-Dream States / Higher Psychic / Kundalini ascension / soul-based

5th Stage Error: Seeking or clinging to subtle lights, sounds, visions, mystical phenomena (Vishnu complex)

- **Yogic** = disciplined breath / subtle energies / kundalini activation

- **Esoteric anatomy** = "inner alchemy" / advanced conductivity

- **Subtle-Deity Mysticism** = low: kundalini ascends chakras; high: One God/dess

6th Stage of Life		**CAUSAL MYSTICISM** Jnani Yogis Arhats Enlightened Sages

6th Stage Characteristics: Deep Sleep / Causal Root (Witness) / True Self

6th Stage Error: Transcendental exclusion of world and Kosmos

- **Witness consciousness** = Turiya / pure awareness; Feeling of Being; Arhat

- **Satori** = Enlightened state: no self (*anatma*) + Emptiness-Void (*sunyata*)

- **No practices** = Liberated state; "Perfect Practice" (early); conscious process

7th Stage of Life		NONDUAL MYSTICISM
		**Enlightened Siddhas** **Buddhas** **Avatars**

7th Stage Characteristics: Nondual Mysticism / Turiya-to-Turiyatita

7th Stage Error: No Error / spontaneous liberated / Divine Consciousness Itself

• **"Open Eyes"** = Sahaj samadhi / "Perfect Practice" (complete)

• **Sunyata-Karunā** = wisdom-compassion; enlightened self in world; Bodhisattva

• **"Outshining"** = Bhava samadhi / "Translation" (after death)

Higher Stages of Life (4 – 7)
Based on the Teaching of Adi Da Samraj
(animal icons selected by Adi Da Samraj[18])

© table by Brad Reynolds

*B*efore reviewing in greater detail some of the sacred scriptures of the Great Tradition based on the Seven Stages of Life model, Adi Da summarizes his Gift to humanity when considering God's Great Tradition of Global Wisdom:

> All the great schools ultimately fulfill themselves in the Seventh Stage disposition. The Way that I Teach, the Way of Radical Understanding or Divine Ignorance, is the Way based on this Seventh Stage wisdom. This Teaching includes a critical commentary on the Great Tradition. We naturally feel that our moment of spiritual culture is built upon or presumes the Great Tradition as its past. Not any one province or segment of the Great Tradition but the Great Tradition as a whole is our tradition. Yet we do not follow that Great Tradition dogmatically. We simply have an affinity for it, based on what we understand, in our consideration, to be the Way. Ours is an affinity based on critical understanding.[19]

A more detailed review of the **Higher Stages of Life** (4–7) are listed in the tables below, followed by a partial **Reading List** selected by the author from the "**Divine Library**" of the World's Global Wisdom Texts that generally correspond to the transpersonal Stages of Life [see following pages]:

4th Stage of Life 	

4th Stage Wisdom Texts – Psychic Mysticism

Stage Characteristics:

- **Nature Mysticism / spiritual devotion / self-surrender** (opening)
- **Shamans / Priesthoods** (priestess/priest) / **Saviors / early Yogis**
- Body-mind integration (integral-centaur) / left to middle heart
- Psychic-intuition wisdom / web-of-life to Cosmic Consciousness
- gods-goddesses as archetypes to the Great Goddess or One God

---

- **Texts** that acknowledge the existence of "The One" Divine Being (Great Goddess, Great Mother, God the Father, etc.) manifesting all forms of existence (gross/subtle) including "the Many" archetypes or deities (gods-goddesses) as the Creator or One God.

- **Texts** of devotional reverence to God (or Supreme Power) by whatever name or conception.

- **Texts** that still recognize a sense of separation from the Divine (hence prayers are most often petitionary or full of praise).

- **Texts** encouraging codes of behavior, morally upright disciplines controlling passions-emotions (or lower human nature).

- **Texts** addressing Afterlife or the journey of the soul: surviving death / immortality, positive reincarnations, going to Heaven, etc.

- **Texts** suggesting Nature-based Mysticism / connection with the web-of-life or Nature as a whole ("Kosmic Consciousness").

4th Stage Wisdom Texts Reading List (partial)

- *I Ching* – "Book of Changes," world's oldest book, cycles in Nature & fortune
- *Rig Veda* – by ancient India Rishis, root text of Hinduism and Vedanta
- *Mahabharata* – Sanskrit epic of ancient India (contains the *Bhagavad Gita*)
- *Ramayana* – Sanskrit epic of ancient India (about the Avatar Rama and Sita)
- *Bhagavad Gita* – "Song of God" devotional text of Hinduism (Avatar Krishna)
- *Rama Gita* – Avatar Rama's nondual message to his brother Lakshmana
- *Devi Mahatmya* – Goddess as Supreme Power of the universe
- *The Dhammapada* – original Teaching-Words of The Buddha
- *What the Buddha Taught* – texts from Suttas and Dhammapada
- *Way of the Bodhisattva* – by Shantideva (685–763) guide to the Bodhisattva way of life (emphasizing compassion and wisdom)
- *Talmud* – central text of Rabbinic Judaism; primary source of Jewish law
- *Holy Bible* – central text of Christianity (with Prophets & Avatar Jesus Christ)
- *Holy Qur'an* – central text of Islam (with the Prophet Muhammad)
- *The Symposium* – by Plato (c. 385–370 BCE) about love and beauty (Eros)
- *The Republic* – by Plato (ca. 375 BCE) about justice in the city-state & in man
- *Dead Sea Scrolls* – (150 BCE–68 CE) recently uncovered texts of the early Christian Essene community
- *Dark Night of the Soul* – by mystic-priest St. John of the Cross (1542–1591)
- *Poems of Rumi* – poems by Persian-Sufi mystic Rumi (1207–1273)
- *Songs of Kabir* – devotional poems by Indian mystic-saint Kabir (1440–1518)
- *The Sacred Pipe* – by Black Elk (1863–1950) Lakota Sioux "Holy Man"
- *Bhakti Yoga* – by Swami Vivekananda (1863–1902) Hindu mystic-teacher who brought Eastern teachings to the West
- *Light on Yoga* – by B. K. S. Iyengar (1918–2014) modern Hatha Yoga
- *The Prophet* – by Lebanese-American writer Kahlil Gibran (1883–1931)
- *A Course in Miracles* – inspirational book by Helen Schucman (said to be channeled from Jesus)
- *Teachings of Krishnamurti* – by Jiddu Krishnamurti (1895–1986), modern Indian philosopher promoted by Theosophy as a "World Teacher" (which he rejected)
- *Three Pillars of Zen* – by Philip Kapleau (1912–2004) American Zen Master
- *Spark of Light: Counseling in the Hasidic Tradition* – by Zalman Schachter
- *The Garden of Truth* – by Seyyed Hossein Nasr on mystical Sufism
- *Zohar: The Book of Enlightenment* – translated by Daniel Chana Matt

5th Stage of Life

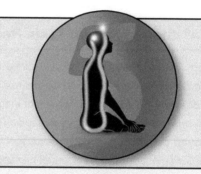

5th Stage Wisdom Texts – Subtle Mysticism

Stage Characteristics:

- **Subtle-Deity Mysticism / higher mind / visionary / dreaming self**
- **Yogis** (low) **/ Saints** (high) / ascension of esoteric anatomy
- Subtle-realm energies / Goddess (*shakti*); middle station of the heart
- One God/dess union-unity (not identity)

- **Texts** addressing the esoteric anatomy of the human being, including subtle energy lines (*nadis*) and centers (*chakras*) involved in the movement of kundalini (life-energy) in the body or conductivity (descent/ascent).

- **Texts** outlining yogic practices, including breathing exercises (*prana-yama*), involved in subtle energy "heat" (cultivation) and movement (such as the sublimation of sexual energy or retention of seminal fluids for "alchemical" or inner-energy/psychic transformations).

- **Texts** addressing Realization of God via opening or oneness with the higher chakras (subtle energy centers) of the inner brain in the ascending hierarchy (or ladder) of consciousness evolution

- **Texts** encouraging yogic and meditative disciplines controlling mind and thoughts; inward turning of attention (away from senses-world).

- **Texts** addressing abstract, archetypal, non-gross or subtle-based phenomena, such as subtle lights, visions, sounds, vibrations, feelings, archetypal (geometrical) shapes or deities (e.g., Tibetan deity meditation, Shabd / Nada Yoga).

© table by Brad Reynolds

5th Stage Wisdom Texts Reading List (partial)

- *The Secret of the Golden Flower* – ancient Taoist text on inner yoga-alchemy
- *Taoist Yoga: Alchemy and Immortality* – by Charles Luk (1898-1978)
- *Awaken Healing Energy Through the Tao* – by modern Taoist Mantak Chia
- *The Interior Castle* – by mystic-nun St. Teresa of Avila (1515–1582) on the stages ascending to God-Realization (union)
- *The Teachings of Don Juan* – by Carlos Castaneda about a Native-American shaman and inner psychic powers
- *Shamanism: Archaic Techniques of Ecstasy* – by world religion scholar Mircea Eliade
- *Yoga Sutra of Patanjali* – original writings on yoga from ancient India
- *Tibetan Book of the Dead* – Tibetan manual for the after-death journey
- *Nag Hammadi Scriptures* – "Gnostic Gospels" early texts on Jesus Christ discovered in 1945
- *Gnostic Gospels* – secret teachings of early Christians about attaining Gnosis
- *Corpus Hermeticum* – by Hermes Trismegistus (2nd c. CE) on raising consciousness
- *The Enneads* – by Plotinus (204/5 – 270) about ascending to The One
- *Sky Dancer* – Teachings by Lady Yeshe Tsogyal (c 777–817), woman Siddha and Buddhist tantric master
- *Flower Ornament Scripture* – Mahayana sutra on interpenetrated realms
- *The Kundalini Experience* – by Lee Sannella, M.D.. modern medical review of kundalini power
- *Kundalini: The Secret of Life* – by modern yogi Swami Muktananda (1908–1982)
- *The Crown of Life* – by Kirpal Singh (1894–1974) modern master of Surat Shabd Yoga
- *Hatha Yoga Pradipika* – classic 15th century Sanskrit manual on hatha yoga
- *The Science of the Soul* – by Swami Yogeshwaranand on esoteric anatomy
- *Raja Yoga* – by Swami Vivekananda (1863–1902) Hindu teacher in the West
- *Tantra Yoga, Nada Yoga, and Kriya Yoga* – by Swami Sivananda (1887–1963)
- *Foundations of Tibetan Mysticism* – by Lama Anagarika Govinda (1898–1985)
- *Six Yogas of Naropa* – Teachings by the Tibetan Siddha Naropa (1016–1100)
- *Power of the Holy Spirit in the Christian Life* – by St. Seraphim of Sarov (1759–1833)
- *An Introduction to the Kabbalah* – by Mosheh Hallamish and translators
- *Kriya Yoga* – by Paramahansa Yogananda (1893–1952) on Self-Realization

 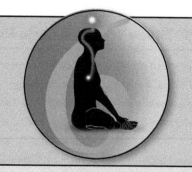

6th Stage of Life

6th Stage Wisdom Texts – Causal Mysticism

Stage Characteristics:

- **Formless Mysticism / Witness Consciousness / True Self** (*Atman*)
- **Sages / Avadhoots / Arhats / Buddhas / Jnanis**
- Causal-Void (*sunyata*) / Godhead / right side of the heart
- No-body Formless Enlightenment / Clear Light Void (Buddhism)

- **Texts** addressing "Emptiness" (sunya) or Liberation (*moksha*) from all gross-subtle forms.

- **Texts** that Witness all states (and stages) arising within the space (emptiness) of Consciousness Itself (*turiya*).

- **Texts** that emphasize "*neti, neti*" ("not this, not that") or the fact there is no logic-rational way to describe (or "know" about) the Divine Condition.

- **Texts** confirming Unity of Atman-Brahman or the inner self (*Atman*) and the One God of the outer universe (*Brahman*) as being "One without a second" (*Atman-Brahman*).

- **Texts** affirming "Thou Art That" (*tat tvam asi*) or "You are God!"

- **Texts** that affirm the Witness Consciousness as being the ultimate "state" of the Divine Condition.

© table by Brad Reynolds

6th Stage Wisdom Texts Reading List (partial)

- **Tao Te Ching** – by Lao Tzu (c. 500 BCE) book (*ching*) of the Way (*tao*) and its virtue (*te*)
- **Upanishads** – numerous authoritative summaries Vedanta ("end of the Vedas")
- **Jnana Yoga** – by Swami Vivekananda (1863–1902) Hindu teacher in the West
- **Vedanta for the Western World** (1945) – edited by Christopher Isherwood
- **Crest Jewel of Discrimination** – by Shankara (8th c CE), epitome teachings on Advaita Vedanta
- **Prabodhasudhakara** – by Shankara (8th c) "Nectar Ocean of Enlightenment"
- **Clear Light of Bliss** – by Geshe Kelsang Gyatso on practice of Mahamudra in Vajrayana Buddhism
- **In Praise of the Dharmadhatu** – by Nagarjuna (2nd c. CE) on Nondual Absolute Reality
- **Mūlamadhyamakakārikā** – by Nagarjuna on "Middle Way" (*Madhyamaka*)
- **Madhyamaka Buddhism** – by Chandrakirti commentary on works of Nagarjuna
- **Book of the Heart** – by Meister Eckhart (1260–1328) nondual Christian teachings of Godhead
- **Yoga Vasishtha** – by Vasishtha, one of seven great Rishi sages of the Vedas
- **Samkhya and Advaita Vedanta** – by Dr. Anima Sen Gupta, comparative study
- **Pearls of Jaina Wisdom** – selections from Jain scriptures about Mahavira
- **Zen Teachings** – by Huang Po (d. 850 CE) Chinese Ch'an Master
- **The Zen Doctrine of No Mind** – by D. T. Suzuki on teachings of Hui-Neng
- **The Practice of Zen** – by Garma C. C. Chang review of Zen philosophy and Enlightenment practice
- **Collected Works** – Ramana Maharshi (1879–1950) on Advaita Vedanta and Amrita Nadi
- **Talks with Ramana Maharshi** – on Advaita Vedanta, *Amrita Nadi*, and the Heart (on the right)
- **Sri Ramana Gita** – Teachings of Ramana Maharshi (1879–1950)
- **Sri Devikalottara Agama** – from the Devi (Goddess) tradition
- **I Am That** – by Nisargadatta Maharaj (1897–1981) answers question from students on Advaita Vedanta

7th Stage of Life

7th Stage Wisdom Texts – Nondual Mysticism

Stage Characteristics:

- **Nondual Mysticism / *Amrita Nadi*** (heart on right to Light above)
- **Jivanmukti / Bodhisattvas / Avatars / Guru-Siddhas**
- Whole-Body Enlightenment / God as Transcendent-Immanent / Conscious-Light / Sahaj Samadhi ("Open Eyes" / "One Taste")

- **Texts** that affirm the Divine as being both transcendent (6th Stage Realization) and immanent (as Kosmos) or Atman-Brahman, Shiva-Shakti, Source-Condition, Ground-Goal.

- **Texts** promoting the "I Am" and "Abiding Thus" Revelations.

- **Texts** that confirm that Enlightenment cannot be gained or "known" through efforts but is only realized (through Grace).

- **Texts** that affirm only no-seeking is the Truth, since all searches for Truth are ego-based soul journeys that are illusory and ultimately deluding (not Enlightenment), including yogic manifestations.

- **Texts** affirming there is Only Consciousness or Pure Awareness, the "natural state" (Dzogchen and Mahamudra)

- **Texts** that announce the heart (particularly on the right) as the source of Divine Consciousness in the human being thus to be heart-open or full of love-bliss and compassion is the Way of the Enlightened Life.

© table by Brad Reynolds

"Premonitory" 7ᵗʰ Stage Wisdom Texts Reading List

- **Inner Chapters** – by Chuang Tzu (396–286 BCE) living life following the Way of Tao (*wu wei*)
- **Vimalakirti Sutra** – by Vimalakirti (c. 500 BCE) ideal Buddhist lay practitioner living nondual Enlightenment
- **Heart Sutra** – short Mahayana text claiming "emptiness is form, form is emptiness" etc., and all is gone beyond (*tathagata*)
- **Ribhu Gita** – Nondual teaching of Sage Ribhu (8ᵗʰ c. CE)
- **Ashtavakra Gita** – by Sage Ashtavakra (ca. 500 BCE) poems of nondualism
- **Avadhuta Gita** – attributed to Dattatreya (from 9ᵗʰ – 10ᵗʰ c. CE) ecstatic nondual praise
- **Tripura Rahasya** – "Mystery Beyond the Trinity" classic of Advaita Vedanta
- **Diamond Sutra** – a Buddhist Prajnaparamita sutra with strong influence on Ch'an / Zen and instantaneous Awakening
- **Lankavatara Sutra** – Mahayana text of primary nondual teaching of Shakyamuni Buddha
- **Mahayanavimsaka** – by Maha-Siddha Nagarjuna on Nondual Reality
- **Platform Sutra of Hui-Neng** – by Sixth Patriarch of Zen, Hui-Neng (638–713) of China

---

SEVEN SACRED SCRIPTURES:
SONGS OF THE SELF SUPREME

Back in the early 1980s after Avatar Adi Da debuted the Seven Stages of Life model, he began introducing some traditional texts as instruction for his devotees that are included in *The Basket of Tolerance* bibliography [see Chapter 2]. As mentioned earlier, a principal talk by the Avatar that introduced these texts of the Great Tradition was titled "The Seventh School of God-Talk" (given on October 5, 1981). It was first published in 1982 as the Preface to a new version of the *Astavakra Gita*, retitled as ***The Song of the Self Supreme: Astavakra Gita***, recently translated by pandit Radhakamal Mukerjee. Here the American-born Avatar highlighted a preference for certain sacred scriptures that he felt reflected the Sixth-to-Seventh Stages of Life or those texts that are ecstatically expressing the state of Divine Enlightenment. Overall, they are confessions by Awakened Adepts of their Enlightened Realization, poetic utterances of the Divine Paradox not manuals of practice needed to attain this Supreme Realization (which are the subject of the earlier Stages of Life).

In another 1982 book, *Nirvanasara: Radical Transcendentalism and the Introduction of Advaitayana Buddhism*, Adi Da discoursed about many of the world's religious traditions and their primary Adepts by placing many of them into the Seven Stage developmental model. Consequently, the global Adept focused mostly on Advaita Vedanta and Buddhism, the most highly evolved esoteric spiritual traditions on the planet (according to Adi Da), as well as the lesser Western Abrahamic religions. In these two books he suggested that several Great Sages, such as Astavakra, Buddha, Nagarjuna, Hui-Neng, possibly even Jesus Christ, were "Seventh Stage" or Divinely Enlightened Adepts, or, at least at times, they confessed the "Seventh Stage of Life" Realization of Transcendental Awakened Wisdom beyond that of Sixth Stage interior inversion. These two 1982 masterpieces—the Preface to *The Song of the Self Supreme* and the book *Nirvanasara*—outlined the best books of the Great Tradition while also introducing "**Advaitayana Buddhism**" or Adi Da's Way of Enlightenment that transcends-yet-includes Advaita Vedanta and the best of Buddha Dharma [see Chapter 10]. This monumental undertaking arises from the Avatar's Enlightened State (not scholarly learning) and is currently updated and integrated, at least in part, in two of the Avatar's five final texts, *The Pneumaton* (2011) and *The Gnosticon* (2010).[20] The depth of Adi Da's spiritual understanding is unparalleled in human history and, as far as I can see, they are certainly worthy of serious investigation and deep study whatever your point of view.

During the following decade (by 1993), especially after his "Divine Emergence" event in 1986, Adi Da began to qualify these assertions about other Adepts and their texts to better accommodate his own Divine Teaching-Work (i.e., his "Only-By-Me" Revelations). Therefore, the Adept-Sage adjusted these traditional texts' placement within the context of his more accurate Seven Stages of Life model. Adi Da now suggests that these high wisdom texts (and their Sages) are more accurately classified as "**premonitory 'seventh stage' literature**" or "intuitions that sympathetically foreshadow" the Seventh Stage Enlightenment which the Avatar now claims that only he has fully manifested.[21] It is not my intention here to argue (or refute) these claims at this time for his overall instruction is still very useful without fully understanding the subtle distinctions being implied [see Chapter 19]. What is important, in my opinion, is how certain esoteric scriptures, usually ecstatic proclamations from the world's most Enlightened Adepts found in the literature of the Great Tradition, do reflect the highest Stage (or Stages) of Life. They give us a real flavor about the divine nature of the God-Realized State (particularly when written down). These texts are not logical philosophical treatises or visionary revelations but are paradoxical pronouncements that transcend language and literature.

Nonetheless, whether **"Sixth Stage"** or **"premonitory" Seventh Stage** is not the point in being able to study the Great Tradition, for these are conveniences of classification. The Sixth Stage of Life *is* Enlightenment too as it has traditionally been defined for it is a genuine awakening to the True Self, our inherent Buddha-Nature or the Divine Nature of Consciousness Itself (gained by completely transcending the self or ego-I). The Sixth Stage of Life, therefore, is not to be diminished in mind games of classification which can never capture the true paradox of this exalted (and "empty") state of nondual consciousness. What is instructive is how these Enlightened Sages and their sacred texts express the Nondual Condition of seeing *Only* God, even if there may be a tendency to view the world as an illusion and hence be introverted (as Adi Da classically defines the **"Sixth Stage Error"**). What is important is that they represent the most highly evolved Great Realizers of human history. They offer us some of the most Enlightened Teachings on our planet appearing within the Global Wisdom Tradition of humankind. Yet, we must read and study—and ultimately *realize* their message for ourselves—before attempting to pronounce final judgment. Therefore, as a scholar-pandit, I have placed certain texts in the Seventh Stage category based on Adi Da's previous distinctions for the sake of clarity and instruction [see Chapter 19 for a further discussion].

As a consequence, Adi Da's publishing house The Dawn Horse Press (in Clearlake, now Middletown, California) published the aforementioned translation of the *Astavakra Gita* by Radhakamal Mukerjee titled as *The Song of the Self Supreme* (1982), a classic text of Advaita Vedanta. This enlightening book includes both an essay by the Avatar (written on August 26, 1981) followed by an extemporaneous talk (given on October 5, 1981). The purpose of this discussion was to introduce seven essential texts or what's now called "premonitory" Seventh Stage of Life literatures (discussed further in *The Pneumaton* and *The Gnosticon*), which, for one, includes the *Astavakra Gita* itself [see detail below].[22] This was an appropriate gesture at the time since the Guru-Adept considers the *Astavakra Gita* to be "among the greatest (and most senior) communications of all the esoteric traditions in the Great Tradition of humankind."[23] This particular *Gita* or "song" is a poetic confession to the "Supreme Self" or Atman-Brahman as *Sat-Chit-Ananda* revealed in God-Realization as given by the ancient Indian sage Astavakra (or Ashtavakra). It was probably composed around the same time as the *Bhagavad Gita* (ca. 6th century BCE), over twenty-five centuries ago, yet it contains the timeless (or perennial) wisdom of Enlightenment, the pinnacle of human possibility.

In the essay and its associated talk, Adi Da presents several other sacred scriptures gathered from the Great Tradition to represent a pure confession of ultimate Realization or Divine Enlightenment. The Avatar feels these texts express in essence the point of view of the Sixth and Seventh Stage of Life or that of Enlightenment Itself.[24] These written records are mostly free expressions of the Enlightened State as seen from that particular Sage's "perspective," not technical manuals of yogic practice or meditation methods or how to realize such a God-Realized Enlightened State-Stage of Life.

As such these sacred texts are mostly spiritual revelations given in ecstatic speech, often paradoxical and sometimes wildly humorous. Adi Da thus clarifies: "Like the *Astavakra Gita*, they do not represent a practice but rather they represent the description or Confession of ultimate God-Realization. They represent the ultimate free point of view of an Adept who teaches others, who are yet practicing in the lesser stages, about the Realization that is the ultimate import of the traditional texts."[25] These seven sacred texts that Heart-Master Da has reviewed are highly recommended for everyone to study in detail. They epitomize the Great Tradition's most Enlightened perspective given to all of us—to the entire world (regardless of culture or race)—from some of the wisest Sages of humankind, whether women or men. They are listed below as they are found in the original Preface of *The Song of the Self Supreme*, thus quotes are from Adi Da's descriptions of these sacred scriptures[26]:

"Premonitory" 7th Stage Wisdom Texts Reading List
Selected by Avatar Adi Da Samraj

(1) ***Astavakra Gita***—the "Song of Astavakra" (c. 500–400 BCE), published in several translations (including *The Song of the Self Supreme*), is a classic Advaita Vedanta scripture that "arose from the ancient Vedic and Upanishadic tradition, as well as the Shaivite tradition in its non-dualistic or Advaitic stage." (40) It is written as a dialogue between the sage Astavakra and Janaka, the king of Mithila, on the divine nature of the soul (Atman), reality, and bondage. This Gita insists on the complete unreality of the external world and absolute oneness of existence yet without mentioning any yogic practices or moral duties, therefore, it is simply an ecstatic confession of the (Sixth-Seventh Stage of Life) or Enlightened "perspective." Adi Da summarizes: "The *Astavakra Gita* is a Confession or Song of such Enlightenment…. It speaks spontaneously in and of the Free Disposition that is the fulfillment of all Ways, even of life itself. Therefore, it speaks of the utter transcendence of discrimination (or mind, whereby independent categories such as self, other, world, God, Nirvana, thought, body, suffering, Liberation, practice, meditation, and so forth are conceived). My advice to you is that you listen well to Astavakra but do not read him indiscriminately." (68)

Astavakra Gita
"Song of Astavakra"
a dialogue between the Sage Astavakra and King Janaka of Mithila on the divine nature of Atman, reality, and bondage

(2) ***Avadhuta Gita*** (or *Avadhoot Gita*)—literally the "Song of the Free Soul" where the first extant manuscripts of this Advaita Vedanta classic comes from the 9th or 10th centuries CE (though it's probably composed earlier). It is an important text of the later Nath Siddha Yoga tradition since it focuses on the devotional relationship and transmission found in Satsang with an Awakened Adept. This Gita, as Adi Da further explains, is "the culminating text of the Dattatreya school, which is characterized by devotion to the

Avadhuta Gita
"Song of the Free Soul"
Advaita Vedanta classic attributed to Dattatreya, the lord of yogis, focusing on the devotional relationship and transmission found in Satsang with an Awakened Adept

God-concept represented by the person of the Adept **Dattatreya** [dates unknown]. In this school, the Transcendental Divine is worshiped as the Eternal Spiritual Master, the God of all the gods." (21)

(3) *Tripura Rahasya*—means "Mystery beyond the Trinity" (or beyond the three states of waking, dreaming, deep sleep), which is also claimed to be narrated by **Dattatreya** (to his devotee Parashurama). It is seen, according to Adi Da, as "the ultimate text of the Devi, Goddess, or Shakti school, the tradition of worship of the Divine Mother or Universal Creative Power... wherein the Adept, in this case, a woman [Hemalekha], brings her devotee and husband [Hemachuda] from a position of relative worldliness and conventional religiosity into the internalized realization of the Sixth Stage [enlightened introversion] and then beyond that limited frame to exclusive Self-Realization into the ultimate or native [or Seventh Stage] God-Realized state (Sahaj Samadhi) in which the world is recognized and tacitly transcended in the Transcendental Self or Ultimate Nirvanic Being of the Devi [called Sri Tripura, the Mother Goddess Chandika]." It was a favorite of Sri Ramana Maharshi as he quoted from it often as being an epitome text of Advaita philosophy. (20)

> **Tripura Rahasya**
> "Mystery beyond the Trinity"
> attributed to Dattatreya, a text of the Shakti school, about transcending the three states of waking, dreaming, deep sleep in the Transcendental Divine named Sri Tripura, the Mother Goddess

(4) *Lankavatara Sutra*—a prominent Mahayana Buddhist scripture in the development of Tibetan, Chinese, and Japanese Buddhism, particularly Zen. It is presented as a dialogue between Gautama Buddha and a bodhisattva named Mahamati ("Great Wisdom)" on the island fortress of Lanka (off of southern India). Adi Da recognizes it as "a culminating text of the Mahayana tradition of Buddhism. To enter into its disposition, one would begin with the Fourth Stage devotional and/or self-transcending disciplines at the foundation of Mahayana (and the Vajrayana) Buddhism. Once the

> **Lankavatara Sutra**
> Mahayana text of a dialogue dialogue between Gautama Buddha and the bodhisattva Mahamati emphasizing Yogachara "Mind-Only" or Consciousness Only Teachings

benign world-attitudes of the Bodhisattva ideal are established, the Fifth Stage yogas of the Vajrayana tradition might be adopted. But the epitome of traditional Buddhist practices is the Sixth Stage exercise of 'mindfulness,' which finally culminates in the [premonitory] Seventh Stage Realization described in the *Lankavatara Sutra*." (21-22). This is one of the most revered texts in the entire Buddhist canon for its wonderful exposition presented with rational language and discourse, yet paradoxically transcending all words and philosophies, thus being exemplary of the Enlightened View. Its principal theme and emphasis is on Consciousness Only (or "Mind-Only").

(5) *Mahayanavimsaka* (or *Mahayana Vimsaka*) attributed to Nagarjuna [but probably not the famous Buddhist sage from the 2nd century CE but one of the 84 Maha-Siddhas from the 7th century CE]—literally means, "Adoration to the Three Treasures." It summarizes the Madhyamika or "Middle Way" philosophy of Buddhism in only twenty verses, thus it's one of the most concise formulations of Mahayana Buddhism; Adi Da explains: "The *Diamond Sutra*, the *Mahayanavimsaka* of Nagarjuna, and the *Platform Sutra* of the Sixth Patriarch are three other remarkable texts from the same basic school of Teaching as the *Lankavatara Sutra*, and they are examples of the same ultimate or [premonitory] Seventh Stage Confession of Truth and Realization." (22)

> **Mahayana Vimsaka**
>
> "Adoration to the Three Treasures"
>
> attributed to the Maha-Siddha Nagarjuna who summarizes the Madhyamika or "Middle Way" philosophy of Buddhism in only twenty verses

(6) *Diamond Sutra*—a Mahayana Buddhist text from the *Prajnaparamita* or "Perfection of Wisdom" collection is one of the most influential Mahayana sutras in East Asia, a key text in Zen Buddhism. It is essentially a discourse of the Buddha given to a senior monk, Subhuti, teaching about *anatman* (or "no-self") and non-attachment (via the emptiness of all phenomena). According to the *Platform Sutra*, this was the sutra that the illiterate

> **Diamond Sutra**
>
> one of the most influential Mahayana sutras in East Asia, a key text in Zen Buddhism, a discourse given by the Buddha to his senior monk Subhuti about *anatman* (or "no-self")

Hui-Neng heard one day while delivering firewood and which initiated his Awakening to Enlightenment.

(7) *Platform Sutra* [or *Sutra of Hui-Neng, The Sixth Patriarch*]—Hui-Neng (638–713 CE) is traditionally viewed as the Sixth and Last Patriarch of Ch'an Buddhism (in China) leading to the development of Zen Buddhism (in Japan). Hui-Neng placed an emphasis on Sudden Enlightenment since such an awakening is realized by "no thought," therefore he tends to be critical of Gradual Enlightenment with its emphasis on meditation and endless practices. Hence it was the Sixth Patriarch of Zen teachings that would evolve into the koan school of Zen, a method that attempts to initiate instantaneous Enlightenment (instead of gradual development).

Platform Sutra

"Sutra of Hui-Neng"
the Sixth Patriarch
of Ch'an (Zen)
Buddhism who
placed an emphasis on
Sudden Enlightenment
since awakening is
instantaneous and
realized by
"no thought," not
philosophy or seeking

These seven sacred scriptures of the Great Tradition, while free expressions of the Enlightened State always take into account, whether explicitly or implicitly, the actual necessity for authentic ego-transcending practice or the discipline of sadhana. In other words, they originate from the "Practicing School" involving authentic Adept-Realizers and Spirit-Transmission (not merely the "Talking School" of pandits and philosophers). In this case, they all honor the importance of their Gurus (or Masters) in serving their Awakening (via the "Practicing School"). Again, as Heart-Master Adi Da clarifies: "The Real process is that wherein Realization is made Real. Everything else is talk."[27] Anything less, the Masters unanimously declare, is just the conceit of the ego, the charade of the self, the illusions of a lifetime (or more) instead of devoted practice and actual Enlightenment.

Truly what could be a Greater Message than this? Enlightenment (or God-Realization) instead of philosophy; ego-transcendence instead of ego-fulfillment. This has *always* been the demand and message of the real Guru-Adepts whether we want to hear it or not. Even science cannot provide such liberating knowledge because its knowledge is only relative, not Absolute. Our true Freedom, our innate Happiness, resides in the Transcendental Truth of

Divine Enlightenment as the Masters have always proclaimed and demonstrated, not in the evolutionary details of relativity.

As a result, the more holistic approach to realizing our full human potential is to *integrate* both: the relative and the Absolute, *samsara* and *nirvana*, the false and the true, the illusory and the real, as being of "One Taste" or One Reality. Because our Consciousness is Divine, is grounded in Prior Unity, we witness the display of the whole Kosmos thus *realizing* Freedom and Liberation in our heart, not with the mind (or via intellectual philosophies). Only when ego-self is transcended is the True Self seen (and known) to be God. It is to That—God-Realization—that we bow down, for only That is Real God or Reality Itself while all else is only temporarily or momentarily "real." Only Reality is "always already the case" and it is to That the great Guru-Adepts point us throughout all of human history in every era. If you look hard enough, you will find It and see for yourself (beyond ego-self)—for, in essence, It IS *you!*

Chapter 3 Endnotes

1. Adi Da Samraj, from the essay "The Great Esoteric Tradition of Devotion To The Adept-Realizer" in *The Aletheon* (2009) Volume 1, p. 161.

2. Richard Schorske, "Accessing the Great Tradition: An Introduction to The Basket of Tolerance" in *The Laughing Man*, 1987, Vol. 7, No. 1, pp. 8-13 [title caps added to the Stages of Life for consistency].

3. Adi Da Samraj, from a Talk given on January 22, 1983, in *The Laughing Man*, Vol. 7, No. 1, p. 13.

4. Adi Da Samraj, April 4, 1987 in *Free Daist*, Vol. 3, No. 4/5, 1992-1993, p. 45; also see: Adi Da Samraj, "I <u>Am</u> One" in *The Aletheon* (2009), p. 1753: "The Universalization of Truth is fundamental to My Divine Avataric Incarnation here—in the context of the prior unity that transcends all 'tribalism', all cultural limitations, all cultural identities (East and West)."

5. Editors, *The Song of the Self Supreme: Astavakra Gita* (1982) translated by R. Mukerjee, p. 28.

6. See: *Meeting Adi Da: A Mandala of Approach to Avatar Adi Da Samraj* (forthcoming) by Brad Reynolds.

7. Adi Da Samraj, April 6, 1987 in *Free Daist*, Vol. 3, No. 4/5, 1992-1993, p. 45.

8. See: Adi Da Samraj [Da Free John], Preface" to *The Song of the Self Supreme: Astavakra Gita* (1982), p. 28.

9. See: Adi Da Samraj [Franklin Jones], *The Knee of Listening* (1973, 2004 revised edition),

10. Adi Da Samraj [Da Free John], "Preface" to *The Song of the Self Supreme: Astavakra Gita* (1982), pp. 29-30.

11. See: Editors to the "Preface" in *The Song of the Self Supreme: Astavakra Gita* (1982) translated by Radhakamal Mukerjee.,

12. Adi Da Samraj [Da Free John], *Nirvanasara* (1982), p. 121.

13. Adi Da Samraj, September 8, 2004 quoted in *The Reality-Way of Adidam* (2010), p. 45.

14. Adi Da Samraj [Da Free John], *Nirvanasara* (1982), pp. 136-137 ["Stages of Life" capped].

15. Ibid., p. 137.

16. Chart of the Seven Stages of Life and corresponding religions was originally created by James Steinberg, Adi Da's principal librarian during the Avatar's lifetime. I have re-drawn and modified it slightly for my purposes here with his permission. Please consult James Steinberg for the official presentation.

17. Adi Da Samraj [Da Free John], "The Seventh School of God-Talk" (essay) in "Preface" to *The Song of the Self Supreme: Astavakra Gita* (1982), pp. 25-26 ["Stages of Life" capped].

18. Animal images for the Seven Stages of Life, as conceived by Adi Da Samraj, originally published in *The Laughing Man* magazine.

19. Adi Da Samraj [Da Free John], "The Seventh School of God-Talk" (essay) in "Preface" to *The Song of the Supreme Self: Astavakra Gita* (1982), p. 67 [title caps added to Stages of Life].

20. Also see: *The Aletheon* (2009) by Avatar Adi Da Samraj, his final and epitome summary Teaching-Word; while *Transcendental Realism* (2010) and *Not Two Is Peace* (2009) complete the "final five" books.

21. See: "The Unique Sixth Stage Foreshadowing of the Only-By-Me Revealed and Given Seventh Stage of Life" in *The Gnosticon* (2010), p. 499ff. Whether or not this claim is true (or not)—i.e., that Adi Da Samraj is the most fully Enlightened human being to ever live on planet Earth—is debatable, of course, especially from the "point of view" of the lesser Stages of Life. However, within the context that he presents the Seven Stages of Life it does make logical (and spiritual) sense, yet, ultimately, I believe such an assertion can only be verified by Revelation, not by the mind, so therefore is beyond this current discussion.

22. See: Adi Da Samraj [Da Free John], "Preface: The Seventh School of God-Talk" in *The Song of the Self Supreme: Astavakra Gita* (1982) translated by Radhakamal Mukerjee; also see: *The Laughing Man*, Vol. 6, No. 2, 1985, which now appears in *The Gnosticon* as "The Unique Sixth Stage Foreshadowings of the Only-By-Me Revealed and Given Seventh Stage of Life," p. 499ff.

23. Adi Da Samraj, *The Gnosticon* (2010), p. 499.

24. As mentioned, Adi Da has revised these "Seventh Stage" texts as actually being "premonitory" of the Seventh Stage of Life, for overall they still tend to exemplify the Sixth, not the fully-realized Seventh, Stage of Life except in a premonitory or foreshadowing manner.

25. Adi Da Samraj [Da Free John], "The Seventh School of God-Talk" (essay) in "Preface" to *The Song of the Supreme Self: Astavakra Gita* (1982), p. 20.

26. See: Adi Da Samraj [Da Free John], Preface "The Seventh School of God-Talk" in *The Song of the Self-Supreme* (1982).

27. Adi Da Samraj, *The Gnosticon* (2010), p. 488.

FOUR

INTEGRAL INTERPRETATIONS:
TALKING SCHOOLS

*So it is that the leading edge of consciousness evolution stands today
on the brink of an Integral Millennium—or at least the possibility of an
Integral Millennium—where the sum total of extant human knowledge,
wisdom, and technology is available to all.*

— **Ken Wilber**, 2000

ith its comprehensive overview of human development, Ken
Wilber's integral perspective shines a new light on many serious matters facing our contemporary global culture, including
a "religion of tomorrow" (the title to one of his recent books).[1]
By taking an evolutionary perspective based on the unfolding of "**basic structures**" or *stages* (i.e., "**fulcrums**") of consciousness development, including the
various *states* of consciousness (plus developmental lines, types, etc.), Wilber's
Integral Metatheory opens up a new and deeper understanding of world history. Without favoring any one culture, the Integral Vision sees all the eras

(and their worldviews) of human history as being **true but partial** in order to embrace the entire inheritance of humankind and all our ancestors without prejudice to any one tradition.

The Integral Approach to human evolution understands the necessity to honor and include *all* the major eras of human knowledge (i.e., the archaic, magic, mythic, rational, etc.) by being based on a healthy integration of the *premodern*, *modern*, and *postmodern* worldviews—an unprecedented accomplishment. Wilber correctly maintains that we do this best by rejecting (or eliminating) each worldview's particular "disasters" ("bad news") or *deficient* modes while maintaining (or incorporating) their "dignities" ("good news") or *efficient* contributions (as Jean Gebser's integral theories also suggest).[2] By doing this, we can recognize the different worldviews that are currently inhabiting the world's various religious systems in order to better jettison each era's errors and fallacies. For example, we can reject both past mythic superstitions as well as the flatland materialism of scientism, yet while including the value of mythic archetypes and the brilliance of modern scientific discoveries and advancements. By relying on free inquiry coupled with discriminative intelligence we can investigate and integrate the various evolving worldviews about reality and our place in it—this is the Integral Vision-in-action.

Unfortunately, however, Wilber has mostly taken a "**Talking School**" approach to spirituality, not one providing Spirit-Transmission and *vertical transformation* of consciousness. Philosophies, even all-embracing integral ones (that even include models of mysticism), always end up falling short of Real Enlightenment because they overlook (or downplay) the "**Practicing School**" of real spiritual life. They talk about God instead of feeling and knowing God. Wilber very effectively offers a *horizontal translation* from the integral stage of awareness, one that does tip its hat to God-Consciousness, but fails to initiate God-Consciousness. Only a genuine Guru-Adept offering Satsang (and Grace) can do this. Only an authentic Transmission-Master can provide actual Spirit-Baptism, a descent of Divine Light into a person's body-mind by opening the heart to higher understandings [see Chapter 3]. Guru Yoga-Satsang, as always, provides this means of authentic transformation that can never be replaced or replicated with Talking School philosophies and psychologies, maps and models, ideas and formulas. It is time we all recognize this greater understanding and *realize* this esoteric fact and simple truth.

Premodern Religions vs. Integral Post-Metaphysics

By taking an attitude of universal appreciation and global tolerance, the integral perspective proclaims that *everyone* is the rightful heir to the world's extant knowledge, technology, and religious-cultural wisdom (much as Adi Da suggests with the "Great Tradition"). Wilber thus announces on the opening page of *A Theory of Everything* (2000), published in the first year of the new millennium this now obvious reality:

> We live in an extraordinary time: all of the world's cultures, past and present, are to some degree available to us, either in historical records or as living entities. In the history of the planet Earth, this has never happened before.... From isolated tribes and bands [archaic], to small farming villages [magic], to ancient nations [magic-mythic], to conquering feudal empires [mythic], to international corporate states [mental-ego], to the global village [pluralistic]: the extraordinary growth toward an integral village that seems humanity's destiny. So it is that the leading edge of consciousness evolution stands today on the brink of an Integral Millennium—or at least the possibility of an Integral Millennium—where the sum total of extant human knowledge, wisdom, and technology is available to all.[3]

In this present era of worldwide communication and an interconnected, interdependent global order it becomes the responsibility of our governments and educational institutions to make sure this collective inheritance is universally available for all nations and peoples. The "**Great Tradition**" of human knowledge is the gift of our ancestors given to us all, the common birthright of every human being born on Earth [see Chapter 1]. As discussed above, this includes making available the Great Tradition's "**Divine Library**" for study and contemplation to inspire everyone's spiritual practice and growth to Enlightenment [see Chapter 2].

Yet it is also important to understand that the Global Wisdom Traditions are only our *collective* inheritance, not the Truth itself. The Great Tradition must be rightly understood and appreciated, not adhered to with blind allegiance since all the different spiritual systems and philosophies naturally contain many errors and falsehoods as well as partial truths. This is an important reason for accessing Adi Da's Seven Stages of Life and Wilber's AQAL spectrum of consciousness developmental models: to recognize the liabilities inherent in each religious and cultural point of view in order to outgrow their errors and confusions [see Chapter 3]. Otherwise, there is a dangerous fallacy in resorting to traditional cultures in today's modern/postmodern world or just reviving ancient religious rituals and practices. This is doomed to fail because, as Wilber emphasizes, they originated in the *premodern* era therefore many traditional views often reject valuable truths uncovered by our current era (such as individual autonomy and basic human rights).[4]

It simply is not constructive or advantageous to regress backwards to bygone eras, as "**retro-romantics**" (in Wilber's words) suggest.[5] Rather, we must *evolve forward* into an Integral Age.[6] While there are certainly many traditional *values* worth keeping, much of the past's ethnocentric bias and superstitious beliefs must be released as being outdated errors from an earlier stage or worldview of development. The integral perspective intends to include the *partial truths* from every era including accessing mythic and traditional truths in addition to those discovered by science and the postmodern mind. Today integral philosophers claim this insight must become the fundamental orientation for any genuine integral theory and world philosophy to emerge.[7] Everyone and *all* cultures have something positive to contribute.

Unlike many of today's "new paradigm" (or "New Age") theorists who often condemn modernity (and reason), Wilber has thoroughly accepted the fact that one of the main problems with the "premodern" Great Wisdom Traditions is that their myths and metaphysics cannot withstand the piercing critiques made by either modern or postmodern philosophers (such as with Kant or Nietzsche). When modern science *demanded* evidence, the exoteric myths of traditional religions were discovered to be inventions and projections of the interior mind (although they too have their proper use and function). Even esoteric metaphysics and some of the speculative philosophies behind the world's great religions have been discovered to be individually and cultural-ly-conditioned, not pre-given truths after all. They are not necessarily based on ontological *pregiven* realities as they usually claim but rather evolve and change due to circumstances and the historical period within which they arise. This strong critique of premodern ideas is what's behind Wilber's so-called "**integral post-metaphysics**," a radical approach that is trying to answer the concerns of advanced post-Kantian and postmodern analyses while still including au-thentic spiritual (or transpersonal) truths. This advance is where, according to Wilber, lies "the religion of tomorrow."[8]

At the same time, I maintain we don't want to lump the Enlightened Ad-epts and their Nondual Wisdom into the same category as religious metaphys-ics, which is an error Wilber (and other scholars) too often promote. Neverthe-less, the integral pandit is correct to note that the contemplative or meditative *core* of the Great Wisdom Traditions does in fact offer verifiable phenome-nological evidence. Not only are they buried in the sacred texts of the Divine Library that can only be "measured" (or verified) by those adequately-trained in the higher Yogas but they reside in everyone's esoteric anatomy (or in the inner spheres of consciousness) as a developmental potential. It is only by resorting to this authentic contemplative and mystical core of the Great Tradition—i.e., by accessing *Sophia Perennis*, not just *Philosophia Perennis* [see Chapter 7-8]—that we can adequately outline the inner contours of the human psyche. It is only by *doing the practice* of mysticism (and meditation)—the "**Practic-ing School**," not simply the "**Talking School**"—can the future of the world's religions ever hope to be revived in the modern/postmodern world.[9] Only by *praxis* (and grace), not *theoria* (or *philosophia*) alone, does *gnosis* dawn. Simply put: we got to walk the walk, not merely talk the talk.

As is well known, ever since the dawn of science in the Renaissance, mo-dernity has rejected premodern religious traditions and their dogmatic, eth-nocentric, and absolutist tendencies, let alone their symbolic-mythic stories stretching fiction into facts. According to modern science, premodern reli-gious and mythological (and "metaphysical") proclamations are asserted without supporting exterior evidence. They are largely imagined projections of the interior mind even if archetypal. They become dogmatic when taken as literal truths. Nevertheless, advanced theories of modern psychology have recognized the value of the imaginal mind and their archetypal representations even if cloaked in myths and metaphysics. This is, however, a perspective Wilber fails to acknowledge adequately, often calling them "prototypes" (instead of archetypes) since they arise from the prepersonal domains without transpersonal significance.[10] Too often the integral pandit claims mythic archetypes simply come from the premodern era so have little use for us today (e.g., often he pokes fun at their more extreme examples of literal interpretation, such as Moses parting the Red Sea and other exaggerated mythic claims).

Nonetheless, postmodernity has rejected both the views of premodernity and modernity by claiming that *all perspectives*, whether metaphysical or scientific, are historically embedded in individual bodies and collective cultures, therefore they're all deluding. A more advanced integral view understands that psychic archetypes or "myths" are illustrations and guideposts to our inner psyche and its potential development, therefore, they serve an important function in psychological health.[11] At its best, Integral Philosophy fully intends to include the partial truths from *all* eras of human knowledge and the entire span of our collective inheritance since they all have valuable truths to contribute, even if some are false if taken too literally. We must learn to discriminate these differences and values.

Another problem with the premodern Great Wisdom Traditions, Wilber points out, is that they mostly focus on individual interiors to the exclusion of exteriors, thus he claims "virtually the entire Great Chain of Being fits into the Upper-Left quadrant [the interiors of individual]."[12] This assertion, however, seems to be an overstatement in order for Wilber to force-fit the premodern spiritual line of development into his AQAL Metatheory. When examined more carefully by incorporating the entire spectrum of culture (especially in places like India and Tibet) the enlightened (or transpersonal) insights of the inner mind also pervade cultural interiors (the Lower-Left quadrant), and therefore influence exterior social systems (the Lower-Right quadrant) as well. Modernity with its flatland materialism, for example, outright rejects the interiors as not being "real" and thus science prefers to shift its focus to exterior forms by relying on objective measurements and experimental observation (in the Right-Hand quadrants). This "flatland" project of scientific materialism intends to scrub the subjective perspective out of our conclusions about reality [see Chapter 1]. This is a major byproduct of the philosophy of modern science that collapses the pluridimensional Kosmos down into a materialistic cosmos of physical-only realities. Such a recommendation is no solution at all to the richness (and spectrum) of human experience.

Another persistent error of many modern people is to associate psi (or psychic) phenomena as being "spiritual" whereas true spirituality is about transcendent *Spirit* not energy states (or even kundalini). While beneficial in many ways, the modern mind is also a disaster for humanity with its stark reductionism of interior values to exterior phenomena. Science alone provides an incomplete philosophy for a Good Life. Both of these limited approaches, the premodern and modern (and postmodern) have weaknesses and liabilities. This is why humanity must evolve *forward* in consciousness development to an "**integral-centaur**" (in Wilber's terms) or whole-body awareness by including interiors *and* exteriors. This "leap" forward is necessary to manifest a genuine Integral Age of global inclusion, for earlier eras (including our own) are insufficient in solving our current predicaments. They are not fully holistic or integral, which is one of Integral Philosophy's principal and salient points.

When postmodernity pointed out the importance of the intersubjective and historical dimensions (Lower-Left quadrant) in influencing our interior worldviews we discovered that these basic structure-stages (or fulcrums) of development have essentially remained unconscious for much of human history, or at least for the average-mode collective. Integral Philosophy attempts to correct this failure by including *all* of these important truths—from the *premodern* to *modern* to *postmodern*—yet by also adding even more: genuine spiritual and *transpersonal* truths. The details and implications of this integral perspective and its revision of philosophy have occupied Wilber's central concerns in the later phases of his writings (since the late 1990s). AQAL Meta-theory intends to include as many partial truths from *all* eras by taking an *all-quadrant, all-level* approach to investigating and understanding the individual and collective branches of the human psyche situated altogether within an evolving universal Kosmos. Nevertheless, I maintain that Integral Theory needs to listen better to the wisdom of the Siddha-Adepts, many situated from within the "premodern" eras, as well as those being born in our modern age. It is only these advanced-tip few, women and men alike, who will be better able to help initiate us into a truly enlightened Integral Age, not just a postmodern era of nihilism and further confusion, or even a post-postmodern era that elevates psychic and mythic ideas to enlightened status, but to a truly New Age of real spirituality for all men and women from all areas of the globe.

"Pop Spirituality" = Consumer Religion

Everybody wants God-Realization to require no effort, no way, no teacher or teaching. To have God-Realization right now is the consumer's ultimate goal.

— **Adi Da Samraj**, 1982[13]

Avatar Adi Da has long been critical of any type of "**pop spirituality**" or "pop religion" or "pop esotericism" (in Adi Da's words) as he explains: "The central problem with conventional or popular religion and philosophy is the substitution of systems of affirmative belief *about* Truth for the self-transcending practice of devotion to the Realization *of* Truth.... 'Pop' religion and philosophy are basically tools of the gross social order. They consist primarily of systems of propagandized belief."[14] I venture to propose that this is true for "integral" philosophy as well including the post-metaphysical AQAL variety even with all its strengths and advantages. Talking or intellectual philosophies are not enough, only genuine spiritual *practices* are adequate. Let's allow the Avatar to vent his "Shout from the Heart" in favor of *authentic* (or vertically transformative) esotericism by critiquing the sophisticated (yet still egoic) philosophers from any time or historical era:

The Truth is reduced to the mortal patterns of psycho-physical inwardness, and the Spiritual Master is abandoned for the "Inner Guide" (or the ego as Master). These conventions of "street wisdom" are combined with bits and pieces of all traditions (such as the Confession of Jesus that "the Kingdom of God is within you") to create the absurd movements of "pop" spirituality (or "pop" esotericism), and these popular movements constantly clash in the streets with the equally absurd "pop" religions (or the "pop" exotericism of all the righteous absolute State religions) and their cultic Idols made of arbitrary beliefs and conventional mythologies....

In the popular un-Enlightened mind, the ego is eternal, good, Divine, and even very God. And mind is sufficient Heaven, or else this mortal Earth-life is the ultimate goal of conscious beings. Such views are not only false, they are the very substance of un-Enlightenment, fear, cruelty, and madness.... And, therefore, it is not only the message of worldly people but the message of ordinary and even extraordinary religious people that must be confronted by Wisdom. The righteous egoic "bite" of "pop" religion (and "pop" politics, "pop" science, and the "pop" mind cults of psychiatric vintage) must be tempered and transformed by righteous love, tolerance, and intelligent understanding.... The Way that is expressive of profound commitment to the Realization of Truth is another order of existence than the common path of the ordinary social [and even integral] personality.[15]

Wilber has also expressed similar reservations about consumer-oriented "spirituality" yet then he makes the error of championing the integral ego over the Enlightened State. He's even gone so far as to upgrade (or "upend") Enlightenment Itself, such as with **"evolutionary enlightenment**."[16] For example, in 1999 (before the Integral Institute) Wilber wrote: "I'm skeptical about the possibility of doing *'pop spirituality'* without its becoming thin and diluted, but it's certainly worth a try, and it can always serve to whet the appetite in a large and hungry audience [for true spirituality]."[17] The problem is that Wilber and many of his advocates (like Andrew Cohen) have corrupted the truths of Guru Yoga by making spirituality about *ideas* and egos (even if integral), thus they try to dispense with the need for an authentic Guru altogether. The pandit goes so far as to suggest that someone like Adi Da, a fully Enlightened Tantra Master, has a "psycho-sexual" line that is underdeveloped.[18] These quasi-practitioner scholars ignore or only express fascination with the potency of Spirit-Baptism (or Heart-Transmission) that any real Guru-devotee relationship is based on. But such is the misguided error of ego (and the mind), even with an "Integral Vision." All mental or "talking" philosophies need to be transcended and outgrown in authentic transpersonal development. I believe it's preferable to use sadhana-Satsang under the guidance of a genuine Guru-Adept as the Great Tradition of Global Wisdom has long taught.

By being influenced by too many ill-fated modern gurus, these postmodern pandits do not differentiate well enough between inauthentic and authentic Gurus nor do they discriminate adequately between the various levels (or state-stages) presented in the higher Stages of Life. Wilber, therefore, seems satisfied to mostly criticize Guru Yoga by offering his philosophical alternatives for the post-postmodern Integral Age. He offers his own "pointing-out instructions" to try to prove that "you" can access these "states" of Waking Up contemplation *without* Spiritual-Transmission or radical life changes (i.e., adapting to sadhana engaged in Satsang). Instead, you get "one-minute modules" and other simplified "integral life practices."[19] The pandit even suggests that if you *go integral* you may become "super-human," among other "first ever in history" utopian idealisms.[20]

Perhaps *if* Wilber had continued to study (and honor) Avatar Adi Da Samraj as an authentic Guru-Adept (after having lavished praise and endorsements on him for decades), and *if* perhaps he would have practiced sadhana in the Guru's Company, *then* he might have realized the inadequacy of the "inner Guru" and "pop" spirituality approach. But unfortunately, he didn't do that. Instead, Wilber turned his back on Adi Da and Guru Yoga by preferring instead his own "Fourth Turning"[21] or integral form of spirituality. This is what Adi Da calls a Talking School method, which Wilber now apparently prefers [see next section]. Wilber proposes his personal form of an integral "Talking School" based mostly on students studying his books and using his AQAL metatheories in addition to doing his suggested "integral practices" of self-improvement (such as with "module" time-slots and mind-based "pointing-out instructions"). While good for psychological health and "Growing Up," this approach has little to do with real "Waking Up" or Enlightenment. For the past twenty years and more Wilber has championed this watered-down approach to "spiritual" life rather than engaging the authentic "Practicing School" based on Guru Yoga-Satsang. This means it misses out on the opportunity to receive actual Spirit Baptism (or *shaktipat* transmission) gained from being in the Company of an Enlightened Adept-Realizer or Avatar.

"Talking School" Philosophy vs. "Practicing School" Spirituality

Since Adi Da Samraj is an authentic Adept, a genuine Siddha-Guru here to Liberate (and Enlighten) human beings, he is interested in actual spiritual *practice* not just talking about it. As Wilber once noted, "What a *guru* does nobody else does, is takes a particular person as a devotee—as a 'client'—and works with them personally…. The Guru eats the karma (or conditioning) of the devotee."[22] Consequently, when the Avatar reviews the Great Tradition, including many of today's psychologists-philosophers and spiritual teachers (including Wilber himself), he turns a critical eye to what he calls the "**Talking School**" approach which, as he defines, is "characterized by talking, thinking, reading, and philosophical analysis and debate, or even meditative inquiry."[23] But this is mostly a mind game, not authentic spirituality.

As a genuine Guru-Adept, Adi Da instead strongly supports the "**Practicing School**" that "involves those who are committed to the ordeal of real ego-transcending discipline under the guidance [and transmission] of a true Guru."[24] The Practicing School, in other words, is the *hard school* of spiritual life demanding discipline and daily meditation, self-surrender and ego-transcendence. Thus this "hard school" of real practice, including self-disciplines and meditation, is highly unattractive to most modern Westerners (and many Easterners as well). Real Gurus who demand and expect actual ego-transcending practice are often ridiculed and thought to be dispensable or outdated in today's egalitarian and consumer-oriented world, an unfortunate claim made by many of the Talking School pandits. The table below lists some of the basic characteristics of each approach (which we will further review):

Talking School	Practicing School
Mind-centered	Body-mind-heart centered
Western "Omega"-mind approach	Eastern "Alpha"-mind approach
Philosophies, science-centered	Religious, mystical-centered
Ego-fulfilling (ego-doubting) debates	Ego-transcending disciplines

There is a modern tendency not only to dismiss authentic ego-transcending practices (such as proper diet and regular meditation) but then to dismiss the external physical Guru in favor of the "Guru within" or the "wisdom inside" (since everyone has interiors). Adi Da, of course, criticizes this tendency of "**self-guruing**" as being ego-based or self-saving "practices of childish, and (otherwise) adolescent, and (altogether) merely exoteric cultism."[25] Adi Da openly complains: "It is in the 'Talking School' of heady practitioners (or self-contained egos) that we hear so much nonsense about the non-necessity of a Spiritual Master. Of course, the Adept is of no use (except perhaps to write books to feed the ego-minds) for those who are self-bound and not interested in the real fulfillment of the Great Way."[26] Talking School scholars like to emphasize self-generated exercises of self-improvement, write books and give lectures, post YouTube videos, podcasts, and lead seminars, instead of declaring the authenticity of genuine Spiritual Masters. They prefer to recommend the "inner Guru" so anyone can follow any path that appeals to them. But this is just a ruse to hide the fact they are fearful of an external Guru who is always demanding preparation, more self-transcendence and active love than most students want to give. They prefer an eclectic smorgasbord approach to spirituality since they're still ego-centered, not a self-transcending entity communing with the Divine Reality. No Adept claims that spiritual life is easy. Yoga scholar Georg Feuerstein (a one-time devotee of Adi Da) noted:

> It is certainly incomparably easier to tinker with spiritual practices on one's own terms than it is to respond to the Guru's incessant appeal for ever more comprehensive self-transcendence. So long as one purports to follow the "Guru within," the tempo of spiritual practice is apt to be comfortable enough for the ego. But the [authentic] Spiritual Master never allows his [or her] disciples to lie back at their ease. Authentic spiritual life consists in the voluntary frustration of one's habitual tendencies toward stasis and self-pleasuring.[27]

Such *authentic* spiritual life needs an *authentic* Adept-Guru. We should be careful about what we criticize for it might be our own reflection in the mirror starring back at us; the error is more likely with us, not Guru Yoga. This criticism of the ego's lazy tendency is one of the important *functions* of the Guru: to provide the push and demand for spiritual surrender into love and self-transcending service to others, to realize God *now* in the present while living daily life. Spiritual life is a "**hard school**," as Adi Da emphasizes, so it's much easier to resist and demure. The frustrations arising from a disciplined life generate "heat," the meaning of *tapas* (in Sanskrit), the "fire" that burns away impurities and egoity. In a famous and popular talk given by Adi Da on July 17, 1978, called "**The Fire Must Have Its Way**" (available in CD and DVD formats), the Avatar clarifies that real spiritual practice is not merely about "feeling good," but is an intense purification on all limits on feeling altogether. This "fire" of purification occurs most directly by coming into contact with the pure radiance of the Spiritual Master as Guru-Adept. Feuerstein acknowledges his own resistance and rigorous doubt, while intellectually agreeing with its age-old principle:

> The Guru is a difficult factor to reckon with. Indeed, the Spiritual Master spells difficulty: That is his [or her] responsibility in the spiritual process. He constantly pushes the devotee beyond all self-imposed and comfortable limits. His efficacy can almost be said to be directly proportionate to his being a disturbance, a turbulence, in the life of the spiritual practitioner.[28]

Avatar Adi Da emphasized this same message during the very first year of opening his Ashram (in 1972): "The Guru is a kind of irritation to his friends. You can't sleep with a dog barking in your ear, at least most people can't.... The

Guru is a constant wakening sound. He is always annoying people with his demand to stay awake, to wake up."[29] Taking on such a powerful and sacred relationship, such as with Satsang and Guru Yoga, can only be handled by serious spiritual practitioners, those who realize the Guru is transforming them in God-Consciousness. This Practicing School based on devotion and meditation is resisted by those who prefer to talk about God and erudite philosophical ideals while they minimize or even shun actual self-transcendence and real transpersonal practice.

When done correctly Guru Yoga becomes a portal to the Divine Abode (in the feeling heart), to see God as All-Pervading and Transcendent to the world-Kosmos. Even in the modern world there is still a great benefit to be achieved by simply *listening* to and *studying* an authentic Adept-Realizer, even if serious practice is postponed. Most of us can't move into an Ashram, though all of us would benefit from taking periodic meditation retreats. Although this is a slower, more gradual approach, it begins by recognizing the true role of the Guru-Adept as being one of the most effective methods of *real spiritual practice.* Guru Yoga-Satsang is not just a Talking School philosophy but devotional authenticity.[30]

True, the work of pandits or spiritual scholars is important even if only to consider and contemplate the Spiritual Master's Call to ego-transcendence. Pandits can effectively translate or explain this radical point of view by facilitating our improved understanding, which in many cases, Ken Wilber has done admirably. But the real work of spiritual practice (sadhana) begins in recognition-response to a true Guru-Adept (in Satsang) so then we come to know and see the Guru as an agent of God transforming us into becoming God-conscious human beings. This is why people bow in respect and devotion, not out of cultic illusion or idol worship, but out of genuine gratitude for living an authentic spiritual life. Wake up to see God as Guru, an Agent of Enlightenment, and find out for yourself.

POINTING-OUT INSTRUCTION:
"I'M A PANDIT, NOT A GURU!"

The heart of Integral Philosophy, as I conceive it, is primarily a mental activity of coordinating, elucidating and conceptually integrating all the various modes of knowing and being, so that, even if Integral Philosophy itself does not deliver the higher modes, it fully acknowledges them, and then allows and invites **philosophia** *to open itself to the practices and modes of* **contemplatio**.... *finally, it is a* **theoria** *that is inseparable from* **praxis**, *on all levels, in all quadrants.*[31]

— Ken Wilber, 1997

The real purpose of the Guru-Adept is not to "talk" people into the ego-transcending process of spiritual life but to insist upon it. The authentic Guru is not your "friend," simply there to console you into complacency or stimulate your mind with spiritual "ideas" but to aggravate you into self-transcending practice so you will learn to find Spirit, to find God or the Transcendental Presence *for real* (with each and every breath). Satsang may be a hard school, even sometimes confusing (or mind-blowing), but it's always full of love and bliss too, endearing affection and devotion. It is the Way of the Heart, not the way of the talking-thinking mind (or self-contraction). Satsang is a *relationship* founded on love and spiritual insight about the ego-transcending process of Divine Realization, not a mindless cultic fascination with some spiritual authority. A person will generally not accept or tolerate self-transcending disciplines without knowing it will be beneficial to them (e.g., such as in sports or the military). Self-transcending growth and development (and even improvement) to God-Realization is also the purpose of submitting to Guru Yoga-Satsang, as millennia of practitioners have proven and testify.

One prime example of a Talking School technique that Adi Da criticizes is the tendency for teachers today *to talk* people into identifying with their base consciousness or awareness, somewhat like the "**pointing out instructions**" used in the Vajrayana Buddhist and Advaitic traditions. Even then, in those traditions they are usually only given to disciples after years of training and dedicated *practice*; they are graduate studies, so to speak, not undergraduate classes. In today's world, however, you can receive these "secret teachings" during a lecture or in a book. While useful (since consciousness is real), they're more effective when given by a God-Realized Guru or Enlightened Lama, not a teacher or pandit.

Wilber acknowledges this is the type of approach he prefers to promote: "Precisely because One Taste is 'always already' present, many people can gain a quick but extremely powerful glimpse of this ultimate state if an accomplished teacher carefully points it out to them. And, in fact, many of the great Nondual schools, such as Dzogchen and Vedanta, have entire texts devoted to these 'pointing out instructions'."[32] This common technique of Talking School enthusiasts, often used by Wilber in his books and public talks, is to engage in an analytical exercise that calls on the listener to identify with the consciousness behind thoughts and actions.[33] We are encouraged, it is suggested, to "witness" all forms (interior and exterior) arising in formlessness awareness. Indeed, such "pointing out" is useful and instructive on any level for conscious awareness is in fact our fundamental reality and mode of knowing.

Such types of popular "**mindfulness**" utilized by the public Talking School approach will, as Adi Da explains, "try to talk people into identifying with consciousness, or merely relaxing their minds, settling into a conscious state that does not have any particular reference to the body-mind, even though it is still associated with it in practical terms."[34] While this is a widespread technique used in today's spiritual marketplace since it helps people relax and possibly experience a short "taste" of what meditation (or stillness of mind) is similar to, it is not earned with daily practice. Then for a person to assume they are now "enlightened," or that they have achieved some type of Jnana Samadhi or Transcendental (Witness) Consciousness simply by identifying with what is "always already the case" is false teaching, according to Adi Da (and other Adepts).

Sure, a popular audience appreciates this style of spirituality since it doesn't demand consistent practice (or sadhana), let alone Satsang, for it can be done in a seminar chair. In truth, this approach is mostly an exercise of relaxation, of releasing attachment to the stream of thoughts (or our "monkey mind") which is positive but definitely not Enlightenment or God-Realization. While "mind-fulness" or being detached from one's ever-changing thoughts and emotional states in repose and relaxation is beneficial in integrating the body-mind into a mild state of equanimity, the necessity to "go beyond" mindfulness becomes a dictum for the "**Practicing School**" (as Adi Da maintains). Awakening to the Divine Nature of Consciousness becomes the practice, not talking about it.

The integral pandit, as one example, provides his own "integral" version of the "Talking" method effectively given to the readers of his books: "I am simply going to point out something that is *already* occurring in your present, ordinary, natural state.… So you push back into the source of your own awareness. You push back into the Witness, and you rest in the Witness.… As you rest in the Witness—realizing, I am not objects, I am not feelings, I am not thoughts—all you will notice is a sense of Freedom, a sense of Liberation, a sense of Release."[35] This "talking" approach or what Wilber also calls "**Big Mind**" (after Gopi Roshi) became a favorite technique used by the integral philosopher in the 2000s. This "always already" pointing-out approach often appears as Wilber's "nondual" last chapter in many of his books.[36] The problem with this method is there is always a "you" or a reader (i.e., an ego-I) who is trying *to do* something, e.g., "*you* rest in the Witness," whereas actual self-transcendence demanded by a bona-fide Guru involves the total surrender of "Narcissus" altogether, the very sense that there's a separate self in the first place. Then you *consciously* commune with God's Spirit-Presence, not simply observe awareness. Such "**ego-death**" is what the Practicing Schools under genuine Guru-Adepts (from whatever tradition) teach and demand and serve by initiating authentic Awakening. Nothing else will do for them, so we too should naturally heed their more advanced Wisdom Call.

At times, Wilber understands this point too such as when he supports *praxis* over *theoria*: "Learning a new concept will not get you to nondual constant consciousness; only intense and prolonged practice will."[37] But in the new millennium, the integral pandit shifted from this emphasis on practice as he relaxed his support for genuine Gurus. He began to promote his own form of "**Integral Buddhism**" (the so-called "Fourth Turning") as being "the first awareness in all of history that is actually competent."[38] Sadly such hyperbole seems to indicate that perhaps Wilber's ego should have listened more closely (and devotionally) to Avatar Adi Da (and other Adepts) instead of just writing and talking about it (as useful as that is for certain horizontal translations).

From Avatar Adi Da's (or an Adept-Realizer's) perspective, Wilber's approach is basically a "talking-writing" method of spirituality that has evolved (or devolved) into one where the pandit discourages (and disparages) practicing with a genuine Guru. While Wilber benefited from several living Gurus and Masters, from several traditions (though mostly Buddhist), such as with Katagiri Roshi and Maezumi Roshi (from Zen), Kirpal Singh (from Shabd Yoga), Kalu Rinpoche, Pema Norbu Rinpoche, and Chagdud Tulku Rinpoche (from Tibetan Buddhism), including offering deep gratitude to Adi Da Samraj (in the pandit's early decades), today he tends to downplay participation in Guru Yoga.[39] Generally, Wilber teaches that Guru Yoga-Satsang is incomplete because it does not see the "hidden maps" or structures of "Growing Up" that filter the Guru's Enlightened Awareness through certain socio-cultural worldviews. Thus he harshly criticizes Guru Yoga and Satsang as being "premodern" and insufficient:

> Humanity *did* produce Awakened or Enlightened individuals—people who followed the path of Waking Up—but they could still be relatively immature in many of their human capacities [of Growing Up]: they might be poorly developed psychosexually (and thus sexually take advantage of their students), or they might not be well developed morally despite their spiritual interests…. They may have been "one with the world," but their capacities in that world remained relatively immature or even dysfunctional and pathological.[40]

This is a very dangerous and mostly deluded assessment to make about such a sacred and time-honored tradition. Even if it is correctly based on a few corrupted Gurus of the modern era (who should be rightly disgraced), he fails to take into account a *genuine* Guru's complete set of functions offered in Satsang. He diminishes the necessity for actual Spiritual Baptism (*shaktipat*), which is a powerful goad to real ego-transcendence and Divine Communion.

The harm of such statements by pandits and scholars, while correct in some instances, betrays the true beauty and Divine Help that an authentic Guru-Adept provides. When it comes down to it, Ken Wilber is an intellectual "Talking School" pandit who is far from an Enlightened Guru, as he himself has often confessed: "A Guru is an enlightened master and teacher. I'm a pandit, not a guru."[41] I suggest he should more readily follow his own advice. I know he knows better but actions speak louder than words.

Unfortunately, even in a sincere effort to learn more, people today tend to prefer these talking meditations and relaxation techniques given by some kind of pseudo-"guru" (with a small "g"). They're often some type of authority from modern psychology offering methods to "awaken you" now, right away. Just sign up for their "webinar" (a seminar held over the Internet), or their slickly promoted class, and usually for a considerable "bargain" fee too. They offer simple techniques instead of emphasizing devotion to God, self-transcendence, and daily meditation. They overlook the hard school of practice and the advantages in finding a genuine Guru or authentic spiritual authority who will push one's boundaries in order to fulfill true spiritual life. Worse, these Talking School advocates overtly forget about the necessity for Spirit-Baptism and Transcendental Transmission (*Hridaya Shaktipat*) that only an authentic Adept-Guru (not an intellectual pandit) can provide to student-devotees. In Wilber's case, this error has become particularly confusing. On the one hand, he is appreciative of Guru Yoga—"Guru Yoga is the most powerful yoga there is"[42]—yet, on the other hand, he's very dismissive at times.[43] By doing this Wilber leads a trail of students who use him more as a "guru" than just a teacher-pandit; I suggest we use both the Avatar and the integral pandit with each serving their appropriate function. They both shower benefit on the inquiring student wondering about authentic spirituality.

The Talking School approach to mysticism (really, an elevated form of Narcissus or the self-contraction) distorts the necessity for ego-transcending and ego-countering disciplines involved in a genuine spiritual lifestyle. As an authentic Enlightened Guru, Adi Da points out this serious fallacy: "The same kinds of advocates are also telling people that there is no real purpose for a Spiritual Master, except to bind yourself to another ego, and so on."[44] Wilber falls directly into this anti-Guru camp when he suggests: "Some of these groups will be headed by people who are highly advanced in state development (of Waking Up), and not at all that advanced in stages of Growing Up…. You might have to resign yourself to simply listening to what this teaching has to say about states [of Waking Up] and pretty much ignore everything else."[45] From my view, this seems like a direct critique aimed at Adi Da himself, which is a true distortion of reality and the function of Adi Da's Teaching-Work and Blessing-Power. I maintain that Wilber's distortion of Guru Yoga is a personal matter and therefore his views are inappropriate for public guru-bashing as honored in the Great Tradition of Global Wisdom. The truth is Guru Yoga-Satsang is one of the most highly regarded methods in the entire esoteric history of humankind. Only time will tell who is right, who is wrong; who is practicing and who is merely talking (or philosophizing).

Chapter 4 Endnotes

1. See: Ken Wilber, *The Religion of Tomorrow* (2017).

2. See: Ken Wilber, *Sex, Ecology, Spirituality* (1995, 2001), *A Brief History of Everything* (1996, 2017), *The Marriage of Sense and Soul* (1998); also see: Jean Gebser, *The Ever-Present Origin* (1949, 1985).

3. Ken Wilber, *A Theory of Everything* (2000), p. 1 [title caps added].

4. See: Ken Wilber, *Integral Spirituality: A Startling New Role for Religion in the Modern and Postmodern World* (2006).

5. See: Ken Wilber, *Sex, Ecology, Spirituality: The Spirit of Evolution* (1995, 2001).

6. See: Ken Wilber, *Sex, Ecology, Spirituality* (1995, 2001), *A Brief History of Everything* (1996, 2017).

7. See: Ken Wilber, *The Marriage of Sense and Soul* (1998); *A Theory of Everything* (2000); *The Religion of Tomorrow* (2017); also see: Dustin DiPerna, *Evolution's Ally* (2015); Steve McIntosh, *The Presence of the Infinite* (2015).

8. See: Ken Wilber, *Integral Spirituality* (2006); *The Religion of Tomorrow* (2017).

9. See: Ken Wilber, *The Eye of Spirit* (1997), *The Marriage of Sense and Soul* (1998), *The Religion of Tomorrow* (2017).

10. See, for example: James Hillman, *The Soul's Code: In Search of Character and Calling* (2017); *Re-Visioning Psychology* (1997).

11. See: for example: C. G. Jung, *The Archetypes and The Collective Unconscious* (*CW*, Vol.9 Part 1, 1981); or Jordan Peterson, *Maps of Meaning: The Architecture of Belief* (1999).

12. See: Ken Wilber, *Integral Spirituality* (2006), *A Theory of Everything* (2000), *Integral Psychology* (1999), *The Marriage of Sense and Soul* (1998), and *The Eye of Spirit* (1997).

13. Adi Da Samraj [Da Free John], "The Seventh School of God-Talk" (talk) in "Preface" to *The Song of the Self Supreme: Astavakra Gita* (1982), p. 46.

14. Adi Da Samraj [Da Free John], *Nirvanasara* (1982), p. 151.

15. Ibid., p. 149, 150, 152.

16. See: Andrew Cohen, *Evolutionary Enlightenment* (2011) with a Foreword by Deepak Chopra, which Wilber claims is "truly one of the most significant books on spirituality written in the postmodern world," probably, to a large degree, because Cohen expresses Wilber's own ideas on how Enlightenment is still evolving through each and every one of us via our born (or inherited) cultural-historical period.

17. Ken Wilber, *One Taste* (1999), p. 132 [italics in original].

18. See: *In God's Company: Guru-Adepts As Agents for Enlightenment in the Integral Age* (2022) by Brad Reynolds.

19. See: *Integral Life Practice: A 21st-Century Blueprint for Physical Health, Emotional Balance, Mental Clarity, and Spiritual Awakening* (2008) by Ken Wilber, Terry Patten, Adam Leonard, Marco Morelli.

20. For example, see: Ken Wilber, *Integral Meditation* (2016), p. 193: "This is the first time, essentially in all of human history, that both Growing Up through developmental levels and Waking Up through developmental states… have all been brought together, practiced together, and realized together, producing a truly super-human Realization in one's very own being." Honestly, and sadly, this is a genuine distortion of the Truth.

21. See: Ken Wilber, *The Fourth Turning: Imagining the Evolution of an Integral Buddhism* (Kindle Edition, 2014).

22. Ken Wilber, *One Taste* (1999), pp. 223-224, to which Wilber quickly added, "That is something that I myself do not wish to do."

23. Talking" School and "Practicing" School definitions from *The Aletheon* Glossary (2009, Volume 8), p. 2162;

24. "Talking" School and "Practicing" School definitions from *The Aletheon* Glossary (2009, Volume 8), p. 2162; also see "What Is Required To Realize The Non-Dual Truth? The Controversy Between The Talking School and The Practicing School of Advaitism" in *The Gnosticon* (2010), p. 385ff [all quotes in this paragraph].

25. Adi Da Samraj, *The Aletheon* (2009), p. 153.

26. Adi Da Samraj, *What Is The Conscious Process* (1983), p. 19.

27. Georg Feuerstein, "Worshiping The Guru's Feet" in *The Laughing Man*, Vol. 4, No. 4, 1984.

28. Georg Feuerstein, "Worshiping The Guru's Feet" in *The Laughing Man*, Vol. 4, No. 4, 1984. In full disclosure, it is true that Feuerstein left Adidam after seven years (of being a devotee) to expand his writing and Yoga Research and Educational Foundation, where he published *Holy Madness: The Shock Tactics and Radical Teachings of Crazy-Wise Adepts, Holy Fools and Rascal Gurus* (in 1991). In this book, Feuerstein is critical of such direct demands and "crazy wisdom" behavior. Nonetheless, Feuerstein remained deeply grateful to Adi Da Samraj until his own death in 2012 (Adi Da died in 2008). Thus, it's easy to understand his comment from the above article: "My own oscillation, stretching over more years than I care to remember, between an affirmative attitude toward the spiritual dimension and a frustrated (and frustrating) skepticism and crypto materialism, allows me to empathize with those who still question the role and function of the Guru in spiritual life." Such honesty is a necessary component to serving the evolution of consciousness.

29. Adi Da Samraj [Franklin Jones], *The Method of the Siddhas* (1973, 1978), p. 152.

30. See: *Meeting Adi Da: A Mandala of Approach to Avatar Adi Da Samraj* (forthcoming) by Brad Reynolds.

31. Ken Wilber, *The Eye of Spirit* (1997), pp. 308-308, 1n.

32. Ken Wilber, *One Taste* (1999), p. 137.

33. See, for example, Wilber's version of pointing out instructions in *One Taste* (1999), pp. 86-88.

34. Adi Da Samraj, *What Is The Conscious Process* (1983), p. 25.

35. Ken Wilber, *One Taste* (1999), p. 87.

36. For example, see the last Chapter in *The Eye of Spirit* (1997) titled "Always Already: The Brilliant Clarity of Ever-Present Awareness"; or the last Chapter in Integral Meditation (2016) titled "The Total Painting of All That Is." This is when the integral pandit likes to dispense with his philosophical "ideas" presented in the earlier Chapters in order to "point to" the "always already" ever-present awareness (or Witness consciousness) that is Real God or Conscious Light (when known in Truth), thus often leaving the reader "in bliss" (at least momentarily) and, hence, more appreciative of the integral ideas he or she has read earlier.

37. Ken Wilber, *One Taste* (1999), p. 133.

38. Ken Wilber, *Integral Meditation* (2016), p. 218.

39. See: Ken Wilber, "Afterword" to *Spiritual Transmission: Paradoxes and Dilemma* (2018) edited by Amir Freimann.

40. Ken Wilber, *Integral Meditation* (2016), p. 2.

41. Ken Wilber, *Grace and Grit* (1990), pp. 156-157; elsewhere, Ken Wilber: "I am a pandit, not a guru," is a line (and explanation) Wilber has "used a hundred times in my life." (One Taste, p. 222) "I do not want to be a guru because I do not want to enter into a therapist/client relationship with people…. I have no plans to get involved with anybody's personal transformation." (*One Taste*, pp. 225-226) Obviously, Wilber has expanded this claim as the 21st century dawned, and he was financed (by millionaires) to establish the Integral Institute

(I-I), for now the integral pandit teaches like a "guru" (small "g") while turning a critical eye on Guru Yoga: "Their Enlightened awareness simply supports their ethnocentric prejudices, because their nondual Suchness looks through the hidden maps of their structure development." (*Integral Meditation*, p. 215) Therefore, Wilber believes he is providing an "Integral Approach" greater than any Enlightened Adept of the past, for he's trying to initiate "the single greatest transformation in human consciousness ever to emerge, anywhere, anytime." (*Integral Meditation*, p. 218) However, unfortunately, I suggest there is more ego talking here than an Enlightened mind.

42. Ken Wilber, *One Taste* (1999), p. 224.

43. I have suggested elsewhere that one of the main reasons Wilber is dismissive of Guru Yoga is because of his ruptured relationship with Adi Da Samraj, who he had long admired personally (and in print as well), but never became a true devotee. See: *The Avatar and Integral Pandit: The Relationship of Two Spiritual Giants at the Dawn of the Third Millennium* (forthcoming) by Brad Reynolds.

44. Adi Da Samraj, *What Is The Conscious Process* (1983), p. 26.

45. Ken Wilber, *Integral Meditation* (2016), p. 212.

FIVE

SATSANG-SADHANA IS THE GREAT TRADITION OF GURU YOGA

True renunciation—and, above all, true Realizers—can rightly serve the possi-
bility of Reality-Realization in ego-bound and "worldly" people only by stead-
fastly refusing to support and engage their illusions (both sacred and secular).

— **Adi Da Samraj**, *The Gnosticon*[1]

CONCEIT OF PRIOR ENLIGHTENMENT: NO GURUS, LITTLE PRACTICE

Avatar Adi Da, in answering the "pointing out instructions" used in the spiritual marketplace, criticizes what he calls "**the conceit of prior Enlightenment**." This "Talking School" approach (in Adi Da's words) often teach that a person needs no Guru and little practice (or only short periods of meditation) for they are "always already" Enlightened (or "I am" God). A genuine Guru-Adept is going to rail against such ideas, as this one from America explains in biting detail:

> The beginner's mind begins to develop a conceit of prior Enlighten-ment. After all (so the beginner reasons), the Adept says that Enlight-enment is the Prior Condition, and we are already established in It, It is the case, and all approaches to It are exercises of that very ob-struction to our Realization. Such reasoning leads to no practice, no spiritual discipline [no Satsang].
>
> Particularly people who are not truly and seriously established in the Spiritual Way of life use the rather wild and humorous confes-sions of Adepts to develop the conceit of no-practice, as if to propose that one need not be involved with meditation or Spiritual Teachers. One acquires such presumptions from popularizers of spirituality, university scholars of spiritual literature, and psychiatrists. Every-body wants God-Realization to require no effort, no way, no teacher or teaching. To have God-Realization right now is the consumer's ultimate goal.[2]

Adi Da Samraj continued this critique until his last writings, where he spoke of an "**Emperor's New Clothes syndrome**" associated with the "Talking School" of ideas and of free "Tantra" sex (with no renunciation). These post-modern and integral advocates of a new and revised spirituality say, yes, there are "premodern" practices like Guru Yoga-Satsang where you "surrender" to a Guru, but such approaches are outdated for the modern mind and are only for those who are "immature" and not yet ripe for the new (integral) version of "pointing out instructions" or "Truth-talking" (in Adi Da's words).[3] These proud listeners of esoteric texts refuse to acknowledge the necessity for counter-egoic practices and then ridicule Guru-devotion, so as Adi Da points out, they "merely 'talk', and think, and 'talk' some more."[4] But this becomes an endless round of non-Realization, of egoic chit-chat no matter how "integral" or wise it may profess to be.

Many readers of popular "spiritual" books like to naively assume they are already enlightened—since Enlightenment is "always already the case"—thus they don't want to do preliminary disciplines and certainly not accept devotion to a Guru. Avatar Adi Da, on the other hand, is an authentic Guru-Adept affirming that spiritual practice and ego-transcendence—or Satsang-sadhana—are absolutely necessary for stable Real God-Awakening. Only a real Guru can help transform your temporary higher states into permanent traits. For someone to simply read some books, or take some drugs, or attend some weekend seminars, or any other "quick-fix" methods, then think they have realized "the Truth," is just another inflation of the ego. While many higher state experiences are indeed blissful, and even ego-transcending (or self-expanding), they are not actual God-Realization. This is true even though they often contain an intuition of the Divine Reality. Indeed, the spectrum of mystical experiences are what the separate self itself experiences (and realizes) in the first Six Stages of Life. Some may be useful, others merely garbage. In Enlightenment the separate self is transcended altogether.

The Avatar, as mentioned, calls this attitude of intellectually assuming God-Realization with critical phrases such as the "**conceit of false Self-Realization**" and the "**conceit of prior Enlightenment**" or the "**conceit of the mind.**"[5] A genuine Guru-Adept will heavily (and rightly) criticize such misguided approaches. Adi Da tells us that those people "who casually assume an attitude or self-idea that mentally presumes Realization, and thus freedom from the necessity to practice as well as [from using] the Teaching Help and Transmission of a fully qualified Adept"[6] are just deluding themselves. He forcefully comments: "The casual reader may imagine that, if he [or she] comprehends or seriously enjoys sympathy with these statements and considerations, he is in fact enjoying Realization. Therefore, he imagines that the Adept Spiritual Master and the process of life-obliging practice are either false or unnecessary for him [or her]. And he leaves these books with a mind full of the ego of Liberation, imagining God, Spiritual Master, and practice to be anachronisms in his 'pure' comprehension."[7] Such an attitude of egoic conceit is far from the realization of the Divine Truth.

People, as you may have noticed, generally react to the demand for self-transcending spirituality by either taking a *childish* attitude of cultic dependence or they get defensive like an *adolescent* fighting for independence from a parent saying they don't need Gurus (or even God). There is nothing wrong in establishing independent autonomy, it is part of Growing Up, but the sacred teachings of Waking Up need to be rightly honored. Adi Da considers resistance to Adepts and their Divine Help as being characteristic of adolescent rebelliousness. Dishonoring the Guru (like one's parents) is an immature attitude of the common ego and modern mind, many of whom doubt God as well. According to the world's Great Adepts, no greater error could be made because real practice (sadhana) with a genuine Guru (Satsang) is our advantage leading to genuine Divine Awakening.

Guru Yoga should not be dismissed even in our postmodern day and age, for if it's engaged correctly (and non-cultically) it will reveal the Truth of Reality, nothing less. But modern people usually prefer instant gratification or to only attend an Internet course (or watch a TV program) or read a book at their leisure. They are unwilling to put in the hard work and devotion necessary for authentic ego-transcending sadhana. To do sadhana or spiritual disciplines and meditation (even if they know it's good for them) a person has to resist their normal habits to simply pleasurize oneself, a hallmark of materialistic consumerism. Most people prefer to party instead of to meditate. To use an authentic Guru correctly a person must readapt to a mature and *spiritual* relationship with their Spiritual Master, not a childish or adolescent one. The Great Tradition of Global Wisdom verifies this truth beyond doubt or argument. Study the wisdom texts for yourself and learn to distinguish what is real from that which is false and deluding. That alone is a test... and demand of maturity.

This conceit of independence from Gurus and sadhana is characteristic of today's tendency to ridicule and degrade the importance of the genuine Guru -devotee relationship. Many teachers and professors stoke our fears of cults and abusive totem-masters, often distorting spiritual truths to increase their bank accounts. Some even claim these Adepts represent only anachronisms of the premodern agrarian past so now it is time to leave these "Masters" behind for a greater, more egalitarian, evolutionary future. However, it is the more evolved individuals *from the past*—the Shamans, Yogis, Saints, Sages, Siddhas, et al.— who are *already* representative examples of our *future* evolution. These are the "**advanced-tip**" individuals, women and men alike, who embody and express the higher (and highest) Stages of Life lying dormant within all of us awaiting to open and evolve. They are not simply heroic relics from the past who have outgrown their usefulness but are beacons to our brighter future. It is not artificial intelligence (A.I.) that will serve and "save" us; it is only Enlightened Intelligence (E.I.)—the choice is ours!

Great Tradition of Global Wisdom: Teaching Satsang-Sadhana

A s only a couple of samples (out of many examples) from the Great Tradition show, many Adepts in history are also critical of the Talking School approach since anti-Guru advocates were alive and active back in ancient days too (just like in modern times). After all the genuine Guru is actively battling the ego or self-identity, a condition always existent in every era (and realm). These brief quotes below are culled from the "Divine Library" of the Great Tradition. Let's begin with the ancient *Mundaka Upanishad* whose wisdom is like a "cutting razor" (from whence its title arises), as sharp and direct today as it was thousands of years ago:

> The Atman cannot be attained through study of the Vedas alone, nor through intelligence, nor through much learning. He who chooses Atman—by him alone is Atman attained. It is Atman that reveals to the seeker Its true nature. (III.ii.3)
>
> In order that he may understand that Eternal Atman, fuel [gifts] in hand, approach a Guru who is well versed in the Vedas and always devoted to Brahman. To that pupil who has duly approached him, whose mind is completely serene, and whose senses are controlled, the wise teacher [Guru] should indeed impart the Knowledge of Brahman [via Transmission and Teaching], through which one knows the immutable and the true Purusha [Divine Person]. (I.ii.12-13)[8]

Or, for another fine example, let's turn to the Mahayana Buddhist text (composed around 350-400 CE or earlier) called the *Lankavatara Sutra* where Gautama Buddha himself is said to have clarified these same concerns:

> In the same manner, those whose minds have been addicted to the discriminations of the erroneous views cherished by the philosophers, which are given over to the realistic views of being and non-being, will contradict the good Dharma and will end in the destruction of themselves and others....
>
> As long as scholars [pandits] remain on their philosophical ground their demonstration must conform to logic and their textbooks, and the memory-habit of erroneous intellection will ever cling to them.... Words and sentences are produced by the law of causation and are mutually conditioning—they cannot express Highest Reality.... Highest Reality is an exalted state of bliss, it is not a state of word-discrimination and it cannot be entered into by mere statements concerning it. The Tathagatas [Enlightened Buddha-Masters] have a better way of teaching, namely, through Self-Realization of Noble Wisdom.[9]

Finally, as one other example (among countless) from the Enlightened Guru-Adepts and Buddhas, let's listen to a sacred song sung by the beloved **Jetsun Milarepa** (1052–1135) who criticizes the "Talking School" when it takes precedence over the "Practicing School" such as given under the enlightened guidance of a genuine Guru-Adept:

> *I bow down at the feet of the supreme Guru....*
> *In realizing that the non-clinging and illuminating mind*
> *is embodied in bliss and transcends all playwords [i.e., Talking Schools],*
> *[then] one sees his mind's nature as clearly as great Space.*
> *This is a sign of the consummation*
> *of the Stage of Away-from-Playwords [i.e., Practicing Schools].*
>
> *Though one talks about the Stage Away-from-Playwords,*
> *still he is declaring this and that;*
> *in spite of illustrating what is beyond all words,*
> *he is but piling words on words.*
> *He then, is the ignorant one....*
>
> *He who says that "all is one,"*
> *is still discriminating;*

In the Stage of One-Taste,
there is no such blindness.

When one talks about Non-Practice [or no Guru-Lama],
his mind is still active;
he talks about illumination,
but in fact is blind.[10]

When understood properly we soon realize that our religious and mystical inheritance bequeathed to us from the world's wisest ancestors came from
authentic "Spiritual Heroes," not merely deluded "premodern" wise guys. Their
message is Eternal, grounded in the actual Truth of our existence, regardless if
a culture measures some facts of the relative world with scientific precision or
not. Hence those Great Gurus who have appeared in our own modern-postmodern times, from Swami Vivekananda to Sri Aurobindo, from the Dalai
Lama to Sri Ramana Maharishi, et al., will still be able serve anyone (any
"modern" person) who turns to them for spiritual guidance and a real "taste"
of the Enlightened State.

And yet it appears no one has come to fulfill and complete the promise of
uniting Eastern wisdom with Western sensibilities with more intensity than
has Avatar Adi Da Samraj. He is here to shine a bright light (the "Brightness")
for our emerging global culture—evolving from the Modern Age to the Integral Age (and beyond)—and for all future generations henceforth. He is not
only a *teacher* of Satsang-sadhana but is the full *embodiment* of that process
by offering his Transcendental Heart-Transmission (*Ruchira Shaktipat*) to all
people, now and into the future. He is a recent example of a genuine "Spiritual Hero," one of similar magnitude to those in the past who have been our
most beloved Masters here to serve our Divine Awakening and devotion to
Real God. Adi Da offers Satsang, real Guru Yoga with no other desire than to
serve *your* Awakening. Yet he always demands *real* practice, not talk. With this
insight we can view the entire religious history of humankind in a new light as
being one long continuous Great Tradition of Guru-Adepts, our sacred inheritance of Global Wisdom.

☆

Chapter 5 Endnotes

1. Adi Da Samraj, from the Essay: "Transcendental Gnosis" in *The Gnosticon* (2010), p. 345

2. Adi Da Samraj {da Free John], Preface "The Seventh School of God-Talk" in *The Song of the Self-Supreme* (1982), translated by Radhakamal Mukerjee, pp. 45-46.

3. See: Adi Da Samraj, *The Gnosticon* (2010), p. 385.

4. Ibid., p. 386.

5. Adi Da Samraj [Da Free John], "The Seventh School of God-Talk" (essay) in "Preface" to *The Song of the Supreme Self: Astavakra Gita* (1982), p. 23, 45.

6. Ibid., p. 23.

7. Ibid., p. 23.

8. *Mundaka Upanishad* (I. iii. 4) in *The Upanishads* (1964) translated and edited by Swami Nikhilananda, pp. 117, 111-112.

9. *Lankavatara Sutra* in *A Buddhist Bible* (1938, 1970), edited by Dwight Goddard, p. 281, 284, 287.

10. Milarepa, *The Hundred Thousand Songs of Milarepa, Volume One* (1962), translated and annotated by Garma C. C. Chang, pp. 98-99 [italics added].

SIX

OUR SACRED INHERITANCE:
GLOBAL WISDOM

I Call all of My devotees to endure this basic education about the Great
Tradition of everybody altogether. One boat, one tradition. That Which
Is Truth Itself, That Which Is Real God, Reality Itself, Remains.

— **Adi Da Samraj**, 2004[1]

here is a Great Tradition of global wisdom encircling this planet. It is the natural inheritance and birthright of every person born here on Earth, now and forever into the future. It is a "**Global Tradition**" that honors no one tradition above another but embraces them all together with one vision of Divine Reality based on Truth that is free of cultural prejudice or historical limitation. Yet it is also a "**Great Tradition**" with limitations since it is built upon the different and progressive Stages of Life, including a spectrum (or hierarchy) of mysticism [see Chapter 1]. As we've seen, Avatar Adi Da Samraj has identified "**Seven Stages of Life**" reflecting the different phases of human growth from infancy to adult Enlightenment, including delineating the varying phases of transpersonal mysticism and spiritual understanding, an invaluable gift for humanity [see Appendix I]. By using the Seven Stages of Life model we can identify in general terms the true function (and level of development) of either Shamans, Saints, Yogis, Sages, or Siddhas (among others) in the higher Stages of Life who have evolved beyond our common (or conventional) level of growth and awareness. This Seven Stage model is the best map around, even exceeding Ken Wilber's AQAL approach (which is partially based on Adi Da's vision), in order to provide us the full perspective of our human potentials and possibilities in the evolution of consciousness.

OUR SACRED INHERITANCE:
GREAT TRADITION OF GLOBAL WISDOM

When seen as a whole this Great Tradition encompasses all the unfolding stages (and states) in the cosmic evolution of any human lifetime, that is, when a person is permitted to realize his or her full potential. When an individual grows to adulthood in body and mind, they have the innate possibility of growing *spiritually* if the ego-self is allowed (or guided) to awaken to its true divine nature. This spectrum of human development has traditionally been the province of religion but ultimately it goes beyond traditional religions for it involves universal truths buried in the psyche of every person. Many of today's modern psychologies, especially Transpersonal and Integral Psychology, are attempting to embrace this entire spectrum of development including the more scientifically-based investigations (such as with brain wave patterns and biochemical functions, etc.). Both of these views, the scientific and spiritual, the ancient and modern, are encapsulated in the bipolar cultures of East and West, in the (inward) Alpha-mind and (outward) Omega-mind tendencies of the ego-I [see Chapter 9]. All views and Stages of Life are united in theory with the *integral* perspective that also adds the "AQAL" approach to its understanding (i.e., by including all interiors *and* exteriors with both individual *and* collectives). It attempts a critical summation of the world's "Great Tradition of Global Wisdom," a point of view that is crucial in our assessment of Guru Yoga-Satsang.[2]

The developmental processes of human maturation, in modern terminology, is called the "**evolution of consciousness**," for it spans the growth from a newborn to a mystic, from a baby to a Buddha (or "Awakened One"), from the unenlightened to the Enlightened.[3] Importantly, it is a journey that is naturally available to all of us if our innate right to "Grow Up" and "Wake Up" is not stunted by cultural conventions or governmental and economic restrictions, which is often the case. It is society's inherent responsibility to provide support and encouragement for the further evolution of consciousness and well-being of all human beings, for each and every person from whatever race, ethnicity, or cultural heritage. This is a reoccurring theme that rings throughout humanity's great span of human history and global wisdom. Everyone is encouraged to develop through the Seven Stages of Life as we grow from an infant to an adult, from a devotee to a Saint or Sage, from a child to a Christ [see Appendix I].

To help us realize our highest potential on this journey of consciousness evolution and higher spiritual development there is a Great Tradition of human spirituality handed down to us all from our wisest ancestors and brightest predecessors [see Chapter 1]. The entire spectrum (or mandala) of consciousness is our sacred inheritance, our global birthright as a human being. It is an incredible resource to tap into, a wisdom treasure trove that needs to be made available to everyone. It is also invaluable in cultivating a true global culture recognizing each person as being part of One Humanity endowed with certain inalienable rights of physical safety, reason, and spiritual awareness.

Yet it does not come easy. It is our responsibility to uncover this global wisdom, often hidden in endless books obscured by historical and cultural context, lost in secret esoteric symbols that often aren't fully understood until you've grown beyond their truths. Not only that, when seen as a whole, many of the sacred texts and spiritual teachers from around the world seem to be communicating slightly different messages about ultimate "Truth" and our relationship to it, especially via the process of Guru Yoga. Some seem to be emphasizing different Stages of Life, different degrees of Realization of God; therefore, even the world's greatest spiritual teachings seem to clash and disagree. What's going on? What are we to do?

These difficulties alone, combined with the wealth of information espousing conflicting conclusions, is why we must be guided not just by books and scholars but by authentic spiritual practitioners and Realizers—true Spiritual Adepts. This is why we must learn to recognize and discriminate the most highly-evolved and enlightened Adepts from the bewildering range of possible mystics and religious personalities.[4] Our premise is that there is a hierarchy of spiritual development exhibiting many stages and states (or state-stages) of consciousness, each offering profound degrees of awareness that still fall short of complete Enlightenment, the pinnacle of human development in any era (regardless of what any philosopher or pandit might say).

There is an embracing mandala of ever-encompassing stages or basic structures mapped out by the world's major religions known as the "**levels of reality**" or "**levels of Being**" (*ontology*) which correspond to the various "**levels of selfhood**" or the "**levels of knowing**" (*epistemology*). Respected world religion scholar Huston Smith delineated this hierarchical structure or traditional "**Great Chain of Being**"—what Wilbert calls "**The Great Nest of Spirit**"—pictured as a "**Mandala of Consciousness**" in the graphic below:

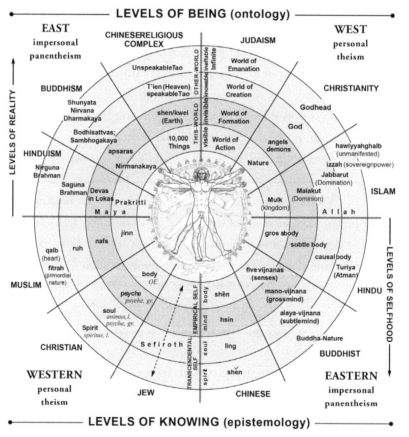

Huston Smith's World Religions as The Great Nest of Spirit
— A Mandala of Consciousness —
© chart by Brad Reynolds

God's Great Tradition of Global Wisdom includes all possible orientations of humankind, from the *stages* of the material to the magical to the mythic to the rational to the religious to the philosophical to the scientific to the holistic to the psychic to the yogic to the spiritual to the enlightened. It includes the *states* of waking, dreaming, sleeping, and altered states, as well as the underlying "Witness" or *Turiya* (in Sanskrit) consciousness. In integral terms this means the Great Tradition includes both knowledge streams arising from the **West**, usually based in science and rational logic, along with the wisdom stream of the **East**, usually based in mysticism and the intuitive mind, the two bipolar approaches to human knowledge and awareness [see Chapter 9]. Whether polytheistic, theistic, or panentheistic, whether East, West, North, South, or shamanic (or even extraterrestrial), let alone materialistic and atheistic, all such views create limitations from the point of view of Divine Enlightenment, the Realization that includes-yet-transcends them all in Prior Unity.

As emphasized, a genuine *integral* approach includes *all* the spheres of existence, from the physical (*physiosphere*) to the biological (*biosphere*) to the mental (*noosphere*) to the spiritual (*theosphere*)—what Wilber somewhat awkwardly calls an "**AQAL**" (or "all quadrants, all levels, all lines, all states, all types") approach—reaching from gross to subtle to causal to nondual awareness. True knowledge is therefore grounded in this *full spectrum of consciousness* where human wisdom is one and whole not partial and incomplete. We find that this psycho-spiritual "map" is altogether an expression of holistic human development outlining the complete evolution of consciousness from babies to Buddhas, from atoms to Atman, from infants to Infinity. What could be a better story than this?

ARCHEOLOGY OF SPIRIT-SELF: EVOLUTION OF CONSCIOUSNESS

By digging through the levels and strata of the Great Tradition, which is like exposing the "archeological" site of the human psyche, we discover that underneath all of the cultural and psychological artifacts scattered from millennia of history there is a universal philosophy, a *perennial* philosophy that reaches across all cultures and centuries [see Chapter 7]. In his masterpiece, *Integral Psychology* (2000), Ken Wilber points to an "**archeology of Spirit**" which is seen as the "**layers of the Self**" or an "**archeology of the Self.**"[5] As the pandit notes, previous transpersonal pioneers—or "advanced-tip" individuals—have explored these higher levels of existence (ontology) and mind (epistemology) to give us the world's sacred teachings that carefully describe the strata of our universal human psyche and inheritance:

> In the extraordinary archeology of Spirit, those [advanced-tip] spiritual pioneers were ahead of their time, and they are still ahead of ours. They are thus voices, not of our past, but of our future; they point to emergents, not exhumations; they urge us forward, not backward. As the growing tip of humanity, they forged a future telos through which the trunk of humanity is now slowly heading, not as a rigid pregiven, but as a gentle persuasion. They [the advanced-tip few] are figures of the deepest layers of our own true Self, layers that whisper to us from the radiant depths of a greater tomorrow.[6]

These are the great Adept-Realizers, from Shamans to Saints to Yogis to Sages to Siddhas, et al., who highlight our potential development into the higher Stages of Life. Yet every human being, even our most noble and Enlightened Heroes first began at "square one" with this precious human birth. This begins the arc of development (in the evolution of consciousness) that lays down the strata in the archeology of the self through the unfolding of our human possibilities. Every born human being needs to be nurtured with the necessary care of family and friends, by our culture and a person's total living environment in order to be successful.

In Wilber's terms, human development is an **AQAL** ("all-quadrants, all-levels, all-lines, all-states, all-types") affair involving *interiors* and *exteriors* based on individual initiative and collective education. Nonetheless, we all follow the same basic patterns regardless of culture or century. Each person unfolds their awareness through universal or "**basic structures**" or "**fulcrums**" (in Wilber's terms) in our growth of body and mind and soul [see Appendix I]. Modern psychology, as well as traditional approaches, has mapped this process with childhood and personal developmental and even transpersonal research, with each stage contributing their own language and insights. Integral Psychology unites them all to sketch out the full range of human development growing from the *prepersonal* (body to early mind) to *personal* (adolescent to adulthood) to *transpersonal* (psychic and soul) structures each with corresponding worldviews and perspectives. From Adi Da's view, these are essentially the "**Seven Stages of Life**" (shown as the outside arcs) which mirror Wilber's basic structures (or state-stages) of growth (the inside arcs) as both models are summarized in the "**Evolution of Human Consciousness**" graphic below:

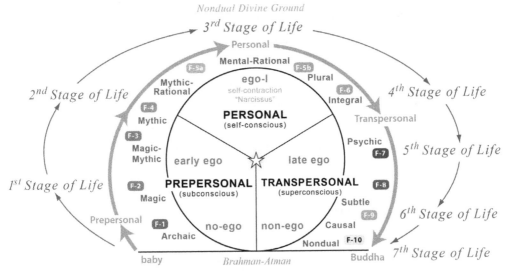

Evolution of Human Consciousness — Baby to Buddha
© chart by Brad Reynolds

Overall, Wilber's Integral Psychology emphasizes that this profound process is a *spiritual* one even in the earlier Stages of Life. It is similar to peeling off the layers of an onion, or the layers of the ego and ignorance, digging through the archeology of the self until there is revealed our True Divine Nature. When we *consciously* know our True Self, we re-awaken and *realize* Divine Spirit, the actual Source-Condition of the whole Kosmos (known as God). Once more, the integral pandit eloquently explains:

> This [shows the] archeology of Spirit, as the more superficial layers of the Self are peeled off to expose increasingly deeper and more profound waves of consciousness. This involves the *emergence* of ever-greater potentials, which therefore leads us forward, not backward, and shows us future evolution and growth, not past evolution and regression. This is an archeology of depth, to be sure, but a depth that plumbs the future, not the past; that reaches into a greater to-

morrow, not a dusty yesterday; that unearths the hidden treasures of involution, not the fossils of evolution. We dig within in order to go beyond, not back.[7]

By "going beyond" our past conditioning, whether individually or collectively, is how Avatar Adi Da uses the metaphor of an archeological site to describe our unconscious psyche and its limitations. In his book *The Way That I Teach* (1978), the Siddha-Guru describes being stuck in the past (i.e., in earlier patterns of maladaptation), often buried in subconscious and unconscious patterns, as being generated from reactions to traumas and stunted growth, from lack of encouragement to ineffective education. These patterns establish our ego-self (as Narcissus), our sense of being a separate "I". Only by *radically understanding* these patterns as our own activity of self-contraction can we transcend them in our ever-present happiness of "always already" Enlightened Consciousness. From his enlightened view, the Adept-Guru opens up the possibility for a more positive and brighter future *if* we realize our innate freedom by not activating past adaptations:

> Everybody here is like an archeological site… because we do not live in an initiatory culture. Each of us is possessed of very complex subjectivity that is made of archaic moments of adaptation…. Any of the strata of old adaptation can come to light at any time—and that is our liability in this world. We must reach a point in our living, in our initiation into life, where we no longer resort to these archaisms. We have a pristine or prior responsibility to love, to remain in communication—in other words, to live in *this* moment rather than an archaic one.[8]

Humanity uncovered the outlines of our future (and higher) potentials when modern scholarship discovered what's called the "**Perennial Philosophy**" or *Philosophia Perennis*, the universal essence buried in all of the world's major religions [see Chapter 7]. This vision shows us our highest potentials as being our deepest truths. Our purpose as born humans is not simply to rummage around reading past texts and cross-cultural expressions, or focusing solely on unconscious and subconscious adaptations, but *to change your life right now* and become love-in-action, to be compassion-at-work. In today's

Third Millennium with the popularity of humanistic, transpersonal, and integral psychologies, coupled with a keen interest in comparative world religions, there has been a growing awareness of the underlying transpersonal or spiritual (as well as biological) unity of humankind. Now verified with the Perennial Philosophy and also a Perennial Psychology (*psychologia perennis*), many modern philosophers and students of spirituality (including Ken Wilber) have relied on its collective wisdom to find our deeper and universal spiritual truths as shared throughout humankind's history. Although traditional religions may be waning in popularity, true spirituality itself will always thrive, even in the halls of science and materialism—for it is *perennial* after all, infinitely deep, existing forever thus *always already* present in our human hearts and psyche.

The reason all traditions and cultures recognize the same spiritual essence is because, despite their differing cultural perspectives and occupations in history, the Spiritual Teachers and Masters of humankind are part of the same human family based upon the same innate esoteric anatomy found in all human beings. Our wisdom inheritance extends down the generations from the mists of prehistory. Our perennialist scholars, such as Frithjof Schuon, Huston Smith, Seyyed Hossein Nasr, Aldous Huxley (among others) maintain we should cultivate a living and vital relationship to this Great Tradition of Global Wisdom, the source from whence Guru Yoga-Satsang arises, lives, and thrives [see next chapter].

It is this perennial or ever-repeating Truth of Divine Wisdom that is the home of all the great Guru-Adepts who have come to serve humankind as a whole. Although their bodies may have died, their wisdom lives on forever. The Perennial Philosophy as well as its fountain of Perennial Wisdom (or *Sophia Perennis*) from whence *philosophia* has its roots, is the beating heart of the Great Tradition pulsing through humanity's veins and arteries circulating the globe living in the Prior Unity of Divine Spirit [see Chapter 8]. Naturally this Perennial Philosophy of the Great Tradition of humankind is a principal guide and map for better understanding our collective historical journey in evolving a better transpersonal global future; hence to this *Philosophia Perennis* we next turn.

Chapter 6 Endnotes

1. Adi Da Samraj, August 19, 2004, in *Adi Da Samrajashram*, Vol. 1, No. 4, p. 29.

2. See: Ken Wilber, *The Religion of Tomorrow* (2017); Adi Da Samraj, *The Aletheon* (2009).

3. As mentioned, an ideal model of human development is Adi Da Samraj's "Seven Stages of Life" [see Appendix I], which is essentially a simplified (yet more comprehensive) model of Ken Wilber's integral developmental model; see: *Growing In God: Seven Stages of Life from Birth to Enlightenment—An Integral Interpretation* (forthcoming) by Brad Reynolds.

4. See: *In God's Company: Guru-Adepts As Agents for Enlightenment in the Integral Age* (2022) by Brad Reynolds.

5. See: Ken Wilber, Chapter 7 "The Archeology of Spirit" in *Integral Psychology* (2000).

6. Ken Wilber, *Integral Psychology* (2000), p. 157.

7. Ibid., p. 102.

8. Adi Da Samraj [Bubba Free John], *The Way That I Teach* (1978), p. 205.

SEVEN

PHILOSOPHIA PERENNIS
PERENNIAL PHILOSOPHY

More than twenty-five centuries have passed since that which has been called the Perennial Philosophy was first committed to writing; and in the course of those centuries it has found expression, now partial, now complete, now in this form, now in that, again and again.... The Perennial Philosophy has spoken almost all the languages of Asia and Europe and has made use of the terminology and traditions of every one of the higher religions.

— **Aldous Huxley**, 1944[1]

UNIVERSAL WISDOM:
PHILOSOPHIA PERENNIS

Perhaps one of the more fortuitous discoveries brought forth in the 20th century by academics or modern scholarship based in archeology, history, and comparative religions is the affirmation there has indeed been a "**Perennial Philosophy**" or universal teaching of Wisdom that cuts across all cultural boundaries regardless of the century or country you've been born into. I believe this discovery may end up being even more important than many of the discoveries of modern science and the incredible inventions of technology. This is because its Wisdom gives us an opportunity to heal the ills of the modern mind corrupted by the destructive power of scientific materialism and unchecked capitalism (and corrupt communism). The notion of a *perennial* or reoccurring philosophy suggests the existence of a universal set of human truths and values, an idea that postmodern philosophers view with skepticism and suspicion.

Today's Integral Philosophy has embraced the basic themes of this universal spirituality as being valid and real although with provisos (hence, for example, Ken Wilber's critique based on an "integral post-metaphysics"). Nevertheless, the evidence is overwhelming (and liberating) that today's diverse global community is deeply interconnected to our wisest ancestors via a shared philosophy grounded in our common (and inherited) human psyche. Indeed, the idea of a Perennial Philosophy has usually appeared whenever there has been a cultural setting of tolerance allowing divergent spiritual practitioners to congregate and interact with the free exercise of mind and spirit, such as in ancient Alexandria in Egypt, or today in California, for instance, and elsewhere in the free world (such as Europe and India). In essence, spiritually-oriented people discover they are talking about the same "thing" when considering what is "God" or "Truth" or "Ultimate Reality" and what Life is really about.

The "**Perennial Philosophy**"—known in Latin as *Philosophia Perennis*—is a term that has been around at least since the Renaissance. This is when the first cross-cultural translations of various ancient philosophical and mystical texts were undertaken by the Medici Italians in Florence. They had retrieved them from Muslim scholars who had protected them for centuries from the persecutions (and burnings) of the Roman Catholic Church. The general thesis is that underneath the *surface structures* or cultural incarnations of the world's religious and mystical paths there are *deep structures* or universal spiritual truths that each system or religious path shares in common. In a very real sense, these "structures" or "state-stages" of human potential are found in the "esoteric anatomy" of each human being, our shared common humanity.

This "**Wisdom of the Ages**" has been recognized in various cosmopolitan centers since ancient times where scholars or scribes and spiritual practitioners could gather in peace, such as in the Great Library of Alexandria (2nd c. BCE–2nd c. CE), or the Persian Academy of Gondishapur, an important medical center of the ancient world (5th–7th c. CE), or at the House of Wisdom in Baghdad during the Islamic Golden Age (7th–12th c. CE), or Córdoba and Toledo, Spain (10th–12th c. CE), or at the esteemed Buddhist center of learning, Nalanda University, in northern India (5th–12th c. CE), among others.[2] Once someone is exposed to different religious traditions and the people who practice them it's easy to recognize that there are common themes to spirituality and wisdom. This includes, as we'll see, a universal recognition of One Divine Reality or Spirit or Ground of Being underlying the entire universe or Kosmos.

This Divine Spirit is the Source or "Ground" of Creation, the "Goal" of existence. Of course, cultural and historical variations have given unique cultural-specific names to this ineffable (unnamable) Divine Condition, such as Tao, Brahman, Yahweh, Allah, God, Ein Sof, Aton, etc. Yet true mysticism transcends all rational signifiers and names, even the thinking mind itself. As the "Old Sage" Lao Tzu (from China) long ago said in the opening chapter to one of the world's wisest and oldest books, the *Tao Te Ching*: "The Tao that can be spoken is not the eternal Tao. The name that can be named is not the eternal name. The nameless is the beginning of Heaven and Earth." Words fail to transmit the Truth; the Truth can only be *realized*, not published.

Nevertheless, scholar-practitioners today emphasize that the Perennial Philosophy is not as uniform as some may profess because there is in fact a *spectrum* of religious and mystical development—from psychic to subtle to causal to nondual states—not one homogeneous soup of soul and spirit everyone agrees on. In other words, not all paths make it to the same mountaintop. Yet when this diverse variation is taken into account and seen from a large enough (or evolved enough) perspective, then there are still certain uniform themes or deep structures running throughout all religious-mystical experiences that warrant them being identified as *"perennial"* or "ever-repeating," occurring year after year, century after century, culture after culture, mind after mind.

The *prior unity* underlying or supporting the idea of a Perennial Philosophy is that we are all human beings sharing a common human psyche and esoteric anatomy composed of various levels and states of awareness regardless of culture or race, time or space. Beyond that, the perennial philosophers claim we are all God *in essence* existing as one whole-part in One Eternal Divine Dance of Reality. The entire spectrum of consciousness and mystical states and stages (or "state-stages") expressed in either Eastern or Western, Northern or Southern, religious language and expression is ultimately embraced in the non-dual awareness of the Enlightened State of God-Consciousness. Such a Perennial Philosophy that ultimately arises from human consciousness lives in the heart, not in ideas or books. The fundamental essence of our humanity unites us with the entire Kosmos as all arising from a single Prior Unity, alive as the radiant light of Divine Spirit. Nothing short of that. This is the "highest common factor" of humankind, uniting us beneath all forms of diversity, constant change, cultural variation, and different stages of consciousness evolution.

PERENNIAL PHILOSOPHY: HIGHEST COMMON FACTORS

This universal commonality among all esoteric religions—called the "**Highest Common Factor**," as one British pundit termed it—began to make its impression on modern scholars of comparative religions once the translation of sacred texts from India began in earnest during the 19th century, which then accelerated in the 20th century. Consequently, by the mid-20th century the novelist **Aldous Huxley** (1894-1962), famed British author of *Brave New World* (1932), published a book titled *The Perennial Philosophy* (1945) as World War II was ending. This best-selling book was Huxley's attempt to thwart any future worldwide conflicts by showing us the common unity of human wisdom and its shared "perennial philosophy." Huxley pointed out in his introduction: "Rudiments of the Perennial Philosophy may be found among the traditional lore of primitive peoples in every region of the world, and in its fully developed forms it has a place in every one of the higher religions."[3] From the most primordial to the most exalted there is a universal cross-cultural spirituality running through all of us. As usual, Ken Wilber states it as succinctly as possible:

> So what are the details of this perennial philosophy? Very simple: the Great Nest of Being, culminating in One Taste—there, in a nutshell, is the perennial philosophy....The core of the world's great wisdom

traditions is a framework we ought to consult seriously and reverentially in our own attempts to understand the Kosmos. And at its heart is the experience of One Taste [of One God]—clear, obvious, unmistakable, unshakable.[4]

In other writings on the subject, the world-renowned scholar-novelist Huxley points out: "Happily there is the Highest Common Factor of all religions, the Perennial Philosophy which has always and everywhere been the metaphysical system of the Prophets, Saints, and Sages."[5] Such a clear awareness of the underlying unity of religious ethics and spiritual thought is one of the great gifts of modern scholarship, reaching back in America (and Europe) to Ralph Waldo Emerson, Henry David Thoreau, and the Transcendentalists who began popularizing recently translated Hindu texts from India.[6] By the late 19th century, Theosophy and leaders of the Theosophical Society, such as H. P. Blavatsky and Annie Besant, called it "**Wisdom-Religion**" and "**Ancient Wisdom**," an idea that influenced thinkers in the East as well as the West. Hindu mystics, such as Ramakrishna and Swami Vivekananda, preached about religious universalism as Vivekananda made headlines throughout the world after appearing at the Parliament of the World's Religions at the 1893 Chicago World's Fair [see Chapter 9].

In the 20th century, the Perennial Philosophy's elucidation has been undertaken by authentic spiritual practitioners, such as with Huxley, Christopher Isherwood, René Guénon, Ananda Coomaraswamy, Titus Burckhardt, Martin Lings, Frithjof Schuon, Huston Smith, Lex Hixon, and many others known as "perennialists" and "traditionalists." Their ideas are supported by spiritual disciplines studied under qualified teachers and Masters, not just theories proposed by academics interested in old books. The *perennial* philosophy, in other words, is a *living* philosophy because it's more about *Sophia* (or Realization) than a mental *philosophia* [see Chapter 8].

| Nicholas of Cusa | Pico della Mirandola | Gottfried Leibniz | Aldous Huxley | Frithjof Schuon |

Although Huxley famously cited Gottfried Leibniz (1646–1716) as the originator of the Latin term *philosophia perennis* (who did use the phrase in private letters) other scholars have pointed out that "the term was probably employed for the first time by Agostino Steuco (1497-1548), the Renaissance philosopher and theologian who... identified [it] with a perennial wisdom embracing both philosophy and theology and not related to just one school of wisdom or thought."[7] Indeed, the discovery (or re-discovery) of a universal Perennial Philosophy during the 16th century helped inspire the European Renaissance, the rebirth of Western philosophy and thought that led to the emergence of science and the modern world. This awakening opened the doors to the Age of Enlightenment or Age of Reason when science and rational thinking broke free from the restrictions of the political and mytho-religious institution of the Christian Church.

The West, by studying the wisdom of the East, and in rediscovering their own wisdom texts from Greece and Rome, realized there's more to mystical thought and experience than what was being taught by the Christian, Jewish, and Muslim authorities. The discovery of a Perennial Philosophy has also helped these traditional Western religions rediscover their own *esoteric* teachings buried in their sacred scriptures as highlighted by the wisdom of their founding Adepts and Prophets. The Renaissance discovery and modern affirmation of the "**Lost Masters**" of ancient Greece—our own "**Western Gurus**"[8] —has been a breakthrough of mystical insight and universal wisdom for everyone to share and learn from [see Chapter 12].

The concept of a Perennial Philosophy was propelled forward by the newly invented printing press (circa 1439 by Gutenberg) and the spread of book reading throughout Europe. It became part of Renaissance Platonism, a philosophical movement incorporating a philological concern with ancient texts that flourished during 16th century Europe. Ancient translations were undertaken to broaden the scope of study during and after the Renaissance. Plato's long-lost dialogues, for example, were translated afresh along with the works of Orpheus, Heraclitus, Hermes Trismegistus, the Pythagoreans, Plotinus, Proclus, Dionysius the pseudo-Areopagite, and others. Importantly, Aristotle's lost teachings that emphasized the investigation of Nature by using the senses (not just metaphysical speculation), inspired many of the new emerging scientists even if they disagreed with him on other topics. These voluminous texts were held to be representative of what was called "**pious philosophy**" which became an alternative to biblical revelation thus freeing thinkers from the domination of the Catholic Church (even helping to initiate the Reformation). From this original formulation of a recognizable universal philosophy spanning centuries, many Renaissance philosophers and later philosophers of the European Enlightenment began to promote a global view about spiritual reality involving the Divine Oneness behind the multiplicity of forms. They discovered that a direct *personal realization* of "The One," an actual *gnosis* (or Nondual awareness) speaks beyond the limited scope of provincial or province-oriented philosophies and inherited tribal-cultural patterns. This is as true today as it was back then (or at any time) or will be in the future.

| Orpheus | Pythagoras | Hermes Trismegistus | Plato | Plotinus |

These wise philosopher-pandits also rediscovered Egyptian and Persian texts as well as the wisdom teachings of ancient India, all of which clearly recognized the unity of humankind in spirit and divine intuition. One of the most attractive translations was that of the *Corpus Hermetica* (that became an alternate Bible for Renaissance thinkers) because, as scholar Linda Johnsen explains: "The ancient Greeks were convinced the *Corpus Hermetica* were authentic transmissions of millennia-old Egyptian wisdom…. [However] modern scholars debate how much of the Hermetic writings are inspired by Egyptian doctrine, and how much represents what Greek speakers simply imagined the ancient Egyptian teachings must have been. In antiquity, however, there was no such confusion."[9] The sacred teachings from Hermes Trismegistus (the "thrice-born"), for example, taught that it is only in discovering the "Divine Awareness" within oneself that peace of mind is finally found.[10]

MODERN VISIONARIES OF THE PERENNIAL PHILOSOPHY

When scholars (or readers) are given access to the world's sacred texts, no matter when written, they soon discover there is a perennial, cross-cultural, esoteric philosophy emanating from these valued spiritual canons bequeathed to us from our wisest Adept-Realizers whether East or West in origin. The same truth is revealed to us in the modern world too if we take the time to read and study the sacred scriptures of the Great Tradition of Global Wisdom and make suitable comparisons [see Chapter 1]. This is also how we may verify the authenticity of our spiritual authorities and Gurus from today. As mentioned, there is a "Divine Library" of wisdom now available for anyone to explore and purchase [see Chapter 2]. Nevertheless, it's important to understand that these sacred manuscripts are never fully (or accurately) understood without actually undertaking the practices and disciplines recommended by them. They are even made clearer when studying under the auspices of an actual Realizer or Guru-Adept.

Huxley's book, which re-ignited the concept of a Perennial Philosophy among modern spiritual thinkers following its publication, is a comparative anthology citing passages from a variety of historical texts, East and West, ancient and modern. He gracefully directs us to quotes from both Oriental Easterners and Occidental Westerners to show the reader the similarities and common themes making up this Perennial Philosophy as well as summarizing its general concepts or tenets. Huxley opened his treatise by defining the *Philosophia Perennis* as "the metaphysics that recognizes a Divine Reality substantial to the world of things and lives and minds; the psychology that finds in the soul something similar to, or even identical with, Divine Reality; the ethic that places man's final end in the knowledge of the immanent and transcendent Ground of all being—the thing is immemorial and universal."[11] Huxley provided a global vision of world unity grounded in spiritual truths which is why these insights still appeal to millions across the generations even now and into the future.

| **René Guénon** | **Ananda Coomaraswamy** | **Alan Watts** | **Huston Smith** | **Ken Wilber** |

Wisely, Huxley was only seeing what five hundred years of scholars had seen as well. In the 15th century, the German Catholic cardinal **Nicholas of Cusa** (1401–1464) recognized "there is a single religion and a single creed for all beings endowed with understanding, and this religion is presupposed behind all diversity of rites"[12] Five centuries later **Frithjof Schuon** (1907–1998), one of our most profound and articulate perennialists, called this universal wisdom "**The Transcendent Unity of Religions**" (the title to his first book published in French in 1953). Such a universal view is most evident in *esoteric* (or "inner-directed") yogas and meditation than they are in *exoteric* (or "outer-directed") rituals and religious thinking, a point the perennialists emphasize (as does Adi Da).[13] The Swiss-born German Schuon studied and was initiated into several world religions, including Hindu's Advaita Vedanta, Islamic Sufism, even being adopted into the Native American tribes of the Sioux and Crow, in addition to being close to the Christian tradition through his devotion to the Virgin Mary and its greatest Saints. No wonder when *The Transcendent Unity of Religions* (1957, in English) first came out T. S. Eliot wrote: "I have met with no more impressive work in the comparative study of Oriental and Occidental religion."[14] Huston Smith, author of the vastly popular *The World's Religions: Our Great Wisdom Traditions* (1958, 1991), simply stated: "The man is a living wonder… I know of no living thinker who begins to rival him…. I consider him to be the most important religious thinker of our [20th] century."[15] In a 1995 interview, soon before his death, Schuon was asked about the title to his famous first book to which he summarily replied:

> Our starting point is the acknowledgment of the fact that there are diverse religions which exclude each other. This could mean that one religion is right and that all the others are false; it could mean also that all are false. In reality, it means that all are right, not in their

dogmatic exclusivism, but in their unanimous inner signification, which coincides with pure metaphysics, or in other terms, with the *philosophia perennis.*[16]

René Guénon (1886–1951) was a French author and intellectual who proposed to show the "universal character" of "Eastern metaphysical doctrines" while adapting them for Western readers so they can remain "strictly faithful to their spirit."[17] Importantly, Guénon denounced occultism and spiritualism popular in the early 20th century including Theosophy (calling it a "pseudo-religion"), claiming their syncretic tendencies along with common Eurocentric misconceptions distorted their interpretations of Eastern doctrines. Guénon was also critical of many modern interpretations regarding symbolism including some of the psychological interpretations proposed by the psychiatrist **Carl Jung** (1875–1961). Nonetheless, the depth and breadth of Jung's writings on many of the world's religions, especially its esoteric Western strains (such as with alchemy and gnosticism), established a proper intellectual basis to promote openness to the study of Eastern spirituality.

Ananda Coomaraswamy (1877–1947) was born in Ceylon and was an early interpreter of Indian culture to the West, focusing on Indian art and its universal symbolism. While in India he was part of the literary circle around Rabindranath Tagore and thus contributed to the early phase in the struggle for Indian independence. Since he was deeply influenced by René Guénon, he became one of the founders of the Traditionalist School (or Perennialism). His books and essays on art and culture, symbolism and metaphysics, scripture, folklore and myth, and other topics, offer a remarkable education to readers working to accept a universal cross-cultural perspective. His writings are filled with references to Plato, Plotinus, Clement, Philo, Augustine, Aquinas, Shankara, Eckhart, Rumi, and other mystics, which lead German Indologist and linguist Heinrich Zimmer to state that Coomaraswamy was "that noble scholar upon whose shoulders we are still standing."[18] By building a bridge between Eastern and Western wisdom, from Vedanta to Platonism, even reviving scholarly interest in Buddhism, he shines a bright light for modern people to see and understand ancient and perennial truths.

Gerald Heard (1889–1971), a good friend of Huxley's and respected scholar who supported the import of the East into the West, simply called this universal wisdom the **"Eternal Gospel."**[19] Heard was an inspiration to a generation of new scholars during the mid-20th century for he had gained modern access to the most secret and esoteric teachings of the East particularly Hinduism and Vedanta (since he studied under the Eastern Guru Swami Prabhavananda). Heard's work was a forerunner of and influence on the consciousness development movement that has spread in the Western world since the 1960s. Ken Wilber calls this group who promoted and supported the Vedanta Society in America, studying under Swami Prabhavananda and living in Hollywood, stalwarts of "the great tradition of **emancipatory writing**, of intellectual light in service of liberation—helping to undo repression, thwart power, and shun shallowness."[20] Heard, author of several brilliant books, including *The Ascent of Humanity* (1929) and *The Five Ages of Man* (1964), was quite instrumental in the founding and flourishing of the Vedanta Society in Los Angeles, even tutoring a young Huston Smith. Next, we turn to some of his emancipatory writing companions.

Christopher Isherwood (1904–1986) was an English novelist, playwright, screenwriter, and translator, but was most importantly a facilitator, a connection between the Vedanta Society of Southern California and famous Anglo-American thinkers, befriending Truman Capote, Dodie Smith, Berthold Brecht, Aldous Huxley, and Gerald Heard, among others. He spent time in Germany when Hitler rose to fame and power then migrated to the USA in 1939 settling in Hollywood. He attended functions with Vedanta Society founder **Swami Prabhavananda** (1893–1976), a monk of the Ramakrishna Order of India, and assisted in translations of *The Song of God: Bhagavad-Gita* (1944), Patanjali's Yoga Sutras titled *How To Know God* (1953), and Shankara's *Crest Jewel of Discrimination* (1947). As Ken Wilber points out, "Isherwood was always struggling, in his own way, for an integral approach that united spirituality with *this* life," searching for a unity of sex and spirit as he became "something of a hero for present-day gays, mostly because of his unflinching acceptance of his homosexuality,"[21] especially in an ascetic tradition like yoga. This was encapsulated in his autobiographical book *My Guru and His Disciple* (1980) where he honestly wrote about his Guru, Swami Prabhavananda, and his own struggles between sensuality and spirituality, worldliness and holiness, sexual abandon and strict discipline; perennial traits and concerns for most of us.

Alan Watts (1915–1973), the British-American popularizer of Eastern religions in the West (especially popular during the 1960s), commented that "in almost every culture there has existed a unanimous, common, and perennial philosophy of man's nature and destiny—differing from place to place only in terminology and points of emphasis and technique.... a single philosophical consensus of universal extent. It has been held by men and women who report the same insights and teach the same essential doctrines whether living today or six thousand years ago, whether from New Mexico in the Far West or from Japan in the Far East."[22] This was a theme running throughout Watts' popular books as another generation of younger Westerners (in the Sixties and even currently) began their spiritual search for deeper truths other than those being offered by the conventional traditions of the West.

Gerald Heard **Christopher Isherwood** **C. G. Jung** **Joseph Campbell** **Duane Elgin**

Joseph Campbell (1904–1987), the popular American scholar of mythology and religion, tells us there is "a great Perennial Philosophy, which, from time out of mind, has been the one, eternally true wisdom of the human race, revealed somehow on high."[23] Campbell taught not only the perennial secrets hidden in myths and their archetypal images, but was also a master at seeing the global arc of human religious history. His books, such as *The Hero with a Thousand Faces* (1949) and the four-volume *The Masks of God* (1959–1968), let alone his monumental *Historical Atlas of World Mythology* (1988), have impressed intellectuals with his insightful generalizations (but not necessarily detailed scholars). His work is an important bridge to East and West, from primordial to ancient to medieval to modern religious thinking, so no wonder he found a *Philosophia Perennis* running throughout them all. His warm nature and excellent teaching skills made him a perennial favorite among students and readers, being a popular feature at the Esalen Institute in Big Sur, California, which played a key role in the Human Potential movement begun in the

1960s.[24] Yet it was journalist Bill Moyer's interviews with Campbell in a six one-hour series called *The Power of Myth* (in 1988) that sky-rocketed him to worldwide fame right after he had passed away (in 1987).

Huston Smith (1919–2016) was a leading scholar of comparative religions bridging the gap between esoteric and metaphysical ideas and the popular mind and for other religious thinkers. Born in China to Methodist missionaries, he came to the United States graduating from the University of Chicago, home to the world-renowned religious scholar Mircea Eliade, ending up at MIT from 1958 to 1973 as a professor of philosophy. While at Washington University in St. Louis (1947–1957) he hosted *The Religions of Man* and *The Search for America* on public television explaining Eastern religions and teaching meditation to large American audiences. His book, at first titled *The Religions of Man* (1958), then later retitled *The World's Religions* (1991), has sold over three million copies (as of 2017) and is still popular in schools and universities. This book introduced many of the world's major religions, including those of Native Americans, with a tolerant attitude and sincere respect for them all. Through his relationship with Heard and Huxley, Smith met Timothy Leary and Richard Alpert (Ram Dass) and experimented with LSD and mescaline as part of the Harvard Project where he claimed, at least for him, these entheogens simulated the mystical experience allowing the religious scholar to *feel* and *realize* what previously he had only known intellectually.[25] He has long been an intellectual defender of the Perennial Philosophy (inspiring Ken Wilber for one) especially with his profound book *Forgotten Truth: The Common Vision of the World's Religions* (1976, 1992); highly recommended to everyone.

Ken Wilber (b. 1949), when he first began publishing, used the idea of a Perennial Philosophy to correlate it with what he called a *Psychologia Perennis*, or "Perennial Psychology," to buttress his "spectrum of consciousness" theories with its universal wisdom. As the integral pandit points out: "The Perennial Philosophy is the worldview that has been embraced by the vast majority of the world's greatest spiritual teachers, philosophers, thinkers, and even scientists. It's called 'perennial' or 'universal' because it shows up in virtually all cultures across the globe and across the ages. We find it in India, Mexico, China, Japan, Mesopotamia, Egypt, Tibet, Germany, Greece. And wherever we find it, it has essentially similar features, it is in essential agreement the world over."[26] Wilber's integral theories and his "spectrum of consciousness" model stand upon the wisdom offered by the universal vision of Divinity and an evolutionary Kosmos of Spirit-in-action[27] [see Chapter 8].

Duane Elgin (b. 1943), author of *Awakening Earth* (1993), and other holistic integral books, affirms the same observation: "There is a perennial wisdom—a highest common denominator—found across cultures, across history, and even in every major spiritual tradition of the world."[28] Historian **Thomas McEvilley** has recently noted in *The Shape of Ancient Thought* (2002): "The relationship between ancient Greece and Indian traditions of thought is the foundational level of comparative philosophy. These two ancient peoples were the first to recognize philosophy as the defining trait of humanity."[29] Most open-minded scholars today, especially if they are spiritual practitioners, come to the same basic conclusion. For example, integral philosopher **Dustin DiPerna** calls it "**The Great Human Tradition**," thus acknowledging Adi Da's influence while brilliantly extending many of Wilber's integral ideas about the future of religion into the 21st century. See his insightful books *Streams of Wisdom: An Advanced Guide to Integral Spiritual Development* (2014) and *Evolution's Ally: Our World's Religious Traditions as Conveyor Belts of Transformation* (2015).[30] This is only a partial list of countless other books reviewing the Perennial Philosophy and the emergence of a global perspective embracing God's Great Tradition of Global Wisdom.

Importantly, anyone can recognize and study for himself or herself the teachings of this inherited Perennial Wisdom Tradition transmitted to us from our ancient Masters and wisest Sages—the Great Gurus in the Great Tradition of Humankind. This "Divine Library" is a bounty everyone should become familiar with so when their spiritual journey begins, they may access it with respect and serious intention [see Appendix II]. Our past Masters will shine a light unto the wisdom lying deep in our hearts awakening us to a better future.

Huston Smith has frequently inserted the title "**The World's Great Wisdom Traditions**" in place of "Perennial Philosophy."[31] Yet he also emphasized it is a "**Primordial Tradition**" to acknowledge its deep, ancient, primal roots in space as well as time, including indigenous cultural traditions.[32] All human cultural traditions, in other words, have contributed to the Perennial Philosophy, from tribes to civilizations, from myths to mysticism, from religion to spirituality. They (and we) are all part of One "Great Tradition" of human spirituality (just as Avatar Adi Da says). Consequently, Professor Smith eloquently explains that the Primordial Perennial Philosophy is the "winnowed wisdom of the human race" for it is, according to him, "the world's religions at their best."[33] As the perennialists have pointed out, "**religion**" has both an *outer exoteric* or institutionalized side, full of "local peculiarities," "rites and legends," as well as its more profound *inner esoteric* dimensions from which all of the world's wisdom traditions plant their deepest spiritual roots. The idea of a Perennial Philosophy, therefore, goes beyond exoteric religion and rites, ceremonies and rituals, as important as they are. The deepest teachings of religions transcend the conventional beliefs of the common masses for its essential esoteric core addresses "That" from which all religions spring forth and flourish in truth and in spirit. The ever-repeating (*perennis*) philosophy (*philosophia*), in other words, is most fundamentally based on Divine Realization (*Sophia*) not just philosophical argument [see Chapter 8].

Wilber emphasizes that not only do mystics and religious people recognize these universal truths but scientists do too, at least some of them share in this perennial spiritual worldview.[34] He points out that the Perennial Philosophy has "formed the core not only of the world's great wisdom traditions, from Christianity to Buddhism to Taoism, but also of many of the greatest philosophers, scientists, and psychologists of both East and West, North and South."[35] This includes many world-famous physicists like Einstein, Heisenberg, Schrödinger, Jeans, Eddington, and others, as Wilber points out in one of his books reviewing their writings.[36] The list of scholars and researchers who claim the validity of a cross-cultural "perennial philosophy" is endless and growing.

Nevertheless, this universal approach also has its critics, especially among postmodernists who claim every view is culturally conditioned.[37] They doubt the authenticity of universalism because for them all religions have different teachings and beliefs. Known as **constructivism**, one scholar summed up this postmodern position:

> The view opposite to perennialism is *constructivism*, which argues
> that culture and assumptions shape mystical experience to such a de-

gree that Buddhist and Christian mystics do not actually encounter the same reality. Some constructivists (hard constructivists) deny that a common substrate of mystical experience even exists. They argue that experience is entirely shaped by culture and assumptions.[38]

While there is some truth to this postmodern observation that culture does influence our interpretation of religio-spiritual experiences, since we all process information and experiences through language and culture, the trans-verbal and trans-personal mystical experiences themselves transcend (or go beyond) the limits of personal interpretation. Wilber concurs: "Radical truth can be *shown* (in contemplative awareness) but never exhaustively *said* (in discursive language)."[39] This transcendence of point of view is what makes them "mystical" or transpersonal experiences to begin with. In any case, there are volumes of sacred texts that offer convincing testimony to the validity of the perennialists' cross-cultural argument and the evidence it offers. Professor **Seyyed Hossein Nasr** (b. 1933) heartily summarizes: "The unity of religions is to be found first and foremost in this Absolute which is at once Truth and Reality and the origin of all revelations and of all truth."[40] Such insight however is best revealed when practice (*sadhana*) is authentically engaged for only then can someone judge for oneself its truth and veracity.

The final conclusions of wisdom are not gained by reading books or thinking and talking about it, as the Talking School of scholars often do, but by engaging in the Practicing School of spiritual life and daily meditation. This is another reason why models of delineating the higher transpersonal stages of mysticism are necessary because all mystical experiences (or samadhi states) are not the same; very few are the ultimate state of Divine Enlightenment.[41] This is why the work of Adi Da Samraj's Seven Stages of Life model supplemented with Ken Wilber's "spectrum of consciousness" and AQAL model are crucial to help us better understand our own developmental potentials.

Even Wilber, once a strong proponent of the Perennial Philosophy has lately become somewhat critical of its thesis since he's worried it has slipped into a static traditional or "traditionalist" worldview with hidden pregiven metaphysics. Wilber maintains the philosophical forms or teachings of *Sophia* continue to evolve so he supports a "**Neo-Perennial Philosophy**,"[42] an updating the traditional Perennial Philosophy with more modern sensibilities and knowledge [see Chapter 8]. Wilber summarizes: "Whereas radical and formless Truth, to the extent it is clearly recognized, is necessarily one and identical in all times and places, nonetheless the forms of its expression are and can only be judged according to the appropriateness for the particular sociocultural context in which they live, and from which their very metaphors and models are drawn."[43] For example, the integral pandit believes teachings on Enlightenment must now include evolution although for past Spiritual Masters this natural process was of little concern.

Next, to summarize, let's briefly review the fundamental doctrines that Huxley highlights as comprising the core tenets of the Perennial Philosophy, a view that unites everyone today and tomorrow in a universal vision of wisdom founded in Real God-Realization and the truth of the Divine Reality.

FUNDAMENTAL DOCTRINES: UNIVERSAL TRUTHS

*A*fter publishing his book with its famous title (in 1945), Huxley made the articulation and dissemination of "**The Perennial Philosophy**" one of his primary tasks for the rest of his life. He delighted in showing us the similarities between the wisdom teachings of the ancients and our current modern Adepts as well as emphasizing the necessity for spiritual practice and meditation. As Huxley taught (and *realized*): "It is only in the act of contemplation, when words and even personality are transcended, that the pure state [*sophia perennis*] of the Perennial Philosophy can actually be known"[44] [see next chapter]. The world-renowned author also wrote introductions for other scholar's books and wrote compelling essays to further define the Perennial Philosophy's main tenets or fundamental doctrines while also giving popular lectures on its all-encompassing thesis. In his introduction to the *Bhagavad Gita* (translated by Swami Prabhavananda and Christopher Isherwood in 1944), Huxley often listed *four fundamental doctrines*—what he called "the Perennial Philosophy in its minimal and basic form" or a "**minimum working hypothesis**"[45] of the "**Highest Common Facto**r" to all world religions—which was quickly followed by a fifth tenet that applies to Guru Yoga (which I paraphrase below by using quotes from Huxley[46]):

Perennial Philosophy's Fundamental Doctrines:

1) <u>Two Truths</u>: relative reality & Absolute Reality:
   (1) <u>relative reality</u> is Immanent Spirit seen as "the phenomenal world of matter and individualized consciousness—the world of things and animals and men and even gods [subtle beings]," also known as "the Many";
   (2) <u>Absolute Reality</u> is "the Divine Ground" or the Transcendent Unconditional Reality which is Consciousness Itself, also called Brahman, Tao, Godhead, et al., known as "The One" from which all conditional relative realities (all possible universes) and states of consciousness arise, exist, and fall away.

2) <u>Divine Enlightenment is possible</u>: Human beings are not only able to *know about* this Divine Ground or Absolute Reality by inference (or mental logic) but they also can "*realize* its existence by *direct intuition*, superior to discursive reasoning" (as well as the scientific method). This realization or awareness called Divine Enlightenment and God-Realization, also known as *gnosis, prajna, satori, wu, moksha rigpa, samyaksambodhi*, et al., is innate in everyone and is the pinnacle of human development.

3) <u>Dual Nature</u>: Human beings have a "double nature":

   (a) <u>phenomenal self</u> or the ego-I that is the self-contracting activity of the separate self-sense which is active in the conditional world of forms but also includes the soul (*atman*) or the subtle entity that reincarnates (or survives death);

   (b) <u>True Self</u> (*Atman*) or "the spark of divinity within the soul" that even transcends the sense of being "within"; it is possible therefore via spiritual practice (sadhana-Satsang) and meditation to identify with this True Eternal Self and to Re-Awaken "with the Divine Ground" of Absolute Reality and thus *realize* Real God (Divine Enlightenment).

4) <u>Goal of Life</u>: *Know God* — *Tat Tvam Asi* or "Thou Art That": The sole purpose of human life is "to identify… with the Eternal Self and so to come to unitive knowledge of the Divine Ground" and be transformed by this Enlightened State as the great Sages and Guru-Adepts demonstrate in person. To reach or realize this Goal it is necessary to practice yoga and regular meditation (*sadhana*) best served by cultivating a sacred relationship (*Satsang*) with an authentic Spiritual Master, a genuine Guru-Adept, in order to fulfill and live this God-Realized process, the essence of True Religion.

5) <u>Guru Yoga</u> IS Real Religion: Huxley wisely emphasized that there are "human Incarnations of the Divine Ground, by whose mediation and grace the worshiper is helped to achieve his or her goal—that ultimate knowledge of the Godhead [Enlightenment], which is a person's eternal life and beatitude."[47] *Satsang* or Guru Yoga is the method of living in an active and sacred relationship with a true Siddha-Guru or Adept-Realizer, which has been practiced for millennia and is the essence of True Religion (and the Perennial Philosophy).

Huxley goes on to mention the vital importance of "**ethical corollaries**" supporting the Perennial Philosophy. These constitute the **moral life** of anyone wanting to learn about and practice authentic spiritual life and their attending disciplines. This approach emphasizes "**Right Life**" (in Adi Da's and Buddha's terms), often based on different degrees of renunciation (or self-transcending discipline) grounded in self-control, non-attachment, and ego-transcendence based in the practice of love, compassion and wisdom. Showing a profound depth of understanding buried in the world's religious traditions, Huxley didn't hesitate to emphasize the necessity for the practice of Guru Yoga and by honoring our Enlightened Adepts. The British pandit wonderfully summarizes:

> An Incarnation of the Godhead and, to a lesser degree, any theo-centric Saint, Sage or Prophet [reflecting the lesser Higher Stages of Life] is a human being who knows *who* he [or she truly] is, and can therefore effectively remind other human beings of what they have allowed themselves to forget: namely, that if they choose to become what potentially they already are, they too can be eternally united with the Divine Ground.[48]

Huxley is also sober enough to recognize that we must do *our own* spiritual work in transcending our self-contracting activity as the ego (and our sense of separation). Although an Adept-Guru can gift us through Grace and Spirit-Transmission to achieve our innate Enlightened State, at least momentarily, our spiritual growth is *our* responsibility. The Grace of the Guru comes from the effective power of Heart-Transmission (*Hridaya Shaktipat*) or Spirit Baptism descending down and opening our heart [see Chapter 1]. Huxley, importantly, also mentions the danger and liability toward cultism and projecting psychological desires and pathologies onto other people as a "Great Other" (such as with an imagined deity or a childish relationship with a Guru-Teacher). Nonetheless, according to Huxley, the benefits of Guru Yoga can only be denied at the peril of aborting our spiritual development.

In addition, the British pandit suggests that the wisdom of the Perennial Philosophy can help temper us in our tolerance for other religions. This means as Huxley explains, "It is perfectly possible for people to remain good Christians, Hindus, Buddhists or Muslims and yet to be united in full agreement on the basic doctrines of the Perennial Philosophy."[49] Avatar Adi Da agrees with this point and maintains one can practice their traditional religion while still practicing the Reality-Way of Adidam Ruchiradam. We honor our born and inherited religious tradition best by practicing the universal truths of the world's Great Wisdom Traditions as expressed in the fundamental doctrines of the Perennial Philosophy.

Wilber also emphasizes this "**trans-lineage**" view since he claims that by understanding our universal drive to God-Realization we can empower our traditional religions to better serve our further developmental growth by acting like "**conveyor belts**"[50] (in his words) to deeper spiritual truths. We can thus see how the Enlightened Wisdom of the Great Tradition and Perennial Philosophy is absolutely necessary for world peace, as Huxley continued to emphasize:

> To affirm this truth has never been more imperatively necessary than at the present time. There will never be enduring peace unless and until human beings come to accept a philosophy of life more adequate to the cosmic and psychological facts than the insane idolatries of nationalism and the advertising man's apocalyptic faith in Progress [scientific materialism] towards a mechanized New Jerusalem [religious provincialism]. All of the elements of this [perennial] philosophy are present in the traditional religions. But in existing circumstances there is not the slightest chance that any of the traditional religions will obtain universal [or global] acceptance.[51]

This is exactly why we need the leadership of the world's first truly Global Adept, a *Jagad Guru*—a Divine World-Teacher and World-Friend—and I submit that one has appeared as His Divine Presence Avatar Adi Da Samraj. Others, such as Avatar Meher Baba (1894–1969) or the incomparable Sri Ramana Maharishi (1879–1950), are also powerful sources of this universal Divine Wisdom and Spiritual-Transmission. Importantly, we may turn to and access any authentic Guru or Spiritual Teacher that our life and our spiritual quest brings to us. Still, I firmly believe it is important to study this American-born Guru-Adept in the context of the entire Great Tradition of the Primordial Perennial Philosophy. As we've seen, Adi Da addresses these issues of the Great Tradition most directly [see Part I]. Only then does it become evident who Adi Da Samraj truly is, what His Message and Method (of *Ruchira Shaktipat*) is all about, and how His Divine Presence *spiritually* initiates people into the

Enlightened State (*sophia perennis*) and the higher Stages of Life.[52]

The Global Avatar has indeed appeared *in our time* at the dawn of the Third Millennium, so now it's up to us to step up and serve and replicate "His" Divinely Enlightened State in our own case. By doing so we embrace all others of our global culture in the mood of spiritual cooperation and tolerance so we may enjoy and participate in world peace, for real.[53] Easier said than done, naturally, but it must be done for true global peace and universal harmony, let alone personal liberation and Enlightenment—yet not to be accomplished as a utopian ideal of unrealistic dreams but as the radiant power of Spirit-in-action manifesting as our higher (and highest) human-spiritual potentials!

Chapter 7 Endnotes

1. Aldous Huxley, "Introduction" in *Bhagavad Gita: The Song of God* (1944, 1987), p. 5.

2. See: *The Map of Knowledge: A Thousand-Year History of How Classical Ideas Were Lost and Found* (2019) by Violet Moller.

3. Aldous Huxley, *The Perennial Philosophy* (1945, 1970, 2009), p. vii.

4. Ken Wilber, *One Taste* (1999), pp. 57-58.

5. Aldous Huxley, "Introduction" in *Bhagavad Gita: The Song of God* (1944, 1987), p. 17.

6. See: *American Veda* (2013) by Philip Goldberg; *How the Swans Came to the Lake: A Narrative History of Buddhism in America* (1992) by Rick Fields; *Coming Home: The Experience of Enlightenment in Sacred Traditions* (1995) by Lex Hixon.

7. Seyyed Hossein Nasr, *Knowledge and the Sacred* (1989), p. 69.

8 See: *Lost Masters: Sages of Ancient Greece* (2006, 2016) by Linda Johnsen is, I believe, one of the best books ever written on the subject for it comes from a practitioner of yoga and meditation, not just an academic scholar. As Ms. Johnsen so wonderfully summarizes (p. 3): "I very much want to introduce you, too, to the great Spiritual Masters of our past, Western 'Gurus' whose traditions, unfortunately, we've forgotten. Their life stories, like those of Sages everywhere, are remarkable. And their distinctive approaches to spirituality will remind you of similar Hindu, Buddhist, yogic, and tantric lineages." Highly recommended book.

9. Linda Johnsen, *Lost Masters* (2006), p. 157.

10. See, for example: *The Hermetica: The Lost Wisdom of the Pharaohs* (1997) by Timothy Freke and Peter Gandy.

11. Aldous Huxley, *The Perennial Philosophy* (1945, 1970, 2009), p. vii.

12. Nicholas of Cusa, quoted in "Philosophy, Theology, and the Primordial Claim," by Huston Smith, *Cross Currents*, Fall 1988, p. 276.

13. See: *The Transcendent Unity of Religions* (1984) by Frithjof Schuon.

14. T. S. Eliot quoted in the "Introduction to the Revised Edition" by Huston Smith, *The Transcendent Unity of Religions* (1984) by Frithjof Schuon.

15. See: Huston Smith, review of *Light on the Ancient Worlds* (1965, 1984) by Frithjof Schuon; and *Foreword to The Eye of the Heart* (1997).

16. Frithjof Schuon, from a transcript of a 1995 interview on WorldWisdom.com (retrieved January 2021).

17. See: René Guénon, *The Symbolism of the Cross* (2001, 2004) via "René Guénon" Wikipedia entry (retrieved January 2021).

18. See: "Ananda Coomaraswamy" Wikipedia entry (retrieved January 2021).

19. See: Gerald Heard, "The Philosophia Perennis" in *Vedanta for the Western World* (1945), p. 294ff.

20. Ken Wilber, *One Taste* (1999), p. 14.

21. Ken Wilber, *One Taste* (1999), pp. 8-9.

22. Alan Watts, *Myth and Ritual In Christianity* (1968), p. 14/15.

23. Joseph Campbell, *The Flight of the Wild Gander* (1969), p. 81.

24. See: *Esalen: America and the Religion of No Religion* (2007) by Jeffrey J. Kripal.

25. See: Huston Smith, *Cleansing the Doors of Perception: The Religious Significance of Entheogenic Plants and Chemicals* (2000, 2008).

26. Ken Wilber, *Grace and Grit* (1991), p. 77.

27. See: Ken Wilber, Sex, Ecology, Spirituality (1995, 2001), A *Brief History of Everything* (1996, 2017).

28. Duane Elgin, *Awakening Earth* (1993), p. 272.

29. Thomas McEvilley, *The Shape of Ancient Thought* (2002), p. xxxi.

30. See: Dustin DiPerna, *Streams of Wisdom* (2014), p. 21; also see: Dustin DiPerna, *Evolution's Ally: Our World's Religious Traditions as Conveyor Belts of Transformation* (2015); Dustin DiPerna and Jon Darrall-Rew, *Earth is Eden: An Integral Exploration of the Trans-Himalayan Teachings* (2016); Dustin DiPerna (Editor) and H. B. Augustine (Editor), *The Coming Waves* (2014).

31. Huston Smith, *The World's Religions* (1991, 2009), p. 5.

32. Huston Smith, "Is There a Perennial Philosophy?" in *Revisioning Philosophy* (1992), James Ogilvy, ed., p. 247, 2n.

33. Huston Smith, *The World's Religions* (1991, 2009), p. 5.

34. See: Ken Wilber, *Quantum Questions: Mystical Writings of the World's Greatest Physicists* (1984, 2001).

35. Ken Wilber, *The Eye of Spirit* (1997), pp. 38-39.

36. See: *Quantum Questions* (1984) edited by Ken Wilber, where Wilber presents selections of the "mystical writings of the world's great physicists" (the subtitle).

37. See: *Psychology and the Perennial Philosophy* (2013), edited by Samuel Bendeck Sotillos; *Primordial Truth and Postmodern Theology* (1989) by David Ray Griffin and Huston Smith.

38. Mario Beauregard & Denyse O'Leary, *The Spiritual Brain* (2007), pp. 204-205.

39. Ken Wilber, *The Eye of Spirit* (1997), p. 59.

40. Seyyed Hossein Nasr, *Knowledge and the Sacred* (1989), p. 293.

41, See, for example: W. T. Stace, *The Teachings of the Mystics: Selections from the Great Mystics and Mystical Writings of the World* (1960), who differentiates different degrees of mysticism; also see: Ken Wilber, *The Religion of Tomorrow* (2017).

42. See: The Neo-Perennial Philosophy," *The American Theosophist*, Special Fall Issue 1983, pp. 349-355 [reprinted in *The Quest*, 1992; now part of Chapter 2: "In a Modern Light: Integral Anthropology and the Evolution of Cultures" in *The Eye of Spirit*, 1997].

43. Ken Wilber, *The Eye of Spirit* (1997), p.64.

44. Aldous Huxley, "Introduction" in *Bhagavad Gita: The Song of God* (1944, 1987) translated by Swami Prabhavananda and Christopher Isherwood, p. 6: "At the core of the Perennial Philosophy we find four fundamental doctrines."

45. See: "The Minimum Working Hypothesis" in *Vedanta for the Western World* (1945), edited by Christopher Isherwood.

46. See: Aldous Huxley, "Introduction" in *Bhagavad Gita: The Song of God* (1944, 1987) translated by Swami Prabhavananda and Christopher Isherwood, pp. 5-17.

47. Ibid., pp. 11-12 [capitalization added].

48. Ibid., p. 12.

49. Ibid., pp. 13, 17.

50. See: Dustin DiPerna, *Evolution's Ally: Our World's Religious Traditions as Conveyor Belts of Transformation* (2018, second edition); Ken Wilber, *The Religion of Tomorrow* (2017).

51. Aldous Huxley, "Introduction" in *Bhagavad Gita: The Song of God* (1944, 1987) translated by Swami Prabhavananda and Christopher Isherwood, p. 16.

52. See: *Meeting Adi Da: A Mandala of Approach to Adi Da Samraj* (forthcoming) by Brad Reynolds.

53. See: Adi Da Samraj *Not Two Is Peace* (2009) by World-Friend Adi Da.

EIGHT

SOPHIA PERENNIS
PERENNIAL ENLIGHTENMENT

With Sophia Perennis, it is a question of the following: there are truths innate in the human Spirit, which nevertheless in a sense lie buried in the depth of the "Heart"—in the pure Intellect—and are accessible only to one who is spiritually contemplative; and these are the fundamental metaphysical truths.

— **Frithjof Schuon**, 1959

UNIVERSAL ENLIGHTENMENT:
SOPHIA PERENNIS

What is it exactly that authentic Awakened Adepts are awake to? And why do they all, at their esoteric core or heart, seem to say essentially the same thing? None, for example, claim that evil or darkness is the primary source of the universe. None. Not that evil and darkness, ignorance and malevolence, are not acknowledged for they certainly are an influential force in human life, so the darker aspects of reality are given their due in the scheme of things. Yet En-Light-enment, as the very word indicates, is an awakening to Divine Light (whatever that may be altogether) for it is "The One" that transcends-yet-includes "the Many" or all things in the Kosmos. Avatar Adi Da simply calls "It" the "Bright" or "Conscious Light" or "Real God," which It IS (once a person *realizes* That). Although there are different degrees or levels of mystical revelation, the *ultimate* Realization of Reality is always the same: indescribable by words or reason, i.e., ineffable and Divine. It has been called "One without a second," Non-Dual (*advayam*), *Sat-Chit-Ananda*, Emptiness-Bliss, *Ein Sof*, Absolute Reality, *Dharmadhatu*, *Tao*, Godhead, etc., to inadequately put "It" into words by anyone from any culture. "It" (God) IS Consciousness. With Enlightenment, paradoxically, the interpreter that is "you" (or mind) is fully transcended. "You" are nothing, gone beyond. But "you" *realize* God, see Buddha-Nature, know the Truth. It is Pure Paradox. This makes it impossible for intellectuals to comprehend, which is why Integral Theory (for one) suggests you must become a Mystic first (as well as being an intellectual) to be truly integral.

It makes no sense (to the logical or scientific mind) but It IS Reality so It makes *perfect* sense (to the Heart).

Silent. Serene. Self-Shining. No-thing. No words. God Only. Reality. As It IS.

Enlightenment—known to the ancient Greeks as *Gnosis* and *Sophia*—claims an intimate and ultimate knowledge of the One Source and Condition or substratum of all existence from which arise all universes, all beings, all possibilities. It *realizes* the Absolute Ground and Goal of conditional relative reality that is (paradoxically) totally Unconditional and Absolutely Transcendent. At its heart, this One Divine Reality transcends all conventions of religion, culture, and language (whether terrestrial or extraterrestrial) for It exists uninterrupted as the Source-Condition of all existence, of all spacetime even before the Big Bang. "What is your 'Original Face' before the Big Bang?" as Ken Wilber likes to rephrase the mind-bending Zen koan.[1] Enlightened people are awake to and aware of the true nature of God, the Godhead, Buddha-Nature, the Absolute Reality of the universe, yet, paradoxically, It IS our own consciousness, which is exactly why it's claimed to be "Consciousness Itself." But "you" must *realize It*—via the schooling of spiritual practice and extensive meditation—for it is not a formula that can be intellectually grasped or known (for it is an "un-knowing").

Thus this Wisdom or "**Divine Ignorance**" doesn't stop there for the Adept-Realizers (and Gurus) universally declare that this One Divine Reality is the Very Truth of who *you* are too. Known currently in English as "Enlightenment" (not to be confused with the "Age of Enlightenment" or the "Age of Reason") it is simply "God-Realization," though no word or phrase does it justice. It is knowing *your* "Supreme Identity," the "Ultimate Wisdom," the "Radical Truth," which is, in simple English: **God**—not the mythic God or Creator or "Intelligent Designer" or "Blind Watchmaker"—but **Real God**. Believe it or not, realizing this inherent Divinity is a genuine human quality and capacity that is part of our inherited psyche and evolutionary potential. Our ignorance, however, cloaks its Realization leaving us in the cave of darkness (as Sokrates-Plato suggest) [see Prologue]. Science remains mute on this mystical possibility of humanity. Hence a Realized Guru-Adept can serve you in this process of Awakening since they have Re-Awakened themselves.

The Great Tradition of mystics and metaphysicians for millennia who have realized this Supreme Reality universally proclaim this Divine Realization is what forms the esoteric core of all true religions. It is these Awakened Adepts or Adept-Realizers (in Adi Da's terms) who are the real root and actual source of all our various world religions and esoteric paths. Religious teachings do not come out of thin air; they come from Adepts. Yet God-Realization comes from God, from *your* primordial consciousness spurred on, perhaps, with the Adept's Help (if you're wise).

Since the mystical revelation of the One Divine Reality goes beyond logic and rationality and metaphysical speculation, then the true province of "philosophy" (*philosophia*) is actually more of a mental activity of analysis, not Divine Revelation. Therefore, religious scholar Frithjof Schuon emphasizes that the idea of a *Philosophia perennis* should more correctly be termed *Religio perennis* or *Sophia perennis* because it is actually founded on *Sophia, Gnosis, Satori, Rigpa*, et al., or actual Divine Realization, not theories.[2] The Swiss-born philosopher points out that what is "perennial" or "re-occurring" is the Unconditional Enlightenment experience not the attending "philosophies" and ideas built upon mental constructs involving the conditions of time, place, history, culture, language... and ego. Schuon, the author of *The Transcendent Unity of Religions* (1957), was a profound mystic himself who was initiated into several religious traditions, from shamanism to Sufism, from Vedanta to Buddhism, thus he stated in his eloquent essay "*Sophia Perennis*":

> *Philosophia perennis* is generally understood as referring to that metaphysical truth which has no beginning, and which remains the same in all expressions of wisdom. Perhaps it would be better or more prudent to speak of a "*Sophia perennis*," since it is not a question of artificial mental constructions, as is all too often the case in philosophy; or again, the primordial wisdom that always remains true to itself could be called "*Religio perennis*," given that by its nature it in a sense involves worship and spiritual realization.[3]

This Divine Wisdom or *Sophia* is ultimately realized *inwardly* (in consciousness) by each individual who transcends egoic self-identification and the limits of their provincial religion and outer exoteric cultural traditions. When realized fully, such a person even *transcends* their identity with their born character and individuated body-mind while simultaneously *including* them as well. They simply *realize* All is One and "The One" is Divine (or "Real God"). For them, the esoteric path involves disciplines of meditative contemplation and absorption, not just religious rituals and ceremonial rites (which are also important). Schuon famously called this aspect of reality the "**Transcendent Unity of Religions**," by which he meant "the unity of the religious forms must be realized in a purely inward and spiritual way and without prejudice to any particular form."[4] Aldous Huxley also reminds us that real *philosophia* is grounded in *Gnosis*:

> The Perennial Philosophy has spoken almost all the languages of Asia and Europe and has made use of the terminology and traditions of every one of the higher religions. But under all this confusion of tongues and myths, of local histories and particularistic doctrines, there remains a Highest Common Factor, which is the Perennial Philosophy in what might be called its chemically pure state [*Gnosis*]. This final purity can never, of course, be expressed by any verbal statement of philosophy... It is only in the act of contemplation, when words and even personality are transcended, that the pure state [*Sophia*] of the Perennial Philosophy can actually be known.[5]

Only in the act of contemplative meditation or self-transcendence can the true and perennial *Sophia* be known. Thus it is from this fountain of ultimate knowledge or wisdom that *philo-sophia* or "loving" [*philo-*] "*Sophia*" [Wisdom] springs forth—as Philosophy. Spirituality begins in the heart when the "Simple Feeling of Being"[6] is awakened (as *Gnosis*), for only then can the mind follow up with a philosophy that speaks and writes words and ideas. Ultimately it is from *Sophia*, not *philosophia*, that the Great Guru-Adepts, male or female, take their stand to transmit this Realization (or Enlightened State) to others who approach them with an open heart and clear mind. It is to these Realizers we should look for the light of true wisdom, not to academic philosophers, psychologists, scientists, or religionists (though pandits can certainly help if "enlightened enough").

For example, Ken Wilber is able to explain, as well as anyone, the perplexing paradoxes that are a perpetual problem for unenlightened philosophers when attempting to "talk about" the ineffable Divine (or One God), as he explains in *Eye to Eye* (1983):

> Reality is *not* holistic; it is not dynamic, not interrelated, not one and not unified—*all* of those are mere concepts about reality.... The Absolute cannot be qualified in any sense.... God is not one thing among many things, or the sum of many things, or the dynamic interaction of many things—God is the condition, the nature, the suchness, or the reality *of* each thing or event or process. It is not set apart *from* any of them, yet neither is it in any way confined *to* them. It is identical *with* the world, but not identical *to* it.... Whatever reality is, it can only, *only* be "seen" upon Satori [*Sophia*], or via actual contemplative insight.[7]

Wilber guides us to realize: "In short, the more consciousness grows and evolves, the more it grows beyond the narrow bounds of the personal ego, the more it touches the transpersonal and universal Divine."[8] This developmental perspective arises by realizing that "Mysticism is not regression in service of the ego, but evolution in the transcendence of the ego."[9] Again, because the pandit embraces the truth of Enlightenment as a genuine Nondual Vision of Reality (not as mythic tall tales), then beyond most of his peers Wilber subtly (and directly) points out: "All things are not ultimately made of subatomic particles; all things, including subatomic particles, are ultimately made of God."[10]

This view, obviously, goes far beyond (yet includes) science. *Sophia*, in other words, can ground *philosophia*, as well as science, in spiritual wisdom if a true Integral Approach is used. In this case, wise pandits, not only Gurus, are very useful. However, it is the Guru-Adepts themselves who are the most useful for they pass on or transmit *Sophia*, not merely *philosophia* (or psychological techniques). As scientific-mind intellectuals, or mythic-oriented religionists, or even vision-logic integralists, we should never forget or overlook this simple truth embodied in the Great Wisdom Tradition of humankind.

NEO-PERENNIAL PHILOSOPHY:
EVOLUTION OF TRADITIONAL METAPHYSICS

One of the great clarifications and contributions given to us by today's Integral Philosophy is the inclusion of **evolution** or progressive development into its metaphysics (and physics). Instead of seeing the physical universe as infinite and eternal, as they did in the past—including Einstein himself until his own spacetime theories changed his mind—integral spirituality sees the pluridimensional Kosmos as an ever-evolving and ever-present expression of the Divine Transcendent-Immanent Condition. This is, of course, a profound paradox beyond the logic of mind or science. However, with a progressive evolutionary view it isn't necessary to postulate a Golden Age in the ancient past or a final Judgment Day in the upcoming future. There's even no longer the need for a strict predetermined "Perennial" Philosophy that always remains the same (except at its core of *Sophia* or Enlightenment).

Only God or the Divine Ground of Being is the *real* or *radical* (meaning "at the root") *truth* that is timeless and whole, transcendent and free; everything else is conditional, including philosophies. The idea that a universal

"Perennial Philosophy" can be modified or upgraded to our current historical standards has been proposed by Integral Theory's leading proponent Ken Wilber who explains why:

> When we speak of the "Ancient Wisdom" [with title caps] as the *philosophia perennis*, there can properly be only one correct meaning, namely, those truths—or rather, That Truth—which is radically *timeless* or *eternal*, one and whole, only and all. That Truth—using "Truth" in the broadest sense as the ultimately Real or Spirit itself—is the essence of the Perennial Philosophy.
>
> In other words, the Perennial Philosophy is not, at its core, a set of doctrines, beliefs, teachings, or ideas, for all of those are *of* the world of form, of space and time and ceaseless change, whereas very Truth [*Sophia*] is radically formless, spaceless, and timeless, encompassing all space and time but limited to none. That One—the radical Truth—is not *in* the world of space and time, except as *all* space and time, and thus it could never be enunciated in formal or doctrinal fashion.... Radical Truth can be *shown* (in contemplative awareness) but never exhaustively *said* (in discursive language)....
>
> Radical Truth itself is formless, timeless, spaceless, changeless; its various forms, however, the various ideas, symbols, images, and thoughts we use to represent it, ceaselessly change and evolve.[11]

With the advent of a detailed evolutionary understanding, Wilber has dubbed this new and improved version of the Perennial Philosophy as the "**Neo-Perennial Philosophy**,"[12] since it is, according to him, "much more finely tuned to present-day needs, ideas, and advances in science."[13] In short, the integral pandit maintains: "The idea of history as devolution (or a fall from God) was slowly replaced by the idea of history as evolution (or growth to God).... God does not lie in our collective past, God lies ahead in our collective future; the Garden of Eden is tomorrow, not yesterday; the Golden Age lies down the road, not up it."[14] This modified version of traditional philosophy inserts evolution as the developmental "engine" or "drive" of a universe that is essentially *spiritual* (or made of Spirit)—known as "**Spirit-in-action**" (in Wilber's words). He is not alone in his assessment, as the integral pandit points out in *The Eye of Spirit* (1997):

This fundamental shift in the sense or form of the Perennial Philosophy—as represented in, say, Aurobindo, Hegel, Adi Da, Schelling, Teilhard de Chardin, Radhakrishnan, to name a few—I should like to call the "**Neo-Perennial Philosophy**." And it is the Neo-Perennial Philosophy—not "old wisdom"—that our present culture so desperately needs.

Thus, at the core of the Neo-Perennial Philosophy is the same Radical and Formless Truth glimpsed by the wisdom cultures of the past… but its outward *form*, its clothing cut in the relative and manifest world, has naturally changed and evolved to keep pace with the progressive evolution of the manifest world itself—and that includes, of course, the very idea of evolution. And whereas "ancient wisdom" [lower case]—meaning in this case the outward doctrines, ideas, and symbols used in past ages to metaphorically represent inward and Radical Truth ["Ancient Wisdom," upper case}—is by and large outdated, outmoded, anachronistic, or simply wrong (even though they were, for their earlier time and place, perfectly phase-specific and culture-appropriate), the form of the Neo-Perennial Philosophy is much more finely tuned to present day needs, ideas, and advances in science.[15]

This integral perspective is best seen when we use science—the "**Eye of Mind**" (or mentality) combined with the "**Eye of Flesh**" (or physicality)—*in combination* with the "**Eye of Spirit**" (or transcendental insight). Then we observe the Kosmos as being a multi-leveled psycho-physical spectrum emerging and unfolding through billions of years of creation. This view is currently called "**Big History**" in academic terms (though it often leaves out Spirit), another cosmological version of the "**Universe Story**" (in Brian Swimme's terms).[16] Evolution *as* Spirit-in-action is today's version of the traditional "**Creation Story**" but told with the facts of scientific observation minus its materialistic reductionism. Once evolution (both before and after Darwin) began to work its way into the modern mind by the mid-19th century, philosophers and scientists, such as Schelling, Hegel, Wallace, Bergson, James, Teilhard de Chardin, Blavatsky, Vivekananda, Aurobindo, Gebser, Swimme, McIntosh, Wilber, among many others, began working with this new thesis and how it might change or upgrade our view of reality and philosophy.[17]

From a strict "scientific" materialistic view, however, one focused mostly on biological evolution as natural selection, the addition of a spiritual purpose or *telos* (or "ultimate aim") seems like hocus-pocus that adds unnecessary ingredients (or theories) to the mechanics of natural processes run by chance and necessity, not by Spirit. Yet integral visionaries see no inherent contradiction by including science's measurements with a spiritual vision of reality; they simply reject the philosophical conclusion of materialism (and chance) as the only determinate factor. Carter Phipps, in his wonderful book *Evolutionaries* (2012) explains:

> [There is] the potential of an evolutionary worldview to serve as a new cosmology, one that provides an authentic meeting point between science and spirit. Evolution, in this respect, has a unique capacity to be a source of spiritual fulfillment, of authentic meaning and purpose, renewing our faith in the possibilities of the future and inspiring us to reach for these higher potentials, individually and collectively. This is perhaps the most profound promise of an evolutionary worldview, with implications as far-reaching as human aspiration itself.[18]

With such an all-encompassing "**Integral Vision**" (as Wilber names it), it becomes critically important to "see" and understand reality not only with the Eye of Science (using the Eye of Flesh with Mind), as moderns do, but also to see reality with the Eye of Spirit, as mystics do. Wilber calls these various modes of knowledge acquisition the "**Three Eyes of Knowing**" (Body, Mind, Spirit) because they acknowledge the physical, mental, and spiritual domains, respectively, as being correlated (or "tetra-meshed") interiors *and* exteriors. Thus the Integral Vision insists we use at a minimum *all three* "eyes" of knowledge, all three modes of knowing, or otherwise we're missing a big part of the whole picture.[19] Now, of course, Wilber has expanded his Integral Theory to include the "**four quadrants**" or the ontological domains of the *interiors-exteriors* of *individuals-collectives*— known as "**AQAL**" (or "all-quadrants, all-levels")—in addition to the epistemological pluralism of the "three eyes" (or all-levels) of knowledge acquisition.

Science doesn't know the whole truth; neither does religion nor does mysticism. We must gain our knowledge from interiors as well as exteriors in order to be whole. The Integral Vision sees all these views or perspectives as "true but partial" (its principal motto) creating an intertwined matrix of wholeness—the Kosmos. Whereas Enlightenment goes even further by integrating-and-transcending *all* domains (or "points of view") in **Divine Ignorance**" (the unknowing that is Ultimate Knowledge). Importantly, the Integral Vision recognizes and philosophically includes this enlightened view as well.

The integration of evolutionary development into our spiritual philosophies, reaching from atoms to amoebas to apes to angels to Atman, from dust to deer to divinity, recapitulates itself—in a "transcend-and-include" manner—within the psychological development of our human psyche. In other words, we are born to *realize* God! Wilber wisely noted as much in *The Atman Project* (1980): "The form of development, the form of transformation—that is constant, as far as I can tell, from the womb to God…. Development is evolution; evolution is transcendence… and transcendence has as its final goal Atman, or ultimate Unity Consciousness in only God."[20] This new spiritual view of evolution is supplemented with the advancements of modern science but not by canceling out Spirit (or God) with reductionistic materialism.

The precise measurements of Nature, down to the very atom (and subatomic particles), even reaching to the origin of spacetime, presents a phenomenal understanding of cosmic evolution that escaped our ancient Seers (although some understood its general contours). The ancient Sages did not have microscopes and telescopes and particle accelerators, etc., nor an understanding of DNA and brain chemistry, and so forth, but they did have consciousness and the capacity to *realize* the Ultimate Truth (*Sophia*), not merely measure relative facts. However, through exploring their interiors they did recognize many of the archetypal patterns creating both cosmos and psyche; in many ways even going beyond science today. The Integral Vision, again, sees all views as "true but partial" and thus offers the world a much broader (and deeper) perspective.

Integral thinkers point out that the Evolutionary Story was not a notion fully understood by our Ancient Masters of the traditional Perennial Philosophy. At least not in detail. But some did anticipate future science in general terms. For example, some Sages from ancient India and Greece, without the benefit of modern science, proposed theories of atoms and the empty void as constructing the fundamental units of solid matter yet formulated without the precision and mathematics of today's general relativity and quantum theories. Integral pioneer Michael Murphy soberly reminds us of this fact in his monumental book on human transformative capacities, *The Future of the Body* (1992):

When the Upanishads, Buddhist sutras, and Tao Te Ching were composed—indeed, when the first teachings of all the great contemplative schools were formulated—their authors did not have our modern knowledge of cosmic and biological development. Though the sacred traditions nurtured understanding of numerous extraordinary capacities, they could not comprehend the history of advances in structural complexity, behavioral repertoire, and awareness among living species.[21]

One of the exquisite beauties offered by the Integral Vision, grounded in *Sophia Perennis* (Enlightenment) or seeing clearly with the Eye of Spirit, is it presents an understanding of evolution that integrates *both* the ancient intuition that we live in a sacred creation in addition to the secular scientific reconstructions about how the universe came into existence and continues to exist. Science's error is in its reduction of everything down to being only processes of physical particles thus being blind to Spirit and the Transcendental Reality. A spiritual-integral understanding, on the other hand, generates its own version a genuine "**Theory of Everything**" (T.O.E.) that *includes* Spirit (and God). This new story of Spirit-in-action working in harmony with science could lead us to a brighter future if we expand our view of knowledge and its acquisition. An important feature of Wilber's Integral AQAL Model is it's "**transcend-and-include**" quality spanning all levels of existence, evolving from matter to mind to soul to Spirit—the **Kosmos** of "**Spirit-in-action**," (in Wilber's words) is best pictured as a mandala of embrace, as the two graphics below simply show:

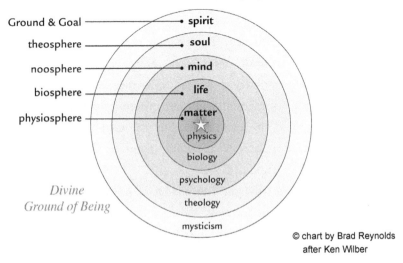

© chart by Brad Reynolds
after Ken Wilber

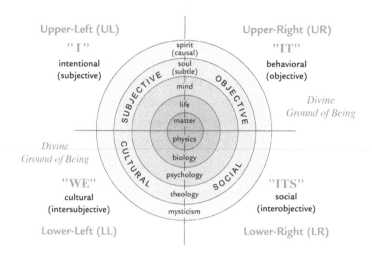

Kosmos: Great Nest of Spirit-In-Action
Levels–Quadrants in the AQAL Matrix
© chart by Brad Reynolds

This "**Great Nest of Spirit**" (Kosmos)—Wilber's updated version of the traditional "Great Chain of Being"—includes what he calls the *physiosphere* (matter), *biosphere* (life), *noosphere* (mind), and *theosphere* (soul-spirit), all the major realms of existence enfolding one another like a giant mandala of increasing embrace.[22] Each level or domain has its place and function in the Mandala of Reality with each sphere interacting with the others yet none being equivalent. Thus Wilber clarifies: "This whole panoply of higher levels generating the lower moment to moment, and of the dazzling interpenetration of each level with the others, and of the extraordinary dynamics between the levels, all occurring in a field of effulgent [Divine] radiance—all this is meant when the Mystic-Sage speaks of *multidimensional interpenetration with nonequivalence*."[23] This interpenetrated Matrix of Reality therefore includes not only the *gross-physical* realm of matter-energy but the *subtle-mental-soulful* domains of etheric-energy and the mind (including the astral and archetypal), even the *spiritual-causal* dimensions all arising in and *as* God, the Transcendent-Immanent Divine Ground of Being.

This is how (and why) the Kosmos of forms and energy are all *included-yet-transcended* in the formless, indefinable Real God of Conscious Light (in Adi Da's terms) or the Clear-Light Void (in Buddhist terms). It is a stunning, beautiful, enlightened—and *integral*—vision of the universe. The ever-changing relative realities (of the Many) are integrated with the Timeless Absolute Truth (of The One) since they all arise from and in It (and *as* It). Wilber noted as much in his integral considerations on the emerging Neo-Perennial Philosophy:

> At the core of the Neo-Perennial Philosophy is the same Radical and Formless Truth ["Ancient Wisdom"] glimpsed by the wisdom cultures of the past (and given such culture-specific and temporal names as Tao, Buddha Mind, Brahman, Goddess, Keter, etc.); but its outward *form*, its clothing cut in the relative world, has naturally changed and evolved to keep pace with the progressive evolution of the manifest world itself—and that includes, of course, the very idea of evolution…. When we descend from this plane of formless, imageless, timeless union-samadhi, we naturally clothe that Realization of formless Truth in the various forms and truth-symbols available to our particular sociocultural milieu.[24]

Instead of the Creation Story being told in mythic time, now the Universe Story is told in measurable time. Instead of just describing the *exterior* evolution of atoms, galaxies, stars, planets, and biological life forms, the integral version of our Evolutionary Story includes the *interior* dimensions of an evolving spectrum of consciousness, from prehension to abstraction to God-Realization. Instead of worshiping God as beyond and above this world, it is realized with Enlightenment that we can *know* God *as being* oneself and *as being* the whole universe. God is the Divine Ground of Being evolving the Kosmos.

Our deepest depth is the Source-Condition of all Nature where the Kosmos is in fact arising as Spirit-in-action. Integral Theory throws out the unnecessary mythical illusions and dogmas of the past, the fancy stories and pictorial metaphors of gods and goddesses (while honoring their archetypal force) as being phase-specific relics of "ancient wisdom" (with a lower case "a"). Yet it retains the mystical or spiritual quality revealed in the heart of "Ancient Wisdom" (with a capital "A") to provide an evolutionary vision for our collective (and individual) future. Wilber continues to clarify:

> There is a confusion of *past forms* of Truth with Truth itself. Once this confusion is made, then "timeless Truth" comes to mean "what

the old folks said." There is a whole tendency to glorify yesterday; they see a greater "wisdom" available in the past than the present; to eulogize ancient Egypt, China, India [and Greece]; to romanticize our ancestors and denigrate our contemporaries; and, on the whole, to see in the manifest realm not an *evolution* of increasing wisdom but a *devolution* of increasing ignorance. And all of this, I believe, is profoundly muddle-headed.

My point is that when we say "our present culture needs ancient wisdom" [lower case "a"], we must be careful to specify exactly what we mean by "ancient wisdom." If by "ancient" we mean "timeless" [i.e., "Ancient Wisdom" in caps], then of course our culture is in desperate need of such wisdom (as have all cultures been in such need). But if by "ancient" we mean "past forms of Truth," then I believe nothing but a reactionary, antiprogressive, antiliberal, anti-evolutionary stance could ever result from such an importation.[25]

This advanced post-postmodern Integral Vision wisely dispenses with the traditional "Creator God" (pictured like in Michelangelo's fresco of a bearded man sitting on clouds) or some type of overarching Parent-Deity or "Intelligent Designer" controlling everything. Rather, this view sees God as transcendent-immanent Spirit-Energy—*Eros* (as Plato and Wilber say) or Divine Light—that creates and sustains evolution and all existence. Evolution *is* Spirit-in-action when *seen integrally*; the universe is not just random chance but a divine dance of immanent relative light grounded in Transcendent Conscious Light while manifesting a whole beautiful Kosmos, from here to Eternity. We can all *see* this, beyond doubt, when the Eye of Spirit is uncovered in Divine Revelation (accompanied by the knowledge that is also seen with the Eye of Body-Mind). Thus the Neo-Perennial Philosophy still reveals the "One God" (or Divine Domain) of the traditional Perennial Philosophy, for the Radical Truth is Unconditional, yet now it sees the Kosmos through the Spirit of evolution. Real Wisdom is timeless, not merely "ancient" or "modern." Real Wisdom (*Sophia*) also transcends evolution. Real Wisdom is Eternal Wisdom regardless of what planet you live on or universe you live in or realm "you" arise from.

Evolving Dharma, Not Enlightenment

As mentioned earlier, the Enlightened Wisdom of the Perennial Philosophy (*Sophia Perennis*) itself does *not* evolve; it is timeless (or eternal), spaceless (or infinite), Radical Nondual Truth (existing beyond words, forms, and measurement). The Formless Godhead is not subject to the conditions of history nor the human ego nor the conditions of matter and energy. Nonetheless, as Wilber has noted, the articulation and teachings—or Dharma—of the Prophets, Yogis, Saints, and Sages themselves have evolved in greater detail during historical time. Even "advanced-tip" individuals continue to evolve within the evolution of collective socio-cultural worldviews and historical periods—from the archaic to magic to mythic to rational to pluralistic to integral to mystical worldviews (in Gebser-Wilber terms).[26] Nonetheless, the Eternal Wisdom they have realized remains free of cultural limits and historical time. Wilber succinctly explains: "The ultimate aim of evolution—the movement from the lower to the higher—is to awaken as Atman, and thus retain the glory of creation without being forced to act in the drama of self-suffering."[27] It is a paradox the logical mind cannot sufficiently comprehend. Once more, only the heart knows for sure.

Consequently, the importance of human development both as "Growing Up" and "Waking Up" has been adequately mapped out by many advanced-tip pioneers of our past collective eras. Recent evolutionary philosophers from Hegel to Aurobindo, from Gebser to Radhakrishnan, from Schelling to Teilhard de Chardin, from Huxley to Wilber, et al., have all proposed that history continues to unfold while human consciousness, individually and collectively, progressively evolves forward so *everyone* may *realize* our inherent Divine Condition. Nevertheless, paradoxically, from the view of Nondual Enlightenment God is Acausal, not created, transcending the entire evolutionary process. Thus we need Guru-Adepts awakened to the Transcendent State to help liberate us from the maze (or maya) of conditional forms and evolutionary processes. Wilber thus wisely noted:

> According to… nondual Sages everywhere, the extraordinary and altogether paradoxical secret is that the Final Release is always already accomplished. The "last step" is to step off the cycle of time [and evolution] altogether, and find the Timeless there from the start, ever-present from the very beginning and at every point along the way. The great far-off spectacular climax… is right now.[28]

In the clothing of the relative world arising in conditional reality, however, philosophical ideas and religious theologies continue to evolve in expression and sophistication, even among its most notable Adept-Realizers. Hence Wilber's Neo-Perennial Philosophy, as we saw, attempts to upgrade the insights of "ancient wisdom" (small "a") or the *old ideas* of traditions and customs by adding the actual perennial Realization of "Ancient Wisdom" (capital "A"), the timeless universals pointed to in the Perennial Philosophy. Wilber wants to distinguish between "ancient wisdom" as "what the old folks said" or "past forms of Truth" from the timeless, formless, spaceless "Ancient Wisdom" of *Sophia Perennis*.

Today this timeless, formless, acausal Sophia-Wisdom has been integrated with the evidence of emergent evolution, such as with the models of recent scholar-pandits who support Enlightenment and science, like Aurobindo, Teilhard de Chardin, and Wilber (among others). Wilber infuses this idea as being the backbone of his current integral "**post-metaphysical**" position, as he philosophically explains:

> Here is my point: we might say that the idea of evolution as return-to-Spirit is part of the Perennial Philosophy, but the idea itself, in any adequate form, is not more than a few hundred years old. It might be "ancient" as timeless, but it is certainly not

"ancient" as "old.".... Whereas "ancient wisdom"—meaning in this case the outward doctrines, ideas, [mythic] symbols used in past ages to metaphorically represent inward and Radical Truth—is by and large outdated...

The point is that the evolution of the *forms* of Truth clearly shows a succession of *increasingly adequate* and *more comprehensive* structures for truth's expression and representation.... The past had the Great Religions. The future will have the Greater Religions.[29]

This position is actually a strong argument for the authenticity of Adi Da Samraj and his Teaching of Radical Understanding and the Way of the Heart. Wilber should know that a "Greater Religion" will only be possible through the presence of authentic Adept-Realizers and genuine Gurus, not through more sophisticated theories and philosophies, even if "integral" (or "AQAL"). It is they who will be "increasingly adequate and more comprehensive," not ideas in books nor with the measurements and theories of science. Each further development in the world's spiritual teachings across the millennia have all arisen from advanced-tip Adept-Realizers appearing in human history, not with the ruminations of scholar-pandits and philosophers (although they may help).

The Guru-Adepts are the ones who express the timeless Ancient Wisdom of *Sophia Perennis* by communicating its truths in a more sophisticated language over the centuries. They are the ones who psycho-physically *transmit* this wisdom and realization to others. *Philosophia* begins with *Sophia*; real philosophy begins with real Enlightenment. In the process the Adept-Realizer often improves and refines the actual techniques of spiritual practice, evolving the yogas and meditations that awaken true devotion to God (or the Divine Reality). In this case, as Wilber proposes: "The Neo-Perennial Philosophy, with its adaptability to modern needs and desires, is and must now be God's witness to the new and rising wisdom culture [such as with an Integral Age]."[30] I maintain this Wisdom Culture can only truly be initiated by a genuine World-Guru, such as with Avatar Adi Da Samraj.

Some say, including Wilber, that our "modern needs and desires" can no longer accept the authority of the Guru-Adept. They believe only "We" can do it—that "the next Buddha will be the Sangha" (as Thich Nhat Hanh suggested)—but this will rely too much on egos and egoic cooperation. While cooperative community (i.e., the Sangha) is very important, one of the "three jewels" of Buddhism (along with the Dharma or Teaching, and the Buddha or Guru-Teacher) it cannot happen in reality without the Buddha and the Dharma coming first, without the Teacher and the Teaching to guide "We," (composed of mostly egos) the Sangha. This alone is the province of the Adept-Realizer, not the average-mode masses of common humanity. We must be cautious in thinking that "We" can do it on our own; that has never worked before and will fail in the future. Idealistic utopias are a product of the ego, not God-Realization.

If the collective—including the entire global culture—is to be transformed into a genuine Wisdom Culture it will be done through authentic sadhana and Satsang via actual spiritual practice and Guru Yoga. The secret is to find and access an authentic (not cultic) Adept-Guru.[31] It is this aspect of *philosophia* or the real love of wisdom that will always remain perennial, timeless, and true. Yet, it does seem to be true that the Adepts themselves adapt to the times as well, so as history evolves forward so does the Dharma-Teaching in certain respects (though at its core it will always already remain Timeless and Unconditional). Wilber long ago affirmed this improved possibility with Avatar Adi Da's Teaching-Work, as he pointed out in a footnote buried in *Up from Eden* (1981):

> This centaur period [our emerging Integral Age] (really just starting) roughly corresponds with the first true and complete understanding of the Svabhavikakaya [nondual mysticism], reached perhaps as early as c. eighth century A.D. in Buddhism (Hui-Neng, Padmasambhava), but which likewise is peaking with certain modern-day sages, especially Sri Ramana Maharshi, Adi Da Samraj, perhaps Aurobindo, Sri Rang Avadhoot, Yogeshwarand [author of *The Science of Soul*, who also identifies the heart on the right as the source of Consciousness like Ramana Maharshi and Adi Da teach].[32]

This "improvement" (or further articulation) of even our most sacred Teachings can be seen in many of the world's religions, for example, in the Judea-Christian tradition it has evolved from Abraham to Moses to Jesus to Eckhart; or the turning of the "Dharma Wheel" in Buddhism from Theraveda/Hinayana (the "lesser vehicle") to Mahayana (the "greater vehicle") to Vajrayana (the "diamond vehicle"); or in Hinduism from Vedanta to Advaita Vedanta to Neo-Vedanta, and so forth. For example, Wilber explains in greater detail:

A clearer examination of the historical record shows, if anything, a continuing evolution and deepening of spiritual understanding, past the axial period [Axial Age, ca. 500 BCE] and right up to (and including) modern times. There is, first, the magnificent growth of Mahayana Buddhism in India, beginning around the second and third centuries CE; the extraordinary growth of Ch'an, T'ien T'ai, and Hua Yen Buddhism in China, especially beginning in the sixth, seventh, and eighth centuries; the exquisite Vajrayana in Tibet, which didn't even get started until the eighth century; Tantric Buddhism in India, which was developed in India between the eighth and eleventh centuries; and Zen in Japan, where the great Hakuin wasn't born until 1685! In Vedanta, Shankara doesn't arrive on the scene until 800 CE; Ramanuja until 1175; Ramakrishna until 1836; and the greatest of all Vedantic sages, Sri Ramana Maharshi, and the greatest of all Vedantic philosophers, Sri Aurobindo, both died only a few decades ago!

I could go on like this, building what I think is an absolutely airtight case: both the *quality* of humanity's spiritual understanding, and the *form* of its presentation, are deepening and becoming *more* adequate in modern times, not less.[33]

In Adi Da's case, in harmony with Ramana Maharshi of the 20th century, this advancement might be indicated in the more intricate Dharma-Teaching about the right side of the heart (not the middle heart usually associated with the heart chakra). This includes the "current of immortal bliss" or *Amrita Nadi* (and *Atma Nadi*) that arises from the heart on the right through the throat and brain core to the Infinite Light above and beyond the crown (transcending all universes and manifestations). This completes the kundalini current and fulfills the esoteric anatomy of all human beings [see Chapter 19]. Although most esoteric Teachings point to the heart as being the source of God-Knowledge in human beings, few point to the "right side" (in the area of the sinoatrial node or "pacemaker"), which is unique to Ramana and Adi Da. This one extended quote from Adi Da's *The Enlightenment of the Whole Body* (1978) indicates a level of detail never before uttered in the literature of the Great Tradition (as far as I know):

The region of the body where the heart appears is the region of the primary root of psycho-physical being. All of the states of manifest awareness—waking, dreaming, and sleeping—have their root in the region of the heart. The heart is also the locus of the primary disposition of the entire body-mind. That whole body disposition is free or unobstructed feeling-attention—which is Love and Divine Communion....

The bulk of the physical heart is in the left of the center of the chest, but the "pacemaker" of the heartbeat is located in the right atrium, or upper right chamber of the heart. It is here that the Radiant Transcendental Consciousness [or God] is continually associated with the impulse of Life in the individual body-mind.... The "pacemaker" (sinoatrial node) is unique among all the nervous structures of the body-mind in that its cells possess an intrinsic rhythm.... It works on its own, in direct association with the Transcendental Force of Life, independently of the brain and all other extended functions of the body-mind....

This locus of the heart, on the right, is the center that must be penetrated, once the body-mind is purified and intensified by regenerative practices and higher contemplation. And only the penetration of this heart-root permits the higher brain and the entire psycho-physical form to be pervaded by the Transcendental Radiance and Bliss of God, beyond all sense of independent self, and beyond all perceptions, subtle or gross. Once that invasion by the Flood of Radiant Life is made, the whole body-mind begins to be Transfigured and Transformed by Divine Love and Humor. [34]

Once more, we can see that Wilber, as a brilliant pandit, has listened closely to the Master-Adepts (particularity Adi Da), grounded in his own realization, thus his Integral Vision realizes: "Transcendent values are not empiric facts revealed to the Eye of Flesh but contemplative and nonverbal insights revealed by the *lumen superius* in the cave of the heart."[35] Evolution, in other words, occurs in the consciousness of human thought and awareness as much as it does in the physical cosmos yet is eternally transcended in the Nondual Divine Ground or the Heart of Real God. This expanded perspective of evolution, from cosmological to biological to psychological to spiritual domains all set within Transcendent Radiance, is an appropriate and valid argument for affirming the authenticity of Adi Da Samraj's new Teaching-Revelation in our current era. Yet, at the same time, his Way of the Heart is in perfect harmony with the Timeless Truth taught by all Enlightened Adept-Realizers from all eras of human history, and, without a doubt, in all of cosmic history regardless of what planet any particular being might manifest or whatever parallel universe might arise, *ad infinitum.*

Chapter 8 Endnotes

1. See: Ken Wilber, *Sex, Ecology, Spirituality* (1995), p. 316.

2. See: Frithjof Schuon, *The Essential Writings of Frithjof Schuon* (1991, Element Books), edited by Seyyed Hossein Nasr.

3. Frithjof Schuon, "Sophia Perennis" in *The Essential Writings of Frithjof Schuon* (1991), edited by Seyyed Hossein Nasr, p. 534 [following Schuon's capitalization of the Latin].

4. Frithjof Schuon, The Transcendent Unity of Religions (1957, 1984), p. xxxiv.

5. Aldous Huxley "Introduction" in *Bhagavad Gita: The Song of God* (1944) trans., by Swami Prabhavananda and Christopher Isherwood, pp. 5-6.

6. See: Ken Wilber, *The Simple Feeling of Being: Embracing Your True Nature* (2004) compiled and edited by Mark Palmer, Sean Hargens, Vipassana Esbjörn, and Adam Leonard; perhaps the best single book presenting Wilber's mastery of the essence of the Great Tradition of Enlightenment.

7. Ken Wilber, *Eye to Eye* (1983, 1990), pp. 171, 172, 177.

8. Ibid., p. 209.

9. Ibid., p. 240.

10. Ibid., p. 167.

11. Ken Wilber, *The Eye of Spirit* (1997), pp. 59-60 [title caps added].

12. See: Ken Wilber, "The Neo-Perennial Philosophy" in *The American Theosophists*, Special Fall Issue, 1983, pp. 349-355, now embedded in Chapter 2: "In a Modern Light: Integral Anthropology and the Evolution of Consciousness," in *The Eye of Spirit* (1997) by Ken Wilber.

13. Ken Wilber, *The Eye of Spirit* (1997), p. 64.

14. Ibid., p. 63.

15. Ibid., p. 63 [title caps added].

16. See: *Origin Story: A Big History of Everything* (2018) by David Christian; *Maps of Time: An Introduction to Big History* (2004) by David Christian; *The Universe Story: From the Primordial Flaring Forth to the Ecozoic Era—A Celebration of the Unfolding of the Cosmos* (1994) by Brian Swimme.

17. See: Carter Phipps, *Evolutionaries: Unlocking the Spiritual and Cultural Potential of Science's Greatest Ideas* (2012); Steve McIntosh, *Evolution's Purpose: An Integral Interpretation of the Scientific Story of Our Origins* (2012).

18. Carter Phipps, *Evolutionaries* (2012), p. 18.

19. Ken Wilber, *Eye to Eye* (1982, 2001); *The Eye of Spirit* (1997, 2000).

20. Ken Wilber, *The Atman Project* (198), p. 79, ix.

21. Michael Murphy, *The Future of the Body* (1992), p. 172.

22. See: Ken Wilber, *Sex, Ecology, Spirituality* (1995, 2001), *A Theory of Everything* (1999, 2001).

23. Ken Wilber, *Eye to Eye* (1983, 1990), p. 132 [italics added].

24. Ken Wilber, *The Eye of Spirit* (1997), p. 64.

25. Ibid., pp. 60-61.

26. See: Ken Wilber, *Up from Eden* (1980); *Sex, Ecology, Spirituality* (1995, 2000); *The Eye of Spirit* (1997, 2000); *The Religion of Tomorrow* (2017).

27. Ken Wilber, *Eye to Eye* (1983, 1990), p. 131.

28. Ken Wilber, *Sex, Ecology, Spirituality* (1995), p. 508.

29. Ken Wilber, *The Eye of Spirit* (1997), pp. 63, 64, 65.

30. Ibid., p. 65.

31. See: *In God's Company: Guru-Adepts As Agents for Enlightenment in the Integral Age* (2022) by Brad Reynolds.

32. Ken Wilber, *Up from Eden* (1982), p. 320n [Adi Da, back when Wilber wrote the footnote, was named "Bubba Free John"].

33. Ken Wilber *The Eye of Spirit* (1997), p. 62.

34. Adi Da Samraj [Bubba Free John], *The Enlightenment of the Whole Body* (1978), pp. 396, 398, 401; I highly recommend studying all of these pages (and more) for an even fuller description of this esoteric processes involving *Amrita Nadi* and "Atma Nadi Shakti Yoga," Adi Da's advanced yogic process of Satsang in His Company and initiated with His Heart-Transmission; also see: *Atma Nadi Shakti Yoga* (2008).

35. Ken Wilber, *Eye to Eye* (1983, 1990), p. 21.

NINE

EAST–WEST:
TWAIN SHALL MEET

Humankind is no longer of either the West or the East.
Rather, now, and forever hereafter, humankind is a global construct
(or re-union) of all—and, therefore, every individual, every brain-
mind, and every nation and culture must intensively and
comprehensively re-adapt to a unified (rather than a bi-polar)
global (and, necessarily, cooperative) order.

— **Adi Da Samraj**, *The Pneumaton*[1]

WAR OF WORLDVIEWS:
OMEGA-WEST VERSUS ALPHA-EAST

Irst published in 1889, a few years before the Parliament of the World's Religions at the Chicago World's Fair in 1893 that changed the dynamic of Eastern wisdom entering the West [see below], an English journalist and writer born in India, Rudyard Kipling, expressed the equality of people even when seen from polar opposites of the globe. In his poem "The Ballad of East and West" Kipling announced:

Oh, East is East, and West is West, and never the twain shall meet,
Till Earth and Sky stand presently at God's great Judgment Seat;

But there is neither East nor West, Border, nor Breed, nor Birth,
When two strong men stand face to face,
though they come from ends of the earth!

Though sometimes ascribed as being racist, the stanzas actually appear as unifying, since the opposite poles of East and West (or North and South) will ever meet , like the two opposing poles of a compass, so instead Kipling was pointing to our common humanity. When two strong men meet face-to-face, regardless of their nationality ("borders"), family ("birth") or race ("breed"), it makes no difference since both are human, universal in desire and need. Since ancient times there has been a tendency for humankind to see one another in bi-polar camps coming from opposing sides of the globe. In reality, we are neither from "**the East**"—traditionally called the "**Orient / Oriental**" (from Latin *oriens* or "where the sun rises")—or from "**the West**"—the "**Occident / Occidental**" (from Latin *occidens* or "where the sun sets"), Kipling's poetic stance is thus sympathetic to both sides, not racist in intent but universal in declaration.

Today, terms such as "Oriental" have become unfashionable in our emerging global society (though they are still used in a scholarly sense). Since slavery legally ended in the United States after 1865, hundreds of years after the worldwide European colonization began in 1492, there has been an effort to eliminate racist-tinged terminologies though much work still needs to be done (as Black Lives Matter shows). Seeing humankind as one human race teaches us to appreciate the diverse streams of knowledge each geographical region has to offer in our quest for global unity and wholeness. In a similar manner both hemispheres of the brain must also learn to work together as a seamless whole although each provides its own perspective.[2] In general, the right-brain, or the intuitive half is more like the East, while the left-brain, or the rational half, is more like the West. We need both halves of the brain and we need both hemispheres of the globe working together in order to be whole.

As the world slowly learns to work together in peace it is *wholeness* (or holism) that needs to be our guiding principle, not divisions nor claims of tribal or national superiority. Consequently, the World-Teacher Adi Da openly proclaimed in the essay: "The Necessity For A Global Unity-Culture To Replace The Ancient Bi-Polar Culture of Separate West and Separate East."[3] Here Adi Da emphasizes that we must discover our "**Prior Unity**" as *one human race* to gain universal tolerance and realize world peace. Once again it is wise to listen to the universal Wisdom of the Adept-Realizers.

Not only have we "inherited" humankind's Great Tradition of Global Wisdom, including its Divine Library of sacred scriptures [see Chapters 1-2], we have also inherited the ancient "bi-polar" tendencies (or strategies) encapsulated in our notions of "East and West." Out of the world's five major and most popular religions, the three "Western" ones, Judaism, Christianity, and Islam are *theistic* with a personal Creator God at the summit, while the two "Eastern" religions, Hinduism and Buddhism, are more *pantheistic* (or *panentheistic*) pointing to an impersonal Absolute spread out everywhere (yet often taking personal form as well). Nevertheless, it is the same Sun (or Light) rising and setting on each shore of the globe as it is the same Sun shining at all times above the clouds of darkness and ignorance. Although the human race no longer lives in the premodern world of the past it still inherits its remnants. The World-Friend Adi Da thus urgently reminds us:

> People today generally no longer represent the "root"-archetypal psychological dispositions that are at the "root" of the ancient great cultural enterprises, East and West. Rather, people today, all over the Earth, are suffering a double-mind brain-confusion of irreducible opposites and unanswered questions.[4]

The world's first "Western"-born Avatar-Guru notes that this bi-polar division is "as if the brain's two hemispheres were at war with one another."[5] Therefore this option is no longer tenable if we are to realize (and evolve towards) a genuine global unity of human wholeness. Because people today still casually (or unintentionally) inherit these bi-polar divisions of culture and mind from East and West embodied in their religious and traditional heritages, then we should more seriously study their unique characteristics. Ultimately, adhering to such unconscious tendencies will prevent us from transcending our bi-polar deficiencies. With an embracing holistic overview, we can move away from these two primary divisions since everyone is a product of circumstance and birth. Wherever we are born we are unconsciously molded by the strategies of being either an Oriental or Occidental, of being a premodern religionist or scientific modernist, whether from East or West. Our goal is to *integrate* these opposing opposites into a thriving wholeness, the aim of a genuine Integral Age.

To be truly spiritual (and integral) we must each intelligently investigate our cultural heritage and psychic tendencies. According to Adi Da, this means a person must "become responsible for 'religious' (and, altogether, human and egoic) conventions your patterning represents.... [thus] you have no choice but to <u>completely</u> inspect your conditions of existence... if you are truly moved to a right 'religious' life."[6] Once again the necessity for *holism*, let alone "right religious life," demands we examine and integrate our competing halves to become one whole human being centered in the Heart. Our split mind, our divided globe, indeed the entire spectrum of consciousness is truly only united in the Heart. This is a principal aim of the integral enterprise for it attempts to *integrate* West and East, to marry Freud and Buddha, to unite science and spirituality in a more holistic solution to life and today's disruptive politics.[7] Come together, indeed, for we are always already One.

In this "New World" of a modernized civilization reaching around the Earth, as we strive toward political and cultural harmony (beyond war), the best way to overcome this ancient bi-polar division is to understand where and how these tendencies arise. To this end, Avatar Adi Da offers a penetrating analysis recognizing, and uniquely naming, these polar opposites coming from each side of the world's ancient cultural divisions: Oriental East versus Occidental West. Overall, they both fundamentally reflect oppositional tendencies of the ego (and human psyche) represented by the two hemispheres of the physical brain. The way of true health and peace is to inhabit and activate the whole body from the heart while embracing the entire globe as One Divine Reality.

To clarify these opposing tendencies Adi Da uses the ancient Greek term *Alpha* (the first letter in the Greek alphabet often indicating a "beginning" or "first" in a series) to represent "the East." He then uses *Omega* (the last letter in the Greek alphabet indicating the "last" or "end" in a series) to represent "the West."[8] **The East**—or the Orient—is called the "**Alpha**" perspective or strategy since it involves a greater orientation toward that which is "beyond" (or behind) Nature and the world of the senses focusing more on "the beginning" of the world. The East, therefore, tends to emphasize the "other world" of subtle soul and causal spirit more than the physical world (which has helped lead to its poverty and caste system). The Alpha-East proposes that we live life

as a positive gesture to what is greater than mere earthly life or physical existence. **The West**—or the Occident—is called the "**Omega**" perspective, the
polar opposite, since it prefers a view more oriented towards "this world," the
"here and now," focusing on improving "the end." The Omega-West, therefore, isn't overly concerned with the realms of existence beyond our senses or
the gross-physical dimension of reality preferring to attack and dominate the
world of Nature. The West works on the outside, the East works inside; our
global Integral Age must do both.

OMEGA–WEST   **ALPHA–EAST**

In this case, the Alpha-East is closer to the **right-brain** tendency of intuition and wholeness while the Omega-West reflects more of the **left-brain** tendency to reason, logic, and fragmentation.[9] Nevertheless, as the global Avatar
makes clear: "Whether Alpha or Omega, it is the *same ego* (or 'self'-contraction)
that makes the path. The same ego turns away from conditional reality [Alpha
strategy] <u>and</u> turns toward it [Omega strategy]."[10] Notice it is still the *same
ego* or self-contraction, the activity into separative self-identity that shows the
qualities manifesting as either Alpha-East or Omega-West. *Both* strategies are
still the same process of *seeking for* instead of *realizing* the Prior Unity and Divine Nature from which East and West, left and right, yin and yang, both arise
co-equally.

Having been born in the West, Adi Da's enlightened perspective is "to Call
humankind to the Great Moment of new understanding, and to the Great
Future of a <u>Single</u> Destiny."[11] The World-Friend, therefore, Calls "humankind
to transcend <u>both</u> the Alpha strategy and the Omega strategy. Neither the one
nor the other should be chosen (exclusively)."[12] Only by using the method of

"Radical Understanding" or transcending the self-contracting ego-I are we able to finally (and presently) heal our divisive tendencies. We do this by feeling from the heart radiating love and light throughout the whole body and universe to Infinity (as the "Feeling of Being"). This understanding (and practice) of Divine Communion serves to heal and evolve our Divine Destiny as One Human Race.

Both of the characteristic tendencies traditionally associated with West and East can be found in either geographical hemisphere especially in today's modern interconnected, overlapping world. For example, the religions of the West acknowledge an afterlife (of heaven and hell) yet their primary orientation to this life is seen as a battle or mighty struggle with the conditions of Nature (and other people), often called a "Fall" from Grace, than it is a metaphysical journey toward Grace. Science completely shifted the focus of the West onto "this world" of solid materiality dispensing with the "metaphysical" and spiritual altogether infamously declaring "God is dead" (as Nietzsche claimed).

In addition, today's world is in the grip of a "Westernization" taking over the entire globe. This includes the nations of "the East" (or Asia) as they accept the exportation of scientific materialism and mass consumerism run by competitive capitalism and a controlling communism (such as in China and Russia). Global travel and worldwide communication supported by a global economy has made the world "smaller" than ever before, demanding better unity and cooperation, but this often fails as past patterns are repeated. Two deadly world wars (and countless smaller ones), the arms race, nuclear weapons, the constant battle for human rights and equitable living, terrorism, religious fundamentalism, ethnocentrism and racism, and so on, prove the divisions are crippling. And, worst of all, our divided nature is destroying the very ecosystem of Earth that gives us life (and a real future). The integral view tries to *transcend-yet-include* these divisions by seeing the value of each and all worldviews, but overcoming their errors and limits. It sees the dignities and disasters of both (and all) without illusion or fault. The Integral Vision recognizes that each is a living part of the whole—each "true but partial"—thus helping us to embrace a greater wholeness not just a heap of fragmented parts.

This divisiveness goes straight into politics and economics too. The **"liberal Democrats"** are progressives wanting to change outer society to support inner growth while "**conservative Republicans**" prefer to change by preserving traditions and the status quo. The liberal-Democrats rely more on science and egocentric modernity while conservative-Republicans rely more on ethnocentric religions and so both are stuck in a constant struggle unable to hear (or listen) to one another. The "**Mystics,**" on the other hand, offer the only viable solution: radical understanding and ego-transcendence. In a telling essay on our political divisions and why people are unfree, Ken Wilber in "Democrats, Republicans, and Mystics" (the last chapter to *Up from Eden*) explains the enlightened view: "The Mystics… find that men and women are unfree because there exists a belief in the experience of a 'true' self in the first place…. We are not to repress or unrepress the self, but rather undermine it; transcend it; see through it."[13] Thus the aim of the Mystics, Wilber points out, "is to deliver men and women from their battles by delivering them from their boundaries. Not manipulate the subject, and not manipulate the object, but transcend both in Nondual Consciousness. The discovery of the ultimate Whole is the only cure for unfreedom, and it is the only prescription offered by the Mystics."[14] The integral pandit summarizes:

> Men and women are potentially totally free because they transcend the subject and the object and fall into unobstructed Unity Consciousness, prior to all worlds but not other to all worlds. The ultimate solution to unfreedom, then, is neither [liberal-Democrat] nor [conservative-Republican], but Buddhistic [enlightenment]: *satori, moksha, wu*, release, awakening.[15]

Wilber's current stance, articulated with Dustin DiPerna, is to promote a "**Deliberately Developmental Civilization**"[16] where evolution and growth is emphasized in both the basic structures or *stages* and *states* of consciousness (the Seven Stages of Life). By engaging in a process of *conscious evolution* we are no longer subject to unconscious inheritances and cultural patterns. This integral approach, our guides explain, "demonstrates that what is needed is a development in BOTH Waking Up and Growing Up."[17] For Integral Theory, this means including psychotherapeutic shadow work and the integration of unconscious elements buried in our psyche—or what's called "Cleaning Up." Thus Wilber-DiPerna conclude:

In our view, a Deliberately Developmental Civilization enables human flourishing through Waking Up, Growing Up, and Cleaning Up (states, structures, shadows).… Ultimately, at its core, a Deliberately Developmental Civilization intentionally creates conveyor belts of transformation (through states, structures, and shadows) leading to a universal culture of the most awake, mature, and integrated human beings possible (which also means, least domineering, least oppressive, least murderous).[18]

I maintain that these truths are adequately integrated by practicing authentic Guru Yoga-Satsang (Waking-Up) and real sadhana (Growing Up). Realization and practice BOTH need to supplement one another in order to create a fully-developed human being, as the Wisdom Traditions have perennially declared. Our future lies in wholeness by healing the divisions of mind and overcome our inherited political and religious worldviews.

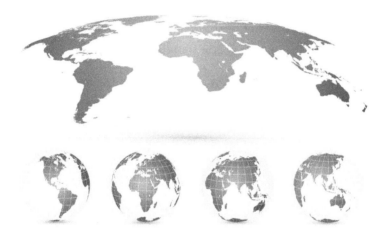

East Is Alpha-Mind — West Is Omega-Mind

In his summary essay "**Alpha / Omega**" (in *The Aletheon*), Adi Da Samraj explains: "Since ancient times, humankind has, in various times and places" taken on *two* characteristic approaches or "*two* primary and opposite motives" to One Reality. The Avatar critically calls them "the two greatest occupational diseases of humankind,"[19] and they both must be transcended (and integrated). A brief review of Adi Da's Teaching on the Alpha-Omega strategies are summarily defined below:

<u>ALPHA</u> strategy / language — **Eastern-Oriental pantheistic approach** = emphasizes **introversion** or turning *inward* so this mindset tends to *turn away* from conditional physical reality by identifying more with the Transcendental (or Non-conditional) Reality.[20]

The Eastern-oriented **Alpha strategist** is primarily motivated to avoid conditional pain and suffering in the physical world by *escaping* into the realms or inner world of the psyche (and the upper or transpersonal dimensions of the Kosmos). Thus the Alpha-mind learns how to better manipulate the physical world by psychic means.[21]

<u>OMEGA</u> strategy / language — **Western-Occidental theistic approach** = emphasizes **extroversion** or turning *outward* so this mindset tends to *turn toward* conditional physical reality by suppressing or excluding the psychic and subtle domains (such as with scientific materialism), especially avoiding the Transcendental (or Non-conditional) Reality.[22]

The Western-oriented **Omega strategist** is primarily motivated to escape conditional pain and suffering in the physical world by *achieving* pleasure and satisfaction. Thus the Omega-mind "must constantly overcome the tendency to presume defeat… or the mortal tendency to lose hope (and to despair)."[23]

These bi-polar divisions of interpreting Reality as two opposing world-views and tendencies, as each view reacts to conditional birth and human life on Earth, are only overcome and healed with an authentic esoteric path of Transcendental Spiritually. Even the *Qur'an* states (Verse 2:115): "to Allah belongs the East and the West. So wherever you turn, there is the Face of Allah." The Reality-Way of Adidam offers such a holistic alternative for it no longer seeks for this world or the other world but stands in the *present* world "always already" in Divine Communion. These polar opposite worldviews and strategies, balanced by practicing the Way of the Heart or Adidam, are briefly summarized in the table below:

Ω	Λ	ᴛ
OMEGA–WEST	**ALPHA–EAST**	**REALITY-WAY of ADIDAM**
Occidental	Oriental	One Reality
"this-world"	"other-world"	present "world"
theism	pantheism	panentheism
physical reality	psychic reality	psycho-physical reality
outer-directed	inner-directed	holistic
left-brained (rational)	right-brained (intuitive)	total brain
descending frontal line	ascending spinal line	Circle of Conductivity (grounded in the heart)
exoteric	esoteric	whole body
esophobic	esophilic	integral
modern	ancient	global
humanistic	mystical	cooperative
form	emptiness	Prior Unity
Immanent	Transcendent	Conscious Light

In general, we can see that the **Alpha** preference is, as Adi Da explains, "for the maximizing of attention, mystical devotion, and meditative surrender to the Transcendental Divine Reality."[24] By placing an emphasis on meditation and contemplative practices, including asceticism and renunciation, the Alpha strategy is more **esoteric** or "inner-directed" (or "esophilic") in its religious outlook (thus it's more often associated with the Fourth and Fifth Stages, and potentially the Sixth Stage of Life).[25]

The **Omega** preference is more of an "anti-esoteric path" (or "esophobic") since, as Adi Da explains, "[this ego] exhibits liberality relative to conditional reality including social relations, social and bodily actions, sex, and functional bodily indulgence of all kinds."[26] Omega-mind therefore places an emphasis on the physical, emotional, and mental realms (most often associated with the first Three Stages of Life). The Omega strategy is more **exoteric** (or "outer-directed") in its religious outlook trying to exercise "control… relative to the Non-conditional (or Divine) Reality (in the form of doubt, lack of interest, and taboos of all kinds)."[27] The Way of Truth requires meditative inversion—the Alpha-orientation—as well as outward disciplines and sacred ritual (or *puja*)—the Omega-orientation—thus both perspectives need to be integrated as a wholeness uniting relative and Absolute truths. This is how we *integrate* the inward and outward: live the Alpha-Omega mind from the egoless One Heart.

Avatar Adi Da continues his observations by explaining that the **Omega-ego** prefers to *descend* into "this world" and life (via the frontal line) by emphasizing the left-brained verbal mind or rational path. The **Alpha-ego** prefers to *ascend* away from "this world" (physical reality) to the "other world" (psychic reality) by emphasizing the right-brained intuitive mind. When the **Occidental-Omega mind** practices religion it does so as a reaffirmation of "this world" by proposing a "Divine Purpose to the cosmos,"[28] or a "Divine Plan."[29] The Western-based ego does this to justify an attachment to the conditional world and its relations, to politics and materialism seeking a utopia on Earth. The **Oriental-Alpha mind** is essentially critical of this world seeing it as an "illusion" (*maya*) not to be trusted, a realm of suffering (*samsara*), thus seeking for Nirvana or release (liberation). Both views are skewed toward one side of the brain, not properly balanced in the Heart. The Enlightened human lives in this world whole bodily, exercising good relations with all without addiction or attachment, while meditatively absorbed in the Heart of God or Reality Itself.

The **Westerner**, as Adi Da explains, "is moved toward the 'world' itself… thus to struggle against the 'root'-psychological tendency to view the 'world' negatively."[30] When Westerners embrace this world, they often become confused by evil and suffering. The **Easterner**, the Da Avatar continues, "is moved to transcend this 'world' with a 'world'-renouncing will… thus is oriented to struggle with… [the potential] to see the 'world' merely positively"[31] thus failing to make constructive changes in the world. Easterners seem more concerned with religious practices, the "other world" in after death or the forces "beyond" this world, thus they are confused by poverty and political power instead preferring to place people in different castes to keep things in place which subverts developmental potential. The **Western mind**, on the other hand, considers it a "sin" (literally, *hamartia* or "to miss the mark") to view this world negatively since Western religions believe this world was "created for Man" by a Creator Deity. The **Eastern mind** considers such a stance to be self-deluded and swept up in false perceptions. From their view, this world is not sinful but an illusion, one to be transcended, not embraced. After all, death wins in the end. The Westerner, therefore, needs to be saved (not liberated).

The merely *exoteric* tendency of the Omega-Westerner is toward the mundane, the material, the physical, and social relations. It does this with a rousing **idealism** bent on overcoming the harshness and stark reality of the conditional world by seeking pleasure and release, for utopia and paradise. Omega-mind, therefore, champions an active **humanism**—an ancient philosophy (epitomized in ancient Greece) where "Man is the measure of all things" (Protagoras, fl. 450 BCE)—in the quest "to achieve a great fulfillment in this 'world',"[32] as Adi Da noted. Omega-mind also encourages a "non-'religious' humanism" (such as with the Western Enlightenment), as Adi Da explains, that "seeks to establish moral propositions on the basis of *collective idealism* (such as 'the greatest good for the greatest number' [Jeremy Bentham]) and *individual idealism* (such as 'enlightened self-interest')."[33] Yet, ultimately, this approach is bound to fail since Omega-mind fails to realize this world is *not* "made by God" (or some outside, controlling Creator), but arises *within* God as an extension of Divine Consciousness Itself (i.e., arising as Light or Spirit-Energy). Hence we need to *integrate* the wisdom of the Alpha-mind as well.

This means, as Adi Da emphasizes, in reality we live in a *psycho-physical* world, not just a materialistic gross-physical realm made only of so-called matter and weight (after all, even "matter" is energy or $E = mc^2$, according to science). Adi Da verifies: "This 'world' of Earth is not merely a physical 'world' made by 'God'. This 'world' of Earth, like all conditional 'worlds', is a psycho-physical 'world' that Inheres in Reality Itself and Truth Itself (Which Is the Only Real Acausal God)."[34] Thus there is a cause and effect dynamic (or *karma*) at play here on Earth (in the Kosmos), a process in motion that must be sacrificed or surrendered in the Transcendental Reality (from which all arises). Only then do we gain true creative freedom where as the *Heart Sutra* summarizes: "Emptiness is Form" so that "Form" (as Spirit-Immanent) is "Emptiness" (as Spirit-Transcendent). If you realize *this*, then "you" are always already Enlightened!

We can therefore see and recognize both the Alpha and Omega tendencies in the world around us (and within us), the bi-polar tensions creating conflict and confusion the world over. Both these poles infect today's modern forms of spirituality as the Omega-West tries to absorb the Alpha-Eastern teachings of meditation and yoga. Sometimes Westerners have difficulty accepting the Transcendent (as an "other world" to the physical), while Easterners tend to reject the necessity for physical (or "this world") improvements. This failure, in my opinion, includes Wilber's "**Integral Spirituality**," which is still heavily Omega-oriented with its unending idealism, an overt reliance on science (and advanced technologies), and other misguided conditional reality concepts such as "evolutionary enlightenment" [see Chapter 4].

Obviously, this bi-polar opposition generates a major conflict between East and West, between the spiritual and material, between religion and science, between justice and politics. This schism cuts deep into our collective psyche as a battle expressed in opposing religious and political perspectives. It's one reason why the West has historically tended to be dominant on the battlefield. It's also why the West tends to only honor exoteric religious rituals of empowerment and not esoteric meditative-yogic practices. However, it should be obvious that *both* views, *both* perspectives, of either the Omega-West or Alpha-East are partial and incomplete. Each favors one side over the other—therefore both are unenlightened (though both claim otherwise). The Enlightened perspective transcends-and-includes both tendencies in whole-body devotion to a Divine Life for everyone (and all of Earthkind).

Only
everybody-all-at-once
can change
the current chaos

The World-Friend, Adi Da
NOT-TWO IS PEACE: The Ordinary
People's Way of Global Cooperative Order

BI-POLAR SPLIT—WHOLE BODY WORLD

Avatar Adi Da strongly critiques the world's "double-mind brain confusion," this "bi-polar ancient 'world' and psyche"[35] because this mindset is inadequate for wholeness and world peace. Yet this split is not so simple to transcend (or make whole) for these dispositions occur individually as well as collectively. Today in our interconnected world these strict divisions of East and West are already dissolving, though not smoothly. The global-envisioning Guru-Adept correctly points out: "People today generally no longer represent the 'root'-archetypal psychological dispositions that are at the 'root' of the ancient great cultural enterprises, East and West."[36] That's because the borders of nations, the boundaries of the world, have spilled over into one another.

A united global identity is already emerging since East and West have met and have discovered what each is lacking. In today's global environment every nation is being "modernized" or "Westernized" under the influence of modern science and current political-economic trends. The liberal progressive movement for political freedom and economic justice is an evolutionary thrust forward. The financial stock market and global trade closes the gap and assures we all are living under one Sun, whether it's rising in the East or setting in the West. Humanity—or **"everybody-all-at-once"** (in Adi Da's words)—sees this possibility more than their leaders, who are heavily invested in conservatively maintaining the status quo and their wealth and influence.[37] Beloved Adi Da clarifies our worldwide situation:

If you are truly moved to a right "religious" life—or, otherwise, eso-teric Spiritual, Transcendental, and Self-Evidently Divine life—you have no choice but to <u>completely</u> inspect your condition of exis-tence. That ordeal is the necessity inherent in the confusion of West-ern-Eastern mind-brain that is the result of the "modernization" (or the universal cultural face-to-face) of the present-day globalized so-ciety of humankind. Therefore, you <u>must</u> grow to understand (and, thereupon, to practice) right "religious" (or, otherwise esoteric) life <u>in</u> <u>Truth</u>. You <u>must</u> become able to differentiate all your casually gener-ated motivations that reflect archaic conventional (and, thus, inher-ently bi-polar) concepts, persuasions, and philosophies.[38]

We are slowly becoming One World. You and I serve this process by evolving ourselves first. We witness our bonding unity with all people in countless ways: from global trade to intercontinental communications, from the "Internet" to the "world wide web," from international travel to United Nations cooperation, the sharing of life-saving medical advances (including vaccines), sharing technology and information, sharing art and music, protect-ing people's information and rights, the rise of democracies in nations of the East while meditation and yoga grow and prosper in the cities of the West, and so on. Then there is also our common humanity so when people meet face-to-face, as Kipling suggests, we are all simply human with feelings and com-mon concerns, families to love and protect, jobs to do, etc. There are countless examples of West and East, North and South, emerging as a global (but not monolithic) culture.

Unfortunately, however, there is mighty resistance as well. Fundamental religionists will not transcend ethnocentric tribalisms where "their people" are right and all others are wrong and thus they're willing to kill and die before changing. Exploitive capitalism still stabs with daggers of discontent for billions of people while only the few benefit and the environment suffers. Corporations and media control information and keep people in webs of illusion manufacturing consent and fueling unrest.[39] The reactivity of ethno-centric tribalism (via terrorism) to a worldcentric modernity is the "bad news" in this clash of civilizations and war of worldviews. Our development, indi-vidually and collectively, is crippled and at risk. This is why the Integral Age demands development, growth, evolution, education and spiritual Enlightenment. Hence the wise Mystic-Adepts tell us this vision of One World will *only* be realized by fully engaging in genuine spiritual life and practices (sadhana). Meditation becomes a prerequisite for overcoming the separative activity of the bi-polar ego transcended in the centering Heart. Ultimately, we need the guidance of a genuine Global Guru, of authentic Mystics (in Satsang).

As a World-Teacher, Adi Da Samraj finds it is necessary to call us out of our partiality and delusional tendencies. According to Adi Da, the bi-polar split of humankind since ancient days can only be overcome by embracing the **"full Circle"** of manifest life, to unite the **"total brain"** via heart-feeling and to circulate the *frontal* and *spinal lines* of **"conductivity"** as the *whole body*, free in the Heart (grounded in the right side). This **"Circle of Conductivity"** (in Adi Da's words) is only accomplished by true surrender to the One Divine Reality uniting "this world" and the "other world" as Conscious Light right here and now (even beyond death). Adi Da summarized this perspective in his magnificent book titled *The Enlightenment of the Whole Body* (1978) where he published with stunning detail insights on the esoteric structure of our human anatomy; I cannot recommend any book more highly. Just one quote clarifies many of the misconceptions about the Enlightened State:

> The Enlightenment of Man is the Enlightenment of the whole and entire body-mind.... Enlightenment is not a higher state of mind. It is not a glorified state of the inward or subjective being. Enlightenment is a bodily Condition. It is a matter of the transcendence of the mind, all inwardness, and all illusions of independent existence. It is a matter of relationship, not inwardness.[40]

The Reality-Way of Adidam sees the bi-polar opposites as one wholeness united in their Prior Unity whether East or West, inward and outward, body or mind, self or Nature. The Avatar openly implores *everyone* to become rightly aligned in tacit recognition of Real God and then embrace both "East" and "West" as a Single Totality. Adi Da will "forever Call humankind to the only Way That Is Single, Whole, and not based on [the bi-polar divisions of] egoity."[41] Although the Transcendental Domain is "senior" or ultimate to the conditional world it is still the same Divine Condition. Samsara *is* Nirvana, once this is *realized*, as the Buddhist *Heart Sutra* long ago proclaimed. The cosmic domain *is* the Divine Domain *right now*, not just after death. Let's listen to the World-Friend with attentive and open hearts:

> I Say the two cannot be separated without deluding humankind and reinforcing the egoity of humankind…. The two are (thus, in practice) presumed in prior unity and dynamic association with one another—and the Non-conditional (or Transcendental…) Reality Is, Clearly, the Senior Dimension (or Source-Condition) of this dynamic pair…. [In the] Reality-Way of Adidam, the conditional reality is proposed and rightly embraced, but… the conditional reality is always surrendered and presently transcended in devotional Communion with Me [i.e., with Real God]…. The conditional and the Non-conditional are not to be conceived apart from one another.[42]

As a person alive today, it is best to recognize and understand the Alpha-Omega strategies in yourself, in your culture, and in the polar dynamics of world politics and religious practices. This is the only way these dissociations are transcended-and-integrated as a whole. To understand the error of rejecting or separating from "this world" (Alpha-mind) or becoming overly attached and addicted to "this world" (Omega-mind) is to adopt a more enlightened perspective. Adi Da has pointed out that *both* Alpha and Omega prescriptions are deficient, incomplete, and distorted, true but only partial thus not whole-body. In other words, unenlightened.

This is why a Western-born Avatar embodying Eastern Wisdom is necessary to unite the whole world. This one did not come to the West in a plane or ship but via the womb. We as global citizens need such an Adept-Guru who fully embodies the Wisdom (and Spiritual Transmission) of the East combined with the insights of Western knowledge and its creative (even scientific) activities. I suggest such a one has appeared with the closing of the "**Kali Yuga**" at the cusp of today's "**New Age**" to help generate a genuine "**Integral Age**" leading to an "**Integral Millennium**," at least as a possibility. Our evolutionary destiny to realize "Whole Body Enlightenment" comes not by preferring one side over the other but living alive as the Heart-center: the Middle Way (as the Buddha might say), holistically integrating East with West.

Such a global vision uniting both East and West, transcending Alpha and Omega, will help lead us out of this double-minded brain-confusion. Only this is what generates a genuine "**Global Unity-Culture**" (in Adi Da's words). The Reality-Way of Adidam Ruchiradam provides such a holistic alternative *if* we are brave enough and wise enough to practice genuine Guru Yoga-Satsang. We would be wise to listen to and hear the wisdom of the Great Tradition of global Adepts. Then we shall see God or the Divine Nature of the universe *right now* and *here*. Then our hearts will love everyone as equal and free beings. Is this not what all people truly desire and need? The World-Friend Adi Da heartily summarizes his call to everybody-all-at-once:

> I Look to Establish a New Global Order of men and women, who will actively establish and sustain a universal new human age of sanity and wisdom. That New Age will not be an age of the occult, the conventionally religious, the scientific, or the technological glorification of humankind. Rather, that New Age will be the anciently expected Universal Age of authentic human existence, wherein human life will be everywhere engaged entirely apart from the tragic history of human ignorance, dissociativeness, bewilderment, and great search....
>
> That New Universal Order and Age of Global Humankind will be always Illuminated by the Intrinsic Freedom of Reality Itself, and it will be always Thus Bright and New.[43]

The Way of Reality grounded in the Prior Unity of Enlightenment addresses the real conditions and circumstances of everyday life. Adi Da's "**Way of the Heart**" shows how to be loving human beings while serving the diverse beauty of Life and Nature. It is to remain both embodied and spiritually awake at the same time. From this Enlightened "Whole Body" perspective each and every thing (or holon) arises in and as the Conscious Light of God evolving as Spirit-in-action. Only this Whole Body Enlightenment resolves the bi-polar confusion (and tension) of our current divisive world. The Ultimate Truth when fully *realized* embraces all relative truths known via either the Omega or Alpha strategies. The indescribable Mystery of One God is realized when, in the Avatar's divinely-inspired words: "Reality Itself (or Truth Itself or Real Acausal God) Simply Stands Eternally Free."[44] To this "Reality" we must awaken beyond the bi-polar dualism of Western-Omega knowledge and Eastern-Alpha wisdom. This is when East truly meets West, where West sincerely meets East as One World, One Heart, One Love, One Destiny.

SWAMI VIVEKANANDA:
EAST MEETS WEST IN CHICAGO (1893)

The first ecumenical meeting in the modern world of the major religions of humankind took place in Chicago at the 1893 World's Fair—known as the World's Columbian Exposition—fortuitously also called the "City of Lights" (for its new electric lights) and the "White City" (for its painted white buildings). It was the largest display of the newly mastered electricity and electric lighting that the world had ever seen with honors going to Nikola Tesla and the alternating current (AC) of Westinghouse Electric who underbid Thomas Edison and J. P. Morgan in the "current war"[45] (between AC and DC). Its vast arrays of lights, searchlights, and a tall tower of light shining from the center displayed for the world what future cities would look like. It would also spark the first great meeting between the Alpha-East and Omega-West as their religious traditions came together in open dialogue.

Marking the 400th anniversary of Christopher Columbus' arrival in the New World in 1492, the Fair exhibited the West's global dominion by highlighting cultures from over 46 countries from around the world. It featured ethnic displays of tribal Indians and native islanders, including arts, music, and cuisine, culminating with the new marvels of European technology and American ingenuity. Covering over 690 acres (the most ever, by far), the 1893 World's Fair was housed in fourteen "great buildings" of predominantly neo-classical architecture surrounded by canals and lagoons, plus a plethora of other buildings and amusements that were nearly all taken down when the Fair ended. The centerpiece of the Fair, held at Jackson Park in Chicago next to Lake Michigan, was a large water pool representing the voyage Columbus took to the New World celebrating the triumph of the West and American industrial optimism. There were world congresses held on medicine, engineering, and women's progress, but all were overshadowed by the universal Parliament bringing together the world's religions for the first time in modern history. It was attended by celebrities and politicians from around the world, including President Grover Cleveland (who flipped the switch on the electric miracle), sparking the imaginations of all who came. Over 27 million people visited during its six-month run influencing and inspiring the future and upcoming new century in countless ways.

One of the prime attractions that garnered the most attention was the Parliament of the World's Religions which ran from September 11 to September 27, 1893. This congregation of the "children of one God" marked the first formal gathering of representatives from Eastern and Western spiritual traditions, from the North and South, ancient and modern. Held off-site at the permanent building of the Memorial Art Palace, now the Art Institute of Chicago, it hosted full-house crowds, a majority of them being women. The original U-shaped building that framed an open court was converted into two assembly halls for this special sacred occasion.[46] Organizers of this interreligious conclave called it "the morning star of the 20th century,"[47] while event chairman, Presbyterian minister John Henry Barrows, clarified:

> Religion, like the white light of heaven, had been broken into many-colored fragments by the prisms of men. One of the objects of the Parliament of Religions has been to change this many-colored radiance back into the white light of heavenly truth.[48]

Another delegate from Zen Buddhism (Shaku Soyen) summarized: "We are not born to fight against another. We are born to enlighten our wisdom and cultivate our virtues according to the guidance of truth."[49] A replica of the Liberty Bell rang out ten times, once for each major religion attending ringing in a New Age of religious tolerance and cooperation (it was hoped and prayed). Some of the organizers wanted to emphasize the disagreements among religions as chairman Barrows explained how doubts to unity were overcome:

> Many felt that Religion was an element of perpetual discord, which should not be thrust in amid the magnificent harmonies of a fraternal assembly of nations [the World's Fair]. On the other hand, it was felt that the tendencies of modern civilization were toward unity.

Some came to feel that a Parliament of Religions was the necessity of the age.[50]

The goal was to create an interfaith dialogue attended by large, adoring crowds, though it was dominated by the Christians and their various denominations.[51] The Jain faith of India was represented by Virchand Gandhi; Swami Vivekananda spoke for Hinduism; Buddhism by Anagarika Dharmapala (for Theraveda or south Asian Buddhism) and Soyen Shaku, the "First American Ancestor" of Zen; the Parsees of India, followers of Zoroastrianism gave presentations; even Confucianism, Taoism, and Shinto were represented; Islam was represented by Mohammed (Alexander Russell) Webb and others; Christianity was represented by G. Bonet Maury (who invited Swami Vivekananda) and other Protestant ministers; by Roman Catholics, such as James Cardinal Gibbons (though the Archbishop of Canterbury declined to attend citing "the Christian religion is the only true religion"), and by an Eastern Orthodox delegation; Christian Science was represented by founder Mary Baker Eddy; Reform Jews attended, including Chicago rabbi Emil Hirsch who titled his talk "Elements of a Universal Religion" declaring "The day of national religions is past. The God of the universe speaks to all mankind."[52] Reverend Henry Jessup spoke for the Bahá'í Faith in the United States; while Annie Besant and William Quan Judge represented the Theosophical Society; other New Religious Movements, such as Spiritualism, were also represented; fortunately, African-Americans sent delegates including the towering figure of Frederick Douglas; however, those religious traditions not represented (until the 1993 centennial Parliament) were Native American religious figures, Sikhs, and other Indigenous and Earth-centered religionists.

Yet, without doubt, the star attraction was the thirty-year-old English-educated Indian lawyer from Calcutta, **Swami Vivekananda** (born Narendranath Datta in 1863), the chief disciple of 19th-century Indian mystic **Ramakrishna** (1836–1886), who was an eloquent speaker for the universalism of Advaita Vedanta [see Chapter 16].[53] Vivekananda, who would extensively tour America and Europe (and India) afterwards, was a key figure in the introduction of the Indian philosophies of Vedanta and Yoga to the Western world.

Clothed in a turban and the orange robes of a renunciate monk, when he began his speech with the opening lines "Brothers and sisters of America," it is said (in the newspapers of the day) he received a two-minute standing ovation from the seven thousand in attendance. When silence was restored, the Indian monk began his address by greeting the youngest of nations on behalf of "the most ancient order of monks in the world, the Vedic order of sannyasins, a religion which has taught the world both tolerance and universal acceptance." He suggested all the world's religions were like different streams, some crooked and some straight but all leading to the one sea where "all lead to Thee!" One journalist responded: "Vivekananda's address before the Parliament was broad as the heavens above us, embracing the best of all religions, as the ultimate universal religion—charity to all mankind, good works for the love of God, not for fear of punishment or hope of reward."[54] Such noble aspirations continue to take time to realize but the vision for these universal ideals for all humankind has been stated and enshrined.

Although Vivekananda's speech was short, its meaning has reverberated around the world for over a century. To this day in India, schoolchildren recite and memorize it. He clearly articulated the sentiments of the Parliament's universalism so the world's newspapers printed its message across the globe. The *New York Critique*, for one, wrote: "He is an orator by divine right, and his strong, intelligent face in its picturesque setting of yellow and orange was hardly less interesting than those earnest words, and the rich, rhythmical utterance he gave them."[55] American newspapers reported Vivekananda as "the greatest figure in the Parliament of religions" and "the most popular and influential man in the Parliament."[56] There was a secret mission in the Parliament by the Protestant organizers to show how Protestantism is the culmination and fulfillment of all religions, but that was dashed when "the coloured guy" spoke. It was noted that so many reporters and women flocked to him that one reporter remarked: "Well, if he can handle those women throwing themselves at him, he is surely a saint." One look at his photos demonstrates this obvious truth. But the humble monk deflected (and reflected) the limelight back to his Guru and the soul of humankind, not for himself.

Vivekananda would become known as the "handsome oriental" and made a huge impression as an orator traveling throughout the United States and Europe often meeting with intellectual dignitaries, including Tesla, the electricity genius, who also shared a fascination with the Hindu's notion of energy and

God (the "akashic" field). Nonetheless, although admired and adored by many, including the rich elites who sponsored him, the compassionate monk still encountered the prejudices of racism, of being a brown man in a white society. He sadly realized that his brown skin was such an obstruction that to bring the Dharma to the West he would have to be light-skinned. He became exhausted from the attention and resistance and so retreated to India before a second tour of the West (between 1899–1902). Yet he yearned for his Mother India to which he would return and soon leave the body altogether (or take his *Mahasamadhi*, as they say in Sanskrit) at the young age of 39; consciously dying while sitting in meditation on July 4, 1902, the holiday of American Independence.

$\mathcal{S}$wami Vivekananda's influence went far and wide, initiating the entrance of Eastern wisdom into the lands of the West. He propagated the essence of the Advaita Vedanta philosophy perhaps best expressed in Adi Shankara (c. 750 CE) which emphasizes the transcendent aspect of the One Divine Reality. In addition, Vivekananda followed his teacher Ramakrishna who taught the Absolute is both transcendent and immanent thus becoming a principal proponent of Neo-Vedanta. Ramakrishna also taught a universalism accepting all religions and faiths as long as they were sincerely devoted to the One God (or Goddess) and yearned for God-Realization or Enlightenment. As one reviewer noted: "For Vivekananda, yoga just meant one thing: Realization of God."[57] Indeed, Vivekananda taught his audiences in oratory and books:

> Each soul is potentially Divine. The goal is to manifest this Divinity within by controlling nature, external and internal. Do this either by work [karma yoga], or worship [bhakti yoga], or mental discipline [jnana yoga], or philosophy [raja yoga]—by one, or more, or

188 | Part I – The Global Wisdom of Guru-Adepts

all of these—and be free. This is the whole of religion. Doctrines, or
dogmas, or rituals, or books, or temples, or forms, are but secondary
details.[58]

Vivekananda was concerned with all the people of the world's nations, especially its poorest and weakest. He believed and taught that the noble ideas of
God-Realization and Yoga could be the light leading people to world peace. He
wrote prolifically and his lectures were printed to steady sales over the past century up to today (and into the future). The Swami also believed his own country
of India needed to benefit from the economic and political strengths of the
West. Being holistic, Vivekananda admired the strong-willed Omega-mind and
its handling of the material world while most of his countrymen lived in dire
poverty. The Alpha-mind strategy of turning away from "this world" by focusing too much attention on the "other world," embodied in India's unfair caste
system, was to be balanced, Vivekananda taught, by integrating the knowledge
and technology of the West with Eastern wisdom. Not only could the West
benefit by turning within, so too could the East benefit by turning without.

These Neo-Vedanta teachings would go on to influence many Indian
nationalists in the 20th century, from Tagore to Aurobindo to Gandhi, who
held that Vivekananda increased his "love for his country a thousandfold."
Indeed, B. R. Ambedkar, an Indian polymath and the father of the Indian
Constitution, said "the Buddha was the greatest person India had ever produced. The greatest man India produced in recent centuries was not Gandhi
but Vivekananda."[59] Vivekananda would go on to influence countless Western
intellectuals as well, from Huxley to Isherwood to Wilber [see Chapter 7],
from J.D. Salinger to Leo Tolstoy to Sarah Bernhardt to Gertrude Stein, from
Nikola Tesla to Max Müller, Lord Kelvin to John D. Rockefeller, and many
others. The Swami's teachings also penetrated popular culture: for example,
over sixty years later the Beatle George Harrison explained: "*My Sweet Lord*
[that] song really came from Swami Vivekananda, who said, 'If there is a God,
we must see Him. And if there is a soul, we must perceive it'."[60] Vivekananda,
who did not live to be forty, changed the world not only with his words but his
mere presence and company.

Perhaps Vivekananda's greatest gift to humanity was the establishment of
the "**Vedanta Society**" in the Western world, a branch of the Ramakrishna

Mission located outside India. The first Vedanta Society of New York was founded by Swami Vivekananda in November 1894 but he then asked Swami Abhedananda to lead the organization in 1897. It would have branches in other American cities, from Boston to Houston to St. Louis extending to the West coast with a Northern California branch in San Francisco. In 1930 Swami Prabhavananda founded the Vedanta Society of Southern California with headquarters in Hollywood. The work of the Vedanta Society is primarily devoted to spiritual, educational, and pastoral activities run by the resident monks and nuns, though many offer social services as well. They maintain temples, give lectures and study courses, teach meditation, and perform religious ceremonies empowering their temples with sacred energy (or *siddhi*). Importantly, their altars display their root Guru Ramakrishna sitting alongside Vivekananda, with the Buddha and Jesus Christ side-by-side.

Significantly, the Vedanta Temple in Hollywood was visited by Adi Da Samraj (then known as Franklin Jones) in 1970, where he noticed it was a powerful "seat of Shakti [the life-energy of the Divine]... as powerful a place as any of the abodes of the Siddhas in India."[61] It was in this temple on September 10, 1970, that Adi Da would permanently Re-Awaken to the Divine Nature of Consciousness, which he noted in his autobiography, *The Knee of Listening* (1972), the first book he published:

> In an instant, I became profoundly and directly aware of what I am. It was a tacit realization, a direct knowledge in consciousness itself.... There was no thought involved in this. I am that Consciousness. There was no reaction either of joy or surprise. I am the One I recognized. I am that One. I am not merely experiencing Him. Then truly there was no more to realize.[62]

The movement of the East to the West was now complete. A Westerner, who had ventured to India from New York City to study under its wisest Guru-Adepts at the time (notably Swami Muktananda, and his Guru, Swami Nityananda), would sit down on the far shore of the Western world, in its most decadent capital of Hollywood, to *realize* God as One Prior Unity and the very essence of consciousness (the same truth taught in all Enlightenment traditions). No longer would an Easterner have to travel West, or vice versa, for the Omega-mind to hear the teachings of self-transcending Enlightenment (though naturally many Yogis and Gurus would do so).

Now the first native-born Westerner from the United States of America would appear to help heal the bi-polar divisions wrought by the world as an Enlightened Guru and authentic Avatar. Teaching in his native English tongue, Avatar Adi Da also offers an extremely potent Heart-Transmission (or *Hridaya Shaktipat*) that itself transcends all nations and cultures, all religions and philosophies for it is pure Spirit-Baptism [see Chapter 20]. The Avataric-Sage would go on to establish his own Ashram in 1972 (now known as Adidam Ruchiradam) so the world could gather in his sacred Company to be with its first truly Global-Guru and World-Friend. No wonder Adi Da would later claim Ramakrishna-Vivekananda to be his deeper-psychic soul motivation for incarnating at this time, in this place, now and forever hereafter.

Next, let's turn to the American-born Adept of the third millennium (and late 20th century) who has appeared to fulfill or complete the entire Great Tradition of Global Wisdom, beyond either West or East, if understood rightly.

Chapter 9 Endnotes

1. Adi Da Samraj, *The Pneumaton* (2011), p. 39.

2. See: Iain McGilchrist, *The Master and His Emissary: The Divided Brain and the Making of the Western World* (2009).

3. See: Adi Da Samraj, "The Necessity For A Global Unity-Culture To Replace The Ancient Bi-Polar Culture of Separate West and Separate East" in *The Pneumaton* (2011), pp. 36ff; also see: *Not Two Is Peace* (2009, 3rd Edition) by the World-Friend Adi Da,

4. Adi Da Samraj, *The Pneumaton* (2011), pp. 39-40.

5. Ibid., p. 39.

6. Ibid., p. 40.

7. See: Ken Wilber, *The Marriage of Sense and Soul: Integrating Science and Religion* (1999).

8. See: Adi Da Samraj, "Alpha / Omega" in *The Aletheon* (2009), Volume One, pp. 279ff.

9. See: Iain McGilchrist, *The Master and His Emissary* (2009); Adi Da Samraj [Bubba Free John], *The Enlightenment of the Whole Body* (1978).

10. Adi Da Samraj, *The Aletheon* (2009), p. 291 [italics added].

11. Ibid., p. 290.

12. Ibid., p. 290.

13. Ken Wilber, *Up from Eden* (1981), p. 333 [title caps added].

14. Ibid., p. 334 [title caps added].

15. Ibid., p. 334 [title caps added].

16 See: *An Everyone Culture: Becoming a Deliberately Developmental Organization* (2016, Harvard Business Review Press) by Robert Kegan and Lisa Laskow Lahey.

17. Ken Wilber and Dustin DiPerna, "Toward A Deliberately Developmental Civilization" in *Purpose Rising: A Global Movement of Transformation and Meaning* (2017, Bright Alliance Publishing) edited by Emanuel Kuntzelman and Dustin DiPerna, p. 25

18. Ibid., p. 22.

19. Adi Da Samraj, *The Aletheon* (2009), p. 315.

20. Ibid.,p. 288.

21. Ibid., p. 312.

22. Ibid., p. 289.

23. Ibid., p. 312.

24. Ibid., p. 288.

25. Adi Da Samraj has generated a new term "esophilic" to describe the Eastern-Alpha mindset of condoning that which is transpersonal or transcendent in nature, while the Western-Omega mind is "esophobic" for it is inherently afraid of or condemns that which transcends conditional knowledge and conditional world. See: Adi Da Samraj, *The Pneumaton* (2011), p. 35.

26. Adi Da Samraj, *The Aletheon* (2009), p. 288.

27. Ibid., p. 289.

28. Ibid., p. 289.

29. Adi Da Samraj, *The Pneumaton* (2011), p. 38.

30. Ibid., p. 39.

31. Ibid., p. 39.

32. Adi Da Samraj, The Aletheon (2009), p. 298.

33. Ibid., p. 300 [italics added].

34. Ibid., p. 301.

35. See: Adi Da Samraj, *The Pneumaton* (2011), "The Western Prohibition Against Higher Knowledge and Realization Versus The Eastern Advocacy of Higher Knowledge and Realization", pp. 33ff; and "The Necessity For A Global Unity-Culture To Replace The Ancient Bi-Polar Vulture of Separate West and Separate East", pp. 36ff.

36. Adi Da Samraj, *The Pneumaton* (2011), p. 39.

37. See: Adi Da Samraj, *Not-Two Is Peace* (2009, 2019).

38. Adi Da Samraj, *The Pneumaton* (2011), p. 40.

39. See, as only one example, Noam Chomsky and Edward S. Herman, *Manufacturing Consent* (1988, Pantheon); it's interesting to note that Chomsky's explanation requires no grand conspiracy but the result of consent simply emerges naturally from the workings of the system; Noam Chomsky, *Media Control: The Spectacular Achievements of Propaganda* (2002, Seven Stories Press; 2nd ed.).

40. Adi Da Samraj [Bubba Free John], *The Enlightenment of the Whole Body* (1978), p. 500.

41. Adi Da Samraj, *The Aletheon* (2009), p. 291.

42. Ibid., p. 293.

43. Adi Da Samraj, *Not Two _Is_ Peace* (2009, 3rd edition), from "I Am Here To Awaken A Bright New Age of Global Humankind," pp. 300-301 [some title caps added].

44. Adi Da Samraj, *The Aletheon* (2009), p. 302.

45. See: *The Current War* (2017 movie) directed by Alfonso Gomez-Rejon.

46. See: Art Institute of Chicago website: "1893 World's Parliament of Religions" essay.

47. See: "Parliament of Religions, 1893" from Harvard University's "The Pluralism Project" (retrieved January 2021, plurism.org/parliament-of-religions-1893).

48. John Henry Barrows, "Parliament of Religions, 1893" from Harvard University's "The Pluralism Project" (https://pluralism.org/).

49. Shaku Soyan, *The Dawn of Religious Pluralism* (1993), p. 352,

50. See: "Parliament of Religions, 1893" from Harvard University's "The Pluralism Project" (https://pluralism.org/).

51. See: Richard Seager, *The Dawn of Religious Pluralism: Voices from the World's Parliament of Religions*, 1893 (1993).

52. Emil Hirsch, *The Dawn of Religious Pluralism* (1993), p. 222.

53. See: *Vivekananda: East Meets West (A Pictorial Biography)* (1995, Vedanta Society of St. Louis) by Swami Chetanananda, Preface by Huston Smith.

54. Quoted from "Parliament of Religions, 1893" from Harvard University's "The Pluralism Project" (https://pluralism.org/).

55. See: "Swami Vivekananda" Wikipedia entry (retrieved January 2021).

56. See: Jyotirmaya Sharma, *A Restatement of Religion: Swami Vivekananda and the Making of Hindu Nationalism* (2013).

57. A. L. Bardach, "What Did J. D. Salinger, Leo Tolstoy, and Sarah Bernhardt Have in Common?" in *The Wall Street Journal Magazine*, WSJ.com.

58. See: Carl T. Jackson, "The Founders" in *Vedanta for the West: The Ramakrishna Movement in the United States* (1994), pp. 33-34.

59. See: "Swami Vivekananda" Wikipedia entry (retrieved January 2021).

60. George Harrison quoted in A. L. Bardach, "What Did J.D. Salinger, Leo Tolstoy, and Sarah Bernhardt Have in Common?" in *The Wall Street Journal Magazine*, WSJ.com.

61. Adi Da Samraj [Franklin Jones], *The Knee of Listening* (1973), p. 132.

62. Ibid., pp. 134-135.

TEN

COMPLETING
THE GREAT TRADITION:
AVATAR ADI DA'S ADIDAM

My Work is Universal. It is World-Work. It is a new Work. It is Avataric Work. Therefore, It does not have a "home" culture. I do not have a "home" culture... My Teaching stands utterly on Its own. It cannot be identified with any tradition on Earth.... It is a totally new Summary World-Teaching.

— **Adi Da Samraj**, "I Am Prior to All Traditions"[1]

In his difficult book *Nirvanasara: Radical Transcendentalism and the Introduction of Advaitayana Buddhism* (published in April 1982), Avatar Adi Da suggested that around three and half thousand years ago (1500 BCE) the sacred Vedic tradition in ancient India, arising from a primordial understanding of "Divine or Spiritual Emanation," had developed into religious "**idealism**" because the Rishis (or "Seers") taught it was necessary to *realize* one's prior unity with the underlying, indivisible

Divine Ground manifesting the whole universe-Kosmos (and self). This developmental goal is reached by engaging the spiritual practices of Yoga, the pinnacle method of mysticism. Contrary to biological evolution in exteriors, the evolution of consciousness involves an *inward* journey (via meditation) in order to transcend the "Atman Project" of "substitute sacrifices" (in Ken Wilber's terms) or the "self-contraction" of "Narcissus" (in Adi Da's words). What is "sacrificed" or surrendered in true mysticism is the sense of being a separate self or entity (a temporary illusion) in order to know Reality as It IS. In *Nirvanasara*, Adi Da pointed out how Vedantists use *positive* terms to assert an "atman" (lower case "a") or inner self (what Westerners call "soul") that contains a spark of the Divine Source called "Atman" (capital "A").

The goal of Yoga (which literally means, in Sanskrit, "to yoke," "to join," or "link") is to find "That" Divine Light said by some Yogis to reside in the crown chakra, or in the "cave of the heart," as the *Upanishads* teach. Only this union (or "re-union") is **moksha** meaning "release" and "liberation" (or Enlightenment). Adi Shankara, the great Sage of Advaita Vedanta (ca. 800 CE) who is considered to be the pinnacle of the Vedic teachings, summarized this view in his brilliant *The Crest-Jewel of Discrimination*:

> The Self-luminous Atman, the Witness of all, is ever-present within your own heart. This Atman stands apart from all that is unreal. Know it to be your self, and meditate upon it unceasingly. Let there be uninterrupted communion with the Atman, free from all distracting thoughts. In this way you will realize, without a doubt, that the Atman is your real nature.[2]

Buddhism, on the other hand, as Adi Da continued to explain in *Nirvanasara*, counters this "idealism" approach by asserting a stark "**realism**" and even materialistic view of human life by focusing on the self's *suffering* caused by unfulfilled desires, disease, and death. There is a tendency (especially in Hinayana Buddhism) to use *negative* terms to negate the attachments of the self. To counter Vedanta's overly positive view, Buddha asserted there is "no self, no Atman"—called *anatma (an* or "no" *atman)*—thus it is only by recognizing the "empty" nature of the illusory self-entity that Nirvana is realized (*nirvana*, in Sanskrit, means literally "to blow out" the ego-self idea). As the *Diamond Sutra*, one of Mahayana Buddhism's most influential and sacred texts, has the Buddha explain to his devotee Subhuti:

> Through the Consummation of Incomparable Enlightenment I ac-
> quired not even the least thing.... *This* is altogether everywhere,
> without differentiation or degree; wherefore it is called "Consum-
> mation of Incomparable Enlightenment." It is straightly attained by
> freedom from separate personal selfhood and by cultivating all kinds
> of goodness.[3]

Yet this approach, as Adi Da clarifies, still tends to generate a *search* for Nirvana in order to discover one's innate Buddha-Nature (*tathagatagarbha*) or Buddha-Mind. The Nondual Mysticism that Avatar Adi Da teaches, however, is based on a *radical understanding* of this self-activity involved in the mystical search of soul for union and release. By understanding that the activity of the ego-I is self-caused (as an activity of contraction), then the search for Enlightenment is transcended at its root (the true meaning of "radical"). This is assisted by *realizing* and living in "always already" communion with Real God *right now*, in the present, not as some future goal. The Enlightened State of the Adept-Realizer (which is ultimately *your* Enlightened State) can *transmit* or magnify this awareness to a practicing devotee which is what the process of Guru Yoga-Satsang is primarily about. Satsang with the Guru, in other words, undoes the need to search for God (or Atman-Nirvana) since the Divine Condition is potentially revealed through the Adept's Heart-Transmission. This then becomes the basis for practice, cultivating a *relationship* with God (as Guru), not a search for God (as separate self).

From this "always already" perspective of Divine Enlightenment, Adi Da confirms that both Vedanta and Buddhism (and all true esoteric religions) have the same goal: liberation of the born being by self-transcendence in Divine Awakening (whatever the name). Thus the Avatar asserts: "Ultimately, the Way of Buddhism Realizes the same Transcendental Reality or Truth that is finally Realized via the Ways built upon the concepts and presumptions of the basic ancient tradition of Divine or Spiritual Emanation [or the Way of the Vedic-Upanishadic traditions]."[4] Whether seen idealistically or realistically, in other words, the Realization of the Transcendental Reality—known tradition-ally as "Enlightenment" (in the East) and "God-Realization" (in the West)—reveals the same reality of "Real God" and "Conscious Light" (in Adi Da's terms) whether seen from the Eastern or Western perspective, Vedantic or Buddhist. When all is said and done it is the same Divine Realization, as Adi Da explained: "All traditions that achieve Completeness ultimately transcend their own original propositions and practices in Transcendental Awakening… and that Awakening can only be expressed (if it is to be described at all) via the ultimate language of Transcendentalism."[5] As the Perennial Philosophy also confers: It IS the One same indescribable, indivisible Radical Truth [see Chapters 7-8].

With authentic spiritual life (or sadhana in Satsang) it is the separate self-sense that is sacrificed (or surrendered) altogether, not just psychological substitutes or patterns projected onto others and objects (which involves the "Atman Project" or activity of Narcissus). Satsang can initiate this self-sacrifice via the Adept's Spiritual Transmission. Most important, therefore, Avatar Adi Da *transmits* his Enlightened State to any spiritual aspirant who will turn to "Him" as Guru-Adept and ambassador of Truth and Reality. This is the true import of Guru Yoga-Satsang and is the most efficient and effective *spiritual* "method" known to humankind. It is genuine Transcendental Spirit-Baptism.

Once God is *realized* via true self-transcendence then the Guru's true function (and nature) is made plainly evident. The relationship with the Guru (in Satsang) continues to grow as the self is purified of previous karmas and re-adapts to ever-present Divine Communion (and Happiness) based on Radical Understanding of the self as an activity of contraction (or "avoiding relationship"). Adidam's Way of the Heart offers a *relationship* in Satsang (with the Guru) that undermines both the idealistic (Vedantic) and realistic (Buddhist) search to fix and heal, to re-unite (Vedanta) and release (Buddhism), the separate self from the problems of ignorance and suffering. Besides, Satsang is a *love relationship* based in the heart, not a goal-oriented mind problem but one of devotion and always already Happiness. Thus it becomes supremely attractive to the awakened heart of the devotee. We can only *be* Happy, not *become* Happy (as Adi Da Teaches in the "Lesson of Life").

The Way of the Heart taught by Beloved Adi Da is the Way of Love-Bliss, of Enlightened Awareness, not the search for these. In *Nirvanasara*, Adi Da situates his contribution as an incarnate Avatar within the overall arc of spiritual history. He has been born to serve the function of a purifier and critic of the Great Wisdom Tradition to focus us on actual self-transcendence and Divine Enlightenment, as he explains:

It is part of My Work to criticize and purify the Great Tradition and realign all traditions to the Truth. An aspect of My purification of the Great Tradition is my criticism of popular religious and philosophical movements of all kinds (exoteric, esoteric, and Transcendental)....

The mind, the body, the world, and the God-idea that supports them are all nothing but the environment and expression of the ego, Narcissus, who is the essence of un-Enlightenment. Unless there is a profound understanding of self, mind, body, world, and the usual God-idea, there is no movement that is self-transcending and oriented toward Enlightenment or God-Truth. The Way of Truth is just such self-transcendence, founded on profound understanding of every feature of conventional existence. And there is no sufficient substitute for the Way of utter self-transcendence....

It is time for all traditions within the Great Tradition to be aligned again to the Realizable Truth that is the matter of value in all schools and all religions. And this realignment to Truth (and the self-transcending Way of practice in the Company of authentic practitioners and Adepts) must humble all traditions, all advocates, and all separate institutions of this world.... This requires continuous self-purification in all institutions, as well as a periodic purification of all [religious] institutions through the Work of Great Adepts.[6]

This is precisely why God's Great Tradition of Global Wisdom teaches God is the Guru (and the Guru is God) because their function (or Agency) serves our Enlightenment and transformation of consciousness by being an active human Agent transparent to the Divine Reality, that is, if they are used properly and not cultically [see Chapter 23]. This is what Guru Yoga-Satsang accomplishes despite fears to the contrary or cultic apprehensions of idol worship.[7] You must study the Great Wisdom Tradition to see for yourself and understand the real message of the Awakened Adepts. Learn to approach them in maturity, not in the mood of childish or adolescent reactivity. True Satsang is *only* about Real God-Realization and ever-present Happiness, not self-contraction (or unhappiness, suffering, and ignorance). It is only from the awakened heart that true worship and devotion arise and when God is truly seen and known.

AVATAR ADI DA SAMRAJ:
COMPLETING THE GREAT TRADITION

lucidating the various planes or pluridimensional fields of manifest
Reality, high to low—traditionally called the "Great Chain of Being,"
or what Ken Wilber calls the "**Great Nest of Spirit**" or "Kosmos" or
"AQAL Matrix," also named the "**Cosmic Mandala**"[8] (in Adi Da's terms)—are
not the point or purpose for an Adept-Guru like Adi Da Samraj. Making models
is not the Way of Satsang or Enlightenment, regardless of how intellectually
interesting and useful they may be. Models and maps are generally the way
of philosophers, scholars, scientists and pandits, not Adepts. In this case, the
global Avatar prefers not to emphasize the levels and possibilities of conditional reality whether as exterior subatomic quantum realms or interior subtle
heavens since he sees how fascinated we are with how things work. We often want scientific (or mythical and metaphysical) explanations for *everything*
desiring magical control over our world and lives. Whereas in truth, as Adi Da
emphasizes, we do not know what anything *is*—a state of "**Divine Ignorance**"
—where the desires and searches of the self are transcended in Reality as It
always already IS. Happiness, Love, Light, Humor, the Truth of Real God is
what Enlightenment reveals, not the mechanics of how things work. Nonetheless, when considering manifest reality, a mandala seems to work best in
mapping the many layers of our pluridimensional existence. Two examples
of mandala models depicting the layers or realms of the universe, from the
gross-physical to subtle energies to formless causal domain all embraced in the
transcendent Divine Domain (of Real God) provided by the Avatar and Integral pandit are shown below:

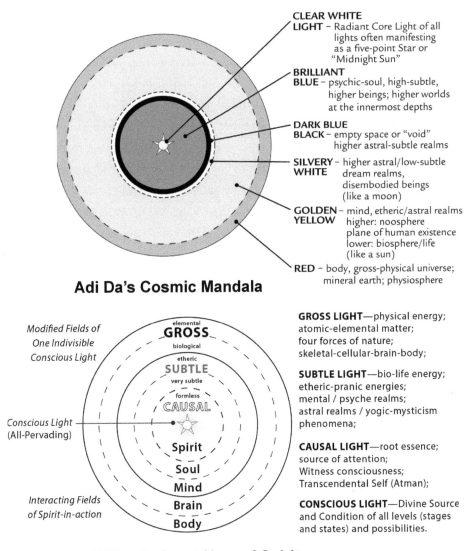

CLEAR WHITE LIGHT – Radiant Core Light of all lights often manifesting as a five-point Star or "Midnight Sun"

BRILLIANT BLUE – psychic-soul, high-subtle, higher beings; higher worlds at the innermost depths

DARK BLUE BLACK – empty space or "void" higher astral-subtle realms

SILVERY WHITE – higher astral/low-subtle dream realms, disembodied beings (like a moon)

GOLDEN YELLOW – mind, etheric/astral realms higher: noosphere plane of human existence lower: biosphere/life (like a sun)

RED – body, gross-physical universe; mineral earth; physiosphere

Adi Da's Cosmic Mandala

Modified Fields of One Indivisible Conscious Light

elemental **GROSS**
biological
etheric
SUBTLE
very subtle
formless
CAUSAL

Conscious Light (All-Pervading)

Spirit
Soul
Mind
Brain
Body

Interacting Fields of Spirit-in-action

GROSS LIGHT—physical energy; atomic-elemental matter; four forces of nature; skeletal-cellular-brain-body;

SUBTLE LIGHT—bio-life energy; etheric-pranic energies; mental / psyche realms; astral realms / yogic-mysticism phenomena;

CAUSAL LIGHT—root essence; source of attention; Witness consciousness; Transcendental Self (Atman);

CONSCIOUS LIGHT—Divine Source and Condition of all levels (stages and states) and possibilities.

Wilber's Great Nest of Spirit

Like the Buddha, who declined to describe the "physics" (or "metaphys-ics") of arising phenomena, these Enlightened Adepts prefer to initiate your own Awakening that transcends mind and ideas, books and rituals, philoso-phies and religions. The "Awakened One" (Buddha) from India preferred that we understand the desiring motives of the self and how to transcend our false sense of separateness (*anatma*). Avatar Adi Da, naturally, takes a similar stance. Though at times Adi Da does describe the structure of the universe from an Enlightened View (such as with his vision of the Cosmic Mandala and Seven

Stages of Life), he primarily insists we *understand* our tendency to seek knowledge about things. This radical understanding of "Narcissus" (or the ego-I) is how the self-contraction into separateness is *transcended*, as Adi Da has constantly clarified. If this is done, if self is released through understanding, then we *see* the Divine Condition of Reality *presently* in the Guru's Company, not in the future or after death. Only then is the mind quieted and the heart set free. Then spiritual practice may be engaged genuinely, not as a search.

This is the only thing Avatar Adi Da (and the Buddha and Shankara, et al.) really care about: your self-transcendence and Awakening to God-Realization (or Nirvana and Atman-Brahman). They want you to *realize* Enlightenment in the heart not through ideas of the mind; to *know* your innate self-luminous condition of "Buddha-Nature" (by whatever name) as "ever-present within your own heart" (as Shankara said). Of course, once realized, the resulting Happiness and sense of Liberation frees attention and energy to allow a person to work in the world more freely, to see how "things" actually are. Even science can be done better once Enlightenment is actualized.

This Realization of Divine Enlightenment is the essence of the "Great Tradition," the primary reason for esoteric religion and spirituality as embodied in the Adept-Realizers who have appeared within human history. As we saw, this accumulated history and wisdom is our common inheritance as human beings born in this "New Age" of global communications [see Chapter 1]. As an American-born Adept, Adi Da arises within the larger historical and global context that preceded him (yet set in a condition which doesn't exceed His Divine Presence or Realization). The Avatar, therefore, has taken extensive steps to present his Teaching and the Seven Stages of Life model within the scope of the entire "Great Tradition of Humankind," especially as epitomized in Advaita Vedanta and the three "vehicles" (*yanas*) of Buddhism expressed as the Ways of the Arhat (Theraveda), the Bodhisattva (Mahayana), and the Maha-Siddha (Vajrayana)[9] [see Chapters 16-17]. Adept Adi Da emphasizes that the Way of Truth, the actual realization of Enlightenment transcends all ideas of ego, time, history, and even all religious differences:

> There is an inherent Sympathy (and necessary equation to be made) between the Buddhist proposition of the "Nirvanic" Condition and the Advaitic proposition of the Brahmanic Atman. This

Sympathy (and this equation) is obvious to all actual Realizers (whatever their tradition may be) of That Which Intrinsically Transcends conditional existence....

The Ultimate Transcendental propositions of Shankara (like the Ultimate Transcendental propositions of Gautama Shakyamuni, and others, within the historical traditions of Buddhism) remain as Self-Evidently True propositions—not based on historical cultural interactions and dependencies, but (rather) based on the undeniable Self-Evidence of Reality Itself.... Both Shankara (with the totality of Indian Advaitism) and Gautama Shakyamuni (with the totality of Indian Buddhism) Ultimately (and equally) declared and demonstrated... the One and Same and Self-Evidently Reality-Truth That Intrinsically Transcends all conditional and merely psycho-physical presumptions, declarations, and Realizations.[10]

First summarized in the incredible book *Nirvanasara* (1982), then in his later books [see below], the Ruchira Avatar revealed his connections with and sympathies for Classical Buddhism and Advaita Vedanta, the supreme mystical teachings of India. Yet he also clearly explains his Teaching has *differences* from them as well. The **Way of Radical Understanding** is not the "**Great Path of Return**" (a point the Avatar has made since the first years of his Teaching-Work[11]). Basically, according to Adi Da, all the enlightened esoteric traditions are speaking about and pointing to the same self-transcending Transcendental Realization [see Chapter 3]. This argument has recently been extended in greater detail in the Avatar's final summary books, *The Pneumaton* (2011), which focuses on Spirit-Baptism (since *pneuma* means "spirit") that begins in the Fourth and Fifth Stages of Life, and in *The Gnosticon* (2010), which focuses on the Great Sages of Transcendental Knowledge (since *gnosis* means "divine knowledge") culminating in the Sixth and Seventh Stages of Life.[12]

Adi Da's *annus mirabilis* ("miracle year") of 1982, when *Nirvanasara* and many other books and talks were published, is a treasure trove of the Avatar's review of the Great Tradition and how his Way of Radical Understanding—the Way of the Heart (now known as Adidam Ruchiradam)—*transcends-yet-includes* all of the previous spiritual traditions of Earth while simultaneously being continuous with them. Only an authentic Avatar would dare to make such statements and have them be true. Ultimately, it comes down to Satsang or cultivating a *spiritual* relationship with the Adept-Realizer in order to transcend self and *realize* God. Hence Adi Da summarized his views below in a discourse given in 2006 on the authenticity of genuine Guru Yoga-Satsang:

> Most of the Great Tradition consists of myths and programs of practice to be applied to oneself, philosophical talk of various kinds, "techniques" of all kinds. Yet, the core and great secret of the Great Tradition is Realization by Grace of the Realizer's Blessing in the course of living the relationship [Satsang] of devotional surrender to the Realizer, to the Master.
>
> I did not Bring that principle to humanity for the first time. That is part of what I am Manifesting here in full Coincidence with the Great Tradition. My Work is a Completing Work, or a Work at the most Full Point of the process that is potential for humankind. As it is said everywhere in the Great Tradition, when there is devotional resort, worshiping the Realizer with your entire being, when you truly surrender to a Master, then you are given Instruction. And, in due course, you are also given Realizations, through direct—and, in the best of cases, Spiritual—Transmission.[13]

Here the Western-born Avatar acknowledges that the "myths and programs" of the "Atman Project" (Wilber's words) hide and obscure the real Atman. A deep study of the Great Tradition's "Divine Library" will make Adi Da's point of view abundantly clear [see Chapter 2]. The Adept is not here to trap you in games of cultism but to help liberate your self in Divine Awakening and ever-present God-Communion. That has *always* been the main mission of the genuine Gurus and Awakened Adepts throughout the millennia. If you believe otherwise then you are mistaken. Only a serious inquiry into the Great Tradition itself will school you appropriately on these important religio-spiritual topics and concerns.

ADVAITAYANA BUDDHISM TO
ADIDAM RUCHIRADAM

Avatar Adi Da's Revelation has become a statement (and challenge) of unending impact. Unfortunately, many critics today still react to his view as being excessive. Yet, indeed, it should be doubted or questioned until proven with your own understanding. Then the full brilliance of Heart-Master Adi Da's Enlightened Realization comes into play as he explains his intentions with a profundity that goes beyond mere scholarship. His insights arise from his Enlightened State not from merely reading books or taking the "Talking School" approach [see Chapter 4]. The Avatar examines in depth the full essence of Buddhism and Advaita Vedanta, the world's two great nondual religions, as well as other major religions (such as Christianity) so he can accurately set his Teaching within and beyond their streams of enlightened wisdom.[14] Avatar Adi Da is about the Truth of God and Enlightenment itself, not the search, as he deftly explains his "**Seventh Stage Way**" or the Way of Divine Enlightenment (offered by Adidam Ruchiradam):

> It is in the Seventh Stage of Life that God is truly proclaimed, not in the conventional mode of Creator, or the Good, but as the Real. God is the Transcendental Truth, Reality, Identity, and Condition of self and Nature. In the Seventh Stage of Life, That is tacitly obvious, and there is not anything that must be escaped or embraced for the Happiness of God-Realization to be actualized. Therefore, the Way that I Teach is not any egoic means for attaining God-Realization. The Way is God-Realization Itself.[15]

Adi Da emphasizes, as mentioned, how the major esoteric mystical traditions of India, Tibet, China, Japan (and Asia) are all pointing to the same fundamental Nondual Enlightened Realization of Transcendental Consciousness. Although not as obvious, the ancient Western traditions also recognize the same Divine Truth [see Part I]. As we saw, the Western-born Avatar has expertly explained how each tradition of India is coming from different propositions: one, **Advaita Vedanta**, is more "**idealistic**" in its orientation by focusing on the True Self or Atman as being God or Brahman, while the other, **Buddhism**, is more "**realistic**" by focusing on criticizing the self as being caught in suffering and illusion.

One calls "It" Atman-Brahman, the other Nirvana; one sees maya, the other samsara; one sees a luminous reality, the other an empty luminosity; one unites with the True Self, the other dissolves self in *Sunyata*; one is Full, the other Empty, etc. Yet, both are simply pointing to the same ineffable and indescribable One Divine Reality (of the True Self-Nirvana), a paradox beyond words or teaching. The table below briefly lists these different approaches to this One Divine Reality of unnamable God:

Advaita Vedanta	Buddhism	Adidam Ruchiradam
Idealism	Realism	Perfect Practice
True Self (Atman)	Nirvana (anatma)	Conscious Light

Avatar Adi Da communicates and actually *transmits* the very same Nondual Transcendental Realization that is recognized by all esoteric world religions; therefore, he stands upon (or is continuous with) both Vedanta and Buddhism but is now present in the Modern Age (and emerging Integral Age). In this sacred manner, "The Reality-Way of Adidam Ruchiradam" is "The Tacit and Prior 'Perfect <u>Knowledge</u>' of Reality Itself",[16] the "Seventh Stage Way" (in his words). It is the Way of realizing Consciousness as being Conscious Light, the "Bright," or Real God.[17] In other words, the Teaching-Revelation and Divine Presence of Adi Da Samraj can accurately be said to fulfill and complete the highest (and most esoteric) Teachings of Buddhism and Vedanta and all religions. This is why the Avatar termed his "Way of the Heart" with the amalgamation "**Advaitayana Buddhism**" and "**Advaita Buddha Dharma**."[18] Once more the Avatar clarifies:

> The Truth, which is associated with the Reality-Teachings of Buddhism, is exactly the same Truth associated with the Reality-Teachings of Advaitism. It is the Truth of Reality Itself, the Truth That Is Reality Itself, which is non-conditional, Transcendental, Acausal in

nature.... They are speaking of exactly the same thing; about exactly the same Realization.... In My Person and Teaching there are no distinctions made between these two traditions, and I Propose them to you as the Root Traditions of Adidam.[19]

Presented in great depth and detail as if given by an erudite scholar, yet spoken with the profound depth of one who knows intimately about that which he speaks, Avatar Adi Da clarifies the religio-spiritual traditions that preceded him as being set within the Seven Stages of Life.[20] Culminating in his summary books *The Pneumaton* (2011) and *The Gnosticon* (2010), and, of course, with *The Aletheon* (2009), as mentioned, the Avatar's review is a tour de force in contextualizing the world's esoteric traditions into a unified whole while simultaneously explaining how his Teaching-Dharma completes and fulfills all previous views. This is why I and others, such as Ken Wilber, highly recommend that everyone should at least study and become a student of Avatar Adi Da Samraj. When you potentially recognize Who He truly IS then you may be moved to become a devotee of The Reality-Way of Adidam Ruchiradam. At least become his student and study, read, and listen to what he says and Teaches.

THE REALITY-WAY OF ADIDAM RUCHIRADAM

The Reality-Way of Adidam Ruchiradam, in summary, asserts that all views, all perspectives are "always already" existing in the Prior Unity seen in Divine Enlightenment. Thus there's no competition between these various enlightened esoteric teachings (contrary to what critics often assume). Then, to top it off, by embodying the pure essence of Enlightenment (from the Sixth to Seventh Stages of Life) in person, Avatar Adi Da clearly and systematically explains how the Reality-Way of Adidam *embraces-yet-exceeds* previous Enlightenment teachings arising (and recorded) from the past. His Teaching eliminates the search for God or Enlightenment by revealing God (or the Divine Nature of Reality) while being in "His Company" (in Satsang) or via his transmission of *Hridaya-Ruchira Shaktipat* [see Chapter 22].

This is a monumental event (and occasion) in the entire history of human spirituality when seen and understood rightly. Whether a scholar or layperson, the Liberation Teaching of Adi Da Samraj makes perfect sense when understood in the context of the entire Great Tradition of humankind. The sacred perspective of Divine Enlightenment sees the *prior unity* underlying all diversity, whether in manifest forms, teachings, religions, or people. Yet ultimately this enlightened understanding arises from the Heart as Love-Bliss, pure and simple, so only the heart knows for sure. In the end, and at all times, there is Only God, God Only. You may discover this truth *personally* since It *is* you (in depth or at root).

This profound matter of why there is such a wide variety of teachings and experiences available and recorded in the "Great Tradition" on Earth is resolved and made most clear with Avatar Adi Da's Heart-Transmission (*Ruchira Shaktipat*) of Divine Grace given via the relationship cultivated in Satsang with the Adept-Guru himself. Significantly, this World-Teacher yet American-born Awakened Adept is one of the first to appear in human history who has had full access to *all* the world's available spiritual literature. His contributions can justifiably be seen as being unequaled to that of any other Adept who has come before limited by their historical time and culture. But again, this is not a competition but a completion and fulfillment, a natural evolution of the Enlightenment Traditions (that truly transcends evolution altogether) [see Chapter 9].

Part of his uniqueness beyond the traditional Global Wisdom Tradition is that Avatar Adi Da provides the fullest descriptions (and Transmission) yet seen about *Amrita Nadi* (or *Atma Nadi*), the current (*nadi*) of Transcendental "Love-Bliss" (*amrita*). This is Divine Conscious Light flowing from the heart (on the right) to the God-Light infinitely Above (and Beyond) the crown of the head and highest chakras [see Chapter 8]. Now reviewed in depth (and detail) in his essay *Atma Nadi Shakti Yoga* (2008),[21] yet revealed throughout all of his Teaching-Literature (from the very beginning), Adi Da has always taught that the "**regeneration of *Amrita Nadi***," the Current of Divine Love-Bliss, is the true "Way of the Heart" of Adidam Ruchiradam. As only one example published decades earlier in *The Way That I Teach* (1978), we find the message (and Realization) of Adi Da has remained basically the same as it was back then as it is today (and will be into the future):

> In [Seventh Stage] *Sahaj Samadhi*, there is a great and Transcendental Yoga that is not described in the traditional texts. It is the yoga of *Amrita Nadi*, in which everything arising is recognized to be only modification of the prior Condition of your apparent condition. Everything arising is without force, unnecessary. If you persist in that meditation or realization in every moment, the limiting or binding force of existence at every level is lost, and you are brought into a transcendental meditation that is the Radiance of the Infinite Being Itself....
>
> In that Realization there is only the absolute projection or Radiance of the Heart felt relative to this gross body as the projected line of Conscious Light that moves out of the Heart, far beyond the crown, far beyond subtle phenomena.... We move into *Bhava Samadhi* or the Divine Domain, which is not describable, which is like that absolute formlessness that we recognize to be our very Condition. It is Bliss.[22]

This great advantage alone ranks Avatar Adi Da Samraj and his contribution of Transcendental Heart-Transmission (*Hridaya Shaktipat*) as being priceless, for he offers these considerations from the perspective of Divine Enlightenment or Real God-Realization [see Chapter 20]. Nothing more, nothing less. He has therefore established the Means and Agency via Adidam Ruchiradam to share this Spirit-Transmission for perpetuity via the commitment and devotion of his devotees in Adidam (his official "Holy Institution"). It is their responsibility to maintain this Agency for all future generations.

Most simply, you become what you meditate on: meditate on God, feel the Guru's Enlightened State (as *your* state) and thus feel and know Enlightenment and God-Realization *right here* and *now* (not as some future goal). But *you* must do the sadhana, you *must* understand and sacrifice self, transcend ego and open your heart; there is no other way. This is the hidden heart-secret that genuine Guru Yoga and Satsang have taught for millennia. Without a doubt, therefore, the incarnation of this American-born Global-Guru is a Divine Advantage for *all* humankind. The Avatar once more emphasizes the beauty and veracity of authentic Guru Yoga-Satsang:

> If there were no one to witness to you, as I do, you would have no way to continue your practice. Because God-Realization is simply true for Me, then if you will give Me your attention, if you will commune with Me, this same disposition will be yours through a process that is much easier than you hearing a philosophical premise and trying to attain it through self-manipulation. You do not have to try to attain it. If you will simply enter into Communion with the Spiritual Master, who is already in the Condition of God-Realization, that Condition will be duplicated in your case.[23]

The Reality-Way of Adidam Ruchiradam, as we've seen, can (and should) be correctly viewed as the epitome of all the world's mystical and spiritual teachings and traditions—the universal Great Tradition of humankind's Global Wisdom—the continuation and fulfillment of all that has come before. This can be known and realized without slipping into cultic belief or iconic delusion for it is about the very nature of your own consciousness as Conscious Light, the Way of the Heart. I can only suggest: please go read and find out for yourself... and *listen* while in God's Sacred Company... in order to *hear* and *see* for yourself while transcending the separative self activity in Divine Communion with the Real Guru.[24] Thus Abiding, Real God is *consciously realized* to be present Here and Now (and Forever Hereafter)! Truly, only the heart knows for sure, since once God is *realized* the heart-mind-soul *knows* the Truth of What IS! May all beings be so blessed! May God (as Guru) Awaken your heart to God Only knows where!

Chapter 10 Endnotes

1. Adi Da Samraj, "I Am Prior to All Traditions: A Communication Offered To Rishi Kumar Mishra" in *Adi Da Samrajashram*, Vol. 1, No. 4, p. 102.

2. Shankara, *The Crest Jewel of Discrimination* (1947, 1975) translated by Swami Prabhavananda and Christopher Isherwood, p. 96.

3. Nagarjuna, *The Diamond Sutra and The Sutra of Hui Neng* (1969) translated by A.F. Price and Wong Mou-Lam, pp. 61-62.

4. Adi Da Samraj [Da Free John], *Nirvanasara* (1982), pp. 65-66.

5. Ibid., p. 137.

6. Ibid., pp. 154-155.

7. See: *In God's Company: Guru-Adepts As Agents for Enlightenment in the Integral Age* (2022) by Brad Reynolds.

8. See: Adi Da Samraj, "The Penetration of the Cosmic Mandala" (from a Talk given on July 20, 1982) in *Easy Death: Spiritual Wisdom on the Ultimate Transcending of Death and Everything Else* (1983, 1991, 2007) for Adi Da's full description and color rendering of the Cosmic Mandala.

9. See: Adi Da Samraj [Da Free John] from "The Three Ways of Buddhism" in *Nirvanasara* (1982), pp. 139-140; also see" "To Realize Nirvana Is To Realize The True Self" in *The Gnosticon* (2010), p. 335ff.

10. Adi Da Samraj, *The Gnosticon* (2010), pp. 341, 378-379 [substituted "Gautama Shakyamuni" for "Gotama Sakyamuni" in Adi Da's text].

11. See, for example: Adi Da Samraj [Bubba Free John], "The Great Path of Return vs. the Radical Path of Understanding" in *The Paradox of Instruction* (1977).

12. These two books, *The Gnosticon: The "Perfect Knowledge" Reality-Teachings of His Divine Presence Avatar Adi Da Samraj* (2010) and *The Pneumaton: The Transcendental Spiritual Reality-Teachings Teachings of His Divine Presence Avatar Adi Da Samraj* (2011), which are the updated versions of *Nirvanasara* (and other writings) are all integrated and summarized in his magnum opus *The Aletheon: The Divine Avataric Self-Revelation Teachings of His Divine Presence Avatar Adi Da Samraj* (2009).

13. Adi Da Samraj, *The Gnosticon* (2010), p. 328.

14. See: Adi Da Samraj [Da Free John], *Nirvanasara: Radical Transcendentalism and the Introduction of Advaitayana Buddhism* (1982, new edition forthcoming); now see *The Pneumaton* (2011) and *The Gnosticon* (2010), specifically the essay "The Unique Sixth Stage Foreshadowings of The Only-By-Me Revealed and Given Seventh Stage of Life" in *The Gnosticon* (2010), pp. 499ff.

15. Adi Da Samraj [Da Free John], *Nirvanasara* (1982), pp. 86-87.

16. See: Adi Da Samraj, *The Gnosticon* (2010), p. v.

17. See: Adi Da Samraj, *The Seventh Way* (2007), book excerpt from *The Aletheon* (2009).

18. See: Adi Da Samraj, *The Gnosticon* (2010), p. 459ff.

19. Adi Da Samraj, 2006 Talk from *The Reality-Teachings of the Buddhist Sages: Renderings and Discourse* CD-2 (2011).

20. See: *Growing In God: Seven Stages of Life from Birth to Enlightenment—An Integral Interpretation* (forthcoming, Paragon House) by Brad Reynolds.

21. See: Adi Da Samraj, *Atma Nadi Shakti Yoga* (2008), also in *The Aletheon* (2009).

22. Adi Da Samraj [Bubba Free John], *The Way That I Teach* (1978), pp. 210-211.

23. Ibid., pp. 212-213 [italics added].

24. See: *Meeting Adi Da: A Mandala of Approach to Avatar Adi Da Samraj* (forthcoming) by Brad Reynolds.

PART II

THE GREAT TRADITION
OF GLOBAL WISDOM
IS GURU YOGA-SATSANG

ELEVEN

AWAKENED GURU-ADEPTS
ARE GLOBAL WISDOM

The tradition of Truth,
the tradition of Spiritual and Transcendental Realization,
is the tradition of the Adept-Realizers.
Apart from the Adepts, there is no tradition of Truth.

— **Adi Da Samraj**, *The Pneumaton*

Avatar Adi Da Samraj has used the phrase the "**Great Tradition**" to identify the world's "Wisdom Inheritance" as being the totality of humankind's religio-spiritual traditions taken altogether, past and present [see Part I]. Specifically, the first Western-born global Adept has defined this "**Great Tradition of Humankind**" as "the total inheritance of human, cultural, religious, magical, mystical, spiritual, and transcendental paths, philosophies, and testimonies, from all the eras and cultures of humanity —which inheritance has (in the present era of worldwide communication) become the common legacy of humankind."[1] In other words, this universal or "perennial" inheritance includes all of the spiritual traditions and paths or yogas ever to exist on Earth from any time period, in every culture, ancient or modern. This evolutionary or developmental process, in both individuals and the collective, includes both the *exoteric* (or "outer-directed") development of "**Growing Up**" as well as the *esoteric* (or "inner-directed") development of "Waking Up" (in Ken Wilber's terms). Avatar Adi Da has been very clear about the responsibility this inheritance now requires from every individual around the globe regardless of his or her native culture today or in the future, as the Heart-Master decidedly explains:

> It is no longer appropriate or even possible for individuals, cultures, or nations to justify absolute independence from other individuals, cultures, or nations—and it is no longer appropriate or possible to grant absolute or ultimately superior status to any historical Revelation, belief system, or conception of how things work. The entire Great Tradition must be accepted as our common inheritance.[2]

As we saw in Part I, other scholars such as Huston Smith, esteemed author of *The World's Religions*, have called the essence of the Great Tradition as being the "**World's Wisdom Tradition**" and "**Primordial Philosophy**," "the winnowed wisdom of the human race."[3] Novelist and philosopher Aldous Huxley called it the "**Perennial Philosophy**," defining it as the universal essence or common metaphysical intuitions behind the worldwide variety of religions and philosophies [see Chapter 7].[4] Wilber has even attempted to update this global inheritance as the "**Neo-Perennial Philosophy**" since according to the integral pandit the "Radical Truth itself is formless, timeless, spaceless, changeless; its various forms, however, the various ideas, symbols, images, and thoughts we use to represent it, ceaselessly change and evolve."[5] The Teaching-Dharma itself continues to evolve to meet the demand of the times [see Chapter 8].

While this primordial tradition is known as the "**Wisdom of the Ages**" this does not mean it contains *only* Enlightened Wisdom for each Teacher and Teaching reflects his or her stage of development and degree of Realization (usually coming from one of the higher Stages of Life). It is all of these traditions taken together that make up our "**Great Tradition**" of human spirituality, therefore each tradition (and worldview) must be valued in a spirit of global cooperation and tolerance. This is what *all* the Spiritual Teachers and Sacred Teachings the world over have in common: they are *all* based in love and compassion for all beings (human and otherwise). They simply want us all to realize God, the Divine Essence of existence; to be Enlightened. Yet it's not so simple since the ego cannot transcend itself by itself. Grace is still necessary but fortunately Grace is freely given (as well as earned), especially through the Agency of the Guru-Adepts.

This Great Tradition of Global Wisdom, as we saw, is everybody's rightful inheritance as a living human being since it has been graciously transmitted to us by our wisest ancestors, women and men alike, from all cultures and races [see Chapter 1]. This sacred knowledge includes all the spiritual and yogic-mystical wisdom handed down to humankind as a global culture, regardless from which country they originated. Avatar Adi Da, however, has made the important observation that this Great Tradition of human spirituality usually involves various forms of *seeking* for the Divine Spirit or Ultimate Reality. Thus most spiritual paths (and Stages of Life) begin with the egoic presumption that we are already separate from God or Ultimate Reality Itself and consequently need to be reunited with it. Indeed, the term *religio*, the root word of "religion," means "to link" or "re-bind," as does *yoga*, which means "to yoke," thus both terms from West and East intend to "link us" back with God or knowing Ultimate Reality. Ironically, however, since we are "*always already*" one with God, right now, then the "linking" or "yoking" involves the transcendence of the very self or ego-I who feels separate from God in the first place. Such a notorious paradox. This egoic error is what generates the profusion of our world religions as we refuse to listen to what the Sage-Founders wanted us to hear and realize.

Since this Great Tradition is our collective inheritance of the world's wisdom, as Adi Da emphasizes, it is to be studied and accessed without giving any preferential status to any one tradition over another. The American-born Siddha-Guru maintains we must "*go to school with the Great Tradition*" as a whole to find out how to rightly value the authentic Guru-devotee relationship—or Guru Yoga-Satsang—and make it into a valuable *transformative* life-changing affair not just a mental philosophy for our entertainment (or temporary release). The Great Tradition is a global gift meant to inspire every generation to take up genuine spiritual life. It's *not* the exclusive province of any one tradition nor should it be used to elevate any one culture or tradition above others. Such "tribal" (or provincial) bickering is to be avoided and transcended in an embrace of compassionate tolerance and a greater understanding exhibited by a truly global worldview, as Adi Da persistently suggests. This fountain of Enlightenment is the wealth of wisdom given by our wisest ancestors to each and every one of us; one to be celebrated and accessed not denigrated or dismissed, including by the knowledge of science.

GREAT TRADITION OF MAHA-SIDDHAS:
SATSANGA + SHAKTIPAT

ne of the most critical instructions that the Great Tradition imparts to every person of any age, of any race, ethnicity, or religious preference, is the importance of having a genuine spiritual teacher or guide. The best of these Spiritual Teachers is a "**Guru**" (literally, "one who dispels darkness") especially a "**Siddha-Guru**" (*Siddha* is a "perfected one") and "**Sat-Guru**" (or "true Guru"), while a "**Maha-Siddha**" is a "Great Guru" (*maha* meaning "great"), all Sanskrit words now used in the West. This is a person, male or female, of ultimate significance and Enlightened Realization assuming a guiding role in a person's life meant to teach their students about true spiritual living known as *sadhana* or "disciplined practices" based on the *Dharma* or teachings of enlightened understanding.[6] This process has been specifically called "**Guru Yoga**" by the Tibetan Buddhists since it is deeply linked with their enlightened spiritual roots in India where the genuine Guru has always been highly valued. All the Dharma-Teachings of Buddhism have descended from the Buddha and his lineage of Enlightened devotees. A Realized Spiritual Master is therefore the most respected person possible for teaching people about authentic spirituality because they have trodden the path of higher consciousness for themselves (having been taught by their own Master-Guru). It is the delusion of the modern mind to believe that Guru Yoga is only about cults and brainwashing.

Called *Satsanga*—or "Satsang"—in India, it literally means "association with the wise" or "right and true relationship," the sacred and devotional relationship between Guru and devotee that becomes an authentic spiritual practice. Almost always it involves a psycho-physical *transmission* of psychic energy—*Shaktipat*—between devotee and Guru that provides the strength and power for real Satsang to begin and grow [see Chapter 3]. Adi Da calls this sacred process the "**Method of the Siddhas**" meaning it involves "the company and conditions generated by the Guru-Adept, one who lives Truth in the world."[7] Avatar Adi Da himself, of course, offers Satsang—a personal, sacred relationship—to all those who will turn to him as Guru-Adept and Avatar (the reason for the Reality-Way of Adidam Ruchiradam). This sacred relationship has been offered in India for thousands of years from countless Gurus and is the root source of the world's wisest wisdom concerning God-Realization. India has been the home base where the veracity and authenticity of the Guru has been most evident and deeply honored for millennia. Knowledge and appreciation of Satsang is the "Great Gift," the "Divine Gift," given by the East to the West (and for all future generations). However, be forewarned: you must learn how to differentiate and discriminate the authentic Master from the poser (even the self-deluded sincere ones).[8] Indeed, genuine Gurus are very rare.

As a whole the Great Tradition of humankind is loaded with different personal relationships between elder Masters, whether women or men, and their usually younger and still learning students (or devotees). Although a Spiritual Master can be younger than their devotees their measure of maturity is in their degree of God-Realization, not their chronological age. The Guru-devotee relationship with a Fully Realized Adept is the most mature form of Divine Agency available for unenlightened human beings. This is why it's so highly esteemed in the esoteric literature of the Great Tradition. Read and study the Great Tradition to find out for yourself.

It is vitally important that we don't lose this invaluable mode of spiritual development regardless of how knowledgeable our sciences or modern (integral) mind might get. These various "**Spiritual Guides**" have arisen from the world's diverse historical cultures including, for example, the **Shamans** of native indigenous cultures reaching from the Americas to Australia to the Arctic to Africa encircling the globe in every millennium. Then there are the **Yogis**, the masters of bodily postures and the internal exercises that move *kundalini* (life-energy) up the spine to awaken the higher centers of the brain; or the **Saints** whose lives are devotionally dedicated to living in communion with the Divine Source, and so forth. As Adi Da and Wilber (and others) have pointed out, as human civilization continued to evolve through the millennia so did the teachings of the "advanced-tip" individuals also evolve in expressing the details (along with the essence) of the sacred path [see Chapter 8].[9]

From this great struggle of human history comes our sacred lineage of Teachers, Shamans, Prophets, Yogis, Saints, Sages, and Siddhas, et al, reaching from Japan to China to Egypt, from India to Europe to Africa to the Americas (and elsewhere), spanning the entire globe affecting every acre of human habitation. This includes many traditions that our examples in the following chapters will not review (due to space constraints), such as Taoism, Jainism, Zoroastrianism, Confucianism, even Rastafarianism, etc. Still, the Guru or Spiritual Master is highly valued in them all, from Lao Tzu to Mahavira to Zoroaster to Confucius to Haile Selassie (Jah Rastafari himself), et al.

In India they say this bounty of Enlightened Adepts comes from the "god" **Vishnu**, the "all-pervading" (or "Preserver") aspect of the One Divine, who has incarnated as the various "**Avatars**" or the ones who "descend" or "cross over" from the Divine Domain to the human world. In the West such evolved human beings have been seen and honored as being a "**Divine Incarnation**," such as with the "**Son of God**" (held to only manifest in Jesus Christ from Galilee). These Avataric incarnations of Vishnu, such as the twenty-two Avatars in the *Bhagavata Purana* follow the contours of biological evolution: Matsya, the fish-man avatar; Kurma, the tortoise avatar (reptiles); Varaha, the boar avatar (mammals); Narasimha, the lion-man avatar (proto-humans); Vamana, the demon-king avatar (warriors), climaxing with the Avatars of Rama, Krishna, Buddha, and Kalki (the future Avatar who, some have said, is Adi Da Samraj).

Obviously, the Great Gurus or "Adept-Realizers" are the engine behind every true religious path, the one who drives true spirituality in every generation with his or her Teaching and bodily demonstration. They are the root source of all the world's religions, as Krishna in the *Bhagavad Gita* (4. 7-8) famously announced:

> *Whenever righteousness wanes and unrighteousness increases,*
> *I send myself forth.*
> *For the protection of the good and for the destruction of evil,*
> *and for the establishment of righteousness,*
> *I come into being age after age.*

To dismiss this sacred function of the Guru-Adepts, as many modern critics now maintain, will surely be an error doomed to place us all at great peril thus to be avoided at all costs. The following chapters in this section are some brief reviews about these awakened beings and their lineage (or descendants) arising from the higher transpersonal Stages of Life in the world's various religions. They come from different eras and areas of human evolution reflecting various cultural worldviews yet some shine brighter than the rest (especially with the Avatars). They appear in every culture during nearly every century over the millennia but with each proclaiming the same essential message: *You are God—Tat Tvam Asi*—and so is everybody else including the entire realm of Nature and the whole Kosmos! With such Awakening to Enlightenment comes a profound responsibility to practice love and compassion to all beings, as the Bodhisattva Vow clearly claims. We all must transcend self to be a more loving person in realizing God. This is the eternal vow to which all enlightened beings sing in harmony and dance in praise showing and showering down their love for all and All.

Since the lineage of Spiritual Masters reaches back deep into the dim mists of prehistory, even before scribes recorded history on paper (or papyrus), this tradition can be seen as the **"Ancient Walk-About Way"** (a phrase from Adi Da Samraj) in order to honor its deep historical (and eternal) lineage. Knowing about this sacred history and highlighting the best of humanity's wisest people is the way to recognize the Enlightened Ones who are found in all the ages of humankind. From Paleolithic hunters to modern city-dwellers, from Neolithic farmers to landed aristocracy, from over the hills and valleys of the countryside to crossing the waves of the mighty seas, their universal message of our innate divinity is the only reality that doesn't change over time because it's the only Truth that will set us Free. These ancient and modern Adepts align with the Perennial Philosophy arising from a reoccurring Sophia or Divine Awakening inherent in Consciousness Itself [see Chapters 7-8]. Fortunately, it is "always already the case" (in Adi Da's words), so all we have to do is "Wake Up!"—to Grow Up, Clean Up, and Show Up (as Wilber-DiPerna say). Won't you join in this blessed journey? Come along in the walkabout? These are human beings to whom we may turn for guidance, love, and help, including Spiritual-Blessing: they are the Awakened Adepts themselves. They are the best friend you'll ever have, your truest guide, your servant (as you are theirs); they are our Beloved.

"ANCIENT WALK-ABOUT WAY"
OF GURU-ADEPTS

The import of the *esoteric* or inner religious teachings is that they lead an individual to a higher yogic understanding of Enlightenment or God-Realization climaxing with a personal and profound experience of the Divine Source-Condition of all life and all multiverses. This wisdom is innate in us all as the very core of our consciousness. Usually this Awakening is initiated by and grounded in the advanced methods or practices of self-transcendence not ones of self-fulfillment (though, overall, this Divine Revelation is felt to be given by Grace not personal effort). This includes the all-important practice of **meditation** or turning attention inward away from the outer ego-I (or our self-identity), so when the body sits still the mind becomes quiet in order to open the heart of the whole body-mind-self to the ever-present Divine Presence that is "always already the case." True meditation is the simple Feeling of Being (or radiant Love-Bliss) arising from the heart and pervading the entire universe to Infinity.

On the other hand, the meaning of the *exoteric* or outer religious beliefs and ritual practices of most religions is used for social associations and cultural cohesion, for optimistic talk (and mythic beliefs), or for providing consoling techniques to help the self feel secure and protected. Both ways have their value and necessity. **Exoteric** "outer-directed" religions give *legitimacy* via horizontal *translations* while the **esoteric** "inner-directed" ones provide *authenticity* via vertical *transformation* (in Wilber's terms).[10] In both cases, people are looking for knowledge and wisdom about what is "Greater" than themselves (as an ego-I). They are trying to find the Way to fulfill life's true purposes beyond survival and social integration. Yet it is only with the esoteric teachings and practices of the Mystics such as in contemplation and meditation that life's deepest needs and possibilities are revealed. This is the spiritual potential inherent in all of us no matter who you are.

Since ancient times people have discovered that the esoteric teachings of wisdom and spiritual transmission comes most directly (and purely) from the Awakened Adepts or Spiritual Masters in whatever country or culture they appear. Sometimes people search the whole world to find the right Adept best suited for them. This process of study and devotion—cultivating a *living relationship* with an awakened human being—is at the heart of real religion. This is the way it has been since the most ancient times even before recorded history. It is an innate characteristic of humanity that makes us yearn for spiritual truth, or at least that's what the evidence amply suggests. Most of us tend to seek no further than our provincial upbringing or the traditional religion that we are most familiar with. Generally, we rely on what we've been taught as children or we blindly accept what our culture and society insist is true. Yet there comes a time to put away childish beliefs *if* you want to grow and know the real truth about real spirituality and meditation. Our parochial attitudes, in other words, generally involve exoteric religion not the esoteric secrets of genuine spirituality and the deeper yogas found in the higher Stages of Life.

To break out of this trend we must go find the true Adept-Realizers and study their teachings directly not just through the interpretation of others (such as scholars and pandits). A good place to start is to become more familiar with the esoteric literature of the Great Tradition of Global Wisdom (the "Divine Library") now collected from around the world telling us about the historical precedents of these Enlightened beings who have lived among us [see Chapter 2]. But you must invest the time in reading and studying. Such an introduction is a primary goal of this book because in most cases there comes a time when an Awakened Adept or genuine Guru becomes a necessary advantage to our spiritual growth in attaining real peace of mind. But we in the West, in particular, have become immune to this possibility of accessing a Spiritual Master mostly since we're afraid of cults; perhaps at our own peril, if history is any guide.

This is one reason why Adi Da Samraj has introduced the phrase the **"Ancient Walk-About Way,"** or simply the **"Walk-About Way,"** an idea that's worth serious consideration.[11] Here the Avatar is not using it as a direct reference to the Australian Aboriginal culture who use the term "walkabout" to reference walking about the landscape following intuition (although, of course, Adi Da includes indigenous cultures too). Avatar Adi Da intends it to mean, as he explains, "the Way of devotion to the Spiritual Master [that] has been practiced in spontaneous response to the Spiritual Master since the most ancient of prehistorical days."[12] Such devotion, or turning to an advanced-tip individual, is a natural response to recognizing someone who is more spiritually evolved than oneself.

Throughout human history people in every generation, or at least a few, have openly recognized the various Spiritual Adepts who appear in their company while alive (not just frozen in mythic tales and fables). Some have been revered as the founders of world religions, while others were put to death. In most cases they were simply ignored or shunned and now are unknown. But when used properly and effectively, as Adi Da summarizes, "The disposition of the ancient Walk-About Way is simply to turn to the Realizer in the very moment of sighting the Realizer."[13] When doing so a person opens himself or herself to that Adept's Transmission of Spirit-Energy and awakening potential to take a step beyond their own egoic tendencies to a Divine Vision of Truth.

As only a few historical examples will illustrate below, we learn that India's most revered (and esoteric) texts, the *Upanishads* (which literally means "to sit at the feet of the Master") honor the Guru-Adept above all others, even more than kings and military leaders. In the *Bhagavad Gita* the Adept-Avatar Krishna implores his devotee Arjuna to simply "**Remember Me**," while in the *New Testament* Jesus's simple yet most difficult command was "**Follow Me**." All of these references indicate the primary impulse that arises when meeting an Awakened Adept: Turn to "Him" (or "Her") to know God for real via their Enlightened State (which is also *your* native state). This hints at the sublime attractiveness of the God-Realized human being through direct experience, not philosophy, the inherent radiance and happiness that emanates from his or her awakened Presence and charisma. This is what the student or devotee is attracted to in the first place, the Divine Presence Itself, not merely the solitary body-mind of the person who is the Master (though that too). When we truly "see" them we ultimately recognize *our own* innate spiritual condition (or Buddha-Nature) freed from the barriers of egoity and cultism.

Such a meeting or "sighting" is called *Darśana* in Sanskrit, also known as "**Darshan**," an "auspicious sighting" of a holy person or Guru-Adept who usually bestows transmission or *Shaktipat* (Spirit-Energy) influencing the person who is now seeing a *theophany* (in Greek) or "vision of the divine" [see Chapter 23]. This sighting or revelation is said in the traditions to be the most auspicious occasion possible for the advancement of a person's Awakening to God. The way to learn about esoteric spirituality (or the secret of Yoga), now and historically, has always been to get instruction (and transmission) from those men and women who have already accomplished these goals in person by simply being in their Wise Company in body or recollection.[14] Yet this is a very rare occasion and so is extremely precious.

In a similar (but lesser) manner, if you want to learn about science you go to the universities and study with scientists; but if you want to learn about spiritual matters you go to a Spiritual Master. Our true teachers are those who know more than we do and are willing to share their insights and wisdom with others (as Plato's cave allegory noted). History proves this is the way it has always been and the way it will always be (now and long into the future). Fortunately, most religious traditions provide such a method to be schooled in the Company of the Wise as do the esoteric sacred texts now being made available to anyone who searches hard enough to look for the answers to their yearning questions. But this **"Method of the Siddhas"** is particularly embodied as the process or relationship of Guru Yoga-Satsang alive as the Great Tradition of Awakened Adepts. Now is the time to avail ourselves to their universal Divine Wisdom for they are our brothers and sisters, our friends and Masters, alive in history and in our hearts.

AWAKENED ADEPTS:
THE HEART OF RELIGION

The true source of Real Religion, the authentic teachers of esoteric or inner wisdom, are the Awakened Adepts or Enlightened Spiritual Masters appearing in all epochs of history and life. They comprise the essence of the Great Tradition of Global Wisdom, as this book maintains, taking on many forms, from Shamans to Priestesses to Yogis to Saints to Sages to Siddhas to Sat-Gurus, et al, each reflecting different Stages of Life. Each of them has realized a certain depth of awareness that transcends the realization of the common average person. They are the **"advanced-tip"** few who often appear to serve the **"average-mode"** masses (in Wilber's words[15]). This great interplay between these two parallel strands of human history is one based on love and right relationship founded in harmony, respect, compassion, and understanding [see Chapter 10].

Guru Yoga is not a master-slave mentality, one of domination or abuse, though false "masters" have also appeared claiming to be what they are not. Such cultic relationships must be warned against and overcome by using discrimination and rational thinking, founded on clear intuition and sincere understanding, using the mind as well as the heart.[16] It helps to understand humanity's history as the unfolding Seven Stages of Life set within the developmental spectrum of consciousness in order to recognize our true Gnostic Giants [see Appendix I]. By using caution and our own understanding and not being misused by "totem-masters" or cult leaders, it is very important we do not shun or overlook the true teachings and divine gifts offered by those who have come to serve our greater awakening and Divine Realization. No reason to throw out the baby with the bathwater, as they say.

Nonetheless, all Adepts and Spiritual Teachers must be understood and critically viewed based on their general Stage of Life and the tradition (or non-traditional means) within which they appear. Only the fully Realized or Divinely Enlightened Adept who transcends all religious and cultural limitations is truly qualified to be the most effective Guru-Adept for us to listen to, follow, and establish a sacred relationship of Satsang or Guru Yoga with. You must become schooled or educated in the Great Tradition of Awakened Adepts (and lesser teachers and Yogis, et al.). Therefore, Adi Da's Seven Stage of Life model is as effective as any you will find (even, in my opinion, exceeding Ken Wilber's and Aurobindo's, or anyone else's). Avatar Adi clearly explains:

> There are all kinds of beliefs that people believe, or say they believe or want to believe, or would like to have be true, but that doesn't mean they are true. If you study in depth and altogether have a comprehension of the nature of the phenomena associated with the traditions, and you can see them in terms of the Stages of Life (the esoteric anatomy of human possibility), you can also see them in historical terms and how they developed in the social and cultural context of human history. Then instead of simply being a naïve believer or a naïve agnostic or naïve atheist or a naïve anything, you transcend the limitations of your own thinking, your own provincialism of mind. You can see any and all traditions clearly. And they all are authentic in the sense they all exhibit dimensions of the Stages of Life and aspects of the esoteric anatomy of human possibility.[17]

Let me now introduce you to the names (and dates) of some of the principal players who have mysteriously and miraculously appeared at certain times and places in the unfolding chapters of human history. They are the Awakened Adepts and true guides to our inalienable spiritual destiny. Notice that while they hail from nearly every culture and country, from every race and every century, still we discover their unity lies in their divine awareness and spiritual understanding. Genuine Gurus are God's greatest Gift to humankind [see Table on the following pages]:

AWAKENED ADEPTS
THE HEART OF WORLD RELIGIONS
AS UNIVERSAL SPIRITUALITY

NAME	DATE	AREA	RELIGION
Cave temple Shamans	Upper Paleolithic	Europe	Cave art initiations
Priestesses	Mesolithic / Neolithic	Europe/West Asia	Goddess religion
Gilgamesh	2700 BCE	Sumer	*Epic of Gilgamesh*
Imhotep	2635–2592 BCE	Egypt	High Priest, pyramid architect
Yellow Emperor	2697–2597 BCE	China	est. Chinese civilization
Abraham	2000–1900 BCE	West Asia	founding Patriarch of Israel
Zoroaster	15th c. BCE (early date)	Persia	Persian Prophet, author of *Avesta*
Rama	16th / 15th c. BCE	India	Avatar-Sage of the *Ramayana*
Rishis (Vedic "seers")	1550 BCE (earlier)	India	est. Vedic religions / *Vedas*
Vyasa	12th / 11th c. BCE	India	Seer-poet compiles the *Vedas*, author of *Gita*

Krishna	12th / 11th c. BCE	India	Warrior-Sage of *Bhagavad-Gita*
Akhenaton	1372– 1354 BCE	Egypt	Pharaoh of Aton (monotheism)
Moses	1300 BCE	Egypt/West Asia	Prophet of monotheism
Sages of *Upanishads*	9th / 8th c. BCE	India	*Upanishad* roots of Vedanta
Kapila	9th / 8th c. BCE	India	Sage est. Samkhya yoga
Dattatreya	8th / 7th c. BCE	India	legendary Sage of *Avadhuta Gita*
Zoroaster	6th c. BCE (late date)	Persia	Persian Prophet, author of *Avesta*
Valmiki	5th c. BCE	India	author of *Ramanyana*
Mahavira	540–486 BCE	India	Sage founder of Jains
Gautama Buddha	563–483 BCE	India	Avatar founder of Buddhism
Badarayana	ca. 500 BCE	India	Shakti-Avatar of *Brahma-Sutras*
Hebrew Prophets	1000–164 BCE	West Asia	Prophetic founders of Judaism
Orpheus	750–700 BCE	Greece	Sage founder of Orphism
Pre-Socratics	5th / 4th c. BCE	Greece	Philosophers of The One
Lao Tzu	500 BCE	China	Sage founder of Taoism
Confucius	551–479 BCE	China	est. Chinese social morality
Sokrates/Plato	469–348 BCE	Greece	Philosophy Sage-founders
Hermes Trismegistus	300 BCE	Alexandria, Egypt	Sage founder of Hermeticism
Patanjali	200 c. BCE or 2nd c. CE	India	founder of Ashtanga Yoga
Jesus Christ	3 BCE–30 CE	West Asia	Avatar-founder of Christianity
Apollonia of Tyana	15–100 CE	Anatolia	Greek Neo-Pythagorean philosopher
Asvaghosa	1st c. CE	India	Buddhist author of *Fifty Verses of Guru Devotion*
Garab Dorje	fl. 55 CE	Oddiyana (Pakistan)	Ati Yoga (Dzogchen) root Guru of Tibetan Nyingma

Shenrab Miwoche	unknown	Tibet	"Buddha" of Bon religion
Nagarjuna	150–250 CE	India	Sage of Madhyamika Buddhism
Plotinus	205–270 CE	Alexandria/Rome	Sage founder of Neo-Platonism
Iamblichus	245–325 CE	Syria	Neoplatonist-Pythagorean
Mani	216–276 CE	Persia (Iraq)	Prophet-founder of Manichaeism
Asanga	300–370 CE	India	Sage of Yogachara Buddhism
Vasubandhu	4th century CE	India	half-brother to Asanga, founder of Yogachara
Hypatia	355–415 CE	Egypt	last priestess at Library of Alexandria
Proclus	410–485 CE	Athens	last classical philosopher
Bodhidharma	470–543 CE	India to China	First Patriarch of Ch'an (Zen)
Muhammad	570–632 CE	Arabia	Prophet of Islam
Hui-Neng	638–713 CE	China	Sixth Patriarch of Zen Buddhism
Fa-Tsang	643–712 CE	China	Sage of Hua-Yen Buddhism
Huang Po	d. 850 CE	China	Sage influences Japanese Zen
Shantideva	7th / 8th CE	India	Sage of Bodhisattva Way
Saraha	2nd century CE	India	founder of Mahamudra; "one who shot the arrow"
Padmasam-bhava	717–804 CE	India to Tibet	Sage brings Buddhism to Tibet
Lady Yeshe Tsogyal	757–817 CE	Tibet	Female Buddha/Tantric Dakini
84 Maha-Siddhas	8th–12th c. CE	Tibet	"Great Gurus" of Tibet
Shankara	788–821 CE	India	Sage reformer Advaita Vedanta
Ribhu	8th-cenctury CE	India	Author of *Ribhu Gita*
Sufi Masters	end of First Millennium	India/West Asia	Mystical (esoteric) Islam
Al-Hallaj	858–922 CE	Baghdad, Iraq	Persian mystic, poet, Sufi teacher ("I Am the Truth!")

Atisha	982–1054	India to Tibet	Second transmission of Buddhism to Tibet
Tilopa	988–1069	India to Tibet	Master of Anuttarayoga Tantra
Naropa	1016–1100	India Mahasiddha	Devotee of Tilopa, Vajrayana 6 Yogas
Marpa the Translator	1012–1097	India to Tibet	Devotee of Naropa, founded Kagyu
Milarepa	1052–1135	Tibet Mahasiddha	Devotee of Marpa, famous Yogi-poet
Ramanuja	1017–1137	India	Sage of Bhakti movement
Gampopa	1079–1153	Tibet	Founder of Kagyu school. devotee of Milarepa
Ibn 'Arabi	1165–1240	Spain to Syria	Arab Muslim scholar, poet, philosopher, mystic (Sunni)
Chu Hsi	1130–1200	China	founder of Neo-Confucian
Honen	1133–1212	Japan	founder of Japanese Pure Land Buddhism
Nichiren	1222–1282	Japan	Buddhist reformer
Gorakhnath	11th /12th c. CE	India	Sage founder of Nath tradition
Meister Eckhart	1260–1327	Germany	Christian mystics
Moses ben Shem	1270–1300	West Asia	Kabbalah text *Sepher ha Zohar*
Longchenpa	1308–1364	Tibet	Adept-pandit of Nyingma
Tsongkhapa	1357–1491	India/Tibet	Sage reformer of Tibet Buddhism
Nicholas of Cusa	1401–1464	Germany	Mystic-author of *Learned Ignorance*
Kabir	1440–1518	India	Islamic-Hindu Prophet-poet
Guru Nanak	1469–1538	India	Saint founder of Sikhs
Martin Luther	1483–1546	Germany	Protestant reformer
St. Theresa of Avila	1515–1582	Spain	Mystic-saint of Christianity
St. John of the Cross	1542–1591	Spain	Mystic-author of *Dark Night of the Soul*
Dadu Dayal	1544–1603	India	Poet-sant and religious reformer

Baruch Spinoza	1632–1677	Holland	Jewish pantheist-philosopher
Baal Shem Tov	1700–1760	Ukraine	founder of Hasidic Judaism
Joseph Smith	1805–1849	USA	founder of Mormonism
Ramakrishna	1836–1886	India	Hindu mystic, saint, and religious leader
Vivekananda	1863–1902	India	brings East to West
Aurobindo Ghose	1872–1950	England/India	est. Integral Yoga
C. G. Jung	1875–1961	Switzerland	Western psychiatrist, psychoanalyst
Ramana Maharshi	1879–1950	India	Sage of Advaita Vedanta
Paramahansa Yogananda	1893–1952	India/West	founder Kriya Yoga in the West (author of *Autobiography of Yogi*)
A. C. Bhaktivedanta Swami Prabhupada	1896–1977	India/West	founder of "Hare Krishna Movement" (ISKCON)
Maharishi Mahesh Yogi	1918–2008	India to Europe	founder of Transcendental Meditation (TM) (The Beatles' guru)
Tendzin Gyatso	(b. 1935)	Tibet/India	His Holiness 14th Dalai Lama
Adi Da Samraj	1939 -- 2008	USA	Avatar founder of Adidam

These are only some among many of the most revered people to ever live on our planet. They comprise an intimate part of our human race and global wisdom inheritance. They were not warriors of iron and blood but warriors of soul and spirit; not conquerors of land and people but conquerors of self and desire. Since their message was one of self-transcendence and surrender, of renouncing worldly things and lustful craving, in a certain sense they stood outside city-life, outside of civilization and its incessant daily activity for survival, profit and pleasure. Yet they did not forego the people of the common average-mode masses for it was out of their compassion and love that they taught the people about esoteric spiritual matters, about Ultimate Reality… and still do.

These figures in the table above are only some of the more well-known, the most famous names that history has dutifully recorded. Out in the forests, up in the mountains, on retreat, in the streets, and in secluded spots of sanctuary there are many, many more of them who through their subtle influences have taught earnest students gathering to hear and practice their sacred teachings. In this case, in ways we'll never know about, they have affected history and the evolutionary progress of One Humanity. These Sages, the Adept-Realizers who became Adept-Gurus, are the mature advanced-tip awakened women and men who only wish to give to others as their Master-Teachers gave to them too. They give back to us in a reciprocal circle of compassion and care.

This book is devoted to all of them and their methods of religious and spiritual offerings for engaging in a sacred relationship as a means to Divine Enlightenment. My main suggestion is that we must go to them and learn, sit at their feet, study their sacred scriptures, awaken devotion and realize that every one of them is our common inheritance of Global Wisdom offering us a path to genuine spirituality. They are the Masters of the Great Tradition influencing all of the world's religions in human history [see Charts on following pages]. Avatar Adi Da Samraj, who has always highlighted the importance of the Guru-Adept, summarizes the situation succinctly when he points out:

> Devotion to the Realizer is the ancient Way of true Spiritual life. Devotion to the Realizer has been the Way since before history was written. Devotion to the Realizer is the "pre-civilization Way," which existed before any recorded history, during a time when human beings were, essentially, merely wandering all over the Earth. Devotion to the Realizer has always been the fundamental Means of human Spirituality, whatever other teachings have been given in the circumstances of devotion to any Realizer.[18]

Next (in the following chapters), let's turn to a brief tour through some of the world's Great Religions to note the high regard the Adept-Realizers have always been held and accorded. This is because the Master-student/Guru-devotee relationship—i.e., **Guru Yoga-Satsang**—is the very essence of religion as well as the best of philosophy. By seeing their Light—and your own Conscious Light—the darkness of the ego and ignorance is dispelled. Interestingly, in reviewing the major world religions of the West (particularly those arising from the lineage of Abraham known as the Abrahamic religions), we must start with the primordial roots of the West itself: Ancient Greece (or Hellas). Here many of Greek's "philosophers" (i.e., "lovers of wisdom") can best be seen as bona fide Adept-Realizers and genuine Gurus, not simply "Pre-Socratics" (or "proto-scientists"), as most modern scholars tend to label them. To them we turn in the next chapter.

Chapter 11 Endnotes

1. Adi Da Samraj "Glossary" definition in *Reality Is All The God There Is* (2008, Rochester, VT: Inner Traditions), p. 193.

2. Adi Da Samraj [Da Free John], *Nirvanasara* (1982), p. 198.

3. Huston Smith, *The World's Religions* (1958, 1991, 2009), p. 5.

4. See: Aldous Huxley, *The Perennial Philosophy* (1945, 1970, 2009).

5. Ken Wilber, *The Eye of Spirit* (1997), p. 60.

6. *Dharma* has several meanings in Indian philosophy, so its context must be taken into account. Hindus usually refer to it as "law, duty, or custom," while the Buddhists (and Buddha), when capitalized, tend to refer to it as the "Teaching of Truth" (as Adi Da also uses it) as Buddha-Dharma.

7. Adi Da Samraj [Franklin Jones], *The Method of the Siddhas* (1973, 1978), p. 23; now see *My 'Bright' Word* (2007).

8. See: *In God's Company: Guru-Adepts As Agents for Enlightenment in the Integral Age* (2022) by Brad Reynolds.

9. See: Ken Wilber, *Up from Eden* (1981, 2007); Adi Da Samraj, a Talk (from July 10, 1978) "The Old Religions, the New Scientism, and the Awakening of the Psyche" in *Vision Mound*, May 1979, Vol. 2, No. 9 and *The Laughing Man*, Vol. 5, No. 4, 1985.

10. See: *Spiritual Choices: The Problem of Recognizing Authentic Paths to Inner Transformation* (1987) edited by Dick Anthony, Bruce Ecker, and Ken Wilber; also see: Ken Wilber, *Eye to Eye* (1982, 2001).

11. See: Adi Da Samraj, *The Ancient Walk-About Way* (2006); *Religion and Reality* (2006).

12. Adi Da Samraj, *The Ancient Walk-About Way* (2006), p. 64.

13. Ibid., p. 67.

14. See, for example: *An Autobiography of a Yogi* (1946) by Paramahansa Yogananda.

15. See: Ken Wilber, *Up from Eden* (1981, 2007); *The Eye of Spirit* (1997, 2001).

16. See: *In God's Company: Guru-Adepts As Agents for Enlightenment in the Integral Age* (2022) by Brad Reynolds.

17. Adi Da Samraj, from a Talk given on August 19, 2004 "The Universals in All 'Religions'" on the DVD *Human History Is One Great Tradition* (2007, The Dawn Horse Press).

18. Adi Da Samraj, *The Ancient Walk-About Way* (2006), p. 80.

UPPER PALEOLITHIC
40,000 – 10,000 BP

EPOCH	PERIOD	AGE	B.P.	EUROPE	EGYPT AFRICA	WEST ASIA	SOUTH ASIA (INDIA)	EAST ASIA (CHINA)	AUSTRALIA AMERICAS

PLEISTOCENE / **UPPER PALEOLITHIC** (side labels) / **STONE TOOL AGE** / **OLD STONE AGE** / **LATE**

40,000 BP — LATE MAGIC TYPHON PERIOD

after 50,000 BP there's a great increase in diversity of artifacts

Homo sapiens sapiens: Europe, Southwest Asia
AURIGNACIAN CULTURE (45,000-28,000 BP)
- oldest known figurine art: **Venus of Hohle Fels**
- earliest known cave art; 3-D figurines
- pendants, bracelets, ivory beads

TOOL KIT: thick flakes of flint, fine chipping; stout scrapers
- warm clothing
- bury dead

GREAT HUNT: WAY OF THE ANIMAL POWERS

Last remaining pockets of *Homo Neandertalensis*

35,000 BP

Last glaciation still at its height

UPPER PALEOLITHIC "ADVANCED HUNTING" CULTURES
"BLADE & BURIN" TOOL KIT: (1) thin, narrow, parallel-sided flint blades;
- primal language   (2) tools for making other implements: chisels, gravers w/ cutting edges
- music & dance: flutes, singing, tribal stories
- bone, antler, ivory implements and art
- Big-Game Hunting: bison, reindeer, horse, mammoths
- seasonal use of caves; snug huts - family groups
- hard clay figurines fired in ovens (32,000 BP)
- bury dead with ornaments
Lion Man (Germany 30,000 BP)

Homo sapiens sapiens MIGRATIONS:
35,000: along N. African coasts
34,000: Zargos mountains (Iran)
32,000: Levant
30,000: Italy / Iberia
28,000: Japan
35,000 – 10,000: "groups of Cro-Magnons with their progressive traditions were spreading from Orient to Occident" – J. Hawkes

30,000 BP

Cro-Magnons: **GRAVETTIAN CULTURE**
Europe, Russia (28,000-23,000 BP)
Venus of Dolni Vestonice (oldest ceramic, 29,000 BP)

GREAT MOTHER   ETHERIC RELIGION

GRAVETTIAN ART
- relief cravings: animal figures, realism / TOTEM CULTS
- FEMALE "VENUS" FIGURINES: grotesque to beauty
- e.g., Laussal, Dordogne   first textile evidence (27000 BP)

succession of cultures indicates a continuous spread from West to East

25,000 BP — LATE MAGIC TYPHON PERIOD

PALEOLITHIC BIG GAME HUNTING
- easy supply of meat
- leisure time
- problem-solving
- barbed harpoons
- eyed needles
- fat-burning lamps
- encampments: half dozen huts
- body ornaments: necklaces, bracelets of shells, teeth, beads of ivory, mother of pearl, stone
Venus of Willendorf (22,000 BP)

SHAMAN
CAVE

GRAVETTIAN ART penetration of Asia: Siberia, Lake Baikal, Goddess figurines

Neandertals now extinct (22,000 BP)

SIBERIAN LAND BRIDGE open: 24,000 - 18,000 BCE
10,000 - 9000 BCE

WORLD POPULATION: 1 million

20,000 BP

Last Glacial Maximum: 18,000 – 15,000 BCE sea levels *lower* than present

18,000 BCE: spear-thrower Advanced Hunting in Egypt and E. Africa
ETHOS
Hunter-gatherers in the forest steppe (20,000 - 12,300 BCE)

SOLUTREAN CULTURE: Europe

MAGDALENIAN CULTURE / CAVE ART (18,000 - 9000 BP)

TEMPLE CAVES: Shaman-Magic Initiations   LATE PALEOLITHIC
Bear Cults

CAVE ART: PALEOLITHIC GREAT HUNT to AMERICAS
Bird-head Shaman of Lascaux (20,000 - 15,000 BCE)
Hall of Bulls, Lascaux (17,000 - 15,000 BCE)
Sorcerer of Trois Frères (15,000 - 11,000 BCE)

15,000 BP — EARLY MYTHIC MEMBER PERIOD

ICE AGE ENDING

REINDEER HUNTERS (12,700-9600 BCE)

EARLY NATUFIAN CULTURE: Levant
- harvesting wild grains with sickle (18,000 - 8000 BCE)
- preparing grains with pestles and mortars
- bow and arrows   (12,500 - 10,800 BCE)

first evidence of possible warfare (13,000 BCE)

WHEAT CUTTING, Zagros Mts. (11,000 BCE)

Late Glacial Interstadial (12,700-10,800 BCE)

12,000 BCE: SIBERIA
11,000 BCE: JAPAN
10,000 BCE AMERICAS:
Clovis
Sandia
Folsom

10,000 BCE

YOUNGER DRYAS (10,800-9600 BCE)   PLEISTOCENE TO HOLOCENE EPOCH

© Brad Reynolds; based on *The Atlas of Early Man* (1993) by Jacquetta Hawkes; *After the Ice* (2003) by Steven Mithen;

© chart by Brad Reynolds

N E O L I T H I C
10,000 BP – 3000 BCE

EPOCH	PERIOD	AGE	B.C.E.	EUROPE	EGYPT AFRICA	WEST ASIA	MESOPOTAMIA IRAN (PERSIA)	INDIA	CHINA

YOUNGER DRYAS   PLEISTOCENE TO HOLOCENE EPOCH

10000 BCE / 10th Mil. BCE — "The Big Freeze" (10,800 – 9600 BCE)

EARLY MYTHIC MEMBER — 9000 BCE / 9th Mil. BCE

ICE MELTING / SEAS RISE (11,000 – 8000 BCE)

Great Flood

LATE NATUFIAN CULTURE: Levant (10,800 – 9600 BCE)
- domesticated cereals & animals (herding)
- hunting/gathering main food source
- increased population; permanent houses
- Neolithic symbolism, trade, pictograms

dog domesticated   Jericho est. 9600 BCE

FIRST FARMERS TO SHARED RELIGION in 1000 yrs: new leaders/elders (9000-8000 BCE)

8000 BCE / 8th Mil. BCE

HORTI — Fertile Crescent — CULTURE — WAY OF THE SEEDED EARTH

FARMERS BEGIN TO COLONIZE through West Asia, Europe

Jericho (7500 BCE) (pop. 2000)
fortified walls
cult of skulls
ancestor cults
vultures/lions

round houses
baskets
wooden vessels
personal oranements
goat domesticated

INDIA'S MYTHIC CIVILIZATION

GREAT MOTHER Cults

SHAMANISTIC-COMMUNAL ELITE

7000 BCE / 7th Mil. BCE

GREAT MOTHER — substantial villages / towns emerging — first fired pottery — FERTILITY

"Classic" Period of Neolithic Development

Nile Delta forms after sea levels stabilize
fusion of hunting/gathering and farming

Catal Huyuk (7500–5400 BCE) (pop. 4000)
religious imagery
shrine rooms
death/burial cults
bull/lion cults

food-producing technology
rectangle houses
Tigris-Eurphrates villages from Zagros to Caucasus Mts.
(e.g. Jarmo, Siyalk)

INDIA'S GOLDEN AGE (Yukteswar) (6700 BCE)

GREAT MOTHER TO — ox domesticated — **Mahegarh** (6000 BCE) (pop. 20,000)

6000 BCE — GREAT GODDESS ETHERIC RELIGION

MID MYTHIC MEMBER PERIOD — 6th Mil. BCE

European Neolithic long houses (6000-5000 BCE)

GREAT GODDESS

farming enters Egypt

small farming settlements in Italy & Iberia

Saharan rock painting

Catal Huyuk
peak (5400 BCE)
decline (5200 BCE)
painted geometric pottery
stylized female figurines
scratch plow fields
(6th mil. BCE)
Dawn of Metals

HALAFIAN CULTURE
(Tigris-Eurphrates)
Neolithic Villages

Inanna (Cosmic Goddess)

INDUS CULTURE
HARAPPAN:
early-food producing (6500-5000 BCE)
regionalization (5000-2600 BCE)
integration era (2600-1900 BCE)

5000 BCE / 5th Mil. BCE

EMERGENCE OF — COPPER AGE (Chalcolithic) — stimulates cross-country trade

megalithic "passage way" tombs & burials ancestor cults

copper mining
copper smelting

TRADITIONAL — GREAT GLOBAL DIFFUSION — AUTHORITY
from the Near East center (J. Campbell)

wheeled cart
potter's wheel

specialized classes emerging
CITY-TEMPLES in SUMER
(4500-3700 BCE)

transition stage (4500-3500 BCE)

4000 BCE / 4th Mil. BCE

AGRICULTURE

MANAGING TEMPLE ESTATES — leads to record keeping / writing

LATE MYTHIC MEMBER PERIOD — 3500 BCE

Predynastic Egypt
large irrigation projects
Egypt writing: "speech of the gods"

FIRST CITIES in SUMER (3700-3200 BCE) (Eridu, Uruk, Ur, Lagash, Nippur)

more towns & villages in NW India preparing for 3rd Mil. BCE
HARAPPAN population explosion

first farmers along Yellow (Huang Ho) and Wei Rivers

Yang Shao farmers

first bronze (3300 BCE)

3000 BCE / 3rd Mil. BCE — TRADE EXPANDING (caravan routes) — RISE OF HIERATIC CITY-STATES

Left-hand vertical columns: EPOCH: NEOLITHIC / HOLOCENE. PERIOD: CERAMIC / ACERAMIC, COPPER. AGE: MESOLITHIC / CERAMIC / COPPER.

RISE of CIVILIZATION
3000 BCE – 1 A.D.

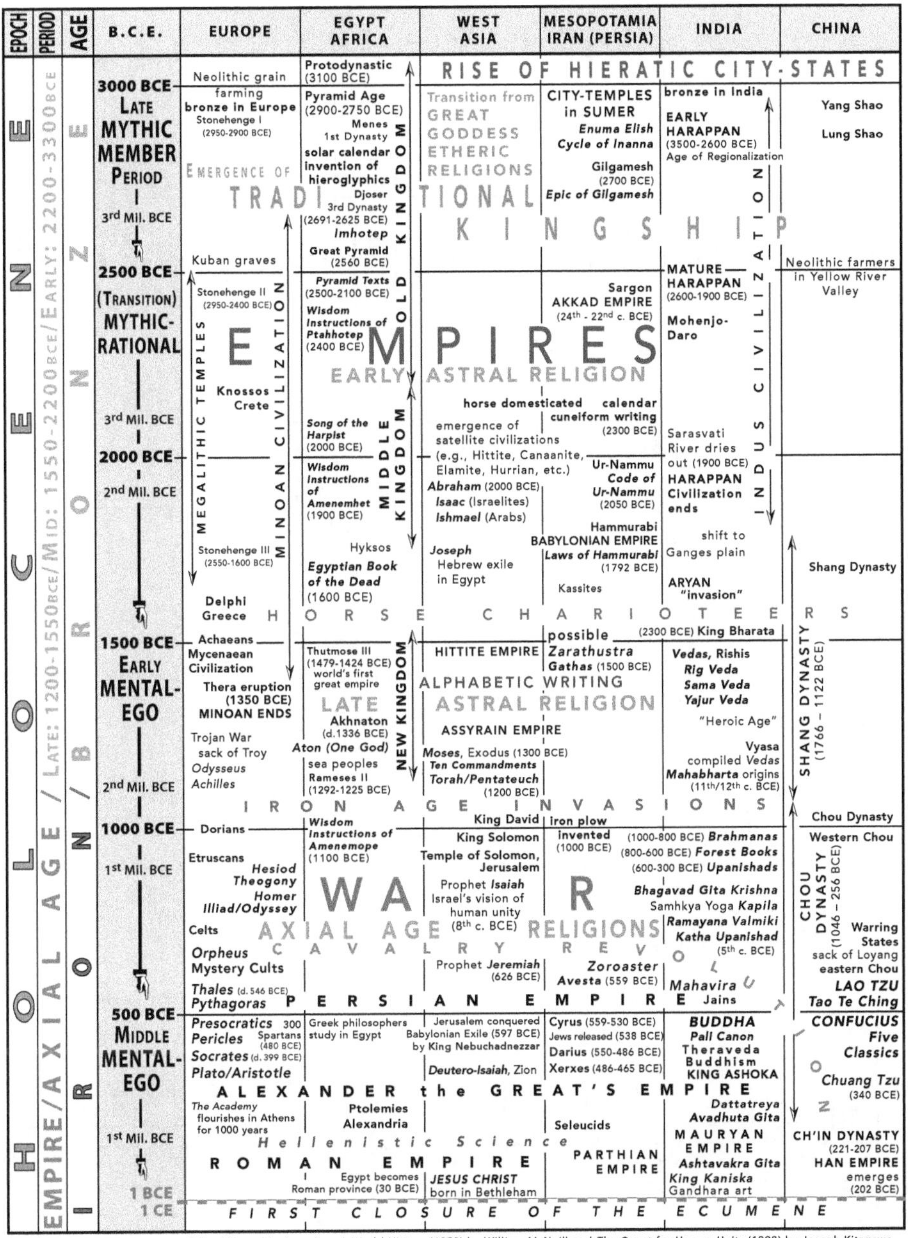

Left margin vertical labels:

- EPOCH: HOLOCENE
- PERIOD: EMPIRE / AXIAL AGE
- AGE scale: LATE: 1200–1550 BCE / MID: 1550–2200 BCE / EARLY: 2200–3300 BCE

B.C.E.	EUROPE	EGYPT AFRICA	WEST ASIA	MESOPOTAMIA IRAN (PERSIA)	INDIA	CHINA
3000 BCE LATE MYTHIC MEMBER PERIOD	Neolithic grain farming; bronze in Europe; Stonehenge I (2950-2900 BCE)	Protodynastic (3100 BCE); Pyramid Age (2900-2750 BCE); Menes 1st Dynasty; solar calendar; invention of hieroglyphics; Djoser 3rd Dynasty (2691-2625 BCE); Imhotep	RISE OF HIERATIC CITY-STATES; Transition from GREAT GODDESS to ETHERIC RELIGIONS	CITY-TEMPLES in SUMER; Enuma Elish; Cycle of Inanna; Gilgamesh (2700 BCE); Epic of Gilgamesh	bronze in India; EARLY HARAPPAN (3500-2600 BCE); Age of Regionalization	Yang Shao; Lung Shao
3rd Mil. BCE	EMERGENCE OF TRADITIONAL KINGSHIP					
2500 BCE (TRANSITION) MYTHIC-RATIONAL	Kuban graves; Stonehenge II (2950-2400 BCE); Wisdom Instructions of Ptahhotep (2400 BCE)	Great Pyramid (2560 BCE); Pyramid Texts (2500-2100 BCE)	EMPIRES EARLY ASTRAL RELIGION	Sargon; AKKAD EMPIRE (24th-22nd c. BCE)	MATURE HARAPPAN (2600-1900 BCE); Mohenjo-Daro	Neolithic farmers in Yellow River Valley
3rd Mil. BCE	Knossos Crete	Song of the Harpist (2000 BCE)	horse domesticated; emergence of satellite civilizations (e.g. Hittite, Canaanite, Elamite, Hurrian, etc.)	calendar; cuneiform writing (2300 BCE)	Sarasvati River dries out (1900 BCE)	
2000 BCE 2nd Mil. BCE	Wisdom Instructions of Amenemhet (1900 BCE)	Wisdom Instructions of Amenemhet (1900 BCE)	Abraham (2000 BCE); Isaac (Israelites); Ishmael (Arabs)	Ur-Nammu; Code of Ur-Nammu (2050 BCE); Hammurabi; BABYLONIAN EMPIRE; Laws of Hammurabi (1792 BCE); Kassites	HARAPPAN Civilization ends; shift to Ganges plain; ARYAN "invasion"	Shang Dynasty
	Stonehenge III (2550-1600 BCE); Delphi Greece	Hyksos; Egyptian Book of the Dead (1600 BCE)	Joseph Hebrew exile in Egypt		possible (2300 BCE) King Bharata	
1500 BCE EARLY MENTAL-EGO	Achaeans; Mycenaean Civilization; Thera eruption (1350 BCE); MINOAN ENDS	Thutmose III (1479-1424 BCE) world's first great empire; Akhnaton (d.1336 BCE); Aton (One God)	HITTITE EMPIRE; ALPHABETIC WRITING; ASTRAL RELIGION; ASSYRIAN EMPIRE; Moses, Exodus (1300 BCE); Ten Commandments; Torah/Pentateuch	HORSE CHARIOTEERS; Zarathustra; Gathas (1500 BCE)	Vedas, Rishis; Rig Veda; Sama Veda; Yajur Veda; "Heroic Age"; Vyasa compiled Vedas; Mahabharta origins (11th/12th c. BCE)	SHANG DYNASTY (1766-1122 BCE)
2nd Mil. BCE	Trojan War; sack of Troy; Odysseus; Achilles	sea peoples; Rameses II (1292-1225 BCE)				
1000 BCE 1st Mil. BCE	Dorians; Etruscans; Hesiod Theogony; Homer Illiad/Odyssey; Celts; Orpheus Mystery Cults; Thales (d. 546 BCE); Pythagoras	Wisdom Instructions of Amenemope (1100 BCE)	IRON AGE INVASIONS; King David; Iron plow invented (1000 BCE); King Solomon; Temple of Solomon, Jerusalem; Prophet Isaiah; Israel's vision of human unity (8th c. BCE); Prophet Jeremiah (626 BCE)	Zoroaster; Avesta (559 BCE); PERSIAN EMPIRE	Brahmanas (1000-800 BCE); Forest Books (800-600 BCE); Upanishads (600-300 BCE); Bhagavad Gita Krishna; Samkhya Yoga Kapila; Ramayana Valmiki; Katha Upanishad (5th c. BCE); AXIAL AGE RELIGIONS REVOLT; Mahavira; Jains	Chou Dynasty; Western Chou; CHOU DYNASTY (1046-256 BCE); Warring States; sack of Loyang; eastern Chou; LAO TZU; Tao Te Ching
500 BCE MIDDLE MENTAL-EGO	Presocratics; Pericles; Spartans (480 BCE); Socrates (d. 399 BCE); Plato/Aristotle	300 Greek philosophers study in Egypt; Ptolemies; Alexandria	Jerusalem conquered; Babylonian Exile (597 BCE) by King Nebuchadnezzar; Deutero-Isaiah, Zion	Cyrus (559-530 BCE); Jews released (538 BCE); Darius (550-486 BCE); Xerxes (486-465 BCE)	BUDDHA; Pali Canon; Theraveda Buddhism; KING ASHOKA	CONFUCIUS; Five Classics; Chuang Tzu (340 BCE)
1st Mil. BCE	The Academy flourishes in Athens for 1000 years; ROMAN EMPIRE	ALEXANDER the GREAT'S EMPIRE; Hellenistic Science; Egypt becomes Roman province (30 BCE)	JESUS CHRIST born in Bethlehem	Seleucids; PARTHIAN EMPIRE	Dattatreya Avadhuta Gita; MAURYAN EMPIRE; Ashtavakra Gita; King Kaniska; Gandhara art	CH'IN DYNASTY (221-207 BCE); HAN EMPIRE emerges (202 BCE)
1 BCE / 1 CE	FIRST CLOSURE OF THE ECUMENE					

EMPIRES & WAR
Sages & the Sword
500 BCE – 500 CE

EAST / WEST

OTHER

BEFORE COMMON ERA / COMMON ERA

"classic" period in Amerindian civilizations begin

Ghana in West Africa

CHINA

Confucius (551-479 BCE)
Warring States (475-221 BCE)
Chuang Tzu (340 BCE)
Mencius (300 BCE)
CHOU DYNASTY (1040-256 BCE)
CH'IN DYNASTY — Shih Huang-ti (221-207 BCE) unites China; GREAT WALL begins
HAN EMPIRE emerges (202 BCE)
Han Confucianism
Ssu-ma Ch'ien, grand historian
"Silk Road" Europe-China international trade
Han Emperor Ming (58-75 CE) welcomes Buddhism
Han Synthesis of Confucianism, Taoism, Yin-Yang, and others creating Pax Sinica
Yellow Turban rebellion, 184
Han Dynasty collapses, 220 CE
Neo-Taoist Synthesis: Buddhism-Taoism dialogues
devasting fall of Lo-yang, 311
North/South China division: both welcome Buddhism
North: Kumarajiva, translator
South: Chih Tun, Neo-Taoist Buddhism; Hui-yuan, Pure Land Buddhism; Gradual/Sudden Enlightenment
HAN DYNASTY

INDIA & SOUTHEAST ASIA

Buddha (563-483 BCE)
First Buddhist Council (400 BCE) Tripitaka
India's 2 Threads: Brahmanism / Buddhism
Alexander's conquest
MAURYAN (322-185 BCE)
King Ashoka (304-232 BCE)
2nd Buddhist Council (250 BCE)
Buddhism spreads throughout India; Brahmanism is transformed
Greco-Buddhist Gandhara art; new Mahayana savior images, e.g., Vishnu, Shiva
King Kaniska, Kusha
spread of Indian culture to southeast Asia; emphasize Maitreya, Amitabha as savior-Buddhas
Mahayana Buddhist Sutras
Nagarjuna (150-200 CE)
Madhyamaka / Yoga Sutras
Patanjali
reinvigoration of Classical Hinduism
Bhagavad Gita added to decimal Mahabharata numbers (esp. to Vishnu) (270 CE)
Asanga Yogachara Buddhism
Lankavatara Sutra
classical Sanskrit Kalidasa
Classical Age of "Hindu India"
Kama Sutra
GUPTA (320-540)
SPREAD OF BUDDHISM AS PAN-ASIAN RELIGION

EURASIAN STEPPE

KUSHANS
HSIUNG-NU
TURKISH DOMINANCE
EPHTHALITES
JUAN-JUAN
Attila, the Hun

WEST ASIA / NORTH AFRICA

Xerxes
PERSIAN EMPIRE
Alexander the Great (356-323 BCE)
MACEDONIAN EMPIRE
PTOLEMIES
SELEUCIDS
PARTHIANS
Hermes Trismegistus / Corpus Hermeticum
Apollonius of Tyana (d.100) Alexandria:
Mithra cults
Mani (216-274) Manicheism: vision of human unity
Sassanian Synthesis (Ardashir I)
SASSANIAN DYNASTY
Persia: (216-274)
Mazdakism movement (reform Manicheism)

EASTERN EUROPE

Seven Sages
Pythagoras
Peloponnesian war
GOLDEN AGE
Socrates (d. 399 BCE)
Plato The Academy
Aristotle The Lyceum
Euclid
Praxiteles
Aristarchus of Samos
Hipparchus
FIRST CLOSURE OF ROME
John the Baptist
Jesus of Galilee
CRUCIFIXION
Jewish revolt: destruction of temple; rise of Rabbinic Judaism
Gospels written
compassion teachings of Savior-Christ spread
Jewish revolt
codification of Greek science: Galen, Ptolemy
Bishop Theophilus burns Library of Alexandria (391 CE)
Hypatia slain (415)
Justinian closes The Academy in Athens (529 CE)
RISE OF ROME

WESTERN EUROPE

Celtic expansion
Persian wars
Protagoras (d. 420 BCE) "Man is the measure of all things"
Democritus
Hippocrates
Gauls sack Rome
Rome unites Italy
Hannibal's war
Lucretius
Cicero
Vergil
JULIUS CAESAR
AUGUSTUS
Apostles
St. Paul
Claudius
Domitian
Tacitus (historian)
Trajan
Marcus Aurelius
civil war and invasion
restoration of Roman empire
Plotinus, Enneads Neoplatonism
CHRISTIANITY BECOMES OFFICAL STATE RELIGION
CONSTANTINE (306-337 CE)
JULIAN (361-363 CE)
Huns
GERMANIC INVASIONS
sack of Rome
St. Augustine, City of God
St. Patrick
Clovis
edict of Theodosius (384) closes Egyptian temples
END of PAGANISM
AGE of PAGANISM
AXIAL AGE

B.C.E./C.E.

500 BCE (5th c.)
400 BCE (4th c.)
300 BCE (3rd c.)
200 BCE (2nd c.)
100 BCE (1st c.)
1 A.D.
CE (1st c.)
CE (2nd c.)
CE (3rd c.)
CE (4th c.)
CE (5th c.)
500 CE

AGE: I R O N A G E

PERIOD: M I D D L E M E N T A L - E G O

FIRST CLOSURE OF THE ECUMENE OF COMPASSION

MEDIEVAL AGES
500 – 1500 CE

EAST

AMERICA / AFRICA
- Polynesian dispersal begins
- end of classic period of Amerindian culture
- Muslim conquests in East Africa
- Aztecs in Mexico
- Incas in Peru
- Chichen Itza in Yucatan

JAPAN
- Buddhism established in Japan
- Hui Neng (638–713)
- Ch'an Buddhism "Sudden Enlightenment" — Nara period in Japan
- Lady Murasaki
- Honen (1133–1212) Jodo School
- Shinran (1173–1262) Pure Land
- Nichiren (1222–1282) Kamakura period (1185–1333 CE)
- Dogen (1200–1253) Soto Zen Japan
- Rinzai Zen

CHINA
- South China: Ch'an Buddhism; North China: Wei kings; Mahayana saviors; Great Canal
- SUI DYNASTY (581–618)
- TANG DYNASTY (618–907)
- China reunited; rock shrines: Sakyamuni/Maitreya to Amitabha/Avalokitesvara (Quan Yin)
- Li Po (major poet)
- printing invented
- Sui-T'ang Synthesis of Confucianism, Taoism, Buddhism greatly influenced by Tantra Buddhism in Tibet; overthrow of Buddhism
- Milarepa (1039–1123)
- compass, gunpowder invented
- SUNG DYNASTY (960–1279)
- Northern Sung (960–1126)
- Southern Sung (1127–1179)
- Neo-Confucian Synthesis: Phase 1 — Chi Hsi (d. 1200) Reason School
- MONGOL INTERLUDE (1276–1368)
- MING DYNASTY (1368–1644)
- Neo-Confucian Synthesis: Phase 2 — Emperor Yung-lo makes Chu Hsi Four Books — Confucian Five Classics state doctrine (1416)
- Wang Yang-Ming Mind School
- Cheng-ho, explorer

INDIA & SOUTHEAST ASIA
- Bodhidharma (5th/6th c. CE) brings Buddhism to China
- GUPTA (320–540)
- Harsa reign (606–647)
- Tantra emerges
- Hsuan Tsang (Chinese translator) Buddhism to China
- Tantra develops
- Shankara (788–820)
- Muslims in Sind
- Hindu Synthesis continues with Advaita Vedanta while Buddhism declines in India
- Ramanuja (1017–1137)
- Raja Raja the Great Tamil Chola Empire south India (985–1014 CE)
- Muhammad of Ghazni; conquest of north India
- Kashmir Shaivism (11th c.)
- Gorakshanath Founder of Nath Tradition (11th/12th c.)
- Tantras & Puranas Shiva to Shakti
- slave sultanate of Delhi
- Bhagavata Purana (13th c.)
- rise of Bhakti
- Yoga Upanishads (14th/15th c.)
- Hatha Yoga Pradipika (15th c.)
- Kabir (1440–1518)
- Sikh Guru Nanak (1469–1539)
- Vasco da Gama discovers sea route to India (1498)

EURASIAN STEPPE
- Chinese control of Central Asia oases
- battle of Talas
- TIBET
- Uighur empire
- Islamic conversion of steppe tribes
- Genghis Khan
- MONGOL EMPIRE
- Tamerlane
- Ivan III repudiates Tatar rule
- TURKISH DOMINANCE

WEST

WEST ASIA / NORTH AFRICA
- SASSANIAN Dynasty — Sassanid Persia (531–579 reign)
- Roman influence / Greek influence
- OMMAYADS
- Prophet Muhammad (571–632 CE)
- Uthman vs. Ali Caliphs
- ISLAMIC CONQUESTS
- Sufis emerge with emphasis on gnosis and teacher's transmission of divine light and falsifah or comprehensive knowledge
- Baghdad est. 762 CE Islamic Golden Age
- al-Hallaj (d. 922 CE) martyred over "I Am Truth"
- ABBASID CALIPHATE 750–1258/1510 CE
- corpus Islamicum
- al-Farabi (d. 950 CE)
- ibn-Sina (980–1037 CE)
- al-Ghazali (1058–1111 CE)
- Omar Khayyam "philosopher of the world"
- Averroes (d. 1148 CE)
- Maimonides (1135–1204 CE)
- 1258 CE Babylon sacked by Mongols
- Rumi (1207–1273)
- Hafiz (1325–1390)
- ibn-Khaldun
- Persian art at its peak
- TURKISH DOMINANCE
- MONGOL DOMINANCE

EASTERN EUROPE
- JUSTINIAN closes the Academy in Athens (529) restoration of Roman Byzantine Empire
- Slav infiltration into Balkans
- Leo III, the Isurian Muslim repulse / iconoclastic controversy
- AVARS
- BULGARS
- conversion of Rus
- Basil II Byzantine recovery
- final East-West schism
- battle of Manzikert
- FIRST CRUSADE
- Hellenic Renaissance
- FOURTH CRUSADE
- Alexander Nevsky
- battle of Kossovo
- capture of Constantinople by Turks
- TURKISH DOMINANCE

WESTERN EUROPE
- St. Benedict
- partial or Austrian invasion
- Muslims in Spain battle of Tours
- iconoclastic reform
- CHARLEMAGNE, Roman emperor
- Viking, Magyar, Arab invasions and raids
- Cluniac reform
- conversion of Magyars and of Norway
- Papal reform
- St. Anselm Abelard
- St. Francis (d. 1226)
- collapse of the Hohenstaufen empire
- St. Thomas Aquinas
- Papacy at Avignon / Dante
- Great Schism
- Hundred Year's war
- ITALIAN RENAISSANCE capture of Granada

C.E.: 500 · 6th c. · 600 · 7th c. · 700 · 8th c. · 800 · 9th c. · 900 · 10th c. · 1000 · 11th c. · 1100 · 12th c. · 1200 · 13th c. · 1300 · 14th c. · 1400 · 15th c. · 1500

AGE: ISLAM / DARK AGES

PERIOD: MIDDLE MENTAL-EGO

MODERN WORLD

WEST   EAST

C.E.	AMERICAS	EUROPE	RUSSIA	WEST ASIA	SOUTH ASIA (INDIA)	EAST ASIA (CHINA)	PACIFIC & AFRICA
1500 16th c.	Columbus	ITALIAN RENAISSANCE / REFORMATION — Leonardo da Vinci, Martin Luther; Machiavelli 1517		ISMAIL SAFAVI; Ottoman-French alliance; SULEIMAN THE LAWGIVER	da Gama; Muslim control of Java; Babur → India		Magellan
	Cortez; Pizarro	HENRY VIII; Calvin; Loyola; Xavier; EMPIRE OF CHARLES V; Counter-Reformation — Copernicus			Chaitanya (1486-1534) Hare Krishna mantra	Macao founded	Portuguese → Japan
	Hawkins brings first African slaves	Michelangelo; Dutch revolt; Vesalius, anatomist; Philip II of Spain	Ivan IV captures Kazan, Astrakhan		fall of Vijayanagar to Muslims		Spanish → Philippines
		Montaigne	Livonian war; Russians conquer Sibir		AKBAR (1556-1605)	Hideyoshi invades Korea	
1600 17th c.	Virginia, Quebec, Massachusetts; New Amsterdam (NYC), established; sugar plantations fix Negro slavery upon New World	Shakespeare; Bacon; Cervantes; Galileo; Henry IV of France; Kepler; THIRTY YEARS WAR; English civil wars; Milton; Harvey "I think, therefore I am"; Descartes; El Greco; Cyril Lucaris; Rembrandt; LOUIS XIV; Molière	Time of Troubles; Polish assult; NIKON AND CHURCH REFORM	Shah Abbas the Great; Kiuprili revival of OTTOMAN EMPIRE	Dutch / English East India companies; Tulsidas (1532-1623); Taj Mahal (1653)	Ricci → Peking; Russians reach Pacific; Tibetans convert Mongols to Lamaism; MANCHU CONQUEST OF CHINA; treaty of Nerchinsk	Dutch ships → Japan; Japan closed to foreigners; West African slave trade
	Dutch driven from New Amersterdam	Newton; Spinoza; Locke; Hobbes; Frederick the Great; decay of Swedish empire; Leibniz; Mabillon	ROMANOV; PETER THE GREAT St. Petersburg new capital	second seige of Vienna; treaty of Karlowitz; loss of Hungary	Aurangzeb, last strong Mughal emperor	*rites controversy*; treaty of Kiakhta	
1700 18th c.		rise of Austria; Newcomen's engine; South Sea Bubble; Watt's engine; partition of Poland	nobles exempted from state service	Nadir shah		Chinese control in Tibet, Mongolia, Turkestan	Berring's voyages
	Franklin; British gain Canada; AMERICAN WAR OF INDEPENDENCE; Jefferson; Madison; abolition of trade monopoly in Spanish empire	Voltaire; Rousseau; AGE OF ENLIGHTENMENT; Adam Smith; Mozart; Linnaeus; Hume; Kant; Herder; Bach	CATHERINE THE GREAT; Pugachev revolt	Russo-Turkish war; treaty of Kutchuk Kainardji	battle of Panipat; British expel French from India	abolition of East India Company monopolies; opium war	Captain Cook's voyages; Spanish found San Francisco; Australia colonized
1800 19th c.	Latin American independence; Thoreau; Emerson; Whitman; UNITED STATES CIVIL WAR; railroad building	Napoleon I; Hegel; Schelling; Schopenhauer; Kierkegaard; railroad building; Beethoven; Congress of Vienna; 1848-49 revolutions; Darwin/Evolution Revolution; Marx 1859; Napoleon III; Cavour (Italy); Bismark (Germany); "God is dead"; Papal infallibility; Nietzsche; automobile; rival alliance systems	CRIMEAN WAR; Alexander I; Puskin; Nicholas I; abolition of serfdom; Dostoyevsky; Tolstoy; railroad building	Serbian and Greek revolutions; Mohammed Ali of Egypt defeats Sultan and Wahhabis; British-Afghan wars; Suez Canal	consolidation of British rule in India; Ram Mohan Roy; Sepoy mutiny	Taiping rebellion; Europeans capture Peking; Russo-Japanese war; Japan rules Korea; Sino-Japanese war	New Zealand colonized; Perry opens Japan (1854); Meiji Restoration; colonial scramble in Africa
1900 20th c.	Panama Canal; mass auto; Wilson movies; airplane; Hubble; *Roaring '20s*; Big Bang theory; GREAT DEPRESSION; F.D. ROOSEVELT; quantum physics; Atomic Energy; CHURCHILL; HITLER; MUSSOLINI; Pearl Harbor; Atom Bomb; rise of USA; Superpower; civil rights (1950s); Vietnam war (1960s); man on the moon (1969); oil crisis (1970s); COMPUTER REVOLUTION / WORLD WIDE INTERNET (1990s)	Einstein; Freud; Picasso; WORLD WAR I; RUSSIAN REVOLUTION OF 1917; LENIN; STALIN; Communist expansion; USSR; WORLD WAR II; division of Europe into Western/Eastern blocs; Berlin Wall constructed (1961); United Nations (1948); Czechoslovakia invasion (1968); Velvet Revolution (1989); European Union; Berlin wall falls (1989) / Glasnost	Russian revolution of 1905; RUSSIAN REVOLUTION OF 1917	Mustapha Kemal; ibn-Saud; rise of OPEC; Iranian revolution; fundamentalist reaction; Taliban / al Qaeda	GANDHI; India independence	Chinese Republic; Sun Yat-sen; Japanese in Manchuria and North China; Chinese Communists to power; China invades Tibet (1959); Atom Bomb	TOKUGAWA SHOGUNATE; EAST MEETS WEST; African states become independent; apartheid ends (1993)
2000 21st c.	9/11; Iraq war						

QUEST FOR GLOBAL UNITY

EUROPEAN OCEANIC VOYAGE OF DISCOVERY

MUGHAL EMPIRE (1526 - 1858)

EAST MEETS WEST

© chart by Brad Reynolds

WORLD RELIGIONS TIMELINE:
THE WORLD'S GREAT GURU-ADEPTS

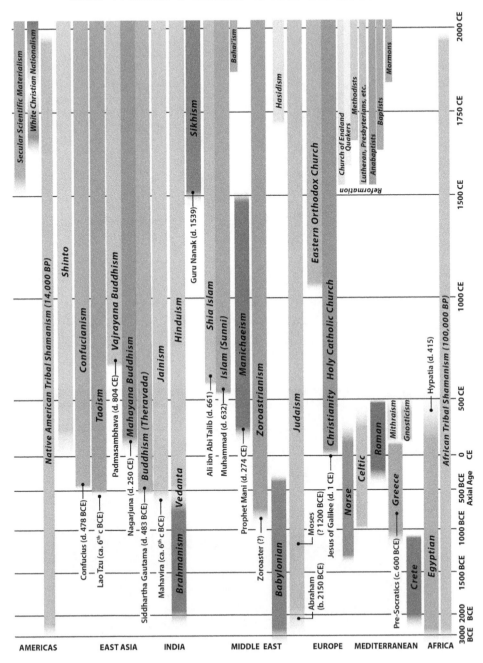

© chart by Brad Reynolds

TWELVE

GURU YOGA-SATSANG: ANCIENT GREECE

GURU YOGA-SATSANG: PRE-SOCRATIC ADEPTS

In the history of the Western World it is seldom understood that at our deepest roots in Ancient Greece there has been a tradition of the Guru-devotee relationship that has been hidden by the shrouds of ignorance and superstition. Since Jesus Christ has always assumed to have been the West's only true Spiritual Master or Adept-Realizer for over two millennia, the Sages and Adepts of Ancient Hellas have only been labeled "philosophers" or "proto-scientists," such as with the term "**Pre-Socratics**" (i.e., those before Sokrates). Yet this only obscures the truth of the West's lost heritage of Enlightened Masters and Awakened Adepts, our "**Western Gurus**" who have been lost and diminished in the pages of history written by unenlightened historians and scholars.

In Ancient Greece, or *Hellas* (in Greek), many of the "philosophers" (from *philosophia*, meaning literally, "lovers of *sophia*") were actually Sages of varying degrees of mystical revelation who were seeking and discovering the deeper truths of life and *kosmos* (a Greek word for the "harmonious order of the universe"). These "**lost Masters**" of the West not only brought their own understanding of Enlightenment (or "Knowledge of the One") to humanity, but many of them were possibly influenced by Enlightened Yogis from the East (a fact unknown to Western historians until recently) as well as being deeply informed by the priesthoods of Egypt and Persia.[1] We can see them as the Western representatives of the Eastern Wisdom tradition thus offering to the West a rich mystical heritage informed by yogic knowledge while still expressing their unique insights as well… yet, hardly anyone knows this. In other words, the West has its own lineage of Adept-Realizers whom we can still learn from and honor.

School of Athens by Raphael (partial), Vatican, Rome, 1510
(left to right) **Parmenides** (yellow shirt); **Sokrates** (green robe); **Heraclitus** (elbow on block)
Plato–Aristotle (center); **Diogenes** (steps)

The so-called "**Pre-Socratic**" philosophers, or those Greek philosophers who were born and taught before **Sokrates** (d. 399 BCE)—include such famous names as Thales, Anaximander, Xenophanes, Heraclitus, Parmenides, Pythagoras, and Democritus (among others)—are more aligned with the tradition of Enlightenment (or God-Realization) than those philosophers who followed in the wake of Plato (himself a disciple of Sokrates). **Plato** (428–348

BCE), and his student-devotee, **Aristotle** (384–322 BCE)—the central figures in Raphael's "School of Athens"—inadvertently set the Western mind on its course of dualism and excessive rationalism thus leading us not only from *mythos* to *philosophia* (a good thing) but also away from *gnosis* (a bad thing).[2] As one perceptive scholar noted: "If Western philosophy is the footnotes of Plato [in reference to Whitehead's famous comment], then the generation of Sokrates and the Pre-Socratics are his bibliography."[3] Nietzsche also emphasized the depth and magnificence of the awakened wisdom tradition of Greece that preceded Plato suggesting the Athenian himself had not one original thought.[4] In *Philosophy in the Tragic Age of the Greeks* (1873), Nietzsche noted:

> Other peoples have Saints; the Greeks have Sages…. In other times and places, the philosopher is a chance wanderer, lonely in a totally hostile environment which he either creeps past or attacks with clenched fist. Among the Greeks alone, he is not an accident.[5]

Before the word "philosopher" was used for those seekers who contemplated the eternal principles (or *arche*) of the living Divine Reality—"The One" (*Hen*) manifesting as the physical cosmos ("the Many")—they were originally called *physikoi* or "those concerned with *physis*" also translated as a "**natural philosopher**" (the term used for a "scientist" until the 19th century). *Physis* (the root word of our "physics" and Latin for "nature"), as the German philosopher Martin Heidegger went to great lengths to demonstrate, was not only seen as "nature" but as the "blossoming emergence" of all things that appear, linger, and pass away within the One Divine Reality.[6] The Pre-Socratics, in other words, were much more than just "proto-scientists" (the category most Western classrooms now teach them as occupying) for they were also full-blown *mystics*, i.e., philosophers with awakened insight into the unfolding nature of existence (*kosmos*).

No longer embroiled in the mythic worldview of earlier generations (instructed by Homer) using myths and stories to explain life in the universe (usually set in poems), these new Pre-Socratic philosophers began using prose to write down their rational inquiry into the Kosmos while still being grounded in mystical contemplation. It's important to note that this pursuit for wisdom was undertaken by both men and women (though mostly men). For example, in Plato's *Symposium* we learn that Sokrates' Guru was **Diotima** of Mantinea (fl. 440 BCE) who taught him the philosophy of Love and Beauty as being ultimate knowledge.[7] During the centuries of the Axial Age (800–300 BCE), each succeeding generation of Pre-Socratic philosophers were taught by a Philosopher-Sage in manner to similar how a Guru would teach, instruct, and discipline a devotee (or disciple) in India. It was a practice built upon *sadhana* or life disciplines, not just ideas. Amazingly, these Greek Adepts now comprise a lineage of Masters and students (partially) recorded in the annals of Ancient Hellas, the roots of Western civilization.

According to some scholars (and the Greek themselves), the Greek's Enlightenment tradition began with **Orpheus** (fl. 7th century BCE), a master yogi who was possibly schooled in India, but certainly learned from Egypt's temples and priesthoods (as reported by the 1st century BCE Greek historian Diodorus Siculus). Orpheus has for ages been considered more myth than man especially since he's preserved in certain Greek tragedies with his bride Eurydice whom he rescues from the underworld of Hades (to lose her in the end). But the Sage who hailed from Thrace (north of Greece in present-day Bulgaria)

Orpheus

had such a major impact on the following centuries of Greek history that the evidence tends to indicate he did in fact exist as a flesh and blood Adept although direct evidence is unavailable. Once again, such sacred teachings do not appear out of thin air (or myths) but come from human Adepts. Yoga scholar Linda Johnsen summarizes:

> Along the banks of the Nile Orpheus would have learned philosophy, ritual, age-old techniques of self-purification, and the mysteries of life after death, a subject of endless fascination for the Egyptians. When Orpheus reappeared in Thrace, he must have seemed like a visitor from outer space. More mature now and fantastically charismatic, he brought back philosophy, science, and ethics beyond anything his countrymen could have imagined….
>
> According to Greek historians, Orpheus taught the twin laws of karma and reincarnation, and the importance of purifying oneself to obtain freedom from the wheel of rebirth. Calm and temperate, he modeled a nonviolent, contemplative lifestyle that included

vegetarianism…. [Some] embraced his new doctrine and lifestyle with fierce commitment. Others felt threatened by his teachings, which promised to overthrow their untamed way of life.[8]

When read from a transpersonal perspective, Orpheus was an Enlightened Sage full of Spirit-Transmission projecting the feeling of Divine Communion (*telete*) to those near him. Legend tells us he even tamed plants and animals with his melodic music and rhapsodic words by transmitting his enlightened bliss through his heavenly lyre (the "electric guitar" of ancient Hellas). Orpheus would become a source of Spirit-Transmission (*Shaktipat*), even influencing others at a distance and through succeeding generations. His words were hammered onto gold plates known as the "**Orphic Tablets.**" For example, one Orphic grave amulet uncovered by archaeologists read: "I am the child of heaven and earth. But my home is in heaven."[9]

The Divine Wisdom of Orpheus would inspire many Greek thinkers and philosophers as well as the common people of the Ancient Greek world (and later, throughout the Western world). The "**Orphic Hymns,**" a collection of eighty-seven hymns, whether composed directly by Orpheus or not (but by his devotees), are now part of our "Divine Library" since they were written down (unlike earlier cults). **Onomakritus** (ca. 530–480 BCE) who brought Orphism to Athens, for example, transformed the earlier myths (in a poem called *Initiation*) so they could be used during Orphic initiation ceremonies to reveal the "Mysteries" of life and death. The Transcendental Teachings of Orpheus would transform the Earth religions of Dionysus and other Nature cults into mystical revelations.

Avatar Adi Da, being born in the West twenty-five centuries later, has proclaimed a deep sympathy with Orpheus who he considers to be the opposite of Narcissus (his archetypal image for the "ego-I" or self-contraction). The Avatar explains: "Orpheus and Narcissus are, characteristically and inherently, opposites—in forever opposition to one another. One of the forever two must die in the eternal struggle—or else neither one can win. Narcissus (or the ego-'I') <u>must</u> die. Orpheus (or the will to ego-transcending Perfection) <u>must</u> win. Or else, the human being—or even the total culture of humankind—will die in contemplation of the mirror that is its own and mortal mind."[10] Adi Da held that the "**Orphic Icon**"[11] reflects true art and life in opposition to the Narcissistic self-centered mode of action and unlove. Hence, in his modern incarnation the

Avatar ecstatically exclaimed:

> I Am Orpheus.
> My Teaching-Work was going to Hades, coming to the common "world".
> I have Accommodated every aspect of ordinary life, but did not look back.
>
> I Am Orpheus.
> My Birth is to wrest you from the results of your conditional preoccupations.
> And I must not look back.[12]

The **Orphic Teachings**, later taught by Orpheus-initiators (*Ophetelete*), directly addressed the death process and the appearance of Light (*Phanes*) that characterizes human souls seeking to be divine and immortal. Set in the atmosphere of the Greek Mystery schools, the Thracian Siddha-Yogi helped transform the Dionysian rituals (such as those at Eleusis and Delphi), which had a long tradition of wild and dangerous ecstasy (*ekstasis*) in archaic Greece, into more disciplined practices of interior contemplation awakened by Apollo (or rationality). The more primitive blood rituals of an earlier age were merged into a more enlightened understanding by the master musician and poet-Adept of Divine Rhapsodies, an initiator with the power to transform.[13] Johnsen again summarizes: "Orpheus was known in ancient Greece as a mystic and religious reformer whose doctrines reshaped Greek spirituality and profoundly influenced the greatest minds of the ancient Western world."[14] The Great Adepts used the symbols of their times to point to the universal *Sophia Perennis* behind (and beyond) the cloak of cultural patterns [see Chapter 8].

Apollo representing the light of reason and cultivated wisdom arrived at these Goddess sanctuaries to tame **Dionysus**, the god of instinctual abandon, through the sacred teachings of Orpheus.[15] This revolution transformed the mystical mind of ancient Greece leading it from *mythos* to *philosophia* into *gnosis*, from religion to philosophy to mysticism.[16] The influence of Orpheus and his strict disciplines for purification, meditation, and right living (including being a vegetarian) was at the heart of the nonviolent mystical tradition of Ancient Greece including those philosophers influenced by the Pythagoreans and other yogic-oriented sects. In *Occidental Mythology*, the scholar Joseph Campbell accurately explains:

> In the Greek world the trend of thought most closely suggesting that

of India was in the line of the Dionysian-Orphic movement, which culminated in the sixth century BCE in the militant puritanism of the Buddha's older contemporary, Pythagoras. In the earlier Orphic system a negative attitude had been assumed toward the world. According to the great Orphic myth, man was represented as a compound of the ashes of Dionysus and the Titans. The soul (Dionysus factor) was divine, but the body (Titan factor) held it in bondage. The watchword, therefore, was *soma sema*, "the body, a tomb." And a system both of thought and of practice, exactly paralleling that of Indian asceticism, was communicated by initiated Masters to little circles of devotees.[17]

These benevolent and esoteric disciplines for the advanced few were taking place during the centuries of Greek wars and warrior-states (involving Sparta, Athens, Corinth, Pergamon, Thebes, and others) fighting amongst themselves and united in perpetual battle with the invading Persians. The clash (and co-operation) between East and West has ancient roots (and is still very active today). Since Orpheus was an important influence on Pythagoras (and other disciples appearing a few generations later), he had a profound impact on Plato as well (who became a Pythagorean during his travels to southern Italy after the death of Sokrates). Once more Johnsen nicely encapsulates: "In the centuries that followed [Orpheus], other Greek Sages continued to explore the mysteries of life, from the origin of the cosmos to the nature of physical reality, from the structure of the soul to the qualities of the Supreme Being…. Like their peers in India, Egypt, Persia, and Palestine, the Greek Sages sought to master both physics and metaphysics."[18] All the wise philosophers of Hellas found inspiration in the original charismatic Master whose wisdom touched the mysticism of India and the mysteries of Egypt, the fountainheads of the Perennial Philosophy [see Chapter 7].

The tradition of Greek Pre-Socratic philosophers, as usually taught in today's universities, began with **Thales** of Miletus (fl. 585 BCE), the first of the "Seven Sages" (or "Seven Wise Men") of the ancient world. Thales initiated a long tradition of succeeding generations of Philosophers teaching and learning from one another in the ancient lands of Hellas and on the coast of Ionia Indeed, it was claimed (by Diodorus) that Thales is credited with the famous saying etched into the walls at the temple of Delphi: "Know Thyself" (*gnōthi seauton*). Thales traveled far and wide to Egypt and the Near East in search of knowledge where he learned about geometry, astronomy, and other early sciences. When he accurately predicted a solar eclipse (in 585 BCE), according to the ancient Greek historian Herodotus, the darkened skies helped end a perpetual war between the Lydians and Medes (in present-day Turkey).

   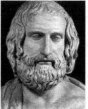 

Thales   Anaximander   Anaximenes   Anaxagoras   Empedocles

Thales' theories were based on keen observation, not experimentation (thus wasn't the scientific method), yet his calculations and measurements made him famous throughout the land. He is the stargazer who supposedly fell into a well since he was looking skyward, the classic absent-mind professor (see Plato's *Theaetetus*, 174A). The brilliant genius founded the Ionian school of natural philosophy developing theories about Nature and the origin of the Earth (though, like the Egyptians, he thought the Earth was flat). From Aristotle's writings it's known Thales claimed "Water" to be the origin (or primordial substance) of all matter probably because it appears in three different forms—gas, liquid, and solid (and since it's the source of life). It's also claimed that Thales thought "all things are full of gods" meaning the world was alive and animated.[19]

His contemporary and most famous student **Anaximander** (fl. 570 BCE), the second great Master of the Milesian school, insisted it was *Apeiron* (the "Boundless" or "Infinite") that was the "First Principle" or fundamental *arche* (ἀρχή). Anaximander believed the Earth was cylinder-shaped with the sun and stars revolving around it. Like Thales, he thought the first living things lived in the oceans and when the sun evaporated some of the seas the ocean creatures came onto land and adapted to new ways of living. Anaximander, in other words, thought humans evolved from sea creatures anticipating the idea of evolution finally proven by Charles Darwin millennia later.

Anaximander then taught his bright student, **Anaximenes** of Miletus (fl. 545 BCE) who was the first to use the word *kosmos*, yet he posited an all-pervading "Air" or *aether* ("Ether") as being the archetypal substance. Anaximenes also draws a connection between this all-pervading "wind" with our breath and soul.[20] Many of these "Pre-Socratics" (or "Presocratics") were attributed by the librarians of Alexandria to have written at least one book they usually called "On Nature" (*Peri Physis*), a comprehensive title ascribed to many of their rational (not mythic) based considerations.[21] Nonetheless, the common presumption of these brightest Hellenes was that reality itself, *physis* (or "nature"), was a living and divine process. Hence the birth of philosophy took place as ***theologoi*** (those concerned with theology or *theos*, "god") transformed first into ***physiologoi*** (those concerned with *physis* or "nature") before becoming philosophers or ***philosophos*** (those who are "lovers of wisdom").

Anaxagoras of Clazomenae (fl. 470 BCE) was a pluralist who believed that because nothing can really come into being, everything must be contained in everything, but in the form of infinitely small parts. In the beginning, all of these particles existed in an even mixture, much like the boundless *apeiron* of Anaximander, but then ***Nous*** ("consciousness"), as the ordering force of the universe, set these particles into a whirling motion. Anaxagoras is importantly credited with bringing philosophy to Athens from Ionia (when he was only twenty years old), living there for thirty years until he was exiled for teaching about lunar and solar eclipses instead of lunar and solar gods.[22] He was the friend and Master-Adept to **Pericles**, the great general of Greece's Golden Age, who fostered Athenian democracy and constructed many of the magnificent temples of Athens including the Parthenon. This esteemed lineage of Master-to-student was actually similar to the Guru-to-devotee relationship and was thus thriving in ancient Greece creating the backbone for Western Wisdom and Real Philosophy. Nonetheless, the depth of transcendental wisdom was still reserved for the advanced-tip few willing to take up the disciplines and learning needed since the average-mode masses still believed in the Homeric myths delighting in the play of gods and goddesses adorning the Greek pantheon and acted out in their public theaters.

Pythagoras of Samos (fl. 540 BCE), perhaps the wisest of them all, was a direct student of Anaximander, who famously claimed he wasn't wise but only a "lover of wisdom," hence he was the first to be called a "Philosopher" (*philosophos*). This well-known Master-Sage and mathematician established his own community on the western Greek island of Samos (off the coast of Italy) based on a religious and philosophical way of life (comparable to an ashram in India). He taught his students to practice many disciplines similar to the Yogis of India, such as vegetarianism, body work, and massage, and inner contemplation, including theories on reincarnation and karma.[23] He is often associated (such as by Herodotus) with "initiation into mysteries, depicting the terrors of Hades, and whose object was to procure a happy state for initiates before and after death."[24] These were probably a combination of knowledge gained from the Egyptians and Orphic initiation cults.

Pythagoras had been schooled by the wisest Greeks and Orphics but also studied with the priests of Memphis (in Egypt), possibly even with the Magi in Babylon.[25] When he returned to Greece after over twenty years in the Egyptian temples, he taught his disciples to explore the harmonious order of the universe (*kosmos*) through mathematical numbers and musical harmonics—the "harmony of the spheres" (*musica universalis*, in Latin).[26] Plato said as much in the *Republic* (530D), "as the eyes are made for astronomy so the ears are made for harmony, and these are sister sciences, as the Pythagoreans say."[27] By using numbers and ratios to understand the universe Pythagoras has been honored as the first true scientist (before Aristotle).

Although Pythagoreans eschewed the written word, this esteemed Master of Samos left a trail of bright students including being an important influence on Plato himself, where he often reworked Pythagorean themes into his dialogues.[28] There was also, for example, **Ameinias** of Elea, who then taught the brilliant **Parmenides** (the great teacher of "The One"); and **Empedocles** of Akragas (fl. 450 BCE), teacher of the "four elements" (Earth, Water, Fire, Air), a doctrine that was taken up a century later by Aristotle thus playing a prominent role in Western thinking up to the Renaissance.

Xenophanes   Parmenides   Heraclitus   Zeno   Democritus

There was also **Xenophanes** of Colophon (fl. 530 BCE), the poet-philosopher who posited there was only "One God," not many gods and goddesses. He famously ridiculed the anthropocentric conceptions of mythology based on the interactions and foibles of human-like supernatural deities as depicted in the

Homeric religion. Xenophanes, who was both a scientist and deeply religious man, complained: "The Ethiopians say that their gods are flat-nosed and black, while the Thracians say theirs have blue eyes and red hair. Yet if cattle or horses or lions had hands and could draw and sculpt…they would depict the gods as having shapes like themselves." Such a strong critique of mythic anthropomorphism struck a blow to the human-like pantheon, even to a Father-like God in the sky (or heavens), yet the philosophers themselves were often ostracized.

Importantly, Xenophanes taught the all-important **Parmenides** of Elea (fl. 475 BCE), whose teaching of "What IS" (or *Hen* "The One") set the tenets of philosophical debate in Ancient Greece for centuries to come. Parmenides is known for only a single treatise, a hexameter poem, that did not wonder about the origin of things but rather asked "What is Truth and how is it different from Illusion and the world of appearances?" In other words, what *is* Being (or the One)? A Goddess chariots him up into the gateways of heavenly light and instructs him on the paradox of Being and illusion (or opinion). Spoken in mythic metaphor the message rings true to the esoteric teachings of Yoga and the Enlightened State, as scholar Linda Johnsen points out: "The Goddess teaches Parmenides to distinguish between eternal unchanging reality and the unstable world of the senses, between the absolute and the relative [the "two truths"]…. In it there is no creation or destruction, no motion of any kind, simply *being* itself."[29] This understanding is similar to advanced meditative *samadhi* states, so it sounds cryptic to those who are not taught by a qualified Adept and engaged in proper disciplines (*sadhana*). However, since the Sage of Elea idealized the eternal Unity as unmoving and unchanging, a problem arose in explaining the relative reality of constant change and motion that was termed "**saving the phenomena**," an occupation that would perplex philosophers for millennia.

Parmenides, in turn, personally taught **Zeno** of Elea (fl. 450 BCE), whose paradoxes became the paradigm of a philosopher's puzzle; both men were questioned by an inquisitive young Sokrates in Athens (see Plato's *Parmenides* dialogue). **Heraclitus** of Ephesus (fl. 500 BCE) was the counterweight to Parmenides' absolute conception (or revelation) of the "One Being" since he emphasized constant change. He was known as "the Obscure" and "the Riddler" because his paradoxical sayings acknowledged a universe in perpetual flux—thus his *arche* was "Fire" or "energy"—while simultaneously teaching a "unity of opposites" governed by *Logos* (or Consciousness Itself). In this case, Heraclitus has often been recognized as the West's counterpart to China's **Lao Tzu**—both living contemporaries in the Axial Age (ca. 500 BCE)—who taught about an elusive *Tao* containing all opposites while paradoxically being One ("The Way" or Tao). Both East and West, in other words, were recognizing the same One and Only Divine Truth (since that is all there really IS).

By the time **Sokrates** was born and schooled (ca. 450 BCE), following centuries of Pre-Socratic Adepts wandering and teaching in Greece, there lived **Leucippus** (fl. 430 BCE), the first real atomist (plus perhaps a pupil of Zeno while being a contemporary of Empedocles and Anaxagoras). He became the teacher to the famous "Laughing Philosopher" (who laughed at silly human follies) known as **Democritus** (fl. 420 BCE), who famously declared: "There are only Atoms and the Void, everything else is opinion" (a proposition not far from that of modern physics). Having studied under many Masters (such as the Persian Magi) from many countries (including Egypt), Democritus wrote encyclopedic treatises on every subject studied in the ancient world (yet, unfortunately, none have survived) where one was supposedly titled the *Great World-System*.[30] The well-traveled "prince of philosophers" is credited as being one of the first strict materialists believing only in physical matter (or solid particles, *atomos*, meaning "uncuttable"), yet this limited perception began with Plato who misinterpreted Democritus' more mystical thinking. Materialism, according to Democritus, is only to be a tool for investigating causality not to be an adequate philosophy of life, a point many modern atomists fail to realize. This Wise Greek Master claimed there was nothing more important than living an ethical life in service to others.

To round off the list let's end with **Diogenes** of Sinope (fl. 400 BCE), "the Cynic," the well-known abstinent-ascetic practicing a renunciate lifestyle in common with disciplined Yogis who lived in extreme poverty yet who were happy and wise. Diogenes is considered a Western example of "Crazy Wisdom" (with stories of him urinating and masturbating in public, for example). This radical method of teaching confounds the conventional mind, yet was done with such brilliance that even **Alexander the Great** (356–323 BCE), soon before he became Emperor of the known world, paid the Crazy Guru a visit to inquire of his Divine Wisdom. As the legend goes the Greek King from Macedonia, who was to become the Ruler of East and West, sought out the cynic for his simple wisdom (or "Divine Ignorance"). When the future Emperor of three continents approached the naked renunciate living in a sewer, the Crazy-Wise Adept bitterly complained: "You are standing in my sunlight!"[31] Diogenes was so unimpressed with the stature of the soon-to-be King of Greece, Pharaoh of Egypt, King of Persia, and Lord of Asia that in response to being in Diogenes' Wise Company, the world conqueror is said to have replied, "If I were not Alexander, then I should wish to be Diogenes." Such recognition-response to an Awakened Adept could not have been more sincere since wisdom is greater than wealth, as conquering yourself is greater than conquering the world.

The point is these Western Sages, whose Wisdom-Teachings are preserved only in fragments (if at all), were practicing a Guru-devotee-like relationship grounded in difficult spiritual disciplines (*sadhana*). In many instances, they seem to have been enlivened with Spirit-Transmission (*shaktipat*) since many were known as healers and purifiers (i.e., if a scholar knows how to recognize this more subtle force). This insight empowers Western history with a genuine lineage of Enlightened-like Teachers and Teachings, a long-lost Wisdom heritage that will only enrich our global future if we can unpack their deeper meanings and truths set within a larger integral context.

The Western scholar of yoga Linda Johnsen, in her excellent book *Lost Masters: Sages of Ancient Greece* (2006, 2016) summarizes: "I believe the time has come to resurrect the ancient Greek Masters, to hear again their perennial wisdom, and to love once more the ageless truths of the active spiritual life they embodied."[32] As wise as it is to study our Ancient Masters living throughout the previous centuries of the Great Tradition, including our "**Western Gurus**," we must also turn our attention to our own modern and current Spiritual Sages and Enlightened Teachers who appear among us in our own time for the very same reason our ancestors did: to help us *realize* the Nondual One *right here* and *now* (and forever hereafter). The history of the past is alive for us to breathe in and receive if only we would listen closely and with free attention. The "Lost Masters" are still "alive" in consciousness and our hearts if we open ourselves to their spiritual transmission and perennial wisdom. But first, let us take a look at how the wisdom of the Masters became fractured moving from mysticism to empiricism as Sokrates' and Plato's famous student, and teacher to Alexander the Great, looked outward more than inward so the West was never the same again.

ARISTOTLE:
FRACTURED FOOTNOTE TO PLATO

ention must be made of the great philosopher **Aristotle** (384–322 BCE), the doctor's son from Macedonia, who taught Alexander the Great and was a pupil-disciple of Plato until Plato's death (in 347 BCE). After that he broke away from Plato's more mystical ideas to establish his own brand of philosophy to influence the Western world even more than Plato since he became an inspiration to science.[33] Because of this, integral philosopher Ken Wilber maintains Aristotle was "the first great fractured footnote to Plato."[34] In other words, Aristotle would dismiss much of the mystical wisdom he inherited from the previous generations of Pre-Socratics (although it's through his better-preserved writings we get much of our knowledge of his philosophical forebears). Like Sokrates, Aristotle was reportedly short and strongly built yet he spoke with a lisp.[35] The trifecta of Sokrates-Plato-Aristotle laid the foundation for the Western world, from Rome to the United States.

Instead of putting his attention on the "other-world" concerns of ideal forms (or archetypes) as taught by Plato, Aristotle shifted his focus on the transformation of natural forms in "this-world." Plato was concerned with *transcendence* (in the "other-world"), while Aristotle focused on *causation* (in "this world") thus representing the fractured dualism of Eastern mysticism and Western science.[36] Consequently, there has been a dynamic debate for over twenty-four hundred years between readers of these two giants of Western philosophy. This was symbolically and beautifully captured by Renaissance painter Raphael's *School of Athens*, where in the center Plato (portrayed as a portrait of Leonardo da Vinci) points upward toward the heavens while the powerful Aristotle holds his hand pointing downward over the Earth.

As a result, Aristotle cannot be considered a mystic Adept and certainly was not an Enlightened Guru although he definitely *intuited* the Divine as the "Prime Mover." He had descended from the lineage of Sokrates and Plato, who had roots reaching back through Pythagoras to Orpheus and the other Pre-Socratic philosophers, many of whom Aristotle strongly criticized for their "other-worldly" leanings. The irony is that although Aristotle is most often associated with "this world," built upon his detailed analysis and classifying of Nature into categories, it was Aristotle's "Ascending God" as a "Prime Mover" (*primum movens*) and "Final Cause" (*telos*) that later St. Augustine (and even Thomas Aquinas) would use to justify Christianity's separation of God from this world of matter. Indeed, since Plato spoke about "this world" as being a "visible, sensible God" (in his *Timaeus*), an emanation of a transcendent "Good," then for Aristotle to refute this mystical notion of Divine Effulgence or Nondual Mysticism is what led Wilber to assert the Unifying Circle of Descent-Ascent was first broken with Plato's brightest pupil (later to be reunited again with Plotinus and other nondual mystics).

Consequently, having inspired aspiring scientists (instead of mystics) down through the centuries the consensus is that Aristotle is "the true father of science and the scientific method, by which we still mean a methodical process of observation, classification, and discovery."[37] This is because Aristotle insisted that reason (and logic) must be linked to the power of observation gained from our senses—it was he who stated "the *fact* is our starting point"[38]— which is why his term for this type of knowledge was *episteme* (later translated into Latin as *scientia* or "science"). Aristotle hardly ever wrote in dialogues, like his teacher Plato, but wrote pioneering treatises on such diverse fields as biology, zoology, physics, astronomy, meteorology, politics, economics, government, aesthetics, poetry, theater, rhetoric, psychology, logic, ethics, and what he called "**first principles**" (later compilers of the Aristotle's works renamed these writings with the word "metaphysics" or "beyond physics" thus distorting Aristotle's original intentions). Aristotle's genius was indeed broad and undeniable, but the transcendent experience (*sophia*) seems to have eluded him.

Plato, on the other hand, saw a static world based on ideal forms and mathematical geometry; Aristotle saw a dynamic one composed of a "Great Chain" of causation that was a combination of matter and form driven by a teleological need to realize its potential (this idea centuries later would inspire

Charles Darwin's evolutionary theories). Oddly enough Aristotle dismissed the Pythagorean ideal that "all things are numbers" or that mathematics was anything other than mental theory (plus he had a disdain for the Pythagorean use of secrecy and cryptic aphorisms). Plato and Aristotle, as Raphael had captured in his huge wall painting, became the defining dualism of the Western world— "this world" versus the "other world." As historian Arthur Herman noted in his magnificent book tracing this dualistic split, *The Cave and the Light: Plato versus Aristotle, and the Struggle for the Soul of Western Civilization* (2013), it was Aristotle who had "an overriding conviction that philosophy must necessarily be an open book, with everything as clear, organized, and straightforward as possible even for the slowest student."[39] This is obviously the point of view of today's modern science and empiricism though empiricism generally rejects Aristotle's notion of substances and essences.

It's ironic, therefore, with today's advanced theories of modern physics based on complex mathematics, such as with Einstein's relativity theories and with quantum mechanics, that Werner Heisenberg (the architect of the "Uncertainty Principle") would conclude: "I think that on this point modern physics has definitely decided for Plato. For the smallest units of matter are, in fact, not physical objects in the ordinary sense of the word; they are forms, structures or—in Plato's sense—Ideas, which can be unambiguously spoken of only in the language of mathematics."[40] Hence, the dualistic debate between Plato's fractured footnotes continues to this day. The West had separated God from this world both in theology and in scientific theory. No wonder the schism in the West is so brutal and debilitating (and in need of dire healing).

This dynamic dualism, however, has driven Western civilization forward through the millennia. There is the idealistic mysticism of Plato, who has inspired artists, romantics, utopians, and mystics throughout the centuries versus the empirical realist Aristotle, who has inspired scientists, theologians, and politicians. Hence author Herman summarily observed:

> Mysticism versus common sense; religion versus science; empiricism versus idealism… two contrasting but highly influential worldviews that have shaped our world, in a perpetual struggle for the soul of Western civilization. Seen in this light, the West's greatest thinkers, theologians, scientists, artists, writers, and even politicians

have found themselves arrayed on one side or the other in a twenty-four-centuries-old battle between the ideas of Plato and Aristotle and the two paths of wisdom they represent....

One path—Plato's path [Ascending or Alpha-mind]—sees the world through the eyes of the religious mystic as well as the artist. It finds its strength in the realm of contemplation and speculation and seeks to unleash the power of human beings' dreams and desires.

The path of Aristotle [Descending or Omega-mind], by contrast, observes reality through the sober eyes of science and reveals the power of logic and analysis as tools of human freedom.... Over the centuries, Plato's and Aristotle's ideas have managed to pull and tug Western civilization in conflicting directions.[41]

These two philosophical giants will spark our imagination and inspiration until we finally heal the fractured footnotes in reaction to Plato's mysticism and awaken to the Nondual Heart of the One Godhead. Only by realizing our *prior unity* will we be able to integrate both the Ascending (other-worldly) and Descending (this-worldly) currents into a view of enlightened wholeness (grounded in an empty-fullness). This is why Wilber concludes the only real solution is the *integration* of both paths of Ascent and Descent:

The One World of Plato/Plotinus fractured into "this world" versus the "other world," and this dualism produced two diametrically opposed and absolutely incompatible World Stances, with two very different (and irreconcilable) views of the "good life," of men and women's ultimate place in the universe, of the object and nature of human destiny... It produced, in fact, two utterly irreconcilable Gods.... The ascending God that takes all things back to the One, or the descending God that delights in the diversity of the Many...

The Nondual answer [of the "unifying Heart"] has always been: do one [ascend], then the other [descend], embracing finally both.... The standard message of all Nondual schools: *transcend* absolutely every single thing in the Kosmos, [then] *embrace* absolutely every single thing in the Kosmos—with choiceless compassion or love.[42]

Our inheritance of the Greek Wisdom Tradition is therefore incomparable to any other in creating our modern world with its dualistic dilemmas. This fractured split shows up everywhere such as with the battle between fundamentalism and democracy, religion and science, mysticism and materialism, or between the Alpha-minded East and the Omega-minded West [see Chapter 9]. This is precisely why students today should study them both closely and learn from whence our own roots arise, and not simply (and arrogantly) dismiss them as "old white guys" (Europeans). As always it is up to each new generation and each person to rediscover for themselves the Divine Heart that unites us all and leads us into the Light by escaping the cave of dualistic darkness and egoic illusions. Such a monumental task that has divided our world (and self) for millennia is best served with help from our Awakened Adept-Gurus who are the link to the Nondual Heart that teaches and awakens us to the Real.

"Golden Chain" — *Philosophia via Praxis*

I n the ancient Greco-Roman world the lineage of Adepts who taught the stream of spiritual knowledge handed down through the generations were known as "**The Golden Chain**" linking us to the Wisdom of the Ages, the *Philosophia Perennis* [see Chapter 7]. In the modern world this movement gave rise to "**secret societies**" in the West (such as with Hermetica sects, Freemasonry, Rosicrucianism, etc.). Their wisdom was not publicly known but was "secret" and often hidden in arcane symbolism, archetypes, and exotic metaphysics.[43] Like the spiritual tradition of India this knowledge and set of practices to realize higher states of consciousness was often passed (or transmitted) from Master to student, from the initiated to the uninitiated, with the utmost care and reverence hidden from public view.

In the West, however, much of this knowledge had to be passed down in secret societies (or cults) outside the Christian mainstream. These "priest-hoods" were often led by a Master-Priest who had risen up the hierarchy of initiation ceremonies for those particular cults. Once the Christian Church rose to power on the waves of political ambition much of these "esoteric" or arcane teachings had to go underground to be hidden from the public and clergy; hence "secret" societies tried to continue the mystical tradition of the West with indoctrinated rituals and esoteric symbols (such as in Western alchemy).

Such linkage to the "ancient" past is like a bright light illuminating its students as they went beyond the limits of Christianity by turning their attention to study and follow the disciplined practices handed down by previous generations of Master-Philosophers who had lived prior to the rise of Christianity.[44] As we've seen, they extended from India to Persia to Egypt, from Orpheus to Pythagoras, from the Pre-Socratics to Plato, from Plato to the Neoplatonists. This Golden Chain of Wisdom flowed past the birth of Christ (A.D.) to influence many great Seers and Philosophers of the past millennia from **Apollonius** (3 BCE–97 CE) to **Plotinus** (205–270 CE) to the luminous **Proclus** (412–485 CE), the last headmaster of Plato's Academy, an institution of learning that flourished for nearly nine hundred years after the Master's death (until the Christians slammed their doors shut). Again, we need to be schooled in the wisdom and history of these Western Masters to reach beyond the exoteric rituals and limited beliefs the Christian Church provides and demands.

PLOTINUS:
BECOMING ONE WITH THE ONE

Perhaps the pinnacle of Greek philosophy peaked with the brilliant **Plotinus** (205–270 CE) who began his career attending the University of Alexandria with its incomparable Library and Museum, in the early 3rd century of the Common Era. In that wonderful cosmopolitan city at the edge of ancient Egypt lying on the shores of the Mediterranean looking out towards Crete and Greece, Plotinus would have had access to the world's cross-cultural currents of intellectual, philosophical, and spiritual teachings. This eclectic gathering ranged from the Goddess cults of Isis and Demeter, the mystery cults of Mithra and the Orphic-Dionysian rituals, much of the Hermetic writings, the Persian Magi, even visiting Yogis from Brahmanic Hinduism and early Buddhism, plus a variety of Gnostic communities, the two most important founders of Christianity, **Clement** (150–215 CE) and **Origen** (184–253 CE), among many others. Alexandria, founded by Alexander the Great in 331 BCE, was where the inquiring student also met his own Guru-Adept, **Ammonius Saccas** (175–243 CE). Plotinus studied with his brilliant Master for eleven years (232–243 CE) before he left on an adventure to India traveling with a Roman army. However, he never made it beyond Persia escaping with his life to finally end up in Rome where he lived until his death (in 270 CE), supported by Emperor Gallienus (218–268).

With such an inherited wealth of wisdom no wonder scholars acknowledge there was no one like the "most divine" Plotinus, such as the respected British philosopher of mysticism W. T. Stace who claimed: "Plotinus was undoubtedly one of the greatest mystics the world has seen."[45] Ken Wilber admirably noted: "Besides being a profoundly original philosopher and contemplative sage, Plotinus was a synthesizing genius of unparalleled proportion… It is only a slight exaggeration to say that Plotinus took the best elements from each school [in the Golden Chain] and jettisoned the rest."[46] Plotinus as much as anyone in Western history (other than Jesus Christ himself) is an example of a Western Enlightened Adept-Realizer teaching about our Divine Condition and the Truth of God ("the Good," in Plato's words). As Wilber recognized: "From Plato the torch of nonduality, the integrative vision, still intact, passed most notably to Plotinus, who gave it one of the most complete, most compelling, most powerful statements to be found anywhere, at any time, in any form, ancient or modern, East or West."[47] Plotinus had directly experienced God and wanted to share it with others so wrote about it as masterly as anyone.

Plotinus not only mastered Platonism and Greek philosophy but was personally enlivened by the "secret" mysticism of Ammonius, who also taught the early Christian scholar (and prolific writer) and ascetic **Origen** (184–253

CE). Ammonius insisted his students swear to secrecy since his transmission was only revealed to the initiated few, not the public (a trait of most Masters, East or West).[48] Plotinus taught about karma and reincarnation and other ideas from ancient India indicating that Indian Gurus also taught in Alexandria. Plotinus, therefore, united the wisdom of East and West by demonstrating the universality of the world's Perennial Philosophy and how we all yearn for God-Realization or *Gnosis-Sophia* [see Chapters 7-8]. For example, he advised his disciples to meditate: "Close your eyes and awaken to another way of seeing. This is a skill everyone possesses but few choose to use."[49] Plotinus' collection of writings *The Enneads* (six sets of nine treatises) was compiled by his principal disciple **Porphyry** (234–305) after his Master's death (in 270 CE). These sacred Western sutras are hard to describe for their range is so great while its pages have inspired generations of mystics and philosophical thought. Even Saint Augustine requested Plotinus' *Enneads* on his deathbed, not asking for the Gospels or Bible.[50]

However, Plotinus himself suffered from bad health for most of his life, reportedly had poor eyesight yet still his concentration was said to be phenomenal, like any Jnani Yogi (from India). Wilber points out that Plotinus had achieved "formless (*nirvikalpa*) samadhi" before experiencing the leap to Nondual Mysticism where he realized "Spirit not only engenders all things; *it is all things*."[51] In this case, the Ascending and Descending currents of the Kosmos (and the individual) are united in the Nondual Heart of "**The One**" (*Hen*). Wilber summarizes the Prior Unity awakened in this Realization: "Flee the Many, find the One [ascent]; having found the One, embrace the Many *as* the One [descent]."[52] Plotinus asks us to ascend (in the mind via contemplation) to the One God that IS Reality to discover our true nature before returning through the intellect (*nous*) to embrace the Many of the Kosmos with love and happiness. This is the Perennial Philosophy taught by all true Masters. Yet Plotinus wrote it down as eloquently as anyone (truly, required reading)— obviously, one of the greatest "Lost Masters"[53] of the West.

Most importantly, as a God-Realized Adept Plotinus' philosophy was a response to his own profound contemplative experiences of the "all-transcending, all-pervading Godhead." Plotinus taught the process of *henosis* (Greek for "union" or "unity") which he defined in his works as a reversing of the ontological process of consciousness via meditation toward no thoughts and no division within the individual being. In other words, his philosophy is *to become* one with The One. Also called **henology**, the process refers to philosophical discourses on The One which appears most notably in Plotinus' writings. The Dominican priest-philosopher Reiner Schürmann describes it as the "metaphysics of radical transcendence" that extends beyond being and intellection.[54] This Neoplatonic teaching has precedents in the Greek mystery religions as well as parallels in Eastern philosophy.[55] But no one in the West reaches the heights of Plotinus on paper (until our current era).

Plotinus taught that from The One the *kosmos* emanates or radiates outward through a stepping down to denser and denser stages (or structures) of existence: from The One down to the higher Intellect (*Nous*) to the World Soul then down to individual souls to Nature and Life then, finally, down to gross or physical Matter. This descending process generates a mandalic hierarchy (or holarchy) of a graded reality that is still ultimately One or a Unity. Wilber openly claims: "It is with Plotinus that the Great Holarchy of Being receives its first comprehensive presentation, although the notion itself, of course, goes back directly to Plato and Aristotle (and earlier)."[56] The great Sage would often confess the paradox of Nondual Realization: "The One is everywhere and yet nowhere."[57] (*Ennead* VI.8.6) Sounds exactly like Zen Buddhism!

Regarding humankind, it was Plotinus who famously observed: "Humanity, in reality, is poised midway between gods and beasts, and inclines now to the one order, now to the other; some men grow like to the divine, others to the brute, the greater number stand neutral."[58] (*Ennead* III.2.8) Evolution or development, in other words, was implicit in Plotinus with his hierarchy of Divine emanation and the turnabout return to The One via contemplative meditation. Wilber therefore observed: "For Plotinus, all development is envelopment,"[59] or better: **"Plotinus temporalized = evolution."**[60] Wilber's Integral Theories on the evolution of consciousness in many ways reflect the timeless wisdom of Plotinus updated to our current times.[61]

We all have descended from the One God through the causal and subtle realms to enter human life and thus we are called to ascend again (beyond the limits of "this-world") in contemplation of the One Nondual Godhead via the evolution of consciousness. In this case Wilber emphasizes that this type of Nondual Mysticism does not reject the world-cosmos (this-world), like the interior-oriented Jnani Yogi will sometimes do (the Sixth Stage Error according to Adi Da), but rather this Enlightened Vision embraces the entire universe and human life—or the Kosmos as a whole—in its divine beauty saturated with compassionate love. In Plotinus, the Descending and Ascending currents of Spirit-in-action are ultimately whole and united in the Enlightened Realization of the One Nondual Heart (to inadequately put it into words).

Significantly, as Wilber strongly notes, Plotinus was interested in rigorous exercises of contemplative meditation on this One Divine Reality, or as he famously stated in the last sentence to *The Enneads*: "The flight of the alone [the individual] to the Alone [The One]." The philosophical system of Plotinus, Wilber emphasizes, is not mere "metaphysics" or a rational mediated "system," but was "the result of actual contemplative apprehensions and direct developmental phenomenology."[62] Plotinus, in other words, hails from the Practicing School, not merely the Talking School [see Chapter 4]. As another scholar summarized: "In the end, Plotinus' system is less of a philosophy than a religion."[63] The Alexandrian Adept himself explained: "Our concern is not merely to be sinless but to be God."[64] (*Ennead* I.2.6) Yet practice and contemplation, according to Plotinus, was to be a "dance" of pleasure and bliss, not one of dread and duty.

The whole point of such philosophy-religion, as all succeeding Neoplatonists emphasize and Arthur Herman explains, is "to be one with God. No one wants to live in the dark cave of illusion. We all want to see the light; and once we discover the true trail, we can retrace the path of the spirit back to whence it came."[65] Plotinus transformed the world of philosophy and people's consciousness to even directly influence the newly emerging Christianity and countless other Western mystics throughout the centuries. He could certainly be counted as a beloved Avatar in human form appearing to teach us about and spiritually transmit the sublime splendor of the Supreme.

After all, it was Plotinus who uttered, "for to be a god is to be integral with the Supreme."[66] (*Ennead* VI. 9.8.) This is why, on his deathbed, when his body was being dropped, his last words (spoken to his attending physician) were: "Try to unite the divinity in yourself with the divine in all things." And so, with his last breath the great Master-Sage of ancient Alexandria and Rome spoke about the goal of yoga: "union with the Divine."[67]

For over two thousand years in the West this enlightening Golden Chain of Wisdom radiated from Orpheus to Pythagoras to Sokrates to Plato and Aristotle to Plotinus, and now to Ken Wilber (among others), who have all been embraced and *transcended* altogether in Avatar Adi Da Samraj. The Avatars and Philosophers, Sages and Saints, indeed, are all speaking to us with the same message about One God. The Golden Chain ultimately leads us all to the One Transcendental White Light free of all chains linking us up in the hierarchy as all forms and conditions swim in Only Light, the Bright.

LOSING AND RE-DISCOVERING *PHILOSOPHIA* IN THE WEST

Tragically this Golden Chain of enlightening wisdom in the West was broken by the ascendency of Christianity, especially after the Roman conquest of Emperor Justinian (482–565) who closed the Academy doors in Athens (in 529), burnt their books, and drove their teachers out of Europe, initiating the backward ignorance of the Dark Ages. Fortunately, the Arabs welcomed many of the homeless philosophers to their academies (such as in Babylon and Jundishapur, in Iraq), wisely preserving many of the Greek's writings. When they were rediscovered centuries later in the libraries of Islamic scholars, their wisdom texts helped initiate the "re-birth" of the Renaissance in Europe as Westerners recovered their lost mystical heritage. This recovered wisdom snapped the West out of its Dark Age of mythic superstition and unenlightened religiosity upheld by the Roman Catholic Church. Soon the Protestant Reformation was set in motion as Christianity (and the secluded priesthoods) had to deal with new ideas and the expansion of knowledge (especially with the rise of science). The Christian West was confused because the wisdom lineage of God-Realized Adepts had been tragically ruptured since Jesus Christ had been deemed the only Awakened Guru worthy of study by the Christian faith [see Chapter 20]; a conclusion I suspect Jesus himself would not have approved.

As we've seen (and will see again in the following chapters), the Great Wisdom Tradition of Enlightened Masters and Adept-Gurus has long existed in other areas around the world. Even today the Yoga lineage of India still thrives with Gurus and Yogis; the Buddha's transmission still lives in their Buddhist Masters and Lamas, and so on; indeed, many practitioners in every tradition are again waking up to recover their esoteric essence in the postmodern world (and emerging Integral Age). New sparks of Divine Wisdom are rekindled in every generation via *Sophia Perennis* leading to ever more astute expressions of *Philosophia Perennis*. Today, our "Golden Chain" is the "Divine Library" of the "Great Tradition"—God's Great Tradition of Global Wisdom—where the Philosophers, Prophets, Shamans, Yogis, Saints, Sages, and Siddhas of world history are now *our* family—our *spiritual* family—whether from East or West, North or South [see Part I]. Let everyone around the globe spend more time even in today's fast-paced world of telecommunications, computers, and digital phones full of mass entertainments (bereft of enlightened teaching), to learn from the fires of wisdom handed down to us from our ancient (and current) Enlightened Masters. They are the Wise Company appearing here to serve our Re-Awakening and God-Realization. We should honor and respect and learn from their fountains of wisdom and divine understanding like our wisest ancestors did.

The parallels between the wisdom taught in ancient Greece (prior to Sokrates) and the Yogis of India is notable, as we saw.[68] Most importantly this divine knowledge (*gnosis*) was based on actual practice (*praxis*) not just *theoria* for it even goes beyond the archetypal theories about First Principles (*arche*) and trying to explain how the Kosmos works. Real practice in ancient Greece (or anywhere) has always involved actual self-transcending contemplative disciplines, including commitments to nonviolence, celibacy, vegetarianism, and sacred rituals (and mantras), thus showing a striking similarity to the practice of Yogis in India. As one modern scholar of an anthology on the lineage of Pythagorean-Platonic-Neoplatonic philosophy put it:

> Platonic philosophy (and especially Neoplatonism [epitomized by Plotinus]) was a spiritual and contemplative way of life leading to Enlightenment; a way which was properly and intrinsically intellectual; a way that was ultimately based on intellection or noetic vision (*noesis*), which transcends the realm of sense perception and discursive reasoning.[69]

Obviously, this sounds similar to the goal of the Eastern Yogas, yet it's only now that scholars in the 21st century are finally realizing the connection that flowed from India to Greece, from East to West long before Alexander the Great brought Hellenic culture to the banks of the Ganges via conquest. As the "Common Era" (CE) dawned after the birth of Christ the **Gnostics**, for example, strove to achieve the goal of *Gnosis* or the knowledge that humanity's true nature is ultimately divine. Yet they too were soon outlawed and destroyed by the emerging Christian Church. They wrote sacred Gospels confessing who Jesus really was (as Christ) but their esoteric knowledge was banned in favor of exoteric political power. Today Gnostic spirituality is still ridiculed as condemning "this world" in favor of the "other world," a bias perpetuated by Western (Omega-minded) thinking [see Chapter 9]. Not surprisingly the *gnosis* of the Gnostics shared a deep affinity with the supreme goal of *samadhi* (or "divine ecstasy") such as spoken about in the *Yoga Sutras* of Patanjali or coming from the transmission of *Satsang* with an authentic Adept-Guru. Again, the Perennial Philosophy arises anew in each succeeding generation because its wisdom (*Sophia-Gnosis*) eternally transcends culture or century [see Chapter 8].

Although extant evidence of this connection is slim, many of the disciplined practices first initiated by Orpheus in ancient Greece (ca. 700 BCE), then followed by others, seems to reflect the yogic wisdom techniques from the East (including from the temples of the Persian Magi).[70] Orpheus, Pythagoras, and other Masters taught methods of purification and detachment from sensual pleasures, as do the Yogis of India. This is done to reawaken us to our innate Divine Condition during this lifetime while subduing the more primitive or primal human passions, like Plotinus said. Importantly, these philosophical (and spiritual) practices were geared to see the Light of God in death—revealing the immortality of the soul—a long-sought goal for many religions and ancient Mystery Schools. These teachings are also similar to what was taught in the inner sanctorum of the Egyptian temples thus showing a universal similarity between all esoteric practices. Many Greek philosophers (such as Orpheus, Thales, and Democritus) journeyed to the Egyptian temples, while others went to Persia, to learn about their "secret" esoteric wisdom which included geometry and other ancient sciences. Others may have ventured as far as India or met their Masters and Yogis along the Silk Road and other extensive trade routes between Asia and Europe.

Indeed, Plato himself clearly declared the true purpose of philosophy was to prepare for death—"the real philosophers train for dying, and to be dead is for them less terrible than for all other men" (*Phaedo*, 67cd)—thus proclaiming our life's goal was to become God-like (*Theaetetus*, 176b). One perceptive modern Hellenic scholar, Algis Uzdavinya, in his excellent book *The Golden Chain* (2004) wonderfully summarizes:

> In the original Orphico-Pythagorean sense, philosophy meant wisdom (*sophia*) and love (*eros*) combined in a moral and intellectual purification in order to reach the "likeness of God" (*homoiosis theo*). This likeness was to be attained by *gnosis* [divine] knowledge…. Thus, the true philosopher was *theios aner*, the divine man, who contemplated the light of the noetic gods [first principles] and tried to live philosophically, i.e., in accord with the divine wisdom.[71]

This points to the fact that the Perennial Philosophy of these highly-evolved Western philosophers was not simply logical or rhetorical discourse, but was, as Uzdavinya points out, "essentially a way of life: not only inseparable from 'spiritual exercise' [*sadhana*] but also in perfect accord with cosmogonical myths and sacred rites."[72] This *philosophia* (based in *Sophia*) is the "Practicing School" of self-transcendence, not the "Talking School" of philosophical pontification. Significantly, these practices were to be undertaken by following the instructions given by the Master to the initiate in order to stimulate (via transmission) genuine *Gnosis* or Divine Awakening in his or her student-devotee. We must not overlook or forget the fact that a Western version of Guru Yoga was alive and active in the misty mystical roots of the West (although most scholars miss that conclusion).

Consequently, the initiatory-teachings found in the inner sanctuaries of the West were (and are) in harmony with the temples and forest retreats of the East. And today these sanctuaries still exist and thrive, most notably, for example, on Avatar Adi Da's island sanctuary of Naitauba (in Fiji) and his other sacred sites in the United States (and elsewhere). This means we can still access this "Wisdom Chain" and its spiritual potency, which I highly encourage everyone to do [see Part III]. Indeed, yoga ashrams and Buddhist sanghas and other spiritual communities are scattered throughout Europe, Asia, Australia, Africa, and the Western hemisphere of the Americas, sprinkled around the world on every continent cultivating greater compassion and Divine Awakening to everyone. India is still a land vibrantly alive with spiritual potency with its many ashrams and Yogi-Saints, Sages, and Siddhas, as Johnsen eloquently explains in closing her book:

> The yoga lineages are still alive, and techniques for translating intellectual knowledge into living experience are still taught there [in India]. Enlightened Masters aren't just inspiring legends; you can still find Saints in India. But, thank God, we don't have to choose between the two traditions [East or West]—we can, if we wish, learn from them both.
>
> Perhaps with the help of Eastern insight, we can forge anew the Golden Chain that was broken when the ancient Greco-Roman academies were closed. Extinguished fires can be relit. In these dark, intolerant times, that ancient light could illuminate the world.[73]

The depth of these insights and the sacred connections between East and West cannot be underestimated. The ancient Greek Philosopher-Sages embody the wisdom of Awakened Adepts standing at the heart of the Western world, the deepest roots of our current civilization, the home of democracy and rationalism. They are in harmony with the best of the East since they reflect the universal *deep structures* of human consciousness. To uncover this sacred stream or "Golden Chain" of Enlightened Wisdom-Teachings that preach about revealing our innate divinity is to align ourselves with the deepest "Wisdom of the Ages," the universal truths inherent in all spiritual exercises leading to Divine Revelation from any time or any place (or for anyone).

The universal and timeless tenets of *philosophia perennis* continue to reverberate in our time as well. We too can *realize* what has "always already" been realized by the world's greatest Philosophers and Mystics: *We are God! Tat Tvam Asi! Know Thyself!* For only this Truth (*aletheia*) sets us free from bondage to the dualistic dread of Narcissus, the ego-I set amidst the fractured boundaries of our socio-cultural existence keeping us trapped in the illusions of politics and a world at war with itself lost in the dark caves of ignorance [see Prologue].

Now is the time, as *all* Adepts have *always* declared, to Wake Up and be Free to love everybody and every little thing as if we're all One since we are! Wisdom Masters from around the world are our sacred link to the Truth, they are our "Golden Chain" to the most Ancient Wisdom of the past and the most Enlightened Wisdom of the present shining a bright light to a better future. *If we heed their Call to Listen, Hear, and See.*

GNŌTHI SEAUTON

Chapter 12 Endnotes

1. See: Thomas McEvilley, *The Shape of Ancient Thought: Comparative Studies in Greek and Indian Philosophies* (2002); Walter Burkert, *The Orientalizing Revolution: Near Eastern Influences on Greek Culture in the Early Archaic Age* (1992); Linda Johnsen, *Lost Masters: Sages of Ancient Greece* (2006, 2016).

2. See, for example: *From Religion to Philosophy* (1912) by F. M. Cornford; *In the Dark Places of Wisdom* (1999) by Peter Kingsley; *The Cave and the Light* (2020) by Arthur Herman.

3. Frank Marrero, "Plato's Inheritance" (2002, unpublished).

4. See: Friedrich Nietzsche, *Philosophy in the Tragic Age of the Greeks* (written ca. 1873; 1996).

5. Ibid, pp. 32-33 [caps added].

6. See: Martin Heidegger, *An Introduction to Metaphysics* (1959).

7. See: Plato, *Symposium* (210a-212b), where in Diotima's view, love (Eros) is a means of ascent to contemplation of the Divine. For this Priestess-Philosopher taught Sokrates (in her Wise Company) that the proper use of love for other humans (i.e., Eros in its many forms, from sexual to aesthetics) is to direct one's mind to the greater love of Divinity.

8. Linda Johnsen, *Lost Masters: Sages of Ancient Greece* (2006), pp. 21-22.

9. Ibid., p. 27.

10. Adi Da Samraj, from the Essay "The Eternal War Between Orpheus and Narcissus: The Culture of ego-Transcendence Versus The Anti-Culture of ego-Reflection" in *Transcendental Realism* (2010), p. 180.

11. Adi Da Samraj has done several Works of Art and Literature using the "Orphic Icon" of "Orpheus" including: *The Orpheum Trilogy* consisting of three transformative novels: *The Mummery, The Scapegoat Book,* and *The Happenine Book*; and a series of abstract artworks portraying the archetypes of Orpheus and Eurydice called Orpheus and Linead (see: Catalog of solo exhibition at Sundaram Tagore Gallery, NYC, 2010).

12. Adi Da Samraj, from "Art Is Love" quoted in *Adi Da Samrajashram* Journal, Vol. 1, No. 3, 2012, p. 46.

13. See: Karl Kerényi, *Dionysus: Archetype; Image of Indestructible Life* (1976), p. 262: "Orphism may be characterized as a kind of private religious exercise…. The figure of Orpheus, who was not only a solitary strolling singer but also an initiator of men and youths."

14. Linda Johnsen, *Lost Masters: Sages of Ancient Greece* (2006), p. 20.

15. See, for example: *The Birth of Tragedy* (1872) by Friedrich Nietzsche; *Orpheus and the Roots of Platonism* (2011) by Algis Uzdavinya; *The Mysteries* (1955) edited by Joseph Campbell; *Eleusis* (1967) by Carl Kerényi; *The Road to Eleusis* (1998) by R. Gordon Wasson, Albert Hoffman, Carl Ruck.

16. See: F. M. Cornford, *From Religion to Philosophy: A Study in the Origins of Western Speculation* (1912, 1991, Princeton University Press).

17. Joseph Campbell, *Occidental Mythology: The Masks of God, Volume 3* (1964, 1991, NY: Arkana), p. 183.

18 Linda Johnsen,*Lost Masters: Sages of Ancient Greece* (2006), p. 28.

19. See: *The Presocratic Philosophers* (1957, 1983, 2nd ed.) by G.S. Kirk, J.E. Raven, M. Schofield, p. 95.

20. Ibid., pp. 158-159.

21. Ibid., p. 102.

22. Ibid., p. 353.

23. Linda Johnsen, *Lost Masters: Sages of Ancient Greece* (2006), p. 35.

24. See: *The Presocratic Philosophers* (1957, 1983, 2nd ed.) by G.S. Kirk, J.E. Raven, M. Schofield, p. 221.

25. Linda Johnsen, *Lost Masters: Sages of Ancient Greece* (2006), p. 39.

26. See: Joscelyn Godwin, *The Harmony of the Spheres: The Pythagorean Tradition in Music* (1992, Inner Traditions).

27. See: *The Presocratic Philosophers* (1957, 1983, 2nd ed.) by G.S. Kirk, J.E. Raven, M. Schofield, p. 214.

28. Ibid., p. 215.

29. Linda Johnsen, *Lost Masters: Sages of Ancient Greece* (2006), p. 48.

30. See: *The Presocratic Philosophers* (1957, 1983, 2nd ed.) by G.S. Kirk, J.E. Raven, M. Schofield, p. 405.

31. See: Cicero for the story of Alexander standing in Diogenes' sunlight; Plutarch reports that both masters died on the same day in 323 BCE, but this is not confirmed.

32. Linda Johnsen, *Lost Masters: Sages of Ancient Greece* (2006), p. 5.

33. See: *Plato & Aristotle: The Lives and Legacies of the Master and Pupil* (2020) by Charles River editors.

34. Ken Wilber, *Sex, Ecology, Spirituality* (1995), p. 349; pp. 320-321: "If Western civilization is a series of footnotes to Plato [as Whitehead suggested], the footnotes are fractured.... These two strategies—denying creation, seeing only creation, the Ascenders and the Descenders—have been the two major forms of fractured footnotes to Plato that have plagued Western civilization for two thousand years, and it is with these fractured footnotes that the West (and not it alone) has deeply and cruelly carved its initials on the innocent face of Heaven and Earth."

35. Arthur Herman, *The Cave and the Light* (2013), p. 42.

36. See: Arthur Herman, *The Cave and the Light: Plato Versus Aristotle, and the Struggle for the Soul of Western Civilization* (2013).

37. Arthur Herman, *The Cave and the Light* (2013), p. 43, following *Introduction to Aristotle* (1967, New York: Modern Library), edited by Richard McKeon, p. xiii.

38. See: Ibid., p. xxi; Aristotle quoted on p. 44: "We must trust the evidence of the senses, rather than theories, and theories as well, as long as their results agree with what is observed."

39. Ibid., p. 43.

40. Werner Heisenberg quoted in *Quantum Questions* (1984) edited by Ken Wilber, p. 51 (from Werner Heisenberg: "The Debate Between Plato and Democritus," 1971).

41. Arthur Herman, *The Cave and the Light* (2013), pp. xxi-xxii.

42. Ken Wilber, *Sex, Ecology, Spirituality* (1995), pp. 355-357.

43. See, for example: Manly P. Hall, *The Secret Teachings of All Ages: An Encyclopedic Outline of Masonic, Hermetic, Qabbalistic and Rosicrucian Symbolical Philosophy* (1928, 2011); also see: F. M. Cornford, *From Religion to Philosophy* (1912, 1991).

44. See: *Lost Masters: Sages of Ancient Greece* (2006, 2016) by Linda Johnsen; Thomas McEvilley, *The Shape of Ancient Thought* (2002); Manly P. Hall, *The Secret Teachings of All Ages* (1928, 2011); among many others.

45. W. T. Stace, *The Teachings of the Mystics* (1960), p. 110.

46. Ken Wilber, *Sex, Ecology, Spirituality* (1995), pp. 332-333.

47. Ibid., p. 331.

48. See: Linda Johnsen, *Lost Masters: Sages of Ancient Greece* (2006, 2016), p. 128.

49. Plotinus quoted in *Lost Masters* (2006, 2016) by Linda Johnsen, p. 141.

50. See: Linda Johnsen, *Lost Masters: Sages of Ancient Greece* (2006, 2016), pp. 142-143.

51. Ken Wilber, *Sex, Ecology, Spirituality* (1995), p. 335.

52. Ibid., p. 326.

53. See: Linda Johnsen, *Lost Masters: Sages of Ancient Greece* (2006, 2016).

54. See: "Henology" in Wikipedia, retrieved February 2021.

55. See: Paulos Gregorius, *Neoplatonism and Indian Philosophy* (2002, SUNY Press).

56. Ken Wilber, *Sex, Ecology, Spirituality* (1995), p. 333.

57. Plotinus, *The Enneads* (1992) translated by Stephen McKenna, p. 691 [all quotes from *The Enneads* are from the McKenna translation, unless otherwise noted].

58. Plotinus, *The Enneads* (1992) translated by Stephen McKenna, p. 188; also see: Ken Wilber, *Up from Eden* (1981), p. ix (first sentence of Wilber's "Preface").

59. Ken Wilber, *Sex, Ecology, Spirituality* (1995), p. 337.

60. Ibid., p. 491.

61. See: Ken Wilber, *Sex, Ecology, Spirituality: The Spirit of Evolution* (1995, 2001).

62. Ken Wilber, *Sex, Ecology, Spirituality* (1995), p. 336.

63. Arthur Herman, *The Cave and the Light* (2013), p. 143, referenced David Knowles, *Evolution of Medieval Thought* (1962), p. 21.

64. Plotinus, *The Enneads* (1992) translated by Stephen McKenna, p. 39.

65. Arthur Herman, *The Cave and the Light* (2013), p. 142.

66. Plotinus, *The Enneads* (1992) translated by Stephen McKenna, p. 705.

67. See: Linda Johnsen, *Lost Masters: Sages of Ancient Greece* (2006, 2016), p. 141; the word yoga means "to be yoked" or "to unite."

68. See: Thomas McEvilley, *The Shape of Ancient Thought* (2002); Mircea Eliade, *A History of Religious Ideas, Volumes 1-3* (1981, 1982, 1988); Joseph Campbell, *The Masks of God, Volumes 1-4* (1964, 2018); Walter Burkert, *The Orientalizing Revolution: Near Eastern Influence on Greek Culture in the Early Archaic Age* (1992); Peter Kingsley, *In the Dark Places of Wisdom* (1999); Georg Feuerstein, Subhash Kak & David Frawley, *In Search of the Cradle of Civilization* (1995, 2001); among many others.

69. Algis Uzdavinya, *The Golden Chain: An Anthology of Pythagorean and Platonic Philosophy* (2004), p. xv.

70. See: Thomas McEvilley, *The Shape of Ancient Thought* (2002).

71. See: Algis Uzdavinys, *The Golden Chain* (2004), p. xv, xvii.

72. Ibid., p. xi.

73. Linda Johnsen, *Lost Masters: Sages of Ancient Greece* (2006), pp. 206-207 [caps added].

Thirteen

Guru Yoga-Satsang: Judaism

Guru Yoga: Abrahamic Lineage

Prior to the Greek worldview that was governed more by the will of men (than by gods) coupled with the first glimmerings of scientific investigation, there were the tribes and nations of the Middle East. This Fertile Crescent was the birthplace of agriculture and villages (Jericho, for example, is one of the world's oldest villages) leading to cities—hence "civilization"—and the rise of monotheism. These diverse peoples (also including Chaldeans, Assyrians, Babylonians, etc.) included the Persians, Jews, and Arabs who would become known for following One God, a Creator God, known as Ahura Mazda, Yahweh, and Allah, respectively. The roots of three of the world's largest religions, Judaism, Christianity, and Islam have descended from the single patriarch known as **Abraham** (originally Abram, meaning "father of many"). Abraham (born in Ur, Sumeria) was the founder of the Covenant between God and the Jewish people (traditionally said to have lived between 2000–1900 BCE). Often these Middle Eastern religions are at war with one another (even today) which is horribly ironic (and tragic) since Abraham's two sons (half-brothers), **Ishmael** (son of Hagar) and **Isaac** (son of Sarah), are the progenitors of the Arab and Jewish people, respectively. It was Isaac's son, **Jacob** (grandson to Abraham), who had twelve children that supposedly evolved into the twelve tribes of Israel. Many of today's warring factions in the Middle East, in other words, are actually blood-related descendants from the same paternal "father" (or ancestor) which makes the tragedy of the war between Arabs and Jews, Palestinians and Israelis, even more disastrous (and deluded).

With its 3000-year-old existence, Judaism is one of the world's oldest living religions. Its monotheism is founded on the belief that YHWH (pronounced Yahweh, sometimes Jehovah), originally a tribal god among many, is the One God, the Creator of all. Therefore, human beings should follow God's "laws" as given to them by his Prophets, Saints, and Sages. Uniquely, according to their tradition, God made a series of covenants with the Jewish people, including a promised Messiah, so they see themselves as "chosen," yet their history calls this into doubt (yet their belief in their special covenant with God carries on indefinitely). Compared to the other Abrahamic religions—Christianity and Islam—there is a greater emphasis on "this world," on their nation, their land, and their traditions, instead of focusing on an afterlife.[1] Only the scientific materialism of the modern West, which dispenses with God altogether, places more emphasis on this physical and political world.

According to the original Jewish oral tradition, Yahweh promised the elder **Abraham** (who was over 70 years old) that he would establish a new nation, **Israel**, in the land of Canaan on the eastern Mediterranean shores. A few generations after Abraham led his tribe to Canaan (land occupied by the Canaanite tribes) to establish Israel (based on Yahweh's promise), resistance to their settlement and famine drove them to Egypt (following **Joseph**) where after some time they were forced into slave labor for massive building projects causing dissension and doubt in their God. **Moses** (ca. 13th century BCE), an Israelite who had grown up as an Egyptian prince, famously led them out of Egypt back to the land of Israel on a delirious forty-year journey known as "**the Exodus**" (according to the Jewish scriptures). Some scientists and geologists today have hypothesized that possibly the eruption of Thera (Santorini) off of Crete (around 1500 BCE) is what generated the so-called twelve plagues (pestilence, frogs, red rivers, etc.) that are now part of the book of Exodus (but the evidence is not conclusive). On the way back to the Promised Land, Moses ascended Mount Sinai (on the Sinai Peninsula) to receive the **Ten Commandments** etched on stone tablets giving the Israelites the "laws of God" that they were to follow religiously with dire consequences if they failed. First among these was to worship no other gods but the "Lord thy God," the One God of Israel. However, the indigenous tribes of Canaan were animistic so there was a constant tension and battle going on between their ancient polytheism and the newly emerging monotheism, even among the Jewish people.

Upon returning to their new homeland to battle the indigenous tribes living there, the Israelites as a confederation of twelve tribes (with a landless tribe, Levi, acting as priests) were ordered by Yahweh through his **Prophets** to kill all the surrounding tribes (including women and children) without mercy to reestablish their ancient kingdom. This covenant to obey Yahweh's laws and commandments for perpetuity lies at the heart of the special relationship between the One God of the Bible and the Jewish people.

| Abraham | Moses | Star of David | David | Solomon |

Unexpectedly, an invading influx of Philistines with iron weapons subdued the bronze weapons of the Israelites prompting an organized army of resistance initially led by **Saul** (reign ca. 1037–1010 BCE), Israel's first king, yet he was defeated and earned God's disfavor. His son-in-law, a shepherd named **David** (the singer of Psalms, slayer of Goliath) became the new king (reign 1010–970 BCE) leading a professional army with iron weapons to end the Philistine threat. The Kingdom of Israel thrived, reaching as far south as Egypt and north to Mesopotamia, and was passed to David's son, **Solomon** (reign 970–931 BCE), who was legendary for his wisdom (and sensual songs) and having many foreign wives, including the Queen of Sheba, possibly from Arabia or even Ethiopia who, as legend has it, stole the **Arc of the Covenant** (holding the Ten Commandant tablets) when she fled her husband. Solomon launched monumental building projects including **Solomon's Temple**, Israel's first permanent house of the Lord (that is currently prophesied to be rebuilt as the Third Temple on the Temple Mount during the future Messianic Age, right where the Islamic Dome of the Rock shrine is located, a perpetual problem for the two religions). This traditional Jewish history is incorporated into both Christianity and Islam making it the backbone of Western religious history.

In 586 BCE, when the Pre-Socratics were thriving in Greece, the Jewish kingdom of **Judah** (where Jerusalem stood) was conquered by Nebuchadnezzar, the new king of the Babylonian Empire. After sacking Jerusalem and destroying their temple, the Jews were exported in exile as captives to Babylon where the term *Jew*, meaning someone from Judah, became common.[2] Without their temple, the books of Moses (that would become the *Torah*) became even more vital as the exiled priests and scribes began to reassess their relationship to Yahweh. They began to write down their oral history to record the **Hebrew Bible**— known to Christians as the *Old Testament*—thus creating the primary sacred texts of Judaism (which would, over time, include a long tradition of commentaries). However, only fifty years later (in 539 BCE), the Persian Emperor Cyrus the Great sacked Babylon allowing the Jews to return to their homeland of **Judea** (now known by its Greek pronunciation). Back in Jerusalem, they rebuilt their temple (the Second Temple) and prospered as a province of the Persian Empire. Some Jews stayed in Babylon where their views appeared to have been influenced by the Persian religion of Zoroastrianism by showing a greater emphasis on the

resurrection of the dead, cataclysms of end times, and a coming new age with a promised redeemer or Messiah.[3]

In 485 BCE, the priest **Ezra** left Babylon with a complete *Torah*, in the form we know today, to return to Jerusalem where he and the governor **Nehemiah** set up a theocratic state with power vested in the priesthood or **Pharisees**. These reforms set forward a new direction for the Jewish religion and people. The Persian Empire was defeated by Alexander the Great in 333 BCE, and after his death (323 BCE), the land of Judea went through an intense Hellenization process (as did the Macedonian's entire empire). Over the next several generations this created tensions between various dynasties sparking several rebellions among the people until Jerusalem was recaptured by **Judas Maccabeus** (in 160 BCE) as worship at the Second Temple was restored (which is now celebrated during the Jewish holiday of Hanukkah). By 63 BCE the Romans took over Judea as a province of Rome led by the native **King Herod** (72–41 BCE) who was appointed King of the Jews in 37 BCE rebuilding the Temple on a grand scale yet creating dissent among the people over his collusion with Rome.

Around 3 BCE, **Jesus from Galilee** was born in Bethlehem, supposedly to become the prophesied Jewish Messiah and free the Jews from Roman rule. However, Jesus was not a political leader but was a Spiritual Master, a Guru-Adept, here to teach about love and worshiping "the Father" (or God) in Spirit and Truth (John 4: 23-24). After just three years of preaching throughout Judea, the Romans (via Pontius Pilate) arrested the holy Sage and condemned him to death by crucifixion, the common method of Roman execution. To quell the rising Jewish rebellion after Jesus was crucified (ca. 33 CE), the Romans destroyed the Second Temple burning Jerusalem to the ground in 70 CE sending Jews once again into an exiled diaspora, many immigrating into Europe and Russia, splitting into **Sephardic Jews** (those moving to the Ottoman Empire after being in Spain) and **Ashkenasic Jews** (those moving to eastern Europe).

Their tradition continued to thrive in population and commerce, however, especially by becoming Europe's bankers (since it was not a sin for Jews to charge interest to non-Jewish people as long as they were honest and fair). Numerous holy men continued to comment on their sacred scriptures, thus inspiring their exiled communities to maintain their tradition and ethnicity (where according to *halakha*, or Jewish religious laws, a Jew by birth must be born to a Jewish mother although conversion is accepted). Nevertheless, anti-Semitic discrimination followed the Jewish people wherever they went, often ostracized into separate communities (called "ghettos") until the 18th century Enlightenment when European countries finally granted civil rights to their Jewish citizens.[4] The Jewish population reached its peak in 1939 (with 17 million world-wide) until the horrific mass murders conducted by the Nazis in the 20th century Holocaust (killing over 6 million). After Germany was defeated (in 1945) the Zionist movement helped established the state of **Israel** (in 1948) with the support of the United Nations giving the exiled Jews their own modern nation but displacing the Palestinians (setting the stage for today's troubles in the Middle East). This long and tortured history of the Jewish people is what helps unite them as a world religion and ethnic group, grounded in their religious practices and sacred scriptures.

JEWISH SACRED SCRIPTURES

The history of the Jewish people is contained in the first 24 books of the Christian ***Bible*** (Greek for "the books"), by far the best-selling book of all time (with an estimated total sale of over five billion copies), the first book printed by Gutenberg's movable type printing press. The Hebrew Bible or *Tanakh*, the most sacred collection of writings for Judaism (the "Old Testament" for Christians), was compiled and written over a period of a thousand years, from approximately 1100 to 100 BCE.[5] The word *Tanakh* comes from the initials of its three divisions: *Torah* (Law), the *Nevi'im* (Prophets), and the *Ketuvim* (Writings).

For the Jews, the first five books (Genesis, Exodus, Leviticus, Numbers, Deuteronomy) are called the ***Torah*** (called the ***Pentateuch*** by Christian scholars) contains the "laws" or "instructions" and early history supposedly written by Moses in Hebrew (but actually written by several authors). Beginning with **Genesis** (the "Creation Story"), God created the universe (starry heavens), the Earth, and all living creatures, then Adam and Eve (the first man and first woman) who were later expelled from God's Garden of Eden, these "books" contains tales stretching from Noah to Abraham to Moses to Elijah, from Jacob to Jeremiah to Ezekiel to Samuel, from Amos to Zechariah, among many others. The Hebrew Bible uses myth and history full of visionary Saints and Prophets, ordinary men and women in their struggle for life and prosperity by recounting Jewish history as led by God's demands for their people. It uses a variety of literary genres incorporating historical chronicles, mythic tales, parables, wisdom literature, song lyrics, prophecies and apocalypses, plus the voices of inspired Prophets who claim they are speaking directly for the One God YHWH.

Over time (from 300 BCE to about 200 CE) hundreds of Jewish religious texts appeared whose authority was later rejected by Jewish scholars, now classified into three collections; *Apocrypha* ("concealed" writings), *Pseudepigrapha* ("writings with false subscriptions"), and **Dead Sea Scrolls** (recently discovered between 1947 and 1960 in the Qumran Valley on the northwest shore of the Dead Sea).[6] During the first five centuries of the Common Era there was a flowering of literary activity among Rabbis generating verse-by-verse commentaries on the *Tanakh*, collectively known as the *midrash*, culminating in the texts of the *Mishnah* and the *Talmud* (a collection of commentaries by Rabbis from 200 to 500 CE), including the *Pirkei Avot* ("Chapters of the Fathers") a vast body of ethical instruction and maxims drawn from the *Torah*.

During the Medieval Ages, after the close of the Rabbinic period, writers still penned their commentaries, the most famous being **Moses Maimonides** (1135–1204) who created thirteen articles of faith that are still a regular part of Jewish prayer services.[7] In any case, true mysticism and knowing God, the Transcendent Creator and Source of all, is not known by simply studying scriptures, tradition, and history, or merely doing rituals—that is the "Talking School" of exoteric religion. Real God is only revealed through the ecstatic mystical experience—call it God-Realization (or Enlightenment)—which comes from the "Practicing School" exhibited only by true Mystics, regardless of time or culture.

ZOHAR:
KABBALAH MYSTICISM

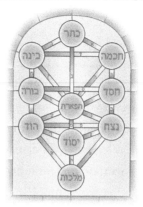

In Jewish mysticism, a principal text is the *Zohar* or "Book of Splendor," the root text for Kabbalistic mysticism written by **Moses de Leon** (1240–1305) between 1280 and 1286 CE. Although Kabbalistic mysticism attempts to reveal an esoteric meaning to the sacred texts of the Jewish people, the idea of *union* with God, let alone *identity* with the Divine, is taboo and generally not part of Jewish mysticism. Most Jewish Prophets, for example, speak of visions and voices—a "Throne Mysticism" (such as with Ezekiel's vision of seeing God on a Throne)—which although profound (and genuine) is a lesser type of mystical experience (typical of the Fifth State of Life), one that still falls short of the ecstatic identity found in Hindu and Buddhist mysticism.[8] There is an acknowledged "joining" with the Divine (known as *devekuth*, which literally means "adhesion") but there invariably remains a sense of distance between the Creator and the creature.[9]

Kabbalah, in Hebrew, literally means "reception tradition," for it is essentially an oral tradition of initiation given by an evolved Master or Rabbi acting as a personal guide into its doctrines and practices to avoid the dangers inherent in mystical experiences. Since the 12th or 13th centuries, this approach has used classical Jewish scriptures to explain esoteric teachings in cultivating a relationship between the unchanging, eternal God (*Ein Sof*) and the mortal, finite universe of God's creation. However, the *Zohar* tends to speak to a narrow Jewish audience, especially in its commentary on many passages from the *Torah*, as it reveals the "hidden" or esoteric meaning behind the words and stories of Jewish tradition. Nonetheless, as inspiring and brilliant as it is to Jewish students and scholars it does not include references to any experience or concept of identity with God.[10]

The *Zohar* teaches about a doctrine of emanation called the ten *sefirot*, but this is not a call to identify with the Divine Condition. Even the attribute of Divine Being called *Ein Sof*, or the formless Infinite, is considered unknowable and ineffable so God is "hidden" and totally incomprehensible to the human mind.[11] Although contemporary scholars are infusing these terms with a more mystical apprehension (based on their own experiences), the Jewish faith itself adheres to its theistic orientation, not to a fully Enlightened (or God-Realized) view. Yet, nonetheless, as world religion scholar and practitioner, Lex Hixon points out: "This mystery of Divine Life lived secretly through human life is revealed in the Jewish mystical tradition of Kabbalah.... While the traditional Kabbalist moves toward this secret union [not identity] with the Divine through esoteric study and contemplation in solitude, the Hasidic Master disappears into God's Life by transforming ordinary daily existence into the holy dance of ecstasy by perceiving God only."[12] This approach of God *only* is difficult to appreciate because of its intense simplicity and thus requires disciplined practice under the guidance of a competent and God-infilled Rabbi.

| Maimonides | Moses de Leon | Shofar | Spinoza | Baal Shem Tov |

The **Hasidic** movement, founded by Rabbi **Israel ben Eliezer** (1698–1760), known as the **Baal Shem Tov**, a Jewish mystic and healer from Poland, comes closer to the Enlightened Vision since it offers a more mystical and joyous approach to Judaism, particularly for the laity.[13] These Hasidic practitioners strive to become "souls on fire," following Moses who said (Deuteronomy 4:24): "For the Lord thy God is a consuming fire," an invitation to an ecstatic embrace of the All-Pervading Divine Presence felt only within.[14] Hixon goes on to clarify: "Any crystallized religious tradition can be melted by the fire of ecstasy, allowing Divine Presence to flow again in all its original power. This release of holy power, this rediscovery of the fullness of Divine Life abiding in the human heart, occurred with dramatic intensity through the Baal Shem Tov, his disciples, and the lineages of soul masters that flows from him."[15] Once again, we can see, regardless of tradition, time, or culture, it is the Awakened Adept who shines God's Light the brightest leading our own soul to touch the "fire" or "Brightness" that is Real God.

Interestingly, although Jewish Prophets had long forecast a "**Messiah**" (or "Anointed One") who would come to establish God's kingdom on Earth, the Jews failed to recognize Jesus himself as their Messiah since he was not a "savior" providing political power but an Adept transmitting spiritual power (*shaktipat*). While Orthodox Jews still believe one day a Messiah will come to rule Jerusalem and rebuild the Temple, other branches of Judaism (such as the **Reform Jews**) lay less stress on the Messianic prophecy by emphasizing their cultural traditions and beliefs by educating the younger generations through study and ritual ceremonies and how to live the moral ethics and law (or *torah*) of the Jewish faith.

Hence the Jewish people continue to prosper in the modern world. Their emphasis on ethical education places importance on charity, respect for life and others ("Love thy neighbor as thyself"), observing the Holy Days (such as the Sabbath, Yom Kippur, Hanukkah, the Festival of Lights, and others), plus honoring their elders (among other customs). Importantly, private prayer lays at the heart of the Jewish faith including using the *siddar*, a Jewish prayer book of blessings traditionally spoken while wearing a small skull cap (*kippa* or *yarmulke*) and prayer shawl (*tallit*). Public prayer and communal rituals are also the center of Jewish life practiced at a *synagogue* (meaning "gathering" of ten or more). An ancient musical horn typically made of a ram's horn, a *shofar*, is often used to open and close religious ceremonies. The most important day of the week is the **Sabbath** ("set apart as holy"), a day set aside for rest and worship (which for Jews is on Saturday; for Christians on Sunday). As with most religions, the cycle of life from birth to death has special ceremonies such as circumcision (on the eighth day after birth for baby boys) and adolescent initiation rituals called *bar mitzvah* (for boys) and *bat mitzvah* (for girls), as well as celebratory weddings of marriage.

Naturally, these religious practices include a special reverence for their spiritual leaders and **Rabbis** (or Ravs "spiritual teacher"). Yet the fullest mystical relationship is cultivated with the great Jewish Teachers, known as Zaddiks or Rebbes, which comes from the fact that these individuals are bearers of *baracha* or the "Blessing of God" (literally, "to kneel, to bless, to adore on bended knee"). Not only can a Jew find direction, guidance, and an example for living from such an ordained person, but they are considered to be a direct means of connection to the Divine Presence.

ZADDIKS:
RIGHTEOUS ONES

Τhis tradition of the **Zaddik** or **Tzadik** (literally, "righteous one,") is a saintly or spiritually-disciplined person who was claimed by the *Old Testament* (Proverbs 10:25) to be "the foundation of the world." The *Talmud*, the central text containing rabbinic laws, ethics, customs, and history, declares that the Zaddik "stood at the very heart of the cosmos and could, by virtue of his meritorious deeds, intervene to remove the decrees of heaven."[16] According to Jewish mysticism it was by virtue of the Zaddik that the world was sustained, thus highlighting the extreme importance of the Master-student relationship in cultivating spiritual understanding in the Jewish community.

It was the later Hasidic movement, as mentioned, begun in the 18th century in Eastern Europe with the saintly figure of the **Baal Shem Tov** that a full and concrete meaning of the term "Zaddik" emerged. In Hasidic Judaism the mystical Zaddik is a divine channel exhibiting such outstanding holiness and piety that each generation has a person who has the potential to become a Messiah, often seen as a miracle worker as well as a mystic. Such a person serves a similar function as a Guru does in India (and now in the West). The Hasidic movement, therefore, brought forward numerous great Masters, or Hasidic "**Rebbes,**" to guide a generation of aspirants seeking for spiritual truth. The term "**Hasid**" means someone who was a "disciple" in a circle of followers gathering around the Hasidic Rebbes or Zaddiks. These exuberant Masters were not just an authority based on rabbinical lineage or scholarship alone but they have cultivated spiritual strength and purity by developing a connection to the Divine Presence, making them special messengers of the One God. Such teachers, or potentially Enlightened-like Masters, are still necessary to fully (and purely) practice the Jewish faith, even in the modern world. Seeing such advanced practitioners in relation to the esoteric Guru-devotee relationship, like in Satsang, shines a brighter light on their potential to serve the transformation of consciousness and enact a more profound relationship with the Transcendent (not mythic) God for serious students and disciples.

On the secular level, there have been numerous famous Jewish intellectuals and philosophers with worldwide influence, such as the philosopher **Baruch Spinoza** (1632–1677), the Dutch-born Jew who wrote about a spiritual rationalism (laid out like mathematical theorems), and the brilliant **Albert Einstein** (1879–1955), the famous 20th century physicist who created the theories of relativity. Politically, for example, there was **Golda Meir** (1898–1978) a Russian-born American who was a young schoolteacher in Milwaukee, Wisconsin when she became involved in the Zionist movement before moving to Palestine to later become Prime Minister of Israel in 1969 (however, it must be noted, she was staunchly anti-Palestinian); or **Ruth Bader Ginsburg** (1933–2020) the second woman and first Jewish woman to sit on the United States Supreme Court having a profound impact on women's rights.

Special mention should be made of **Rabbi Zalman Schachter-Shalomi** (1924–2014, born in Poland) who fled the Nazis arriving in the United States as a teenager to become a well-known founder of the **Jewish Renewal** movement, which began in the early 1970s, intending to invigorate Jewish life with greater spirituality and celebration. Reb Zalman has long participated in interfaith dialogues, including a famous trip to India in 1997, along with a group of other Jewish leaders, to speak with the Dalai Lama. Even **Bob Dylan** (b. 1941 as Robert Zimmerman), widely regarded as one of the greatest and most popular singer-songwriters in American history (winner of the Nobel Prize for Literature in 2016), was born a Jewish-American, and although he has studied and honored his Jewish roots, at one time he became a Christian convert, yet generally is considered to be more spiritual than religious. Overall, Dylan has used his music to explore religion and man's relationship with God (or a higher spiritual power) while himself admitting that music is his conduit to faith, his way of praying. All of these Jewish people, plus many more, have helped change the world for the better.

In today's world, however, many (or most) modern Jews do not strive to realize their genuine divine potential but rather consider such aspirations eccentric relics of a past religious tradition or as an import from the East. They prefer to put their faith in the One God (or Creator) and their traditional beliefs or in their economic and military-political power. Being traditional defenders of monotheism, new generations of Jewish people are becoming more nonsectarian—for example, some call themselves **JewBu** (a "Jewish Buddhist") since they've embraced the universalism (and enlightened wisdom) of Buddhism (beyond its religious rituals)—while others strive to be more integral in order to promote world peace and tolerance for all religious faiths and people regardless of ethnicity (including for the Palestinians). Amen to that!

Barak

Chapter 13 Endnotes

1. See: *Scriptures of the World's Religions* (2018) by James Fieser and John Powers, p. 322.

2. Ibid., p. 323.

3. Ibid., p. 324.

4. Ibid., p.327.

5. Ibid., p.327.

6. Ibid., p.329.

7. Ibid., p.331.

8. See, for example: W. T. Stace, *The Teachings of the Mystics* (1960), p. 221.

9. See: Gershom G. Scholem, *Major Trends of Jewish Mysticism* (1954), p. 5.

10. See: W. T. Stace, *The Teachings of the Mystics* (1960), p. 223.

11. Ibid., p. 223.

12. Lex Hixon, *Coming Home: The Experience of Enlightenment in Sacred Traditions* (1978, 1989), pp. 110-111.

13. See: *Scriptures of the World's Religions* (2018) by James Fieser and John Powers, p. 326.

14. See: Elie Wiesel, *Souls on Fire: Portraits and Legends of Hasidic Masters* (1972).

15. Lex Hixon, *Coming Home: The Experience of Enlightenment in Sacred Traditions* (1978, 1989), p. 111; it is notable, in my opinion, that during his lifetime Hixon discovered Adi Da Samraj (then Bubba Free John) and was so impressed with his Spiritual Transmission or "Fire Baptism" that he hosted and introduced the film about Adi Da's early Teaching-Work and ecstatic Transmission intensity titled *A Difficult Man* (1975).

16. *Talmud* quoted in *Love of the God-Man* (1990), by James Steinberg, p. 158, which quoted Arthur Green, "Typologies of Leadership and the Hasidic Zaddiq," *Jewish Spirituality*, Vol. 1 (New York: Crossroad Publishing Co., 1987), p. 132.

FOURTEEN

GURU YOGA-SATSANG:
CHRISTIANITY

GURU YOGA:
CHRISTIAN DESCENT

hristianity acknowledges there is only one true Guru-Adept in the figure of **Jesus Christ** who they proclaim is the "Son of God" (who himself claimed to be the "Son of Man"), thus he's the object of Christians' contemplation and prayer. Keeping attention on the Master is in fact the method of Satsang; however not for the purpose of living in heaven forever or surviving the end times as mythic Christianity preaches. Jesus can be rightly seen as an Adept-Guru, for after being Baptized with Holy Spirit (an initiation of *shaktipat* or Spirit-Baptism by the ascetic John the Baptist), then after fasting for forty days and nights and overcoming all temptations to acknowledge Only God, he went to Galilee where the people "saw a great light" in his Company (Matthew 4:16).

The Teaching-Work of Jesus had been initiated so he began to call forth his first two disciples, Peter and Andrew, to "Follow Me, and I will make you fishers of men" (Matthew 4:19); then he issued the same call to James and John: "Follow Me!" (Matthew 4:21). This is a disciplined call to devotional renunciation—"For whosoever will save his life shall lose it: and whosoever will lose his life for My Sake shall find it" (Matthew 16:25). By recognizing their Master's Divine Presence they dropped their conventional living and work to enter Satsang with their Guru. Soon Jesus's circle of disciples numbered a dozen (according to the "New Testament" in *The Bible*).

As previously mentioned, the relationship between Jesus and his twelve disciples (later known as the twelve Apostles) exemplifies the Guru-devotee relationship. The Divine Adept calls everyone to strict discipline (*sadhana* or "spiritual life"), such as when he says: "Sell whatsoever thou hast, and give to the poor, and thou shalt have treasure in heaven; come, take up the cross, and Follow Me" (Mark 10:21). Such a hard school (*Satsang*) is the same call that all genuine Gurus make, including Adi Da Samraj. They expect their disciple-devotees to be prepared for the esoteric teaching about Real God awakened with Spirit-Baptism and developed through yoga and meditative contemplation (*sadhana*).

Jesus Christ   **Saint Peter**   **John the Beloved**   **Saint James**   **Saint Matthew**

On an exoteric level, however, within the Christian faith there has been a tradition of "spiritual guidance," where a member of the priesthood or clergy, often called a "spiritual director" or "minister," will advise aspirants and their congregation on sacred and secular matters. This is the exoteric (or "outer") wing of the Christian faith, a very valuable one for the community and social cohesion and thus it is a *legitimate* (via "horizontal translation" as opposed to *authentic* "vertical transformation"[1]). Spiritual guidance during times of tragedy and normal life events (such as with birth, dying, funerals, marriages, family crisis, etc.) is invaluable as a way to serve people during hard times and difficulties. Tragedy and suffering, losing loved ones and enduring hardships, are a fact of life, often throwing into question the belief in a benign and loving God, therefore, counseling by religious authorities often helps maintain "the faith" (and the role of the Church). There have been many "spiritual guides" for the average masses throughout Christian history as they provide moral and ethical direction rather than explicit Spirit-Transmission or Awakening Power. Thus, while the spiritual guide, priest, or minister helps direct people in their personal lives, it is still Christ (or the Holy Spirit) that provides the overriding inspiration and authority for a Christian.

A true Christian mainly follows (in theory) the Teachings of Jesus, their enlightened Sat-Guru, or "**Christ**" (*Khristos*, Gk.) the "**Anointed One**" sent by God to give guidance in realizing spiritual understanding of "the Father" (or God). Unfortunately, Jesus's Teachings are often distorted by myths and other Church rules, whether Catholic or Protestant, thus they too often stray from the Master's original intent. Nonetheless, the words of Christ, such as his divine utterances known as the "**Sermon on the Mount**," provide comfort and profound enlightened love and insight, especially when people read the first four Gospels of the *New Testament* for themselves (and thus directly listen to Jesus's purportedly recorded words). The remaining books, including the letters and teaching of St. Paul, and especially the "Book of Revelation," are another matter altogether (and will not be discussed here).

Desert Fathers **Desert Mothers** **St. Anthony** **St. Augustine** **Thomas Aquinas**

In the esoteric (or "inner") wing of Christianity, there is the monastic and celibate tradition that has produced powerful spiritual authorities based on their ascetical and yoga-like practices grounded in intense devotion to God through the Adept Jesus Christ. This includes, for example, the **Desert Fathers** (along with the **Desert Mothers**) who were the elders, hermits, and monks among a group of early Christian ascetics living in the Egyptian, Palestine, and Syrian deserts beginning in the 4th century CE, which continued for centuries.

The most famous of these desert fathers was **St. Anthony** (d. 356 CE) who was traditionally considered Christianity's first monk and thus inspired the millennial-old tradition of Christian monasticism. Yet Christianity as a faith and philosophy was not built upon ascetics who were usually only an inspiration, at best, to the ecclesiastical clergy and congregations of the average masses. The fact is the Christian Church, whether Catholic or Protestant, has never fully understood the esoteric message given by Jesus of Galilee as a Guru-Adept with his call to God-Realization via Spirit-Baptism. They only acknowledge it in ritual and perhaps in hidden theological discourse.

The famous **Augustine of Hippo** (354–430 CE), also known as Saint Augustine, was an important early Church Father whose writings helped establish the philosophical foundation of Western Christianity by integrating Platonic philosophy. Nonetheless, he could not be considered an Enlightened Adept simply because he felt (and taught) the sense of feeling separate from God. He strove for *union* or communion but not mystical identity with God through faith in the miracle of Jesus Christ. Augustine lived at the end of the Greco-Roman world as Rome fell to the invading barbarians so he showed a depth of doubt and individual conscience not seen before in the ancient world as he openly confessed his sins and limitations in his writings. His famous book *Confessions*, which inspired Christians for millennia, still missed the mark of mystical realization. His utopian tome titled *The City of God* provided a vision of a Heavenly City (not an Earthly City) and so created a mythological and exoteric interpretation of Jesus's Teaching, not an esoteric one.

Nearly a thousand years later, **Thomas Aquinas** (1225–1274 CE) was another Christian Saint who used rational philosophy based on the newly rediscovered writings of Aristotle to justify religious faith (consequently he integrated Aristotelian philosophy into a Church worldview that had, up to that time, been mostly influenced by Platonic thought). Nonetheless, he too failed to realize *identity* with the Divine which is the true purpose of real religion. While these were profound philosophers and inspiring forces for the good (what we would call the Fourth Stage of Life, according to Adi Da), these noble minds still distracted people from realizing the Divine for themselves, the error of the Western-Omega mind [see Chapter 9]. The realization of the **Saint**, which is based on devotion to God, still feels separate from God which is why devotional faith is needed. The **Sage**, on the other hand, realizes *identity* with God (a heresy for Christians).

Over the centuries Christian Saints would struggle with different levels (or states) of consciousness revealing either *union* with a personal God or *identity* with the nondual Godhead (as known by the Sage). Out of the monastic Christian tradition there arose several Saints whose degree of God-Realization transcended their mythic religious heritage (i.e., the exoteric limits of the institutionalized Church) thus making them genuine Mystics. However, such mystical status in Christianity often led to being criticized and jailed and, at times, condemned to death, even burned at the stake, especially with comments advocating any identity with God Almighty. According to Church doctrine, only Jesus is permitted to confess: **"I and the Father are One"** (John 10:30), a statement of the Enlightened State realized by the Adept of Galilee. Church officials, who tend to be more concerned with wealth and rituals (or exotericism), prefer to see mystics or people who *realize* God through direct experience as being dangerous to their ecclesiastical authority. This is part of the reason for the taboo against Gurus to this day in the West because it is part of the West's Judeo-Christian heritage that influences secular culture as well.

| St. Francis of Assisi | Meister Eckhart | St. John of the Cross | St. Teresa of Avila | Giordano Bruno |

Other important Saints of Christianity include **St. Francis of Assisi** (1181-1226), the ecstatic ascetic and patron saint of animals and the environment who founded the Order of Friars Minor (known as the Franciscans), who believed commoners should be able to pray to God in their own language; **Meister Eckhart** (1260-1328), the German mystic-theologian who was condemned as a heretic by Pope John XXII but who was one of the greatest and most articulate mystics the West has ever produced; **St. Teresa of Avila** (1515-1582), a prominent Spanish mystic and co-founder of the Carmelite order, along with her contemporary **St. John of the Cross** (1542-1591), author of

Dark Night of the Soul were major mystic figures in the Catholic Reformation, both of whom inspire people to this day (whether Christian or not). There was also **Giordano Bruno** (1548-1600), an Italian Dominican friar, mathematician, and philosopher who proposed the infinity of the universe, yet he was burned at the stake by the Roman Inquisition for heresy; nevertheless, his martyrdom helped inspire the European Age of Reason. Such Saints, however, were restrained by the Church's limited views on mysticism only to be appreciated and honored by later generations through their exquisite writings and thus canonized into "saints" long after their death.

| Eastern Orthodox Jesus Christ | St. Seraphim of Sarov | Father John of Kronstadt | Saint Silouan | Our Lady of Vladimir |

In addition, there is the **Eastern Orthodox** "subtradition" of Christianity especially prominent in Russia, which required an aspirant to place himself under the guidance of a "**spiritual father**" or *staretz*, a charismatic spiritual leader whose wisdom of God stems from ascetic discipline and intensive prayer and contemplation. The guidelines for this relationship calls for full submission to the spiritual authority of the staretz, who would serve their student-disciple's connection to Divine Grace Itself.

The most famous staretz of modern times was the Russian mystic **St. Seraphim of Sarov** (1759-1833), who is remembered for extending the monastic teachings of contemplation and self-denial to the average layperson and who also taught that the purpose of Christian life was to acquire the Holy Spirit.[2] There were also other eminent figures, such as the Russian **Father John of Kronstadt** (1829-1909), a striking and somewhat unconventional figure who was also deeply pious, immensely energetic and beloved; plus the modern-day Greek "Monk of Mount Athos," **St. Silouan** (1866-1938), an Eastern Orthodox monk whom Thomas Merton has described as "the most authentic monk of the twentieth century." We would do well to study the lives and teachings of these great Christian Masters, ideal examples of the higher Stages of Life (especially the Fourth to Fifth Stages of Life) grounded in Divine Communion with the Holy Spirit (or Presence of God).

Nonetheless, there has generally been a strong resistance in the Christian tradition to attribute Divine Awakening or Enlightenment to anyone other than Jesus Christ. This, therefore, places a severe limitation on the West's understanding of the true Guru-devotee relationship. In fact, due to the predominance of myths about salvation in the afterlife and such dire prophecies like Armageddon and the Rapture, etc., the true Spiritual Power of Christ (or *Christus*, L.) as Enlightened Consciousness is diminished and corrupted. Yet once a person of faith puts their attention on the life and teachings of Jesus himself as an Avatar or Divine Incarnation of the One Supreme Reality (or "Real God"), and listens to Christianity's greatest Saints as being sincerely devoted to their Guru-Adept from Galilee, they will see the template of the genuine Guru-devotee relationship in action. They will find that this sacred relationship should be honored and instructive in cultivating real spiritual life and in establishing a loving relationship with an authentic Siddha-Guru or Awakened Adept.

SAINT JESUS OF GALILEE: DEVOTIONAL MYSTICISM

Jesus Christ from the region of Galilee—and from the city of Nazareth— born in 3 BCE (in Bethlehem) is the Awakened Adept standing at the root of the Christian tradition and religion, and for good reason. At one time (in 1982) Adi Da admitted: "I would say that there is a basis in the

'Confessions' or self-descriptions of Jesus [such as 'I and the Father are One'] that Jesus had himself entered into the Realization of the [Enlightened] Seventh Stage of Life, and there is some indication in the *New Testament* that he may have Taught the Non-Dualistic Wisdom to at least a few others (such as Nicodemus)."[3] Yet, this is not how Jesus is generally perceived in today's most populous world religion where he is perceived as a "Savior," which to a large degree is an egoic point of view hoping to be "saved" so the separate self can exist forever and live in heaven after death with deceased family members and friends based just on their belief.

This Savior myth is, however, not true esoteric religion but simply exoteric belief and faith. Adi Da goes on to explain: "In any case, Jesus of [Galilee] has historically been more mythologized than remembered. And he has been blatantly transformed into a symbol for justifying worldly activity and social-political power, whereas he was a Spiritual Master who passionately called his hearers to repent of all worldly ambitions and follow him into the Mysterious Domain of Divine Being."[4] As is often the case the worldly exoteric religion (or political power) corrupts the actual Teachings of the Adept so we must learn to distinguish the difference. This is why we as humankind need to study God's Great Tradition of Global Wisdom and embrace its entire breadth as our universal inheritance. We need to see past mythic religion and convert to True Religion. Only then can we sift the esoteric teachings (and practices) from the chaff of exoteric myths.

Jesus is obviously a Great Adept; an Enlightened "God-man" sent to serve us all to enter the "Kingdom of the Lord" but in *esoteric* (not mythic) terms. His teaching-demonstration of compassion and love to others and deep devotion to God has inspired billions throughout the centuries. As Jesus is recorded to have openly taught in several Gospels of the *New Testament* (Matthew 22: 34-40; Mark 12:30-31; Luke 10: 25-28): "Thou shalt love the Lord thy God with all thy heart, and with all thy mind, and with all thy strength. This is the First Commandment. And the Second is like it, namely, 'Thou shalt love thy neighbor as thyself.' There is none other commandment greater than these." Precisely. But how many truly listen?

Nevertheless, like with all the Abrahamic religions, these types of phrases are reduced to address the position of the separate self as moral instruction, not as encouragement for direct union (or identity) with the Lord. This is why Adi Da later reassessed Jesus to be more as a Realized Saint (predominantly of the Fourth and Fifth Stages of Life), a compassionate guide for the masses not necessarily a Guru-Adept offering ultimate Divine Enlightenment. Adi Da explains:

> Jesus himself (even as he is shown in the "New Testament" Gospels) stood outside institutionalization, yet (paradoxically) he became the most institutionalized and the most mythologized human being in history. Consequently, there are countless versions of "Jesus of Galilee" in everybody's thinking (and in everybody's talk)....
>
> Jesus of Galilee (as the principal figure of the "New Testament" Gospels) should be understood to be a Spiritual Master of the Fifth Stage degree. He stood apart from institutions and the institutionalization of his function. He was a simple itinerant, a wanderer. He spoke very critically of many things, and was, essentially, simply Blessing people—with his healing Blessing, his teaching Blessing, and (in the case of those who were sufficiently prepared) his Spiritual Blessing.
>
> There is a tradition that suggests Jesus Transmitted his Spiritual Blessing privately, to an "inner circle" of those of his followers who were most prepared to receive the (Fifth Stage) esoteric instruction and the Spiritual Transmission that would enable them to participate in Divine Communion through the internally "Up"-turned psycho-physical process of Spiritual development and Spiritual Ascent.[5]

Only if we look deeply beyond the inherited tradition of the Christian religion and its mythology does Jesus become the real Christ leading us to full God-Realization in union with the Nondual Godhead. This is because Jesus's esoteric teachings have been hidden or destroyed, such as those ttaught in the Gnostic Gospels, for example, which were banned and outlawed by the early Christian Church (especially after the Nicaean Council of 325 CE, and later in 381 CE). The real spiritual teaching of Christ was diminished when canonized into the Gospels of the *New Testament* as Jesus's true religion was corrupted to become a religious cult with worldwide political as well as social reach. The rest, as they say, is history.

Jesus Christ | **Paramahansa Yogananda** | **Adi Da Samraj**
(from Shroud of Turin) | (1893–1952) | (1976)

Jesus's true teachings can be best understood in their spiritual essence only if you turn to other God-Realized Adepts who can help explain their deeper meaning. For example, I have found great benefit in studying the interpretations offered by Paramahansa Yogananda (1893–1952), author of the highly popular and influential *Autobiography of a Yogi* (1946), a book where he interprets the esoteric teachings of Jesus as presented in the *New Testament* with stunning clarity and insight. Yogananda (as taught by his Master-Guru Sri Yukteswar), who is reflecting the view of Yoga (and Spiritual Ascent), saw the Christian "Trinity" as being: (1) "**God the Father**" is the Transcendental Absolute (*beyond* vibratory creation); (2) "**God the Son**" is "Christ Consciousness" or Enlightened Awareness (existing *within* vibratory creation); and (3) as the "**Holy Ghost**" which *is* the Spirit of God manifesting creation.[6] All three are aspects of One God, as Sri Yukteswar clarified: "It is the Spirit of God that actively sustains every form and force in the universe; yet He is transcendental and aloof in the blissful uncreated void beyond the worlds of vibratory phenomena."[7] According to the Yogis, we all have the potential to *realize* our Christ Consciousness—or knowledge of God—in this lifetime and thus become a "Son [or Children] of God" ourselves, as Yogananda explains:

> All [humans] have been divinely created, and must someday obey Christ's command: "Be ye therefore perfect, even as your Father which is in heaven is perfect" (Matthew 5:48). "Behold, what manner of love the Father hath bestowed upon us, that we should be called the sons [children] of God" (I John 3:1).... The millions have not utilized their "one lifetime" to seek God, but to enjoy the world—so uniquely won and so shortly to be forever lost! The truth is that man [humankind] reincarnates on earth until he [or she] has consciously regained his [or her] status as a son [or daughter] of God.[8]

Yogananda collected his esoteric considerations in a magnificent two-volume set titled *The Second Coming of Christ: The Resurrection of the Christ Within You* (2004). This highly recommended masterwork of inspiration takes the reader on a profoundly enriching journey through the four Gospels, verse-by-verse, illuminating the universal path to oneness with God taught by Jesus to his immediate disciples. Although perceived by most to be a great Saint and Savior, which he certainly was, the great Sage from Galilee, when seen rightly, is indeed an Awakened Adept, an Enlightened Guru in full Communion with God the Father (the Transcendental Absolute). Seen with spiritual eyes, Jesus is a wonderful example of Ascended Mysticism where God is Guru; Guru is God, a true "Son of God"—"I and the Father are one" (John 10:30). The Christian Church itself is founded on Jesus's divinity as a man, even if they do not quite understand what that means (but have only mythologized its meaning). This is the real reason why his Spirit-Transmission is still powerful today, opening the hearts of countless believers. Yogananda makes this clear by distinguishing between "Jesus" and "Christ" in the following passage from his introduction:

> There is a distinguishing difference to be made between *Jesus* and *Christ*. His given name was Jesus; his honorific title was "Christ." In his little human body called Jesus was born the vast Christ Consciousness, the omniscient Intelligence of God omnipresent in every part and particle of creation. This Consciousness is the "only begotten Son of God," so designated because it is the sole perfect reflection in creation of the Transcendental Absolute, Spirit or God the Father.[9]

Overall, as a Teacher for the average-mode masses (in Adi Da's Seven Stages of Life model) Jesus is best seen as an epitome representative of the Fourth and Fifth Stage of Life, one of real devotion in *ascent* to the Transcendent Divine. Jesus was a true Saint, an extremely laudable approach, as millions of followers of Jesus know. The "descent" of the Holy Spirit (represented by the image of the dove) is the reception of Divine Blessing and Awakening, a Fourth Stage characteristic. His "Ascension" to God after his crucifixion represents the Fifth Stage phenomena of yogic-kundalini ascent where the cross represents the body and his crucifixion the sacrifice of self (or "ego-death"), thus he's seen as an Ascended Saint or Yogi. At best, his Transfiguration represents "translation" into the Divine Light of God's Transcendental Radiance (hence the potential for Seventh Stage Enlightenment).

Worship of Jesus among Christian believers mostly involves (Fourth Stage) Devotional Mysticism, not Yogic (or Fifth Stage) Mysticism, nor is it Enlightened (Sixth and Seventh Stage) Mysticism [see Appendix I]. Unfortunately, most Christian believers today still are associated with magical and mythic (or prepersonal) stages of development, not transpersonal ones of true awakening and awareness. They all too often, therefore, make Christ into a cultic figure. Christianity was hijacked by the mythic mind generating cultic behavior for the masses while turning scientists away and leaving Mystics out altogether. This disaster of Western religion can only be overcome by listening to the wisdom of other true Adepts, such as provided by Paramahansa Yogananda and Adi Da Samraj (among others, including some within the Christian tradition, such as with Meister Eckhart and Teresa of Avila).

Madonna & Child	**Jesus at 33**	**Crucifixion**	**Transfiguration**
(Raphael)	(Heinrich Hofmann)	(Raphael)	(Raphael)

Jesus does offer hope for traversing the trials and tribulations of a difficult human life by transcending the sufferings of samsara and sin in an evil world (which, according to Biblical myth, has been condemned ever since "the Fall" from God's Grace in Eden). When Jesus is said to offer "Salvation" from "this world" by going to the "other world" (or Heaven) this is a dualistic (and unenlightened) interpretation. Nondual Mysticism, on the other hand, sees the Kingdom of God *on* Earth *as* Earth by *transcending* Earth (or the gross physical domain). Jesus did seem to teach this Nondual Mysticism to his closest disciples (or devotees), yet few have understood. Although the Church tends to portray Jesus in Fourth and Fifth Stage terms, at the deepest levels, I believe, he is a God-Realized human being and genuine Guru-Adept (reflecting the Sixth and Seventh Stages of Life), an authentic Avatar.

Since Adam and Eve "missed the mark" (the literal meaning of "sin" or *hamartia* in Greek) to send humanity down the wrong path by refusing to commune with God in "Paradise" or on Earth (as "Eden"), it is taught that Jesus took on the burden of humankind's evil ways to be crucified on the cross to sacrifice his body and blood for our sake. This is the basic mythic teaching of Christianity, a literal teaching based on published words, not Spirit-Baptism. Although these mythical allegories represent esoteric yogic processes and profound human truths, when seen correctly, most Christians take the myth literally. They want *their* ego to be saved, not sacrificed (in God); they want evil to magically disappear thus they put all their hope in one man, even if an Adept. This comes close to the definition of a childish cult praying to a Parental Deity who will hopefully take care of them—not true religion.

Jesus died a criminal's death before rising from the dead in a "Transfigured" state to enter the Divine Light thus proving life exists after death and that God is Real, according to the Gospels. In truth, however, Jesus didn't sacrifice himself so people could live in a magical heaven for eternity. His sacrifice is a symbol for our own sacrifice of self that is required to surrender (or transcend) our ego (the activity of the self-contraction). Jesus didn't die to mythically erase "our sins" but to show us how we can stop sinning *now* when we "miss the mark" and turning away from God's Love. Christ lived and died so we can learn for ourselves how to enter the Kingdom of God *within* and to *be love* as a self-sacrifice in Divine Communion. These esoteric interpretations are not part of the common Christian understanding but are only clarified by Awakened Adepts (similar to Jesus).

The worldly Church religion has misrepresented these esoteric matters given by a real Guru-Adept thus reducing them down into political and exoteric propaganda. This often happens in the common world (of average-mode consciousness). This is very dangerous for it creates unnecessary wars both within and without. Today this distorted view is used by religionists and charismatic individuals, radio hosts and megachurch preachers, and other mythic believers, to exploit people's ignorance, misunderstandings, and fears. This approach often degrades into cultism and fundamentalism numbering in the hundreds of millions, a condition far from the sacred teachings of Jesus the Christ. It even influences political forces usually in the negative (and cultic) manner. Adi Da criticized this tendency of the ordinary ego to seek for refuge (and to be saved) in the exoteric sanctity of common religion:

> The popular Myth of Jesus is an Idol of mass religion. It was created
> by the exoteric Christian Church when it moved to legitimize itself
> in the eyes of the secular State of Rome… The popular Myth of Jesus
> is founded on archaic cosmological archetypes…. The man Jesus is
> popularly believed to be God, the Creator of the Universe, and his
> death is glorified as a necessary Cosmic Event that somehow makes
> it unnecessary for any believer to suffer permanent death…. None of
> this Idolatry was the teaching or the intention of Jesus or any of the
> other great spiritual Adepts of the world.[10]

This helps us to understand that there is a profound difference between faith and belief in God and actual *realization* of God as your inherent nature or True Self. By attentively studying the Great Tradition of Global Wisdom, by making yourself available to the teachings of *all* the Great Adepts, not just any "One and Only" Adept or Teacher, we come to *realize* our true prior unity with the Divine Reality, not just one based on egoic faith or belief in certain roles and rules. Hence Adi Da affirms: "All the 'Holy Books' are *our* books, and all of us must go to school and be transformed in our minds by the Great Tradition."[11]

In one of his final revelation books about devotion to and ascension of Spirit, *The Pneumaton* (2011), Adi Da Samraj devotes several chapters (Part Five) on "The Non-Conformist Moral, Devotional, and Spiritual Teachings of Saint Jesus and The Conventional Public Religious Message of Institutional Christianity" (very highly recommended). In these pages, the Western-born Avatar reviews his teachings about Jesus throughout his nearly forty-year career where he clarifies the important differences between exoteric ("outer-oriented") Christianity and the true esoteric ("inner-directed") teachings of Jesus of Galilee. That is, at least as far as we can gather from the historical record since Jesus himself never wrote anything down (for we have only the writings of his disciples and followers). These Gospels are then combined with an Avatar's Awakened insight as Adi Da clarifies the true teaching of Jesus:

> Jesus himself apparently did not believe the popular myth that God
> is spatially above the physical sky. On the contrary, Jesus affirmed
> God is "Spirit" (or "Breath-Energy")—All-Pervading, and within
> human beings…. Jesus taught and practiced mystical (or Yogic)
> Communion with the Spirit of God (or the Spirit That Is God)….

Jesus taught the Way of God <u>As</u> Spirit, or the Way of Salvation (or Real-God-Realization) through descent (or Fourth Stage reception) of the Spirit, ego-transcending (Fifth Stage) mystical ascent via the Spirit, and (Fifth Stage) mystical absorption in the Spirit.[12]

We need only turn to the right passages from *The Bible* to discover this for ourselves since Jesus famously tells us (in John 4: 23-24): "Those who are real worshipers will worship the Father in Spirit and in Truth. Such are the worshipers whom the Father wants. God is Spirit, and those who worship Him must worship in Spirit and Truth." This is the *true* message of Jesus Christ as a devotional (Fourth Stage) Savior-Saint and esoteric yogic (Fifth Stage) Adept highlighting ascension to God by opening the heart to awaken the mind in Spirit-Baptism [see Chapter 20]. It is only by surrendering self in Divine Communion, via breath and spirit (*spiritus*, in Latin, literally means "breath," as does *psyche* in Greek), that we are really "saved" or "hit the mark" (i.e., do not sin) and *realize* our true Divine Condition. Yet most of us cannot figure this out on our own; we need an Adept's Help and Spirit-Transmission. Again, Avatar Adi Da expounds upon the true message of the Christ, the Messiah, the "Anointed One," for he too is an Adept of equal character pointing to God Only, as are others in recorded world history. Beloved Adi Da, therefore, summarizes the esoteric Message of Jesus (and all Adepts) for everyone to hear:

> The <u>physical</u> "Ascension" of Jesus never happened… But Jesus did Realize a Spiritual Ascension. The true Christian (and non-Christian) Ascension is the Fifth Stage mystical ascent to the brain core (and the "sky of mind") via the "ladder" (or the "cross") of the nervous system (in the line of the spinal column)….
>
> Therefore, all the ancient secrets must be told—everywhere, and to all who will listen. The Great Tradition (as a whole) must, by this education, inform its separate and provincial parts. And humankind must, once again, be schooled (and Awakened) by True and Free Realizers of the Living Divine.[13]

Generally, you will not hear this "secret" message in your local Church. The Great Tradition is our repository of Global Wisdom from (Fourth Stage) devotion to (Fifth Stage) yoga to (Sixth and Seventh Stage) Enlightenment. Whatever Sage, Saint, Yogi, or Prophet you identify with the most, probably the one whose culture you were born into, you need to realize they are all part of our one human family. We are all united in the Prior Unity of Real God, the esoteric Realization of all Awakened Adepts. Yes, our born culture in history tends to prefer one religion over another, yet they are in truth each and all part of one global sacred inheritance—God's Great Tradition of Global Wisdom. Let us all learn to follow Jesus as a genuine Adept-Realizer—to "Follow Me"—by living in a sacred relationship to a real Guru-Adept so you may receive actual Spirit-Baptism.

AMEN

Chapter 14 Endnotes

1. *"Legitimacy"* via *"horizontal translation"* at a certain stage of consciousness development versus *"authenticity"* via *"vertical transformation"* between stages of development are definitions used by Ken Wilber to designate different processes of developmental growth in consciousness evolution. See: Ken Wilber, *Eye to Eye* (1983, 2001); *Spiritual Choices* (1987); also see: *In God's Company: Guru-Adepts As Agents for Enlightenment in the Integral Age* (2022) by Brad Reynolds.

2. See: Adi Da Samraj [Franklin Jones], *The Spiritual Instructions of Saint Seraphim of Sarov* (1973).

3. Adi Da Samraj [Da Free John], *Nirvanasara* (1982), p. 76; however, it is important to note that Avatar Adi Da revised this assessment in later years (during the 1990s), nevertheless, for practical purposes I do believe it is accurate enough and that Jesus Christ is an Awakened Adept-Guru at the highest stage of life.

4. Adi Da Samraj [Da Free John], *Nirvanasara* (1982), p. 76.

5. Adi Da Samraj, from the Essay "The Forgotten Spiritual Esotericism of Saint Jesus and The Christian Social Exotericism That Succeeded It" in *The Pneumaton* (2011), pp. 251-252 ["Stages of Life" capped].

6. See: Paramahansa Yogananda, *Autobiography of a Yogi* (1946, 1979), p. 169n.

7. Sri Yukteswar, quoted in *Autobiography of a Yogi* (1946, 1979) by Paramahansa Yogananda, p. 168.

8. Paramahansa Yogananda, *Autobiography of a Yogi* (1946, 1979), p. 199n.

9. Paramahansa Yogananda, *The Second Coming of Christ: The Resurrection of the Christ Within You* (2004), p. xxi.

10. |Adi Da Samraj [Da Free John], *Scientific Proof of the Existence of God Will Soon Be Announced by the White House!* (1980), p. 211,

11. Adi Da Samraj [Da Free John], *Nirvanasara* (1982), p. 199.

12. Adi Da Samraj, *The Pneumaton* (2011), pp. 229-230 ["Stages of Life" capped].

13. Ibid., pp. 230, 235 ["Stages of Life" capped].

FIFTEEN

GURU YOGA-SATSANG: ISLAM

GURU YOGA: THE PROPHET OF ISLAM

he third of the Abrahamic religions of the West is **Islam**, which like the other two religions of the Middle East (Judaism and Christianity), does not accept the possibility of achieving a state of consciousness identical with the Divine Condition as some of their best-known mystic Sufis did. Islam's principal figure **Muhammad ibn 'Abdullāh** (ca. 570–632)—also known as **Muhammadun Rasūlu l-Lāh**, the "Messenger of Allah" or simply **Muhammad**—is considered to be more like a **Prophet**, such as with Moses, Isaiah, Jeremiah, a voice or mouthpiece for Allah (or God) rather than someone who is an Adept-Realizer fully identified with God-Consciousness. Technically, the word *islam* derives from *salam* (*s-l-m*) which primarily means "peace," but secondarily means "surrender," so in full it means "the peace that comes when one's life is surrendered to God."[1] This is why Islam is often associated with just "surrender," so a *muslim* is one who "submits to Allah." However, it is true self-surrender (or "ego-death") that leads to Enlightenment (or God-Realization), not simply self-submission. Thus, in theistic religions where God is seen as separate, the self is actually submitting to traditional laws and customs as a way to honor God. This is the mythic (and unenlightened) mind of Western religions that perpetually feels itself divided from God or the Divine Reality. Thus God is to be feared, while being grateful for one's life, yet this is not knowing Allah as being one's own consciousness.

Adi Da bluntly criticizes this dualistic problem with unenlightened theism found in all three Abrahamic religions of the West:

> Whenever theism or religion becomes the base for political and social order, it inevitably becomes the base for knowledge and power in the material world.... Theism is, at its base, egoic and fitted to worldly concerns.... This is evident in the popular theistic (and now almost exclusively exoteric) cultures that have come out of the Semitic tradition of the Middle East. Judaism, Christianity, and Islam are the principal theistic religions (in terms of worldly power and numbers), and they are all based on similar idealistic conceptions of God and creature and salvation, but each of these [religious] cults has also historically sought and achieved the general power to command the social order.
>
> And, in the process, each of these [religious] cults became a political State, controlling the forms of knowledge and power. As a result, over time these religions developed more and more of a secular, materialistic, and worldly character.... [so that] the historical conflict among these three (and between their claims and the equally absolutist and absurd claims of other and atheistic or non-religious systems, such as communism, democratic capitalism, and technological scientism) has now become the basis for the idealistic State politics and political conflicts all over the world. And the seemingly more important or esoteric matters of spiritual wisdom, mystical knowledge, and the [spiritual] power of sainthood or Adeptship are as much in doubt and disrepute in the common religious circles of theism as they are in scientific and atheistic circles.[2]

Truly, only an Adept can clarify these difficult matters pushing us beyond our preferred religious provincialisms [see Chapter 1]. **Muslims**, or followers of Islam, always turn to the *Qur'an* (sometimes spelled "Koran"), the revealed word of Allah through the Prophet Muhammad to receive their divine understanding and wisdom as well as social mores. They say their Holy Book can only be rightly read in Arabic, which they believe comes directly from Allah, not Muhammad (thus making translations incompetent). The laws or instructions in the *Qur'an* and *Hadith* are used more for religious beliefs and social order, not for mysticism (or attaining the Enlightened State). This is one of the main reasons there has been a contentious history in Islam with sects fighting sects, such as between the Sunnis and Shi'a, over various interpretations of the *Qur'an* by the Caliphate authorities that goes on to this day. Thus, not many Muslims engage in the ecstatic practices of the Mystics, which for Islam are the Sufis [see below].

Islam, for most Muslims, is founded on the "**Five Pillars**" where the first (and most important) claims: "There is no God but Allah, and Muhammad is his messenger" (*shahada*). As one scholar put it: "Muhammad, the Founder of Islam, is best understood as the last of a long line of earlier prophets who proclaim the One True God and the need for total submission to Him."[3] All the previous Prophets, including Jesus, had been authentic (for their Stage of Life), but Muhammad claimed to be their culmination, hence he was titled "The Seal of the Prophets." Muhammad was also a warrior and general who led armies fighting in battles (killing people with the sword), activities foreign to all other founders of major world religions.

In this case, Muhammad disavowed any divine status for himself since he still felt separate from Allah and was only to be the devoted servant and mouthpiece for Allah's revelations to the Arabs as recorded in the ***Qur'an***—literally *al-qur'an* (in Arabic). Professor Huston Smith explains the significance of the Book of Allah: "The *Qur'an* is perhaps the most recited (as well as read) book in the world. Certainly, it is the world's most memorized book, and possibly the one that exerts the most influence on those who read it."[4] Unlike other major world religions, like Buddhism and Christianity, the sacred text of Islam is attributed directly to their Founder (who was speaking for Allah), not recalled years later by disciples. Muhammad claims God authorized him as Prophet to speak in His Name as part of the prophetic tradition of Israel and the Old Testament including building upon the message of Abraham and Jesus. Muhammad's message in the Qur'an is direct and simple: There is One God who is the Creator and Giver of Life and since people can recognize His Wonders (in Nature) they are duty-bound to submit and live in accord with the revelation of God's special messengers.[5] To do so will save a person on Judgment Day and guarantee rewards in Heaven.

Once again, right from the start, we can see Islam, like the other Western Abrahamic religions, see themselves as separate from God. They seek the right *relationship* to God instead of *realizing* or knowing their *identity* with God directly from within. Thus no one can gain union or direct knowledge of Allah (i.e., seeing Him "face-to-face"), like the esoteric yogic traditions of the East claim is a potential for every person. The mythos-religious scholar Joseph Campbell explains this profound difference between West and East, between monotheism and mysticism:

> Gods and Buddhas in the [East] are, accordingly, not final terms—like Yahweh, the Trinity, or Allah, in the West—but point beyond themselves to that ineffable being, consciousness, and rapture that is the All in all of us. And in their worship, the ultimate aim is to effect in the devotee a psychological transformation through a shift of his [or her] plane of vision from the passing to the enduring, through which [they] may come finally to realize in experience (not simply as an article of faith) that [we] are identical with that before which [we] bow. These are, then, *religions of identity*. Their mythologies and associated rites, philosophies, sciences, and arts, are addressed, in the end, not to the honor of any god "out there" but to the recognition of the divinity within.[6]

The influence of Islam on world history, the second most populous religion on the planet, is profound and will be so far into the future. This is an important reason why as a global culture we must become tolerant of all world religions and faiths by seeing them as inhabiting one Great Tradition of humankind. Religious diversity demands there is no "one true religion" (but only a *sophia perennis*), for only by seeing our prior unity—as one human race and by realizing our oneness with the Transcendent Godhead—will there ever be enough cooperation and tolerance to achieve world peace (through true self-transcendence and sacrifice in love). In this case, the true Awakened Adepts call everyone to *realize* God for themselves, not just through intermediaries (whether Gurus or Prophets or Saviors). Thus, the One True Divine Reality (that *is* Reality) is not simply to be believed or surrendered to without question via one's inherited traditional religion or whatever we've been taught. God may actually be known and *realized* through spiritual disciplines of love and compassion, and via the Grace of the Spiritual Master, where everyone and every little thing is seen to be nothing but God, Allah Only, Only Allah.

Muhammad:
Prophet to Politician

Muhammad—meaning "highly praised"—was born in Mecca (in Saudi Arabia) around 570 CE to a clan that traced their lineage back to Ishmael (Abraham's first son). An orphan at an early age, he was raised by his uncle where as a young man, naturally bright and of a gentle disposition, he led trade caravans where he met a wealthy widow, **Khadija** (fifteen years his senior) who was an important supporter (and mother of his children). Around 610 CE (when he was 40 years old) on a solitary religious retreat in a cave, Muhammad has a series of life-changing visions—the "**Night of Power**" (*Laylat al-Qada*)—where the voice of the Angel Gabriel said to him "Proclaim!" He was to proclaim Allah's direct word and instruction to the Arabs (and all humankind). Yet Muhammad doubted his abilities, wondering if he was a prophet or mad, until his wife confirmed to him it was true so she became his first convert. Following Gabriel's orders, Muhammad gave his life over to the One God of Allah (above all other gods) so his words, written down by others around him, became the Holy *Qur'an*—"the Recitation" (in Arabic).

Pre-Islamic Arabia was a vast tribal, desert area that practiced **animistic polytheism** worshiping supernatural *jinn* or nature spirits and demons. The god Allah was already worshiped in Mecca but not as the only God yet a powerful one, although certain contemplatives, called *hanifs*, which Muhammad was one, exclusively worshiped only Allah.[7] Arabia's largest city, **Mecca**, had 360 shrines (one for each day of the year) where people worshiped different deities, idolized objects, stones, symbols, and fetishes so it was a very profitable business. Allah, Muhammad felt, was greater than his countrymen knew, so he was determined to proclaim: *La ilaha 'llah!*—"There is no god but Allah!" Muhammad's uncompromising message of monotheism that Allah alone was *the* God—the One and Only—without rival, made him enemies as well as converts. In addition, the Prophet provided a strict moral code, such as no gambling, no drinking, no adultery or promiscuous sex, no infanticide (a common practice, especially with daughters), no lying, thieving, eating pork, etc., that went against centuries of popular behavior. Nonetheless, these disciplined practices had transforming effects on the Arabs as they found their lives improved, so gaining even more converts to his new religion.

Not being very popular in Mecca after three years, with resistance to One God being intense, a group of elders from Yathrib (north of Mecca) convinced Muhammad to come be their leader since they would follow his laws and only worship Allah. The exodus from Mecca to **Medina** (Yathrib was renamed by Muhammad as Medinat al-Nabi, the "City of the Prophet") in 622 CE, is now called the **hijrah** (or *hijra* and *hegira* meaning "migration"), an event that is so important it starts the Islamic calendar and is considered by Muslims to be a turning point in world history.[8] Muslims see their contribution of monotheism as unique in world history. The Jews, for example, had One God (Yahweh) but his teachings were confined to the people of Israel. Christians, on the other hand, compromised their monotheism by deifying Christ, according to the *Qur'an*.[9] Only Islam, which accepts converts, gave the entire world One God, Allah, to believe and have faith in.

In Medina, Muhammad established a new theocratic "city-state" (*umma muslima*) where the primacy of religious authority superseded land and tribal authorities of the past (by following the "laws" of the Prophet).[10] This would become the prototype for the union of the state and religion that dominates the Islamic ideal. Muhammad then became chief of state, more than Prophet, yet his rule was gentle and merciful, even against his enemies.[11] The State of Islam intends to be the perfect marriage of religion and politics. Obviously, this approach violates the laws (and rights) of other religions and the modern Western world where a sharp division is made in the separation of Church and State allowing for greater religious diversity since no one religion is considered supreme (which annoys some Christians, who are in often the majority).[12] The original Muslim city-states, and the *Qur'an*, were only at times tolerant to other religions, especially with monotheistic Judaism and Christianity who were called "People of the Book" (Islam's religious predecessors). After Muhammad's death, Islam went on a mission to first convert or conquer the Persians (of Zoroastrian dualism) and the Europeans (of Christian trinitarianism) with its perceived superior message about the One God, Allah, the Beneficent, the Merciful. Unfortunately, if someone was an infidel (or a nonbeliever in Islam), mercy was not often granted, according to the annals of history. Muslims conquered and oppressed as well as provided for the faithful.

Such strong (egoic) belief that only their religion is true and complete puts them in constant conflict with other religious groups, either through taxation (*jizyah*) or battle. In a theocratic state, all people are expected to follow their religious laws and spiritual teachings, so no quarter is given to those who resist such strict regulation, making Islam a perpetual problem for a unified global society unless they themselves better adapt to modern values of religious diversity. This is true for all three of the major Abrahamic religions, a conflict perpetual that needs to be transcended with a deeper and more universal spiritual understanding and Enlightened Realization. Either that or the acceptance of the democratic principle based on the actual separation of Church and State where civil authority is not influenced by religious belief, and where religious preference is protected by law (unlike in communism). Then everyone may practice the religion of their choice (or not practice any at all).

After several battles with the armies of Mecca, Muhammad gained moral and military victories (even when outnumbered) so his converts increased, yet not among the Jews or Christians. This led to the Arabic elements in his religion to be emphasized, such that Muslims would pray facing Mecca, not Jerusalem, and Friday became the official day of rest, not Saturday (Jewish) or Sunday (Christian).[13] After five years in Medina establishing sacred and social laws, Muhammad and his army again approached Mecca, first trying to negotiate a compromise, but then marching on the city whose leaders responded by surrendering to avoid bloodshed. Entering in victory, Muhammad rode to the **Ka'ba** (also spelled *Ka'bah* or *Kabah* and *Kaaba* meaning "The Cube")—a black stone sanctuary believed to be the navel of the world, supposedly consecrated by Abraham and Ishmael—where with his own hands the Prophet-General destroyed its 360 idols declaring: "Truth has come and

falsehood has vanished," thus claiming it for only Allah, the One God.[14] All of Mecca converted with no resistance. The *Ka'ba* (now covered with a black silk and gold-trimmed curtain) is the principal site for pilgrimage by all Muslims. In ritual ceremony everyone (regardless of rank or race) wears white robes and performs *tawaf* ("going about") to circumambulate (seven times in a counterclockwise direction) the Black Stone of Mecca in prayer. On the tenth year of his migration from Mecca (in 632), Prophet Muhammad stood at the Ka'ba proclaiming his mission was complete, he had established a new religion, given them the Book of Allah, which they were to follow religiously and spread Islam around the world. Shortly thereafter, he died… and the rest is history.

Although the Prophet had founded a new religion and social order, the larger social community (*umma*) of Islam (*muslima*) was not yet fully realized. The first task after Muhammad's death was to appoint a successor, or **Caliph**, a political leader but not a religious or prophetic one. Right from the beginning there was dissention and conflict. **Ali** (or **Ali ibn Abi Talib**), Muhammad's cousin and son-in-law, was expected to take on the leadership role but others selected **Abu Bakr** (573–634), a general in Muhammad's army, as the first Caliph. Two other Caliphs ruled before Ali finally took over (reigning from 656–661), whom the Shi'a Muslims ("separate party") consider to be the first rightful Caliph, but he was soon assassinated.[15] The third Caliph Uthman, a member of the Umayyad clan (and son-in-law to Muhammad), who was also assassinated, began the Muslim military expansion into the Persian and Byzantine empires, spreading into Arabia, Persia, and North Africa before moving onto Europe. Centuries later Muslims marched into India bringing conquest more than conversion. Professor Kitagawa summarizes:

For one hundred years following Muhammad's death in 632, the Islamic community enjoyed phenomenal expansion. During the final ten years of Muhammad's life, he exerted his influence widely on the Arabian peninsula. Soon Syria, which had been part of the Byzantine empire, fell to the Islamic community. Jerusalem followed in 638. The Islamic forces then invaded Egypt, defeated Sasanian Persia, and pacified North Africa. In 711, aided by oppressed Jews, they defeated the Visigoth kingdom on the Iberian peninsula. The Islamic attempt to subdue France was blocked by Charles Martel in 732 at the Battle of Tours, but their successful efforts in Spain—or *Al-andalus*, as it was called by the Muslims—turned Spain into the most highly civilized region in Europe…. Thus, the seeds of internal disunity began being sown within the Islamic community [with its vast expansion and diverse territories].[16]

By the 10th century, like their Christian counterparts (with their own competing Popes), the Islamic community was theoretically united but was split politically with three rival Caliphs located in Baghdad, Iraq, in Cairo, Egypt, and in Córdoba, Spain. Over the next thousand years, the Caliphate exerted authority under several dynasties: **Umayyad Dynasty** (661–750 CE) and **Abbasid Dynasty** (750–1285 CE), centered in Baghdad—where "the splendor of Baghdad under the Abbasid Caliphate was reputed to be second only to the magnificence of Constantinople"[17]—and then the **Ottoman Empire** (1300–1922 CE), centered in Istanbul which ruled until the modern age.[18] In 1924, the idea of a single Caliphate exercising supreme religious authority was abolished by the Turkish National Assembly, inheritors of the Ottoman Empire. However, claims of an all-ruling Caliphate has been revived by radical Muslim groups, such as ISIS or the Islamic State (IS), terrorist organizations not supported by the vast majority of Muslims.

Although Muhammad had originally envisioned a united theocratic state based on the principles of Allah's holiness and justice to establish a society founded on religious faith, after their military expansion and conquests Muslims were forced to acknowledge other religions and beliefs. Islam therefore divided the world into: (1) regions under their control (*dar al-Islam*) and (2) regions not yet converted to Islam (*dar al-Harb*) also known as *kafir* or "infidels" (literally "unfaithful," or better, "one who lacks thankfulness").[19] This idea of a divided world into Muslims and non-Muslims has often been radicalized and used to justify violence and terrorism, a practice not condoned by the original teachings of Muhammad's Islam.

People in the countries controlled by the Caliphate were encouraged to embrace Islam, of course, yet were generally left to their own beliefs as long as they paid a poll tax (*jizyah*). It was assumed that sooner or later the Islamic synthesis was destined to dominate the world, a vision still shared among the more radical and fundamentalist Muslims. Therefore, the religions (descended from Abraham) and the political systems (descended from Greece and the European Enlightenment), now encircling the globe, seem destined to remain at perpetual war until the traditional religions themselves are transcended in a greater understanding of the One Real God, or Transcendental Divine Being of Conscious Light (in Adi Da's words), where the history of each worldview is seen from a more integral (and embracing) perspective.

ISLAMIC LAWS AND ORDER

Islam, for most Muslims, is a religion that follows the laws and ethical guidelines outlined by the **Caliphates**, or religious authorities, in obedience to Allah. Importantly, Muhammad accepted the Old Testament (or Jewish history) as precursors to his revelation, so their Prophets, including Jesus, have become enfolded into Islamic religious belief as reinterpreted in the *Qur'an*. The religion of Islam that Prophet Muhammad gave the Arab people was thus very similar to the monotheistic religions of Judaism and Christianity that preceded him. All of the Abrahamic religions accept One God as ruling over all of Creation, that the history of humankind began with Genesis and will end on Judgement Day when God's Truth will be revealed.[20] Islam integrates their religious values directly into the political affairs of the state more than perhaps any other world religion, especially in the modern world. This is based on their belief that this world is mostly lived in preparation for the next world (after death); therefore, an individual, male or female, must be directly responsible for his or her other-worldly destiny.[21] This makes the community and state, as well as their religious laws and dictates, vital to Muslim life.

The laws or instructions for proper Muslim conduct have been compiled in a book of commentaries called the *Hadith*, which literally means "talk" or "speech" since they are thought to be short narratives about Muhammad's life that came from his early contemporaries. These stories of instruction were used by later generations to develop the Islamic legal systems, finally being systematized in the 9th and 10th centuries by some of Islam's greatest scholars, including **Ibn Al-Hajjaj** (d. 875). Both the Sunnis and Shi'a have their preferred collections. *Hadith* has been called "the backbone" of Islamic civilization since the authority of the Hadith is a primary source for religious law and moral guidance ranking second only to the *Qur'an*.

By strictly following their religious laws, the Arabs and Islamic converts propelled themselves into a world religion (now with nearly two billion followers). But soon after Muhammad's death they split into two major denominations: **Sunni** (now 80–85%, roughly 1.5 billion people) and **Shi'a** (15-20%, roughly 240–340 million people). **Shi'a** (originally "Shiat Ali" or the "Party of Ali") are the majority in Iran and Iraq (with large communities in other Arab countries), while **Sunnis** (from the phrase "Ahl al-Sunnah" or "People of the Tradition") are the majority in Saudi Arabi, Syria, Egypt, Jordan, the West Bank and Gaza (with large communities in other Arab countries). Sunnis recognize the first three Caliphs as the true successors to Muhammad and follow the four schools of Islamic law (*madhhab*) developed in the 8th and 9th centuries, while Shi'a only accept Ali (the fourth Caliph) as the true successor to Muhammad. Sunnis believe the Caliph should be elected, whereas Shi'a believe a Caliph should be an **Imam** (or "spiritual teacher") chosen by God. The Iranian revolution of 1979 launched a radical Shi'a Islamist agenda that was perceived as a challenge to more modern Sunni regimes, particularly in the Gulf nations. Tehran's policy of supporting Shi'a militias and radical parties beyond its borders was countered by Sunni-ruled Gulf states. Today, many conflicts in the region have strong sectarian overtones including the contentious relationship with Israel over the Palestinian displacement.

Contrary to popular belief in the West, Islam introduced rights for women where few had existed previously in tribal Bedouin culture. Before Muhammad, women were treated as property, and female infants were often buried alive; marriage contracts were loose and temporary always favoring the husband, and inheritance to women was forbidden. Muhammad, in establishing a new way of life, outright condemned infanticide and required daughters to be given a fair share of inheritance; in addition, women were allowed the right to give consent in marriage while divorce became more difficult.[22] Islam, however, does permit a plurality of wives, as long as the husband can take care of them, but it's only in marriage that the sexual act is sanctioned. Nonetheless, death by stoning for adultery is permitted, and according to strict Islamic law, social dancing (and other forms of entertainment) are proscribed, yet in most Islamic nations the civil laws of the State take precedent. The problem though is that Islamic society has not kept pace with the advancement of women's rights in the West, which have also proceeded at an exceedingly slow rate (for example, only gaining the right to vote in the 20th century), yet the difference is striking (especially in places like Saudi Arabia).

Life in Islamic society resides in the *sharia* (law) given by God through the divine words of Allah recorded in the *Qur'an* and the tradition of the *Hadith*, which have been developed by legal experts (*fiqh*) with the consensus (*ijma*) of the community (*umma*).[23] Islam places an emphasis on the self's individuality and responsibility, though it colors this through condemnation on Judgement Day, a constant threat in the *Qur'an* where heaven and hell realms are described "in vivid, concrete, and sensual imagery."[24] This emphasis on a series of *exoteric* ("outer-directed") social practices, like all Abrahamic religions, leads to a developmental weakness in individual-oriented or *esoteric* ("inner-directed") practices that promote mysticism and full God-Realization. Prayer in Islam is usually canonical prayer giving thanks with gratitude yet done by following specific rules and rites, not as a self-transcending practice of communing with the Divine Presence.

The principal aim of Islam is to live a righteous life by following the **Five Pillars of Islam** (*arkan ad-din*):

(1) **Faith** by sincerely believing in the creed: "There is no God but Allah, and Muhammad is his messenger" (*shahada*);

(2) **Praying** five times a day facing Mecca (*salat*);

(3) **Charity** as almsgiving for the needy (zakat);

(4) **Fasting** during the month of Ramadan (*sawm*);

(5) **Pilgrimage** to Mecca to pray and worship at the Ka'ba once in a lifetime, if possible (*hajj*).[25]

What has been called a "sixth pillar" of Muslim obligation is *Jihad* or "holy war," which is the struggle for Allah's cause and religion.[26] Jihad is supposed to rely on missionary activities, but when necessary the use of armed force aims to gain political control and submission over a society to then be governed by Islamic principles. Obviously, such aggressive conversion theology (historically practiced by Christians as well) is an antithesis to the democratic (and even communist) political and economic systems of the modern world often placing Islamic nations in conflict with modern Western nations.

However, the need for self-preservation and independence, intertwined with economic co-dependence in an interconnected global economy (especially rich with oil resources), has created a political stalemate between the West and Islamic nations (such as with Saudi Arabia, Egypt, Iraq, Iran, Syria, Turkey, and others). Yet minor and sometimes major wars continue to erupt in the twentieth and twenty-first centuries, the most critical being the world-changing event of 9/11, 2001 when Islamic terrorists attacked the World Trade Towers and Washington D.C. With Judaism mostly aligned with the Christian

West, a viable world peace seems far off thus the potential for another world war is a perpetual possibility, especially with Russian influence and interference. One of the root causes for instability, as mentioned [see Chapter 12], is the Israeli-Palestinian conflict (since 1948), but it is also embedded in Islam's ideals of religious conversion and world domination through offering what, for them, is a better (or more true) religion.

Truly, only Enlightened Wisdom (exemplified by Adept-Realizers) gained via transcendence of the egoic-self and one's inherited traditional provincialisms and ethnocentric nationalisms will ever relieve these types of religious and political antagonisms. Only a **trans-lineage** approach or trans-religious understanding will heal centuries of religious war and embittered hatred. This is the profound task confronting all future generations, whether from East or West, North or South, in our search for global unity and peaceful cooperation. May God or the Radiant Transcendental Being (by whatever name) truly bless humanity in its elusive quest for world peace and the true fulfillment (and Realization) of Happiness. Yet, until *everyone's* rights, man and woman, child and elder, religious or not, is honored and made real, then conflicts are bound to be the result. I believe, therefore, that only the Awakened Adepts, not Prophets or Saviors alone, are capable of leading us out of this quagmire to a better and more enlightened (and integral) future.

As proven time and time again, when the mythic (or exoteric) dimensions of orthodox religions are not transcended (and properly integrated) then the stories and fables, the beliefs and faiths, themselves are made into objects of cultic devotion for the ego. Truth be told, many people's relationship with their traditional religions is cultic, based only on a degree of *legitimacy* (in terms of horizontal *translation*), not *authenticity* (based on the vertical *transformation* of consciousness).[27] Therefore, much harm has been done over the centuries, including countless wars and killing, murder, executions, torture and terrorism, since people identify so strongly with their "tribe" or ethnocentric heritage at the exclusion of others.

By being deeply attached to their own unique "Holy Book" and ethnocentric tribalism, rather than on the Transcendental Divine of Awakened Consciousness, the true abode of the Heart, they "miss the mark" (or commit sin, *hamartia*). Releasing attachments and transcending religious obsessions and personal parochial preferences and ego-identities is, therefore, a principal focus (and purpose) for engaging in genuine meditation and true mysticism founded on Satsang, an authentic relationship with an Adept-Realizer.

FALSAFAH:
INTEGRAL ISLAMIC PHILOSOPHY

slam was not just a proselytizing religion looking for riches and conquest since the Islamic Empire offered regions of tolerance and learning among all religions including the rationally-oriented thinking and dialectic of scholars influenced by ancient Greek sources, especially at certain cities at certain times in world history. World religion historian Joseph Kitagawa called this open-ended approach a "**corpus Islamicum**, a multiracial, multinational cosmopolitan syntheses that provided the best common denominator for the peoples of Asia, North Africa, and Europe."[28] Naturally, this expansive investigation among some leading-edge Islamic scholars generated tensions with the orthodox scholastics or "people of the Tradition (*hadith*)." Greek influence, when escaping the oppression of their philosophers and destruction of their Academy by the Holy Roman Catholic Church, encouraged the growth of rationalism among the Arab elite scholars (not the masses), particularly stimulated by the writings of Aristotle. Professor Kitagawa explains:

> Originally, Muslim were not noted for culture and education, but they were eager to learn from neighboring peoples and were superb translators of Greek, Latin, Persian, and Sanskrit. In both Sicily and Spain, Jewish intellectuals served as cultural intermediaries between Muslims and Christians, and Aristotle became as much a favorite of Muslims as of Christians. Persia also contributed to Islamic culture.... Broader than a philosophical system per se, the *falsafah* attracted natural scientists, practicing physicians, and philosophers.[29]

The Greek influence, from the Pre-Socratics to the Neoplatonists, including Plato, and his student Aristotle (and also Plotinus, whose writings were mistaken for Aristotle's), impacted the Islamic scholars in their search for knowledge beginning with what had been learned in the ancient world. The Muslims conquered Egypt's Alexandria in 641 gaining access to its remaining ancient libraries (though much had been destroyed by the Christian zealots centuries earlier). This led to the development of *Falsafah* meaning "philosophy" (the Greek pronunciation of *philosophia* became *falsafah* in Arabic) which became a "system of comprehensive knowledge that included both humanistic and [ancient] natural scientific learning."[30] This stimulated a rationalist form of Islamic theology called *Kalam* (literally, "science of discourse") that was criticized by orthodox Muslims, such as by Al-Ghazali in his book "The Incoherence of the Philosophers" (*Tahafut-al-Falasifa*).

Nevertheless, their investigations were not pursued for the sake of knowledge alone since Muslim scholars tended to use the ancient sources to support the religion of Islam itself. As one scholarly source noted: "It was common for Muslim philosophers to think of Plato, Aristotle, Plotinus, and other great figures of Greek philosophy as monotheists who would have become Muslims if they had been exposed to the Qur'anic revelation."[31] Overall, like most philosophers at any time, we could say they represent the "Talking School" of engaging the mind more than transcending it in transpersonal understanding (such as with the "Practicing School" of enlightened spirituality) [see Chapter 4].

Beginning with Al-Kindi (died 873), the "father of Arab philosophy," to Averroes (died 1198) these several centuries became known as the "**Golden Age of Islam**," often called the Peripatetic (or Aristotelian) Islamic school. After this flourishing period, particularly strong in Muslim Spain, Islamic philosophical activity declined significantly but not before leaving its indelible influence on Christian Europe. The Arabic translation of ancient texts of learning, such as Euclid's treatise on geometry, *The Elements*, or Ptolemy's text on astronomy, *The Almagest*, and Galen's medical texts, along with many of the ancient Greek philosophers and Pre-Socratics, were preserved by Islamic scholars before being translated back into Latin (in the eleventh and twelfth centuries) and distributed across the cities and new universities of Europe snapping it out of its own Dark Ages.[32] For example, there was Toledo, Spain that would become "the most important center for the transmission of scientific knowledge between the Muslim and Christian worlds"[33]; and Córdoba, Spain ("one of the most advanced cities in the world"); as well as Baghdad at its height with its famous "**House of Wisdom**" (during the seventh and twelfth centuries) and its "Grand Library" sponsored by the Abbasid Caliphs. Such cosmopolitan openness was absent in Europe until Florence opened the gates to a "Rebirth" (Renaissance) when they discovered the Islamic treasures of philosophical literature balanced by a renewed proliferation within the arts.

This tradition of *falsafah* included the aforementioned **Al-Kindi** (801–873 CE), often called the first *falasuf*; then **Al-Farabi** (872–951), called "the Second Teacher" (Aristotle being "the First Teacher"), who wrote prolifically in the fields of political philosophy, metaphysics, ethics, and logic while being a scientist, cosmologist, mathematician and music theorist. **Ibn Sina** known as "Avicenna" (980–1037) is regarded as one of the most significant physicians, astronomers, and writers of the Islamic Golden Age, the father of early modern medicine. **Ibn Rushd** known as "Averroes" (1126 –1198), born in Córdoba, Spain, a devotee of Aristotle, *par excellence*, authored more than 100 books and treatises on philosophy, theology, medicine, astronomy, physics, psychology, mathematics, linguistics, Islamic jurisprudence and law. The famous Jewish philosopher-physician **Moses ben Maimon** known as "**Maimonides**" (1135–1204), physician to the court of Saladin and devotee of *falsafah*, was one of the most prolific and influential Torah scholars of the Middle Ages who also wrote his widely popular *Guide for the Perplexed* (still read to this day).[34]

By the 12th century, these Muslim philosophers had a profound influence on the Christian Scholastics, such as **Thomas Aquinas** (1225–1274) and **Albertus Magnus** (1200–1280), whose Aristotelian writings contributed to the development of the universities in medieval Europe setting the stage for the scientific revolution. Yet, some scholars point out that Islam lost the dynamic tension between Plato-Aristotle by favoring the rationalism of Aristotle (via Averroes and Avicenna, et al.). By turning their backs on the mystical side of Plato, Arthur Herman in *The Cave and the Light* (2013) explains: "Instead of the constant creative tension between speculation and science that arose in the Christian West, Islamic Platonism retreated to the religious sidelines of Sufism, where it contemplated the mystical and divine and little else."[35] Once more, it was the separation of Church and State in the West, begun with Galileo, that was needed for science to be able pursue its own goals and investigations without concerns about religious domination, a course of events that took centuries to realize (and still is in debate today).

For the West and the modern world, therefore, perhaps one of the greatest gifts Islamic scholars have given to us all as a global culture is that they preserved and saved the ancient Greek philosophers from extinction after the Christian Church condemned them as pagans. Interestingly, the last three books of Plotinus' *Enneads* were credited as the *Theology of Aristotle* influencing the development of the more mystical side of Islam (such as with Sufism).[36] Of course, the **Christian Crusades** against the Muslim world (1096–1291) in their attempt to regain Jerusalem interrupted this exchange of ideas leading in time to the expulsion of Muslims from Spain (in 1492). Then there were the Muslim incursions into India (after 1000 CE) bringing havoc and brutal bloodshed. This is when conquest preceded conversion as **Mahmud of Ghazni** (971–1030), known as the destroyer of idols, plundered northern India nearly twenty times between 1000 and 1027 CE.[37] By 1197, a fresh wave of invasions led by **Muhammad Ghori** (1149–1206) destroyed the famous Buddhist monastic university of Nalanda killing thousands of monks effectively ending Buddhism in India. Tragically, the pacifism of the Hindu population allowed a relatively small number of Muslims to rule the non-Muslim Indian majority for centuries (who remain bitter rivals to this day).

The exception to this animosity came with the famed Mughal emperor **Akbar the Great** (1542–1605), who adopted a more tolerant policy of religious cosmopolitanism. Akbar brought together various religious leaders of his

day in an attempt to foster peace and unity among all religions (it was ultimately unsuccessful, especially after his death). He was illiterate but became a commanding general so that, as Kitagawa explains, "during his fifty-year reign he brought more of India under his sway through conquest and alliance than had ever been ruled by one man... he surrounded himself with persons of talent and quality, carefully balancing between Hindus, Muslims, Afghans, Turks, Iranis, and Turanis."[38]

Akbar

Akbar permitted all religions to thrive, even moving away from his native Islam into a universal mystical view. He erected (in 1575) a **"House of Worship"** (*Ibadat Khana*) where different spiritual teachers could gather for the purpose of worship and discussion, integrating the rational with the devotional.

Akbar's vision for the unity of humankind rested on his belief that at the core of the human quest was a spiritual need and yearning. He even proposed a **"Divine Faith"** or **"Faith of the Divine"** (*Din-i-Ilahi*) which was a syncretic religion that intended to merge the best elements of all religions gathered together in his empire. His political rule was fair and just as well, ending harsh practices such as *sati* (cremation of the widow), excessive dowries, slavery, and the loss of inheritance due to the conversion from one faith to another.[39] Naturally, such a broad and forward-thinking integral vision was doomed to decline after he died but his efforts helped stimulate a Hindu religious revival. Once Muslims had entered and conquered much of India after the second millennium began, the influence of Hinduism and Yoga waned yet its sacred teachings (and Adepts) went on to influence many Muslim mystics, such as the ecstatic yet faith-bound Sufis.

WHIRLING SUFIS: ESOTERIC MYSTICS

$\mathcal{S}$ince human beings, born anew in every generation, always yearn for the higher truths of mysticism, it took a new movement (or sect) in Islam called **Sufism** (followers are known as **Sufis**), often defined as "Islamic mysticism," to bring forward the esoteric and mystical aspects of Islam, a trend that arose alongside the traditional orthodoxy of Muhammad's new religion. Neo-Platonism, in particular through the writings of Plotinus and Proclus, had a profound influence on the development of Sufism by emphasizing a mystical union with God ("The One"). Nonetheless, they "encouraged faith in a broad spiritual path that sought truth and meaningfulness in every aspect of life."[40]

The name *sufi* comes from the word for "wool" (*suf*) probably used for the woolen garments these ascetics wore setting them apart as "knowers" (or *gnostics*) of God or the Divine Ground of Being.[41] One scholar nicely notes their mood and intentions: "Their love of God took the form of a one-pointed yearning for union with Him, for the 'vision of His Face'; and their writings [usually poems] often resembled the arduous outpourings of a lover to his beloved. For the Sufis, the path of love is the Way by which the soul makes the involute journey to the awareness of her own true identity."[42] Ecstatic Sufi poetry,still read and deeply appreciated today, became a principal mode of written teaching and inspiration, outside of the direct relationship with a Spiritual Master or wise teacher. The whole point was to turn within beyond external rites and symbols: "Love the pitcher less and the water more!" they cried.[43] Even Avatar Adi Da directly addresses this issue:

> The dominant "religions" of the present-time are, fundamentally, exoteric traditions that exists in order to serve social purposes—the purposes that are of interest to the State and to the human public collective as a whole…. Sufism, for example, is associated with the tradition of Islam—yet, many exoterically acculturated Muslims oppose Sufism because of its esoteric tendencies. Some "orthodox" Muslims even regard Sufism to be heretical—yet, Sufism is always there, fully within the total tradition of Islam.[44]

As a result, the Sufis cultivated a sacred relationship with an elder known as a **Shaykh** (commonly rendered as *Sheikh* or *Sheik*), meaning an "elder" or "wise old man," i.e., the semblance of a Guru. This helps create a more direct link with the Divine through a personal relationship with an authentic practitioner of contemplative disciplines, therefore emulating the Guru-devotee relationship (depending, of course, on the Shaykh's level or degree of Realization). The Sufi Spiritual Master is also known as **"Pir"** or **"Murshid"** (Arabic for "guide" or "teacher"), who is characterized by *dhikr* or "Remembrance of God" supported with disciplined asceticism. This serves the disciple to realize the **"Supreme Identity"** (or our innate oneness with God). As Swami Abhayananda correctly explains: "It is best to obtain the guidance of one who has already attained that awareness—a Guru, or a Pir—who could guide them correctly to the attainment of Truth."[45] In other words, it is not through scripture or books—or "The Book"—that mystical knowledge is gained, a perennial message in the annals of the Great Wisdom Tradition of humankind. As mentioned, the most effective method is Spirit-Transmission from a Guru-Adept, not intellectual understanding alone [see Chapter 3].

| Rabia Basri | Suhrawardi | Mevlevi Mysticism | Avicenna | Bayazid Bastami |

No precise date can be given for the origins of Sufism, though it was during the 9th century CE that it rose in importance to reach its Golden Age in the 10th century.[46] They would continue at a high level for several centuries before declining in the 15th century but still it is a vibrant mystical view of Islamic theology. Amazingly, one of the earliest and most admired Sufis was an escaped slave-girl from Egypt, **Rabi'a al-'Adawiyya** or **Rabia Basri** (717–801) whose key contribution was her unconditional love of God (*mahabbah*), paralleling the Hindu *bhakti* movement arising in India around the same time.[47] Among other of the best known and revered of the early Sufis were **Hasan al-Basri** (642–728), an ascetic Muslim preacher born in Medina; **Dhul-Nun al-Misri** (796–859), the Sufi Saint known as "The Egyptian"; and **Abu Yazid al Bistami** or "**Bayazid Bastami**" (804–875) the Persian known for promoting the state of *fanā*, the notion of dying in mystical union with Allah and who declared God was in his soul, thus horrifying the orthodox authorities by ecstatically exclaiming: "Glory to Me! How great is my Majesty."[48] There was **Abu al-Husain al-Nuri** (840–908), the Iraqi or "Saint Nuri" known for saying, "I love God and God loves me!"; all were great lovers of God, and each of them greatly influenced the mystical mood of their time.[49]

Indeed, Muslim mystics (almost always Sufis) seemed to be wilder and more extreme than their more sober Christian counterparts in uttering their ecstatic or "intoxicated" language about their Divine Oneness and Realization. Perhaps they acted out this form of "Crazy Wisdom" because there was no strong central religious authority like that of the Roman Catholic Church in Christianity.[50] As another example showing the utter transcendence of self (and subtle visions) in ecstatic union with God as the Heart, the 9th century Sufi **Abmad b. al-'Arabi,** who wrote a book on ecstasy (*Kitah al-wajd*) exclaimed: "Ecstasy in this world comes not from revelation, but consists in the vision of the Heart and realization of the truth."[51] **Avicenna** (d. 1037), the Persian polymath and father of early modern medicine, offered this explanation: "The gnostic [Sufi] passes away from himself and contemplates only the Divine Glory and if he looks upon himself, it is only as the one contemplating, and when he has come to this, he has attained complete union with God."[52] Such Beatific Visions, however, are the province of the advanced-tip few (not the average-mode masses), the contemplative mystics, yet, nonetheless, they perennially arise around the globe wherever they appear. Sadly, orthodox Islam martyred many of their Mystics, as did their Christian counterparts, for claiming their oneness with the Divine (by whatever name) due to its rigid adherence to monotheism (always feeling *separate* from God) and its strict dependency on laws and order.[53]

| Murshid teacher | Rumi | Sufi Whirling Dervishes | Al-Hallaj | Ibn-Arabi |

Several "intoxicated" Sufi Mystics became martyrs and world famous, such as **Al-Hallaj** (858–922), who was flogged, mutilated, and burned for heresy by ecstatically exclaiming his identity with the Lord crying out "I am the Absolute!" (*ana'l Haqq*).[54] Al-Hallaj explained, "When the mystery of Realization that the mystic is one with the Divine—is revealed to you, you will understand that you are no other than God."[55] Although Al-Hallaj was like everyone in our deepest essence, he was killed for realizing this truth and claiming it out loud (and in public); such political corruption of authentic spiritual life has been a perpetual problem for many people in the Abrahamic faiths, creating a condition of disbelief in actual God-Realization that pervades the Western mind to this day. Sadly (and tragically) these attitudes have led to constant warfare, conquest, and bloodshed in the name of religion thus betraying the essence of true religion (as any mystic would claim). There was also the martyred "Murdered Master" (at the age of thirty-eight) named **Abu al-Najib Suhrawardi** (1153—1191), a Persian philosopher and founder of the Iranian school of **Illuminationism**, an important school in Islamic philosophy that claimed "Light" is the source of knowledge about God:

> The Essence of the First, the absolute Light, God, gives constant illumination, whereby It is manifested and brings all things into existence, giving life to them by Its rays. Everything in the world is derived from the light of His Essence, and all beauty and perfection are the gifts of His bounty. To attain fully to this illumination is salvation.[56]

The Sufis have maintained a highly-respected tradition of mysticism producing many revered mystics, some known in the West even today. For instance, the famous Muslim mystic and poet-scholar **Ibn 'Arabi** (1165–1240), whose writings have become well-known outside the Muslim world, is a beacon to the perennial Light of Truth. The talented young Ibn Arabi (who met the aging Averroes) first came under the tutelage of two women well-versed in mystical teachings. When he was twenty, he was initiated into the Sufi path. In his late twenties, he traveled several times to Tunis in North Africa and studied under a number of Sufi *Shaykh* elders.[57] In 1200 CE, when he was thirty-five, Ibn Arabi had a vision leading him on a sacred journey to various cities where he ended up in Mecca to write his magnum opus, *Meccan Revelations*, only affirming his growing reputation as a Divine Master. In 1230, he wrote the acclaimed *Bezels of Wisdom*, possibly writing over 250 books during his lifetime. His writings are dense, however, yet contain bright gems of mystical insight leading one scholar to claim: "Because Ibn 'Arabi represents an early attempt to convey a rational formulation of the vision of Unity that he must be accounted as one of the most influential thinkers of Sufism in any history of mystical thought."[58] Importantly, he emphasizes that *Haqq*, or the transcendent state of God-Realization, is identical with *Khalq*, or the immanent appearance of God in the world.

The Sufis practice spiritual techniques (including meditation) to stimulate ecstatic union with Allah called ***dhikr*** or "Remembrance" of God. Different

Sufi orders achieve *dhikr* through different methods including using prayer beads, chanting, music, poetry, and dancing. The famous Sufi Muslim mystic-poet Rumi started a form of dancing meditation called *sama*, the well-known "**Whirling Dervishes**" of the **Mevlevi Order** of mysticism who spin themselves into a contemplative trance. The Persia-born Rumi living in Konya (then the capital of the Turkish Seljuk Empire) told his followers, "There are many roads which lead to God. I have chosen the one of dance and music." He would fast, meditate and then dance to reach a state of unparalleled ecstasy to feel and remember God.[59] The most renowned sect of whirling Sufis are the Mevlevi order where dance participants are called *semazen*. Although it might look like a trance-state to the uninformed, it is an elevated state of consciousness in which the self is transcended but awareness is clear and awake. Yet to conceal their intentions and be more respectable in the eyes of the Islamic orthodoxy, the Sufis would use metaphors like "madness," "drunkenness," and "intoxication" to describe their "crazy" (yet more direct) relationship with Allah. They did this to deflect criticism in order to not seem like they were making exaggerated egoic claims for what's considered to be only God's privilege—Divine Realization.

Again, like Christianity, Islam tends to condemn those Mystics who have developed further than mythic devotion and faith by professing God-Realization or ecstatic union with the Divine (even if temporarily). Therefore, these advanced-tip Mystics often face persecution and death by opening the inner doors to esoteric truths (beyond exoteric beliefs). This taboo is so strong in Islam, for example, that images of the Prophet himself are not tolerated, since they are considered blasphemous (and an insult to their religion), sometimes even evoking murder to those who print his image. Such cultic and mythic intolerance, however, is exactly what is transcended with higher (and true) spiritual development.

The call of True Religion, therefore, as Adepts throughout history (including Adi Da) point out, is about the transcendence of self (and its limited ideas) to *realize* Real God directly for oneself (*as* oneself)—this is what true self-surrender (not merely self-submission) is all about, i.e., if one's listens attentively to God's Great Tradition of Global Wisdom (not merely to any one religion).

Strict adherence to orthodoxy seems to be a perpetual error in all three of the Western theistic religions descended from the Abraham lineage, but Islam seems to be the most extreme, especially in regard to their treatment of Mystics.[60] The American-born yet global Adept Adi Da directly addresses this dilemma that must be overcome for world peace and religious freedom to truly exist on Earth:

> The strategic purpose of exoteric "religion" is always to subvert the intrinsic and deep esoteric and Transcendental motivations of humankind, and to systematically subordinate humankind to the intrinsically fruitless perennial search for the illusory goals of "worldly", ego-bound, and otherwise mortal psycho-physical "self"-fulfillment.
>
> Therefore, the authentic Wisdom of humankind is in transferring of human endeavor from the exoteric [outer] domain to the esoteric [inner] domain.[61]

Since Islam is a religion of faith (not God-Realization or Enlightenment), we do not often find the appearance of Fully-Realized Adepts (the Sixth and Seventh Stages of Life) within any of the Abrahamic religious traditions (as descended from the founding father Abraham, and even Adam). There are exceptions, of course, such as with Sufism and the few Christian and Jewish Mystics. In this case, most people are not allowed culturally (or theologically) to develop into the higher transpersonal Stages of Life (such as beyond the devotional Fourth or yogic Fifth Stages of Life). Study of the Global Wisdom Tradition, however will assist one in understanding that a sacred relationship to an already Awakened Adept is essential in helping us realize the Enlightened State of God-Realization.

As integral pandit Ken Wilber would put it, although the Biblical Prophets had evolved (ascended) to the higher, transpersonal stages of life (exhibiting Theistic Mysticism); they had not yet attained ultimate nondual Enlightenment (realized in Formless or Nondual Mysticism), except in special cases.

Their relationship was defined by feeling separate from God, not living in union with "the Father" (whether named Yahweh and Allah). Such Prophets claim to be intermediaries using the mind or instructions from God to speak to "his people" (or tribes) claiming they had heard His Voice. This was the case with Prophet Muhammad, who heard Allah through the Archangel Gabriel to give Muslims the holy *Qur'an*. For Muslims, the *Qur'an* is literally the "Voice of Allah" speaking directly to them (through their messenger Prophet Muhammad). This was the case with Moses and the other Prophets of the *Old Testament* as well. Yet few (if any) would claim like Jesus of Nazareth did in the *New Testament* that "I and the Father are one." Nonetheless, those Adepts have said, as did Jesus and many others, to "Follow Me" and see for yourself.

RUMI & KABIR: DEVOTIONAL POET-MYSTICS

The lamps are different, but the Light is the same;
It comes from beyond.

— **Rumi**, Sufi Mystic

Rumi
(1207–1273)

Kabir
(1398–1448 or 1440–1518)

One of the most famous Adept-Realizers arising from the culture of Islam (born in present-day Afghanistan) was today's extremely popular Persian poet **Jala ad-Din Rumi** (1207–1273), or simply **Rumi**, the world-renowned mystic who would powerfully influence the mystical Sufi tradition and become known and respected throughout the modern world. Called "Mawlana," meaning "our Master,"[62] our scholar Swami Abhayananda explains: "Rumi's verses are full of imagery of love, but it is the love of the soul for God. Rumi is the epitome of the mystical lover; but he is also knew [for himself] the 'union' with his Beloved, and speaks with rare beauty of this mysterious 'marriage' of the soul to God."[63] Rumi's poetic masterpiece, the *Masnavi* (or *Mathnawi*), is composed of twenty-six thousand verses written in Persian that are often called "the Qur'an in Persian," one of the most influential works of Sufism. Rumi was an aristocrat, a lavish and vibrant writer with tremendous learning, whereas Kabir (a couple of centuries later) was a peasant, a lower-class weaver who lived in poverty most of his life, speaks more fiercely and directly. Rumi leads with the tender love of God, while Kabir emphasizes the side of God that howls for everyone to Wake Up![64]

Rumi's relationship with his own Master, **Shams Tabrizi** (d. 1228) is famous for the overwhelming love they had for one another and the Divine Being. As the God-infilled devotee sings in his ecstatic poetry for everyone to hear:

> Choose a Master, for without one
> the road on this journey is
> full of hazards, fear and danger....
> Only the Master's shadow of Love
> kills the self.
> Do not let go of your devotion
> to Him who kills the self.

Kabir or **Kabir Das** (either 1398–1448 or 1440–1518) was born a Muslim (in Varanasi, India) but studied under the Hindu bhakti leader and ascetic **Ramananda** (14th century). Kabir, however, was a married householder earning a living as a poor weaver, yet became one of the most influential figures in northern India to be hailed as the "Father of Hindi literature." Kabir was critical of both Hinduism and Islam, claiming followers of both were at times misguided by the *Vedas* and *Qur'an* as he questioned, for example, their meaningless rites of initiation such as the sacred thread and circumcision, respectively. Consequently, he was threatened by both Hindus and Muslims but by the time he died both claimed him as being one of their own. Kabir was reacting against the increasing formalism of the orthodox cults of both religions, including the intense intellectualism of the Vedanta philosophers (pandits) and the exaggerated monism of orthodox Islam. His poetic songs are now an important part of the Sikh scripture the *Adi Granth* (or *Guru Granth Sahib*) [see below].

Kabir was following the revival movement began by **Ramanuja** (1017–1137 CE) in India that emphasized the mystical "religion of love" or devotion to God, the new Bhakti movement of Hinduism [see Chapter 16]. Kabir's Guru Ramananda was preaching religious tolerance since India was full of Hindus, Muslims, Christians, Yogis, and other spiritual seekers all trying to live together. Yet it is in Kabir's mystical poetry that he also lives for people today, part of the great lineage of Persian mystic-poets, including Rumi, **Fariduddin Attar** (ca. 1145–1220), **Saadi Shirazi** (1210–1291), and **Hafiz** (1315–1390), who's collected works are regarded by many Iranians as a pinnacle of Persian literature. It is Kabir's intense devotion to the One God, beyond religious provincialism, that sings out for our emerging global culture:

> Hari is in the East: Allah is in the West.
> Look within your heart,
> For there you will find both Karim [of Islam] and Ram [of Hinduism];
> All the men and women of the world are His living forms.
> Kabir is the child of Allah and of Ram:
> He is my Guru, He is my Pir.[65]

The sincere devotion to a Guru, however, is lost on most modern people who read and enjoy this ecstatic Persian poetry (including the immensely popular Rumi). But it is their relationship with an authentic Adept-Realizer, their Guru and Spiritual Master, who is a genuine "channel" (or Agent) to the Divine that lies at the heart of their spiritual life and Awakening to God-Realization. These intoxicated mystic-poets ecstatically exclaim that the embodied reality of the God-State is present right here and now on Earth, not waiting for us in some future paradise or vision. Kabir knows also that he came to this mystical vision of Prior Unity with help from his beloved Guru:

> O Brother, my heart yearns for that true Guru, who fills the cup
> of true love, and drinks of it himself, and offers it then to me.
> He removes the veil from the eyes,
> and gives the true Vision of Brahma.
> He reveals the worlds in Him,
> and makes me hear the Unstruck Music.
> He shows joy and sorrow to be one.
> He fills all utterance with love.

Kabir says: "Verily he has no fear, who has such a Guru
to lead him to the shelter of safety!"[66]

Contemplation of the Master and his image, the spiritual relationship between *shaykh* (guru) and *murid* (disciple), is a primary practice of the Sufis.
They are honoring many of the basic principles of the Guru-devotee relationship or *Satsang* (as long practiced in India). As the twentieth-century Chishti
Sufi **Nawah Gurdri Shah Baba** declared:

> The contemplation of the Murshid [Master] is the first step towards
> mysticism…. When the image of the Murshid takes its abode in the
> heart of the murid [disciple], his heart will be filled with light and un-
> der the influence of the Murshid the mind will find Enlightenment.[67]

As in all the esoteric traditions of the world's religions, the Light of Truth
(*sophia*) is eternal (and perennial) and thus will always become evident with
sincere practice and devotion (for it is "always already the case"). In this case,
Awakened Adepts and Sat-Gurus, continue to appear throughout the centuries
being born anew when darkness and ignorance overshadows the traditional
religions thus to spark the birth of new Adepts for new times and new generations, as we'll see next.

SIKHS: ONE GOD UNITY

A well-known saying in India (and throughout the Perennial Philosophy)
is that in dark times a special Adept will appear to bring the light
of Wisdom to a struggling humankind. This happened in the 16th
century in India while the West began to emerge from their own Dark Ages
and began to colonize the world (and eventually India). The warfare and
bitter quarreling between the factions of native Hinduism and invading Islam

created deep animosity and the constant potential and actuality for violence to erupt at any time (as it often does still today). Unfortunately, with staunch monotheists (who believe in no gods but their One God), and with religions like Islam and Christianity made even more dangerous by being founded on a future Judgment Day, this has usually led to intolerance among their mythic followers who believe only they hold the "Truth." Yet, in reality, the One Truth of God is universal and "belongs" (or can be revealed) to everyone, one and all, for it is not beholden to any one tradition. Thus Adept-Realizers who have been freed (or liberated) from identity to any one tradition or religion must appear anew in succeeding generations to teach and remind us of this simple (yet most profound) truth.

In India, following in the footsteps and universal wisdom of Kabir [see above] there came an Adept-Guru who would become the founder of the Sikh religion, the fifth most popular religion in the world today. Known as **Guru Nanak** (1469–1539), he was the first of "Ten Gurus"—the "First Guru" or *Adi Guru* (the "primal Guru")—who would establish the Sikh religion which is thriving in the modern world. In 1499 (at age 30), Nanak, who was disgusted with the persistent conflicts between local Muslims and Hindus, had a mystical experience of God's prior unity (or oneness) after bathing in the Bein River in the Punjab of northeastern India. Awakened, he announced: "There is neither Hindu nor Muslim, so whose path shall I follow? I will follow God's path for God is neither Hindu nor Muslim." This universal message would become the foundation for his teachings and writings often sung in poems so he became known as the "Singing Guru."[68] Guru Nanak would emphasize that God was greater than any one religion, as scholars James Fieser and John Powers powerfully explain:

> Throughout his life Guru Nanak worked to reconcile Hindus and Muslims, to teach them that God is everywhere and continually calls His creatures to experience Him directly and intuitively. This cannot be accomplished by those who rely on external religious observances. Rather, God is found only by practitioners of pure devotion who open themselves to the divine call and experience mystical union. Nanak taught that devotion is the highest form of religious practice, but also the most difficult. The ego is a powerful force in human beings, and it causes us to recoil from the experience of union in which

all sense of individuality is swept away by a transcendent vision of the divine presence.[69]

Guru Nanak traveled widely teaching the truth of his new religious message attracting many followers throughout the villages of India; some say he even traveled to Mecca.[70] Nanak had originally belonged to a group of mystics known as *Sants*, who also stressed the unity of God beyond all exoteric rituals and ceremonies since one of their greatest teachers was Kabir. Nanak, like Kabir, emphasized God's two unified aspects: (1) the *immanent* aspect or God as *saguna* meaning "with qualities," and (2) the *transcendent* aspect or God as *nirguna* meaning "without (or beyond) qualities."[71] Guru Nanak died in 1539 after gathering together a small group of *Sikhs* (from *śisya* meaning "student" or "disciple"), who were both Hindus and Muslims that recognized their Guru was transcending their own sectarian divisions.

Guru Nanak   **Arjan Dev**   **Khanda**   **Ninth Guru**   **Tenth Guru**

Before he died, Guru Nanak designated his devotee **Angad** (1504–1552) as his successor, the Second Guru, who further established the Sikh path (*panth*) initiating a lineage of succeeding Gurus. Next came **Amar Das** (1479–1574), another personal devotee of Nanak, the Third Guru from age 73 to his death at 95, and who founded the city of **Amritsar** (in the Punjab), where his son-in-law **Ram Das** (1534–1581), built the **Golden Temple** (*Darhar Sahib*), the Sikh's holiest shrine still revered to this day. The Fifth Guru, **Arjan Dev** (1563–1610) set about to compile the Sikh's sacred teachings, ranging from Kabir to Nanak to other devotional poet-saints, called the *Adi Granth* (the "primal book"). This sacred text is now the central focus of the Sikh religion where copies are placed on pedestals in the center of each Sikh temple called a *gurdvara*, literally, "door to the Guru" (holding the book of the Awakened Adepts' ecstatic songs). Guru Arjan's tenure, however, brought about a serious challenge to the Sikh approach since the surrounding Muslim Mughal regime controlling northern India began persecuting other religious groups, including the Sikhs.[72] Arjan was captured and tortured to death in prison since he would not renounce his faith. He advised his son, Guru **Hargobind** (1595–1664) to "sit fully armed upon the throne," thus this group of devotional mystics began stressing combat readiness and willingness to fight—and die—to defend the Sikh faith.[73] This is why the symbol of the Sikhs, called the *khanda*, has two curved swords or *kirpans* (on the outside) protecting the two-edged sword in the center representing freedom and justice with a circle symbolizing unity or the oneness of God and humanity.[74] Indeed, as one of our supportive scholars explains:

> It is ironic that Sikhism, which began as a movement dedicated to reconciling different faiths, was pushed by historical circumstances to become a tradition that stressed the differences of its members from other religious groups and that was determined to defend itself against hostile opponents.[75]

The next several Gurus ruled during increasing tensions between the Sikhs and Mughal emperors. The Ninth Guru **Tegh Bahadur** (1621–1675) was martyred since he refused the imposed tax on non-Muslims and so was executed. His son, **Gobind Singh** (1666–1708), the Tenth Guru, became the last Guru, but perhaps the most important. For one, he further developed the institution of the *Khalsa*, the community of Sikh believers that would defend their faith against all enemies. Then, realizing the title and office of Guru made it a target, as he lay dying from an assassin's wounds, declared that the *Adi Granth*, the Holy Book, would be the future Guru, now to be called the *Guru Granth Sahib*, a Collection of Sacred Wisdom of the Gurus. As the wise pandit-sage Huston Smith explains: "Only in a secondary sense was Guru Nanak a *guru*. The only True *Guru* is God. Others qualify as *gurus* in proportion as God speaks through them."[76] Truly, the Real Guru agrees.

In addition, the Tenth Guru instituted what are called the "**Five Ks**" that all Sikhs should follow expressing their faith and unity: (1) *kes*, hair, so Sikhs do not cut their hair or beards; (2) *kangha*, a comb, to keep the hair neat; (3) *kirpan*, a short sword symbolizing the warrior ethos of the Khalsa; (4) *kara*, a steel wristband; and (5) *kachch*, short pants. Many Sikhs wear turbans as a way to manage their long hair, and many have also changed their family name to Singh, meaning lion, as a symbol of their devotion to their Guru.[77]

Sikh theology always stresses the One God "without a second" and that this Transcendent Divine Reality (*Ik Onkar*), or "Timeless Being" (*Akal Purukh*), is only known through mystical union. One of their main methods of meditation is "remembering the Name" (*nam simran*). They also believe reverently in community, working hard, and serving others (by offering free vegetarian meals, giving alms, by living the good life, etc.). As one scholar pointed out: "Extending the ethic of service to the whole of humanity is one example of an important principle in Sikh morality. Sikhs believe that all of humanity was created by God and therefore all of humanity is equal."[78] This has led the Sikhs to be successful in communities throughout the modern West (including in Europe and the United States) displaying a tolerant and beneficial attitude to all, regardless of race, gender, or belief. Unlike most world religions, their sacred writings, contained in the *Guru Granth Sahib*, include writings from people outside their own faith. For Sikhs, as real religion and cooperative community prove, it is possible to extend the oneness of God to embrace the oneness of all humankind, a trait our entire world direly needs. They have also learned how to honor the role of the genuinely enlightened Guru (and Gurus). For, as noted, Awakened Adepts continue to appear, especially when needed.

MANI: PERSIAN PROPHET OF LIGHT

As one more example arising from the land of Persia (not Arabia) is the Prophet **Mani** (ca. 216–274 or 277 CE) who would establish a religion known as **Manichaeism**. Mani taught an elaborate dualistic cosmology that described the struggle between a good, spiritual world of light, and an evil, material world of darkness, yet the spark of divine light in each person gives them their possibility for salvation. The previous dominant religion in Persia was Zoroastrianism, founded by **Zoroaster** or **Zarathustra** (dates unknown, possibly 1500–1000 BCE or 650–500 BCE), whose sacred scripture is the *Gathas*, 17 hymns that make up the core liturgy of the *Avesta* (in the Avestan language, an old Iranian language group). One of the world's oldest living religions, Zoroastrianism is still practiced to this day (perhaps 200,000 members), a minor religion in parts of Iran and India.

The influence of Zoroastrianism throughout the Middle East was significant; not the least of which was how the Jewish exiles in Babylon seem to have been thoroughly impregnated with Zoroastrian ideas as they wrote down the *Old Testament*, consequently influencing all the Gnostic religions—Hermetism, Gnosticism, and particularly Christianity.[79] Zoroaster's message of reform is based on the idea that people are free to choose between good and evil, a struggle set up by **Ahura Mazda** ("Wise Lord"), the Creator of all and uncreate Spirit (or Light) in constant battle with **Angra Mainyu** ("destructive spirit") the creator of death and evil. In Zoroastrianism cosmology the end of four three-thousand-year periods came to a close with the coming a savior. Mani considered himself the final Prophet in the line beginning with Adam which also includes the Buddha, Zoroaster, and Jesus.

Zoroaster
from Parsi statue

Ateshkadeh Zoroastrian
fire temple, Yazd, Iran

Mani studied in Babylon and traveled throughout India studying Hinduism and Buddhism until he returned to the Sasanian Empire and was received favorably by King Shapur I (died 272). Although in competition with Zoroastrianism, Mani attempted to establish an independent religion with a universal message that he hoped would replace all existing religions, including Christianity (thus he was considered heretical by the Christian Church). It's hard to underestimate its importance, although today hardly anyone knows about Manichaeism, as world religion scholar Joseph Kitagawa explains: "From the perspective of the unity of humankind, Manichaeism marked an important page in the history of the human race. Mani believed that it was possible to unite people of diverse backgrounds with a syncretic method that combined the faiths of different religions."[80] Being intensely missionary-oriented, Mani gathered followers throughout Central Asia, China, Europe, and North Africa; even Augustine was once an adherent.

Manichaeism popularity grew rapidly so that for a brief period it was the main rival to Christianity in the competition to replace classical paganism before the spread of Islam in the tenth century drove its headquarters in Persia to Samarkand (in southeastern Uzbekistan, one of the oldest continuously inhabited cities in Central Asia). Mani's religion had a world-wide influence, as scholar David Snellgrove summarizes:

> If we measure world-wide extent by the vast number of different languages in which his teachings spread from their original Iranian dialects in translated versions throughout western Asia, thence westwards to the then limits of the Roman Empire, Egypt and North Africa, and eastwards across Central Asia to China. Regarded as a form of Christian heresy by the Church authorities, Mani's religion was practically obliterated by the sixth century in the West, although valuable manuscript remains have been preserved in Egypt in Coptic.
>
> Meanwhile it continued to thrive throughout Central Asia in association with Buddhism and Nestorian Christianity, even becoming for a short while in the 8th and 9th centuries the state religion of the Uigurs, the Turkish tribe who then dominated much of the whole vast area. It survived in southern China side by side with Buddhism and Taoism until the 14th century, when the murderous Mongol invasions led to its eventual extinction. Maybe it is salutary to reflect that a great religion does not necessarily last forever.[81]

Similar to other gnostic religions, Mani taught the world is full of evil and misery but there was a spark of divine light in every person that needs to be cultivated so they may become beacons of the good, practicing love and compassion for all beings. Manichaeism suggests it is only through the special wisdom of *gnosis* that this salvation or knowledge of the Light may be attained. Kitagawa summarizes in his excellent *The Quest for Human Unity* (1990): "Mani advocated the perfectibility of human beings through *gnosis*, fasting, almsgiving, and purity of thought, word, and deed. Enjoining a rigorous asceticism, he preached the importance of love, both of the Godhead and of every human being, each of whom bears the divine element. Under his beliefs, this world would hopefully become one huge, unwalled monastery."[82] However, as is always the case, without the actual (and personal) experience of *gnosis* or Enlightenment, usually only gained under the guidance of an authentic Adept-Guru (via *Satsang*), supported by genuine spiritual practices and serious meditation (*sadhana*), such ideals are not fully realized, unfortunately. This is another reason why this book claims that we must learn to appreciate the true function of the Awakened Adept-Realizer even in the modern age. It is important that we not dismiss what has driven the Founders of all world's religions who make up God's Great Tradition of Global Wisdom.

BAHA'I FAITH:
UNITY OF ALL RELIGIONS

Shrine of the Bab
Bahai gardens in Haifa, Israel

Religious Unity

ne of the most recent attempts to unite all religions under one religion began in 1844 when a merchant's son living in Persia (present-day Iran) named **Sayyed 'Ali Muhammad** (1819–1850)—to be known as the **Bab** meaning "Gate" or "Door"—prophesied the coming of a great Prophet., similar to Moses, Jesus, or Muhammad. In 1859, a Persian nobleman and follower of the Bab had a mystical revelation that it was "He Who God Shall Make Manifest" and so he was accepted as **Baha'ullah** ("The Glory of God") (1817–1892), the one who the Bab had foretold.[83] That did not go over well with the majority of Muslims. Thousands of his followers were executed by the Islamic Persian authorities for their beliefs, where Baha'ullah ended up in a prison city of Akka (in present-day Israel) until he died in 1892. His burial site is now a destination of pilgrimage for followers of the **Baha'i Faith** near the **Baha'i World Center** in Haifa, Israel, where there is a gold-domed shrine surrounded by beautiful green gardens where the Bab himself was also laid to rest in 1850. After Baha'u'llah's death, his eldest son, 'Abdu'l-Baha (1844–1921) became the leader known as the "Head of Faith" and "Center of the Covenant." When he was released from prison (in 1908), he led a life of traveling and teaching to maintain the Baha'i communities centered mostly in Iran and the Ottoman Empire, but also spreading into Asia and Africa, even finding a foothold in Europe and the Americas. The Baha'i Faith has 5–7 million followers but is still intensely persecuted in Iran (its place of origin).

Baha'u'llah was a prolific writer producing a vast body of writings known as **Tablets**, including sending many letters to world leaders, covering everything from spirituality to politics, thus forming the main scriptures of the Baha'i Faith. Born at a time when the colonized world was beginning to recognize the universal principles that unite all religions—such as with the 1893 Parliament of the World's Religions [see Chapter 9]—the Baha'i Faith proposed such a global unifying vision. For example, their temples, such as the Lotus of Bahapur in Delhi, India, have nine sides surrounding a central dome to represent the prior unity of all religions and humankind. The Baha'i Faith is essentially founded on three main principles:

(1) There is One God and all faiths essentially worship the same Divine Reality, whatever they call It (which is unnamable).

(2) There is One Religion since all faiths draw from the same spiritual truths revealed in the human psyche, which have been taught by one descending line of "Manifestations of God," including Moses, Buddha, Krishna, Jesus, Muhammad, et al., including Baha'u'llah.

(3) There is One Humanity since everyone, regardless of culture or century, is created by the One God so therefore everyone is a member of one worldwide family.[84]

As one scholar summarizes: "The Baha'i Faith aims to unite this [human] family, overcome the differences that divide us, and so bring salvation for both individuals and for the world."[85] However, as Huston Smith noted: "Baha'i, which originated in the hope of rallying the major religions around the beliefs they hold in common, has settled into being another religion among many."[86] Yet, this universal religion born amidst the conflicts of the Middle East and

Europe, grounded in the Abrahamic religions, yet transcending them all, still points to the Perennial Philosophy (and *sophia perennis*) where all religious impulses are seen to be universal and innately human [see Chapters 7-8].

The Baha'i writings maintain that all human beings have a "rational soul" providing our species with a unique capacity to recognize God or the Source-Condition of the universe, and that humanity can cultivate a sacred relationship with this Divine Presence.[87] Importantly, they also maintain that every human being has a responsibility (and capability) to recognize God through God's Messengers, the Adept-Realizers (and Guru-Adepts), and to follow their teachings through study and practice (not mere belief). As we have seen, this is a universal (and perennial) message that rings throughout the centuries, throughout the millennia, regardless of race, culture, gender, or traditional heritage. Ultimately, it is up to each of us to "Wake Up!" to this universal truth, as this book hopes to highlight. Again, this approach of real mysticism has long been taught by the "hidden" (or esoteric) Teachings of the East, found most deeply in the heart of India (as we'll see next).

AMEEN

Chapter 15 Endnotes

1. See: Huston Smith, *The World's Religions* (1958, 1991), p. 222.

2. Adi Da Samraj [Da Free John], *Nirvanasara* (1982), pp. 83-84.

3. David Snellgrove, *Religion as History, Religion as Myth* (2006), p. 111.

4. Huston Smith, *The World's Religions* (1958, 1991), p. 231.

5. See: David Snellgrove, *Religion as History, Religion as Myth* (2006), p. 111.

6. Joseph Campbell, *The Flight of the Wild Gander* (1951, 1990), p. 198 [gender-neutral terms substituted].

7. See: Huston Smith, *The World's Religions* (1958, 1991), p. 225.

8. Ibid., p. 229.

9. Ibid., p. 236.

10. See: Joseph Kitagawa, *The Quest for Human Unity: A Religious History* (1990), pp. 106, 110.

11. See: Huston Smith, *The World's Religions* (1958, 1991), p. 229.

12. See, for example: Randall Balmer, *Solemn Reverence: The Separation of Church and State in American Life* (2021).

13. See: James Fieser and John Powers, *Scriptures of the World's Religions* (2018), p. 531.

14. Ibid., p. 531.

15. See: Joseph Kitagawa, *The Quest for Human Unity: A Religious History* (1990), p. 109.

16. Ibid., pp. 109-110.

17. Ibid., p. 109.

18. See: James Fieser and John Powers, *Scriptures of the World's Religions* (2018), p. 533.

19. See: Joseph Kitagawa, *The Quest for Human Unity: A Religious History* (1990), p. 110; also see: Huston Smith, *The World's Religions* (1958, 1991), p. 239.

20. See: Joseph Kitagawa, *The Quest for Human Unity: A Religious History* (1990), p. 107.

21. Ibid., p. 108.

22. See: James Fieser and John Powers, *Scriptures of the World's Religions* (2018), p. 554.

23. See: Joseph Kitagawa, *The Quest for Human Unity: A Religious History* (1990), p. 108.

24. See: Huston Smith, *The World's Religions* (1958, 1991), p. 241.

25. See: James Fieser and John Powers, *Scriptures of the World's Religions* (2018), p. 561.

26. Ibid., p. 563.

27. See: *Spiritual Choices: The Problem of Recognizing Authentic Paths to Inner Transformation* (1987) edited by Dick Anthony, Bruce Ecker, and Ken Wilber; Ken Wilber, *Eye to Eye* (1982, 2001).

28. Joseph Kitagawa, *The Quest for Human Unity: A Religious History* (1990), p. 111.

29. Ibid., pp. 111, 112

30. Ibid., p. 112.

31. See: "The Rise of Falsafah: The Philosophical Tradition" at encyclopedia.com (retrieved June 2021).

32. See: Violet Moller, *The Map of Knowledge: A Thousand-Year History of how Classical Ideas Were Lost and Found* (2019).

33. Ibid., 121.

34. See: Joseph Kitagawa, *The Quest for Human Unity: A Religious History* (1990), p. 112.

35. Arthur Herman, *The Cave and the Light* (2013), p. 561.

36. See: Joseph Kitagawa, *The Quest for Human Unity: A Religious History* (1990), pp. 112, 115.

37. Ibid., p. 129.

38. Ibid., p. 161.

39. Ibid., p. 162.

40. Ibid., p. 112.

41. See: Swami Abhayananda [Stan Trout], *History of Mysticism: The Unchanging Testament* (1987), p. 240; also see: Huston Smith, *The World's Religions* (1958, 1991), p. 258.

42. Swami Abhayananda [Stan Trout], *History of Mysticism: The Unchanging Testament* (1987), pp. 240-241.

43. See: Huston Smith, *The World's Religions* (1958, 1991), p. 258.

44. Ad Da Samraj, "Exoteric and Esoteric: The Public and The Secret Dimensions of Religion" in *The Pneumaton* (2011), p. 41.

45. Swami Abhayananda [Stan Trout], *History of Mysticism: The Unchanging Testament* (1987), p. 357.

46. See: W. T. Stace, *The Teachings of the Mystics* (1960), p. 201.

47. See: *Scriptures of the World's Religions* (2018) by James Fieser and John Powers, p. 599.

48. See: W. T. Stace, *The Teachings of the Mystics* (1960), p. 201.

49. See: Swami Abhayananda [Stan Trout], *History of Mysticism: The Unchanging Testament* (1987), p. 240.

50. See: W. T. Stace, *The Teachings of the Mystics* (1960), p. 202.

51. See: Margaret Smith, *Readings from the Mystics of Islam* (1950, 1994), 10.

52. See: W. T. Stace, *The Teachings of the Mystics* (1960), p. 207.

53. See: W. T. Stace, *The Teachings of the Mystics* (1960), Chapter 7: "Islamic Mysticism."

54. See: Joseph Kitagawa, *The Quest for Human Unity: A Religious History* (1990), p. 112.

55. See: W. T. Stace, *The Teachings of the Mystics* (1960), p. 212.

56. Quoted in Annemarie Schimmel, *Mystical Dimensions of Islam* (1976, 2011), p. 261.

57. See: Swami Abhayananda [Stan Trout], *History of Mysticism: The Unchanging Testament* (1987), p. 268.

58. Ibid., p. 269.

59. See: Cara Tabachnick, "Here's what you should know before attending a whirling dervish ceremony in Turkey" (in *The Washington Post*, April 12, 2019).

60. See: W. T. Stace, *The Teachings of the Mystics* (1960), Chapter 7: "Islamic Mysticism."

61. Adi Da Samraj, "The Wisdom of Esotericism" in *The Pneumaton* (2011), p. 45.

62. See, for example: *The Way of Passion: A Celebration of Rumi* (2000) by Andrew Harvey; *The Essential Rumi* (New Expanded Edition, 2004) translated by Coleman Barks.

63. Swami Abhayananda [Stan Trout], *History of Mysticism: The Unchanging Testament* (1987), p. 279.

64. See: Andrew Harvey, *The Way of Passion: A Celebration of Rumi* (2000); *Turn Me to Gold: 108 Poems of Kabir* (2018).

65. Kabir, *Songs of Kabir* (1915, 1977), translated by Rabindranath Tagore, p. 112.

66. Ibid., pp. 71-72.

67. See: *The Lord as Guru: Hindu "Sants" in Northern India* (1987) by Daniel Gold, p. 193, quoted from *Love of the God-Man* (1990) by James Steinberg, p. 168.

68. See: *The Singing Guru: Legends and Adventures of Guru Nanak, the First Sikh* (Mandala Publishing, 2015) by Kamla K. Kapur.

69. James Fieser and John Powers, *Scriptures of the World's Religions* (2018), p. 171.

70. See: *Religions: Belief, Ceremonies, Festivals, Sects, Sacred Texts* (NY: Metro Books, 2016) by Philip Wilkinson, p. 210.

71. See: *Scriptures of the World's Religions* (2018) by James Fieser and John Powers, p. 172.

72. Ibid., p. 173.

73. Ibid., p. 173.

74. See: *Religions: Belief, Ceremonies, Festivals, Sects, Sacred Texts* (2016) by Philip Wilkinson, p. 213.

75. James Fieser and John Powers, *Scriptures of the World's Religions* (2018), p. 174.

76. Huston Smith, *The World's Religions* (1958, 1991), p. 390.

77. See: *Scriptures of the World's Religions* (2018) by James Fieser and John Powers, p. 174.

78. Philip Wilkinson, *Religions: Belief, Ceremonies, Festivals, Sects, Sacred Texts* (2016), p. 218.

79. See: R. C. Zaehner, *The Concise Encyclopedia of Living Faiths* (1959, NY: Hawthorne Books), p. 209, referenced in Joseph Kitagawa, *The Quest for Human Unity: A Religious History* (1990), p. 22.

80. Joseph Kitagawa, *The Quest for Human Unity: A Religious History* (1990), p. 103.

81. David Snellgrove, *Religion as History, Religion as Myth* (2006), pp. xi-xii.

82. Joseph Kitagawa, *The Quest for Human Unity: A Religious History* (1990), p. 103.

83. See: *Religions: Belief, Ceremonies, Festivals, Sects, Sacred Texts* (2016) by Philip Wilkinson, p. 280.

84. Ibid., p. 280.

85. Ibid., p. 280.

86. Huston Smith, *The World's Religions* (1958, 1991), p. 385.

87. See: McMullen, Michael D., *The Baha'i: The Religious Construction of a Global Identity* (2000).

SIXTEEN

GURU YOGA-SATSANG: HINDUISM

GURU YOGA:
RISHIS TO FOREST YOGIS

India is the heart (and root) of the world's esoteric spirituality—it even looks like a heart dangling down from the middle of the Asian continent—for it has produced two of the world's most advanced religious systems: Hinduism-Yoga and Buddhism, as well as several others (such as Jainism and Sikhism). From the mists of the dim past it appears that Adept-Realizers, or certain individuals exhibiting advanced stages in the evolution of consciousness, from Rishis to Yogis to Siddhas, came forth to bring the world its first teachings on Yoga and how to attain Awakened Realization of what IS (beyond all names and forms). No one less than the quintessential American humorist Mark Twain (1835–1910), who (unknown to many) extensively traveled this vast ancient land, claimed that "India is the cradle of the human race, birthplace of human speech, mother of history, grandmother of legend, great-grandmother of tradition." Even today, every era and stage of human civilization is alive in India: from the magic to mythic, from the mental to the transpersonal, from the scientific to the religious, from Priests to Yogis to Saints to Sages to Siddhas, from villages to towns to metropolitan cities, from farmers to craftsmen, from the free to those bound in poverty and disease.

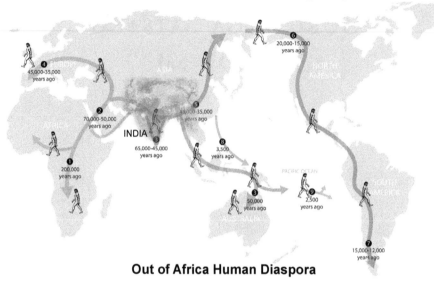

Out of Africa Human Diaspora

The India subcontinent was one of the first stopping places of early *Homo sapiens* in their migrations out of Africa, probably around 65,000 years before present (BP). In other words, the first people into India were Black people, which is still evident by the darker skinned Indians who still live in the southern and southwestern coasts. Although the exact dates of the first successful African migrations are disputed, and whether they are "pre- or post-Toba" (referring to the globe-altering supereruption of volcano Toba in Indonesia, around 75,000 years BP) is not clear. After entering India, the wandering Africans first settled in the tropical rainforests on the southwestern edges of the Asian subcontinent. In time, further migrations progressed into south and southeast Asia eventually leading people eventually over to Australia (ca. 40,000 years BP). People also spread out north from Motherland India to cover much of Asia and Europe (changing into different races and skin colors as environmental adaptation demanded). Many of today's languages are derived from the ancient Proto-Indo-European language group (including most European ones). No wonder historian Will Durant wisely noted: "India was the motherland of our race and Sanskrit the mother of Europe's languages. India was the mother of our philosophy, of much of our mathematics... In many ways, Mother India is the mother of us all." And so she is, spiritually as well.

Once the Neolithic (or agricultural) revolution took place after the Last Glacial Period (ca. 10,000 BP), historians have subdivided the history of India into the following Ages[1]:

1. **Pre-Vedic Age** (6500–4500 BCE) — evidence of an early Neolithic town called **Mehrgarh** in western India (present-day Pakistan) grew in size to 20,000 individuals (which is huge for that period) being an industrious marketplace and center of innovation with pottery and terra-cotta figurines (by 2600 BCE); leading to the **Indus-Sarasvati** River Valley civilization, including its two largest cities of **Mohenjo-dara** and **Harappa** (3rd mil. BCE).

2. **Vedic Age** (4500–2500 BCE) — the wisdom-tradition culture (including the indigenous "**Dravidians**" of the Indus-Sarasvati civilization [in Pakistan]) captured in the four *Vedas* (composed orally perhaps in the 5th to 4th millennium BCE or later) was disrupted first, by the drying up of the mighty Sarasvati River (by 1900 BCE) that caused a civilizational shift to the banks of the Ganges River (in India), and second, with the "invasion" or assimilation of the Sanskrit-speaking Vedic "**Aryan**" culture from the northern steppes (perhaps Anatolia) who wrote down the *Vedas*. This period ended with the famous war remembered in the *Mahabharata* with King Bh arata (traditionally dated at 3102 BCE), also said to be the beginning of the so-called Kali Yuga or "Dark Age" (that the Hindus [and Adi Da] say we're still in).

3. **Brahmanical Age** (2500–1500 BCE) — after moving to the Ganges River (and her tributaries) and shifting to a hierarchical society (based on the caste system), the *Brahmana* literature (including Vedic sciences, such as astronomy astrology, geometry, mathematics, etc.) was created, including the *Aranyakas* (ritual texts for forest-dwelling ascetics), plus the *Sutra* literature dealing with legal and ethical issues and the arts.

4. **Upanishadic Age** (1500–800 BCE) — with the earliest *Upanishads* the yogic ideal of turning inward or "internalizing ritualism"—an "inner sacrifice" (*antar-yajna*), a hidden trend in the *Vedas*—becomes the principal practice of free-wandering **Yogis** based upon intensive meditation and renunciation (*sannyasa*) that culminates with the non-Vedic traditions of **Jainism** (started by the Adept Mahavira) and **Buddhism** (begun by Siddhartha Gautama Shakyamuni, the Buddha) both around 500 BCE.

5. **Epic Age** or **Pre-Classical Age** (1000–100 BCE) — along with the growing canon of the *Upanishads*, there emerged the classic epics of the *Mahabharata* and the *Ramayana* (introducing the Adept Rama) depicting the earlier era involving the great war of the Pandavas and Kauravas from which also came the *Bhagavad Gita* (introducing the Adept Krishna and his warrior-devotee Arjuna), the earliest complete **Yoga** work clarifying the extreme importance of the devotional Guru-devotee relationship.

6. **Classical Age** (100 BCE–500 CE) — is when the classical schools of Hindu philosophy and Yoga were further codified, including the *Yoga Sutra* of Patanjali, the *Brahma Sutra* of Badarayana, and the *Samkhya Karika* (from disciples of the Adept Kapila); it is also the period when Mahayana Buddhism emerged (following Hinayana or Theraveda) [see Chapter 17] creating an active dialogue between Buddhists and Hindus culminating with the **Advaita Vedanta** Adept Shankara (8th century) who integrated the views of Buddhism into the Vedanta tradition.

7. **Post-Classical** or **Tantric/Puranic Age** (500–1300 CE) — the time when the *Puranas* were compiled, huge encyclopedic compilations weaving together sacred histories, philosophies, mythologies, and ritual knowledge. It was also when the revolution of **Tantra** or Tantrism took place promoting a spiritual lifestyle that elevates and integrates the feminine psycho-cosmic principle (*shakti*) to profoundly influence not only Hinduism, but Buddhism and Jainism.

8. **Sectarian Age** (1300–1700 CE) — the rediscovery (or highlighting) of the feminine-shakti principle of Tantra initiated the *bhakti* movement in India which emphasized religious devotionalism and an emotional response to the Divine Presence (through various symbols), notably with the **Vaishnavas** (worshippers of Vishnu and his Avatars) and the **Shaivas** (worshippers of Shiva and his Siddhas), thereby increasing the attention paid to Guru Yoga and Satsang or the importance of the Guru-Adept for awakening God-Realization, such as with the **Nath** and **Siddha** traditions

9. **Modern Age** (1700–present) — with the collapse of the Muslim Mughal empire (first half of 18th century) and global colonization by Europeans, Britain began to officially rule India in 1757 until she gained independence in 1948 after the nonviolent (*satyagraha*) movement led by Mahatma Gandhi (in the first half 20th century).

The scribes of India speaking and writing in ancient Sanskrit called all of these instructions from ancient India and her Gurus as being *Sanatana Dharma* or the "Eternal Teaching," for they are as true today as they were way back then, thus giving us the essential doctrines of what scholars now call the "Perennial Philosophy" [see Chapter 7]. Dr. Feuerstein agrees: "Hindu religion is referred to as *sanatana-dharma* ('eternal law'), which corresponds to the Western notion of *philosophia perennis*."[2] The "eternal" teaching about discovering or knowing God revolves around the Great Gurus, the Adept-Realizers of human history, actual living people pointing the way for all of us to follow.

However, what is important to understand is that all of the Sages and Adepts, Yogis and Saints, or any spiritual person tends to reflect the basic structure or stage of consciousness development (Stage of Life) that they have adapted to—one's "**center of gravity**" (in Wilber's terms). Most people who are not serious spiritual practitioners (the average-mode masses) are still involved with the first Three Stages of Life involving ego development and social adaptation. Those people entering the spiritual path, or beginning to appreciate the necessity for ego transcendence and devotion to God (or the Spirit-Power of the universe), are entering the Fourth Stage of Life [see Appendix I]. The transpersonal stages (Wilber's psychic to subtle to causal "state-stages") are those of spiritual and yogic development representing the higher Stages of Life (Four through Six) until complete Nondual Divine Enlightenment (Seventh Stage of Life). Note: both Adi Da's and Ken Wilber's developmental models of human growth reflect this basic pattern (with variations, of course, especially in terminology). Their models are an extremely useful way to understand the Teachings (and practices) of the world's various religions and their Shamans, Saints, Yogis, Sages, Siddhas, Avatars and Buddhas, et al., as Avatar Adi Da summarizes:

> Certain spiritual or sacred traditions are relatively or basically complete, in that they are represented by many schools which, if viewed collectively, express all of the Stages of Life in one form or another. The various schools within any such tradition may stand in conflict with one another, because each is limited to the point of view of one or another of the Stages of Life, but the Great Adepts see them all in terms of a progressive unity, culminating in the Seventh Stage of Life [Nondual Divine Enlightenment].... We could argue for the relative completeness of almost any tradition, if we would only examine every aspect of it, every school, every moment, every Adept within it.[3]

Of course, Adi Da has modified his stance somewhat in regard to the "Seventh Stage of Life," but we do not need to be concerned with these elusive distinctions here [see Chapter 19]. For our purposes, Wilber's model of generally recognizing the "Sixth Stage of Life" as Causal or Formless Mysticism (*nirvikalpa samadhi*) [Overmind] and the "Seventh Stage of Life" as Nondual Mysticism (*sahaj samadhi*) [Supermind] will allow us to review the history of India's Adept-Gurus as reflecting a progressive movement of unfolding conscious awareness. Indeed, this distinction between "inverted" formless Witness consciousness (Sixth Stage) and "open eyed" nondual Awakened consciousness (Seventh Stage) is basically how Adi Da refers to these stages in the source book we will be using and quoting from in this chapter.[4] Either way it is a brilliant and enlightened way to understand our religious inheritance and God's Great Tradition of Global Wisdom.

YOGA:
ESOTERIC ROOTS OF INDIA

ost people know that Yoga and meditation developed to its highest degrees in India, from the most ancient days to today. How did this come about? Adi Da (and others) suggest that Yoga evolved from Shamanism since each involves an ascension of consciousness (from the gross to subtle realms). This seems natural since both have methods to alter one's awareness in order to enter nonordinary realms of reality or altered states of consciousness that go beyond the waking state of the "average-mode" masses. Both Shamans and Yogis use specific psycho-spiritual techniques, such as drumming, chanting, fasting, and psychoactive substances (*entheogens*), to achieve these new vistas of vision and awareness. The Shaman and Yogi, therefore, are considered "advanced-tip" individuals (in Ken Wilber's terms) although their practices are available to anyone willing to undertake the proper schooling since humanity's highest potentials are innate in everyone's anatomy. Nonetheless, they are only activated with disciplined practices and superior guidance, such as from am Elder or Guru or Spiritual Master.

Shamanic ecstasy is generally concerned with an inward "soul flight" or "journeying" and "out-of-body experiences" (OBE) in order to gain some special (and sacred) knowledge used to serve the tribe (or community) and for healing.[5] The environment for the **Shaman**, therefore, is the subtle realms of existence and the etheric energies of Nature (where they often encounter "spirits" and "animal powers" seen in vision quests). The **Yogi**, on the other hand, attempts to go beyond the subtle realms, even to transcend the mind and individual identity altogether, in order to *realize* the Transcendental Being behind (and the Source-Condition of) *all* the realms of existence.[6] The Shaman is a sacred technician who usually acts on behalf of the tribe whereas the Yogi is oriented more toward an individual revelation seeking "liberation" (*moksha*) from the ever-changing and temporary conditions of Nature and the ego-self (and all conditional realms). As Yoga scholar Georg Feuerstein (whom Wilber calls "the foremost authority on Yoga today") summarizes: "The condition of illumination, or enlightenment, is to the *yogin* what the magical journey into other realms is to the shaman."[7] The Shaman, in this case, operates in the tribal magic-mythic structures accessing higher transpersonal "psychic" states, while the Yogi is associated more with the emerging mental-ego and "subtle-causal" state-structures as Yoga first emerged during the Axial Age (800–300 BCE).[8]

Yoga is, as the term implies, most interested in the "union" of the individual self (*jiva-atman*) with the Supreme Self (*parama-atman*). As is often noted, the word **yoga** comes from the Sanskrit word *yuj* meaning "to link, to join, or unite," which is related to "yoke," like the yoke of an oxen.[9] As Wilber plainly reveals:

> The essence of Yoga is very simple: It means *yoking* or *joining*. When Jesus said, "My yoke is easy," he meant "My Yoga is easy." Whether East or West, Yoga is the technique of joining or uniting the individual soul with absolute Spirit. It is a means of liberation. And it is therefore fiery, hot, intense, ecstatic. It will take you far beyond yourself; some say it will take you to infinity.[10]

Feuerstein continues to explain: "*Yoga* is thus the generic name for the various Indian paths of ecstatic self-transcendence, or the methodical transmutation of consciousness to the point of liberation from the spell of the ego personality. It is the psycho-spiritual technology specific to the great civilization of India."[11] In India, these psycho-spiritual techniques have developed into the various schools of Yoga, such as Ashtanga Yoga, Hatha Yoga, Laya Yoga, Raja Yoga, Kriya Yoga, Jnana Yoga, and so forth. Importantly, as the Perennial Philosophy affirms, the actual state-stages of higher realization and Enlightenment (or God-Realization) itself are not only corroborated from thousands of advanced-tip Yogi-Adepts from India but by the testimony of Mystics from around the world [see Chapter 7]. They each, as Adi Da points out, tend to reflect or emphasize one or the other of the higher Stages of Life (from the Fourth to the Seventh) [see Appendix I].

In a sense, as scholars have noticed, the root word of *yoga* is analogous to the Latin word *re-ligio* (*ligare*) from whence our word "religion" comes from also meaning "to link back or bind." However, as Joseph Campbell clarifies: "[In the West] religion, *religio*, refers to a linking [that is] historically conditioned by way of a covenant, sacrament, or *Qur'an*, whereas yoga [in the East] is the psychological linking of the mind… what is linked is finally the self to itself, consciousness to consciousness; for what had seemed, through *maya* [illusion], to be two [duality] are in reality not so [nondual]; whereas in [Western] religion what are linked are God and man [as a separate creature], which are not the same [as the Eastern goal of Yoga]."[12] In other words, with Yoga one discovers that "I Am God," "I and the Father are one" (in Jesus's words), known in Sanskrit as "*Tat Tvam Asi*" or "Thou are That," and "*aham brahma-asmi*" or "I am the Absolute!" Real Yoga—or Real Religion—is about Divine Realization as a *direct experience* for oneself (not through the intermediary of a priesthood), nothing else, regardless of the various paths or methods offered to realize this final and ultimate truth. The potential for such Awakening is the great Gift offered to everyone through God's Great Tradition of Global Gurus and Adept-Realizers.

GURU SATSANG: TRANSMISSION-INITIATION

*Y*oga, like all forms of esoteric mysticism (in all religions)—as this book attempts to show—insists that a Spiritual Master needs to be present to initiate and guide a student (disciple or devotee) in the proper cultivation and use of these hidden and difficult psycho-spiritual

354 | Part II – The Great Tradition IS Guru Yoga-Satsang

techniques of Yoga Historian of religion Mircea Eliade in his classic study *Yoga: Immortality and Freedom* (1973) explained: "What characterizes Yoga is not only its practical side, but also its initiatory structure."[13] Yoga is never a do-it-yourself enterprise, but out of necessity it takes a teacher (*guru*) to not only guide one in the proper practice of the disciplines, but also to initiate one via spiritual transmission (*sancara*), activating *shaktipat* to awaken consciousness by stimulating kundalini energy arousal and a heart opening to love-bliss (i.e., a feeling for the Divine).

God is seen or recognized to be real and true when the heart opens (beyond the mind) by aligning with the Awakened State of the Enlightened Guru (who is in a higher Stage of Life). Feuerstein explains: "Such transmission, in which the *guru* literally empowers the student through a transference of 'energy' or 'consciousness' (corresponding to the 'Holy Spirit' of Christian baptism), is the fulcrum of the initiatory process of Yoga."[14] This sacred method (beyond words or scriptures) is precisely why this book emphasizes the vital importance of Guru Yoga-Satsang in establishing an authentic sacred relationship with a Guru-Adept. We are all personally called to this sacred process.

As we saw, Adi Da Samraj acknowledges the primordial wisdom tradition of being attracted to a sacred relationship with a Realizer of God, or a genuine Guru, with his unique title "**The Ancient Walk-About Way**"[15] [see Chapter 11]. The method and teachings of the Adept-Gurus, based upon their own Divine Enlightenment (or particular Stage of Life), is what perpetuates and extends the religious impulse in others down through the generations since the origins of humankind.[16] Avatar Adi Da clearly explains:

> Though there are many historical traditions of "religion" and Spiri-
> tuality, there is, in Truth, a single Great Tradition. In fact, that Great
> Tradition is far older than the recorded history of humankind. There
> is a prehistorical background to all the historical traditions of "reli-
> gion" and Spirituality. That background tradition, which I call the
> "Walk-About tradition", existed long before there were concentrated
> bodies of civil society where human beings became highly organized
> in large numbers. Even anciently, people were being "religious" and
> Spiritual. In fact, ancient peoples were, as a general rule, being every-
> thing that human beings are being now. Thus, even the prehistoric
> peoples are part of the Great Tradition.[17]

We all feel a teleological drive or urge to fulfill our highest potential, so we turn to those who have realized that Truth for themselves, male or female. Although we do require their assistance and guidance, especially their Spirit-Transmission, to initiate us into the higher (and highest) Stages of Life, ultimately, it is *we* who must *do the yoga* by turning to the Guru [see Chapter 20]. This is what Real Religion is all about: knowing God. The contemporary and global Avatar Adi Da succinctly summarizes:

> The primary force and "root" of all the esoteric traditions of humankind are the Adept-Realizers, those who actually Realize (to one or another degree) the Spiritual and Transcendental Nature of Reality. ...The tradition of Truth, the tradition of Spiritual and Transcendental Realization, is the tradition of the Adept-Realizers. Apart from the Adepts, there is no tradition of Truth....
>
> The Spiritual Master is a Transparent Reminder of the Divine Reality, a Guide to the ecstatic Realization of the One Reality in which all conditions arise and change and pass away. The Spiritual Master is not to be made into a merely "objectified" idol of a cult, as if the Divine Being were exclusively contained in the "objective" person and "subjective" beliefs of a particular sect. Rather, right relationship to the Spiritual Master takes the form of free devotional response to the Spiritual Master's Radiant State.[18]

This Guru-disciple relationship, according to scholars, goes back at least until the **early Vedic period** (4500–2500 BCE), but probably earlier (in more rudimentary forms).[19] As Adi Da suggests with the Ancient Walk-About Way, the sacred relationship to an advanced-tip practitioner goes back to the times of Paleolithic Shamans up to those of Axial Age Yogis, from Prophets to Sages, from Saints to Siddhas showing deep primordial roots extending back to the earliest stages of *Homo sapiens sapiens* evolution when religion first dawned.[20] As Adi Da's editors point out: "The function of the Awakened Master, or Guru, has appeared in every genuinely Truth-Realizing form of sacred practice. From Buddhist masters and Hindu gurus to Jewish rebbes and zaddiks, Christian Spiritual fathers, and Muslim shaykhs, the transformative relationship to the Illumined guide is testimony to the universal truth of the 'Ancient Walk-About Way'."[21]

Such ancient history, of course, is hidden in the fading mists of time, especially prior to agriculture, for the inward journey does not fossilize into artifacts uncovered by archaeologists. The spiritual evolution of consciousness involves a *living* energy to be explored by each and every person if they choose to engage in the disciplines and advanced psycho-spiritual techniques of "**Real Religion**" (as Adi Da calls it). In short, Divine God-Realization, we are told, always involves the discovery of the "fearless Light" (*Rig Veda* 6.47.8) which is Real God or "Conscious Light" (as Adi Da says), but you must *find out* for yourself.

VEDIC MYSTICISM:
WORLD'S OLDEST SCRIPTURES

What has come to be known in the West as "**Hinduism**" (a mispronunciation by the Persians over a thousand years ago of "Sindhu" or the Indus River) is based on certain psycho-physical practices that were codified into written form when the indigenous traditions of India came in contact with the "invading" **Aryans** from the northern steppes. Although there is scholarly contention about how much the northern Aryans supplemented the indigenous population of the older Indus Valley **Harappan Civilization** (that included cities like Mohenjo-daro and Harappa), the yogic origins of Hinduism were certainly preceded by ancient shamanic cultures reaching back to the Upper Paleolithic.[22] Using an "idealistic" and pantheistic view of life that posits the "Divine Emanation" of a Supreme Being (seen as "outside")—called *Brahman*—and the True Self (seen as "inside") —called *Atman*—are actually *realized* to be "One without a second" (as the *Upanishads* often say). These ancient Sages have always taught about this Divine Reality (*Atman-Brahman*) which can be known through right effort and understanding via meditation and a right relationship (and devotion) to a genuine Guru-Adept.

Ascetic yogic disciplines involving intensive meditation (taking hundreds of hours of practice) offer an authentic route to transform a person's consciousness until God-Realization awakens. Importantly, this evolution of consciousness was found to be most effective when it was based around the Guru-devotee relationship (now called *Satsang*). The state-stage of development gained by the Adept-Realizer could, since ancient times, directly influence those who came around him or her because Satsang invokes the "super-physics" of the Kosmos and the subtle energies circulating throughout the esoteric anatomy of human beings.[23] Most important, yet least understood in the West, is the reality of Spirit-Transmission (*shaktipat*) or a literal Spirit Baptism, the most sacred method (or blessing) offered by a genuine Guru-Adept to a student-disciple [see Chapter 3]. And thus it has been since most ancient times. Modernity cannot erase this truth (and reality) so it's time for us to give credit where credit is due.

The *Vedas* (meaning "Knowledge") are some of the world's oldest spiritual scriptures, written in one of the world's oldest languages: Sanskrit. The writing down of these teachings, however, must be remembered to have originated centuries (or millennia) earlier and were initially passed down orally from Master to student. The ideas or esoteric understandings implicit in the *Vedas* are themselves much older than the written evidence going back to where time fades away. These ancient sacred texts of holy India are divided into four major **Vedas**:

(1) *Rig Veda* = the oldest (and most important) is a collection of Vedic Sanskrit hymns and instruction (most popular in the West);

(2) *Sama Veda* = a liturgical text of chants and melodies;

(3) *Yajur Veda* = prose mantras for worship and rituals; and

(4) *Atharva Veda* = procedures for everyday life, including rites and spells, especially for healing.

The *Vedas* are *śruti* ("what is heard") from the mouth of a Sage, thus distinguishing them from other religious texts called *smrti* ("what is remembered"), coming from the inner Self. Hindus consider the *Vedas* to be *apauruseya* meaning they are "not of a man, but are superhuman," that is, "impersonal, authorless" for they are inner revelations of sacred sounds and teachings heard and seen by the ancient Seers after intense inward meditation.

Overall, it has been noted the Vedic religion is a "**sacrificial mysticism**" since sacrifice (*yajna*) is at the heart of their beliefs and religious activities.[24] The *Vedas* have various sections of instruction, such as *karma-khana* (good actions), *upasana-khana* (devotional service), and *jnana-khana* (esoteric knowledge of self-transcendence and Brahman). The Vedic hymns were composed by their Adepts called **Rishis** (*rishi*) or "Seers," as Feuerstein explains: "To compose a hymn means to envision it in a state of contemplation… the hymns are expressions of the deep spirituality of the Vedic Aryans."[25] As such, the "Proto-Yoga of the *rishis* contains many of the elements characteristic of later Yoga: concentration, watchfulness, austerities, regulation of the breath… devotional invocation… visionary experience… [and] the encounter with a [Divine or spiritual] Reality larger than the ego-personality, and the continuous enrichment of ordinary life by that encounter."[26] The Rishis, in other words, were the ecstatics, the creative visionaries, while the ancient Brahmins, the orthodox priesthood, were the conservative arm of Vedic religion.

Since ancient times the Vedas were authoritatively transmitted by an oral tradition called *sampradaya*, given from father to son or from teacher (*guru*) to student (*shishya*) down through the generations. The great American philosopher, Ralph Waldo Emerson (1803–1888), one of the first Westerners to read the *Vedas*, exclaimed: "It is sublime as heart and night and a breathless ocean. It contains every religious sentiment, all the grand ethics which visit in turn each noble poetic mind… It is of no use to put away the book."[27] The sacred teachings initiated by the Rishi-Seers heard the primordial sounds or **mantras** in deep meditation which then stimulated inner consciousness evolution (by opening the higher brain centers beyond the ordinary mind). Only a living tradition, not one learned by books but embodied by living Masters, can impart the correct pronunciation of the mantras and explain their hidden meanings in a way that "dead and entombed manuscripts" can never do.

One of humanity's first and oldest written spiritual texts, the **Rig Veda** contains more than a thousand hymns that probably arose during the third millennium BCE (yet often dated by Eurocentric scholars as between 1500-1100 BCE). One commentator noted that a single phrase from the *Rig Veda* constitutes the core of Vedic religion and philosophy: "The Sages make their voices heard with hymns" (Hymn 64: 16).[28] Again, Gurus or the "Enlightened Seers" (of God)—Adept-Realizers—are found at the very root of real religion [see Chapter 11]. However, in India only the Brahmin priestly class could fully access the sacred Vedas that were handed down orally by memory, prior to written texts. They are still chanted and memorized until this very day taught to priests from childhood. The average person did not (and does not) receive the esoteric teachings, just the rituals, particularly the most important fire sacrifice (*agni-shtoma*), which is practiced in the home as well as outdoors in public places led by priests.

As mentioned, these orally-transmitted scriptures were borne from the steppe Aryan horsemen from the north as they merged with the ancient indigenous farmers of the Harappan civilization, whether by invasion or assimilation.[29] Whatever the exact historical interplay, it was the Rishi-Seers or Adept-Realizers who described the cosmic order of the universe in a myth-ic-poetic language full of symbols and metaphors representing spiritual and natural processes, activated by sacramental rituals, both internally and exter-nally. The indescribable depth of detail and sacred understanding they reveal is mind-boggling. They describe an exotic and archetypal play of gods and goddesses (such as with Agni, Indra, Surya, Brahma, etc.) as all being embraced within the ultimate unity of the One Supreme God (Brahman). The *Vedas* famously proclaimed: "Reality (or Truth) is One but the wise call it by differ-ent names" (*Rig Veda* 1:164:46), a core tenet of the Perennial Philosophy, the universal wisdom of humanity. Today exoteric or mythic conventional religion seems to forget this simple truth claiming their preferred religion is best.

Brahma	**Vishnu**	**Shiva**
"Creator"	"Sustainer"	"Destroyer"

Once these natural and psychic forces were combined with local indige-nous spirits these inner archetypes took on multiple names and identities cre-ating a vast pantheon of deities (including many popular ones still used today, such as Ganesh, Lakshmi, Shiva, Vishnu, et al.). What has often been perceived as polytheism by Westerners was actually the monotheism of Brahman cloaked in multiple forms. First of all, **Brahman** as the formless, effulgent One God was subdivided into a trinity (*Trimurti*): (1) **Brahma** the "Creator," (2) **Vishnu** the "Sustainer," and (3) **Shiva** the "Destroyer" (actually more like a "Re-Creator" thus is known as **Shiva-Nataraja**, the "Lord of the Cosmic Dance"). This cosmic-energy dance is seen as "*Prakriti*" or the feminine and *immanent* form of the transcendental Divine Being, while "*Purusha*" is the "Divine Person" or the Supreme God of *transcendent* Consciousness within which all possible universes appear and disappear. This is the *Shakti-Shiva* principle used by other Sages and pandits which are symbols pointing to the manifesting aspects of the indescribable, indivisible Prior Unity of the One Divine Reality that simply IS. These are, again, the "two truths" of relative reality and Absolute Reality [see Chapter 7].

This apparent dualism expressing the two experiential aspects of the One Divine Reality (as being transcendent and immanent) seems to have first been taught by **Kapila** (6th to 7th century BCE), the founder of **Samkhya Yoga** (or philosophy). Less enlightened pandits, however, have misunderstood the true meaning behind seeing *Purusha* as Transcendental Consciousness and *Prakriti* as its relative manifestations, thus claiming it to be dualistic. However, *Prakriti-Purusha* simply portrays the two complementary aspects of one indivisible Reality. Kapila's Samkhya philosophy had a vast influence on later thinkers in India, though many distorted this singular vision of Nondual Unity since they themselves had not yet experienced this Unity Consciousness.[30]

| **Prakriti** | **Shiva-Nataraja** | **Purusha** |

Hidden in the mythic-symbolic mind of the *Vedas*, these Wise Seers were singing about the perennial Wisdom handed down from a complex oral tradition appearing in each generation as the Eternal Divine Being which is singular (*eka*) and unborn (*aja*), yet given many names.[31] These insights were rising, as Adi Da explains, from our innate spectrum of consciousness or "**esoteric anatomy**" that is possessed by all human beings reflected in the potential Seven

Stages of Life [see Appendix I].[32] Often, as the *Vedas* attest, their knowledge was initiated by "**Soma**" (the "ritual drink") in order to better see the Light of the Lord (*Rig Veda*, 8.48.3). Scholars today propose this was a psychedelic or psychoactive substance (or medicine), an *entheogen*, helping to reveal God within.[33] Arising from shamanic ascension (or "sky magic") often based in plant medicine and fasting, the new yogas began to rely more on breathing exercises and stillness meditation thus internalizing the sacrifice rather than using ritual ceremony alone. Only with actual Divine Revelation or *direct experience* does one ever attain **moksha** or liberation from the illusions of **maya** (the conditional world) and from **samsara** (the cycle of death and rebirth or reincarnation), as the Sages have long taught. Feuerstein clearly explains:

> The Vedic Seers won their sacred visions by their own hard inner work—their austerities and their deep impulse toward spiritual enlightenment. They regarded themselves as "children of light" (*Rig Veda* 9.38.5) and had their hearts set on reaching the "heavenly light," or ultimate Light-being (*Rig Veda* 10.36.3).[34]

The illumined (or highly-evolved) Rishis were the first Great Gurus of India, women and men, who went on to establish the Way of Truth on Earth. Yet, we must be clear: these Teachings and Transmissions arose in and from the psyche of real, living, flesh-and-blood human beings, not from gods or deities. Although often depicted in the literature and scriptures as supernatural beings with supernatural powers, they were originally humans. All the Great Sages and Seers, perhaps with names representing several authors instead of a single person—such as Kapila, Rama, Sita, Krishna, Vyasa, et al.—were men and women, even if now they are spoken about in legendary (if not mythological) terms. Nevertheless, they were always living breathing human beings with the same anatomy as each of us. Yes, they often developed special psychic powers (*siddhis*) which can also be our potential *if we do the yoga* (although that is not the point). Therefore, everyone is always capable of seeing and knowing exactly what they knew and saw, as they teach and tell us every time. The Adepts are real, not just figments of our imagination. Their Teachings come from the mouths (and hearts) of real people, not out of thin air or from voices from the sky. Thus, when we bow down at their feet in gratitude for their Divine Gifts we are actually bowing to our own innate wisdom not yet fully realized.

UPANISHADS:
SITTING AT THE MASTER'S FEET

he pinnacle of the ancient wisdom of India is not clearly found in the mythic-spoken but deeply insightful Vedas, even with their esoteric inclinations. The supreme knowledge of Brahman and God-Realization is first clearly articulated in the sacred texts called **Upanishads** (ca. 800–500 BCE), which literally means "to sit near one's Guru" or "at the feet of the Master." As Professor Stace commented: "The *Upanishads* have always been the supreme source of Indian spirituality."[35] These simpler and directly-stated scriptures, though complex in cosmology, appear a thousand years after the earliest *Vedas* (meaning more than half a millennium before Christ). They mostly transcend mythic images and rituals for these meditating Sages were less concerned with gods and goddesses or the forces of Nature but with the Supreme Self or Ultimate God. They put their attention on the Indescribable Source-Condition from which *everything* arises. They wanted to transcend the subtle mind to discover the causal Witness consciousness, the True Self, found in the heart (on the right). This is why, no doubt, German philosopher Arthur Schopenhauer (1788–1860) starkly said: "The study of the *Upanishads* has been the solace of my life. It will be the solace of my death." With the new translations of the Sanskrit *Upanishads* finally being made available to the West (in the 19th century), the wisdom of the Great Tradition began to penetrate the materialism of the modern mind. By doing so they initiated a spiritual revolution in the Western world ruled by the monotheism of Abraham's tribal God (of Yahweh and Allah) who is always set apart from His creatures.

Scholars tell us that at the dawn of the Upanishadic Age (around 1000 BCE) there were small groups of outcasts, such as the *Vratya* brotherhoods, or the solitary *munis*, whom all pursued the spiritual quest living on the margins of Vedic society.[36] The *Rig Veda* (10.136), for example, had a "Hymn of the Long Hair" describing long-hair ascetics who remained close to the ancient shamanic heritage outside of Vedic orthodoxy. They were noted for breath control (*pranayama*), mastering the life-force (*prana*) to arouse the *kundalini-shakti*, which is pictured as a "coiled serpent" lying at the base of the spine waiting to rise up (via the *chakras* or "wheels" of energy) to awaken the brain with God-intoxication. The Vratyas had a vital relationship with the *kshatriya*, the warrior class (not the Brahmin priesthood), as Feuerstein explains: "At the time of the *Upanishads*, the wisdom tradition, with its emphasis on ecstatic self transcendence and Self realization, was often transmitted not by Brahmins, but by members of the warrior estate."[37] In this way, the Upanishadic Sages initiated an ideological revolution by internalizing the Vedic rituals in the form of intense contemplation or inward-turning meditation.[38]

With practices of self-restraint (*sadhana*), these ascetic Sages used yogic techniques (such as breathing exercises and fasting) to stoke the inner heat of the body. By restricting sexuality (celibacy) and retaining semen flow they performed the "inner fire" sacrifice. They sought esoteric inner wisdom that would lift them beyond ordinary conditional life to realize or directly know the Unconditional Reality (called *Brahman*, from the verbal root *brih* meaning "to grow," thus denoting the vastness of the Supreme Being).[39] Feuerstein continues: "Most significantly, the Upanishadic Sages turned unanimously to meditative practice, or inner worship (*upasana*), as the chief means of obtaining transcendental knowledge."[40] Knowledge of Reality as an eternally unchanging single Divine Being (*Purusha*) was already acknowledged in the *Vedas*, though not openly, yet it was honored through sacrificial rituals (conducted by Brahmin priests). Now individuals, willing to take up the required practices of Yoga (which involve years of strict discipline and countless hours of meditation) learned only under a qualified competent Master-Guru, could realize for themselves what the Rishis had seen. Sitting at the feet of the Master—*Upa-ni-shad* (*upa* "near," *ni* "down," *shad* "to sit")—is how their esoteric words of wisdom were whispered by India's Adepts to deserving devotees instead of being proclaimed aloud in public places.

All the *Upanishads* teach one essential theme: "**Atman is Brahman**," i.e., your inner self-soul (*atman*, with a small "a") is an illusory (or relative) manifestation of the One True Self (*Atman*, with a capital "A"), which is God Itself (*Brahman*). Ultimate Realization of Atman-Brahman is characterized with the Sanskrit phrase "*Sat-Chit-Ananda*," meaning, respectively, "Existence, Consciousness, Bliss," indicating it is an ecstatic, ineffable state of consciousness. *Mundaka Upanishad*, a concise text whose name means the "sharpness of a razor" repeats the same nondual teaching found in all the *Upanishads* given by the most wise:

> He who knows all and understands all, and to whom belongs all the glory of the world—He, Atman, is placed in the space in the effulgent abode of Brahman.... He dwells in the body, inside the heart. By the knowledge of That which shines as the blissful and immortal Atman, the wise behold Him [Brahman] fully in all things.[41]

Importantly, such Enlightenment or Divine Wisdom is *realized* in the heart (beyond the mind) once the "knots" of the heart (caused by egoic self-contractions) are "untied" and released (*bhidyata hrdaya granthih*). As *Katha Upanishad* (II.2.14-15) states: "When all the desires that dwell in the heart fall away, then the mortal becomes immortal and here attains Brahman. Then all the knots of the heart are severed here on earth, then the mortal becomes immortal. This much is the teaching."[42] *Brihad-Aranyaka Upanishad*—the "**Great Forest Text**"—the earliest of them all, is very clear about this. Its main Adept Yajnavalkya, pointing to his chest on the right, explicitly explains: "In what does the truth [of Brahman] find its support? The heart, for through the heart one knows the truth; therefore it is in the heart that the truth finds it support. (III.9.23)."[43] Or *Katha Upanishad* (I.2.20): "Atman, smaller than the small, greater than the great, is hidden in the heart of all living creatures. A man [or woman] who is free from desires beholds the majesty of the Self through tranquility of the senses and the mind and becomes free from grief."[44] The heart is pointed to in all the major *Upanishads*, not the brain (or mind). What is revealed in the heart is the "great, unborn Self," the "Light of all lights." *Brihad-Aranyaka Upanishad* (IV.4.15-18) continues:

When a person following the instructions of a Teacher [Guru] directly beholds the effulgent Self, the Lord of all that has been and will be, he no longer wishes to hide himself from It.... Upon that immortal Light of all lights the gods meditate... that very Atman I regard as the Immortal Brahman. Knowing that Brahman, I am immortal.[45]

The numerous *Upanishads* (with thirteen principal ones) are considered the "end of the Vedas," which is what "**Vedanta**" literally means. Thus, their nondual ("not-two") teachings about the union of Atman-Brahman are called ***Advaita Vedanta*** (*advaita* meaning "nonduality"). These are considered the supreme Teaching-Revelations of India. Feuerstein points out: "The earliest clear articulation of the notion of Self-Realization, or the realization of the Absolute (*Brahman*), can be found in the oldest *Upanishads*... these expound the original insights about the identity of the person's essential being [*Atman*] with the essential nature of the universe at large [*Brahman*]."[46] These more philosophical treatises, written in rational-oriented prose instead of myth-ic-laced poetry, characterize the emerging mental structure of consciousness.[47] The sacred *Upanishads*, as mentioned, focus more on inner meditation, rather than mantras and ceremonial rituals. They aim to quieten the mind through calming the breath, stopping all thoughts, summarized centuries later in Patanjali's *Yoga Sutra* (1.2): ***Chit vriti nirodha*** meaning "Yoga is restraining the mind from taking various forms" (in Vivekananda's words). First the mind is stilled, the breath set at ease, the ego-self transcended, for the heart to open and realize its Divine Source (Atman) thus attaining *samadhi* (or "Divine ecstasy"), the goal or highest "limb" of Patanjali's Way of Yoga. Only by *doing the yoga* will a person awaken to the truth of Reality, the essence of true religion, hence the necessity for a qualified Guru-Adept, whether modern or ancient.

Chakras   **Kundalini Ascension**   **Enlightenment**

Once again, the highly revered scriptures teach us that to sit at the feet of the Spiritual Master (or be in their company) is the easiest and most direct way to receive the "sacred knowledge" (or *veda*) of Ultimate Reality. It is not revealed simply by reading books or ancient texts, certainly not by offering blood sacrifices. *Mundaka Upanishad* (III.2.3) clearly states: "This Atman cannot be attained through study of the *Vedas*, nor through intelligence, nor through much learning. He who chooses Atman—by him alone is Atman attained. It is Atman that reveals to the seeker Its true nature."[48] Only the disciplined practices of Yoga and meditation, guided by the Guru, allow the esoteric anatomy, rooted most deeply in the heart, to open and be purified so Brahman (God) may be revealed. India's spiritual teachings fully understand that the spiritual process cannot be truly undertaken without the guidance of one who has already completed the path. Guru Yoga-Satsang is the Way to re-discover the Absolute Reality beyond the coverings of the separate self-sense or ego-I temporarily living in Nature, otherwise destined after death to recycle (or reincarnate) through many lifetimes. Only by seeing beyond life and death does one enter the "Way of Immortality" (as we just heard).

Katha Upanishad, as another example, the sacred text said to be given by Yama, the Lord of Death, to his inquiring disciple Nachiketa, explains that the Way to Eternal Life (or "Immortality") is best served via the Grace of the Guru. Yet it is a very difficult path, like walking on a razor's edge:

> Many do not even hear of Atman [God within]; though hearing of Him, many do not comprehend. Wonderful is the expounder [Guru] and rare the hearer [devotee]; rare indeed is the experiencer of Atman taught by an able preceptor [Guru]. (I.2.7)

Atman, when taught by an inferior person, is not easily compre-
hended, because It is diversely regarded by disputants. But when it
is taught by him who has become one with Atman [the Sat-Guru],
there can remain no more doubt about It. Atman is subtler than the
subtlest and not to be known through argument. (I.2.8)

Arise! Awake! Approach the great Illumined Teachers [Guru-
Adepts] and learn. Like the sharp edge of a razor is that path, so the
wise say—hard to tread and difficult to cross. (I.3.14)[49]

Once more, we see that it is the Guru-Adept who leads the way to this
sacred understanding since we cannot learn this wisdom alone. *Mundaka
Upanishad* (I.2.13) affirms: "In order that he [the devotee] may understand
that Eternal [Brahman], let him, fuel in hand [gifts], approach a Guru who is
well versed in the Vedas and always devoted to Brahman. To that pupil who
has duly approached him [the Guru], whose mind is completely serene, and
whose senses are controlled, the Wise Teacher should indeed rightly impart the
Knowledge of Brahman (via teaching and transmission), through which one
knows the immutable and the true Purusha [the Divine Person or Consciousness Itself]."[50] Remember, these are the same words of wisdom spoken nearly
three thousand years ago but now given from the Spiritual Masters to you alive
today. The sublime *Mundaka Upanishad* continues to reveal this plain (yet
hidden) truth:

The Atman becomes one with Brahman... Know that non-dual
Atman alone and give up all other talk. He is the bridge to Immortality. (II.2.5)... He, Atman, is placed in the space in the effulgent
abode of Brahman. He assumes the forms of the mind and leads the
body and the senses. He dwells in the body, inside the heart. By the
knowledge of That, which shines as the blissful and immortal Atman,
the wise behold Him fully in all things. (II.2.8)... It is the Light
of lights; It is That which they know who knows the Self.... When
He shines, everything shines after Him; by His Light everything is
lighted. (II.2.10)[51]

This blissful state of nondual awareness is the ultimate goal of Yoga—
or "how to know God"—the *samadhi* or ecstasy of Divine Enlightenment.
Svetasvatara Upanishad (VI.4) confirms: "He who attains purity of heart by

performing actions as an offering to the Lord, and merges *prakriti* [cosmic energy] and all its effects in Brahman [*purusha*], realizes his true Self [*Atman*] and thereby transcends phenomena."[52] Thus the search or seeking for God-Realization, the "**Great Path of Return**"[53] (in Adi Da's terms), became the basis for India's esoteric religious tradition sprouting numerous variations including countless Spiritual Masters up until the present day. In India, all paths to God are accepted within the tolerant embrace of Hinduism—thus *practicing* what they preach. The different path a person takes—whether Karma Yoga, Bhakti Yoga, Jnana Yoga, Raja Yoga, and so on, all embraced within Guru Yoga—depend on the temperament and circumstance (and karma) of the individual. Thus all are accepted and honored in India where no one religion is claimed to be better than any of the others. Such tolerance is a noble ideal our entire global culture should aspire to.

ADVAITA VEDANTA:
NONDUAL MYSTICISM OF THE HEART

The culmination of India's Vedic-Upanishadic "Eternal Teaching" (*Sanatana Dharma*), in the opinion of most (as already mentioned), is known as **Advaita Vedanta**—*advaita* is "nonduality" ("*a*" is "non-" and "*dvaita*" is "duality") and *vedanta* ("*veda*" is "knowledge" and "*anta*" is "end")—thus it is the "ultimate or end-knowledge of the Vedas." Again, the *Vedas* are the oldest hymns in the sacred canon of Hinduism (ca. 1500 BCE but probably older) given to the world by the *Rishis* ("Seers") and thus are regarded as "Revelations" (*shruti*). They were (and still are) handed down orally by the Brahmins (*brahmana*) or the priestly class of India, although they have been written down for millennia (yet not widely available until the 20th century). At their heart, of course, is the Enlightenment of the Guru-Adepts—the source of God's Great Tradition of Global Wisdom.

As we saw, the earliest *Vedas* deal with ritual ceremonies more than philosophy, spoken more in mythic language (with gods and goddesses) than with metaphysics (though those topics are addressed indirectly). The metaphysics of Vedanta, therefore, culminates with the *Upanishads* (ca. 800–500 BCE), the collection of scriptures stripped of mythic language and spoken with rational logic and directions for realizing Atman (in the "cave of the heart"). All of the *Upanishad* texts acknowledge the necessity for a Guru or a Master-Adept or one who has already realized Atman for themselves so they will be an effective guide for others.

After the *Upanishads* were written down (authors unknown), Vedanta as teachable philosophy was first systematized by **Badarayana** with the *Brahma Sutras* (traditional dates of 500–200 BCE, but perhaps 200 CE) which summarizes the wisdom of the Upanishadic texts. Importantly, after the first millennium of the Common Era, there appeared **Gorakhnath** (or **Goraksanath**, dates uncertain, perhaps 9th or 10th century CE), a famous Hindu Yogi-Saint who was an influential founder of the Nath monastic movement and Shaivism, where Shiva is held to be the First Guru as well as being a great master of Hatha Yoga. The *Gorakh-Bodh* ("Illumination of Gorakh") is a Hindi text that is supposed to be a dialogue between Gorakhnath and his Guru, **Matsyendra** (early 10th century CE) a revivalist of Hatha Yoga (focused on bodily postures and breathing exercises for meditation). Gorakhnath was a Maha-Yogi (a "Great Yogi") who championed spiritual disciplines and an ethical lifestyle more than metaphysical theory of any particular Truth.

A thousand years after the Vedantic *Brahma Sutras* were first written down there appeared Vedanta's best known and most influential school taught by **Adi Shankara** (ca. 788–820 CE)—*acharya* or "Teacher"—who only lived to be 32 years old yet has been a major influence on India's Nondual Mysticism for over a thousand years (and, no doubt, for millennia more). A precocious child said to have mastered the *Vedas* by the age of eight, Shankara's

Shankara

Guru is traditionally said to be **Govinda Bhagavatpada** (ca. 7th century CE), who was the devotee of the revered **Gaudapada** (ca. 6th to 7th century CE), both esteemed scholar-Sages of Advaita Vedanta. Shankara is one of the most famous and celebrated Guru-Adepts of India, since as Feuerstein points out, "his expositions of Advaita Vedanta, as preserved in many extant works of great erudition, were mainly responsible for the renaissance of that ancient tradition [during] the decline of Buddhism in India."[54] Shankara was influenced by the teachings and popularity of Mahayana Buddhism, particularly Madhyamaka, and its insistence that phenomena and the self inherently lack any separate essence or reality. Shankara's argument, however, relies more on the ancient teachings of the *Vedas* and *Upanishads* to revive the transcendental, nondual message inherent in Vedanta. As Adi Da points out, the Vedic-Upanishadic Teachings rely on a more "idealistic" (positive) approach than the more "realistic" (negative) approach of Buddhism [see Chapter 10].

Shankara's commentaries on classic Vedantic texts, such as the *Brahma Sutra*, the *Bhagavad Gita*, and the principal *Upanishads*, among others, are a favorite of modern translators and fairly easy to understand since Shankara places an emphasis on practice and meditation (the "Practicing School"), not merely philosophy and scholarship (the "Talking School"). Among his best-known original works are *Atma Bodha* ("The Knowledge of The Self"), *Upadesha-sahasri* ("The Thousand Teachings"), and *Vivekachudamani* ("The Crest Jewel of Discrimination"), an all-time favorite among many (including myself), as Swami Abhayananda [Stan Trout] wonderfully notes:

> Shankara's little book, *The Crest Jewel of Discrimination*, is undoubtedly one of the clearest and most persuasive accounts of mystical philosophy ever written. It is cast in the form of a dialogue between a Master and disciple and serves its reader as an unerring guide to Enlightenment. This short book, among all the spiritual guides and philosophies ever written, must certainly be regarded, as its title implies, as the crown-jewel of all knowledge, and the consummate pinnacle of its expression. In the field of Enlightenment literature, there is nothing to compare with it.[55]

Shankara taught what is called **Kevala-Advaita** ("absolute nondualism") since once a person is awake to the True Self (Atman) the manifest universe

(Brahman) then appears as nothing but the Nondual Heart of Atman-Brahman. As Ken Wilber has noted: "For by the truth of nonduality, to know God is to be God: the two are not at all separate."[56] Adi Shankara is also attributed with one of the most concise (and easiest to understand) definitions of "nondualism" ever penned, often used by such luminaries as Sri Ramana Maharshi (and others), including Wilber who nicely summarizes the formula below:

> Sri Ramana Maharshi (echoing Shankara) summarizes the "viewpoint" of the ultimate or Nondual realization:

> ### The world is illusory;
> ### Brahman alone is Real;
> ### Brahman is the world.

> The first two lines represent pure causal-level awareness [Sixth Stage], or unmanifest absorption in pure or formless Spirit; line three represents the ultimate or nondual completion (the union of the Formless with the entire world of Form) [Seventh Stage]. The Godhead *completely transcends* all worlds and thus *completely includes* all worlds. It is the final within, leading to a final beyond—a beyond that, confined to absolutely *nothing*, embraces absolutely *everything*.[57]

Ironically, it is often asserted by modern scholars that Shankara was mostly a *jnani* or one who practiced the "Yoga of Wisdom" (in contrast to the **bhakti** or the "Yoga of Devotion") thus being more like the ascetic Shiva (the pinnacle archetype of renunciate Yogis). This is because he placed an emphasis on constantly discriminating Absolute Reality from relative unreality, or the True Self from the false self (of ego-I), as if distinguishing a snake from a rope, therefore this view often criticizes or sees the world as illusion (*maya*), as the *Upanishads* taught. However, some scholars (myself included) do not interpret Shankara's view in such strict dualistic terms, as Swami Abhayananda once more clearly explains:

> Shankara's sole message is that "nothing exists but Brahman." It is the conscious Self (Atman) within everyone, and It also constitutes all appearances of diversity. When Brahman is directly realized, then one knows, "I am Brahman; I am the Consciousness from which all this universe arises." The world itself, including one's own body,

is then realized to be an image in Brahman's cosmic light-show, an undifferentiated sea of Energy in which various separate forms are indistinguishable. This light-show, this vast sea of living Energy [*prakriti-shakti*], is projected from the Absolute, from Brahman [*purusha-shiva*]; [the universe] is His own, but it is not Brahman-as-Absolute. Looked at from a different perspective, as nothing else exists but Brahman, the world too is Himself. From the first perspective, the world is illusory; from the second, the world is nothing but Brahman Itself manifesting in form. Both [or all three] perspectives are true. The world-appearance [maya] shines forth magically from the Ever-Unchanging; it is He, but it is not He.[58]

Some people are more *jnani*-**oriented** by temperament for they prefer to identify with the Eternal Self via understanding (and control of the mind); while others are more *bhakti*-**oriented** since they more easily identify with feelings (and the heart) and so want to relate to the Eternal Self more like a child to a father, or as a lover to a beloved. Some practice both paths according to the inspiration of the moment since both are valid. As a consequence, a couple of hundred years later the Sage **Ramanuja** (1017–1137 CE) founded **Vishishta-Advaita** ("qualified nondualism"), based more on Vishnu (than Shiva), establishing the medieval *bhakti* movement of ecstatic devotion to the Divine. Ramanuja has been seen as the chief opponent to Shankara's philosophy since he taught the Absolute is not merely impersonal and transcendental but is a personal God (*Ishvara*) that includes (not excludes) the phenomenal world.[59] In Shankara's defense, he sees the world as being transparent to the Divine, thus includes but also transcends it.

Ramanuja

Ramanuja rejected the idealist notion that the universe is unreal or illusory (*maya*) but that it is the immanent "body" of the Transcendent Divine. Thus, those who turn to the Divine through heartfelt devotion (*bhakti*) will receive God's favor (*prasada*). For many people (if not most), this is an easier and more direct path or practice to Self-Realization, especially when supplemented by a Guru-Adept's Grace (and Transmission). As Feuerstein points out: "For

Ramanuja, *bhakti* is not a state of emotional effusiveness but one of wisdom (*jnana*)."[60] Such an approach of bhakti-devotion, therefore, would go on to form and influence the foundation for Guru-devotion that was to be revived during the centuries after Shankara (such as with the Sant Mat and Nath tradition). This view recognizes the formless Divine as being incarnate in the form of one's chosen Master-Guru. In the end, however, what is revealed is only Jnana or Wisdom and Knowledge (actually "Divine Ignorance") of the unspeakable and unknowable Divine Being (*purusha*), the "Radiant Transcendental Being" (in Adi Da's words), which is truly "nondual" since it transcends-yet-includes all descriptions, forms, or qualities.

In this case, whether known as **bhakti-yoga** (the "path of devotion") or **jnana-yoga** (the "path of wisdom"), or **karma-yoga** (the "path of work or service") or **hatha-yoga** (the "path of the body"), or *raja yoga* (the "royal yoga" that includes them all), or any of the other many *yogas* of Hinduism (such as *kriya-yoga, kundalini-yoga, mantra-yoga, nada-yoga, shabd-yoga*, etc.), the main purpose is always "to yoke or harness" via spiritual disciplines and exercises (*sadhana*), specifically meditation (*dhyana*), the small self of the  deluded "ego-I" with the True Self (*Atman*) of Ultimate and Absolute Reality (*Brahman*) or That which is "always already the case" (as Adi Da says). Only this awareness awakens *moksha* or "Liberation" and Enlightenment via *samadhi* ("ecstasy" or "enstasy," i.e., turned within), the final "limb" or goal of all Yoga. This is God-Realization and Divine Enlightenment, as we've been using those terms. However, Adi Da criticizes this *seeking* for God in any form as being the "Great Path of Return,"[61] thus he offers another more direct alternative with Satsang in Adidam Ruchiradam where God is known from the beginning not found at the end [see Chapter 11].

INDIA'S ETERNAL GURUS:
"SONGS TO GOD"

I ndia has thus given us—the global culture of humankind—a vast wealth of spiritual literature and psycho-spiritual techniques (including yoga and meditation) in addition to a deep reverential appreciation of the Guru. From Kapila to Krishna to Vyasa, from Rama to Ramakrishna to Ramana Maharshi, from Aurobindo to Vivekananda, from Shankara to Yogananda, from Maharishi Mahesh Yogi to Swami Prabhupada, from Shirdi Sai Baba to Neem Karoli Baba, to so many, many more, they all point to the same universal One Truth: the *Sanatana Dharma* or Eternal Teaching and Wisdom of the Ages. Even if their paths and teachings vary, reflecting different Stages of Life (as Adi Da has pointed out), they are all moved by a heart response to the very Divine Condition in which we all inhere.

Each Adept offers their own "**Song to God**"—*gita* means "song"—so that all of our different ears (and minds) can hear what we need to hear at our stage of development, to discover what will Awaken us to know Only God, God Only. As Huston Smith eloquently noted:

> The way the religions [of the world] are related likens them to a stained glass window whose sections divide the light of the sun into different colors. This analogy allows for significant differences between the religions [and Stages of Life] without pronouncing on their relative worth. If the peoples of the world differ from one another temperamentally, these differences could well affect the way Spirit [the One Light] appears to them; it could be seen from different angles…. for

God to be heard and understood divine revelations would have had
to be couched in the idioms of its respective hearers.[62]

In the ancient world, many of India's Gurus laid down the foundations
and sacred teachings that would inspire generations of seekers looking for God.
Many spoke of devotion (Fourth Stage), others of subtle energies and inner
visions (Fifth Stage), others of the formless Witness (Sixth Stage), and a few
Abiding as That which is ultimately revealed (Seven Stage). From their own
words or from the written records of their devotees (who often reached a similar or lesser stage of Realization), there has emerged India's sacred scriptures.
They have been called *sutras* meaning "thread" or "string" (English, "suture")
since they bind together in written words what was previously an oral tradition. The term is also descriptive since the works were written on leaves or
pressed bamboo slats which were bound together with a string (binding them
like a book). At other times, as mentioned, they are called *gitas* or "Songs"
of the Adept, sung by men and women alike, some expressing their ultimate
identity with That (*Brahman*), others yearning to see the Supreme Self within
(*Atman*). Let's review a few of these divine dancers and singers.

First, there is the difficulty, as scholars say, of knowing now thousands of
years later which Adepts existed historically as an actual person and which are
legendary figures, perhaps existing as several people but now known to us under one name. For example, there was **Dattatreya** (perhaps 8th or 7th century
BCE), a paradigmatic renunciate monk (*sannyasi*) and considered one of the
lords of Yoga, an Avatar of Lord Vishnu. The medieval Nath tradition (meaning "Great Master") centered around the esoteric Hatha Yoga of Shaivism
reveres him as the **Adi-Guru** (First Teacher), while he is often iconographically
depicted with three heads representing Brahma, Vishnu, and Shiva, the three
"gods" (or archetypes) of Hinduism [see above]. Yet, he was very probably a
real human being for he has several *Upanishads* dedicated to him including
one of the most important texts of Hinduism, the ***Avadhuta Gita*** (literally,
"song of the free soul"). Although generally, as Adi Da explains: "The Dattatreya tradition… is originally a Fourth Stage tradition. It begins with a God-
idea that is the subject of devotional and ceremonial worship. It is thus a cult
of God-worship, particularly associated with the idea of the Spiritual Master
as God. Dattatreya is presumed to be a historical personality and the original

Guru."[63] From the most ancient days, the special radiance (or charisma) and spiritual transmission of any highly-Realized Adept-Guru was recognized and highly revered.

Nonetheless, the point of view of the *Avadhuta Gita* itself is an ecstatic fulfillment of that tradition expressing a higher Stage of Life, as Avatar Da confirms: "This school culminates in a version of Advaitic Wisdom communicated in the *Avadhuta Gita*, in which the ultimate Realization of the Transcendental Self [Sixth to Seventh Stages of Life] is proclaimed completely independent of any kind of yogic exercise or conditional mystical experience [Fourth to Fifth Stages]."[64] The American-born Avadhoot, himself a Free-Realized being, continues to clarify:

> The mast [pronounced "must"], a kind of crazy man or woman who has no concern for the world, is typical of the character that is worshipped and venerated in the Dattatreya tradition.... You must understand, however, that the ultimate school of the Dattatreya tradition is represented by the *Avadhoot Gita*, which has a direct affinity to and association with the Advaitic tradition and the ancient tradition of Upanishadic non-dualism, whereas the Fifth Stage schools of the Dattatreya cult are very much associated with the tradition of Nathism, Shaivite yoga, and Fifth Stage phenomenal [yogic] attainments. The ultimate Dattatreya school is associated with the Sixth to Seventh Stage point of view described in the *Avadhuta Gita*, and is more directly aligned with the ancient tradition of Upanishadic non-dualism, such as found in the *Ashtavakra Gita*, and the Advaitic tradition of Shankara and others.[65]

The *Ashtavakra Gita* (composed around 5th to 4th century BCE), based on a dialogue between the sage Ashtavakra and the famous King Janaka, is a slightly later cousin of the *Bhagavad Gita*, yet is similar in its message proclaiming the ultimate reality of the Supreme Self.[66] Avatar Adi Da holds it in the highest esteem: "The *Ashtavakra Gita* is the Confession or Song of such Enlightenment. It stands in the supreme tradition of the spiritual literature of the ["premonitory"] Seventh Stage of Life. It speaks spontaneously in and of the Free Disposition that is the fulfillment of all Ways, even of life itself.... My advice to you is that you listen well to Ashtavakra, but do not read him indiscriminately."[67] A few stances of Ashtavakra's wisdom will prove this point:

> Burn the forest of ignorance with the fire of certitude that "I am the non-dual and pure consciousness"; abandoning sorrow, be blissful. [9]
>
> In that pure, supremely blissful consciousness the universe appears as illusory, like the snake apprehended as the rope. Live in that consciousness. [10]
>
> O child, you are ever bound by the fetters of the ego sense. With the axe of wisdom—"I am pure consciousness"—rend asunder the fetters and become happy. [14]
>
> You encompass the universe as the universe enters into you. You are in reality the embodiment of pure consciousness. Do not give way to the pettiness of the (finite) mind. [16][68]

Remember, these words of wisdom were whispered thousands of years ago, epitome statements from the Axial Age (800–300 BCE) and God's Great Wisdom Tradition affirming the truth of Self-Realization and God-Knowledge that has been known perennially. This **Ultimate Knowledge**—actually more like "**Divine Ignorance**"—can never be exceeded but is only waiting to be *realized* by each and every one of us now and forever into the future. Without this wisdom living in our hearts, we are doomed to a life of evil, ignorance, and intolerance. But the Sages have given us a way out, the means to know the Truth for real—we need to listen and hear them now!

Dattatreya   Vyasa   Kapila   Patanjali   Badarayana

Another legendary Adept (or several people) who is recorded as having produced some of the most sacred scriptures of Advaitic-Upanishadic wisdom is the incomparable **Vyasa** (perhaps 10th century BCE or later), another Vedic Rishi regarded by tradition as the arranger of the *Vedas*, as well as being the author of eighteen *Puranas*, and perhaps the early *Brahma Sutras*, in addition to being credited as chronicler of the epic *Mahabharata*, possibly even composing the *Bhagavad Gita* (literally "Song of God") thus introducing us to the Avatars of Rama (and his wife Sita) and Krishna (and his consort Radha). By any account, obviously, Vyasa is one Great Guru or Maha-Siddha.

One figure who is generally acknowledged by scholars as being historical is **Kapila** (ca. 8th or 7th century BCE), also famed as a Vedic Sage or Rishi who composed the **Samkhya Sutra** thus founding the crucial school of Samkhya Yoga that would influence many generations of Spiritual Teachers in India, including Mahavira of Jainism (ca. 600 BCE) and the Buddha (ca. 500 BCE). Another historical figure was **Badarayana** (ca. 500 BCE to 200 BCE) who compiled the later **Brahma Sutras** in the form known today as well as the *Vedanta Sutra*. And the amazing **Patanjali** (dates unknown, perhaps 2nd century BCE or 2nd century CE) who compiled the well-known *Yoga Sutras*, the most important early text of Yoga practice and theory outlining the eight "limbs" or practices of Ashtanga Yoga. The list goes on and on.

Shaivism is a major tradition of Hinduism, originating in Kashmir—i.e., **Kashmir Shaivism**—said to worship Shiva but more accurately sees the Enlightened Guru (who Shiva represents) as being an agency to Divine Self-Realization. **Shiva** is the ultimate Yogi from the Himalayas (specifically Mt. Kailash), sitting in the lotus posture on tiger skin absorbed in the meditative stillness of the Heart, the kundalini serpent fully awakened sprouting out of the top of the head, like a fountain. This approach of Guru Yoga inspired later traditions, such as the Naths who honor the "**Siddhas**" or "perfected ones" (meaning "liberated" or Enlightened beings). This honoring of the Guru is similar to **Vaishnavism**, which worships **Vishnu** as Supreme Being, the one who incarnates as the world's various "**Avatars**" or "one who crosses down" from the Divine Domain to come teach human beings about the ultimate truth of Reality. Modern-day Avatar Adi Da Samraj clarifies that various Stages of Life are being activated in these great pandits and Sages, therefore, even many advanced Yogis do not necessarily attain Supreme Enlightenment but remain seekers for higher yogic attainments and visionary experiences:

> **Shaivite yogis** are generally inclined to regard certain kinds of higher yogic [Fifth Stage] phenomena to be Enlightenment.... Basically, it is a school of Fifth Stage yogic idealism, the highest attainment of which

is transcendence in the form of *nirvikalpa samadhi* ["formless mysticism"].... The Siddhas of the Fifth Stage schools of the cults of Shiva and Dattatreya do not commonly communicate the point of view of the Sixth and Seventh Stage Realization. They do not communicate the Transcendental Realization (beyond discrimination, beyond the conceits of experience and knowledge), nor Self-Realization (in the sense communicated in the Advaitic tradition), nor Nirvanic Realization (as communicated in the Buddhist tradition). In general, the popular cults of the Dattatreya tradition and the Shaivite traditions are limited to Fourth and Fifth Stage ideals and peculiarities.[69]

Nevertheless, certain of their Adepts, such as Ashtavakra and the Sage of the *Avadhuta Gita*, do communicate the highest attainments of the Sixth and Seventh Stages of Life, as Adi Da concedes. As one fine example, there is the *Ribhu Gita* or *Song of Ribhu*—probably composed around 500 BCE by the Adept **Ribhu**—a favorite text of twentieth-century Sri Ramana Maharshi. The *Ribhu Gita* is, as one scholar explains, "a dialogue between an Enlightened One and his disciple... just as the *Bhagavad Gita* represents the highest most exalted declaration of Vishnu [via Krishna], the *Ribhu Gita* represents the purest and most sublime declaration of Shiva [via Sage Ribhu]."[70] Adi Da explains: "I thought originally that the *Ribhu Gita* would naturally belong to this category [of the 'premonitory' Seventh Stage], but it is full of 'Abide as this, abide as that.' It is telling you how to realize the ultimate stage. It also instructs you relative to use of the discriminative faculty [of the higher mind]. Although primarily a Sixth Stage text, it is based in Seventh Stage wisdom."[71] As just one example of its Enlightened Wisdom clearly shows:

> Everything is the Supreme Spirit, which is Being-Consciousness-Beatitude [*Sat-Chit-Ananda*], and I am That. By constantly cultivating this pure thought, get rid of impure thoughts.
>
> Then, my son, discarding even that thought and always inhering in the State of Fullness, you will become the non-dual and undifferentiated Supreme Being and attain liberation.[72]

Again, Adi Da points out: "The *Yoga Vasishtha* is also a great text in this same ultimate tradition, but its extensive consideration of the 'how' and 'why' rather than the pure 'is' of Realization also qualifies it as a general text on the ultimate Way rather than a specific 'confession' of Realization."[73] All these sacred "songs" now make up our "Divine Library" of Global Wisdom and can be accessed by any interested reader [see Chapter 2]. But they must be read and studied, contemplated and considered, hopefully to inspire the reader to take up the necessary practices (or Yoga) to realize the Enlightened State for oneself.

Another powerful text is the ***Guru Gita*** ("Song of the Guru"), a favorite of Swami Muktananda, a lesser-known cousin of the *Bhagavad Gita* (possibly composed slightly later). Its several hundred verses praise the Guru as being even greater than God because it is only through the Guru's Grace and Teaching that a devotee can come to know God for real (and in truth). The *Guru Gita* (said to be written by Vyasa) contains instructions given by **Lord Shiva** to his consort the **Goddess Parvati** where the Guru first explains that the Truth cannot be fully told in words but only imparted (or transmitted) by one who has already realized this Truth, thus showing the necessity for a living Guru. According to this splendid exposition, the Guru in human form is the supreme servant to humankind for he or she only exists to teach about (and transmit) the Light inherent in the devotee's own heart (as their very consciousness which is God itself).

This is why the ultimate truth given to Parvati is the secret heart of Enlightenment: "**Thou Art That**"—known in Sanskrit as ***Tat Tvam Asi***—the universal truth declaring "I Am God" or "You are God." Therefore, in truth, "the Guru is God or Brahman," as the *Guru Gita* constantly affirms, since "the Guru shows the supreme state of Brahman."[74] These types of short phrases of the God-Realized State, scattered throughout the *Upanishads* and Hindu's sacred scriptures, are called ***Mahavakyas*** or "great sentences" that utter the

Enlightened View in a few short words, such as:

- "I am Brahman" (*aham brahmasani*);
- "This Atman is Brahman" (*ayam atma brahma*);
- "Consciousness is Brahman" (*prajñanam brahma*);
- "The Self is Brahman" (*ayam atma brahma*), and so on.

Only a Guru, however, can impart their true meaning through serving your awakening in consciousness. Even then *you* must *do the yoga*, engage the sadhana (spiritual disciplines), and not expect the Guru to do it for you. If you do not approach the Guru with the right attitude and devotion you will not be open to their sublime Gift [see Chapter 24]. For this simple fact alone the *Guru Gita* points out how the Guru is more important than God because as its verses explain:

> Meditating on the Guru one acquires real knowledge. One should then strongly feel: "By the instructions of the Guru I am liberated!"
>
> [Translator] Note: This kind of meditation leads to Mukti [liberation]. The injunction to meditate on the Guru… is the same as the Guru's instructions conveyed in the Mahavakya "*Tat Tvam Asi*," etc., and the consequent realization: "I am Bramham—*Aham Brahmasmi*". The Guru says "*Tat Tvam Asi* [Thou Art God]" and the disciple asserts and feels "*Aham Brahmasmi* [I am God]."[75]

For modern people to think they can dispense with this time-honored tradition of Guru Yoga-Satsang and this valid (or authentic) method of Enlightenment is ignorance parading as wisdom. We must learn to adequately access the Guru-Adept in the right and proper manner, and not cultically, since this method of Guru-devotion is only here for our own advantage and benefit. The Guru is God's Grace-in-action. When we evolve our personal consciousness then our collective society also evolves. The true Guru is not a cultic icon but the means for our salvation and liberation in God-Realization, which is the only true way to world peace, as Ken Wilber once noted:

> The aim of the Mystics is to deliver men and women from their battles by delivering them from their boundaries. Not manipulate the subject, and not manipulate the object, but transcend both in

Nondual Consciousness [or Enlightenment]. The discovery of the ultimate Whole is the only cure for unfreedom, and it is the only prescription offered by the Mystics [as Guru-Adepts].[76]

The **Hindu Tantras**, a later development in India's esoteric teachings (around 500–1000 CE), also reverentially exalt the Guru-Adept as the necessary means (and agent) for cultivating Divine Enlightenment. For example, the *Kularnava Tantra*, a major Tantric scripture, extols the necessity of the genuine Sat-Guru (or "True Guru") with these words:

> At the root of *dhyana* [meditation] is the form of the Guru; at the root of *puja* [sacramental worship] is the feet of the Guru; at the root of *mantra* [vocal incantation] is the word of the Guru, and at the root of all liberation [Enlightenment] is the Grace of the Guru. (Verse 90)[77]

It is obvious that in the East, far more than in the West (with its Abrahamic religions), the culture of India honors the supreme value of the Siddha-Guru or Adept-Realizer as being an Agent of God's Grace [see Chapter 23]. This is because the East, from Japan to China to Tibet to Southeast Asia to India, has had countless living examples of the Guru-function, whereas the West has basically one (Jesus). When this universal "method of the Siddhas" (*Satsang*) is fully understood, we in the West would do well to learn from the East, to study and listen attentively and discover for ourselves the Guru's authentic veracity for your own God-Realization. Yes, even in India there have always been the cultic (and mythic) tendencies of the ego (even the religious ego) to grant undue authority to Guru figures and create cultic objects of religious obsession. The ego is always seeking for fascinating objects (or subjects), even spiritual ones, including those with political or social power, just to prevent itself from fully surrendering and *realizing* the ever-present Divine Reality. This is just as true in modern times as it was in times past, thus it's an error that must be overcome by right understanding and right relationship to the genuine Adept-Guru.

Cultism around the Guru, in other words, must always be undone by true ego-transcendence, whatever your religion. What is realized culminates in actual God-Realization supported by genuine *sadhana* or spiritual practices.

Only by actively practicing and meditating with a surrendered (or opened) heart and awakened mind in real Divine Communion are we truly Free. Meditation and right devotion (or Right Life), practiced on a daily basis by following the instructions of one's Guru becomes the key to unlocking these inner secrets. But *you* must make the right approach and *do the yoga* of devotion on your own.

BHAKTAS:
DEVOTEES OF GOD AS GURU

The celebration of the Gitas or "Songs" to God-Realization sung by various Yogis and Adepts continued throughout the history of India, far too many to go into detail here. But a few examples follow below. In the 16th century there lived many illumined Saints in India that are still known and talked about today due to their *bhakti* or devotional enthusiasm (Fourth Stage) leading to yogic ascension (Fifth Stage), and, potentially, even greater Realization (Sixth and Seventh Stage). There was **Chaitanya** (1486–1533), the love-intoxicated *bhakta* of Bengal known for his gentle "Divine Madness," a tall, muscular man who considered himself the bride of Krishna often dancing in public drawing others into his God-Communion with his entranced dance. There was **Vallabha** (1479–1531), a mystic-philosopher and *archarya* ("teacher"), who founded the Krishna-centered Pushti sect of Vaishnavism in the Braj region of India emphasizing a Pure Nondualism. Also, **Sant Eknath** (1548–1609) an Indian Hindu saint, philosopher and poet, a devotee of Krishna who was a major figure of the Warkari tradition. These are actual figures documented in the historical record (though often embellished with legendary tales).

Chaitanya   **Vallabha**   **Sant Eknath**   **Dadu Dayal**

Perhaps most amazing of all, however, was a special poet-saint from Gujarat, India who taught a universal message given with simple clarity.[78] **Dadu Dayal** (1544–1603), like Kabir and Nanak [see Chapter 15], stood between the quarrelling factions of Islam and Hinduism proclaiming: "All the Saints are of one mind; it is only those in the midst of the way who follow diverse paths. All the enlightened [Sages] have left one message; … It is only those in the midst of their journey who hold diverse opinions."[79] Born with the Muslim name Allahdad, he became known as "Dadu" for "brother" and "Dayal" meaning "the compassionate one," so his group of followers formed a sect known as *Dadupanth* (the "path of Dadu"). His recorded verses are known as the *Dadu Anubhav Vani* (a compilation of 5,000 verses) that would sing about the spontaneous "open eye" bliss (*sahaja*) arising from supreme devotion to God. Since Dadu preached that pure devotion to the Divine Reality should transcend all religious or sectarian divisions his devotees became known as *Nipakh* or "non-sectarian."

Dadu was a married householder with four children (two sons and two daughters) and had a trade involving cotton, but soon gained a reputation as a holy man attracting a following of devoted disciples. Like Kabir, whom he greatly admired, Dadu had experienced the One Divine directly so he saw no reason to be associated with being either a Muslim or a Hindu since his Awakening transcended all religious frameworks.[80] He encouraged everyone from both religions, and from all religions, to reconcile their differences by recognizing their common pursuit to know God, yet not through beliefs or rituals alone but directly through realizing the mystical state of God-Realization.

Although the 16th century seemed to be flush with Awakened Adepts (of various Stages of Life), according to some scholars, they seemed to diminish during the following centuries.[81] Notably, there were exceptions, such as

Ramprasad Sen (1718–1778), the Bengali poet who worshiped the female aspect of the Divine as Kali, the Mother Goddess with intense devotion being an exemplar of Bhakti Yoga (Fourth Stage of Life). Also, **Sant Tukaram** (1598 or 1608–1649/1650), a bhakti by nature and a farmer by trade, bequeathed to posterity many wonderful devotional songs, chants, and poems in praise of sadhana and the Divine. This apparent scarcity of Mystics seemed to change in the 19th century.

Gorakhnath   **Ramprasad Sen**   **Sant Tukaram**   **Akkalkot Maharaj**

There was the venerated **Swami Samarth** (died 1878), also known as **Akkalkot Maharaj** (since he resided at Akkalkot for 22 years after traveling far and wide, even to China), who passed from Fourth Stage devotionalism to become as Fifth Stage Siddha, according to Adi Da's review:

> Those who would Realize the Truth via this point of view [Guru Yoga] pass through the Fourth Stage worship of Dattatreya and his incarnations, among whom are various Fifth Stage Siddhas (such as Akkalkot Swami, Sai Baba of Shirdi, and Rang Avadhoot), on the basis of which they go on to enter the esoteric tradition of Hatha Yoga associated with Gorakhnath [early 11th century CE] and the Yogi Siddhas. This school culminates in a version of wisdom communicated by the *Avadhoot Gita*, in which the ultimate Realization of the Transcendental Self is proclaimed completely independent of any kind of yogic exercise or conditional mystical experience.[82]

Recognized as being a reincarnation of Dattatreya, **Akkalkot Swami** (another of his names) was unpredictable with his "Divine Madness" or "Crazy Wisdom" behavior, yet credited with many miracles. Importantly, he treated Muslims, Christians and Parsees all alike, and his kindness was bestowed on the poor, needy and those at the lowest rung of the society.[83] It is also said that Swami Samarth and Shirdi Sai Baba were the manifestations of the same Divine Spirit in two different gross-physical bodies.

There are so many more Yogi-Adepts, even in the 20th century, that I cannot begin to do them justice. Let me mention a few more names, remembering that each stood and breathed the same air as we do, each part of their time and place, dramatically influencing those around them with their higher development in the Stages of Life. Each of them and their *leelas* ("stories") and Teachings now belong to the whole human race; that's the role of the Guru's Work.

Totapuri   **Shirdi Sai Baba**   **Narayan Maharaj**   **Meher Baba**

For example, there was **Totapuri** (b. 1780?), affectionately known as "Nangta Baba" (Naked Baba), because as a renunciate he did not wear any clothing, and who regarded the gods and goddesses (and all of their rituals) as dualistic fantasies of the mind. Upon arriving in Dakshineswar, Totapuri (in 1864) taught Ramakrishna [see below] Advaita Vedanta by emphasizing its formlessness, until Ramakrishna achieved *Nirvikalpa Samadhi* (the disappearance of individual identity in the Absolute) nearly instantly (whereas it took Totapuri forty years). The great wandering Yogi (who never remained in one place for three days) became a devotee of Ramakrishna staying with him for eleven months. **Shirdi Sai Baba** (1831?–1918), also known as Sai Baba of Shirdi, considered by his devotees to be a manifestation of Dattatreya [see above], was revered by both his Muslim and Hindu devotees as he condemned the distinction of castes and taught about the Realization of the Self. There are many temples dedicated to Sai Baba throughout India and even throughout the world. **Narayan Maharaj** (1885–1945) was a Hindu spiritual master considered by his followers to be a Sadguru ("True Guru"), who lived in luxury in a palace with a silver throne provided by his devotees but he was uncommonly unselfish giving to the poor as his motto was "Treat every one as God." **Meher Baba** (1894–1969) was considered an Avatar or God in human form for his era. He was a major spiritual figure of the 20th century with followers estimated in the hundreds of thousands to the millions (including famous rock stars, like Pete Townshend who dedicated The Who's rock opera *Tommy* to him; or Bobby McFerrin's 1988 Grammy Award-winning song "Don't Worry, Be Happy" was inspired by Baba's adage). Most of his followers were concentrated in India yet had a significant number in the United States, Europe and Australia. Importantly, from July 1925 to his death in 1969, he took a vow of silence that he never broke, though he wrote a popular book called *God Speaks* (1955) read religiously by those in the "Meher Baba Movement" who consider him a fully God-Realized being. And these are only a few. The list could go on and on, especially when we consider those Gurus from India who came to the West (particularly after the 1960s) bringing their teachings of meditation and Yoga with them.

Ramakrishna-Vivekananda: One Who Was To Come

A special mention must be made of the incomparable 19th century Saint and Guru-Adept **Ramakrishna Paramahansa** (1836–1886), who was Guru to Swami Vivekananda [see Chapter 9], both of whom would have a deeper psychic connection with Adi Da Samraj. A son of a poor Bengali brahmin, Ramakrishna, as Feuerstein notes, "is widely recognized as one of the greatest spiritual geniuses of modern Hinduism."[84] He was an celibate ascetic married to **Sarada Devi** (1853–1920), a notable saint and mystic herself, so he saw his wife as the Goddess incarnate and she looked upon her husband as her *guru*. Ramakrishna lived the life of a renunciate temple priest at a Kali temple in Dakshineshvar (near Calcutta), yet his influence spread far and wide, even into the West.

Ramakrishna

The Goddess-worshiping Yogi was prone to ecstatic reveries since a child, going into samadhi states for extended periods, sometimes twisting his hands in *mudras* (or exaggerated gestures), even being photographed with the newly invented camera. The beloved Saint, however, was typically oriented to Fourth and Fifth Stage phenomena, generally puritanical, devotional, and exhibiting "conventional dualism" (in Adi Da's terms).[85] He was revered for being a "fool for God" since he was oriented more toward mystical experiences than book learning. Nonetheless, he was very articulate and appealed to a wide variety of spiritual seekers including advanced Yogi practitioners, who surrounded him as he instructed them on the path to realizing the One God (or Goddess)—whether Hindu, Christian, or Muslim—going to the heart of all religions.[86] Sri Ramakrishna ecstatically exclaimed:

> If any sincere practitioner, within whatever culture or religion, prays and meditates with great devotion and commitment to Truth alone, Your Grace will flood his [or her] mind and heart, O Mother. His particular sacred tradition will be opened and illuminated. He will reach the one goal of spiritual evolution. I long to pray with sincere Christians in their churches and to bow and prostrate with devoted Muslims in their mosques! All religions are glorious![87]

Importantly, like Kabir and Guru Nanak centuries earlier, Ramakrishna cultivated tolerance and praise for all the religious traditions congregated in India, including Christianity and Islam, proclaiming "all paths lead to the same end"—God-Realization. Being a preacher of religious tolerance in an emerging global world (India was then ruled by Britain) Ramakrishna is heralded today as one the world's greatest Saints and Guru-Adepts. His **Ramakrishna Mission** was dedicated to providing charity, social work and education for all who needed it. He had many devotees but it was the world-renowned Swami **Vivekananda** (1863–1902) who would shine the brightest after leaving his Mother India to travel to the West (in 1893) and bring in person the tolerant religious wisdom of the East to Westerners at the first-ever Parliament of the World's Religions [see Chapter 9].

At one point, according to reports, shortly before Ramakrishna dropped his body the Adept poured his spirit-energy transmission into his beloved disciple Vivekananda so the young man would be empowered to approach the West and walk straight into the gates of materialism.[88] By doing so, it is said, the "two became one force, one person at the deeper self… [representing] eons of Masters of the highest order."[89] As powerful as Vivekananda's presence was in the West, and it changed the course of history, he became frustrated with the racism he encountered realizing his impact could only go so far. Vivekananda seemed to understand that his universal work for humanity required a submission of the Eastern soul to be directly reborn in the West as a Caucasian. On July 4, 1902 the Swami, who had already predicted his early demise, sat down and intentionally departed his body. He was not yet forty.

Ramakrishna   **Sarada Devi**   **Vivekananda**   **Aurobindo**   **Mirra Alfassa**
"The Mother"

Adi Da Samraj has suggested that his own incarnation born as an Avatar in the West was in part caused by the deeper personality of Ramakrishna-Vivekananda in creating an opening for a World-Teacher to appear who would be capable of mastering (and transcending) both orientations of Alpha-East and Omega-West.[90] Avatar Adi Da makes it plain: "Swami Vivekananda was My Forerunner here. He prepared the world (and Himself) for My Avataric Divine Manifestation in the West."[91] Consequently, Adi Da's appearance is a unique event—for as Ken Wilber once said: "He is destined to be recognized as the first Western-born Avatar (World Teacher) to appear in the history of the world."[92] For the Eastern mind to deeply enter the West it must come from the inside and move out, not get on a plane or ship and travel to a foreign land. To actually manifest a fresh Teaching and Spirit-Transmission of Divine Enlightenment unique to our times during the unprecedented emergence of a global culture, the Wisdom of the East had to *be born* in the West via Western parents and their cultural heritage. Adi Da then submitted to this limitation (of Omega-mind) as a child and young adult, transcended it at age thirty (in 1970) with his Divine Re-Awakening at a temple dedicated to Ramakrishna, and now has given the world a unique and universal Teaching (the Reality-Way of Adidam Ruchiradam) uniting East and Wes in a prior unity:

> Particularly in the time in which we now live, when the ideas of all
> the provinces of Earth are now gathering together for the first time in
> human history, and all the absolute dogmas find themselves casually
> associated... the complex mind of Everyman is remembering itself all

at once. Therefore, we are obliged to discover the Truth again by penetrating the bizarre consciousness of all the races combined as one....

My Work in the world is to communicate that summary of religious and Spiritual Wisdom, so that humankind may again be devoted to the Way of Life in Truth, even now that all religious and
spiritual cultures confront us collectively and at once.[93]

In this case, we can see the importance of Vivekananda's preparatory work
by the fact that, for one, Adi Da was Re-Awakened at a Vedanta Society temple
in southern California that the Swami's organization had erected to worship
Ramakrishna. The East had become the West so the One Truth inherited from
all the world's religions, felt most deeply in the land of India, could beat as the
heart of a new cooperative world order. Adi Da Samraj is the Integral Age's true
Root-Guru—Wake Up and see!

INTEGRAL YOGA: ENLIGHTENED EVOLUTION

Another way the East entered the West was through Eastern Yogis who
had received a Western education (as had Swami Vivekananda). During
the early twentieth century, **Aurobindo Ghose** (1872–1950), educated
in Cambridge, England, incorporated the newly discovered concept of evolution (uncovered by Charles Darwin a few decades earlier) to apply its idea of
unfolding development to individual consciousness. He saw the evolution of
consciousness as involving the descent of Spirit down into the world (and human body) to give us the opportunity to live not only a thoroughly human but
also a "**Divine Life**."[94] Aurobindo gave the world a highly sophisticated and
updated version of the timeless Wisdom of India he called "**Integral Yoga**"[95]
(an inspiration decades later for Ken Wilber's Integral Theories). Aurobindo
summarizes his new approach to Yoga, which still contains the idealism of the
Fourth and Fifth Stages of Life, which is its principal error (in Adi Da's view):

I am concerned with the Earth, not with worlds beyond for their own
sake; it is a terrestrial realization that I seek and not a flight to distant
summits. All other Yogas regard this life as an illusion or a passing
phase; the Supramental Yoga alone regards it as a thing created by the
Divine for a progressive manifestation and takes the fulfilment of the
life and the object for its object. The supramental [Supermind] is sim-

ply the Truth-Consciousness and what it brings in its descent is the full truth of life, the full truth of consciousness in Matter.[96]

Both Vivekananda and Aurobindo taught that science has given us a powerful tool in understanding the evolutionary processes of Nature and the human being, even on an esoteric level. By combining the wisdom of the East with the scientific knowledge of the West the workings of Spirit can become even more illumined (when not reduced by scientific materialism). Aurobindo's Integral Yoga, and his community at Auroville, was extended and carried on by his wife after his death, **Mirra Alfassa** (1878–1973), known as "The Mother," thus introducing many young Westerners to an integrated way of living.[97] They suggest that the clear, rational thinking of the scientific Omega-mind could counterbalance the tendency of Alpha-Eastern metaphysics to escape this world in otherworldliness. This way the material Earth of Nature and all her living creatures and plants, including her flesh-and-blood humanity, are seen as all being expressions of Spirit and thus evolution itself is simply the unfolding of "Spirit-in-action" (in Wilber's words).

Ramana Maharshi

Without a doubt, the greatest Guru-Adept to appear in India during the 20th century, or at least the best known and honored, was **Ramana Maharshi** (1879–1950), the Sage who was featured in a lead article for *Life* magazine (written by William Sargeant in the May 30, 1949 issue). Born in Tamil Nadu, India, at the age of 16 (in 1896) the precocious youngster laid down, after a relative had died, and had a "death experience" (or "ego-death") during which he realized the True Self (Atman) that he called "the Heart," as this one example shows: "The Heart is the only Reality. The mind is only a transient phase.

To remain as one's [True] Self is to enter the Heart."[98] Ramana was soon attracted to the holy mountain **Arunachala** (honored as a manifestation of Lord Shiva) at Tiruvannamalai (in southern India), where he took on the role of a *sannyasin* (or renunciate). The Sage of Arunachala spent years meditating in a small cave on the mountainside until he came down after his mother died where devotees were so attracted to him that an ashram (or spiritual community) grew up around him. During his several trips to India, Adi Da Samraj visited Ramana's ashram, **Sri Ramanasramam**, next to Shiva's holy mountain Arunachala, where the young American Avatar paid homage by spending time in the very cave where Ramana often meditated.

During his time alive, people regarded Ramana as an authentic God-man with a beautiful divine radiance, so they would approach him for *darshan* (or "the sighting of God") to receive his spiritual transmission by simply being in his company (which was very potent). As American scholar Lex Hixon explains: "Those who experienced the power of Ramana's gaze have reported that the initiation was so clear and vivid they could never again seriously doubt that the Guru was none other than their own primal conscious being."[99] The wise Heart-Master taught a method of **self-inquiry** ("Who is the I?") as being the principal means to remove ignorance and abide in awareness of the Self, the Heart. He could speak freely, as any genuine Guru can, about the ancient sacred spiritual texts of India and their true esoteric meanings with a felicity as if he had written them himself.

Visitors from around the world came to see Ramana and to ask endless questions, where many of his responses have been collected and published (along with his poems).[100] Ramana is one of the most articulate spokesmen for Advaita Vedanta ever recorded, easy to understand and direct, influencing many Westerners including Ken Wilber and Adi Da Samraj. In a foreword to *Talks with Ramana Maharshi* (2001), Wilber claimed the humble Guru "is the greatest Sage of the twentieth century and, arguably, the greatest spiritual realizer of this or any time."[101] Adi Da also found him to be as clear as any Sage he had read or studied, taking *The Collected Works of Ramana Maharshi* with him (with only two other books) on his third visit to India in May 1970.[102] The Avatar's review of the *Sri Ramana Gita* suggested, "though it clearly contains the point of view of the ['premonitory'] Seventh Stage, it answers the question of an aspirant who wants to know how to realize it. Thus, it is basically devoted to the point of view of the lower stages. The clear point of view about the transcendence of the discriminative intelligence appears only here and there, is only suggested."[103] Nonetheless, Ramana's Realization was obvious to the American-born Guru, thus, in a sense, he was a precursor to Adi Da's Way of the Heart.

Importantly, Ramana taught and spoke about *Amrita Nadi* (the "conduit of immortality") as being an esoteric structure in the human body-mind that extends from the head down to the heart (in the pacemaker chamber on the right). Adi Da later clarified that it then extends up in an S-curve to Infinity (above and beyond the crown chakra), what he called "the regeneration of *Amrita Nadi*."[104] Rarely mentioned in the Great Tradition, this current (or *nadi*) is said to complete the circuit of kundalini running up from the base of the spine (*sushumna-nadi*) into the inner brain exiting the crown of the head before dropping down to the heart on the right, a process confirmed by Avatar Adi Da. Indeed, although they never met in person, at one time Adi Da called Ramana his "twin brother" due to both of their emphasis on *Amrita Nadi* (or *Atma Nadi*) grounded in the Heart (on the right) [see Chapter 19].

As fascinating as these esoteric figures are, and their stories (*leelas*) may be, the importation of Guru Yoga from East to West (beginning in the 20th century) must be understood from a level of true maturity and stable ego development on part of the devotee or student. Gurus from the East can't simply be "saviors" for childish-thinking people wanting a "Big Parent" to tell them what to do. Rather, only with real maturity and discriminative intelligence based on true practice and meditation can the root dualism of the West, the felt separation of the self from the Divine, be released into the esoteric practices of Real Religion. True human growth to Enlightenment or God-Realization seems to have best manifested in the Eternal Teachings of India whether expressed in the language of Vedanta or Buddhism, Jainism or Samkhya Yoga, or a variety of other paths, such as Tantra. The West, unfortunately (as our survey shows), barely touches upon this type of True Religion. Each of India's roads to God-Realization has had their deepest roots in the ancient *Vedas* given to humankind by the Great Seers, the Rishis, the Maha-Gurus for everyone to now receive as our common global inheritance. This is why the backbone of India stands in the knowledge of Vedanta where the Realization of Nondual Mysticism is the eternal fountain of India's Divine Wisdom and perennial source of her Enlightened Gurus.

AVATARS OF ATMAN:
"REALIZE ME"—GOD AS GURU

As the literature of the Great Gurus of India spread throughout the first millennium BCE and into the Axial Age it became embodied in her famous "**Avatars**" or "one who crosses over" from the Divine Domain (or Enlightened Consciousness) down into the human domain. Avatars are seen as "divine incarnations" of Vishnu (the "all-pervading" or "preserver" aspect of the Brahman trinity). For example, these Maha-Gurus include the legendary Adepts of **Rama**, the spiritual hero of the epic story-poem *Ramayana*, and also **Krishna**, the spiritual hero of the *Bhagavad Gita*, literally, the "Song of God," often called the "Hindu Bible." (Krishna would become widely known in the West via the "Hari Krishna movement" begun by Swami Prabhupada in the 1960s, with famous devotees like George Harrison of The Beatles). **Buddha**, too, according to this tradition was a prophesied Avatar of Enlightenment, an incarnation of Vishnu. Significantly, each of these Great Gurus or Maha-Siddhas were usually paired with a tantric wife-consort, such as **Sita** (with Rama) and **Radha** (with Krishna), women who had also attained divine insight and devotional understanding. Yes, the record of Enlightened Masters includes women as well as men, though one has to look harder in the literature to find them, generally being written by men-scribes (and brahmins). Nevertheless, it is commonly acknowledged that women can often be the best devotees in recognizing the true value of the Guru since they seem to more naturally live from the heart (instead of being overly obsessed with the mind, like males tend to do, especially in ancient days).

These well-known examples are among many of the stories (or *leelas*) known to us through fable and legend coming from ancient India, including warrior-hero devotees such as **Hanuman**, the "monkey-man," a powerful master of yoga who was a prime example of being devoted to his Guru beyond everything else. He will do anything for his Guru, since his Guru gives him everything (i.e., Divine Awareness). These stories or mythic tales are often performed as plays (and now in films) as an important means of instruction and acculturation whether in the rural villages or modern cities of India.

Devotee Hanuman in devotion to Guru Rama-Krishna

The ***Bhagavad Gita*** is a 700-verse scripture that focuses on Lord Krishna teaching Prince Arjuna to "fight and remember Me" as instruction for doing one's duty (*dharma*). The *Bhagavad Gita* is, of course, the best-known Hindu scripture in the West. **Ralph Waldo Emerson**, the Sage of Concord, "a *Rishi* in Concord,"[105] upon discovering the newly-arrived translations from the lands of India in a journal entry wrote (in 1831): "[The *Bhagavad Gita*] was the first of books; it was as if an empire spake to us, nothing small or unworthy, but large, serene, consistent, the voice of an old intelligence which in another age and climate had pondered and thus disposed of the same questions which exercise us… the very oldest of thoughts cast into the mould of these new times."[106] It was also **Henry David Thoreau**'s constant companion as "the Buddha of Walden" secluded himself in the woods at Walden Pond (in 1845) with a borrowed copy from Emerson's library. Thoreau famously exalted: "In the morning I bathe my intellect in the stupendous and cosmogonal philosophy of the *Bhagavad Gita*, since whose composition years of the gods have elapsed, and in comparison with which our world and its literature seems puny and trivial."[107] Also **Walt Whitman**, "the Bhakti Bard" inspired with his own ecstatic poetry of divine bliss led Emerson to call *Leaves of Grass* (1855) "a mixture of the *Bhagavad Gita* and the *New York Herald*."[108] Yet it couldn't all be good news, naturally, since nearly a hundred year later **Robert Oppenheimer**, the "father of the atomic bomb," is reported to have uttered a verse during the first atomic bomb explosion at the Trinity test site where the only thing that flashed through his mind as the sky filled with blazing light (and radiation) as the earth shook was:

> Now I am become Death, the destroyer of worlds (11.32)
> If the radiance of a thousand suns were to burst at once into the sky,
> that would be like the splendor of the Mighty One (11.12).[109]

Gandhi, the peaceful warrior who freed India from Britain's shackles, also found solace and inspiration from its pages declaring in his *Autobiography*: "Truth is the sovereign principle, and the *Bhagavad Gita* is the book *par excellence* for the knowledge of the Truth."[110] One of Krishna's best-known appearances in this Holy Book is when he showed His All-Magnificent Manifesting Transcendental Form as the Creator of all universes to his devoted disciple **Arjuna** who was a powerful warrior leading an army into battle. When Krishna, as Divine Lord of the universe, reveals a multi-armed and multi-storied magnificent apparition shining brilliant 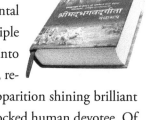 "like a thousand suns," it utterly overwhelmed his shocked human devotee. Of even greater significance, however, is the fact that Krishna had been previously incarnated as the two-armed form of Arjuna's loving human Guru. Avatar Adi Da poetically relayed this sacred sighting with his free-rendering of Chapter 11 from the *Bhagavad Gita*, which he called "**The Free Standing Man**":

> The Master of Life [Krishna] said to His devotee: "Look and see. The entire Realm of Nature arises in Me. Whatever may be desired is experienced in Me." And He gave insight to the man, with mystical Vision to conceive the Form of God. (7-8)
>
> [Arjuna remarked:] "When I stand again and see You There, stretched between Heaven and Earth in a Rainbow of all the colors blazing bright… my inward soul begins to shake with the great fear, my mind becomes unsteady, and I fail to be Your Heart in this moment of Vision. (24)
>
> "Even so, I am thrilled to see what Man has never seen before!

Now, Divine Master of this body-mind, be kind to me, and show me your two-armed form again." (45)

The Divine Person spoke to His devotee: "Stop all of this unmanly trembling, and this mood of fear. What does it matter if you see this Vision of Me, projected in the Realm of Nature? It is only Me. I am the Radiant Heart of Love, Eternally Free of fear. Now see Me again in my human form, as Your Spiritual Master, your friend in love." (49)

Then the Great Person [Guru] restored the true heart of His devotee, and set his breathing free....
Now the devotee beholds his Master from the heart. Now he only sees the Free Standing Man. (50-51)[111]

Krishna & Arjuna

The *Gita's* erotic cousin, the ***Bhagavata Purana*** (also known as the *Shrimad Bhagavata* from the 10th century CE *bhakti* movement), is where it's told Lord Krishna attracts thousands of *gopis*, the cowgirls who leave their husbands to spend adoring time in the company of their Guru. The *Bhagavata Purana*, therefore, explains how single-minded devotion (first activated in the Fourth Stage of Life) is the supreme means to reach liberation (*moksha*). Adi Da clarifies the benefit of honoring the spiritual path of Guru Yoga-Satsang, and yet how it also falls short of proclaiming direct *identity* with the Divine Person:

> The *Bhagavata Purana* and the *Bhagavad Gita* ultimately instruct people toward a perfect, transcendental, even Seventh Stage point of view based on a practice that is primarily devotional and that has the quality of Fourth Stage idealism. Thus, neither the *Bhagavad Gita* nor the *Bhagavata Purana* can strictly be said to be an example of the genre of the ["premonitory"] Seventh Stage confession to which the *Ashtavakra Gita* belongs.[112]

Since all of the transpersonal Stages of Life can be activated by anyone who takes up the Yoga, Krishna reveals in the *Bhagavad Gita* the supreme value of Guru Yoga-Satsang with the Adept-Realizer—"**Realize Me**" and know God:

> Not through sacred lore,
> penances, charity, or sacrificial rites
> can I been seen in the form
> that you saw Me.

> By devotion alone can I, as I really am,
> be known and seen
> and entered into, Arjuna.

> Acting only for Me [your Guru], intent on Me,
> free from attachment,
> hostile to no creature, Arjuna
> a person of devotion comes to Me.[113]

Yet, truly, each "Song of God" only makes sense when studied under the tutelage of an Awakened Adept. For then the words on paper (or heard orally) are transmitted into the heart and mind of the devotee so their meaning is truly heard and understood. These sacred *gitas* or "songs" of the Gurus express the dominant philosophical traditions within Hinduism that comprise her various schools and perspectives. All the Yogas, each in a different voice, point to the same "One without a second." Feuerstein therefore notes: "The spiritual path [Stages of Life] is a movement in consciousness through progressive levels of the hierarchy of existence [gross to subtle to causal], until the original Consciousness (*cit*), or transcendental Self [*Atman*], is realized. That Self experiences itself as an integral part of the ultimate Reality [*Brahman*]."[114] Always already there is Only God, God Only.

Truly, in Divine Awakening all words and ideas fall away and only paradoxes remain since the self itself is utterly transcended. Thus the duality of the seer and the Transcendental Reality are only resolved or transcended in the Absolute Nondual Awareness of the Heart. Books are closed, silence is Real, nothing need be said (only Bliss be had). The mind alone will never know, which is why devotion to God via Guru Yoga-Satsang with an Awakened Realizer becomes the safest way to know for sure what cannot be known at all (in Divine Ignorance). Thus God's Grace is most alive in the genuine Guru and the relationship of Satsang.

As a result, as the true esoteric teachings of India understood, and as do all the Great Gurus everywhere affirm, everyone and everything *is* always already the Indivisible Oneness of Real God or Brahman (*Ein Sof* or *Allah* or *Tao* or Buddhahood, et al.); always already one with the "Bright" Clear Light Void of the Nondual Godhead (Atman-Brahman) whether incarnate or not. All and all always already exists in Prior Unity where none is above nor below but only Awake to Reality as It IS, centerless, boundless, Free. This is the Divine Love-Bliss "Brightness" that is truly ineffable and beyond description of any kind, even beyond scriptures and songs, eternally shining outside of life and death, beneath and behind the dark underground caves of walled ignorance as the Eternal Love of the Radiant Transcendental Being. Nothing else can be said (or printed); "It" can *only be realized!*

Om Namah Shivaya!

("O salutations to Lord Shiva [the primordial Great Guru]!")

Next, let's compassionately turn the page to the world-renowned Guru-Adept who is best known for simply *being Awake!*—Fully Enlightened—known as the "Awakened One," literally, the Buddha, who also came from the heart of holy India.

AUM

Chapter 16 Endnotes

1. See: Georg Feuerstein, *The Yoga Tradition: Its History, Literature, Philosophy and Practice* (2002 new edition), pp. 82-86; much of this section is based upon the research and incredible writings of Dr. Feuerstein (1947–2012), a friend and literary mentor to the author.

2. Georg Feuerstein, *The Yoga Tradition* (1998), p. 96.

3. Adi Da Samraj [Da Free John], "The Seventh School of God-Talk" (essay) in "Preface" to *The Song of the Self Supreme: Astavakra Gita* (1982), pp. 19, 22 ["Stages of Life" caps added].

4. See: Adi Da Samraj [Da Free John], "Preface" in T*he Song of the Self Supreme: Astavakra Gita* (1982) translated by Radhakamal Mukerjee.

5. See: Roger Walsh, *The Spirit of Shamanism* (1990), p. 10.

6. See: Georg Feuerstein, *The Yoga Tradition* (1998), pp. 124-127 for many of these parallels between the Shaman and Yogi.

7. Georg Feuerstein, *The Yoga Tradition* (1998), p. 127; Ken Wilber's quote is from the Foreword where he points out (p. xiii) that with Feuerstein it is "rare, indeed, to find a scholar who is also a practitioner [having studied, for one, directly under the guidance of Adi Da Samraj]."

8. See: Jean Geber, *The Ever-Present Origi*n (1984); Georg Feuerstein, *Structures of Consciousness* (1987); Ken Wilber, *Up from Eden* (1982).

9. See: Joseph Campbell, *The Masks of God: Oriental Mythology* (1962), p. 13.

10. Ken Wilber, Foreword to *The Yoga Tradition* (1998) by Georg Feuerstein, p. xiv.

11. Georg Feuerstein, *The Yoga Tradition* (1998), p. 7.

12. Joseph Campbell, *The Masks of God: Oriental Mythology* (1962), pp. 13-14.

13. Mircea Eliade, *Yoga: Immortality and Freedom* (1973), p. 5.

14. Georg Feuerstein, *The Yoga Tradition* (1998), p. 11.

15. See: Adi Da Samraj, "The Ancient Walk-About Way" in *The Gnosticon* (2010), pp. 736ff; "Adept-Realizers Are The Esoteric Root of All Esoteric Traditions" in *The Pneumaton* (2011), pp. 189ff.

16. See: Ken Wilber, *Up from Eden: A Transpersonal View of Human Evolution* (1982, 2007).

17. Adi Da Samraj, September 8, 2004 quoted in *The Reality-Way of Adidam* (2010), p. 45.

18. Adi Da Samraj, "Adept-Realizers Are The Esoteric Root of All Esoteric Traditions" in *The Pneumaton* (2011), pp. 189, 191.

19. Georg Feuerstein, *The Yoga Tradition* (1998), p. 12.

20. See: Adi Da Samraj, *The Ancient Walk-About Way* (2006); also see, for example: Mircea Eliade, *From Primitives to Zen: A Thematic Sourcebook of the History of Religions* (1967, 1977); Mircea Eliade, *A History of Religious Idea, Volumes 1–3* (1978, 1982, 1985; Robert Bellah, *Religion in Human Evolution: From the Paleolithic to the Axial Age* (2011).

21. Editors, *The Reality-Way of Adidam* (2010), p. 45.

22. See: Georg Feuerstein, Subhash Kak & David Frawley, *In Search of the Cradle of Civilization* (1995, 2001); Thomas McEvilley, *The Shape of Ancient Thought* (2002).

23. See: Adi Da Samraj, "The Super-Physics of Divine Enlightenment" in *The Aletheon* (2009).

24. See: Georg Feuerstein, *The Yoga Tradition* (1998), p. 134.

25. Georg Feuerstein, *The Yoga Tradition* (1998), p. 139.

26. Georg Feuerstein, *The Yoga Tradition* (1998), p. 140.

27. Ralph Waldo Emerson, *Journals of Ralph Waldo Emerson*.

28. *Sacred Writings: Volume 5: Hinduism: The Rig Veda* (1992, NY: Book-of-the-Month Club) translated by Ralph T. H. Griffith, p. ix.

29. See: *In Search of the Cradle of Civilization* (1995) by Georg Feuerstein, Subhash Kak & David Frawley, for a full accounting of the competing theories.

30. See: Swami Abhayananda [Stan Trout], *History of Mysticism: The Unchanging Testament* (1987), pp. 30-34.

31. See: Georg Feuerstein, *The Yoga Tradition* (1998), p. 135

32. See: Adi Da Samraj [Bubba Free John], *The Enlightenment of the Whole Body* (1978); also see: "God-Talk, Real-God-Realization, Most Perfect Divine Self-Awakening, and The Seven Possible Stages of Life" in *The Aletheon* (2009), *The Gnosticon* (2010), and *The Pneumaton* (2011).

33. See: *Soma: Divine Mushroom of Immortality* (1972, 1988) by R. Gordon Wasson; *entheogen* is ancient Greek meaning "seeing the Divine within," the term is often preferred over the colloquial "psychedelic"; also see: Aldous Huxley, *The Doors of Perception* (1954, 2009); Huston Smith, *Cleansing the Doors of Perception: The Religious Significance of Entheogenic Plants and Chemicals* (2000).

34. See: Georg Feuerstein, *The Yoga Tradition* (1998), p. 135

35. W. T. Stace, *The Teachings of the Mystics* (1960), p. 49.

36. See: Georg Feuerstein, *The Yoga Tradition* (1998), pp. 160-163.

37. Ibid., p. 141.

38. Ibid., p. 168.

39. Ibid., p. 169.

40. Ibid., p. 169.

41. *Mundaka Upanishad* in *The Upanishads* (1963) trans. by Swami Nikhilananda, p. 114.

42. *Katha Upanishad* in Ibid., p. 82.

43. *Brihadaranyaka Upanishad* in Ibid., p. 218.

44. *Katha Upanishad* in Ibid., p. 73.

45. *Brihadaranyaka Upanishad* in Ibid., p. 236.

46. Georg Feuerstein, Subhash Kak & David Frawley, *In Search of the Cradle of Civilization* (1995), p. 177.

47. See: Jean Gebser, *The Ever-Present Origin* (1984); Georg Feuerstein, *Structures of Consciousness* (1987); Ken Wilber, *Up from Eden* (1982, 2002).

48. *Mundaka Upanishad* in *The Upanishads* (1963) trans. by Swami Nikhilananda, p. 117.

49. *Katha Upanishad* in Ibid., pp. 71-72, 76.

50. *Mundaka Upanishad* in Ibid., p. 112.

51. *Mundaka Upanishad* in Ibid., pp. 114-115.

52. *Svetasvatara Upanishad* in Ibid., p. 139.

53. See: Adi Da Samraj [Bubba Free John}, "The Great Path of Return vs. the Radical Path of Understanding" in *The Paradox of Instruction* (1977); also see: "The Seven Stages of Life—and The Intrinsic Transcending of All of The First Six Stages of Life In The Seventh Stage Way of Adidam" in *The Aletheon* (2009).

54. Georg Feuerstein, *The Shambhala Encyclopedia of Yoga* (1990), p. 327.

55. Swami Abhayananda [Stan Trout], *History of Mysticism: The Unchanging Testament* (1987), pp. 192-193.

56. Ken Wilber, *Eye to Eye* (1983, 1990), p. 314.

57. Ken Wilber, *Sex, Ecology, Spirituality* (1995), p. 302.

58. Swami Abhayananda [Stan Trout], *History of Mysticism: The Unchanging Testament* (1987), p. 193.

59. See: Georg Feuerstein, *The Shambhala Encyclopedia of Yoga* (1990), p. 287.

60. Ibid., p. 287.

61. See: Adi Da Samraj [Bubba Free John], "The Great Path of Return vs. the Radical Path of Understanding" in *The Paradox of Instruction* (1977); also see: "The Seven Stages of Life—and The Intrinsic Transcending of All of The First Six Stages of Life In The Seventh Stage Way of Adidam" in *The Aletheon* (2009).

62. Huston Smith, *The World's Religions* (1958, 1991), p. 386.

63. Adi Da Samraj [Da Free John], "The Seventh School of God-Talk" (talk) in "Preface" to *The Song of the Self Supreme: Astavakra Gita* (1982), p. 48 ["Stages of Life" is capped].

64. Ibid., p. 21.

65. Ibid., p. 49 ["Stages of Life" capped].

66. See: *The Song of the Self Supreme: Astavakra Gita* (1982) translated by Radhakamal Mukerjee with a Preface by Adi Da Samraj [Da Free John].

67. Adi Da Samraj [Da Free John], "The Seventh School of God-Talk" (talk) in "Preface" to *The Song of the Self Supreme: Astavakra Gita* (1982), p. 68 ["Stages of Life" capped].

68. Astavakra, *The Song of the Self Supreme: Astavakra Gita* (1982) translated by Radhakamal Mukerjee, pp. 105-109.

69. Adi Da Samraj [Da Free John], "The Seventh School of God-Talk" (talk) in "Preface" to *The Song of the Self Supreme: Astavakra Gita* (1982), p. 51 ["Stages of Life" capped].

70. Jason Brett Serle, *Abide as That: Ramana Maharshi & The Song of Ribhu* (2019, Winchester, UK: Mantra Books), p. 3.

71. Adi Da Samraj [Da Free John], "The Seventh School of God-Talk" (talk) in "Preface" to *The Song of the Self Supreme: Astavakra Gita* (1982), p. 42 ["Stages of Life" capped].

72. Jason Brett Serle, *Abide as That: Ramana Maharshi & The Song of Ribhu* (2019, Winchester, UK: Mantra Books), p. 50.

73. Adi Da Samraj, "The Seventh School of God-Talk" (essay) in "Preface" to *The Song of the Self Supreme: Astavakra Gita* (1982), p. 42 ["Stages of Life" capped].

74. *The Guru Gita* (Verse 59) translated by Swami Narayananda (1972), p. 21.

75. Ibid., p. 21.

76. Ken Wilber, *Up from Eden* (1981), p. 334.

77. Quoted in *Love of the God-Man* (1990, The Dawn Horse Press) by James Steinberg, p. 153.

78. See: Swami Abhayananda [Stan Trout], *History of Mysticism: The Unchanging Testament* (1987), p. 377.

79. Dadu Dayal quoted in *A Sixteenth Century Indian Mystic* (1947, Lutterworth Press) by W. G. Orr, p. 191.

80. See: Swami Abhayananda [Stan Trout], *History of Mysticism: The Unchanging Testament* (1987), p. 378.

81. Ibid., p. 392.

82. Adi Da Samraj [Da Free John], "The Seventh School of God-Talk" (essay) in "Preface" to *The Song of the Self Supreme: Astavakra Gita* (1982), p. 21 ["Stages of Life" capped].

83. See: "Shree Swami Samarth" at http://www.shreeswami.org/swami-samarth-of-akkalkot/ (retrieved June 2021).

84. Georg Feuerstein, *The Shambhala Encyclopedia of Yoga* (1990), p. 286.

85. See: Adi Da Samraj, "The Place of Ramakrishna and Swami Vivekananda in the Great Tradition, and Their Unique Function in Preparing the Vehicle of My Avataric Divine Incarnation" in *The Knee of Listening* (2004 enlarged and updated edition), p. 464.

86. See: Lex Hixon, "The Tantric Way of the Goddess Kali: Ramakrishna of Bengal" in *Coming Home: The Experience of Enlightenment in Sacred Traditions* (1978, 1989).

87. Ramakrishna quoted in *Great Swan: Meetings with Ramakrishna* (1992) by Lex Hixon, p. 15.

88. For a full account of this incident, see: *The Life of Swami Vivekananda, Volume 1* (1979), by his Eastern and Western disciples, pp. 182-198.

89. Carolyn Lee, *The Avatar of What Is* (2007, 2017), p. 18.

90. Ibid., p. 22.

91. Adi Da Samraj, "The Place of Ramakrishna and Swami Vivekananda in the Great Tradition, and Their Unique Function in Preparing the Vehicle of My Avataric Divine Incarnation" in *The Knee of Listening* (2004 enlarged and updated edition), p. 464.

92. Ken Wilber, "The One Who Was To Come Is Always Already Here" in *Vision Mound*, Vol. 2, No. 9, May 1979, p. 28.

93. Adi Da Samraj [Da Free John], "Preface" to *The Song of the Self Supreme: Astavakra Gita* (1982), p. 29.

94. See: *The Life Divine* (1939) by Sri Aurobindo.

95. See: Sri Aurobindo, *The Integral Yoga* (1993); also see: *A Greater Psychology: An Introduction to the Psychological Thought of Sri Aurobindo* (2001) edited by A. S, Dalal, foreword by Ken Wilber.

96. Sri Aurobindo, *The Integral Yoga* (1993), p. 68 [some title caps added].

97. For example, Michael Murphy, co-founder of the Esalen Institute and a key figure in the Human Potential Movement visited Auroville before opening Esalen; see: *Esalen: America and the Religion of No Religion* (2007) by Jeffrey J. Kripal.

98. Ramana Maharshi, *Talks with Ramana Maharshi* (1955, 1994), p. 210.

99. Lex Hixon, *Coming Home* (1978, 1989), foreword by Ken Wilber, p. 46.

100. See: *The Collected Works of Sri Ramana Maharshi* (2015); also see: *Talks with Ramana Maharshi: On Realizing Abiding Peace and Happiness* (2001) foreword by Ken Wilber.

101. Ken Wilber, Foreword "The Sage of the Century" in *Talks with Ramana Maharshi* (2001), p. ix.

102. Adi Da Samraj [Franklin Jones}, *The Knee of Listening* (1972), p. 122.

103. Adi Da Samraj, "The Seventh School of God-Talk" (essay) in "Preface" to *The Song of the Self Supreme: Astavakra Gita* (1982), p. 41 ["Stages of Life" capped].

104. See: Adi Da Samraj, "Atma Nadi Shakti Yoga" in *Atma Nadi Shakti Yoga* (2008), also in *The Aletheon* (2009).

105. See: Philp Goldberg, *American Veda* (2010), p. 32; I cannot recommend this book more highly for a wonderful and lively introduction of the East entering the West in the United States, and especially how it shaped the New England Transcendentalist movement.

106. Ralph Waldo Emerson quoted in *American Veda* (2010) by Philp Goldberg, pp. 32-33.

107. Henry David Thoreau quoted in *American Veda* (2010) by Philp Goldberg, p. 39; here Goldberg calls Thoreau "the Buddha of Walden."

108. Ralph Waldo Emerson quoted in *American Veda* (2010) by Philp Goldberg, p. 41; here Goldberg calls Whitman "the Bhakti Bard."

109. See: James Temperton, "'Now I am become Death, the destroyer of worlds'. The story of Oppenheimer's infamous quote," August 9, 2017, *WIRED*.

110. Mahatma Gandhi quoted in *The World's Religions* (1958, 1991) by Huston Smith, p. 13.

111. Adi Da Samraj [Bubba Free John], "The Free Standing Man: A free rendering of portions of the eleventh chapter of the Bhagavad Gita" in *The Enlightenment of the Whole Body* (1978, Middletown, CA: The Dawn Horse Press), pp. 75-76.

112. Adi Da Samraj [Da Free John], "The Seventh School of God-Talk" (talk) in "Preface" to *The Song of the Self Supreme: Astavakra Gita* (1982), p. 54 ["Stages of Life" capped].

113. *Bhagavad Gita* (11.53-54) in *The Bhagavad-Gita: Krishna's Counsel in Time of War* (1986) translated by Barbara Stoler Miller, p. 108.

114. Georg Feuerstein, *The Shambhala Encyclopedia of Yoga* (1990), p. 10.

SEVENTEEN

GURU YOGA-SATSANG:
BUDDHISM

GURU YOGA:
BUDDHA'S THREE JEWELS & FOUR NOBLE TRUTHS

Buddhism as a "religion" begins with a truly Enlightened Guru-Adept or Awakened Realizer, an authentic Maha-Siddha and world religion Avatar: the royal prince born as **Siddhartha Gautama** (Siddhattha Gotama in Pali), also known as **Shakyamuni** (of the Shakya tribe in Lumbini, now in southern Nepal). This flesh and blood man (born ca. 563 BCE, a hundred years before Sokrates) became known as *Buddha* (in Sanskrit) or "**The Buddha**," which, literally, means "one who is Awake" (or Divinely Enlightened). When asked after his Enlightenment what he had gained or what he knew, Siddhartha simply replied, "I am Awake."

The life story of the Buddha becomes a lesson on how to become Enlightened, to not get lost in trance states or mystical visions or ascetic extremes but simply to be *aware* as Consciousness Itself. All living beings already have "**Buddha-**

Nature" (the "Suchness" of *Tathāgatagarbha*), according to the Buddha; thus a person must simply Re-Awaken to their natural enlightened state. As Buddha, he was also named *Tathagata* (another of his esteemed titles), meaning "one who has gone beyond" the sufferings of the ego-I or the illusions of *samsara* to realize *Nirvana* (literally, to "blow out" the separate self-sense). Famously, the Buddha did not teach about an all-powerful God (or Deity) but rather pointed to Consciousness Itself (Buddha-Nature) as being the Supreme Reality.

| Buddha Born | Before Enlightenment | During Enlightenment | After Enlightenment | Buddha Teaching |

Gautama Buddha (ca. 563–483 BCE)—who flourished around 500 BCE, that is, 500 years *before* Jesus Christ—offers a path based on a "realistic" (not "idealistic") view of life as the starting point of his Teaching (or Dharma). According to legend, in his early life Siddhartha was sheltered in his father's (King Suddhodana) palaces from the sufferings of the world until in his twenties when he discovered the ills of human life: sickness, old age, and death. Consequently, the young prince left his royal life (his wife and new-born child) to become a yogi-ascetic living in the surrounding forests searching for Truth and the end to suffering. He at first became a strict ascetic studying under several Gurus but never attaining Enlightenment. He found that harmony comes from being like the string of an instrument that is neither too taunt, nor too loose, but is just right to be in tune.

After discovering that neither sensual pleasures nor severe asceticism is the true way, he followed and taught the "**Middle Way**" or "**Middle Path**" (*Madhyama-pratipadā*) as being the best and most practical path to Liberation (*Nirvana*). After years of profound discipline, he sat down in meditation under the *bodhi* (or *bo*) tree at Bodh Gaya (in northeastern India) for days, confronting and transcending temptations and past karmas (and desire and death itself in the form of the god Mara), until the Yogi touched the earth (as his witness) to Wake Up and realize Enlightenment to become Buddha or "Awake."

At first, The Buddha preferred to just sit in serene silence, profoundly happy and at peace. Once convinced by others he should teach (instead of remaining silent), the Buddha's first sermon—revealed in the *Dhammacakkappavattana Sutta* meaning "**Setting in Motion the Wheel of the Dharma**"—was at Deer Park (in Sarnath) where the Awakened One began by teaching the "**Four Noble Truths**":

(1) **First Noble Truth**: "Truth of Suffering/Dissatisfaction" (*dukkha*)— all conditional existence is suffering since all things (and the self) are impermanent;

(2) **Second Noble Truth**: "Truth of Causation" (*samudaya*)—egoic reactivity as desire or aversion is the root cause of all suffering;

(3) **Third Noble Truth**: "Truth of Extinction" (*nirodha*)—it is possible to end (with a cessation of) our negative reaction to suffering by transcending self and realizing Nirvana (*nirodha* or *nibbana*) which is Ultimate Reality, our innate Buddha-Nature;

(4) **Fourth Noble Truth**: "The Path" (*magga*) of disciplines to be practiced to achieve this state of Nirvana (and cessation of *dukkha*) called the "**Eight-Fold Noble Path**" listed below:

1. **Right View:** understanding the 4 Noble Truths 2. **Right Intentions:** (resolve) we must want to change	***Prajna*** (wisdom)
3. **Right Speech:** tell the truth, speak positive words; politeness (no coarse language, etc.) 4. **Right Conduct:** (action): do good, not evil; be kind, non-violent, courteous, helpful, etc. 5. **Right Livelihood:** have a good job, no cheating, no violence, no slavery, cruelty, or exploitation, etc.	***Sila*** (ethics)
6. **Right Effort:** (resolve) cultivate self-knowledge and self-discipline; do yoga, meditate 7. **Right Mindfulness:** avoiding extremes of emotions and action (Middle Way); cultivate equanimity via meditation and stillness 8. **Right Meditation:** (concentration) advanced sadhana in stillness with samadhi states; One Taste	***Samadhi*** (awareness)

In his second sermon—recorded in the *Anattalakkhana Sutta*, meaning "**No-Self Discourse**"—he even criticized the search for Atman within by claiming in reality there is "no-self" (*anatta*, Pali; *anatman*, Sanskrit). Rather, the sense of self comes from its constituents (*skandhas*) that are impermanent (*anicca*) thus being subject to suffering (*dukkha*). The third sermon, known as the "**Fire Sermon**"—preserved in the *Adittapariyaya Sutta*—is when Buddha preached about achieving liberation from the "fire" of suffering through detachment from the five senses and the mind (the *skandhas*). In Gautama's view, born existence is "on fire" stoked by the "**three poisons**" of greed, hatred (anger), and ignorance. However, the fire is not necessary because it can be cooled (or relieved) and ultimately quenched (or transcended) with the cool wind of Nirvana (which means, literally, "to blow out").[1] Originally, as the Theravada Buddhists point out, the Buddha made a clear distinction between the sufferings of the separate, relative self (as *samsara*) and reaching "the other shore" (of *nirvana*) beyond the self.

Remarkably, the Buddha's Teaching went beyond the popular expressions of the ancient Vedic Teachings (of Hinduism) and their ritualistic tradition since he discovered the Truth anew for himself (even going beyond his own Yogi-Gurus). The Buddha maintained it was not by doing rituals that one is liberated, but by looking inside and understanding the mind. He did not want his followers to simply practice based on devotion to him as Guru, but to use their own rational mind and assess for themselves whether what he Teaches is true or not.

Buddha accomplished his own Enlightenment by transcending the illusion of being a separate self within the field of consciousness or "**Buddha-Mind**" (the natural enlightened state), what's called *Dharmata* (the Real) or the "intrinsic nature of everything, the essence of things as they are," and also *Dharmakaya* or "absolute reality, the true nature of the heart-mind."[2] We all innately possess Buddha-Mind so it is not gained but *realized* by becoming free of the afflictive emotions and desires that obscure it. Since the Buddha transcended the spiritual desires of yogic asceticism, he taught a path of balance and equanimity—the "**Middle Way**"—as the means to cultivate the "ground" (or foundation or right view) for entering the "path." By following the Eightfold Way, we may bear the "fruit" (or goal) of Enlightenment. The "Ruchira" ("Bright") Buddha uniquely reviews:

> Gautama's Teaching developed spontaneously from his own Samadhi. (Such is also the case with My Own Teaching and the Teaching of all Great Adepts.) His Great Argument is not merely a call to discipline, or to blow cool breathes on the fire of self. Such is only a lesser aspect of his Teaching—or that part that first attracts the gross personality. Gautama's Great Argument is basically a call to Samadhi, or Nirvana Itself, which is Oblivious to the born self and all conditional possibilities, but Awake to the Inherent Bliss of the Transcendental Reality (or That which is Obvious in the Samadhi of utter self-transcendence.[3]

Consequently, the Buddha termed his Awakened Realization "**Consummation of Incomparable Enlightenment**" (according to the *Diamond Sutra*), though it is beyond words (as he always emphasized) because this naked awareness is actually a *tacit* understanding, not an acquisition of mental knowledge. Thus, the Buddha confessed: "Through Consummation of Incomparable Enlightenment I acquired not even the least thing... It is straightly attained by freedom from separate personal selfhood and cultivating all kinds of goodness."[4] Thousands of years of Buddhist history, embodied by countless Adept-Realizers and Siddha-Gurus, would all realize the same inherent awakened awareness of Divine Consciousness (*prajna*, in Sanskrit; *rigpa*, in Tibetan), since this is our natural state or condition revealing the "Empty-Full" Nondual Truth of Incomparable Divine Enlightenment [see Chapter 18].

For hundreds of years the Buddha was not
pictured as a man (until the influence of the Greeks)
but was portrayed as "empty" footprints or with symbols.

The "**Buddha**" has thus appeared on Earth to help guide everyone on the path to Enlightenment by giving his "**Dharma**" or Teaching of Truth. This has been done successfully for over twenty-five centuries sharing the Enlightened State with more people than any other world religion. In this way, the "**Sangha**" or community of monks and nuns (and all other practicing Buddhists) are capable of realizing the same Enlightened State that the Buddha himself achieved since it's everybody's native (or universal) condition or Buddha-Nature. In the Buddhist religion, the beginning of the path starts when monks and nuns (or even lay people) take an eternal vow in sincere dedication to the "**Triple Refuge**" or "**Three Jewels**" of Buddhism:

(1) *Buddha*—the Sat-Guru;

(2) *Dharma*—the Teaching of Truth;

(3) *Sangha*—the Community of assembled practitioners.

These are simply: the Guru, the Teaching, and the Cooperative Community (in Adi Da's words). This **"Triple Gem"** is what a person needs, both individually and collectively, in order to transcend the illusions of the suffering ego-I (or self-contraction) that occurs during our born existence arising in the rotating "**Wheel of Life**" (*bhavachakra*). Reincarnation may sling us from lifetime to lifetime, as many Masters say, but that is not an article of faith necessary to make good use of the Buddha's Enlightened Teaching. What's most important is a lifestyle of right living, meditation, and compassionate service to all beings (including non-humans), led by a competent Master-Guru, in order to correctly practice the precepts of the Buddha-Dharma. Sooner or later, suddenly or gradually, Enlightenment is realized as a *direct experience* of awakening (not simply a philosophy or system of beliefs), the true essence and heart of Buddhism.

BUDDHISM:
TURNING THE DHARMA WHEEL

| The Dharma Wheel | The Wheel of Life |

Buddhism, as an effective *esoteric* religion, has continued to evolve its presentation of the Dharma (or "Teaching of Truth") for over 2,500 years as other Enlightened "Buddhas" have appeared in history to criticize (and correct) the degradation of the Eight-Fold Noble Way in their own generation and historical period. The Awakened Adepts (or "Buddhas") do this to re-establish "right practice" and "right view" in order to purify and refresh the tradition and stay aligned with the actual Enlightened State of the primordial Buddha. As all religions tend to do, people can easily slip into the *exoteric* aspects of ritual and egoic seeking, even within monasteries and among certified lineage Masters. Only Realized Adepts are capable of rightly aligning and restoring an esoteric wisdom tradition.

Consequently, there have been a succession of *Yanas*, meaning "vehicles" or "rafts" or "ferries"[5]—the **"Turning of the Dharma Wheel"** (*Dharmachakra*, in Sanskrit)—that indicate a shift in emphasis on the practices and teachings of Buddhism as the centuries unfolded, yet while still maintaining the Buddha's Enlightening Truth at its core. Although taking centuries for the different versions to appear, the Buddha is said to have given all of the *yanas* or traditional "vehicles" of Buddhism during his lifetime in order to serve different people at various stages of practice along the Way to Enlightenment. Consequently, throughout historical time the different *yanas* were revealed by an emerging lineage of Adepts where, according to legend, some found hidden texts or sutras (called *termas*, in Tibetan) that were often obscured for centuries until they were finally uncovered. More than likely, however, they were written anew by Adepts appearing in those generations who then attached legendary status to them to gain further authenticity. In this case, the three major "Vehicles" of the Buddha's Dharma each have their own emphasis on an Enlightened Master, called the **Arhat** (in Hinayana), the **Bodhisattva** (in Mahayana), and the **Maha-Siddha** (in Vajrayana). The Ruchira Buddha clearly summarizes:

> In the Buddhist tradition there are three primary Ways—the Hinayana, Mahayana, and Vajrayana or the Ways of the Arhat, the Bodhisattva, and the Maha-Siddhas.
>
> The **Hinayana Way** of the **Arhats** is the Way of the transcendence of sympathetic (and, ultimately, sorrowful) attachment to conditional self, its relations, and its world of experience. It is the "masculine" Way of uncompromising abandonment or transcendence of the motives of sympathy or desire.
>
> The **Mahayana Way** of the **Bodhisattvas** is the Way of the transcendence of angry rejection of the conditional self, its relations, and its worlds of experience. It is the "feminine" Way of self-surrender and compassionate service.
>
> The **Vajrayana Way** of the **Maha-Siddhas** is the Way of the transcendence of both sympathetic attachment and angry rejection, or all the positives and negatives relative to the conditional self, its re-

lations, and its worlds of experience. It is the magical [psychic] Way of the powers inherent in the male-female unity (or the unity and equanimity of polarized opposites).

Behind and beyond these is Enlightenment Itself, or Realization of the Transcendental [Prior Unity] that is, under one Name or another, the Ultimate Goal of all the Wisdom traditions.[6]

In the early centuries after the Buddha's death, in gathered councils relying on the clear memory of devotees (such as Ananda, one of his closest disciples), the Buddha's sermons were codified into the **Pali Canon** or the earliest collection of Shakyamuni's original words. Often beginning with the phrase, "Thus have I heard" (Pali: *Evam me suttam*), these *sutras* (literally, "string or thread," in Sanskrit) were short aphoristic statements of the Tathagata's Teachings bound together with string until they were later expanded into prose manuscripts. One of the most widely read texts from the Pali Canon is known as the *Dhammapada*, a collection of the Buddha's sayings from various occasions presented in verse form intended to appeal to the laity, thus making it popular for Westerners as well. The subdivisions of the Pali Canon are known as the *Tripitaka*—the "**Three Baskets**" or "**Triple Basket**":

(1) *Vinaya Pitaka* — "Discipline Basket" — dealing with the rules or discipline of the Sangha (or Buddhist community);

(2) *Sutta Pitaka* — "Sutra/Sayings Basket" — mostly containing the discourses and sermons of Buddha;

(3) *Abhidhamma Pitaka* — "Systematic Philosophy" Basket — or treatises that elaborate on various Buddhist doctrines.

From the early Buddhist community in India there emerged what is known as *Theravada*, literally, the "**Way of the Elders**," Buddhism's oldest existing school, also called *Hinayana* or the "**Lesser Vehicle**" and "Little Raft" (later so named by the Mahayana or "Greater Vehicle" Buddhists as a derogatory term). The **First Buddhist Council** or Congress convened in 483 BCE (soon after the Buddha's death) was where the original Pali Canon was constructed with its collection of scriptures and discourses said to be given by Gautama.

The **Second Buddhist Council** was held in 383 BCE, a century later (there were a total of six councils over the next several hundred years). Theravadins rely more strictly on the "Buddha's Words" and thus focus more on the individual Enlightenment of the **Arhat** (meaning "to deserve"). The later Mahayana Buddhists would emphasize the Enlightenment of all humanity (and all beings)—the **Bodhisattva** ideal (*bodhi* is "enlightenment," in Sanskrit, while *sattva* is "sentient being"). The Bodhisattva is often personified as the goddess **Avalokiteshvara**, the Great Goddess of Compassion (known as Quan Yin, in Chinese); a deity whom the Dalai Lama is said to be an incarnation of in human form.

Hinayana, therefore, places more emphasis on wisdom (*bodhi, prajna*) while the Mahayana perspective highlights compassion (*karuna*) that arises from wisdom; Vajrayana would go on to integrate both (in Tantra). World religion scholar Huston Smith explains: "Whatever progress those in [Hinayana] make is the fruit of wisdom—insight into the cause of suffering and its cure. The other [Mahayana] held that compassion is the more important feature of Enlightenment, arguing that to seek Enlightenment by oneself and for oneself is a contradiction in terms. For them, human beings are more social than individual, and love is the greatest thing in the world."[7] The modern-day Adept Adi Da Samraj offers his analysis:

> From the Hinayana point of view, the primal error that produces conditional existence is desire.... The language of Gautama seems to call for such an attitude. Life is suffering because it is generated

by desire, and desire leads us into association with the phenomenal states that are always changing, that never last, and that frustrate our fundamental force of being. Since life is simply suffering, then we must find a way out of it, and the way out of it is to transcend desire. The method, therefore, is to observe everything, to see it as undesirable, to transcend the process of desiring, to transcend desirableness, and thereby to force the outgoing energy of attention to return to the base, the Self, Chit, the fundamental Consciousness wherein the Nirvanic Condition Awakens.[8]

Hinayana Buddhism (emerging around the 3rd century BCE in India) later migrated into Southeast Asia (where it thrives today). Its teachings are based on the *"Abhidhamma"* metaphysical system which comes from an intuitive knowledge based on a close study of the Buddha's Teaching combined with **mindfulness** meditation (*vipassana*). Vipassana is being aware of the stream of thoughts by not attaching to them, just letting them float by like clouds in the sky. As mentioned, this monastic lifestyle of following the Buddha's *Dharma* emphasized the **Arhat** or one who cultivates a "solitary" Enlightenment (yet still accomplished under the guidance of an elder acting as a Guru authority). The dedicated *Arhat* is one who has "laid down the burden" of the suffering self (which is ultimately "empty") to realize the goal of *Nirvana* or reaching "the other shore," as they metaphorically say. Once again, Avatar Adi Da clarifies and critiques the limitations (and strategy) of this "Lesser Vehicle" Hinayana with its often negative (or "realistic") view of life seeking to escape this world of *samsara* (meaning "wandering" or "cyclic existence"):

> The primary form of meditative practice in the Hinayana school is called the "way of mindfulness" or *vipassana* meditation. It is based on the tradition of Buddhist logic called "Abhidhamma," or the analysis of the constituents of existence [*skandhas*], which, when introduced into the setting of meditation, sees conditional life as suffering, only changing, and without a substantial self or basis.... But the traditional exercise generally superimposes a negative psychology on the process of observation, so that one is not only supposed to see what is arising and transcend it, but also supposed to interpret it as loathsome, horrible, disgusting, putrid, terrible, terrifying, and so forth....

I criticize this problem-based ["realistic"] approach of Buddhism for this reason: It is unnecessary.... The Way can be practiced in another form. The life-negative psychology is not part of the context of our practice [in the Reality-Way of Adidam]. It is in itself to be understood, not only as a strategy peculiar to Buddhism, but as a strategy common to people generally that is to be understood and transcended. Ultimately what is to be Realized is not negative. Real meditation is not meditation on loathsomeness. What is to be Realized is Bliss, Freedom, Transcendental Happiness. That is what Gautama Realized.[9]

One of the central teachings of Theravada, based on the Buddha's direct Teaching-Word, is the doctrine of *anatta* (in Pali; *anatman*, in Sanskrit), which literally means "no-self" (i.e., "no atman"). The sense of being a separate self, therefore, comes from the five *skandhas* or "aggregates" and "groupings":

(1) **physical form,**
(2) **sensation,**
(3) **perception/impulse,**
(4) **emotion/image ("dispositions"),**
(5) **symbolic/conceptual mind.**

These modes of existence are indeed relatively real via the interdependent co-arising of phenomena—also called "**codependent origination**" (*pratityasamutpada*)—that gives us the sense of being a separate self, however, they do not constitute a real, enduring self (according to the Buddha). This insight of relativity helps the practicing Hinayana Buddhist to transcend one's attachments to the skandhas and our sense of being separate self. However, Adi Da makes clear: "The Hinayana tradition is limited because it stands on realism or the criticism of phenomena. It is very much involved, therefore, in the problem of the body and the self and the ego, rather than That which always already transcends the body and mind and the ego and the world."[10] As Ken Wilber explains (in one of his most brilliant, and longest, footnotes he ever wrote) in reviewing the history of Buddhism:

This no-self or *anatman* doctrine was particularly leveled against the Brahmanical and Samkhya doctrines of a permanent, unchanging, absolute Subject of experience (Purusha, Atman). And against the Atman tradition, the Anatman doctrine was wielded with much polemical force: in place of substance, flux; in place of self, no-self; in place of unitary, pluralistic; in place of cohesive, discrete. Thus, the Abhidharma accepted the reality of momentary, pluralistic, discrete, and atomistic elements (*dharmas*) and accepted the causal effects as real (codependent origination).[11]

According to Abhidharma (and the Buddha), this illusory self is driven by fear and desire (aversion or attachment) leading to a life of pain and suffering (*duhkha*). However, once it's realized that this apparent self is ultimately an illusion or "empty" (*sunya*), one discovers the wisdom of liberation via self-transcendence (*bodhi*). However, the Mahayana (or "Greater Vehicle") and the Vajrayana (or Tantric Vehicle), while conceding Abhidharma was a

good starting point, teach it wasn't enough. Mahayana and Vajrayana, as Wilber explains, "aggressively attacked *both* [Hinayana's] capacity to cover relative or *phenomenal* reality *and* its inability to indicate *absolute* reality.... Thus, Nagarjuna [a Mahayana Adept] launched a devastating attack on the reality of the *skandhas* and *dharmas* themselves (they have apparent reality only), and the general Yogachara and Vajrayana tradition lambasted the *skandhas* system because it only dealt with 'coarse'-level reality (the gross realm, or Nirmanakaya) and did not cover the 'subtle' and 'very subtle' [causal] realms (which Vajrayana identified with the Sambhogakaya and Dharmakaya)."[12] And so the Dharma Wheel rolled on to produce the various versions or views (and practices) of Buddhism.

MAHAYANA EMPTINESS:
BODHISATTVA'S YOGA

Next, in the second turning of the Wheel, over five hundred years after the Buddha's death, there arose (during the 1st to 2nd centuries CE) the so-called "Greater Vehicle" of **Mahayana Buddhism**, which emphasized the *Bodhisattva* ideal or one who cultivates Enlightenment for the benefit of all beings (under the guidance of the Mahayana Sutras and Gurus). By the latter half of the first millennium in the Common Era, Buddhism had trekked over the Himalayas to enter China and Tibet, as well as other parts of eastern Asia (from Java to Japan). With the Muslim invasions into India (especially after 1000 CE), with its monasteries burning, Buddhism expanded further to evolve into the "Diamond Vehicle" of **Vajrayana Buddhism** which highlights the *Maha-Siddhas* (or "Great," *maha*, "Perfected Ones," *siddhas*), the legendary Adept-Realizers of the Himalayas [see Chapter 18].

With the third turning of the Dharma Wheel (Vajrayana), the Buddhist path began to actively incorporate *Tantra* (meaning "weaving together"), which had originated in northern India, to merge the nondual union of *samsara* (the relative world) and *Nirvana* (the Absolute), the "two truths" of the profane and sacred. But first, the second turning of Mahayana was needed to emphasize that not only did the Absolute *transcend* phenomena but in a vital sense it is *immanent* or identical with phenomena as well.[13] The modern-day Indian pandit T. V. R. Murti clarifies: "Sunyata [Emptiness] and Karuna [Compassion] are the two principal features of the Bodhicitta [awakened mind]. Sunyata is Prajna, [Wisdom or] intuition, and is identical with the Absolute. Karuna is the active principle of compassion that gives concrete expression to Emptiness in phenomena. If the first is transcendent and looks to the Absolute, the second is fully immanent and looks down towards phenomena."[14] Or as Wilber once deliciously put it: "Bliss cognizing Emptiness arises as compassion."[15] The Mahayana view, in other words, took a different approach based on the Buddha's Teachings, as Avatar Adi Da distinctly explains:

> The Hinayana Buddhists argue so heavily against the existence of a separate self or "atman" that they also want to argue against the Transcendental Paramatman, or Transcendental Nirvanic Being, although it is clearly the Transcendental Being that is Realized in the Buddhist tradition.... Gautama does not describe it. Yet clearly he is Realizing and pointing to, not annihilation, not the destruction of karmic existence with nothing left over, but the transcendence of conditional or karmic realism in Transcendental Being....
>
> In the greatest Mahayana texts there is no reluctance to point toward the Transcendental Reality in some basic way. It is not so explicitly defined as in the Advaitic tradition, but it is pointed to. It is referred to as Mind [or Consciousness Itself in the *Prajnaparamita Sutras*]. The reluctance in the Hinayana literature to point to and presume the Transcendental Being does not exist in the Mahayana literature. Yet, even so, the Mahayana literature is clearly giving expression to an orientation that is implicit in the original, or Hinayana, Buddhist tradition. In that sense, therefore, a direct relationship exists [via the Buddha's Teaching] between the Mahayana and Hinayana.[16]

This transition was revolutionary. By emphasizing a radically Nondual perspective (grounded in transcendental Enlightenment), it is maintained that words or ideas can never grasp its truth; *only* Realization (Prajna) can.

Wilber explains: "In short, *both* the cohesive self and the momentary states are relatively real, but *both* are ultimately Empty: the absolute is neither self nor no-self (nor both nor neither), neither momentary nor permanent (nor both nor neither), but is rather the 'Thatness' disclosed by nondual Prajna or primordial awareness, a 'Thatness' which, being radically unqualifiable, cannot be captured in any concepts whatsoever."[17] It was the emphasis on "Emptiness" (*Sunyata*) that distinguishes Mahayana-Madhyamika Buddhism from Hinayana, in addition to the Bodhisattva ideal. Yet, its "drawback" or limitation was that its strong dialectic *via negativa* as **neti, neti** ("not this, not that") could not adequately account for the Absolute. Professor Murti, therefore, explains: "This may be said to constitute the drawback in the Madhyamika conception of the Absolute: The Absolute is nowhere *explicitly* shown to be *in* things constituting their very reality. The relation between the two is not made abundantly clear."[18] And this "drawback" is precisely what the later Yogachara and Tantra, and even later in Advaita Vedanta (via Shankara), would set about to redress in creating a more direct "bridge" to the Absolute with the union or "One Taste" of samsara and Nirvana. It is a nondual union of the universe and God, not one where the Creator is set apart from the Creation (as in the Abrahamic religions). Nonetheless, the revolution instigated by Nagarjuna and Madhyamika was monumental and can never be underestimated (or overlooked), as Wilber makes crystal clear:

> Scholars are still arguing about the exact influence of Nagarjuna on subsequent Eastern thought, but most agree that the Nondual Madhyamika was a profound revolution that, to one degree or another, influenced virtually all succeeding schools of Asian thought (either directly or indirectly). Because Emptiness was not a realm *apart* from or divorced from other realms, but rather was the reality or Suchness or Emptiness of *all* realms, then nirvana was not, indeed could not be, sought apart from the phenomenal world. This, indeed, was revolutionary.[19]

Adi Da, naturally, with his "**Advaitayana Buddhism**" [see Chapter 10] has no hesitation in describing the Absolute or "Real God" in glowing bright and positive terms since his view stands upon God-Realization or Divine Enlightenment, not on philosophical debates between various traditional schools. In this case, he clearly acknowledges that Divine Realization Itself, as recognized by all traditions of Enlightenment, arise from the same Transcendental (and Immanent) Source-Condition, which is, as the Buddhists and Vedantists (and all Adept-Realizers in the Great Tradition) say, is Consciousness Itself, as this extended quote from the Avatar confirms:

> Consciousness is Realized in Its Real Status, not as one of the "dharmas" or constituents (whether absolute or conditional) of phenomenal existences, but as the "Dharma" or Truth or Real Condition or Transcendental Identity. It is not a matter of consciousness extroverting toward objects or introverting upon itself. It is a matter of consciousness directly and intuitively Realizing Itself as the Transcendental Condition of all phenomenal conditions....
>
> It is Consciousness as it *is*, always already, whether or not phenomenal conditions arise in the forms of apparent self and/or not-self. Consciousness as Reality is not merely appearing in the form of phenomena, or as a phenomenon exclusive of or unlike other phenomena. It is simply Itself, always and already—and all phenomenal conditions are appearances or merely apparent, unnecessary, and non-binding modifications of Itself....
>
> [Consciousness Itself] is the Condition and ultimate Substance of self and world. It is not merely Spirit-Energy (which is the phenomenal Matrix of the phenomenal world). It is the Condition or Truth and Reality of the Spirit-Energy, of Light, and of all lights and sounds and heavens and hells and worlds and embodied beings. It is the Condition or Truth and Reality of all Nature, of all "dharmas," of the phenomenal self (or body-mind), of the presumed soul (or "atman"), of phenomenal consciousness (or "Purusha"), of all that is phenomenal but not consciousness (or "Prakriti"), and of all the forms and ideas that are called God, or "Purushoattama," or the Eternal Creative Other. Consciousness is ultimately Realized and Proclaimed to be Transcendental Being, the Condition of all phenomena and even the All-Pervading Energy that is the Creative Matrix and Mover of all phenomena....

That Consciousness is not an object to us, nor is It merely within us. It has no *necessary* relationship to phenomena. It is simply the ultimate or Real Context of the phenomenal self and world (in any of the gross or subtle planes of cosmic Nature). The tacit Realization of Transcendental Consciousness as the Obvious Condition is the natural or native Realization of Reality, Self, Being, Love-Bliss, or Radiant Happiness. [20]

Nothing else need be said… *only* be Realized.

But here we go again.

As Buddhism evolved from Hinayana to Mahayana to Vajrayana, Buddhism increased its reliance on the Siddha-Guru or Spiritual Adept or "*Buddha*" ("one who is Awake") where his or her transmission of the Enlightened State is given in a secret and esoteric manner. The Realized Master-Guru of Buddhism (whether as Elder, Lama, Rinpoche, Roshi, et al.), as in Hindu India, has always been considered critical in guiding a person's practice and keeping the Sangha-Community aligned with the true Dharma-Teaching of Gautama Buddha's Realization. In the individualistic-oriented West, however, this view has been called into question, where even Ken Wilber suggests that his "Integral Approach" and "Integral Buddhism" is now the actual "**Fourth Turning**"[21] of the Dharma Wheel (an assertion that is very questionable). Nonetheless, most Western "gurus" are more like Teachers, not fully Realized Adepts (including Wilber), therefore we must be cautious about changing what has worked so well for millennia. Remember, an authentic Adept has attained Nirvana by extinguishing all attachments (and desires) to the conditional self or ego-I and worlds, so only such a one is truly capable of critiquing and transmitting the

Enlightened Truth of Wisdom to another.

In Theravada, it was the ***kalyanamitra*** or "Spiritual friend" (usually a dedicated monk or renunciate) that is the characteristic guide of the Hinayana Buddhist tradition. Consequently, Hinayana Buddhists somewhat downplay the importance of the Guru by relying on what was reported to be Buddha's dying words: "Be lamps unto yourself; work out your salvation with diligence."[22] As Buddhism developed over the centuries the importance of the Guru-devotee relationship continued to become more explicit, especially as the practices became more esoteric (and tantric) in nature. By the time Tibetan Vajrayana Buddhism emerged during the opening centuries of the second millennium, **Guru Yoga** was deemed the highest and most direct practice possible for one's Enlightenment or Realization of Nirvana (or "blowing out" the separate self-sense).

In Vajrayana, the advanced esoteric practices of Tantra were given (and must be done) under the guidance of a genuine Guru or ***Lama*** (in Tibetan), the "diamond guru" of Guru Yoga [see Chapter 18]. Paradoxically, as

the Buddha was recorded to have said in the Mahayana text of the *Diamond Sutra*: "I tell you truly, Subhuti, there is no formula by which the Buddha attained it. The basis of Tathagata's attainment of the Consummation of Incomparable Enlightenment is wholly *beyond*; it is neither real nor unreal…. Buddha teaches that all things are devoid of selfhood, devoid of personality, devoid of entity, and devoid of separate individuality."[23] In this case, although the world of human existence is embraced and served with love and compassion by all Awakened Buddhas and Bodhisattvas, the physical world and self are still utterly transcended (while simultaneously being integrated) in a Transcendental Realization radiating beyond all forms of mind and states of awareness (whether in waking, dreaming, or deep sleep, even transcending death itself). And so the Dharma Wheel rolls on and on in the spokes of Infinity.

PRAJNAPARAMITA SUTRAS:
MOTHER'S MILK FOR BUDDHAS

By the first century BCE, four hundred years after the Parinirvana or Mahasamadhi (bodily death) of Gautama Buddha (ca. 483 BCE), the originating texts (*sutras*) of **Mahayana** Buddhism began to appear.[24] As just reviewed, Mahayana emphasized a universal social gospel of love and compassion (*karuna*) in addition to enlightened wisdom (*prajna*) called the "**Way of the Bodhisattva**," referring to any person supremely dedicated on the path to Buddhahood. They also began to invoke a powerful dialectic denying any argument could be made for the existence or non-existence of the Absolute, for it can *only* be *realized* in Prajna or the Enlightened State. Only from the position or insight of Enlightenment can Nirvana and Samsara said to "be the same" (for by definition they are opposites). Only a Buddha "knows" for sure.

Hence, these new Sutras were referred to as the ***Prajnaparamita*** or "the Perfection of Transcendent Wisdom" or the "Supreme Essence of Transcendental Wisdom"[25] (combining the Sanskrit words *prajna* "transcendent wisdom" with *paramita* "perfection"). Pandit-scholar Lex Hixon summarizes: "This precious Sutra revealing the Bodhisattva Way has created spiritual cultures in India, Tibet, China, Mongolia, Korea, Japan [and Southeast Asia], just as the Bible and Qur'an have in Europe, Africa, the Middle East, Southeast Asia, and the Americas."[26] Buddhist scholar T. R. V. Murti explains in *The Central Philosophy of Buddhism* (1955): "The *Prajnaparamitas* revolutionized Buddhism, in all aspects of its philosophy and religion, by the basic concept of Sunyata ["Emptiness"]… [Yet] the *Prajnaparamitas* are not innovations; they can and do claim to expound the deeper, profounder teachings of Buddha."[27] Once again, *prajna* or the Enlightenment Awakening experience (beyond all experiences of the self) is the primary emphasis, the foundation, yet not just to realize it for oneself but for the benefit of all beings: the Bodhisattva ideal. Such compassion embracing reality as a whole impresses any genuine spiritual person since the vow to gain Enlightenment is to help all other beings do the same, not just to gain some "knowledge" for oneself. It is a exalted ideal, as integral philosopher Ken Wilber once commented:

> Ultimately, in the compound individuality of the [Enlightened] Sage, all the lower levels are allowed to participate in absolute Enlightenment and bathe in the glory of Spirit. The mineral, as mineral, the plant, as plant, and the animal, as animal, could never be enlightened—but the Bodhisattva takes all manifestation with him to Paradise, and the Bodhisattva vow is never to accept [Final] Enlightenment [or Translation] until all things participate in Spirit. There is, to my mind, no nobler conception than that.[28]

This new view of the "**Greater Vehicle**" (literally, *maha* "great" plus *yana* "vehicle") was expounded in the original text called ***Great Mother: Prajnaparamita of 100,000 Lines***—sometimes called *Mother of the Buddhas* since she gives birth to Awakened Buddhahood. Hixon, who wrote a new and brilliant interpretation titled *Mother of the Buddhas: Meditation on the Prajnaparamita Sutra* (1993), noted they are "the mother's milk of transcendent insight," the "tender wet-nurse… for every past, present and future Buddha or Awakened One."[29] Buddhist scholar Robert Thurman further explains: "[The *Prajnaparamita*] purports to record the full audience given by Shakyamuni Buddha on Vulture Peak [the mountain top of many of his discourses] with the greatest explicitness and completeness, though even it falls short of a full record, which would have run to many hundreds of thousands perhaps millions of lines. Over the centuries various abridged versions have emerged [such as *8,000 Line*, the *18,000* or *20,000 Line*, and *25,00 Line Sutras*, or the very short *Heart Sutra*, for example]."[30]

These important Mahayana scriptures changed the direction of Buddhism for they initiated, as Hixon reveals, "a gentle revolution in Buddhist thinking, a vast maturing in the Buddhist mind and heart after five hundred years of intensive meditation and realization."[31] This advanced school produced not only the rich wealth of the *Prajnaparamita* texts, but also the sutras of the *Inconceivable Liberation Sutra*, the *Lotus Sutra*, the *Heart Sutra*, the *Diamond-Cutting Sutra*, *The Holy Teaching of Vimalakirti Sutra*, the *Lankavatara Sutra*, the *Surangama Sutra*, and the Pure Land Sutras, among others.[32] As Thurman continues to explain: "These perfect wisdom texts served as the foundation for a systemic curriculum developed over many centuries in the Mahayana Buddhist monastic universities, among the earliest universities on the planet."[33] We would all do well to continue this enlightened education, even if on our own, since these amazing texts are now available for anyone to study (yet it's best done, of course, under the guidance of a competent Buddhist Master and disciplined lifestyle). In the West, probably the two best-known are the *Diamond Sutra* and the very short *Heart Sutra*, sacred scriptures worthy of anyone's study and attention.

Legend has it that they were given to a great Adept from South India named **Nagarjuna** (ca. 150–250 CE) by undersea dragons called *nagas* (hence the Master's name) after they heard one of his lectures at the monastery of Nalanda. Through these sacred scriptures, though, of course, they were actually written (and orally transmitted) by flesh-and-blood Adept-Realizers, is how the universal and liberating message of the Buddha launched new psychic pathways of understanding to transcend cultural and even instinctual conditioning. From this rich field of the Enlightened Buddha-Mind the wisdom of the Awakened Buddhas continues to

Nagarjuna

arise even today. They guide not only the vowed monks and nuns in the monastic Sangha, with their practices and ceremonies of peace and insight, but also serve lay people as well. Through these Wisdom Texts, but more importantly from the Spiritual-Transmission they inspire, Buddhism is active all around the globe thriving in East and West, North and South. Let's allow our pandit-guide Professor Thurman (also known as "Buddha Bob") to explain their far-ranging influence:

> This ancient curriculum opened the minds of millions of practi-
> tioners for a thousand years in India. Around 1000 CE, it was trans-
> ferred to the Tibetan monastic universities and six hundred years
> later to the Mongolian institutions, wherein it flourished until the
> present day....

> In East Asia, it seems clear that *Prajnaparamita* served as the basis
> of the Ch'an and Zen traditions. Some might think this controver-
> sial, since Ch'an tends to refer to itself as the "Sutra-less tradition," in
> contrast with the T'ien T'ai school based on the *Lotus Sutra*, the Hua
> Yen school based on the *Garland Sutra*, and the Pure Land school
> based on the *Land of Bliss Sutra*. But the *Prajnaparamita Sutra* re-
> fers to itself as the "teaching that is no teaching," its understanding as
> the "understanding by way of nonunderstanding," its attainment as
> "attained by not attaining," and so on and on. The bottom line is that
> perfect wisdom is the direct teaching of the highest enlightenment
> of all the Buddhas, radical, uncompromising, emphasizing absolute
> reality over relative reality, the definitive meaning-teaching over all
> interpretable meaning-teaching.[34]

Nagarjuna   **Asanga**   **Avalokitesvara**   **Vasubandhu**   **Shantideva**
Bodhisattva

Buddhism was undeniably served by all the great Guru-Adepts of the Mahayana, but its foundation was laid with the incomparable Nagarjuna, mentioned above, who uncompromisingly emphasized **"Emptiness"**—*Sunyata*—
thus allowing Buddhism to reach another pinnacle of manifestation known
as *Madhyamika* (literally, "Middle Way"). As one respected scholar put it:
"*Sunyata* (Doctrine of the Void) is the pivotal concept of Buddhism. The entire Buddhist philosophy turned on this."[35] Another modern Buddhist pandit
simply stated: "If there is one teaching that is peculiar to Buddhism alone

among the world's religions, I would say it is the principle of *Sunyata* (Voidness or Emptiness). If I were to choose the one doctrine among others that best represents the core of Buddhism, I would also choose the principle of *Sunyata*."[36] Essentially, the teaching of "Emptiness" (*Sunyata*) emphasizes the insubstantiality of all phenomena, including the emptiness of the individual self (i.e., *anatma* or "empty of atman"), thus indicating that even the soul is an illusion to be transcended. This Eastern (Alpha-mind) teaching is, obviously, far from the world-clinging mind of the Western (Omega-mind) culture. The global Avatar Adi Da makes clear the advancement in this view:

> In the Mahayana tradition, That which is directly pointed to is given various names, such as Mind, not meaning the discriminative mind, or thoughts, but what in the Advaitic tradition is called the Self [or Atman]. It is also called *Sunya*, or Void, meaning "beyond dualities," "beyond the conventions of the discriminative faculty of mind." Perhaps, along with the concepts of Void and Mind, the direct pointing to the Reality is the principal advance of Mahayana over Hinayana Buddhism.[37]

Nevertheless, "Voidness" or "Emptiness," as Professor Thurman implores, "does not mean nothingness… The voidness [of Sunyata], far from annihilating everything, is the *necessary condition* for all relative existence. In other words, voidness here is not 'the void' we imagine in microspace or macrospace, a dark nothingness in which galaxies or atoms are contained; nor is it a substratum. It is Infinity, which is only a term for the ultimate ineffability of the relative reality to which we can see no ending or beginning."[38] This teaching was brilliantly articulated by many of the Mahayana Sutras penned by the prolific Nagarjuna, such as "Fundamental Verses of the Middle Way" (*Mulamadhyama-kakarika*) and "In Praise of Dharmadhatu" (*Dharmadhatustava*), two of his best known and certainly worth the effort of dedicated study, even today.[39] These sutras teach that all things (including the self) only arise due to cause and effect relationships or the patterns of conditional phenomena, known as the **"Law of Causation"** or **"Dependent Origination,"** since all things (or holons) are impermanent, temporary and ever-changing. According to Adi Da, all the Stages of Life find fuller expression in the Mahayana Dharma, as his fully Enlightened (Seventh Stage) perspective recognizes:

> I do not think we should seriously believe that the Mahayana texts are transcripts of actual talks of Gautama given to hearers different than those to whom he was speaking in the Pail literature of the Hinayana. Nevertheless, the Mahayana literature develops considerations that are only implicit in the Teaching and Realization of Gautama. A great deal more is added. Of course, a great deal of philosophizing and references to Fourth Stage [devotional] practices and meditative traditions that cannot be seen to be direct extensions of Gautama's Way. But what is fundamental in this Mahayana literature of the [Sixth Stage and "premonitory"] Seventh Stage is also fundamental in original Buddhism and represents that aspect of original Buddhism with which I [in the Reality-Way of Adidam] feel a clear affinity....
>
> Buddhism in general has the flavor of the original world-negating disposition, yet the Buddhist tradition is always in one fashion or another showing signs of wanting to break away from that limitation and point to Reality directly, even to give it a name somehow [e.g., *tathagatagarbha*], as the idealistic Hindu traditions do [e.g., *Atman-Brahman*]. Thus, out of the Buddhist tradition there comes also the [Sixth Stage and "premonitory"] Seventh Stage paradoxical point of view that is expressive of ultimate Enlightenment. Gautama himself was a ["premonitory"] Seventh Stage Adept, although his instructions are primarily examples of the Sixth Stage point of view of realism.[40]

By the time the great Tibetan pandit and Maha-Siddha **Tsong Khapa** (1357–1419) came along in the 14th century to reawaken and restore the various schools of Buddhism in Tibet (and establish his own school, the Gelugpa), the *Prajnaparamita* Sutras were still the foundation of its highest Buddhist philosophy [see Chapter 18]. Professor Thurman (himself the Je Tsongkhapa Professor of Indo-Tibetan Buddhist Studies at Columbia University) deftly explains:

Tsong Khapa reinterpreted and revitalized the perfect wisdom insight so masterfully, he came to be regarded by millions of followers over centuries as a living incarnation of the bodhisattva **Manjushri** [the oldest and most significant bodhisattva in Mahayana literature wielding his ignorance-cutting sword of wisdom]. The essence of his insight was that voidness does not mean nothingness, but rather all things lack intrinsic reality, intrinsic objectivity, intrinsic identity or intrinsic referentiality. Lacking such static essence or substance does not make them not exist—it makes them thoroughly relative. Once they are so thoroughly relative, there is no limit to their being

Manjushri

creatively reshaped by enlightened love. So the *via negative* of the *Prajnaparamita* does not annihilate things; it frees them from entrapment in negativity, opening them up to a creative relativity.[41]

As a means of teaching, for example, Nagarjuna's dialectical philosophy of nonduality used not only *via negativa—neti, neti* or "not this, not that" to point to the "Emptiness" of all phenomena (including the self), but he also emphasized the discriminative power of the "**Two Truths**," a common universal found in the Perennial Philosophy [see Chapter 7]. Ken Wilber explains: "Nagarjuna relies on the 'Two Truths' doctrine—there is [1] **relative**, or conventional, truth, and there is [2] **absolute**, or ultimate Truth. Relative truth can be categorized and characterized, and is the basis of disciplines such as science, history, law, and so on…. But ultimate Truth cannot be categorized at all (including that statement)."[42] Thus we have, by (our limited) definition:

(1) **relative truth** (*loka-samvriti-satya*) based on the duality of the conditional universe;

(2) **Absolute Truth** (*paramarthika satya*) grounded in the nonduality of Emptiness (*Sunyata*).

In this case, Enlightenment is *realized* when the relative self is transcended and awakened to see that the absolute *Sunyata* or "Emptiness" of all phenomena reveals our inherent liberation from all suffering and death. Henceforth one recognizes that the self's own inherent "emptiness" is actually he Ultimate Reality that is "the emptiness of emptiness."[43] This paradox (or seeming contradition) can boggle the mind (which then becomes a teaching method in transcending self), so my words here are practically useless. Pandit Hixon once more succinctly summarizes: "Relative truth and absolute truth must remain in subtle balance or even in perfect unison,"[44] since both are One or Nondual (i.e., "not-two").

Paradoxically, by realizing the nondual equation, as famously codified in the *Heart Sutra*: "form is emptiness, emptiness is form; consciousness is emptiness, emptiness is not different from consciousness"—or as Buddha Bob Thurman has it: "Matter is not void because of voidness; voidness is not elsewhere from matter. Matter itself *is* voidness. Voidness itself *is* matter."[45]—then the conditional world (samsara) is not to be excluded or rejected (as the many interior-oriented Yogas of Hinayana and Vedanta suggest) but is embraced and integrated (or honored). Wilber summarized nicely: "For Nagarjuna, the deconstruction of relative truths leaves not nihilism but Emptiness: it clears away the conceptual rubble in the mind's eye and thus allows the space of nondual intuition to disclose itself… if you don't want to be a complete self-contradiction, then you must come to rest in infinite Emptiness… which alone sets the soul free on the ocean of infinite Mystery."[46] Get it?

Yogachara Fullness:
"One Taste" of Consciousness Only

The Two Truths of Mahayana means that *everything* (including the self and all others) are simply transcended-yet-included as "**One Taste**," known as "**Nondual Mysticism**" (in Wilber's words). Or, in Western terms: "Everything *is* God!"; there is God Only, Only

God! Just as Wilber once said: "All things are not ultimately made of subatomic particles; all things, including subatomic particles, are ultimately made of God [Empty-Fullness]."[47] As the integrally-enlightened pandit would later wisely reveal:

> There is only One Taste in the entire Kosmos, and that taste is Divine, whether it appears in the flesh, in the mind, in the soul. Resting in that One Taste, transported beyond the mundane, the world arises in the purest Freedom and radiant Release, happy to infinity, lost in all eternity, and hopeless in the original face of the unrelenting mystery. From One Taste all things issue, to One Taste all things return—and in between, which is the story of this moment, there is only the dream, and sometimes the nightmare, from which we would do well to awaken.[48]

This Nondual philosophy (grounded in Enlightenment) was a revolutionary understanding provided by the most-advanced Buddhist Adepts. It was an awareness that transcends-yet-integrates the Atman-Realization of Vedanta, since too often the Hindu Sages *exclude* the phenomenal world as being illusory (the Sixth Stage error, according to Adi Da). For an enlightened Buddha or Bodhisattva, however, both self and world and all living beings are united as Transcendental Consciousness or "**Mind-Only**," which is ultimately "Empty" as the "**Clear Light Void**," but also is paradoxically "Full" as Light and Bliss or "**Clear Light Bliss**,"[49] a major tenet of the Yogachara school. Professor Murti further explains: "Accepting the Sunyata of the *Prajnaparamita*, and even protesting that they interpret it correctly, they [Yogachara Buddhists] modify the *Sunyata* of the Madhyamika; they give substance to the *sunya* by identifying it with Pure Consciousness that is devoid of duality."[50] It seems the Tibetan Tantra Buddhists more clearly understood this, as contemporary Buddhist teacher-author Lama Surya Das clarifies:

> Tibetan Buddhism says that at the heart of you, me, every single person, and all other creatures great and small, is an inner radiance that reflects our essential nature, which is always utterly positive. Tibetans refer to this inner light as pure radiance or innate luminosity; in fact, they call it *ground luminosity* because it is the "bottom line." There is nothing after this, and nothing before this. This luminosity

is birthless and deathless. It is luminescent emptiness [*Sunyata*], called "clear light," and it is endowed with the heart of unconditional compassion and love.[51]

Such a wonderful radiant nondual paradox is, as Zen likes to say, "plain yet marvelous," arising as "eternal spontaneity," or, simply (but paradoxically) put: "the ordinary mind is Tao."[52] Nothing more, nothing less, utter Divine Realization, here and now. See "It"? Another Buddhist Zen Master, **Shen Tsan** (devotee of **Pai-Chang** [720–814]), beautifully uttered the pure simplicity of this radiant nondual truth with these poetic phrases:

> Singularly radiating is the wondrous Light;
> Free is it from the bondage of matter and the senses.
> Not binding by words and letters,
> The Essence is nakedly exposed in its pure eternity.
> Never defiled is the Mind-nature [Consciousness Itself];
> It exists in perfection from the very beginning.
> By merely casting away your delusions
> The Suchness of Buddhahood is realized.[53]

I could go on with countless examples like these from the Mahayana literature of the "Divine Library," so I wholeheartedly encourage you to explore for yourself.[54] Read them from the heart (not just the mind).

In China, during this prolific Mahayana period, there also emerged **Hua-Yen Buddhism**, known as the "**Mind-Only**" doctrine, primarily based on the *Avatamsaka Sutra* (in Sanskrit) or the *Flower Garland Sutra* (in English). This Buddhist "**Teaching of Totality**" holds that no element of the universe has a separate and independent existence apart from the whole. Hua-Yen Buddhism highlights the interconnected and infinite *Dharmadhatu*, the Filed of Reality—also known as "**Indra's Net of Jewels**"—the Transcendent Unconditional Reality as a living, intertwined Matrix where all points or perspectives of conditional existence are reflected in each other.[55] Once again, we see Mahayana Teachings pointing to Reality as being a "Fullness" (*tathagatagarbha*) arising within "Emptiness" (*sun-ya*), paradoxically both, as Nondual Oneness. Or, as Adi Da has called it, the "Radiant Transcendental Being," or "Conscious Light," or simply "the 'Bright'." Whatever the words (which all fail), it is Only Real God as our Buddha-Nature.

This further refinement of Buddha-Dharma, made by a succession of Adept-Realizers over the centuries of the Common Era, continued forward with the aforementioned **Yogachara Buddhism** (literally, "yoga practice"), per-haps the most evolved of all Buddhist Teachings. Legend has it that an Adept named **Maitreya** (270–350), whose name is linked with the future Buddha (popular in the *Amitabha Sutra* and the *Lotus Sutra*), is the one who founded Yogachara, and whose historicity is now generally accepted.[56]

Nonetheless, Yogachara was principally established by the brilliant two half-brother Indian monks **Asanga** and **Vasubandhu** (of the 4th century CE) with their series of Sutras and commentaries.[57] Yogachara and the Hua-Yen (or Hwa Yen) school of Mahayana, as mentioned, places an emphasis on "Consciousness" (or "Mind-Only") to balance the Emptiness doctrine empha-sized by Nagarjuna's Madhyamika. In the Buddhist universities of the first mil-lennium CE, such as with Nalanda, pandits and Adepts would engage in long (and heavily attended) debates arguing over these subtle distinctions based on their own Realization and understanding of the sacred Sutras. Since Yogachara later influenced Zen, one modern Zen teacher explains:

> Vasubandhu's ability to integrate his extraordinary understanding of both Abhidharma and Mahayana thought and practice, and to express them in his numerous writings, helped give birth to the new tradition of Yogachara…. Yogachara arose as an attempt to integrate the most powerful aspects of the earliest Buddhist teachings and the later Mahayana teachings. There was growing sectarian argumenta-tion between the proponents of these two bodies of teachings, and Yogachara sought to show how the teachings were not actually in

conflict and to allow for practitioners to access the profound transformative benefits of both traditions.[58]

The realization of pure Consciousness (beyond ego-self) as being Divine
(or Empty-Full)—our innate Buddha-Nature—is the same Nondual Enlightenment found in both "realistic" Buddhism and "idealistic" Vedanta, the two
greatest Nondual traditions on Earth. Adi Da confirms (using his Seven Stage
model): "The only significant difference between the basic traditions of ultimate Realization according to the Vedic and the Buddhist (or non-Vedic)
traditions is the language of the Way *toward* Realization. The Upanishadic
schools of Advaita Vedanta are the principle Sixth to Seventh Stage schools
of Vedic spiritual idealism. And the schools of Buddhism are the principle
Sixth to Seventh Stage schools of non-Vedic materialistic realism. But both
traditions are oriented toward and originally based upon the same ultimate
Transcendentalism."[59] It is also the same *Gnosis* or *Sophia* (or *Prajna*) appearing throughout the highest mysticisms of the Perennial Philosophy, i.e., when
properly understood via the Stages of Life [see Chapter 8]. Only an Avatar
familiar with both great Enlightenment traditions from India, but ultimately
based on his own Realization, can clearly explain its ultimate significance:

> The Enlightenment that is the fulfillment of the life of Gautama,
> and the Hinayana tradition, is the Seventh Stage Enlightenment. It is
> the same Enlightenment that is the fulfillment of the Advaitic tradi-
> tion, except that the Hinayana or Buddhist tradition is based on the
> realistic point of view, concentrating on the dharmas or conditions
> of existence, and the Advaitic tradition of Vedanta is based on the
> idealistic point of view, typical of Hinduism in general, that affirms
> from the beginning the Transcendental Reality....
>
> When that Transcendental Realization occurs, it inherently tran-
> scends the discriminative mind [of the lower Stages of Life], which
> [in the Sixth Stage of Life] distinguishes between Self and not-Self,
> and which sees a difference between the subjective being and its ob-
> jects or the world. Discrimination also tends to be part of the psy-
> chology of the Hinayana tradition. The orientation toward the ulti-
> mate subjective Truth, as distinct from, as discriminated from, the
> objects of the self, is an aspect of the Sixth Stage limitation in general

[the Sixth Stage error]. In the [Enlightened] Seventh Stage, this discriminative effort that dissociates Self from not-Self and identifies exclusively with the essence of self is transcended, and samsara, or the realm of objects, is not strategically avoided.[60]

In the Mahayana, as mentioned, it was the monk or nun who vowed to become a *Bodhisattva* for the sake of all beings, not just for oneself (such as with the Arhat) that became the ultimate ideal for Enlightenment. This enlightened compassion and love for all beings was summarized by **Shantideva** (685–763 CE) in his poetic text *The Way of the Bodhisattva* (*Bodhicharyavatara*). Shantideva once more reflected the "two truths" doctrine by emphasizing "**absolute bodhichitta**" (the wisdom of emptiness) coupled with "**relative bodhichitta**" (the aspiration to attain the highest good of Buddhahood).[61] Let's allow the Ruchira (or "Bright") Buddha to further clarify:

> The Bodhisattvas are said [by Western scholars] to put aside their Enlightenment until all other beings are Awakened. They are not truly putting aside their Enlightenment. They are putting aside Bhava Samadhi [i.e., "Outshining" or "Translation," in Adi Da's terms, the final phase of Enlightenment]. At least they are said to do so in the descriptions of the Bodhisattva ideal. Clearly, the best service to pay to all other beings is to pursue Enlightenment with absolute vigor [*bodhicitta*]—to pursue it for the sake of all beings, not to prevent it for the sake of all beings, is the highest service.[62]

In addition, as to be expected, these evolved vehicles of Buddhism pay sincere reverence to the necessity of Guru Yoga and the Awakened Adept as guide and Master-transmitter of the Enlightened State. As a consequence, the sadhana or spiritual practices of advanced meditation and Tantra Yoga were able to establish a remarkable lineage of recurring Guru-Adepts each teaching new generations of dedicated practitioners. They do this by appealing to those who were (and are) willing to take up the necessary disciplines (as they also had to do by following the admonitions of their own Adept-Masters). This "lineage" or linkage of *spiritual transmission*—an energy exchange of Enlightened Consciousness— from Master to devotee is the essential ingredient needed to fully initiate our own personal practice as well [see Chapter 11].

However, the vital importance of Guru Yoga-Satsang is often overlooked by Western scholars and casual practitioners (particularly today). As always, it is the "Practicing School," not the "Talking School," that is the only true Way taught by all the authentic Buddhas, Maha-Siddhas, and Master-Adepts [see Chapter 4]. The Guru is absolutely necessary, not an anachronism, regardless what some modern teachers might profess. The historical record—God's Great Tradition of Global Wisdom—verifies this truth; look for yourself. See for yourself what the Buddhas teach and listen well. Thus have I heard.

ZEN: DIRECT ENLIGHTENMENT

Development of Buddhism in China (begun in the first half of the first millennium CE) evolved into **Ch'an Buddhism**, which went to Korea, then to Japan (in the second half of the first millennium) to become **Zen Buddhism**. "Zen" is Japanese for the Chinese word "Ch'an" that (in Sanskrit) is *dhyana*, which means "meditation," its most fundamental practice. As Ch'an Buddhism developed during the Tang Dynasty (618–907 CE)—the Golden Age of Buddhism in China—the living Adepts there integrated Buddhism with mystical Taoism creating two major schools. There was the **Northern school** of China that emphasized "**Gradual Enlightenment**" (based on disciplined sadhana under a Guru-Master) and the **Southern school** that emphasized "**Sudden Enlightenment**" (also known as subitism) which is initiated with *kensho* and *satori* (the Enlightenment experience of no-self). Both attempt to attain awareness of one's own innate Buddha-Nature, as did the Buddha himself realize.

Nonetheless, in its essence, the primary experience of actual Enlightenment (via "ego-death") is always *sudden*, immediate and tacit. It is known as **Wu** (in Chinese) and *satori* (in Japanese Zen) or **kensho** (or "seeing one's essential nature"), the *direct experience* of (or awakening to) our innate Buddha-Nature, also called seeing our "Original Face" (in Zen). This awakening experience is the "goal" yet "ground" of Buddhism—actual Divine Enlightenment transcending the boundaries of the ego-I—as the Buddha long ago taught. Awakening will always be Buddhism's true essence, the fountain from which all philosophies, teachings, writings, and schools (or *yanas*) of Buddhism arise. Buddhism, in other words, is based on Awakening, not theology; Buddhism is not a religion, as its practitioners often claim, it is a way of life by understanding the truth of life and existence. Ruchira Buddha Adi Da points to this silent Realization:

> In a famous scene in the Mahayana literature, in response to some query about Enlightenment, Gautama is said to have held up a flower [without saying a word] and thereby Enlightened the individual to whom he showed it.... Here is a *direct pointing* to Reality that we find in the Mahayana tradition, particularly in the Ch'an or Zen school, *directly pointing* to Reality, Happiness, Freedom, That which is not describable by the mind but which is nevertheless the import of the Way.
>
> Thus, the Zen tradition does not emphasize the superimposition of the negative psychology on the practitioner [as does the Hinayana tradition]. Clearly there are some very strict monastic approaches to the Japanese Zen or Chinese Ch'an Way, but there is also much of this humorous, playful pointing and the use of paradoxes [such as with koans].[63]

Most importantly, the Adepts of Ch'an (in China), then Zen (in Japan), were shedding the weight of academic and literary Buddhism (in India) to place more emphasis on the *direct experience* of Enlightenment itself, not its scholarly interpretations. As we've said, it's the difference between the "Talking School" of the mind and the "Practicing School" of real sadhana-Satsang or "a special transmission outside the scriptures" (as Bodhidharma famously declared). It's about authentic Divine Realization under the guidance of a genuine Guru-Adept, not self-guruing [see Chapter 4]. This is why extensive meditation and a sacred relationship with a Zen Master or qualified Adept-Realizer is the true essence of Zen (and real Buddhist) practice (as Westerners soon discover).

Such Realization is not gained via an easy weekend seminar or drug experience or spending ten minutes a day "meditating," but arises from a dedicated lifestyle (and "right view") before Real Enlightenment dawns. Yet, even then, Enlightenment (or God-Realization) is always *sudden*, instantaneous, tacit, ineffable, an ungraspable event, as all Zen Masters constantly emphasize. This understanding supposedly led the Soto Zen monk **Suzuki Roshi** (1904–1971), who was teaching in the United States, to simply state: "Gaining Enlightenment is an accident. Spiritual practice [and meditation] simply makes us accident prone." In other words, although God-Realization is ultimately a matter of Grace (i.e., being totally unpredictable), when sadhana-Satsang is undertaken with an Awakened Adept this increases the probability of Grace occurring. Zen scholar (and practitioner) Garma C. C. Chang clarifies this slippery paradox in *The Practice of Zen* (1959), one the best books I know explaining the mysterious truths of Zen:

> Since Zen is not, in its essence and on its higher levels, a philosophy, but a *direct experience* that one must enter into with his [or her] whole being, the primary aim should be at the attainment and realization of the Zen experience. To realize this supreme experience, known as the "Wu experience" ["wu" is Chinese for *satori*, a Japanese word] or "Enlightenment," one needs to rely completely on an accomplished Zen Master... for none is better qualified than these accomplished Masters to deal with the subject of practical Zen....
>
> Zen represents a teaching which may well be considered as the

pinnacle of all Buddhist thought, a teaching that is most direct, profound, and practical—capable of bringing one to liberation and perfect Enlightenment....

The ultimate *Prajna*-Truth that Zen tries to illustrate is, itself, ungraspable and indefinable in nature. Zen is a very practical teaching in that its main object is to bring individuals to Enlightenment by the quickest and most direct route; and as each disciple differs in disposition, capacity, and state of advancement, a Zen Master must give instructions in different ways and from different levels of approach in order to make his [or her] Zen practice effective.[64]

Bodhidharma—a name meaning "*dharma* [teaching] awakening [*bodhi*]" (known as Daruma in Japan)—who established Buddhism in China (ca. 520 CE), is often claimed to be the twenty-eighth Patriarch in a direct lineage from Shakyamuni Buddha. More importantly, he is also considered the First Patriarch of Zen because his brand of Buddhism emphasized *dhyana* ("ch'an") or serious meditation. According to legend, the Hindu monk was so dedicated to achieving Enlightenment that while living in China (at Elephant Trunk Mountain above a Shaolin Monastery) he spent nine intensive years meditating in a cave so his shadow was impressed on the cave's wall. It is said Bodhidharma's favorite sutra was the *Lankavatara Sutra* ("the only sutra," in his words) known for its emphasis on a "turn-about" in consciousness and the "Mind-Only" doctrine of Yogachara. Combining the naturalistic (and more atheistic) quality of Taoism, in contrast to the polytheism of India and the animistic spiritism of Tibet, Chinese Buddhism took on a unique quality and character.[65]

By the time the illiterate **Hui-Neng** (638–713), the Sixth Patriarch of Ch'an/Zen (who purportedly attained Enlightenment merely by hearing a recitation of the *Diamond Sutra*) appeared on the scene, he ultimately had little use for the extensive literature of the Mahayana *Sutras*. He preferred to emphasize the truth of "Emptiness" and the "self-realization of Mind-essence" (as taught in the *Lankavatara*). Consequently, he established the Southern "Sudden Enlightenment" School in China, yet, ironically, he composed one the most famous sutras in all of Buddhism: *The Platform Sutra of Hui-Neng* (also known as *The Platform Sutra of the Sixth Patriarch*). Adi Da explicitly explained: "The *Platform Sutra* shows a ["premonitory"] Seventh Stage Adept teaching and criticizing and urging toward the Transcendental point of view, in which even the Self is not discriminated from the world or phenomena."[66] This unique blending of the various elements of Buddhism with the naturalism of Taoism gave Chinese Ch'an and Japanese Zen their unique characteristic form and spirit, which was more concerned with immediate awakening than theory and gradual practice.[67] Buddhist scholar Dwight Goddard, who worked with D. T. Suzuki, summarily explained:

> Hui-Neng was deeply influenced by his inherited and personal ac-
> quaintance with Taoism…. The term he used for Ultimate Reality,
> and made much of, was Mind-essence. A self-realization of *this* was
> all the Buddha cared about. It was *Dharmakaya* and *Buddhahood*
> and *Nirvana* and *Tathata* and *Prajna* [i.e., Enlightenment Only]. To
> Hui-Neng [and Zen], perfect Enlightenment and self-realization of
> Mind-essence and Buddhahood were the same thing…. In his mind,
> all scripture and all teachings were subordinate to the self-realization
> attained suddenly by earnest Dhyana and Samadhi.[68]

The **Rinzai** School, or Southern "Sudden" School, modeled after Hui-Neng (and his devotee, Shen-Hui), therefore relies on *koans* and other instantaneous awakening practices. Actual Awakening, in this case, is known as **"a special trans-mission outside the scriptures"** since it goes beyond words and letters, rules and training, for it's based more on a transmission of consciousness from Master to disciple, one that directly points the mind (or consciousness) to one's innate Buddha-Nature. Still, an unprepared mind will not have the breakthrough experience so even transmission must be cultivated properly. Zen students are not initiated until they are ready. True Enlightenment is very rare and hard to attain (since it also takes Grace) because the mind or stream of thoughts must completely cease (or be transcended). While the rigorous use of *zazen* or "seated meditation" is a commonly known practice of Zen, *sanzen* defined as "the face-to-face training under a Zen Master is the core Rinzai practice."[69] Sudden Awakening or *satori* (*kensho*) is the fundamental *direct experience* of Enlightenment required for authentic Zen to begin (associated with the same experience Buddha had under the bodhi tree). Easier said than done, naturally, because you can't get there from here (as Adi Da likes to joke).

| Hui Neng | Huang Po | Budai
Laughing Buddha | Han Shan | Dogen |

In contrast to the "Sudden Awakening" school, when the Northern school of China moved over to Japan flowering into Zen, it branched out into the **Soto** School, established by **Eisai** (1141–1215), who deemphasized the koans (of sudden enlightenment) to focus more on *zazen* or the "sitting meditation" (of gradual enlightenment). His devotee, the famous Master **Dogen** (1200–1253), continued focusing on meditation and tranquility (such as with the tea ceremony) based on strict practice and surrender of ego (to become more "accident prone"). Contrary to this calmer approach, the Rinzai Masters (of the Southern School) would often act "crazy" in sudden surprising ways, sometimes shouting or hitting their students to shock them out of their egoic trance and complacency. Nonetheless, both schools stressed the necessity for "sitting on the cushion" in hours of concentrated meditation under an Awakened Master's tutelage and guidance. Consequently, since both Rinzai and Soto Zen ultimately emphasize *kensho-satori*, or direct insight into one's Buddha-Nature, it is important to follow this sudden awakening experience with post-satori practices in order to integrate awakened awareness with the stabilization of gradual enlightenment.

This points to an oft-misunderstood aspect of Zen (and Buddhism in general) by Westerners. It involves two main principles called (by their Chinese names still used by Japanese Masters): (1) *chien* is "View" as in "seeing reality," and (2) *hsing* is "practice" as in "the work" or "the action." ***Chien***, the Right View, is gained with *Satori* or *Wu* ("original enlightenment"), while ***Hsing*** transforms an enlightened person into *Samyaksambodhi* or final and perfect Enlightenment. As our guide Master Chang clarifies: "In other words, after one has attained *Satori*, he should cultivate it until it reaches its full maturity, until he has gained great power and flexibility."[70] Westerners typically like to be goal-oriented, to *search for Satori*, trying to gain it, thus failing to appreciate the long haul of practice even after sudden Awakening. Thus, Zen places its main emphasis on the Awakened "View" (*chien*) as being its true essence. Then real practice (*hsing*) begins, not before, as Master Chang confirms:

> The spirit as well as the tradition of Zen is fully reflected in its emphasis on *chien* rather than *hsing*. Therefore, though Satori *is merely the beginning, it is nevertheless the Essence of Zen. It is not all of Zen, but it is its Heart.*[71]

From this rich resource of Enlightened Teaching-Transmissions, handed down by Adepts generation after generation, there arose a plethora of brilliant Zen Masters who were scattered throughout China, Korea, and Japan, etc., some living as hermits in the mountains, like **Han Shan** of Cold Mountain (9th century CE), while others were head of monasteries, such as **Huang Po** (d. 850 CE). It is a rich and marvelous history worthy of deep study. From the graceful gifts of these many time-honored Adept-Gurus and Maha-Siddhas, Masters and Roshis, the Buddha's Dharma (and Awakening) has continued to generate Enlightenment in human beings, women and men, for thousands of years up to the present day (and will far into future).

In all Zen schools, it is the relationship with the "**Roshi**" (literally, "elder master") that becomes the all-important aspect of one's practice and spiritual life, even more than meditation alone. Without the Master-Adept, meditation will never be fully successful since it is the self who tries to meditate that must be transcended. It's a paradox not understood until *Satori*. As one scholarly encyclopedia points out: "It is the task of the *Roshi* to lead and inspire students on the way to Enlightenment (*kensho* and *satori*), for which, naturally, the prerequisite is that he himself has experienced profound Enlightenment."[72] Once a student awakens to *satori* (causal-nondual insight) the relationship with the *Roshi* often changes from master-student to be more like brother-brother (or sister-sister, sister-brother), where all are equal in Realization (if not in mastery).[73]

Zen Master Garma C. C. Chang wonderfully explains: "Zen only *begins* at the moment when one first attains *Satori*; before that one merely stands outside and looks at Zen intellectually. In a deeper sense, *Satori is only the beginning, but is not the end of Zen*."[74] Such is the case in Adidam Ruchiradam as well, for only *after* "seeing" Adi Da as an authentic Agent of Divine Grace embodied as the Siddha-Guru, that is, when seeing with Right View (*chien*)— or the Enlightened State—does the Way of the Heart truly begin. Then practice (*hsing*)—or Satsang-sadhana—becomes the heart's recognition-response to what is revealed, not a goal to be sought.

OX-HERDING "EMPTINESS": TAMING MIND TO ENTER THE MARKETPLACE

𝕿he Zen Buddhist approach of disciplined practice and meditation or "taming the mind" is always done in sacred relationship with a qualified and authentic Adept-Realizer or "**Roshi**" (in Japanese). Zen takes practice and more practice: *zazen* to *sanzen* to *satori* to gain the Right View (*chien*) or Awakening. This process is cleverly depicted in the famous "**Ten Ox-Herding**" brush paintings, authored by the Sung Dynasty Zen Master known as **Kakuan Shien** (12th century), which are based on another Zen Master who used only five paintings.[75] The final steps show the student (now a Master) as "re-entering" the world *after* attaining *Satori* or Absolute Emptiness depicted by the circle of whiteness, the eighth frame—the circle of "Emptiness"—also known as *Wu* (in Zen). This state of formless emptiness (*sunya*) is comparable to the introversion of the Sixth Stage of Life (in Adi Da's terms) or "Formless Mysticism" (in Wilber's terms). Nevertheless, it is still a genuine Awakening beyond self (and the bull or ox).

After Satori comes the final stages (the ninth and tenth frame) where, according to Zen, living in the world becomes easy, spontaneous, and free—known as *Wu Wei* (from Chinese Taoism meaning "not doing" or "effortless action," or simply "going with the flow" of Tao). This is *living* in the present with the Right View of the Enlightened State or perspective—seeing Reality with "open eyes" or in the Seventh Stage of Life (*sahaj samadhi*)—which itself allows further maturity and deeper purification of remaining personal "leftover" karmas (*prarabdha karma*). Such "practice" (*hsing*)—the "Perfect Practice" (in Adi Da's words)—is what allows Enlightenment to fully bloom beyond its immediate suddenness. As another Zen Master poetically expressed:

> Even beyond the ultimate limits there extends a passageway,
> whereby he comes back among the six realms of existence;
> Every world affair is a Buddhist work,
> and wherever he goes he finds his home air…
> In whatever associations he is found he moves leisurely unattached.[76]

This is also nicely summarized with the famous phrase "**chop wood, carry water**,"[77] which comes from Zen Buddhist **Pang Wen** (740–808): "carrying wood and fetching water are miraculous performances."[78] Daily activities, ordinary life, ordinary mind are all miraculous *after Satori*, as Professor Chang explains: "For the awakened Zen Buddhist holds the Essence of God, the Heart of Buddha, in his hand."[79] Holding it in his heart is more like it, since, of course, this is where original Buddhahood resides when Right View is *realized*. For example, *The Planform Sutra of Hui-Neng* explains: "As to the

Dharma, this is transmitted from heart to heart, and the recipient must realize it by his [or her] own efforts. From time immemorial it has been the practice for one Buddha to pass to his successor the quintessence of the Dharma, and for one Patriarch to transmit to another the esoteric teaching from heart to heart."[80] Huang Po also made plain: "All the Buddhas and sentient beings are nothing but one's Mind… It is here now! But as soon as any thought arises you miss it right away! It is like space, having no edges, immeasurable and unthinkable. Buddha is nothing else but this, your very Mind [Consciousness]!"[81] I could go on and on presenting quotes like this; read and see for yourself!

The ten ox-herding paintings famously depict this process of gradual enlightenment by first taming the wild and wandering mind (symbolized by the ox or bull) which must be mastered by the Zen practitioner in meditation and living Right Life. Usually unfolding in stages of development, the student goes from searching for, then catching the bull (i.e., the mind), to taming the bull, to riding the bull, and so on (the first seven sequential frames of the painting). Yet, after Enlightenment finally awakens (pictured as an "empty" circle) depicting "bull and self transcended," then the enlightened one "enters the marketplace" (or conventional world) with "open hands" to live life "in the world" but as an Awakened One, as a "Buddha," living spontaneous and free of self illusions—*Wu Wei!* The ten-stage sequence is shown below:

Searching for the Bull Finding the Footprints Perceiving the Bull Catching the Bull Taming the Bull

Riding the Bull Home The Bull Transcended Bull and Self Transcended Reaching the Source In the World

Ten Ox-Herding Zen Paintings
(original paintings by Kakuan Shien)

This "return to the marketplace," however, does not mean simply "re-entering the world" as it was known prior to Satori. It is important to understand, therefore, that this does not literally mean samsara and Nirvana are the same, for they are *not* according to their definitions. **Samsara** is the illusions created by the self-contraction; **Nirvana** is samsara's release or transcendence into the natural state of Buddhahood. Only from the point of view of Enlightenment, not prior to it, are "samsara and Nirvana the same," as Nagarjuna paradoxically declared. Adi Da, from his Seventh Stage perspective makes plain what is a perpetual confusion in the Great Tradition, especially among Western interpreters: "The mind that makes differences [the discriminative mind] is transcended altogether in Enlightenment.... From that point of view, samsara is not discriminated from Nirvana. Manifest conditions are not seen to be other than the Self.... The Seventh Stage point of view that Brahman is the world is the same point of view as that samsara and Nirvana are the same."[82] Only from the "view" of Enlightenment are all things seen and *realized* to be Only One Divine Reality, always already the case... One Taste, nothing less.

Avatar Adi Da, therefore, points out that the formula "Nirvana and samsara are the same is similar to the **Advaitic formula**: (1) The world is unreal; (2) Only Brahman is real; (3) Brahman is the world, or even 'Thou art That' (*Tat Tvam Asi*) which means 'The atman (or the essence of the individual self) and the Paramatman (or the Transcendental Self) are identical'."[83] Adi Da assists us in understanding this important point:

> Truly, these formulae may be affirmed to represent the point of view of Enlightenment—but only those who have Realized Enlightenment can affirm them. Otherwise, the process of Awakening must somehow be entered into—since the Truth of the traditional formulae cannot be affirmed by the un-Awakened.[84]

Clearly, to most of us who are unenlightened, then samsara *is* samsara: a life of suffering and dissatisfaction (*dukkha*) perpetuated by desire (*tanha*) and ignorance (*avidya*) resulting in our *karma* and the repeated cycle of birth, mundane existence, and dying again (via reincarnation). Nirvana, on the other hand, as the word signifies, means something else: the end of theses repeated cycles of rebirth and suffering (and ignorance) by attaining the liberation gained only in Divine Enlightenment. So the Masters do in fact teach. Obviously, then, samsara and Nirvana are *not* the same from the perspective of our conventional (unenlightened) view.

FIRST SIX STAGES OF LIFE:
SAMSARA AND NIRVANA ARE NOT THE SAME

There is a popular misconception perpetuated by Western scholars (including Ken Wilber) and unenlightened beings that "samsara and nirvana are the same" based on Nagarjuna's famous dictum (countering all dualistic distinctions): "There is no distinction whatsoever between samsara and nirvana; there is no distinction whatsoever between nirvana and samsara. The limit of nirvana and the limit of samsara: one cannot find the slightest difference between them."[85] Yet this is simply one of Nagarjuna's dialectics where he persistently counters *all* definitions as being products of dualism, not of Nondual Awakening. Such statements must be understood, therefore, in their proper context. It's one thing to utter these phrases logically; it is another thing altogether for them to be *realized* in truth. The fully-Realized Adept Adi Da Samraj clarifies:

> The equation (or "sameness") of "Nirvana" and "samsara" is *not* factually the case. It is not a conventional truth, nor is it in any sense obvious to the egoic mind. In the un-Enlightened condition [in the first Six Stages of Life], Nirvana and samsara are the ultimate opposites. The declaration (or Confession) that they are the same is truly made only by those who have transcended the limits of ego and phenomenal appearances [in the Seventh Stage of Life]....
>
> Those who are not thus Enlightened or perfectly Awake must clearly understand (and take heed of the fact) that Nirvana and samsara are *not* the same. A conventionally worldly life, egoically attached to the merely apparent or perceptual "realities" of phenomenal existence, is not in any sense Nirvanic.[86]

For Buddhists, Hinayana Buddhists in particular, the wish to extinguish the sufferings of the self caught in samsara, to escape the realistic inequalities of the world in Nirvana, or complete cessation—"**Formless Mysticism**"—is the goal of the **Sixth Stage of Life**. Indeed, Adi Da calls it the "**Sixth Stage Error**," since as he explains, "[The Sixth Stage] conceives of a path or method for Realizing a state of exclusive identification with consciousness. That Realization is considered to be liberation or Truth, since it separates consciousness from the phenomenal not-self and thus effectively solves the apparent 'problem' of egoic suffering. And that Realization is based on meditative inversion of the phenomenal being."[87] Consequently, "the principal limitations of the Sixth Stage type that have become identified with traditional Buddhism are the tendency to consider existence exclusively in the terms of phenomenal realism and the tendency to view manifest existence as a problem to be solved."[88] Mahayana and Vajrayana attempt to overcome this limitation, as Adi Da also notes:

> The philosophical origins of the Vajrayana demonstration of Enlightenment are in the Mahayana Equation or the Realization of samsara, or phenomenal existence, in the context of Nirvana, or the Transcendental Condition, rather than in the context of egoic bondage. Thus, the Vajrayana philosophy is basically that of the Mahayana schools of "Mind Dharma" [Yogachara] or the Transcendental Idealism expressed in the Mahayana equation of Nirvana and samsara [are the same].[89]

In this case, as Westerners tend to do, they simply use such radically nondual statements—"samsara and Nirvana are the same"—as a way to avert real disciplined practice (*sadhana*) and forego study under a realized Adept. Such "pop spirituality" is promoted in the spiritual marketplace as a shortcut to Enlightenment, which never works since it's foundation is in egoity [see Chapter 4]. Therefore, Avatar Adi Da critically addresses this confusion, as not only being a "Sixth Stage Error" but the perpetual error of egoity in *all* the Stages of Life:

> In the domain of "pop" Buddhism, the Enlightened Confession "Nirvana and samsara are the same" is reduced to the idea that discipline and transcendence are unnecessary… The same tendencies are evident in "pop" Hinduism, where, according to the conventional belief in the sameness of atman and Brahman, the ego is regarded

to be Divine, the Truth is reduced to the mortal patterns of psycho-physical inwardness, and the Spiritual Master is abandoned for the "Inner Guide" (or the ego as Master).[90]

There is in fact an important distinction to be made between samsara and Nirvana or otherwise the Buddha would not have distinguished them. **Samsara** is the experience of the separate self in "relative" reality (which the Buddha claimed is ultimately illusory)—perpetuated by what Adi Da calls the activity of the "self-contraction" (or Narcissus)—whereas **Nirvana** is the Absolute Transcendental Reality (or Buddha-Nature) that sets the ego-self free (for it "blows out" the illusions and feeling of separateness). Thus, in actuality, samsara (phenomenal relative reality) arises *within* Nirvana (Absolute Transcendental Reality), so only in that sense are they the same. Otherwise, there is a huge difference between samsaric (or egoic) suffering and the bliss of Transcendental Nirvanic Liberation. This is the actual Enlightened perspective on such terms, regardless of their Prior Unity in Transcendental Realization.

Samsara is based on dualism, whereas in truth Reality Itself is nondual or "not-two" (or "One without a second"). If this view is *realized* in Nondual Mysticism, then, indeed, "samsara and Nirvana are the same"; if not, as is generally the case with the vast majority of us, then there is a huge gulf between the self's experience of samsara and the liberation gained in *realizing* Nirvana. Indeed, this is the whole purpose of sadhana in Guru Yoga-Satsang (done in relationship to competent Spiritual Masters or Buddhas). In fact, it's the whole point of human life altogether, according to Buddhism is to overcome this illusion between seeing things dualistically and seeing things as they really are—as Nondual Nirvana (or the Transcendental Reality)! Let's allow Ruchira Buddha Adi Da Samraj, to set us straight on Buddha's true Dharma with this extended quote:

> This is the ultimate logic of [Hinayana] Buddhism: Neither "samsara" (conditions) nor "Nirvana" (the absence of conditions) can be happily and finally embraced or attained.... The proposition of pleasurable fulfillment (even at the risk of painful frustration) is the proposition of "**samsara**." The proposition of dissociation and escape from conditional states is the proposition of "**Nirvana**." Therefore, both samsara and Nirvana are conventional propositions of the mind.... The trend of Buddhist philosophy is to criticize mind

and all propositions of mind as artificial and binding artifices…. And Enlightenment is, therefore, a matter of the transcendence of mind (and thus the conventional self-idea as well as all other limiting and binding conceptions)….

The Awakening associated with Enlightenment in the traditions of Buddhism is an Awakening to the native and natural state of awareness prior to identification with mind [small "m"]…. Once the position of simple awareness is established as the native state [e.g., with Dzogchen] (rather than the conventions of the body-mind-self), then the ultimate "Nature" [*tathagatagarbha*] of mind and body and world events suddenly becomes obvious in the form of a tacit or "mindless" intuition [*prajna*]…. In that native or natural state, which is unqualified or, as a Buddhist would say, Void or Empty [*sunya*] (since it adds nothing to what is spontaneously arising), there is blissful clarity in which the "Nature" of Nature is obvious.[91]

Only with this Awakening (epitomized in the Seventh Stage of Life) are "samsara and Nirvana the same"—One Taste, Nondual Prior Unity. With this understanding, therefore, it would be an error to think that the Enlightened being simply "returns" to the conventional world—or "enters the market-place"—as just a better person, more playful perhaps, after Enlightenment. Rather, the conventional mind of ego-I has been totally transcended so self-identity radically changes. "You" do not return; "you" (the ego-I) has been liberated from previous illusions and ignorance. "You" now know God or Buddha-Nature or Consciousness Itself as Divine and Transcendental (as *tathagata* or "gone beyond"). Enlightenment (or God-Realization) is about recognizing that samsara (the gross-physical world) is ultimately arising *within* Nirvana, of seeing its nonbinding power, its non-necessity. Therefore, it is not simply a matter of returning to the conventional world as a regular person (with the same ordinary desires after Enlightenment). Sure, the same phenomena of the world are seen to arise spontaneously, but there is not the normal (or average-mode) reactivity of the ego that is involved. Rather, love and compassion are freely given in the embrace of reality as It IS, which at its heart is Love-Bliss.

The "Talking School" of unrealized scholars, especially in the Omega-West, might like to equate (or reduce) these esoteric formulae into a "nondual" soup of "oneness" or "sameness" based on reading certain texts as a justification for merely accepting the world as it is. Which means, unfortunately, not having to seriously practice sadhana or engage in Guru Yoga and to really *discipline* the self in renunciation, but rather to simply "follow our bliss" (in Joseph Campbell's words). However, it's *only* in (and *after*) the Enlightened State is realized that Nirvana and samsara are seen (and known) to be "the same" (or "not-two")—One Taste—though by definition they are total opposites. Therefore, only a Seventh Stage Adept-Realizer can truly enlighten us about this paradoxical quagmire:

> The Seventh Stage of Life is not what one might feel is suggested from the literature of ["premonitory"] Seventh Stage Adepts. One might expect at least in some cases or on some occasions, some sort of return to the conventional world. A great deal of ill-considered scholarly literature strives to interpret wisdom as some sort of return to the conventional involvement with samsara.
>
> In the Seventh Stage Awakening the Self, the Transcendental Reality, or Nirvana, is not discriminated from objects, from samsara, from conventional existences, from the ego. Rather, samsara, the ego, the body-mind, and all relations are tacitly recognized to be nothing but the Nirvanic Self, nothing but a moment of It. What is unique in the Seventh Stage of Life, therefore, is the *recognizability of samsara, not the return to samsara*.[92]

Overall, as we've seen, the tradition of the Guru-devotee relationship—grounded in Enlightenment or Nondual Mysticism—is absolutely fundamental to Buddhism (as it is in Hinduism) for this is how we learn to be grounded in disciplined spiritual practices coupled with serious time sitting quietly in meditation (or being still). Both the outer and inner life must be integrated with Right Action and Right Life founded in Right View. Therefore, true Buddhism that is based in Right Devotion (*bodhicitta*) is dedicated with a serious ego-transcending commitment (under vows) to tame the mind and calm the emotions. As all Zen students and Buddhist practitioners quickly find out (especially in Western countries) this is difficult and concentrated work (*sadhana*) though it's also pervaded by humor and love. Obviously, then, the assistance of a Spiritual Teacher and Master, a genuine Guru-Adept, becomes indispensable for there is no more difficult task than transcending the ego and the illusions of samsara (and maya).

Adi Da, once again, brilliantly offers his enlightened insight on these topics taking us far beyond the conventional mind or even the research of university-trained scholars:

> [In Enlightened Buddhism] "samsara" is not a problem, and, there-
> fore, "Nirvana" is not needed as a solution. In place of conventional
> attachment to phenomena ("samsara") or the absence of phenomena
> ("Nirvana") there is the native state of no-contraction, no-reaction,
> no-mind, no-clinging, no-aversion. And the "mood" of such En-
> lightenment is naturally associated with the native state of being. It
> is the blissful mood of innate freedom, in which phenomenal con-
> ditions are naturally or spontaneously permitted (neither sought nor
> suppressed) as a pure or mere event, without binding implications.
> On the basis of this pre-mental [or trans-mental] and pre-egoic [or
> trans-egoic] equanimity, the intuition ultimately arises that all phe-
> nomenon are a display or spontaneous modification of inherently
> Radiant Transcendental Being [or Real God and Buddha-Nature].[93]

Zen Buddhism—as representing the Enlightened person in the world—is about being a natural human being living with graceful creativity and tolerant compassion arising from the Awakened or Enlightened State-Stage of aware-ness—*Wu Wei*. The Master-devotee relationship, whether with Guru Yoga (in Tibet), Satsang (in India), or with Zen (in China-Japan), and also with Adidam Ruchiradam, etc., arises from Divine Enlightenment as being the fundamental moral compass or ground, not just a far-off goal. Being Divinely Awake as the Heart is what best guides the entire process of living a human life on Earth—living a Divine Life—until the day we die… and beyond. Indeed, we might say, it is living in the Pure Land—or "Buddhaverse"— present right now.

POPULAR BUDDHISM:
PURE LAND BUDDHA

Naturally, Buddhism became an exoteric religion for the "average-mode" masses as well, not just esoteric disciplines practiced by "advanced-tip" individuals cloistered in secluded monasteries or mountain caves. By the 3rd century BCE, a few centuries after Buddha died, the northern Indian emperor **Asoka** (reign 268–232 BCE) of the Mauryan dynasty converted to Buddhism after renouncing the violence that had gained him his empire [see Chapter 16]. Consequently, he helped spread Buddhism throughout India by building temples and shrines, including his famous stone pillars etched with Buddhist edicts and inscriptions proclaiming the Dharma far and wide to guide the common people toward benevolence and wisdom. Within centuries the popularity of Buddhism had spread to Southeast and Northern Asia, while now it encircles the globe and has even penetrated the Western mind.

Pure Land Buddhism, based mostly on the *Lotus Sutra* (written ca. 100–200 CE), became very popular in East Asia among the common people stretching from Kashmir to Mongolia to Tibet, from China to Japan and Korea, from Sri Lanka to Laos, Cambodia, Thailand, Vietnam, Indonesia, and other neighboring countries. Today it is the most widely practiced form of popular Buddhism in Asia with its ceremonial rituals and chanting (as prayers), even reaching into the lands of the West, especially among emigrant Asians. Its moral precepts, such as giving, morality, patience, energy, concentration, and prayers, are highly valued to maintain an honorable and peaceful community from village to nation-state.

Interestingly, Pure Land Buddhism also has a deity—a "personal" God—called *Amitabha*, a celestial "Buddha of Immeasurable Light and Life" who is radiant and all-pervading (hence will "answer" prayers or positive intentions). This visionary archetype is behind many exoteric rites and ceremonial prayers in the conventional and larger Buddhist community throughout Asia and the Western world. Radiant light-filled images and statues, shrines and temples of

Amitabha abound throughout much of Buddhist Asia. Amitabha is known for his attribute of longevity, the magnetizing red of fire and pure perception grounded in the deep emptiness of all phenomena thus possessing and dispensing infinite merits to which the people call upon and pray. Based on the *Larger Sutra of Infinite Life*, as it's known throughout East Asia, this popular and conventional form of Buddhism is based on the desire to be reborn in Amitabha's "**Pure Land**" heaven realms until Buddhahood is finally achieved.

In Japan, **Nichiren Buddhism** established by **Nichiren** (1222–1282) uses the chant "***namu myōhō renge kyō***" to gain prosperity and benefit, thus it has gained popularity in the West and among celebrities. Once again, this approach appeals more to exoteric fulfillment and desires for peace rather than an authentic esoteric transformation of consciousness. Grounded in the Pure Land's *Lotus Sutra* that claims people already have Buddha-Nature thus everyone can be enlightened in this lifetime, it is a noble aspiration, indeed, yet in reality this takes more than chanting or positive prayers.

Buddhism, like other religions, includes both *exoteric* (or "outer-directed") religious forms for the average-mode conventional masses to use, while also maintaining an *esoteric* (or "inner-directed") form for advanced-tip practitioners of meditation, whether done in people's homes or in monasteries or on mountaintops. The Buddha, one of the most revered and loved figures in human history continues to teach and enlighten generation after generation of living beings on how to fulfill their highest potential and be free of suffering. Indeed, it is said, the Buddha and celestial Buddhas everywhere—"more than all the grains of sand on the banks of the Ganges" (as their *Sutras* like to say)—teach the Dharma in all universes endlessly until all beings are Enlightened to exist in the Pure Land of Infinite Light forever hereafter. Thus have I heard.

The importance of Buddhism as adapted by many Westerners, however, has been to focus more on the philosophical (and esoteric) aspects of this great Enlightenment Tradition. Now, in the 21st century, any individual can access and use these various visions and teachings about re-discovering our innate Buddhahood. Meditation proliferates; Sanghas expand and grow; new generations learn the Timeless Wisdom. They have been handed down from the wise and compassionate Buddhist Masters, the Guru-Adepts and Rinpoche-Lamas, et al., to further one's spiritual growth until Enlightenment or Buddhahood is finally (and permanently) achieved and fully realized. Nonetheless, we must always remember that the entire breadth and span of worldwide Buddhism originated from the simple, natural enlightened mind and compassionate heart of one Awakened Adept-Guru, Shakyamuni Gautama Buddha, a once-living human Avatar, a baby, a prince, an ascetic, a Buddha. To this great Gift of Wisdom-Transmission handed down through posterity from all Enlightened Buddhas, we reverentially prostrate. Thus have I seen.

Mindfulness: Wisdom-Training

In the modern West, Buddhism appeals to millions simply because of its strong ethical and moral "**mind-training**" exercises, such as **Mindfulness** (which is very popular today, even in the corporate business culture). These practices develop compassion and loving kindness, wisdom, and understanding by releasing afflictive emotions and strong attachments to mind-stuff, all qualities the modern world (and modern self) needs in abundance. For example, part of Buddhism's universal appeal that is common to all religions is its ethics of concern, compassion, and love for others (humans and non-humans). This approach involves the basic ethical practices found within the Buddha's **Eightfold Noble Path** (the "Fourth Noble Truth") summarized below as including:

- **Wisdom Training** (*Prajna*): (1) Right View, (2) Right Intentions;
- **Ethics** (*Sila*): (3) Right Speech, (4) Right Action, (5) Right Livelihood;
- **Meditative Awareness** (*Samadhi*): (6) Right Effort, (7) Right Mindfulness, and (8) Right Concentration (i.e., Meditation).[94]

Buddhism, in other words, is not just about "Buddhism" as a religion, or even the "Buddha" as a person, nor about bringing in converts to the faith for it has no evangelical aspect beyond acknowledging that people need to see beyond illusions and awaken to our true nature (which is "God" or "Buddha-Nature," by whatever name). If you want to be like Buddha, do like Buddha! This is what studying "**The Buddha**," the great Axial Age Adept-Realizer provides anyone, even in today's emerging Integral Age (perhaps, the second Axial Age). Now, in the modern global culture of the 21st century, the opening of the Third Millennium, the Buddha is again being recognized as one of the world's primary Guru-Adepts or Enlightened World-Teachers of human history. Buddhism as a religion includes the vast community of monastic monks and nuns (the Sangha), as well as hundreds of millions of laypeople, who are all trying to practice compassion and meditate on wisdom (and self-transcendence) even in today's interconnected world of consumerism and economic-politics, the "**Internet of Jewels**," so to speak.

This is a large part of the reason for Buddhism's eager acceptance in the West today. In prophetic terms, it has been said the "swans" of the East—the Enlightened Adepts of Buddhism—have come to the "lakes" (or lands) of the West since Buddhism now thrives in North, South, and Central America, in Europe and Russia, even in the Middle East and Africa, let alone Australia and New Zealand, as well as in Asia (and elsewhere throughout the world), wherever human beings live and interact.[95] The Dalai Lama thus summarized: "We must complement the human rights ideal by developing a widespread practice of universal human responsibility. This is not a religious matter. It arises from what I call the '**Common Human Religion**'—that of love, the will to other's happiness, and compassion, the will to other's freedom from suffering."[96] The Light of Buddha touches all (and everyone) who looks for Light and Truth, as any genuine Guru shall do too, for they highlight our own Buddha-Nature, our Divine Condition, and the truth of who we really are.

The Buddha as a global icon and humble monk also demonstrates the role of a World-Teacher, or *Jagad Guru* (in Sanskrit), an Enlightened Spiritual Master of the highest attainment teaching millions of modern people. Some who do not even believe in traditional religions because they are scientifically-oriented and rational, find themselves attracted to Buddha. Yet this is not a contradiction because Buddhism has no problem with science as a method of knowledge acquisition (as the Dalia Lama shows); it is only critical of scientism as a reductionistic philosophy of materialism. Buddhism is, therefore, a *universal "religion"* because its precepts involve *universal truths* (or deep structures) that apply to everyone pursuing their inner development to Divine God-Realization (or Enlightenment).

For more than twenty-five centuries we have seen a peaceful lineage of Enlightened "Buddhas"—or Adept-Realizers—who have left a long trail of Enlightened Teachings currently being translated into numerous languages for all people regardless of culture, race, or creed to read, study, and practice long into the future. These are the sacred "jewels" in the Divine Library of the Great Tradition of Global Wisdom, the wisdom texts of the world's inherited Perennial Philosophy. Such gifts are the god-like signs of a real authentic Great Guru born over twenty-five centuries ago appearing in human existence to Enlighten everyone the world over. It's a fraternity which the Buddha helped establish as one of its leading lights spawning countless other "Buddhas" (or Awakened Adepts) to follow him—and it is a lineage, I maintain, to which Avatar Adi Da Samraj also rightly belongs, the Ruchira ("Bright") Buddha, born over two and a half millennia later to bring the same essential Dharma of Enlightenment to all beings, to everyone (as we'll see in Part III). But first, let's turn to the Buddha's profound influence on the high plateau of Tibet.

SĀDHU

⬡

Chapter 17 Endnotes

1. See: Adi Da Samraj [Da Free John], *Nirvanasara* (1982), p. 173.

2. Lama Surya Das, *Awakening the Buddha Within* (1997), p. 105.

3. Adi Da Samraj [Da Free John], *Nirvanasara* (1982), p. 175.

4. Tathagata Buddha, *The Diamond Sutra* (1969) trans. by A.F. Price and Wong Mou-Lam, pp. 61-62.

5. See: Huston Smith and Philip Novak, *Buddhism: A Concise Introduction* (2003, SF: HarperSanFrancisco), p. 65.

6. Adi Da Samraj [Da Free John], "The Three Ways of Buddhism" in *Nirvanasara* (1982), pp. 139-140 [bold added].

7. Huston Smith and Philip Novak, *Buddhism: A Concise Introduction* (2003), p. 65.

8. Adi Da Samraj [Da Free John], "The Seventh School of God-Talk" (talk) in "Preface" to *The Song of the Self Supreme: Astavakra Gita* (1982), pp. 60-61.

9. Ibid., pp. 60-61.

10. Ibid., p. 57.

11. Ken Wilber, *Sex, Ecology, Spirituality* (1995), pp. 691-692, 1n.

12. Ibid., p. 692, 1n.

13. See: T. R. V. Murti, *The Central Philosophy of Buddhism* (1955), p. 86.

14. Ibid., p. 264; also see: Ken Wilber, *Sex, Ecology, Spirituality* (1995), pp. 696-697 [where I have used Wilber's bracketing].

15. Ken Wilber, *One Taste* (1999), p. 107.

16. Adi Da Samraj [Da Free John], "The Seventh School of God-Talk" (talk) in "Preface" to *The Song of the Self Supreme: Astavakra Gita* (1982), pp. 57-59.

17. Ken Wilber, *Sex, Ecology, Spirituality* (1995), p. 695, 1n.

18. T. R. V. Murti, *The Central Philosophy of Buddhism* (1955), p. 237.

19. Ken Wilber, *Sex, Ecology, Spirituality* (1995), p. 696, 1n.

20. Adi Da Samraj [Da Free John], *Nirvanasara* (1982), pp. 135-136.

21. See: Ken Wilber, *The Fourth Turning: Imagining the Evolution of an Integral Buddhism* (2004, Kindle only); *Integral Buddhism and the Future of Spirituality* (2018); *The Religion of Tomorrow: A Vision for the Future of the Great Traditions* (2017).

22. Gautama Buddha quoted in *Buddhism: A Concise Introduction* (2003) by Huston Smith and Philip Novak, p. 65.

23. Gautama Buddha, *The Diamond Sutra* (1969) trans. by A.F. Price and Wong Mou-Lam, p. 53.

24. See: Robert A. F. Thurman, "Foreword" in *Mother of the Buddhas: Meditation on the Prajnaparamita Sutras* (1993) by Lex Hixon, pp. x-xi.

25. See: *The Divine Library* (1992) by Rufus Camphausen, p. 91.

26. Lex Hixon, *Mother of the Buddhas: Meditation on the Prajnaparamita Sutras* (1993), p. 3.

27. T. R. V. Murti, *The Central Philosophy of Buddhism* (1955, New Delhi, India: HarperCollins), p. 83.

28. Ken Wilber, *Up from Eden* (1982), p. 311n [Adi Da's terms have been added to assist in clarification].

29. Lex Hixon, *Mother of the Buddhas: Meditation on the Prajnaparamita Sutras* (1993), p. 4.

30. Robert A. F. Thurman, Foreword in *The Mother of the Buddhas: Meditation on the Prajnaparamita Sutra* (1993) by Lex Hixon, p. xiii.

31. Lex Hixon, *Mother of the Buddhas: Meditation on the Prajnaparamita Sutras* (1993), p. 6.

32. See: Robert A. F. Thurman, "Foreword" in *Mother of the Buddhas: Meditation on the Prajnaparamita Sutras* (1993) by Lex Hixon, p. xiii.

33. Ibid., p. xiii.

34. Ibid., p. xiv.

35. T. R. V. Murti, *The Central Philosophy of Buddhism* (1955), p. 58.

36. Garma C. C. Chang, *The Buddhist Teaching of Totality: The Philosophy of Hwa Yen Buddhism* (1994, Pennsylvania State University Press), p. 60.

37. Adi Da Samraj [Da Free John], "The Seventh School of God-Talk" (talk) in "Preface" to *The Song of the Self Supreme: Astavakra Gita* (1982), p. 62.

38 Robert A. F. Thurman, *The Holy Teaching of Vimalakirti* (1992), p. 2.

39. See: *In Praise of Dharmadhatu by Nagarjuna* (2007) translated by Karl Brunnholzl; *The Fundamental Wisdom of the Middle Way* (1995) translated by Jay Garfield; *Verses From the Center* (2000) by Stephen Batchelor.

40. Adi Da Samraj [Da Free John], "The Seventh School of God-Talk" (talk) in "Preface" to *The Song of the Self Supreme: Astavakra Gita* (1982), pp. 59, 62 ["Stages of Life" capped plus "Sixth Stage and 'premonitory'" has been added to conform with Adi Da's later revisions to the Sixth and Seventh Stages of Life descriptions; see: Chapter 19].

41. Robert A. F. Thurman, "Foreword" in *Mother of the Buddhas: Meditation on the Prajnaparamita Sutras* (1993) by Lex Hixon, p. xvii.

42. Ken Wilber, The Religion of Tomorrow (2017), p. 23.

43. See: Nagarjuna, *Mūlamadhyamakakārikā (Sanskrit) or Fundamental Verses on the Middle Way* (various translations).

44. Lex Hixon, *Mother of the Buddhas: Meditation on the Prajnaparamita Sutras* (1993), p. 9.

45. Robert A. F. Thurman, *The Holy Teaching of Vimalakirti* (1992), p. 1.

46. Ken Wilber, *Sex, Ecology, Spirituality* (1995), p. 723, 4n.

47. Ken Wilber, *Eye to Eye* (1983, 1990), p. 167; *Quantum Questions* (1984), p. 27n.

48. Ken Wilber, *One Taste* (1999), p. viii.

49. See: *Clear Light of Bliss* (1982, 1995) by Geshe Kelsang Gyatso.

50. T. R. V. Murti, *The Central Philosophy of Buddhism* (1955), p. 107.

51. Lama Surya Das, *Awakening the Buddha Within* (1997), p. 18.

52. See: Garma C. C. Chang, *The Practice of Zen* (1959), p. 13, 17.

53. Shen Tsan, in Garma C. C. Chang, *The Practice of Zen* (1959), p. 20.

54. See, for example: *A Buddhist Bible: The Favorite Scriptures of the Zen Sect* (1938, 1963, 1970, 2010), edited by Dwight Goddard, is a wonderful collection and very readable; being first published 1938 it was a favorite text for the emerging Beat generation in the 1040s and '50s, such as for Jack Kerouac, Alan Ginsberg, Gary Snyder, et al.

55. See: Garma C. C. Chang, *The Buddhist Teaching of Totality: The Philosophy of Hwa Yen Buddhism* (1994).

56. See: T. R. V. Murti, *The Central Philosophy of Buddhism* (1955), p. 107.

57. Ibid., p. 106.

58. Ben Connelly, *Inside Vasubandhu's Yogacara: A Practitioner's Guide* (2016), pp. 2, 4.

59. Adi Da Samraj [Da Free John], *Nirvanasara* (1982), p. 71 ["Stages of Life" are capped].

60. Adi Da Samraj [Da Free John], "The Seventh School of God-Talk" (talk) in "Preface" to *The Song of the Self Supreme: Astavakra Gita* (1982), pp. 59, 63 ["Stages of Life" capped].

61. See: Shantideva, *The Way of the Bodhisattva* (1997) translated by the Padmakara Translation Group, p. 3.

62. Adi Da Samraj [Da Free John], "The Seventh School of God-Talk" (talk) in "Preface" to *The Song of the Self Supreme: Astavakra Gita* (1982), p. 66.

63. Ibid., pp. 61-62 [italics added].

64. Garma C. C. Chang, *The Practice of Zen* (1959), pp. 7-8, 11, 15 [italics added].

65. See: Dwight Goddard, *A Buddhist Bible* (1938, 1970), p. 671.

66. Adi Da Samraj [Da Free John], "The Seventh School of God-Talk" (talk) in "Preface" to *The Song of the Self Supreme: Astavakra Gita* (1982), p. 43.

67. See: Dwight Goddard, *A Buddhist Bible* (1938, 1970), p. 674.

68. Ibid., p. 674 [italics added].

69. See: Meido Moore, *Hidden Zen : Practices for Sudden Awakening & Embodied Realization* (2020, Boston: Shambhala Publications), p. 2, 281.

70. Garma C. C. Chang, *The Practice of Zen* (1959), p. 52.

71. Ibid., p. 54 [italics in original].

72. *The Encyclopedia of Eastern Philosophy and Religions* (1994) by Shambhala Publications, p. 292.

73. See: Ken Wilber, et al, *Spiritual Choices* (1987), p. 249.

74. Garma C. C. Chang, *The Practice of Zen* (1959), p. 51 [italics in original].

75. See: D. T. Suzuki, *Manual of Zen Buddhism* (1960), pp. 127-128.

76. Ibid., p. 128.

77. See: *Chop Wood, Carry Water: A Guide to Finding Spiritual Fulfillment* (1984) by Rick Fields.

78. Pang Wen quoted in *The Practice of Zen* (1959) by Garma C. C. Chang, p. 54.

79. Garma C. C. Chang, *The Practice of Zen* (1959), p. 54.

80. *The Sutra of Hui Neng* (1969) trans. by A.F. Price and Wong Mou-Lam, pp. 19-20.

81. Huang Po quoted in *The Practice of Zen* (1959) by Garma C. C. Chang, p. 18.

82. Adi Da Samraj [Da Free John], "The Seventh School of God-Talk" (talk) in "Preface" to *The Song of the Self Supreme: Astavakra Gita* (1982), p. 64.

83. Adi Da Samraj [Da Free John], *Nirvanasara* (1982), p. 220.

84. Ibid., p. 221.

85. Nagarjuna from *Mulamadhyamakakarikah*; see: *The Experience of Buddhism: Sources and Interpretations* (1994, Wadsworth Publishing) by John S. Strong.

86. Adi Da Samraj [Da Free John], *Nirvanasara* (1982), pp. 148-149 [italics added].

87. Ibid., p. 131.

88. Ibid., p. 108.

89. Ibid., p. 161.

90. Ibid., p. 149.

91. Ibid., pp. 209-211 [emphasis added].

92. Adi Da Samraj [Da Free John], "The Seventh School of God-Talk" (talk) in "Preface" to *The Song of the Self Supreme: Astavakra Gita* (1982), pp. 43-44 ["Stages of Life" capped; emphasis added].

93. Adi Da Samraj [Da Free John], *Nirvanasara* (1982), pp. 209-211.

94. See: Lama Surya Das, *Awakening the Buddha Within* (1997), p. 93, for an excellent summary of these Buddhist practices for modern people.

95. See: Rick Fields, *How the Swans Came to the Lake* (1981, 1992).

96. Dalai Lama quoted in *How the Swans Came to the Lake* (1981, 1992) by Rick Fields, p. 379, from remarks on accepting the Raul Wallenberg Congressional Human Rights Award, June 1989, in Buddhist Peace Fellowship Newsletter, Fall 1989, p. 4.

EIGHTEEN

GURU YOGA-SATSANG:
TIBETAN VAJRAYANA

GURU YOGA:
MAHA-SIDDHAS

In Tibet the "Guru" becomes the "*Lama*" (Tibetan for "unsurpassed" or "none above") as their history is resplendent with enlightened beings who show their students how to achieve Enlightenment then go on to grace succeeding generations. The most powerful Gurus and Lamas, in both India and Tibet, have been called the "**Maha-Siddhas**," literally, "Great Adepts" (*maha* is "great," in Sanskrit). A *Siddha* or "perfected one" is an individual, both women and men, who has achieved not only Enlightenment but who has also acquired *siddhis* or psychic powers and special spiritual abilities. These are only gained through a strict regime of *sadhana* ("spiritual practice") under the guidance of a thoroughly competent Guru-Adept. Importantly, many Maha-Siddhas were *Tantrikas* or practitioners of yoga and tantra initiated under the guidance of their revered Lama or Guru. Throughout the Medieval Period of Buddhism (3rd –13th century CE) the historical influence of these Great Adepts spread throughout the Indian subcontinent and Himalayas to reach mythic proportions codified in colorful hagiographies (*namtars*) and embodied in their ecstatic songs of Enlightened Realization.[1]

Mount Kailash   **Potala Palace**, Lhasa, Tibet

It was the Maha-Siddhas of **Tibetan Vajrayana Buddhism** who established Dzogchen and Mahamudra, for example, some of the most esoteric traditions in all of Buddhism (and the Great Tradition). **Tibet** (probably from the Mongolian word *Thubet*)—also called "Kangchen" or "the Land of Snows"—is the highest country on the planet located in the Himalayas with an average elevation of 14,300 feet; people live at an average of 8,900 feet (2700 meters), and Lhasa, its capital since ancient times, is 11,995 feet (3600 meters) above sea level. **Mount Everest**, the highest point on Earth (29,031 feet; 8848 meters;), is located in Tibet, as is **Mount Kailash** (21,778 feet; 6638 meters), the abode of Shiva for the Yogis of India and the land of many meditation caves for the Maha-Siddhas. Circumambulating the sacred mountain of Kailash is a pilgrimage of a lifetime, a journey towards Enlightenment (if undertaken with the right guidance).[2] American Buddhist scholar Robert Thurman reveals: "For a thousand years, Kailash has been a magnet for Tantric Practice, the special, accelerated path designed for the extremists of the Dharma."[3] The previous capital of Tibet (until the Chinese invasion of 1950) was **Lhasa** where the Potala Palace, the winter palace of the Dalai Lamas from 1649 to 1959, is located. It is (or was) one of the most stunning temples on Earth.

Tibetan culture evolved into one the most highly-revered and sacred nations of humankind (until the China takeover systematically attempted to destroy its culture). Their Buddhist religion covers the full range of consciousness: from shamans to mystics, from farmers to priests, from monastic renunciates to lay people to eccentric tantrikas, from herding to craftsmen, etc., a unique admixture of the world's highest teachings, as Swami Abhayananda summarizes: "Tibetan Buddhism was compounded of the shamanism of [the tribal folk religions, such as with the Zhang-Zhung], the mythology of the Vedas, the non-dualism of the Upanishads, the ideals of the Buddha, and the disciplines of Yoga and Tantra."[4] Mixed together, that is, with the genius arising from some of the world's brightest Guru-Adepts or Maha-Siddhas.

These "Great Adepts" of India and Tibet have come down to posterity as the "**Eighty-Four Maha-Siddhas**" (a list first compiled by the 12th century Indian scholar Abhayadatta Sri) accompanied with intriguing, inspiring biographies of their incredible lives and dedication to Enlightenment. There have certainly been more since, as one scholar explains: "[They] can be seen as archetypes representing the thousands of exemplars and Adepts of the tantric way."[5] Significantly, these Master-Adepts arose from a remarkable diversity of social roles and family backgrounds, from kings and ministers, priests and yogis, poets and musicians, craftsmen and farmers, housewives and whores, men and women (*dakinis*).[6] Professor Thurman clarifies their historical significance:

> It was in the second half of the first millennium CE, when the Enlightenment movement, which had always maintained the value of the individual, clearly took a new turn. A new breed of spiritual heroes and heroines arose in India: the world-transforming Maha -Siddhas, or Great Adepts.

The Great Adepts, whether kings or washermen, began as people who had reached a point in their evolutionary progress where they were excruciatingly aware of the priceless opportunity of a human lifetime. They were intelligent enough to know that a life lived just for the sake of eating, working, procreating, and seeking sense pleasures is a waste of time... They sought to attain Buddhahood in the immediate context of this life.

The Buddha is said to have manifested in special male and female forms [Maha-Siddhas] to teach such urgent bodhisattvas the esoteric Tantric Vehicle or Diamond Vehicle [Vajrayana Buddhism], the technological or apocalyptic vehicle of immediate revelation and immediate transformation.[7]

Thurman, for one, calls them "psychonauts" (similar to astronauts but exploring the interior spaces of the psyche)—the "**World-Taming Adepts**"—who practice an "Inner Science" (*adhyatmavidya*) of advanced yogic and meditation practices.[8] The American Buddhist pandit explains: "By becoming a being of radiant blissfulness, a Bodhisattva is a living instrument that can effectively bring about the aim of all true love—the happiness of infinite beloved others. This goodwill moves to tame the whole society, the whole world, even the universe so that it becomes a place in which the maximum number of people can attain the highest level of happiness—a Buddhaland or Buddhaverse."[9] Thurman calls for everyone to follow in their footsteps to generate an "inner revolution," the only true way to world peace and happiness, as he wonderfully explains in his book *Inner Revolution: Life, Liberty, and the Pursuit of Real Happiness* (1998):

The enlightened individual is called a buddha. Shakyamuni Buddha was not simply a historical figure who lived and taught 2,500 years ago—he is an example of the full flowering of human potential, reached by undergoing inner revolutions, coups of the spirit in which the power of negative impulses and emotions is toppled and we are freed to be as happy, good, and compassionate as we can evolve to be. The Buddha developed an inner science for achieving this revolution [in consciousness and culture].[10]

In Buddhism, the "Buddha" appears in all levels of existence, in all three major sheaths (or "bodies") and states of consciousness. This is the *Trikaya* doctrine or "three bodies" or *kayas* ("bodies," in Sanskrit) representing the gross-physical, the subtle-dreamlike, and formless causal dimensions or manifestations of Reality (a doctrine somewhat similar to Vedanta's five *koshas* or sheaths):

1. <u>Dharmakaya</u> (causal-deep sleep state) — formless causal body, the "Truth" body of Reality Itself, referring to Ultimate Reality (*Dharmadhatu*), Buddha-Nature, Pure Being, Emptiness, akin to Nirguna (formless) Brahman; realm of all the Buddhas (and Enlightened beings);

2. <u>Sambhogakaya</u> (subtle-dreaming visionary state) — subtle realm body, the "Enjoyment (or Bliss)" body, the sixth "third eye" (*ajna*) to seventh crown (*sahasrara*) chakras, referring to higher subtle and visionary realms of the inner mind, akin to Saguna (with form) Brahman; deity Buddhas, archetypal forms used in Deity and Dream Yoga;

3. <u>Nirmanakaya</u> (gross-physical waking state) — physical human body, "Transformation (or Appearance)" body, the historical Buddha; living human Adept-Realizers, and Siddha-Gurus manifesting in gross-physical form for the transformation of consciousness in others.

4. <u>Svabhavikakaya</u> (nondual integration) — Ken Wilber (along with Mahayana-Vajrayana) likes to use this term to indicate the nondual union (or embrace) of all three bodies possessed by a Buddha.

Strictly speaking, the Dharmakaya refers to the causal meaning unmanifest emptiness, beyond form, the Ground of Being (of Buddha-Nature), pure formlessness, thus indicating the very subtle difference between the formless causal realm of the Witness and the nondual realm of One Taste (where "samsara and nirvana are the same"). These gross-to-subtle-to-causal bodies are the esoteric secret behind Guru Yoga-Satsang: the **Nirmanakaya Guru** is the physical person with personality, conditioned by culture and birth, who can have faults or weaknesses (e.g., getting sick, injured), etc.; the **Sambhogakaya Guru** works in dream and visionary states that activate subtle energy channels in the esoteric anatomy of the devotee-practitioner; the **Dharmakaya Guru** reveals the Transcendental  Truth (arising from the "clear light" in "the indestructible drop of the heart") beyond form or historical manifestation. This is why, for example, when Adi Da (or any Guru) says meditate on "Me" or "turn to Me" he is referring to the Dharmakaya body, the Reality beyond and behind (and embracing) all forms, the Prior Unity of Divine Being as Conscious Light.

These Mind-Taming Adepts, in full flight with all three "bodies" of the Trikaya, practice not only as disciplined renunciates but they also use advanced methods such as **Dream Yoga** or other subtle realm visualization techniques like with **Deity Yoga**, yet all these practices are set within the context of **Guru Yoga**. Importantly, they often pursued these radical practices outside the settled monasteries, abandoning the monastic life to practice in the mountain caves and wild forests surrounding the villages of India and Tibet, sometimes being lay people (leaving jobs and families).[11] They often were itinerant wanderers and mendicants viewed by most people as marginalized failures or "crazy."[12] It is from them that the phrase "**Crazy Wisdom**" comes from, even still used today. Avatar Adi Da Samraj, therefore, rightly puts them in their place:

> Some Adepts in the [Sixth and "premonitory"] Seventh Stage [of Life] have a kind of "crazy" aspect. They behave in an unconventional manner as a sign of their transcendence of the discriminative mind

that is always differentiating between what is Spiritual and what is not, what is Nirvana and what is samsara, discriminating between interior and exterior, mind and body, subtle and gross. Just as the unique literature of the ["premonitory"] Seventh Stage is playfully and humorously free of all the conditional approaches of the earlier Stages [of Life], similarly the biographies of Adepts of the Seventh Stage very often describe "crazy wisdom."

The behavior of such individuals, in other words, seems to betray the earlier stages, does not seem to take seriously the rules, the disciplines, the point of view, the philosophies of the earlier Stages of Life. Of course—the transcendence of all of that is what God-Realization is about! But these Adepts have not ceased to be spiritual. The Adepts must be understood, yet they cannot be understood directly. They can be valued within a traditional context that values ultimate wisdom [like Vajrayana Buddhism], but you cannot understand them without transcending yourself.[13]

Notice, the American-born Adept tells us that "you cannot understand them without transcending yourself." This is a call for everyone to *do the yoga*, to take up the practice (or sadhana) of Guru Yoga-Satsang and engage the Realization of Enlightenment (or God-Awareness), not just be amused by their outrageous stories. Adi Da continues: "In the play of the Crazy Adept with devotees, they are simply confounded, not dissuaded from their disciplines, but attracted toward its ultimate fulfillment."[14] Indeed, the path of ego-transcendence and Enlightenment is a difficult road—like treading "a razor's edge" (as the *Upanishads* say)—thus this process is not generally acknowledged (or appreciated) in the conventional world, even among religious seekers who tend to be *exoteric* or "outer-directed" (involved with the lesser Stages of Life) and "following the rules" (of the rule/role or traditional/religious mind) [see Appendix I].

Nevertheless, only the true Enlightened Way of the Heart

reveals the Truth to life and existence, not just exaggerated eccentricities. Everyone is called to *realize* for oneself, to know God for real—not just via ideas, beliefs, or faith—but as a *direct experience* (verified by the community of the like-minded). The great Guru-Adepts, the uncompromising Maha-Siddhas and their biographies and "Crazy" Teachings are meant to inspire, to humor one beyond self-boundaries, but first you must listen and hear… then you may see the truth behind their Crazy Wisdom.

CRAZY WISDOM ADEPTS

From these Maha-Siddhas, who initially arose from northern India to later become highly honored in Tibetan legends, came the "**Crazy Wisdom**" tradition often talked about today in arousing fears and suspicion of certain Guru's spiritual authenticity. Humorously, many of the Eighty-Four Maha-Siddhas, women and men alike, had "crazy" titles attached to their names, such as the "Avaricious Hermit," the "Rejected Wastrel," the "Handsome Fool," the "Free Lover," old "One-Eyed," "Siddha Two-Teeth," the "Lucky Beggar," the "Revitalized Drone," the "Envious God," the "Wise Washerman," "Tiger Rider," "Exiled Loud Mouth," "Peasant Guru," "Royal Hedonist," "Enlightened Moron,"

Bodhidharma

and so on. Both the Indian Hindu and Tibetan Buddhist traditions honor the number "eighty-four" with some overlap between the two lists. Importantly, for the most part they lived outside the monasteries so were unconventional or "crazy" to those in conventional society (even in Tibet).

Their powerful siddhis and psychic powers make for compelling stories and life lessons as well as making their way into thangka paintings created in the monasteries. Consequently, many of the meditative methods and yogic practices used by these "Crazy" but Enlightened Adepts were codified into the "**Tantras**" of Buddhist literature and practices. Their methods might be unorthodox or seem like madness but they arise from great human freedom and humor as well as with deep love and compassion. Thus, Crazy-Wise Adi Da explains:

> The Maha-Siddhas, the "Crazy" Siddhas, are humorous, not only about ordinary life, but also about extraordinary life. They are humorous about miracles and humorous about lunch. Even so, the point of view that is of greatest or most fundamental value in the disposition of the Maha-Siddhas is this [Enlightened] freedom. They are simply, paradoxically, humorously playing with individuals to point to this ultimate freedom.[15]

Even so, in every case, no aspect is more crucial to the Vajrayana Buddhist tradition than the supreme importance of the genuine Guru, the Enlightened Master. They were all powerful Yogis and blazingly compassionate (even if "crazy") Adepts demonstrating the true efficiency and efficacy of Guru Yoga needed to generate enlightened divine insight in others. Nonetheless, we must learn to discriminate the various Stages of Life each of these Adepts tend to teach from. Although most all them are always pointing to the highest state-stage of Nondual Mysticism (Sixth and Seventh Stage), many naturally address the devotional Fourth Stage and yogic Fifth Stage practices and phenomena [see Appendix I]. Western scholar Keith Dowman, in his amazing book *Masters of Mahamudra* (1985), reviewing each Maha-Siddha one-by-one, explains the esoteric meaning (and practice) of true Guru Yoga:

> Without exception the legends [of the Maha-Siddhas] stress the importance of the Guru. The Guru should not be viewed simply as an extraordinary human being with certain special knowledge to be transmitted, although this will be the preconception that the supplicant brings to him [or her]. It is essential, incidentally, that the disciple approaches the Guru as a supplicant [devotee]; for, bound by his own tantric commitment, the Guru can only give precepts to those who approach him with respect, and who requires initiation and instruction at a propitious moment and an appropriate juncture. But initiation [via Spirit-Transmission] radically alters the Guru/disciple relationship, destroying all the initiate's preconceptions.[16]

| Tilopa | Naropa | Marpa | Milarepa | Niguma |

One lineage of Maha-Siddhas from North India that had a profound influence on Tibetan Buddhism descended from the Tantra Master **Tilopa** (988–1069) to his student **Naropa** (1016–1100), then to his disciple **Marpa the Translator** (1012–1097), then to his devotee the famous poet-yogi **Milarepa** (1052–1135), as well as the yogini (female practitioner) **Niguma** (10th or 11th century). These are some of the best known and dearly loved among Tibetans and are now known throughout the Western world. Milarepa is author of the well-known and highly-praised *The Hundred Thousand Songs of Milarepa* (first translated into English by Garma C. C. Chang in 1962[17]). Milarepa is known for overcoming many obstacles to study under his Guru Marpa, who tested his devotion (such as building and rebuilding three stone towers) before revealing the secret tantra teachings, and who also became famous for climbing Mount Kailash. Adi Da, who often uses Milarepa as being an exemplar devotee, clarifies the various Stages of Life exhibited by the Vajrayana Adepts:

> *The Hundred Thousand Songs of Milarepa* and *The Life of Milarepa* are written in terms of the ["premonitory"] Seventh Stage orientation, but if you examine those books, you will see that they are dominated by the Fifth Stage point of view. Fifth Stage yogic idealism is primary in the Vajrayana Buddhist tradition, and, although obviously I understand and appreciate the yoga of the Vajrayana tradition, which is not remarkably different from the Fifth Stage practices of Hindu Tantra and Shaivism, it is not this Fifth Stage yogic idealism which I feel an ultimate affinity in the Vajrayana tradition [but with its Sixth to Seventh Stage orientation].
>
> The literatures of the Vajrayana and the remarkable biographies, including the life of Milarepa, although gesturing toward and ultimately representing the Seventh Stage Realization, are teaching texts,

devoted largely to communicating a Way of Realization that is dominated by Fifth Stage yogic practices and yogic idealism.[18]

Naturally, most Tibetan people themselves are not practitioners of higher yogas and meditative practices. Grounded in the indigenous culture of the tribal Bön, who lived in Tibet long before Buddhism arrived, the average-mode masses were devotional advocates of their exoteric ("outer-directed") religion, as are most people in other religions. They rely on ancient mythic thinking, superstitions and prayers, spirit powers and dreams, and other ritualistic methods to express their relationship with the Wheel of Life including the possibility of Buddhahood, even as lay people. Yet, they still honor their monasteries, their Lamas and Siddhas, even those outside the orthodox traditions. The entire spectrum of consciousness is alive in Tibetan culture (at least prior to the Chinese invasion). Again, Adi Da's developmental model effectively conveys this importance:

> In addition to Fifth Stage yogic practices, the Vajrayana tradition also gives place to Fourth Stage devotional exercises of various kinds and the development of compassionate service to the world, rather than inversion upon the self [as in the Sixth Stage]. However, implicit in the Vajrayana literature are the Sixth and ultimately the Seventh Stage [of Life] traditions.... Thus, the Vajrayana tradition allows for the point of view of Seventh Stage Adepts in its "Crazy" form, in the appearance of Enlightened Siddhas, or individuals who entered into the Seventh Stage on the basis of Awakening that [then] developed Fourth, Fifth, and Sixth Stage characteristics.[19]

As another example of an important Maha-Siddha from India going to Tibet is the beloved **Atisha** (982–1054), author of the well-known *The Great Path to Enlightenment: The Seven Points of Mind-Training* and *The Great Path of Awakening*.[20] Atisha was a Bengali Buddhist Master from the Indian subcontinent who helped spread Mahayana and Vajrayana Buddhism throughout Asia and inspired Buddhist thought and practice from Tibet to Sumatra. The list is long and colorful if one takes the time to investigate and study and read their translated texts and lively biographies full of rich spiritual instruction.

Yeshe Tsogyal   Atisha   Gampopa   Longchenpa   Tsong Khapa

Tibet, of course, has had its own tradition of indigenous Maha-Siddhas born from its various regions and schooled in the various schools of Tibetan Vajrayana Buddhism. One of the original Masters of Bön Dzogchen was **Tapihritsa** (7th–8th century CE), the 34th Adept of the Zhang Zhung Nyen Gyu lineage who is a shining example of one who achieved the rainbow body, hence he is often pictured a as white body in a meditation posture emanating rays of the rainbow (the five pure lights). **Gampopa** (1079–1153) was a devotee of Maha-Siddha Milarepa, a tantric Adept and physician who codified his master's teachings to establish the Kagyu school of Tibetan Buddhism. Gampopa authored the *Jewel Ornament of Liberation*, the first Lamrim text combining Mahamudra and Dzogchen and assimilating the monastic strand of teaching into his work.[21] **Longchenpa** (1308–1364), another realized pandit considered one of the three main manifestations of Manjushri (along with Sakya Pandita and Tsong Khapa), from the Nyingma tradition, was instrumental in establishing the esoteric transmission of Dzogchen.[22] His monumental work, *Seven Treasuries*, encapsulates the previous 600 years of Tibetan Buddhism highlighting Ati Yoga. Another example is the all-important **Lady Yeshe Tsogyal** (c.757 or 777–817 CE), the "Mother of Tibetan Buddhism" from Kharchen, Tibet (originally the wife of Emperor Trisong Detsen). The highest female in the Nyingma Vajrayana lineage, she famously became the consort to Guru Padmasambhava from India who was the founder-figure of the Nyingma tradition of Tibetan Buddhism. The list, of course, exceeds the confines of this book.

One of the most important (and revered) Tibetan-born Maha-Siddhas was the brilliant genius **Je Tsong Khapa** (1357–1419), who revised and purified many of the Tibetan Buddhist monasteries. Simply known as "Je Rinpoche," he is considered an emanation of Manjushri (the sword-wielding Bodhisattva of Wisdom), he strongly critiqued the egoic tendencies of the Buddhist monastic universities by placing an added focus on devotional practice and effective meditation instead of rote learning. In Adi Da's terms, he advocated for the "Practicing School," not merely the "Talking School" [see Chapter 4]. The American-born Je Tsongkhapa Professor of Indo-Tibetan Buddhist Studies at Columbia University, Robert Thurman explains: "Tsong Khapa reinterpreted and revitalized the perfect wisdom insight so masterfully, he came to be regarded by millions of followers over centuries as a living incarnation of the bodhisattva Manjushri."[23] Manjushri's flam-

Manjushri Tsong Khapa

ing sword of wisdom cuts through all deluding dualities of egoic ignorance to blossom forth transcendental insights and awakened compassion.

Part of the lineage descended from Nagarjuna (fl. 2nd century CE), the originator of Mahayana Madhyamaka [see Chapter 17], Lama Tsong Khapa was the Guru to the First Dalai Lama, who five hundred years later manifested for our emerging global civilization as His Holiness the Fourteenth Dalai Lama, **Tenzin Gyatso** (b. 1935), a beacon of authentic Buddhism for people all over the world. Under Tsong Khapa's tutelage and transmission, the Tibetan tradition was able to prosper under reliable spiritual guidance, proving once again the Buddha has produced a fountain of gnostic awakening fused with selfless love for countless beings.[24] This fertilization of Buddhism into Tibet led to a series of schools or various branches of Vajrayana Buddhism in the perpetual turning of the Dharma Wheel.

| Tapihritsa | Machig Labdrön | Tantric Deities | Tsangnyön Heruka | Drukpa Kunley |

Again, it is important to distinguish where each Adept falls within the Seven Stages of Life model (in Adi Da's view), which state-stage their "center of gravity" tends to rotate around (in Wilber's integral terms), whether or not they personally attained the highest (or most ultimate) Realization (or Divine Enlightenment). Adi Da makes this clear:

> The Vajrayana tradition is a good example of how the Sixth and Seventh Stage points of view [of Enlightenment] may be communicated through Fourth and Fifth Stage teachings, particularly teachings of the [yogic] Fifth Stage…. There is an implicit criticism of cosmic bondage, or the attainment of higher cosmic or subtle states for their own sake in the Vajrayana literature, and yet books like Milarepa's biography are filled with descriptions of associations with subtle deities and higher worlds. Such descriptions appear because nothing in the tradition prohibits subtle experiences. However, the idealism that seeks such experiences, or settles for them for their own sake, is constantly criticized.[25]

A few other notable examples are **Machig Labdrön** (1055–1097), a female Maha-Siddha who was a founding figure of the Chöd lineage. There is **Drukpa Kunley** (1455–1529), the "Divine Madman of the Dragon [*Drukpa Kahgyu*] Lineage" (now known with a famous translation by Keith Dowman), also known as "The Saint of 5,000 Women" since women would seek out his blessing in the form of sexual intercourse—"I can have sex with many women because I help them to go the path of Enlightenment…. Outwardly I am a ragged beggar and inwardly a blissful Buddha"[26]—yet, nonetheless, he first attained Buddhahood through arduous, highly disciplined training in a Tibetan monastic academy being empowered by his Lamas and Tantra initiations.

There is **Tsangnyön Heruka** (1452–1507), the "The Madman Heruka from Tsang" best known as the compiler of the Milarepa's Songs and biography; plus several others with profound historical influence.

...moving through Kashmir

Let's be clear in this brief survey, I am not covering all of the streams of wisdom hidden in the Great Tradition of humankind, especially in the peaks and valleys of the Himalayas, for they are too numerous. But mention should be made of **Kashmir** in the northwestern edge of the Indian subcontinent, traditionally situated around the Kashmir Valley (north of the Punjab in India), tucked up into the Great Himalayas (now involved in territorial disputes with Pakistan). By the first half of the first millennium CE, Kashmir had become an important land for Hindu Yogis, especially with Shaivism (the worship of Shiva, the archetypal Yogi) coming down from his abode on Mt. Kailash, then later incorporating advanced Mahayana Buddhism practices (such as Dzogchen and Mahamudra). By the 9th century CE there emerged what is known as **Kashmir Shaivism**, a nondual Tantric Yoga that relies on the kundalini-Shakti force for energy transformation, thus also attracting *Yoginis* or female practitioners. Kashmir became a vital and thriving intersection of trade routes bringing many great spiritual seekers together from all around Asia, as Western Tantra Master Daniel Odier respectfully explains:

> Kashmir was a paradise, a welcoming land. It was traversed happily by travelers, merchants, mystics, Ch'an adepts, Hindus, Buddhists of various schools, and later by Sufis in a great intellectual, poetic, musical, and philosophical effervescence. Kashmir was a location where the boundaries of religious structures could be transcended by yogis and yoginis during grand celebrations, where all the religious taboos could be forgotten in mystical fervor. Kashmir and Tantrism attracted Brahmins as well as monks from various forms of Buddhism. They

would seek out initiation with yoginis who had extraordinary powers that provided them with access to the heart of Mahamudra in the most direct way—a path where everything was brought together and reserved for the "heroes" (*vira*) [or Maha-Siddhas] for whom Kashmir became the chosen land.[27]

Obviously, therefore, the stories of Kashmir's ancient history are endless, deep, and profound (as Led Zeppelin once sung about). In other words, as Adi Da suggests: "Let the traditions be your entertainment,"[28] that is, listen to and contemplate the wisdom stories of the Great Adepts found in God's Global Wisdom Tradition for there is no better way to be schooled and enlightened at the same time. Indeed, I highly recommend that creative artists, filmmakers, movie directors (and scriptwriters), musicians, and others do a deep dive into the Divine Library of the Great Tradition and bring these lively characters and their incredible stories to the public eye. Perhaps there could be no greater service for humanity's further growth. Let's next follow that long and winding road back into Tibet's ancient and sacred history.

BRIEF HISTORY OF TIBETAN BUDDHISM

One of the great ironies of Tibetan Buddhism is that Buddhism's first contact with Tibetans (6th to 9th centuries CE) was from invading armies of the Yarlung dynasties and their emerging empire of "Red Faces" or Tibetan soldiers who painted their faces with red ochre and savagely attached Buddhist institutions in India and China.[29] Before the rise of the Tibetan Empire, Tibet had mostly been a gathering of tribes and small

kingdoms living in the southern half of Tibet since the north half is a virtually uninhabited desert called the Jangtang (Northern Plain). Tibet became a
kingdom influenced by three religious traditions: (1) the "folk religion" of the
common average-mode people; (2) the Bön religion that was there prior to
Buddhism but then incorporated many Buddhist practices; (3) the Mahayana
and Vajrayana branches of Buddhism that came into Tibet from India and
China. It is a common misconception that Tibetan Buddhism is simply a
shamanistic form of Buddhism (inherited from the indigenous Bön) but this
is a distortion of Tibet's complex history.[30] Buddhism itself officially entered
Tibet under the invitation of its Yarlung Kings in various phases, the first major
phase brought in Guru Rinpoche **Padmasambhava** (8th century), then after
an "era of fragmentation" and persecution (9th to 10th centuries), the second
phase (the "second dissemination") was established by **Atisha** and other
Maha-Siddhas (11th century onward). From then to the twentieth century,
Tibet went through phases of relative independence, Chinese influence, and
Mongol dominance where some of their rulers, including **Kublai Khan** (1215–
1294), converted and then protected Buddhism.

| Kublai Khan | Songtsen Gampo | Trisong Detsen | Santaraksita | Padmasam-bhava |

The Yarlung Dynasty and Tibetan Empire arose from a series of tribal
kings coming from the Yarlung Valley until becoming a united empire with a
strong army in the 7th century. King **Songtsen Gampo** (ca. 617–650 CE) was
the thirty-third king of the Yarlung dynasty (rulers since ca. 500 BCE) which
adhered to the native Bön religion using exorcists, shamans, and royal priests
for ritual ceremonies to appease spirits and demons to benefit and protect the
people.[31] According to legend, sometime during the 4th century CE, the first
Buddhist scriptures appeared by falling from the sky although more than likely
they came from India. The Bön priests, however, at first resisted the imported
Buddhist religion. Unlike his predecessors, Songtsen Campo created a power-

ful empire and army that attacked India to the south and China to the east, as he established his capital at Lhasa and built the Potala Palace (on the Red Hill). Later the "religious king" came to appreciate Buddhism, as legend has it, from his foreign wives who were devout Buddhists, so he started to build temples and create a written Tibetan script so they could translate Sanskrit Buddhist scriptures into their own language. This changed everything.

The second great religious king of the Yarlung Empire was King **Trisong Detsen** (reign 755–797), who became a committed Buddhist making it the state religion, and thus began a wide-scale restoration of Buddhist temples overcoming the resistance of the local **Bönpo**. Most importantly, he invited two notable Indian Buddhist monks; first was **Santaraksita** (725–788), a philosopher of the Madhyamaka school who studied at Nalanda University and became the founder of the first Buddhist monastery in Tibet named Samye—thus he was known as the "Bodhisattva Abbot." And, most important of all, was **Padmasambhava** (exact dates unknown), whose name means "Precious Teacher," also called Guru Rinpoche, who arrived in Tibet under the king's invitation in 747 CE. Padmasambhava, an Indian

Padmasambhava

tantric Adept, was known for his charismatic personality and subduing demonic forces, including convincing the Bön priests with his *siddhis* (or psychic powers) to embrace Buddhism, thus he was able to stabilize his religion in Tibet with additional monasteries and widespread popular appeal. Importantly, Guru Rinpoche did not suppress the indigenous religion and their spirits but rather incorporated them into Buddhism's more enlightened worldview. He became the root Guru for the Nyingma school or the "Ancient" order of Tibetan Buddhism. Also, he and his wife-consort **Yeshe Tsogyal** are said to have written important Buddhist scriptures called *termas* ("hidden treasures") that were concealed for future discoveries by **Tertöns** or "Treasure Masters" [see below].

The third and last great Yarlung king was **Tri Ralpachen** (reign 815–838) who made a treaty with China and furthered Buddhist dissemination until his assassination in 838, which fractured the dynasty. His elder brother took the throne but began a violent persecution of Buddhists (as he was a strong supporter of the Bön faith). A Buddhist monk, during a theatrical play, fatally wounded the king with a well-aimed arrow forgoing his vows (not to kill) in order to save thousands.[32] Tibet was then shattered into small fiefdoms overseen by warlords and Buddhism declined over the next century or so.

| Atisha | Marpa | White Tara | Tilopa | Naropa |

In the eleventh century, Buddhism in Tibet was reawakened and revived—known as the "**second dissemination**"—largely due to the arrival of **Atisha** (982–1054) from India who reached the western kingdom of Guge in 1042 CE. Atisha spent the last twelve years of his life traveling throughout Tibet spreading the Dharma far and wide attracting many disciples who would establish the Kadampa order of Tibetan Buddhism. Most notably, Atisha wrote several sacred treatises, one of the best known being the *Lamp for the Path of Awakening*,[33] that is still an excellent summary of the Buddhist path bringing together the two streams of the scholastic Mahayana and radical Tantra teachings with the systematic path of "mind-training" *(lamrim)*.[34] Atisha's tutelary deity was **Tara**, the "Mother of Liberation," the female bodhisattva-buddha of Vajrayana (probably brought to Tibet via Padmasambhava). Among the various Tara forms are her White Tara form (from China), known for compassion, long life, healing and serenity; her Green Tara form (from Nepal), as protector from fear and obscurations; Yellow Tara, for abundance; Black Tara, associated with power, and so on.

Contemporary with Atisha was **Marpa Lotsawa** (1012–1097), known as "Marpa the Translator" [mentioned above], who traveled to India to gather sacred texts and study with several Indian Buddhist Adepts. Marpa's root Guru was the former abbot of Nalanda University, **Naropa** (1016–1100), an important holder of transmissions from the Mahamudra Teachings. Naropa had become a tantric yogi studying under the Adept **Tilopa** (988–1069), before teaching his principal student Marpa who had arrived from Tibet seeking Enlightened Wisdom. The Bengali Brahmin became known throughout Tibet (and history) as the teacher of the "**Six Yogas of Naropa**," a set of tantric practices that focus on the "inner heat" (*tummo*) yoga (or conducting the kundalini Life-Force) to awaken higher states of consciousness. Although aimed at the highest revelation of Buddhahood or Enlightenment (the Sixth and Seventh Stages of Life), the tantric practices such as the Six Yogas basically represent the Fifth Stage of Life, as Adi Da explains in detail:

> The Fifth Stage of Life is the basic stage of ascent into the cosmic domain above and beyond the material or lower elemental planes of Nature. It is the stage of life that represents the limit of fulfillment by conventional mystical means. The "dharmas" of this stage include all of the technical yogas of mystical ascent via progressively subtler techniques of psycho-physical self-sacrifice. And the results include the various conditional "samadhis" attainable during human embodiment (such as the visionary "**savikalpa samadhi**" and the ascended or conventional and conditional form of "**nirvikalpa samadhi**," which is associated with the transcendence of all mental forms or images).
>
> The "dharmas" of this stage include all kinds of yogic techniques, such as "Hatha Yoga" (in its complete classical form), "Kundalini Yoga," the mystical form of "Kriya Yoga," "Mantra Yoga," "Nada Yoga" (or "Shabd Yoga"), "Tantra Yoga" in all its forms, and the "Six Yogas of Naropa."[35]

The tantra text *Six Yogas of Naropa* is an ideal summary of advanced tantric practices, including Dumo Yoga (or Tummo) or "inner heat" practices, Dream Yoga (including lucid dreaming) and Light Yoga, the essence of the path, among other sophisticated Fifth Stage Yogas.[36] The yogas of the Fifth (and Sixth) Stage of Life, it must be realized, are some of the highest and most evolved spiritual teachings and practices on the planet. They often evoke special psychic powers or *siddhis* that make their practitioners appear superhuman, so to speak, especially in legend. Yet, as the most advanced Buddhist and Advaita Vedantists Adepts (including Adi Da) maintain these powers and states of consciousness are not the most evolved Realization of Enlightenment or complete Liberation (from the self). I could offer countless statements from Adepts of the Great Tradition confirming this view, especially from Ch'an/Zen and Dzogchen Masters, but let's allow Avatar Adi Da to summarize this point of view:

> The Six progressive Stages of Life are finally fulfilled in the Seventh Stage of Life ["**sahaj samadhi**"]. All of the "dharmas" or yogas of progressive practice are forms of self-transcending mind-control that are finally fulfilled in the transcendence of conditional attention (or self-based awareness) in the Realization of Perfect Identification with the Love-Bliss of Radiant Transcendental or Divine Being ["**bhava samadhi**"].[37]

During the 13th and 14th centuries, with various political treaties established with the invading northern Mongol Empire (that began under Genghis Khan) ruling most of Central Asia (including China), even reaching into Europe (bringing with it the Black Plague), the Sakya order of Tibetan Buddhism became the prevailing political power as they struck deals with the Mongols who guaranteed peace for submission.[38] Buddhism's leading advocate at the time was **Sakya Pandita** (1182–1251), traditionally said to be an emanation of Manjushri (archetypal Bodhisattva of Wisdom) due to his impressive scholarly achievements and knowledge of Sanskrit, and thus he became a bridge between the Tibetans and Mongol court. It is said that he so impressed Genghis Khan's grandson, **Godan Khan** (also Khodan, 1206–1251), after he had already invaded Tibet killing hundreds of monks that the Mongol ruler converted to Buddhism.[39] In 1253, **Kublai Khan** (who had also converted to Buddhism) invited Sakya Pandita's nephew, **Chogyal Phagpa** (1235–1280) of the Sakya school to the Mongolian court, and as a result Buddhism was declared the state religion. Instead of invading Tibet with death and destruction, the Mongol ruler created a special "priest-patron" relationship where the "Sakya Lamas would become spiritual preceptors of the Mongol Khans,"[40] thus bringing peace to Tibet for another century or more. If only this type of benign conversion could happen with some of our world leaders today! This led to the period of "Sakya supremacy" in both the political and spiritual life of Tibet while the other Buddhist orders receded until a renaissance was born a couple of centuries later bringing about the ascendency of the Gelugpa school with their Dalai Lamas (in the mid-17th century).

Godan Khan
Mongol Buddhist

Sakya Pandita
Sakya Order

Lobsang Gyatso
5th Dalia Lama

Thubten Gyatso
13th Dalai Lama

Tenzin Gyatso
14th Dalai Lama

Mongol rule waned over the next century or so as a powerful succession of Tibetan royal families were able to secure relative independence for Tibet between the 14th and 17th centuries. During the 14th century, a new cultural awareness grew among Tibetans permitting the resurgence of the other orders of Tibetan Buddhism attempting to revive the glory of ancient Tibet. This took firm hold with the rise of the reformist pandit **Je Tsong Khapa** (or Tsongkhapa, 1357–1419), who founded the Gelug order that would lead to the rise of the Dalai Lamas ruling Tibet from 1642–1959. The precocious and brilliant Tsong Khapa studied under Lamas from all the various Buddhist sects to create a lucid and synthetic vision of Buddhist philosophy and practice.[41] His works have been translated into a variety of well-produced texts, including *The Splendor of an Autumn Moon: The Devotional Verse of Tsongkhapa* (2011) and the three-volume set of *The Great Treatise on the Stages of the Path to Enlightenment* (2000s).[42] Tsong Khapa emphasized the necessity for an ascetic monastic lifestyle (harking back to Atisha and Gautama) based on strict ethical values thus attracting a wide following of many devoted devotees who would carry on his work for the next several generations. Tsong Khapa's disciples established several monasteries in Central Tibet while founding the "Gelug" ("Virtuous") order that became the ideal school for Tibetan Buddhism into the future, now its most dominant school. Importantly, it was from the Gelug order that the reincarnated Dalai Lama lineage arose from the title "*Ta-le*," the Mongolian word for "ocean" or "big" (*gyatso* in Tibetan), which is now written as "Dalai," plus *laa-ma* meaning "Master or Guru."[43]

However, it wasn't until the Fifth Dalai Lama, **Lobsang Gyatso** (1617–1682), that they were enthroned with both temporal and spiritual power over all of Tibet (with Mongolian support). The "**Great Fifth**," as he was known, traveled throughout Tibet inspecting and improving the various monasteries while administrating the various provinces and unifying Tibet under the "Ganden Phodrang" (or Ganden Podrang), a Tibetan governmental body founded in 1642 in Lhasa (with a standing army). Generally acknowledged as a wise and benevolent ruler, the Fifth Dalai Lama brought back a sense of national unity visible in the grandeur of his Potala Palace.[44] Over the next several centuries, the Dalai Lamas, and the Gelug order, benignly ruled Tibet until they closed their borders in the 19th century as imperial European and Asian powers encroached on their self-contained spiritual society.

With the twentieth century, and two deadly World Wars involving both the European West and Asian East, Tibet was breeched as the Thirteenth Dalai Lama, **Thubten Gyatso** (1876–1933), warned about the impending forces of modernity coming from its threatening neighbors of British India to the south and an unstable China to the east. By the time of the Fourteenth Dalai Lama, **Tenzin Gyatso**, was born in 1935, Tibet was being thrown into the modern world whether they wanted it or not. Fortunately, the young Tenzin was eager to learn about the West, fascinated with science, so was growing up fast as he was enthroned at the age of fifteen while Tibet's borders were brutally invaded by the communist Chinese. After succumbing to a communist revolution led by **Mao Tse Tung** (1893–1976), China invaded Tibet in 1950 on the pretext that Tibet had always belonged to China (a false assertion).

An uneasy truce existed until 1959 when His Holiness the 14th Dalai Lama had to flee the Potala Palace after a popular uprising against the Chinese occupation tragically resulted in the murder of thousands of monks and nuns and wholesale destruction of countless Buddhist monasteries and temples by the atheist communists. In 1966, Red Guard troops, representing communist China's "Cultural Revolution," poured into Tibet to eradicate the "Four Olds" (ideology, culture, habits, customs) of Tibet with an official policy of "merciless repression" (according to China's then security chief).[45] In fairness (and for justice), I feel I need to quote some of the atrocities committed to the Tibetan people and culture so it will never be forgotten:

Lacking even the limited restraint exercised by the soldiers of the People's Liberation Army [in 1959], the Red Guards held mass executions, engaged in torture on an unprecedented scale, and rampaged throughout the countryside destroying monasteries, forcing monks to urinate on sacred texts, placing religious images in latrines, scrawling graffiti on the walls of temples and monasteries, and subjecting religious and political leaders (even those who collaborated with the Chinese authorities) to thamzing. The Red Guards also struck fear into the populace with marauding bands of young soldiers who staged mass gang rapes randomly throughout the countryside. International human rights organizations estimate that thousands of women of all ages were raped, often in public, with their parents, children, and neighbors being forced to watch.

The reign of terror lasted for almost a decade until Mao's death in 1976. By the end of the Cultural Revolution, tens of thousands of Tibetans had been murdered, and millions more had suffered extreme physical and mental abuse. It also brought economic devastation on such a scale that when Mao was succeeded by Deng Xiaoping the new supreme leader had to acknowledge that "mistakes were made." A more accurate assessment was offered by Alexander Solzhenitsyn [the Russian Gulag author-dissident], who stated that China's rule in Tibet is "more brutal and inhumane than any other communist regime in the world."[46]

The exiled Tibetan Buddhist community settled in Dharmsala, India, and other places, such as Bhutan (with strong support from the West), to establish a thriving (and peaceful) resistance to Chinese rule while disseminating Tibetan Buddhism to Westerners and spiritual seekers. Ironically (but impossible to justify), by having to flee Tibet and take refuge in India, Tibetan Vajrayana Buddhism has now entered the West bringing its wise Lamas, Rinpoches, and enlightening Dharma to the global community. The current Dalai Lama has become one of the most respected spiritual leaders in the world today, while still maintaining his spiritual responsibilities to his Tibetan people, showing both wisdom and compassion like a true Bodhisattva emissary of the Buddha's Enlightened Dharma. He first visited the West in 1974, and was awarded the Nobel Peace Prize in 1989, while continuing to push for reconciliation with the Chinese government as his predecessors often did in the past. Westerners have taken vows as monks and nuns to become committed Buddhists, while hundreds of Buddhist centers are thriving. Importantly, Tibetan Buddhist literature has offered an untold benefit to our "Divine Library" of Global Wisdom [see Chapter 2]. In many ways, as is often noted, it appears that a long ago prophecy attributed to Guru Rinpoche Padmasambhava (in the late 8th century) has now appeared to become true:

> When the iron bird flies and horses run on wheels the Tibetan people will be scattered like ants across the face of the earth, and the dharma will come to the land of the red man.[47]

What arose from the ancient lowlands of Vedic India to reach the highest mountains of the Himalayas, the roots of Tibetan Buddhism have spread far and wide encircling the planet and touching the hearts of millions... now and far into the future.

TIBETAN ROOTS-MUDRAS

bviously, Tibetan Buddhism did not arise in a vacuum nor did Buddhism enter the high plateau to encounter an empty land. They entered a land that had been occupied by various tribes since the arrival of human beings into the Central Asian continent. Following the ancient history of Tibet is still controversial (as it is in India) so only the briefest outline is offered here. But Buddhism seemed to have found a fertile and receptive culture of shamanism and small kingdoms that already had a sacred history, especially with the indigenous Bön culture that appears to have been already influenced by the wisdom of India in various forms. In any case, the foundation for Tibetan Buddhism as a political as well as spiritual authority was laid down by the Tibetan culture itself, as Adi Da also noted:

> The native Tibetan schools developed institutional organizations (both of the ascetical and the non-ascetical variety) that were designed to maintain ordinary social order and political power in the period before the recently grossly destructive China invasion of the closed society of Tibet. Therefore, the "**Bodhi-Siddha**" [Adi Da's original term for a Bodhisattva-Siddha] of the traditionally organized Tibetan culture came to be identified more or less exclusively with the endlessly reincarnating magical "tulkus" and high Adepts who were said to be always embodied in the ecclesiastical authorities of the traditional Vajrayana organizations [such as with the Dalai Lamas]. This more or less exclusive identification of Enlightened Adepts with ecclesiastical hierarchies is an ordinary or popular device of social, cultural and political power.[48]

The **Bön** religion as practiced by **Bönpos** (or *bon-po*) included ritual priests and shamans that has been historically interpreted by Western scholars as being the indigenous-shamanic culture of Tibet, yet this appears to be a misconception according to current studies. Bönpos view their tradition as being distinct from Buddhism although it contains many similar elements. Perhaps their fundamental difference is they do not consider the Buddha (6th century BCE) to be the originator of their religion but rather they have their own "Buddha" (or Enlightened Adept) named **Tonpa Shenrab Miwoche** or **Shenrap** (dates unknown). Although the Bön tradition dates him much earlier than Gautama Shakyamuni, some even suggesting 18,000 years ago to give him authority over Buddhism, he more than likely lived around the 6th century CE before the rise of the Tibetan Empire (though his historical facts are unknown and controversial).

Evidence indicates that Shenrab came from the land of the **Zhang Zhung**, an ancient tribal region in western Tibet surrounding Mount Kailash and the cradle of the Tibetan civilization. Tonpa Shenrab is said to have taught three successive cycles of teachings where the last cycle includes Sutra, Tantra, and Dzogchen. Importantly, to this day Bön retains the richness and flavor of its pre-Buddhist roots as well as its Buddhist influence, as His Holiness the 14th Dalai Lama has recognized: "Bön is Tibet's oldest spiritual tradition and, as the indigenous source of Tibetan culture, played a significant role in shaping Tibet's unique identity. Consequently, I have often stressed the importance of preserving this tradition."[49] The complex interaction of Bönpos and Buddhists in Tibet has given the world a rich source of Enlightened Wisdom that will serve global peace if we would only listen and study… and practice what is learned.

Bön claims to have been based on advanced meditative practices, such as Dzogchen, which then influenced Buddhism as it entered Tibet centuries later. Hence, they are classified as the pre-dynastic "**Old Bön**" including the folk religion (prior to 8th century CE), the "**Eternal Bön**" or the divine dharma (emerged 10th to 11th centuries), and the "**New Bön**" or Bön dharma (from 14th century in eastern Tibet), where each has their own scriptures and practices similar to Buddhism.[50] The early historical evidence indicates "bön" was a priest who would propitiate local spirits for the benefit of the people and serve the dead in the afterlife. More than likely it was only after Buddhism entered Tibet that Bön become associated with Buddhist-like practices (such a Dzogchen), yet both the Bönpo and Buddhists have revised their histories to honor their own tradition, thus it's really hard to say. The Tibetan folk religion continued to involve magical-animistic rituals full of powers and spirits instead of being concerned with enlightened liberation like the Buddhists.[51] As scholar John Powers points out, "historical evidence indicates that Bön only developed as a self-conscious religious system under the influence of Buddhism."[52] Nonetheless, the integration of Bön with Buddhism is a large part of what gives Tibetan Buddhism its distinctive and unique character. Arising out of this confluence of spiritual practices there are several important ones that are highlighted in the Vajrayana Buddhism of Tibet briefly reviewed below.

Dzogchen (*rdzogs chen* in Tibetan) means "Great Perfection" or "Great Fulfillment" since it focuses on the "natural state" or what is "always already the case" (in Adi Da's words) as being the basis for real practice, not in achieving a goal. Consequently, Dzogchen is considered to be the definitive and most secret teaching of the Awakened Buddha. In this sense, Dzogchen methods focus more on a direct breakthrough experience to *realize* the ultimate nature of Consciousness and Being, similar to the Ch'an Buddhist of China and the Japanese Zen tradition.[53] Dzogchen is known as **Ati Yoga** (or "utmost yoga") because it is ultimately about discovering the primordial ground and state of existence (*ghzi*, "basis") or one's nondual Buddha-Nature. This ultimate ground is said by Dzogchen to have the quali-

Dzogchen "A"

ties of purity or "emptiness," luminous clarity, and compassion (or love)—or "Clear Light Bliss."[54] The practice of Dzogchen, therefore, is the direct discovery of this divine ground of Being realized in *rigpa* (in Tibetan, "knowledge of the ground," similar to *prajna*, in Sanskrit, or *gnosis* in Greek). Then this Enlightened awareness becomes the basis for practice making it the pinnacle of all meditation, the various vehicles, views, and goals of Buddhist practice. This is also why its transmission of Awakening (or the Enlightened State) is so dependent on a Realized Lama and Guru Yoga.

According to Buddhist tradition, Dzogchen first arose with the primordial Buddha or **Adi Buddha** or "First Buddha"—also known as **Vajrasattva** the "Primordial Buddha whose essence is the diamond or thunderbolt" meaning the Incorruptible Consciousness of the Awakened One—yet Bön religion attributes its practice to the founder of Bön, Shenrab Miwoche [see above]. Over time, the realization-practices of Dzogchen have been integrated into all the major schools of Tibetan Vajrayana Buddhism, particularly with the oldest school Nyingma ("Ancient School") who also claims the semi-historical figure of **Garab Dorje** (ca. 665 CE) as being the original transmitter of Ati

Vajrasattva

Yoga or Dzogchen. It is also said that **Padmasambhava** (ca. 8th century CE) introduced Dzogchen to Tibet when he came from northern India.

Dzogchen claims that Enlightenment or the "natural state" is always already present so the practice is actually a matter of recognizing the mind's innate purity of Buddha-Nature (beyond all illusions of the separate self). Naturally, as suggested, there is controversy over the precise historical origins of this ancient practice which in no way effects its purity or current practice by Buddhist practitioners today (since it transcends all mental categories). In many ways, I believe, a valid argument can be made that Dzogchen, especially with its reliance on Guru Yoga and the "always already" nondual state, is most similar to Adi Da's Reality-Way of Adidam Ruchiradam since ultimate Realization or "Seeing" (God-Realization) is necessary *from the beginning* in order for the Way to be undertaken properly (and not as a program of seeking).

Mahamudra (*phyag chen* in Tibetan) means "Great Seal" or "Great Imprint," which is similar to Dzogchen in that its practice begins with Awakening or re-discovering one's natural state or Buddha-Nature, the "moment-to-moment recognition of the manifest objects as the transcendental Reality."[55] Yoga scholar Georg Feuerstein continues to explain: "The attitude of seeing the absolute identity of the phenomenal world and the transcendental Reality creates an inner immunity to all fear and doubt. It established practitioners in their authentic being, which is sheer bliss."[56] Like a wax seal stamped on legal documents, the "Great Seal" of Mahamudra meditation is affixed on authentic practice to ensure Enlightenment for the benefit of all beings. French Tantric Master Daniel Odier explains:

hand mudra with dorje
Padmasambhava

> The distinctive characteristic of Mahamudra meditation is to focus on mind itself and on its intimate relationship with the conventional world of appearances and its relationship with emptiness (the void). The fact of not being aware (being ignorant) of this relationship and the confusion around this ignorance drives our disturbing emotions and our compulsive karmic behavior, bringing in suffering and constant problems. Mahamudra meditation is an extremely effective method for attaining liberation from all that, and, ultimately, attaining Enlightenment, but only when we carry it out based on a solid foundation, which implies exhaustive preparatory training.[57]

Deity Yoga is another commonly used practice among Tibetan Buddhists to invoke the Enlightened State through symbolic forms or *yidam*, one's chosen deity. These subtle realm states are contacted through meditation or in the dream state where the practitioner of Vajrayana enters a living relationship with an enlightened deity, such as Chenrezig, Kalachakra, Heruka, the various Tara Goddesses (and dozens of others), or focuses on seed syllables and mandalas, etc., all visionary exercises until identification awakens higher states of consciousness. Mandala sand paintings, for instance, are a creative practice of concentration which is brushed away as dust symbolizing the impermanence and "emptiness" of all forms. Instead of a dualistic attitude of overcoming evil or the body for the transcendent good (such as in the Abrahamic religions and Theravada), a nondual approach of integrating the arising forms of the world and mind into an enlightened wholeness becomes the practice. Buddhist scholar Stephen Batchelor summaries:

> The often bewildering array of deities [seen] in Tibetan temples and monasteries personify the multifaceted phenomena of enlightenment that are utilized and developed in the Vajrayana. Some deities depict peaceful aspects of Buddhahood, smiling with encouragement and love. Others show its wrathful side, urging the practitioner to overcome his or her hesitation and engage in the awesome, compassionate dance of liberated consciousness….
>
>
> **Heruka**
>
> There are two stages involved in this process of transformation. First, it is necessary to rid oneself of delusive ideas and perceptions of who one is and what reality is. On the tantric path this is achieved by imagining oneself as a deity and the world as the mandala of that deity…. In the second stage the practitioner uses his or her powers of imagination and concentration to free and rechannel the subtle energies that are the physical basis of psychic life. This gives him or her access to the founding stratum of existence, which is known by a number of descriptive terms: clear light, primordial Buddha, Great Perfection, and others.[58]

Strong ethical rules and practices are always maintained, however, so these tantra practices are not simply means for the ego to do what it pleases or indulge in sensual pleasures. Being instructed under the auspices of Guru Yoga and a qualified teacher are absolutely necessary since they are grounded in the precious Buddhist tradition based on thousands of years of advanced Adepts and their instruction. We would be wise to heed their wisdom and *realize* the inherent love-bliss of our natural state (beyond egoic contraction and self).

Padmasambhava and Lady Tsogyal
in Tantric Maithuna

As mentioned, many great and powerfully Enlightened Maha-Siddhas (or "Great Adepts") historically appeared during the first millennium, such as the "mad monk" **Bodhidharma** (early 5th century CE) who brought a more mature Buddhism to China, and **Padmasambhava** (ca. 8th century CE) who brought Buddhism into Tibet where it progressed to even further stages of flowering known as the "Diamond Vehicle" of **Vajrayana Buddhism** [see below]. The establishment of Buddhism in Tibet in successive waves or phases was followed by a succession of important Maha-Siddhas, as we reviewed, such as the famous "Eighty-Four Maha-Siddhas" who used methods similar to the forest-dwelling Shaivite Yogis that were radically different than the practices found in the common Buddhist monasteries to further establish **Tantra Buddhism**—including the practice of Deity Yoga, Mahamudra, the "Great Seal," and Dzogchen, the "Great Perfection" [see above]. Avatar Adi Da also recognizes and acknowledged the advanced phases of Tibetan Vajrayana Buddhism and their esoteric practices as involving the Sixth and Seventh Stages of Life (whether in a fully Realized or "premonitory" manner):

> The Free Adepts, or those who are moved to Truth and Awaken by whatever trial of means, are the real heart of the Vajrayana tradition of Bodhisattvas (as well as all other traditions), and even though such beings may have also appeared in the form of authorities in the traditional Tibetan hierarchy, it is the tradition of spontaneously appearing Adepts that grants fundamental authenticity to the Vajrayana Way.... [Similarly] it is the Transcendental philosophy (expressed in

the "**Mahamudra**" version of the Mahayana philosophy of mind and Enlightenment), rather than the magical-mystical yogic philosophy [of the Fourth to Fifth Stages of Life], that is the reason the Vajrayana is an authentic form of Buddhism [the Sixth to Seventh Stages of Life], rather than merely a species of the Fourth to Fifth Stage yogism.[59]

Now let us turn our attention to the various schools of Vajrayana that appear in the historical unfolding of Tibetan Buddhism, the highest practice of esoteric mysticism found on the highest plateaus surrounded by the highest mountains (the Himalayas) on Earth. Let us sit with elders of a gentle race, with ancient ones whom this world has seldom seen, as we talk for days and sit and wait, for all will be revealed.[60]

Vajrayana Vehicles: Tibetan Guru's Gifts

Vajrayana Buddhism is technically a branch of Mahayana but with its conjunction with Tantra, emerging in northern India and the **Pala Empire** (which controlled the northern and eastern Indian subcontinent from the 8th to 12th century), it is seen as its own branch or *yana* ("vehicle"), another spoke in the ever-turning Wheel of the Dharma. *Vajra* in Sanskrit means "thunderbolt" and "diamond," which was originally the thunderbolt-lightning of Indra, the god of thunder in the *Vedas*, who is often mentioned in early Pali Buddhist scriptures.[61] Mahayana, however, turned the Buddha into a cosmic figure so the thunderbolt became Buddha's diamond scepter, a *dorje*, a kind of battle club of hardness and invincibility, thus Huston

Smith explains, "the diamond transforms the thunderbolt, a symbol of nature's power, into an emblem of spiritual authority."[62] The diamond is the hardest of all stones (a hundred times harder than any other rock) as well as being the most transparent, therefore, Vajrayana Buddhism—the "**Diamond Way**"—is the method of lucid strength combining the Buddha's penetrating wisdom with his luminous compassion.[63] Consequently, the word *vajra* signifies the lightning-bolt power of Enlightenment and the absolute, indestructible reality of *sunyata*, ("emptiness"). Thus, we see the visual icon of the masculine vajra club (*dorje*), along with the feminine bell (*ghanta*), form a principal symbol of the tantric elements found in Tibetan Vajrayana Buddhism, which are often used by Buddhist Lamas in ritual ceremonies and for meditation twirling them in hand mudras.

Vajrayana is usually considered the "**third turning**" of the Dharma Wheel since it combines the insights of Mahayana (particularly Madhyamika and Yogachara) with the practices of Tantra (usually emphasized with the Maha-Siddhas of India and Tibet). The energy released and mastered in Tantra, which combines form and emptiness, samsara and Nirvana, via powerful skillful means (*upaya*)—based in disciplined sadhana and Guru Yoga—gives Vajrayana its unique flavor which has been embraced most fully by the various schools of Tibetan Buddhists. Our world religion scholar confirms: "It was the genius of the great pioneers of Tantra to discovers *upayas* ("skillful means") for channeling [psycho-]physical energies into currents that carry the spirit forward instead of derailing it."[64] Tantra [see below], when viewed properly as it was originally intended, is not simply to use sexual practices and other non-ascetical means for personal enjoyment but as a means for self-transcendence and entering higher states (or state-stages) of transpersonal consciousness development (including the Fourth to Sixth Stages of Life).

Bhagavan Adi Da Samraj, in his far-reaching analysis of the "Three Ways of Buddhism" in *Nirvanasara* (1982), which I have liberally quoted from, once more situates these profound teachings within his Seven Stages of Life model [see Appendix I]:

> The Vajrayana tradition of *practice* has its roots in the tantric tradition of India and the Taoist tradition of China, both of which traditions are basically oriented toward the psycho-physical yogism of the Fifth Stage of Life. And it is this Fifth Stage connection (as well as the motives toward institutional popularization and social power) that are the source of the unique characteristics and the lesser or limited formulations of the Tibetan Vajrayana tradition.
>
> The techniques of the Vajrayana schools are typically either Fourth Stage devotional and exoteric disciplines [such as chanting, prayer wheels, full-body prostrations, etc.] (intended to purify and concentrate the mind) or Fifth Stage yogic disciplines comparable to the psycho-physical yogas of India and China) intended to develop powers or "siddhis," visionary and other forms of super-sensory contemplation, and, ultimately, Nirvana-like samadhi (that is virtually identical to the ascended "**nirvikalpa samadhi**" of all the ancient schools of shamanistic "sky-magic" or mystical ascent).
>
> Therefore, the Vajrayana system of means is generally mapped out along the lines of the contemplative phenomenal mysticism associated with the goals of the [yogic] Fifth Stage of Life. But these means are, in the best of the Vajrayana schools, considered to be secondary or "helping" yogas, preliminary to the ultimate "Mahamudra" [and Dzogchen] yoga of mind-transcendence (rather than mind-development).[65]

One of the first Maha-Siddhas credited with founding Vajrayana Buddhism is **Saraha**, "The Archer" (7th–8th century CE), particularly important in establishing the Mahamudra tradition. Tradition suggests Saraha was the Guru to Nagarjuna (which would place him in the 2nd century CE), but the consensus is he lived later influencing the emergence of Vajrayana in Tibet. Saraha was known for being a wandering Yogi and Avadhoot engaging in behaviors that overturned the social norms of caste,

Saraha
"The Archer"

social class, and the gender hierarchies of the time. It is said that two of Saraha's important teachers-consorts were women (yoginis) who were lower than him in caste, class, and gender, yet was an equal (or above) on the path of spiritual practice leading him further in his own spiritual development. Saraha is also associated with the arrow and arrow-making, an important art of Mongolian shaman-mystics, coming to mean one who has shot the arrow of nonduality into the heart of duality to awaken Nondual Mystical states.[66]

The penetrating arrow, the most important weapon and tool of the world's tribal shamanic cultures, later evolved into the masculine *dorje* to symbolize the bliss of Enlightenment while the feminine *ghanta* bell represents emptiness. These two handheld symbols of Vajrayana are often manipulated by tantric deities and priests performing Buddhist ceremonies. Indeed, the intersection of Tantrism, Kashmir Shaivism, and Vajrayana was often transmitted and taught by female Yoginis, masters of Mahamudra and Dzogchen as well as the highest Tantras, living outside the temples in the sanctuary of Nature with the mountains and lakes.[67] The tradition of the Maha-Siddhas [see above] descends down through the generations after the 8th century bringing the "Diamond Vehicle" or "Thunderbolt Way" to Tibet and the Buddha's Divine Dharma. Its piercing insight and strength still has the power to transform consciousness when used rightly (and under the guidance of a competent Awakened Adept-Guru). Consequently, several schools of Vajrayana Buddhism emerged in Tibet, which we'll briefly review next.

Yellow Hat Gelugpa monks
in Lamayuru monastery in the Indian Himalayas

The Tibetans established several main branches or sects with their version of the Buddha's Dharma, including four (or five) principal schools centered around the Teachings of different Guru-Adepts that then became the variants of **Tibetan Vajrayana Buddhism**:

(1) <u>Nyingma</u> (Nyingmapa) or "Ancient" school is the oldest tradition (known as the "Red Hat" sect) that descended from Garab Dorje (fl. 7th century CE) and Padmasambhava (fl. 8th century CE) by focusing on tantric practices and the transmission of Dzogchen ("Great Perfection") Buddhist teachings.

(2) <u>Kagyu</u> school (which translates as "Oral Transmission") descended from the lineage of the Maha-Siddhas (known as the "White Hat" sect) founded by Tilopa down through Naropa, Marpa, Milarepa, and yogini Niguma (and others); they focus on the Six Yogas of Naropa and practice Mahamudra (the "Great Seal") Buddhist teachings; the head of the Kagyu is called the Karmapa.

(3) <u>Sakya</u> (Sakyapa) school (one of the "Red Hat" sects) was founded by Drogmi Shakya (11th century CE), the smallest of the four schools that emphasizes the clerical-textual side of Tibetan Buddhism over Tantrism by focusing on Lamdre (the Path and its Fruit) thus creating a balance between study and meditation.

(4) **Gelug** (Gelugpa) school is the newest (and largest) school (a "Yellow Hat" sect) founded by Tsong Khapa (14th century CE) that established the Dalai Lama tradition focusing on strict monastic disciplines and prohibitions while valuing the esoteric practices of Vajrayana (but limiting tantra and magical rituals).

(5) **Kadam** (Kadampa) school, associated with Atisha and his main devotee Dromtön (1005–1064), emphasizing strict Dharma practice (and *bodhicitta* or "enlightenment-mind"), not the sexual yoga of the Tantra, yet was later integrated into the Gelugpas by Tsong Khapa.

Obviously, the Tibetan tradition of Buddhism is highly complex and profoundly deep, far beyond what a brief history here can do justice.[68] The "folk religions" of Tibet (connected with the shamanism of Mongolia, where the term "shaman" originates, *šaman*, meaning "one who knows") were based on indigenous "Earth religions" using "Earth Magic" (in Adi Da's terms) or ceremonial rituals of "magic" (psycho-physical manipulations) to bring mundane benefits to the tribe and people, such as protection from harm, good crops, healthy livestock, health, wealth, eliminating plagues, etc. The Tibetans, as all indigenous tribal people worldwide, were fascinated with spirits and supernatural forces living in the natural environment (including ancestor spirits) so they performed rituals for good mana and to repeal bad taboos.[69] In the merging of the magical animistic-shamanic cultures of ancient Tibet (such as the Zhang-Zhung), including the unique advances of Bön religion, with the monastic Buddhism and Tantras of India, Tibetan Buddhism developed a unique flavor incorporating ritual practices (*puja*) with advanced meditation and empowerment practices, always under the guidance or influence of Lamas and Enlightened Guru-Adepts. To situate the Vajrayana Buddhist tradition within the scope of Adi Da's Seven Stages of Life, let's allow the Avatar to clarify his perspective:

> The Vajrayana tradition basically extended the list of "means" whereby Enlightenment could be pursued. The Mahayana schools also added [Fourth Stage of Life] ceremonial and devotional practices to their lists of means whenever they expanded their influence into the popular domain.
>
> Therefore, whereas the original Buddhist tradition generally limited its list of means to those that were compatible with the strictly Sixth Stage orientation [of Formless Mysticism], the Mahayana tradition extended those means in order to provide a framework for practice in the terms of the first Four Stages of Life. And although there was some development of Fifth Stage yogic means in the Mahayana tradition, it was largely the Vajrayana tradition that grafted the mystical yogas of the Fifth Stage of Life onto the traditional list of means [such as with Tantra and the Six Yogas of Naropa, etc.] associated with Buddhism. Therefore, it is with the Vajrayana tradition that we see the Buddhist tradition return full circle to the shamanistic, animistic, and Emanationist orientation from which Gautama originally recoiled.[70]

Vajrayana thus integrated all the forms of yoga and meditation for the service of its Enlightenment tradition. They incorporated the indigenous Bön religion with Taoism from China, Tantra from India, and Mahayana from the Maha-Siddhas of Buddhism's greatest Adept-Realizers. No wonder it was such a potent mystical brew! Adi Da insightfully summarizes: "At its best, Vajrayana represents a true development of Buddhism, although, as was the case with the Mahayana, the popular institutionalization of the Vajrayana as well as its Fifth Stage mystical tendencies have produced a range of limitations and false (or at least) conventional views."[71] Hence new Awakened Siddhas are always needed to rightfully align institutional hierarchies with the truth of Transcendental Enlightenment.

In addition, the Vajrayana Adepts developed the ideal of the **Bodhisattva** into a more complete and esoteric conception than the popular Mahayana view [see Chapter 17]. As their histories suggest, many of these Vajrayana Bodhisattvas had extraordinary psychic powers or *siddhis* gained either through tantric yogic practices or as spontaneous results of their Realization where they were uniquely effective in serving others toward Enlightenment. Adi Da has called these special Seventh Stage Adepts "**Bodhi-Siddhas**," combining "*Bodhisattva*" with "*Siddha*" (or "Perfected Ones"). The American-born Adept explains: "The Mahayana tended to support a popular idea of the Bodhisattva as the bearer of an ideal attitude toward the world. Thus, the Mahayana Bodhisattva ideal tends to align itself toward the popular motives of the social ego rather than toward the radical Realization of Transcendental Enlightenment. The Vajrayana schools continued this line as part of their popular Teaching, but they otherwise promoted the idea of Bodhisattvas as Enlightened Siddhas who intentionally remain in the phenomenal planes of existence in order to Help un-Enlightened beings."[72] Therefore, we discover these Great Bodhi-Siddhas appear throughout the Great Tradition, as our Avatar acknowledges:

> The principal examples of such true Bodhi-Siddhas in the Vajrayana tradition are the Indian Maha-Siddhas and the Crazy Wisdom Adepts of Tibet. And their likeness may also be seen in the Awakened Adepts and "Avadhoots" of Advaitism—such as may be sometimes found in the "Devi" school, the Shaivite school, and the Dattatreya school—who, like the Buddhist Siddhas have transcended both the subjective and the objective tendencies of mind.
>
> Such individuals behave in an unconventional fashion as an expression of the true understanding of Enlightenment. They are frequently non-ascetical and non-celibate masters of yogic tantrism, and they are also frequently associated with super-normal powers of the Fifth Stage yogic variety. However, the significance of the Crazy Wisdom demonstration of Enlightenment is not self-indulgence or attachment to subtle powers and states. Rather, it's significance is the spontaneous communication of the attitude of transcendence (in the form of non-preference).[73]

By the end of the first millennium of the Common Era, after Buddhism had planted it roots in Tibet (and throughout Asia), it was invigorated by the emergent tradition of Tantra, a unique version of esoteric yoga and spirituality that thoroughly combines Nirvana and samsara, as if they are absolutely the same One Reality (since they are).

TANTRA:
PATH OF "ONE TASTE"

nother major trend in the unique development of Tibetan Vajrayana Buddhism, as we've indicated, was the incorporation of **Tantra**, which first arose in northern India before making its way into Tibet (and China). In Tibet, through its transmission by the various Maha-Siddhas and "Crazy-Wise" Adepts, Tantra blossomed and influenced the various monasteries and schools of Buddhism. Tantra originated with the "84 Maha-Siddhas" and other Enlightened Yogi-Adepts, often outside the monastic setting, who passed on their secret teachings only to select disciples. These advanced-tip Yogis developed a psychic and spiritual sadhana of channeling subtle energy currents throughout the body, brain, and heart by using inner alchemical processes to activate their esoteric anatomy (including sexual yoga and intoxicants) that were generally taboo in monasteries. Such a tantric path to Enlightenment was supposed to be quicker than ordinary Hinayana or Mahayana methods but it was also more arduous and difficult to maintain properly.[74] Hence, again, the extreme necessity for instruction under a competent Lama-Guru.

Tantra, as a word, has two Sanskrit roots: (1) is "extension" meaning they were added to both the Hindu and Buddhist corpus of sacred texts as secret and esoteric methods; and (2) as "interpenetration" or "weaving" since Tantra focuses on the interrelatedness of all things, gross and subtle and causal, arising within the *Dharmadhatu* (or Ultimate Reality) involving the "always already" union of emptiness (*sunya*) and form, the prior unity of samsara and Nirvana.[75] As one scholar explains: "One of the main goals of Tantric Buddhist practice is to realize the innate perfection of the world by visualizing the world as a celestial mansion (*mandala*) and all beings as divine."[76] As Feuerstein rightly points out:

> **Tantra** is a practical path geared to transform human consciousness until the transmental (*amanaska*) Truth stands out as the obvious. What all Tantric schools have in common is the affirmation that this transcendental Truth is to be discovered in the human body itself, not somewhere else. This affirmation expresses the fundamental doctrine of the Mahayana tradition that the world of change (*samsara*) is co-essential with the ultimate Reality, whether called *nirvana* ("extinction") or *sunya* ("void").[77]

Importantly, Tantra uses the energy of Nature and the human body to generate transformation, not just mystical ideas or turning inward away from the world and the body. *Tantrikas* (or practitioners of Tantra) used these practices to help transmute base consciousness into the Enlightened State. One of our scholars explains: "Tantra is the unique combination of mantra, ritual, worship and yoga on an absolutistic basis. It is both philosophy and religion, and aims at the transmutation of human personality, by tantric practices suited to the spiritual temperament and needs of the individual, into the Absolute."[78] Yoga pandit Feuerstein confirms: "Tantric Buddhism, or Vajrayana, is an esoteric ritualism that includes a vast variety of paraphernalia and the ceremonial worship and internalization of male and female deities, as well as the philosophy of spontaneity (*sahaja*)."[79] In other words, ultimately the Transcendental Reality is not merely found in the external manipulation of body or even the mind but is simply intuited to be one's native Condition. The externals then become blissful play balanced with disciplined sadhana grounded in Right View and Right Life. Feuerstein confirms this understanding in *The Yoga Tradition* (1998):

> The great Tantric formula, which is fundamental also to Mahayana

Buddhism, is "*samsara* equals *nirvana.*" That is to say, the conditional or phenomenal world is coessential with the transcendental Being-Consciousness-Bliss. Therefore, Enlightenment is not a matter of leaving the world, or of killing one's natural impulses. Rather, it is a matter of envisioning the lower reality as contained in and coalescing with the higher reality [of Spirit-God], and of allowing the higher reality to transform the lower reality. Thus, the keynote of Tantra is integration—the integration of the self [ego] with the Self [Atman].[80]

Although originally developed as an underground movement coming from northern India and the caves of the Himalayas, Tantra was integrated into the later schools of Vajrayana Buddhism. Sometimes called "**Tantrayana**," it involved a set of difficult disciplines, self-control, and strict obedience to the qualified Lama or Guru. The different schools of Tibetan Buddhism categorized the various tantric scriptures and practices into various classes leading to increasing levels of bliss awareness to finally focus on the "emptiness" of "**Clear Light Bliss**" (*prabhasvara* which literally means "brilliance") arising from "the eternal indestructible drop of the heart."[81] These practices therefore stimulate the inner anatomy of the body-mind, including the cerebrospinal fluid, the endocrine system (where *chakras* correspond to the various glands), the nervous system, as well as the subtle energy channels (*nadis*), including the central channel (and other corresponding channels), the inner brain (including the "third eye" or *ajna chakra*), all of which Adi Da calls the "**esoteric anatomy**" of the human being. Therefore, chanting, mudras, meditation, and other practices (especially advance tantric disciplines), stimulate and purify these currents circulating throughout the body-mind-soul. Tulku Urgyen Rinpoche explains: "Ultimately everybody has to travel the path themselves and purify their own obscurations.... There is no other way to reach Enlightenment than by recognizing Buddha-Nature and attaining stability in it."[82] This begins with *rigpa* or Awakening (similar to *prajna* in Sanskrit; *satori* in Japanese, etc.) where the aim of Dzogchen is to integrate this primordial awareness into daily life. As *Progressive Stages of Meditation on Emptiness* outlines:

> *The mind of clear light is the foundation of all other minds.* When the gross and subtle minds and winds dissolve into the indestructible drop at the heart [pure Ascent], you perceive only the clear light and

it is from this clear light that all other minds—each one more gross than the one it follows [from causal/very subtle to subtle to gross]—are generated [pure Descent].[83]

The Sarma or newer schools (Kagyu, Sakya, and Gelug) divided these tantras into four classes, while the Nyingma or "Ancient" school divides the last class into three separate subdivisions, topping off with "Highest Yoga Tantra" (Anu Yoga) and Dzogchen (Ati Yoga). I think it's important to note that Avatar Adi Da Samraj, in developing the Reality-Way of Adidam Ruchiradam (which was not based on scriptural study but his own Enlightenment and Divine Emergence), has practices very similar to these tantras, such as with Radical Devotion, Right Life, the "Five Reality Teachings," the "Perfect Knowledge" series, and, ultimately, the "Perfect Practice" (which is similar to Dzogchen). These are available to any serious practitioner willing to take up his Way of **Atma Nadi Shakti Yoga** (as taught by Adi Da), yet without the artifice of Buddhist traditions, which, from the beginning of practice (in Adidam), reveals (or intuits) "the 'Bright'" Condition (or the Reality of Real God).

Over time, therefore, the tantric practices of Vajrayana Buddhism were subdivided into the "external" or "**Lower Tantras**" that emphasized acts of external rituals and purifications (right diet, etc.) and interior practices (including Deity Yoga)—called:

(1) **Kriya** or "Action" tantra (external ritual practices and disciplines);

(2) **Charya** or "Conduct" tantra (external-internal deity practices, including mudras or hand gestures);

(3) **Yoga** tantra (integrated meditative practices)—all generally reserved for the monasteries and for practitioners of varying levels of practice (beginning, middle, mature).

Then come the "internal" or "**Higher Tantras**," which are the tantra divisions that work with the subtle energy systems of the body (chakras, channels, winds, etc., of the gross, subtle, and very subtle [or causal] bodies, etc.), including the "clear light" level of the root mind or consciousness (the very subtle level) in the heart—then comes **Anuttarayoga** tantra or "**Highest Yoga Tantra**"[84] including the "bliss of being in union," which the Nyingma school subdivides this stage into:

(1) **Maha Yoga** or the "Father tantras" of the "generation" stage emphasizing the practice of blissful awareness;

(2) **Anu Yoga** or "Mother tantras" of the "completion" stage emphasizing the further development of enlightened "clear light" (*prabhasvara*) awareness; and finally,

(3) **Ati Yoga** or Dzogchen (the "Great Perfection"), a non-gradual method that focuses on the innate purity of Consciousness Itself.

Ultimately, Dzogchen speaks of attaining the "**rainbow body**" which involves the transformation of the physical body into energetic states or after death when the gross body is dropped materializing into a body of light. In all cases, very importantly, these Tantras were always given under the guidance and instruction of a qualified Guru-Adept or Maha-Siddha (known in Tibet as Lama or Rinpoche), one who has already completed the Tantra. This tradition has tried to become established in the more liberal (and less disciplined) West with varying degrees of success (and failures).

People in the West who use "tantra" for their own personal (egoic) pleasure, especially with sexual encounters, almost always dismiss the need for Guru Yoga and the Awakened Adept thinking they can do it on their own, thus corrupting this ancient time-honored tradition. Professor Smith notes: "Tantric sexual practice is pursued not as a law-breaking revel, but under the careful supervision of a *guru* (spiritual teacher) in the controlled context of a nondualistic outlook, and as the climax of a long sequence of spiritual disciplines practiced through many lives."[85] This means the many years (and decades) of practice, as well as renunciation, that are involved. Once again, scholar-pandit Miranda Shaw clearly explains in *Passionate Enlightenment* (1984):

> **Tantra** is a path that uses passion as a basis for self-transformation through ecstatic beatitude. Therefore, passion (*raga*) and desire, specifically amorous or sexual desire (*kama*), are essential for both male and female Tantrics....
>
> Tantric texts agree that the sexual yoga for transforming passion to divine ecstasy should be performed in a state of meditative awareness that is free from lust, ordinary attachment, and conceptual thought. This presumes both a passionate temperament and tangible progress toward cultivating a pure heart and clear mind.[86]

In this case, maturity and practical experience will sooner or later turn the sincere practitioner to the proper training and instruction that they require. This is why Adepts—including Avatar Adi Da Samraj—appear to serve all humankind and their serious students. But we must first learn to turn to them and sit at their feet with respect and devotion.

Tantra is based on the disciplines and philosophies found in the sacred texts called *Tantras*, yet these exotic practices were always accomplished under the guidance of a genuine Tantric Master-Adept. This relationship has always been vital since these esoteric practices would often use restricted accessories, such as liquor, meat, and sex, but they were done in a sacred ritualistic context (not for self-indulgence). Instead of shunning the world as illusion the *tantrika* transforms the conflicting world of opposites into the prior unity of "**One Taste**" (*samarasa*) enacting the nondual unity of samsara and nirvana. Feuerstein notes: "Tantra is more 'value-free' than the non-Tantric traditions; that is, it permits practices that are ordinarily considered taboo in spiritual life… Tantra is body-positive and anti-puritanical."[87] This obviously confuses casual Westerners. Yet this is also what makes such a "short-cut to Enlightenment" so dangerous, thus needing close instruction from a competent Siddha-Guru.

As Wilber points out, this process of Tantric practices—replicating the evolution from Hinayana to Mahayana to Vajrayana—involves the (Ascending) *Paths of Renunciation* "where defilements are exterminated in cessation" (exemplified in Samkhya Yoga and Theravada), which then evolved into the (Descending) *Paths of Transformation* "where the defilements are seen to be the *seeds of corresponding wisdoms*, since nirvana and samsara are ultimately not-two" (exemplified in Mahayana, Vajrayana, and Tantra) that turned into the (Ascending-Descending or Nondual) *Paths of Self-Liberation* "where the defilements are seen to be *already* self-liberated just as they are, and just as they arise, since their basic nature is *always already* primordial Purity [or] pure Emptiness in pure Presence"[88] (exemplified in Dzogchen, Mahamudra, and Adidam Ruchiradam).

In Tantra, the Supreme Reality (*Dharmadhatu*) is seen to contain the relative conditional world as the consummation and unity of masculine and feminine principles (*shiva/shakti*) transforming into Nondual Oneness. This is why Tantra paintings (called *thangkas*) often depict an Adept in sexual embrace or coitus (*maithuna*) united with his adoring consort as they both merge into the empty oneness of their innate Buddha-Nature. Buddhist scholar T. R. V. Murti summarizes this view in *The Central Philosophy of Buddhism* (1955):

> It is *Sunyata* that provided the metaphysical basis for the rise of Tantra. With its phenomenalizing aspect, *Karuna* [compassion], the formless Absolute (*Sunyata*) manifests itself as the concrete world. But the forms [of samsara] neither exhaust nor do they bring down the Absolute [Nirvana]. It is through these forms again that [the human] ascends and finds his [or her] consummation with the universal principle [of Buddha-Nature or Enlightened Consciousness—Clear Light Bliss].[89]

As mentioned, many of the "secret teachings" of Tantra were often revealed in what the Tibetans call **terma** or "hidden treasures" since they were supposedly planted in the earth (or minds of receptive future Adepts) by Guru Rinpoche Padmasambhava (in the 8th century CE)—often assisted by his enlightened consort Lady Yeshe Tsogyal—only to be found when the time was ripe for their revelation. Their dissemination was delayed since they usually involved teachings from the highest yoga tantra level, therefore practitioners had to be ready for their sacred transmissions. In Tibet, they were discovered by **Tertöns** or "Treasure Masters," most often in the ancient Nyingma lineage, which is thus sometimes referred to as the "Treasure Text tradition."

The movement of Buddhism into other Asian countries, from Southeast Asia to China to Japan and Tibet, was undertaken by a series of profound (and well-educated) scholar-pandits and Adept-Realizers carrying with them their translations of the Indian Sanskrit Buddhist *Sutras* and *Tantras*. Like a lotus bud growing up from the muddy bottom of the lake to bloom when it reaches the light, Buddhism continues its growth and influence spreading beauty, wisdom, and compassion throughout the Kosmos. These living "Buddhas" and "Bodhisattvas"—or "Bodhi-Siddhas" (in Adi Da's terms) have appeared in every generation expressing themselves with eloquent articulation and rational intelligence giving humankind, up to this very day, the great variety of Buddhist Tantra *Sutras* we now know about (too numerous to mention here).[90] Yet, remember it was always a Realized Adept who was at the root-source of this wisdom that further evolved Buddhism throughout the centuries (the ceaseless "Turning the Wheel of Dharma").

Importantly, this evolution of Dharma (or "Teaching of Truth") is based in oral and textual as well as spiritual *transmissions* handed down from Master to devotee in a personal and well-earned sacred relationship founded on *direct experience* (not simply book learning). According to these Great Adepts, their lineages reach back to the primordial Buddha, the ***Adi-Buddha*** (or "First Buddha") who is, historically speaking, the human being Siddhartha Shakyamuni, the founder of Buddhism, but who mythically (and mystically) exists since the beginning of time (and in all universes). Adi Da Samraj offers such sacred practices and Yogas as well, for not only does he Teach about Enlightenment but is here to Transmit (via his *Ruchira-Shaktipat*) the "Clear Light Bliss" of the "Bright" to all who turn to him as Siddha-Guru and Divine Avatar, the Primordial Adi Buddha.

Seventh Stage Nondualism:
Samsara and Nirvana ARE the Same

As we saw in the previous chapter, only an Awakened Adept can clear up the misunderstanding around such nondual phrases as "Samsara and Nirvana are the same" (in Nagarjuna's words) expressing the nondual perspective of Nondual Mysticism (in Wilber's words), or that "form is emptiness, emptiness is not different than form, neither is form different from emptiness, indeed, emptiness is form" (in the words of the *Heart Sutra*). From our relative (conventional) point of view, samsara and Nirvana are certainly *not* the same because **samsara** is the dissatisfaction/suffering of the separate self—or "self-contraction" (in Adi Da's words)—while **Nirvana** is the Transcendental Reality (also known in our terms as Real God and Buddha-Nature) [see Chapter 17]. This Mahayana view of Nirvana, beyond Hinayana's conception, goes beyond cessation (or formlessness) since it is the "infinite space" from *within* which samsara (the phenomenal universe) is arising. Adi Da, therefore, notes the development of Mahayana-Vajrayana into an "idealism" similar to Vedanta beyond the "realism" of the original disposition taught by Hinayana:

> The Mahayana [and Vajrayana] path is based on an "idealistic" conception in which conditional or phenomenal existence (or samsara) is understood to inhere in (and not to be separate from or causally related to) the Transcendental Reality (or Nirvana). And that path stands in contrast to the original Buddhist path which was based on a purely "realistic" analysis of phenomena (or self and not-self), and which view Nirvana as an utterly independent and relationless Transcendental Realization (not related to phenomena via causation,

not at all coincident with phenomena or phenomenal consciousness, and, therefore, attainable only in the event of the utter cessation of phenomenal arising).[91]

This means, then, that in the Grand Scheme of Things, samsara (as the separate self) and Nirvana (as God) are not exactly the same, although from the Ultimate View they are in fact precisely "One without a second," "not-two," i.e., Nondual. Wilber identifies this move from causal unmanifest formlessness (such as in *nirvikalpa samadhi*) to a nondual embrace of reality (such as in *sahaj samadhi*) with the term "**Nondual Mysticism**" giving us the "**Nondual traditions**" (such as with Advaita Vedanta, Yogachara, Vajrayana, and Tantra). This is the next (and final) evolutionary step beyond Formless Mysticism— where, as Wilber says, "the great Nondual traditions, East and West, attempt to integrate both the Ascending and the Descending path…. To balance both transcendence and immanence, Emptiness and Form, nirvana and samsara, Heaven and Earth."[92] In *The Eye of Spirit* (1997), Wilber made plain: "The realization of the Nondual traditions is uncompromising: there is only Spirit, there is only God, there is only Emptiness in all its radiant wonder…. And this simple recognition of an *already present* Spirit is the task, as it were, of the great Nondual traditions." To his great credit, Wilber himself has been uncompromising in promoting this Nondual perspective. However, I believe he was always emboldened to take this stance, not only from his own *satori* (or Nondual Realization), but also upon Adi Da's Teaching that emphasizes the "*always already*" Condition of Real God.[93]

In his own unique brilliance, Wilber also summarized this Nondual stance using Plato's/Plotinus' words (showing again the universality of the Perennial Philosophy, East and West) by stating: "Flee the Many [samsara], find the One [Nirvana or Sixth Stage formlessness]; having found the One, embrace the Many as the One [Seventh Stage Nondual Realization]. Or in short: Return to One [Nirvana], embrace Many [samsara]."[94] In Buddhist terms, as we've discussed: Flee the phenomenal self and world of suffering (samsara), find Nirvana; having discovered (or *realized*) Nirvana, embrace the self and world as Nirvana (or the Transcendental Reality). Avatar Adi Da explains in depth how this nondual view appeared to Buddhism:

The later Mahayana schools proclaimed, in contrast to Gautama, that phenomena are inherently egoless. This attitude was expressed in the Madhyamika view that "nirvana and samsara are the same." The same view was later expressed (in the *Lankavatara Sutra* and in the Teachings of the Yogachara or Vijnanavada school) via the "idealistic" Buddhist view that "Consciousness," or the Transcendental and Unconditional "Buddha-Mind," is the Source and Condition and truth of all conventional, conditional, and conceptual "dharmas" or apparent "realities."

And the persuasions associated with this original Mahayana tradition provided the basis for the Vajrayana conception of Enlightenment as **"Coemergent Wisdom"** [Tantra] or the unconditional Samadhi that is inherent in the transcendence of the idea of a difference between Nirvana and samsara. The central thrust of these philosophical trends in later Buddhism is in the direction of conceiving a path that is most basically about the transcendence of concepts, or the conditional mind.... that Condition was conceived to be the inherent Condition of conditions (or causes and effects, great or small in the scale of Nature).[95]

As we discussed [see Chapter 17], the way that the **"Mahayana Enlightenment Equation"** (in Adi Da's words) is true is when we realize that samsara arises *within* Nirvana, for only in that sense are they "the same." It is only in Enlightenment that samsara is recognizable as Nirvana and known to be empty, void, free, boundless, formless form. I always liked the way the pandit-Bodhisattva Lex Hixon translated the *Heart Sutra*'s verse:

> Universal transparency is what manifests as both form and consciousness. Material forms are empty of the slightest substantial self-existence, and luminous emptiness of self-existence is precisely what is manifest as material forms. In the same way, conscious states are empty of the slightest independent self-existence, and luminous emptiness of self-existence is precisely what is manifest as conscious states.[96]

Samsara arises *within* Nirvana (*as* Nirvana) thus they are the same when seen from the view of Nondual Enlightenment. Buddha Bob Thurman got it right when he said: "That's the Bliss that everything is made of (in the Tantric vision). That's why Nirvana and samsara are the same—because in a way, samsara is made of Nirvana… [but] of course, you can't fully understand that unless you become a perfect Buddha."[97] Yet everybody, especially Western pandits (including Wilber), like to throw the Buddha's sayings around as if we are all Perfect Buddhas… well, not yet. As Adi Da warns: "In the mode of 'pop' Buddhism, formulae such as 'Nirvana and samsara are the same' are reduced to slogans that justify the conventions of egoity in the lesser Stages of Life."[98] We need to *realize* the truth of the Nondual View by first engaging in genuine Guru Yoga in order to *realize* God or Buddha-Nature for ourselves before making such utterances. Ultimately, we must make the sacrifice (of ego) and do the work; the Buddha-Guru can only help lead the way.

Part of the reason for this perpetual confusion between samsara and Nirvana, as we've seen [see Chapter 17], comes from Theravada's (Hinayana Buddhism's) emphasis that **Nirvana**—from the prefix "*nir*" meaning "without" and "*vana*" meaning "desiring, grasping, craving"—as the goal of practice, therefore, implying the complete extinction (or "blowing out") or utter transcendence of samsara. Thus Wilber points out: "According to some schools, there is even an end limit, or 'extreme' form of Nirvana, called *nirodh*—complete cessation—where neither consciousness nor objects arise at all, and that might be thought of as an infinite formlessness of pure freedom ['Formless Mysticism']. Be that as it may, the goal [of Hinayana] is clear: get out of samsara and into Nirvana."[99] In Adi Da's terms, this version of Nirvana is seen as the **Sixth Stage of Life**, which is epitomized with **Nirvikalpa** (or "formless") **Samadhi**, the causal Witness detached from all forms just "witnessing" them rise and fall, which is itself a profound realization, yet it is ultimately incomplete, according to the Nondual Sages [see Appendix I].

Mahayana Buddhism, in contrast, saw this individual-oriented interiorization of absolute emptiness (*sunyata*) as still falling short of the true nature inherent in the Buddha's Realization, the purity of the **Seventh Stage of Life** that ultimately reveals the Heart of Love and Compassion as being the Truth of our Divine Condition realized in **Sahaj** (or "Open Eye") **Samadhi**. *Prajna* reveals not just Emptiness (*sunya*) but a Divine Fullness (*tathagatagarbha*), the *Dharmadhatu* or "Buddhaverse" (in Thurman's terms), not merely nihilistic nothingness (or cessation), as the Yogachara Buddhists realized and taught. Of course, these are closer to the original definitions of the Sixth and Seventh Stages of Life [see table below] that Adi Da first used which Wilber then picked up on (in the late 1970s) because they fit with his model and reasoning in distinguishing between the Causal (formless) and Nondual (One Taste) domains. However, by the mid-1990s, Adi Da modified his definitions slightly by referring to traditional Enlightened Adepts as being "premonitory" (or "preliminary") Seventh Stage since they tended to *teach* from the earlier Stages (Fourth to Sixth) following their traditions, for example, with the Buddha's emphasis on "realism" and Emptiness (Sixth Stage) [see Chapter 19 for more detail].

Stage of Life	Fourth Stage	Fifth Stage	Sixth Stage	Seventh Stage
Domain	Low Subtle	High Subtle	Casual	Nondual
Samadhi	Bhakti	Savikalpa	Nirvikalpa	Sahaj / Bhava
Advanced-Tip	Saints	Yogis	Sages	Siddhas
Error	Separate from Divine	Ascending mysticism	Introversion cessation	No error: En-Light-enment

The Buddha's (and our) Awakening is one of nondual embrace, a view that, as Wilber wonderfully explains, "would ring out from the Nondual Heart: the Many returning to and embracing the One [in Formless Mysticism] is Good, and is known as *wisdom*; the One returning to and embracing the Many [in Nondual Mysticism] is Goodness, and is known as *compassion*."[100] Thus Mahayana offers a more socially and compassionate embrace of samsara with its Bodhisattva ideal for transforming the entire Kosmos into Nirvana manifested (and realized). Adi Da agrees: "It should be clear, then, that both the ultimate Mahayana idea (of Enlightenment as the equation of Nirvana and samsara) and the ultimate Mahayana ideal (of the Enlightened Bodhisattva) are conceptions born of the Transcendental Wisdom of the Seventh Stage of Life."[101] Our trustworthy pandit Georg Feuerstein precisely explains:

> In keeping with this reorientation, *nirvana* was no longer conceived as a goal "out there" but as the ever-present substratum underlying phenomenal existence. The famous Mahayana formula is *nirvana* equals *samsara*, that is, the immutable transcendental Reality is identical with the world of impermanence, and vice versa. What this means is that the realm of changeable forms is inherently empty (*sunya*) and that *nirvana* must not be sought outside *samsara*.[102]

In Tibetan Vajrayana Buddhism, as we've seen, this formula of integrating the apparently dualistic relative reality within the nondual Absolute Reality was achieved and epitomized by **Tantra** with its embrace of ordinary human existence (and desires) as a method of consciousness transformation into Enlightenment (Nirvana), not its extinction. This highlights the different perspectives uncovered by the revolving Dharma Wheel of Buddhism and the Buddha's Teaching. This is precisely why we need Adept-Realizers, such as today's World Teacher Adi Da Samraj, who reveals what is really going on:

> The original idea expressed in the form of "Nirvana and samsara are the same" is an expression of Enlightened freedom from egoic and phenomenal bondage. Therefore, in that formula. "Samsara" simply means "phenomenal existence." It does not mean bondage. (That is to say, the equation does not mean Nirvana, or Enlightenment, and bondage are the same.) It is only in the original or Hinayana concept of "samsara" that the term means both "phenomenal existence" and

"bondage." (Therefore, in the Hinayana view, Nirvana is absolutely not samsara.) The Mahayana formula views "samsara" (as a general term for phenomenal existence) from the Enlightened or Seventh Stage point of view... [therefore] the **Mahayana Enlightenment Equation** should be regarded as the expression of a point of view that will be possible for them [Hinayana Buddhists] only in the event of their spiritual maturity.[103]

Chopping wood, carrying water becomes marvelous (enlightened) activities when not seen as the self's burden in samsara. It is to "to see a world in a grain of sand and a heaven in a wild flower, hold infinity in the palm of your hand and eternity in an hour" (in William Blake's words). This is why, no doubt, Avatar Adi Da named his form of Advaitayana Buddhism with the unique term "**Nirvanasara**," the Perfect knowledge of Nirvana united (in prior unity) with samsara:

> When there is no self-contraction [ego], the Realm of Nature is Obvious as it *is*.... Transcend the self-contraction via radical understanding until the Awakening of the Seventh Stage of Life [of Perfect Nondual Mysticism], wherein self and not-self are equally and simultaneously transcended and ultimately Outshined in the One that *is* Love and Happiness and the Peace of Bliss. This is "**Nirvanasara**," the Essence of the Teaching of Nirvana, or Radical Transcendentalism.[104]

Nirvanasara is where we live now, in other words. Nirvana-samsara, Absolute-relative, transcendent-immanent, heaven-hell—it's all up to our mind (and heart) and how we interpret our present reality. This is why the Buddha appeared; this is why the lineage of Adepts continue to Teach every generation; this is why the Avatar was incarnated; this is why the Guru-Siddhas are born to offer genuine Guru Yoga-Satsang to all who will listen, hear, and see that we all are really Divine even in the midst of this material realm and psycho-physical universe of suffering, madness, and death. We live in a Kosmic-Mandala of Divine Radiance but we must each Wake Up and see just that... otherwise we are living in samsara (maya). Which do you choose? It *is* your choice. Choose well and be diligent in your practice and devotion to Right View and Truth, as the Buddha (and Avatar) suggest.

EMPTY OR FULL:
MADHYAMAKA VS. YOGACHARA DEBATE

his ongoing "debate" or confusion between viewing or transcending "Samsara" and "Nirvana" is, as I maintain, truly only clarified by the Enlightened understanding of a Realized Adept or Awakened Buddha, such as Adi Da has done above. Such Enlightened insight also clears up a very subtle debate that has gone on within the Tibetan Buddhist schools that can be effectively cleared up (and integrated) with the Reality-Teachings of Avatar Adi Da Samraj and his distinction between the Sixth and Seventh Stages of Life [see Appendix I]. In the Mahayana Buddhist philosophy of **Madhyamaka** founded by its greatest proponent Nagarjuna [see Chapter 17], they claim that all phenomena and self are ultimately "empty" (*sunya*) of any enduring essence. The Tibetans call this **Rangtong** (*rang stong* or "empty of self-nature") and it was defended rigorously by the famous pandit-Adept Tsong Khapa (who founded the Gelug sect). Nagarjuna, as we've seen, emphasized that both self and phenomena are simply "empty," therefore, *sunyata* has no need to point to anything beyond that. This is the mainstream Tibetan interpretation of Madhyamaka. In essence, this corresponds to the Realization of the Sixth Stage of Life, as Adi Da explains:

> In the Sixth Stage mode, Buddhism sees self as not-self (or only phenomenon rather than noumenon), and so it by-passes the false view of soul (or a permanent non-phenomenal self) and the implied necessity of phenomenal existence. But it also is bound to a problematic struggle with phenomenal existence and a reluctance to admit the always

present Reality that always already Outshines self and world.[105]

This Sixth Stage view of "Formless Mysticism" (in Wilber's terms) was later countered, or expanded, by the Tibetan Adepts of **Yogachara** based on their own innate Realization of Buddha-Nature (or Dharmakaya, since names do not matter) where they suggest, yes, it is true that phenomenal relative reality (and the self) are *sunya* ("empty") but that Absolute Reality is itself not empty but is "truly existing." This view is called **Shentong** or **Zhentong** (*gzhan* "other," *stong* "empty," or "other-emptiness") which agrees that the *rangtong* understanding of Emptiness (*sunya*) does destroy false concepts (of self and relative reality) but that ultimately Enlightenment involves the fullness of realizing an eternal essence or Buddha-Nature (known as *Tathagatagarbha* or *Dharmadhatu* or *Buddhadhātu* or *Buddhajnana*, and so on) which can be described in positive terms (such as luminous clear light, love-bliss, etc.). This view was systematized and expounded by **Dolpopa Sherab Gyaltsen** (1292-1361), whose views are summarized by modern-day pandit Cyrus Stearns in his wonderful study *The Buddha from Dolpo* (1999):

> In brief, Dolpopa considered the Buddha-Nature to be naturally luminous radiant light, which is synonymous with the buddha-body of reality (*dharmakaya*), and a primordial, indestructible, and eternal state of great bliss inherently present in all its glory within every living being.... Whereas the veils of temporary defilement are empty of self-nature (*rang stong*), the Buddha-Nature is empty only of phenomena other than itself (*gzhan stong*).[106]

Relative reality is in fact "empty," only existing as a vast matrix of co-dependent (and interdependent) arising, as the "realistic" Buddhists say, but so does the Absolute Reality or the True Self (*Atman-Brahman*), as the "idealistic" Advaitists say, exist as a Radiant Transcendental Being of *Sat-Chit-Ananda* (Existence-Consciousness-Bliss)—or Real God (in Western terms). Once more, modern-day Avatar Adi Da precisely explains and integrates both views by pointing to the Seventh Stage of Life Realization that reveals the "Bright" of "Conscious Light" (from the beginning) which transcends-yet-includes the Transcendental Realization of "emptiness" (realized by Sixth Stage of Life):

It is from this conventional "realism" [of Hinayana] that the great tradition of Buddhism gained and inherited its limitations as well as its virtues. And that original Buddhist view is focused on the basic proposition that the phenomenal self is unnecessary and thus inherently transcendable. Even the later Buddhist schools [of Mahayana and Vajrayana] maintain the tendency toward analysis of the phenomenal self (and all phenomenal events) as *merely* or exclusively phenomenal events (or merely phenomenal ideas). Thus, the ultimate Buddhist conception is flavored by this conventional phenomenal context of consideration. All apparent entities are ultimately viewed to be not-self, non-entities, Void of self-essence.

Some Buddhist schools (such as the Vijnanavada [Yogachara]) tended to give positive metaphysical status to that phenomenal Void (calling It Mind, Consciousness, and so forth)... Even so, all characteristically Buddhist conceptions are, to one or another degree, founded in phenomenal realism, and, therefore, traditional and conventional Buddhist orthodoxy tends to feel uncomfortable with the affirmation of an ultimate noumenal Reality.[107]

The Sixth Stage limitation, or "error," is ultimately only transcended in the Seventh Stage Realization of Complete Divine Enlightenment or, as Adi Da says, "the affirmation that the phenomenal self and the phenomenal not-self are not merely Void of a phenomenal essence but Full of the Transcendental Essence, Consciousness, or Self-Existing Being."[108] In any case, these type of subtle debates *must be* based on actual Divine Realization or Ultimate Enlightenment since their very subject matter transcends the observing subject (and its discriminative mind) altogether. Hence, only Awakened Adepts truly understand and are capable of making such precise pronouncements, though we should all be schooled to what they are pointing to. Part of the reason I am pointing to them here, in this brief overview, is to acknowledge what I feel is Avatar Adi Da's complete and total understanding of the highest and most enlightened traditions of humankind. Indeed, I believe he is offering a culmination and summary of all that has come before, thus setting the stage for a new Integral Age of enlightened understanding [see Chapter 10]. Let's end this section by allowing the Ruchira Buddha to speak for himself in this extended quote from his unparaelleld *Nirvanasara* (1982):

Buddhism and Advaitism represent the two basic ancient traditional approaches to Transcendental Realization. As such, these two traditions are really streams of one tradition. That single tradition is the ultimate stage of religious and spiritual philosophy. It is a tradition that is principally associated with the orientations of the Sixth and Seventh Stage of Life. Therefore, the total tradition of Transcendental Realization stands either in contrast to or as an advancement beyond the traditions that pursue the various goals of the first Five Stages of Life.

However, this tradition of Transcendental Realization itself bears certain historical limitations. And those limitations originate in the conceptual limitations of the Sixth Stage of Life ["Formless Mysticism"]. My Own Work is the ultimate development of the tradition of Transcendental Realization. My Teaching stands in positive but critical relation to the entire Great Tradition, including all the schools of the first Six Stages of Life.

I view the traditions of Buddhism and Advaitism to be the ultimate, most advanced, or Sixth to Seventh Stage dimensions of the Great Tradition. But My Work is also to reconsider and purify what we have inherited from the Great Tradition as a whole, and, therefore, My Work stands in critical relation to the Buddhist and Advaitic traditions themselves.... Therefore, I Teach a Way that epitomizes the Great Tradition and that stands entirely on the basis that is the Free Transcendental point of view of the ["Nondual" or "Prior Unity"] Seventh Stage of Life....

The Way That I Teach is the Seventh Stage Way of natural, inherent, or always prior Abiding as the Radiant Transcendental Being, free of the self-based or inherently contracted tendency toward phenomenal extroversion or noumenal introversion.... All of that inheres in the Transcendental Being without qualifying the Bliss or Radiance of Consciousness even to the slightest degree.

The Way That I Teach is to Abide in this Awakened Realization of the Transcendental or unborn Being or Consciousness, recognizing all that arises in It, tacitly allowing the manifest world and self [samsara] to be spontaneous expressions of the Radiant Self [Nirvana], until that very Divine Self or Reality Outshines all noticing of conditional existence.[109]

Importantly, as all the Adepts and Avatar Adi Da persistently insist, you too can *realize* this Transcendental Condition or Enlightened State of Real God since it is always already the truth. But first you must understand the egoic self-contraction and do sadhana (spiritual practices) by turning to authentic Guru-Adepts in genuine Guru Yoga-Satsang so you may clearly recognize your innate Buddha-Nature—or the Truth of Reality—which is "always already the case" (as Adi Da consistently says). Let's next turn to Tibetan "Guru Yoga" in our brief survey.

TIBETAN GURU YOGA

Importantly, as I've indicated, each school of Tibetan Buddhism emphasizes the all-important role of the Guru or Lama, a practice that has often been deemphasized as Buddhism enters the West and clashes with the individualistic, egalitarian, democratic, modern worldview (of the Omega-mind). Nevertheless, the importance of "**Guru Yoga**" cannot be overlooked; yet still, such "Buddhas" (or Spiritual Masters) must be understood from a mature point of view if the Dharma and Sangha are to remain strong and vibrant in the modern global culture. Guru Yoga itself has a specific practice in Tibetan Buddhism where the devotee "becomes" the Guru (and thus the Buddha) through various meditation and visualization practices. Buddhist scholar Keith Dowman expertly explains:

> The heart of the initiation is the Guru's revelation of himself as the Buddha and the initiate's experience of identity with this Guru/ Buddha. Thereafter, the initiate's basic practice is to reproduce this ultimate experience of oneness and to assimilate it fully into

his everyday life. Identifying the Guru/Buddha's body with all human beings and all appearance whatsoever, and his speech with all human speech and all sound whatsoever, and his mind with the all-pervasive, pure, non-dual awareness, he effectively identifies himself with the Guru. So, although the initiate will always retain respect for the human individual in whom the Buddha manifested at initiation, gradually his notion of the Guru expands to include all beings without exception, including himself. The Siddha is a man [or woman] with such a vision.[110]

Centered around a living Lama, or a past Maha-Siddha, there are many varieties of Tibetan Guru Yoga (*la-may nal-jor*), for according to a respected authority like the Dalai Lama, its practice has always been widespread with numerous manuals exclusively devoted to its veracity.[111] Most basically, Guru Yoga is founded on a relationship where the Guru leads the devotee to Enlightenment by having them practice the required disciplines by keeping attention focused on the Lama's (and Buddha's) Enlightened State. By turning one's attention to the Lama, to your authentic Guru—to "Me"—it is easier to replicate the Lama's enlightened awareness, which is ultimately your own innate awareness—the same method used in the practice of Satsang (from India) as well. It is exactly similar to the type of sacred relationship offered by Adi Da Samraj in the Reality-Way of Adidam Ruchiradam.

Guru Yoga includes, for example, visualization techniques such as seeing the Lama floating above one's head and radiating light to the devotee or with the feet of the Lama standing in one's heart. Although at times described as "preliminary" practices, as the practitioner matures it actually becomes the core practice in replicating the Lama's Enlightened State. Thus, once again, we see that the stage of development and Realization attained by one's own Guru is of utmost importance for they need to be truly Enlightened or have realized the highest Stages of Life (the Sixth or Seventh Stages, in Adi Da's scheme). Supplemented by "**pointing out instructions**" (that help guide a practitioner to higher states of consciousness beyond ego) the fundamental practice still remains the same: Meditate on the Guru or Lama who is recognized as the Buddha in the state of Nirvana.

The modern Buddhist teacher Dilgo Khyentse summarizes: "Essentially, the practice is to remember the Guru in all our activities, whether in meditation or in post-meditation."[112] Or, as Avatar Adi Da likes to point out: *you become what you meditate on* (a universal principle of consciousness), thus it's best to meditate on the Enlightened One or the Guru-Adept as an embodiment of Conscious Light (or the Clear Light Void) because that *is* their Enlightened State as well as being *yours* too [see Chapter 22]. Perhaps, then, it's easier to understand why giving an authentic Adept-Realizer your attention (and studying their Teachings) may be the most potent spiritual practice possible, which is what I am suggesting in this book. Yet, it is your personal Guru, your chosen Master, whomever he or she might be that will work best for you in determining your progress and success. As Westerners, we must be careful not to dismiss such time-honored (and proven) techniques, simply because negative reaction to them comes from our fear of cults (which are only sometimes justified) and the delusions we have inherited from our provincial traditional religions.[113] The Dzogchen Master **Jigme Lingpa** (1730–1798) from the Nyingma school, a pillar of the tradition, put it like this:

> [Guru Yoga is] the finest method for realizing the innate wisdom within oneself. It is accomplished through one's own faith and by the grace or blessing of the Spiritual Guide. All Fully Awakened Beings abide inseparably in the expanse of Primordial Awareness, and all are in essence one. The Spiritual Master is the embodiment unifying all wisdom, compassion and power of an Awakened Being. Understanding this with strong devotion and belief will lead to a direct experience of the essence of the path. By these means the emotional defilements are purified and the accumulation of merit and wisdom is perfected.[114]

This is exactly why **Sakya Pandita** (1182–1251), for example, a moment before entering the clear light of death, placed his hand on the head of his young nephew and dharma heir **Chogyal Pagpa** (who was destined to be the spiritual tutor of Kublai Khan), to point out: "Practice Guru Yoga, the one path followed by all the Buddhas."[115] He then assumed the full meditation posture, held a dorje and bell together at his heart, and entered the clear light of death. Only a true Maha-Siddha can enact and live such esoteric processes grounded in unwavering devotion and transcendental wisdom. Guru Yoga is, most simply and directly, the real heart and true essence of God's Great Tradition of Global Wisdom, as this book has tried to show. Another modern Buddhist scholar, once again, makes this point crystal clear:

> Guru Yoga [Satsang] purifies one's awareness through practices that involves visualizing the teacher as an embodiment of the pure, exalted wisdom of Buddhahood.... The Guru transmits Buddhist teachings, instructs us on their proper application, and provides an example of a person who puts them into practice; thus the relation of a tantric practitioner with the Guru is much more intimate than relationships with Buddhas.
>
> Imagining one's Guru as a Buddha provides a concrete example of the awakened state one is trying to achieve.... Successful Vajrayana practice requires the ability to see the Guru as a Buddha, and to understand that any apparent faults the Guru might have are only reflections of one's own inadequacies.... One who views the Guru as a Buddha actualizes the innate potential for Buddhahood.[116]

Mention should also be made of the Tibetan *tulkus* who are reincarnate custodians—or an "incarnation body" (*tülku*)—of a specific lineage in Tibetan Buddhism. These are Adepts who supposedly reincarnate in succeeding generations to be sought out by their traditions, and then after being discovered as young children are raised and taught in an academic environment balanced by unconditional love. High-profile examples include the Dalai Lamas, the Panchen Lamas, the Karmapas, Khyentses, and the Kongtruls. Only in Tibet, it seems. What a precious jewel for this planet in honoring the power (and authenticity) of Guru Yoga-Satsang.

GURU YOGA DEVOTION

Guru Yoga has been practiced by enlightened Buddhas (and Adepts) for thousands of years helping to transform people from simple humans to awakened human beings, from one enlightened Buddha to another, generation after generation; this is the *lineage* so highly spoken about in Tibetan Buddhism. Nonetheless, it is still *our responsibility* to do the work, engage the yoga, practice the disciplines, for the Guru cannot do the sadhana for us, as the Buddha reminded us (on his deathbed[117]). Nonetheless, neither can we do it alone by ourselves. Buddhist pandit John Powers confirms: "All schools in Tibetan Buddhism emphasize the necessity of finding a qualified teacher. Such a teacher is one who has successfully traversed the path and attained the highest levels of Realization. Because of this, the Guru can guide students around the pitfalls they will encounter, warn them of dangers, correct their errors, and skillfully help them to actualize this potential Buddhahood. It is stated throughout Tibetan meditation literature that one cannot successfully follow the path of Tantra without a Guru."[118] This is precisely why I am directly pointing to Avatar Adi Da Samraj and the Reality-Way of Adidam Ruchiradam as being a viable alternative to even such a great and respected tradition as Tibetan Vajrayana Buddhism: He will help you realize your innate Buddhahood. Simply, directly, with Heart-Transmission and Perfect Wisdom, but first you must "turn to Him."

As the Great Wisdom Tradition maintains, Guru Yoga (*Satsang*) is a sacred and *spiritual* process that cannot and should not be erased or dismantled (or even diminished) as being outdated or irrelevant in our modern times. By accessing the "Divine Library" of our inherited wisdom, we must use our discriminative intelligence wisely to be sure the Lama-Guru is worthy of such a sacred responsibility and relationship. If not, it's better to choose a more appropriate Guru, not abandon the practice altogether. Buddhism has always affirmed the necessity for a qualified Guru-Adept to transmit the primordial state of Enlightenment (*bodhi*) to the student-devotee in order to help Awaken them to their true nature (or Consciousness Itself). But first the disciple must be prepared and purified before receiving the innermost transmission effectively, which often takes years of disciplined practice and meditation (*sadhana*).

This process and the need for authenticity has become especially relevant in today's modern world since some Buddhist Lamas and Rinpoches have come to the West needing to readapt to the different worldview and cultural milieu of the modern world. Some have failed to make the transition properly which has tarnished the idea of Guru Yoga as being appropriate for modern Westerners.[119] Yet still, we must avoid the tricks and illusions of the ego not willing to take on the practice of real sadhana-Satsang. Henceforth, I maintain, if used rightly Guru Yoga is as relevant today as ever! By studying the history of the Maha-Siddhas and Buddhist Masters we will see the efficacy, and indispensable nature, of Guru Yoga-Satsang. Indeed, as we've seen, Avatar Adi Da has instructed us as thoroughly on this sacred matter of Guru Yoga as any esoteric tradition on how to use the function of Satsang correctly without being cultic or deluded.[120]

| Manjushri | 14th Dalai Lama | Chagdud Tulku Rinpoche | Kalu Rinpoche | Ruchira Buddha |

As another example, before most significant initiations in Vajrayana Buddhism the practitioner is initially given instruction on Guru Yoga since it is ultimately the most fundamental—and quickest—practice to Enlightenment.

Indeed, Vajrayana has added the **Rinpoche** (Tibetan for "greatly precious") or Siddha-Guru as being the "Fourth Jewel" of Buddhism since contemplating the Guru and receiving his or her Grace is the most direct means to Awakened Realization. Importantly, this is accomplished by a sacred transmission from Lama-to-disciple, such as with initiation rituals including the powerful **Kalachakra Tantra**, an empowerment ceremony given so the devotee may begin the esoteric practices of the Kalachakra Tantra in the service of attaining Buddhahood. Perhaps one of the most intriguing and extremely authentic recent Rinpoches was the venerable **Kalu Rinpoche** (1905–1989), one of the first Tibetan Masters to teach in the West bringing these sacred initiation ceremonies to well-prepared Westerners (such as to Ken Wilber and Lama Surya Das). Another of my favorites, who radically altered my life after massaging his feet one evening, was the great Dzogchen master, **Chagdud Tulku Rinpoche** (1930–2002), who was, as Wilber noted, "one of only a handful of Tibetan masters giving the entire Dzogchen teachings, A to Z."[121] Consequently, nothing matches the authentic spiritual-transmission (*Shaktipat*) given from a genuine Guru-Lama to the aspiring devotee-student. As one Buddhist Tantra succinctly states:

> A hundred thousand visualizations of a deity's form, performed a hundred thousand times [a common Buddhist practice], are no match for one unwavering visualization of the Guru's form.[122]

It was also from Tibetan Buddhism that the well-known but small text *Fifty Verses of Guru-Devotion* was written by **Ashvaghosa** (ca. 80-150 CE) to help bring this practice into clear focus by establishing the fundamentals of Guru Yoga (based on the similar tradition of Stasang found in India). Once again, such devotion is not to be used in a cultic fashion but is for advanced spiritual growth and the transcendence of egoic tendencies (such as clinging to objects and persons and desires as well as to their aversions). In other words, the Guru is here only to help you realize your own Divine Condition and that of the Kosmos or "Buddhaverse," the *Dharmadhatu* (in Buddhist terms). They are here to serve the transcendence of ego, not infatuate the ego with cultic illusions.

As a result, a point which Adi Da also emphasizes, is that the essence of this important Buddhist scripture can be summarized in the short stanza: "Do whatever pleases your Guru and avoid doing anything that he [or she] would not like. Be diligent in both of these" (verse 46).[123] In this case, do whatever is necessary to make the Guru, and the Transmission of his or her Enlightened State, available to you. It's as simple as that. The genuine Guru is here to awaken the Buddha-Nature that you already are (but fail to realize), yet it takes a mature relationship based on ego-transcending disciplines and meditation which allows this Divine Realization to reach its fullest potential. Nevertheless, we must be on guard for fake or deluding Gurus too, even those with good intentions (but who have not yet acquired fully authentic qualifications).[124] Therefore, we must not only know about this sacred process, we must study and *practice* it to preserve it in each generation! Indeed, we are encouraged to become an active participant in this sacred lineage ourselves.

Such intense devotion may seem foreign or even unwarranted to the average Westerner, even by one impressed with the philosophy of Buddhism, especially in its milder Western forms (which often focuses on compassion and calming the mind and our negative emotions). Yet, if understood within the proper context of the genuine Guru-devotee relationship—such as the one offered by the Ruchira Buddha Adi Da Samraj—then the time-honored techniques like those found within Tibet's Guru Yoga is an affirmation of its authenticity, not just cultic fascination with a charismatic personality.

To *realize* and then live Enlightenment is no easy matter as all the esoteric traditions testify the world over. In most cases it is only with a genuine Guru or Guide—or one who has realized the Divine Nirvana for themselves—will we be able to suddenly experience our own Re-Awakening and then accomplish the necessary transformations (and purifications) needed to maintain it (via gradual post-Enlightenment practices). Yes, Enlightenment may rise spontaneously (given by Divine Grace, not self-effort), but that is very rare. Ultimately our God-Realization is *our responsibility*, not the Guru's, for it is our own ego-contraction, our own obscurations and defilements, that must be understood and transcended. No one else can do this for us. We *must practice*, actually do the yoga!

We must want to see God or *realize* our Buddha-Nature and yearn (or need) to know the truth of our Divine Condition for it to be revealed and *realized*. You won't get it from watching TV! Many of the world's religions declare this sacred process is the true purpose of this precious human life, yet most of us are too busy to do much about it. Ideally there is not a moment to waste. The Guru's call to "Follow Me!" is as immediate now as it was in the past. Therefore, the Guru or Lama is our best friend, our Spiritual Guide, not a cultic object of blind worship. They have realized the very State in which we too will awaken (since we are always already IT). But, first, we must understand and turn to the Agency of our own Enlightenment: the Buddha-Guru, our Beloved Lama-Masters. Thus have I heard (and seen).

BUDDHA'S UNIVERSAL TRANSMISSION

For the modern global culture I personally believe there is no other traditional world religion that offers more for everyone on the planet in developing the highest spiritual awakenings inherent in each individual than that of Buddhism. The Teachings of Buddhism (or the *Dharma*, in Sanskrit, and *Dhamma*, in Pali) originally came from a Fully Enlightened Guru-Adept, their "**Root Guru**" (as the Tibetans say) or primary Adept-Realizer. As mentioned above, this was **Siddhartha Gautama Shakyamuni**, who became the "*buddha*" or "Awakened One" living during the Axial Age of the 6th century BCE (500 years *before* Jesus Christ). Now, twenty-five centuries *after* Jesus, I believe, we have had another Avatar incarnate in our midst, born in the modern West—he is named **Adi Da Samraj**—who has come for the same purpose: to Awaken!

The universal appeal of Buddhism comes from the fact that it does not consider itself a religion or something to be believed in with faith alone but rather is about a *process* of coming to know oneself, of discovering the truth of one's own mind (and self) and our clinging to objects and others which then creates suffering. The same can be said of Adidam. Buddhism (and Adidam), in other words, is about the unfolding awakening of Enlightenment (via the Seven Stages of Life), whether sudden or gradual, as being an evolutionary or developmental potential inherent in every living human being… no matter what religious culture (or tribe) you were born into. Everyone can be Enlightened! Although it is true Buddhism does not believe in a Ruling Deity or "God" like Westerners do, it does assert a "Supreme Reality," as we've mentioned, that is the essence of our own consciousness, what Buddhists call "Buddha-Nature" (*tathāgatagarbha*) or *Dharmadhatu* ("Absolute Reality"), mere signifiers for the ineffable. Buddhism is therefore one of the most *universal* "religions" ever to appear on our planet. What a person becomes "Awake" to is Reality Itself, one's own true nature (as the Masters often say), not just ideas or belief systems. "This" is precisely what Adi Da offers everyone, if you will only "turn to Him."

This is precisely, in Tibetan Buddhism, what **Dzogchen** (*rdzogs chen*) is all about: to discover or have *direct* experiential knowledge of one's own true primordial condition, to Awaken to one's Buddha-Nature or Divine Condition. And this almost always involves a *direct transmission* from Master to devotee, usually given in secret (not in public) although paralleling the teachings of official Buddhist doctrines. This is precisely what real Tantra is all about at its heart: the transmission of the Enlightened State of the Master to the devotee who are each equal in Buddha-Nature. The modern-day Dzogchen Master **Chögyal Namkhai Norbu** (1938–2018) explains: "The Dzogchen Teachings are linked to a Transmission, which resides in the Master, and which is of fundamental importance for the development of the knowledge and Realization of the disciple."[125] He goes on to point out: "When a Dzogchen Master teaches, he or she transmits the state of knowledge through three types of transmission: oral, symbolic, and direct…. But in fact the three transmissions are all inseparable from the Master, and they themselves are the 'path'."[126] I could go on and on with countless examples from the sacred texts of Tibetan Vajrayana Buddhism verifying the same simple truth: the Spiritual-Transmission of the Guru-Adept, of one who has Awakened to the Enlightened State, is the core secret in the Enlightenment Traditions, the heart of God's Great Tradition of Global Wisdom. Thus, the stage of Awakening achieved by the Master is of primary importance, as this book keeps emphasizing. Go read the literature for yourself and discover what is revealed when this clue has been uncovered and set in its proper context.

Becoming a "buddha" or awakened human being is a real possibility for any person, thus Buddhism appeals to the evolution of consciousness that can be unveiled by anyone for himself or herself when served by an Awakened Master. This occurs not by merely believing in certain metaphysical descriptions of Reality but in discovering your innate *oneness with* Reality, which is Consciousness Itself—what the Buddhists often call "Mind-Only" (as we've pointed out). It is the ultimate state-stage of conscious awareness (called *nirvana*) that stands beyond the delusions and desires of the separate self (called *samsara*). This possibility arises because we are all human beings, each with an innate esoteric anatomy with the inherent potential for Enlightenment. Such potential is nullified, however, if people believe that *only one person* in the distant past is the *only one* who can achieve the highest mystical goal of God-Realization, as some religions teach. Instead, everyone should realize that *anyone* can be Enlightened, like Buddhism does. Our world would be more peaceful, loving, and compassionate if more people would simply Wake Up (as well as Grow Up, Clean Up, and Show Up, as Wilber-DiPerna suggest).

Naturally, Buddhism also has its cultural traditions and traditional modes, varying from country to country, century to century, which have all contributed to the richness and variety of Buddhism as a world religion active in numerous nations (as we've reviewed). But its essence is about discovering (or re-discovering) your own divine nature, regardless of race, religion, caste, social status, or sexual orientation. The essential teachings of Buddhism adapt well to all cultural circumstances, as history proves. The Buddha clearly explained in the *Diamond Sutra*: "What is called 'the Religion given by Buddha' is not, in fact, Buddha-Religion…. Buddha teaches that all things are devoid of selfhood, devoid of personality, devoid of entity, and devoid of separate individuality."[127] Because of this trans-cultural appeal Buddhism is described as a "**universal religion**" since it not only transcends the boundaries of state and nation but also of self and conditional Nature.

Put simply, it is the Buddha's Dharma-Teachings, not necessarily Buddhist rituals, that are pointing to the Truth—not just opinion, not conventional truths, but to Absolute Truth revealing the "Emptiness" of the "Clear Light Void," our Ultimate Reality. And it does this by encouraging calm, rational investigation of these truths before adapting them to one's spiritual practice, a hallmark of Buddhism's wisdom and seriousness. Consequently, the original Buddha and all of the Enlightened Adepts or Sat-Gurus, Maha-Siddhas and Bodhisattvas who have followed in the Buddha's footsteps offer the world a Teaching of Truth (*Dharma*) that transcends the negative tendencies of the separate self and its provincial religions by practicing compassion, love, and transcendental wisdom.

This is exactly, what the world-famous Tibetan chant *Om Mani Padme Hum* is about as well, the mantra of the Goddess of Compassion, Avalokitesvara, who is said to incarnate as the Dalai Lamas. It is the mantra that the Tibetan people chant as they circumambulate the residence of the Dalai Lama's Potala Palace (or used to) to focus their minds with the goal of eventually attaining his level of wisdom and compassion.[128] *Om Mani Padme Hum* literally means "the jewel" (*mani*) in "the lotus" (*padme*) surrounded on both sides by *Om*, the sacred vibration of the universe, and *Hum*, the "spirit of enlightenment." The lotus is an important symbol throughout Asia representing purity and spiritual Awakening since it is born in the muck and mud at the bottom of the swamp, or the gross-material world, to rise up to the surface of the water to touch the light and open into the shimmering, beautiful petals of a luscious, gorgeous flower representing the Enlightened Mind. Professor Powers wonderfully illustrates its significance:

> Just as the lotus arises from the bottom of a swamp, so Buddhas were formerly humans, immersed in the negative thoughts and actions in which all ordinary beings engage: the strife, wars, petty jealousies, and hatred to which all humans, animals, and other creatures are subject. Through their meditative training, however, Buddhas have transcended such things, and like lotuses have risen above their murky origins and look down on them unsullied by the mud and mire below…. Because Buddhas do not simply escape the world and look down on others with pity or detached amusement; rather, like the lotus, which has roots that still connect it with the bottom of the swamp, Buddhas continue to act in the world for the benefit of others, continually manifesting in various forms in order to help them, to make them aware of the reality of their situations, and to indicate the path to the awakening of Buddhahood, which can free them from all suffering.[129]

However, one does not have to convert to Buddhism as a religion since technically it is not based on beliefs but on rational understanding (even going beyond mythic-psychic rituals and prayers). By understanding the principal teachings of Buddhism about the self (being "empty") and the need to purify the monkey-mind and its endless thoughts, it's also possible to become more deeply and truthfully involved with one's born or chosen religion because such understanding is based on insight into the self-contraction or ego-I (the source of suffering). This penetrating (and liberating) insight is what matters the most, regardless of your parochial upbringing. By understanding the desires and clinging, aversions and anger, hurt and wounds, of the self-activity we can awaken to the esoteric core behind all religions—recognizing the Perennial Philosophy grounded in *Sophia Perennis*—that transcends mythic and personal beliefs provided by any one culture or provincial tribe [see Chapters 7-8]. With such a universal perspective it's possible to appreciate all of the various artistic expressions and ethnic diversities and cultural heritages the world over. To see the endless plethora of cultural diversity held together within a Prior Unity is a true blessing! True religion, in other words, embraces all religions.

Such a universal approach of wisdom and compassion acknowledges that we have all inherited a global culture of enlightening yogas and spiritual practices which can unleash the awakening potential inherent in all people. By doing so, this becomes a fundamental key to world peace and global harmony. Such processes of inner psychology, of inner awakening, are not about religious or ethnic-cultural identification but about being liberated from the shackles of the self (in samsara) activated by each person's inherited political provincialisms and personal patterns (or karma). Once liberated (or awakened) then we have reached the other shore of Nirvana.

This is also a principal message, for example, behind Avatar Adi Da's call for everyone to access and be educated by the world's "Great Tradition" of Global Wisdom [see Part I]. This is the way the human family can finally come together in our Prior Unity so we may live in peace and tolerance with one another. However, trying to elevate one's own religion or nation above all others does not work and never has. Followers of the Buddha's Teachings can live in *any* culture, even in the modern/postmodern world, even as a concerned scientist (or atheist). This is done by following the principles taught by this humble Awakened Adept who lived during the first Axial Age of humankind (ca. 500 BCE). This Buddha-Guru can be accepted and honored by any traditional religious person to help them re-connect to the deeper mystical truths of Reality. Such a vision and lifestyle is the true goal of all esoteric mysticism regardless of birthplace or inheritance, whether ancient or modern, postmodern or integral. This, then, I believe, would be the real dawning of a Bright New Integral Age.

OM MANI PADME HUM

Chapter 18 Endnotes

1. See: John Myrdhin Reynolds, "The Mahasiddha Tradition In Tibet" (chinabuddhismencyclopedia.com).

2. See: Robert Thurman and Tad Wise, *Circling the Sacred Mountain: A Spiritual Adventure Through the Himalayas* (2000, Bantam Books) an incredible tale of Dr. Thurman (and his friend Tad Wise) encircling the sacred mountain while reciting and studying the ancient sutra *The Blade Wheel of Mind Reform* composed by Master Dharmarakshita (10th century CE) who was a teacher of the great Indian master Atisha (982–1054).

3. Ibid., p. 31.

4. Swami Abhayananda, *History of Mysticism: The Unchanging Testament* (1987), p. 216.

5. See: Keith Dowman, "Introduction," *Masters of Mahamudra* (1985).

6. See: Ibid.

7. Robert Thurman, *Inner Revolution* (1998), pp. 196-197.."

8. See: Robert Thurman, "Buddhist Psychonauts and Their Yogic Technology" – Tibet House Podcast Episode 189, November 10, 2018; also see: Robert Thurman in *The Cakrasamvara Tantra: The Discourse of Sri Heruka* (2007, 2019) edited by David Gray, pp. ix-x; Robert Thurman, *Inner Revolution* (1998), Chapter 7: "The World-Taming Adepts."

9. Robert Thurman, *Inner Revolution* (1998), pp. 195-196.

10. Ibid., pp. 25-26.

11. See: John Myrdhin Reynolds, "The Mahasiddha Tradition in Tibet" (chinabuddhismencyclopedia.com).

12. See: Judith Simmer-Brown, *Dakini's Warm Breath: The Feminine Principle in Tibetan Buddhism* (2002), p. 127.

13. Adi Da Samraj [Da Free John], "The Seventh School of God-Talk" (talk) in "Preface" to *The Song of the Self Supreme: Astavakra Gita* (1982), p. 44 ["Stages of Life" capped].

14. Ibid., p. 44 ["Stages of Life" capped].

15. Ibid., pp. 47-48.

16. Keith Dowman, "Introduction," *Masters of Mahamudra* (1985), pp. 13-14.

17. See: *The Hundred Thousand Songs of Milarepa, Volumes One–Two* (1962) translated by Garma C. C. Chang.

18. Adi Da Samraj [Da Free John], "The Seventh School of God-Talk" (talk) in "Preface" to *The Song of the Self Supreme: Astavakra Gita* (1982), p. 47.

19. Ibid., p. 47.

20. See: Atisha, *The Great Path of Awakening* (1987, Boston: Shambhala Publications) translated by Ken McLeod; also see: Ken Wilber, *Grace and Grit* (1991), p. 250: "Ken [McLeod] translated a key Tibetan text on the practice of tonglen—*The Great Path of Awakening*—that I highly recommend if you are interested in this practice."

21. See: *The Divine Library: A Comprehensive Reference Guide to the Sacred Texts and Spiritual Literature of the World* (1992) by Rufus Camphausen, p. 153.

22. See: *The Life of Longchenpa: The Omniscient Dharma King of the Vast Expanse* (2013, Snow Lion) compiled and edited by Jampa Mackenzie Stewart.

23. Robert A. F. Thurman, "Foreword" in *Mother of the Buddhas: Meditation on the Prajnaparamita Sutras* (1993) by Lex Hixon, p. xvii.

24. See: Lex Hixon, *Mother of the Buddhas: Meditation on the Prajnaparamita Sutras* (1993), p. 8.

25. Adi Da Samraj [Da Free John], "The Seventh School of God-Talk" (talk) in "Preface" to *The Song of the Self Supreme: Astavakra Gita* (1982), p. 53.

26. See: *The Divine Madman: The Sublime and Songs of Drukpa Kunley* (1980, London: Rider) translated by Keith Dowman.

27. Daniel Odier, *Crazy Wisdom of the Yogini: Teachings of the Kashmiri Mahamudra Tradition* (2021), pp. 15-16.

28. See: James Steinberg, "Pure From the Beginning: Beloved Adi Da's Call for the Universal Acceptance of the Great Tradition As the Common Inheritance of Humankind" in *Adi Da Samrajashram*, Vol. 1, No. 4, 2015, p. 28.

29. See: John Powers, *Introduction to Tibetan Buddhism* (2007), p. 143.

30. See: Stephen Batchelor, *The Tibet Guide: Central and Western Tibet* (1998), Foreword by the Dalai Lama, p. 29.

31. See: Ibid., p. 12.

32. See: Ibid., p. 14.

33. See: *Atisha's Lamp for the Path To Enlightenment* (1997), Commentary by Geshe Sonam Rinchen, translated and edited by Ruth Sonam.

34. See: John Powers, *Introduction to Tibetan Buddhism* (2007), p. 158.

35. Adi Da Samraj [Da Free John], *Nirvanasara* (1982), pp. 188-189 ["Stages of Life" capped; bold added].

36. See: Garma C. C. Chang, *The Six Yogas of Naropa and Teachings on Mahamudra* (1963, 1977, Ithaca, NY: Snow Lion Publications); also see: Glenn H. Mullin, *Readings on the Six Yogas of Naropa* (1997, Ithaca, NY: Snow Lion Publications).

37. Adi Da Samraj [Da Free John], *Nirvanasara* (1982), p. 191 ["Stages of Life" capped; emphasis added].

38. See: Stephen Batchelor, *The Tibet Guide: Central and Western Tibet* (1998), p. 16.

39. See: John Powers, *Introduction to Tibetan Buddhism* (2007), p. 159.

40. Ibid., p. 159.

41. See: Stephen Batchelor, *The Tibet Guide: Central and Western Tibet* (1998), p. 17.

42. See: *The Splendor of an Autumn Moon: The Devotional Verse of Tsongkhapa* (2011) translated and edited by Gavin Kilty; also see: *The Great Exposition of Secret Mantra: Yoga Tantra, Volumes 1-3* (2016, 2017) by Tsongkhapa with a Commentary by the Dalai Lama, translation, editing, and explanatory material by Jeffrey Hopkins; *The Great Treatise on the Stages of the Path to Enlightenment: Lam Rim Chen Mo: Volumes 1-3* (2000-2002, 2014-

2015) by Tsong-khapa, translated by The Lamrim Chenmo Translation Committee, Joshua W. C. Cutler, Editor-in-Chief.

43. See: Stephen Batchelor, *The Tibet Guide: Central and Western Tibet* (1998), p. 18; also see: John Powers, *Introduction to Tibetan Buddhism* (2007), p. 164.

44. See: Stephen Batchelor, *The Tibet Guide: Central and Western Tibet* (1998), p. 19.

45. See: John Powers, *Introduction to Tibetan Buddhism* (2007), pp. 208-209.

46. John Powers, *Introduction to Tibetan Buddhism* (2007), p. 208; Alexander Solzhenitsyn quoted in Anne Klein, "Contemporary Tibet: Cultural Genocide in Progress," *White Lotus* (Ithaca: Snow Lion, 1990), p. 45.

47. Padmasambhava quoted in John Powers, *Introduction to Tibetan Buddhism* (2007), p. 213.

48. Adi Da Samraj [Da Free John], *Nirvanasara* (1982), p. 162.

49. His Holiness the XIV Dalai Lama, from the Foreword to *Wonders of the Natural Mind* (2000, Snow Lion; new edition) by Tenzin Wangyal Rinpoche.

50. See: John Powers, *Introduction to Tibetan Buddhism* (1995, 2007), p. 497.

51. See: John Powers, *Introduction to Tibetan Buddhism* (2007), Chapter 16: "Bön: A Heterodox System."

52. Ibid., p. 497.

53. See: Stephen Batchelor, *The Tibet Guide: Central and Western Tibet* (1998), p. 35.

54. See: *Clear Light of Bliss: The Practice of Mahamudra in Vajrayana Buddhism* (1982, 1995) by Geshe Kelsang Gyatso.

55. Georg Feuerstein, *The Yoga Tradition* (1998), p. 243.

56. Ibid., p. 243.

57. Daniel Odier, *Crazy Wisdom of the Yogini: Teachings of the Kashmiri Mahamudra Tradition* (2021), p. 130.

58. Stephen Batchelor, *The Tibet Guide: Central and Western Tibet* (1998), pp. 34-35.

59. Adi Da Samraj [Da Free John], *Nirvanasara* (1982), p. 162 ["Stages of Life" capped].

60. Free-rendering of the lyrics to "Kashmir" by Led Zeppelin (Songwriters: John Bonham / Robert Anthony Plant / James Patrick [Jimmy] Page) from their double album *Physical Graffiti* (1975).

61. See: Huston Smith and Philip Novak, *Buddhism: A Concise Introduction* (2003), p. 105.

62. Ibid., p. 105.

63. Ibid., p. 105.

64. Ibid., p. 109.

65. Adi Da Samraj [Da Free John], *Nirvanasara* (1982), p. 161 ["Stages of Life" capped].

66. See: Peter Kingsley, *A Story Waiting to Pierce You: Mongolia, Tibet, and the Destiny of the Western World* (2010, Point Reyes, CA: The Golden Sufi Center), where the author makes the case of the arrow-caring Mongolian Shaman Abaris "Skywalker" (claimed by the Greeks to be from northern Hyperborea) as bringing his mystical wisdom to Pre-Socratic Greece, particular transmitting his wisdom to Pythagoras.

67. See: Daniel Odier, *Crazy Wisdom of the Yogini; Teachings of the Kashmiri Mahamudra Tradition* (2021) from a modern-day practitioner taught by a woman Yogini-Adept in the ancient tradition of Mahamudra-Dzogchen during the 1970s.

68. See, for example: *Ancient Tibet: Research Materials* (1986, Berkeley, CA: Dharma Publishing) by Tarthang Tulku; *Introduction to Tibetan Buddhism* (1995, 2007 revised, Ithaca, NY: Snow Lion Publications) by John Powers.

69. See: Ken Wilber, *Up from Eden* (1981, 2007).

70. Adi Da Samraj [Da Free John], *Nirvanasara* (1982), pp. 158-159 ["Stages of Life" capped].

71. Ibdi., p. 159 ["Stages of Life" capped].

72. Ibdi., p. 159 ["Stages of Life" capped].

73. Ibdi., pp. 159-160 ["Stages of Life" capped].

74. See: Stephen Batchelor, *The Tibet Guide: Central and Western Tibet* (1998), p. 34.

75. See: Huston Smith and Philip Novak, *Buddhism: A Concise Introduction* (2003), p. 106.

76. Miranda Shaw, *Passionate Enlightenment: Women in Tantric Buddhism* (1994), p. 84.

77. Georg Feuerstein, *The Yoga Tradition* (1998), p. 235.

78. T. R. V. Murti, *The Central Philosophy of Buddhism* (1955), p. 109.

79. Georg Feuerstein, *The Yoga Tradition* (1998), p. 234.

80. Ibid., p. 455.

81. See: Geshe Kelsang Gyatso, *Clear Light of Bliss* (1982); also see: Daniel Cozort, *Highest Yoga Tantra* (1986).

82. Tulku Urgyen Rinpoche, *The Dzogchen Primer: Embracing the Spiritual Path According to the Great Perfection* (2002, Boston: Shambhala Publications), Compiled and edited by Marcia Binder Schmidt, p. 43-44.

83. Khenpo Tsultrim Gyamtso Rinpoche (author), Lama Shenpen Hookham (translator), *Progressive Stages of Meditation on Emptiness* (1986), p. 76 [italics in original]; the [brackets] are added from Ken Wilber, *Sex, Ecology, Spirituality* (1995), p. 702, 1n.

84. See: Ken Wilber, *Sex, Ecology, Spirituality* (1995), pp. 700-705 for an excellent review of the history of Buddhism including Anuyoga or "Highest Yoga Tantra" and Atiyoga or Dzogchen, the "Great Perfection."

85. Huston Smith and Philip Novak, *Buddhism: A Concise Introduction* (2003), p. 108.

86. Miranda Shaw, *Passionate Enlightenment: Women in Tantric Buddhism* (1994), p. 169.

87. Georg Feuerstein, *The Yoga Tradition* (1998), p. 235.

88. See: Ken Wilber, *Sex, Ecology, Spirituality* (1995), p. 696, 1n.

89. T. R. V. Murti, *The Central Philosophy of Buddhism* (1955), p. 109 [emphasis added].

90. See: Kogen Mizumo, *Buddhist Sutras: Origin, Development, Transmission* (1982, 1995).

91. Adi Da Samraj [Da Free John], *Nirvanasara* (1982), p. 146.

92. Ken Wilber, *A Brief History of Everything* (1996), p. 12.

93. Since Wilber's very first book, *The Spectrum of Consciousness* (1977). he has liberally used Adi Da's fairly unique phrase "always already the case," such as with that book's last chapter

titled "That Which is Always Already" where he notes, "Whether we realize or not, it is always already the case," where he footnotes Adi Da's [Franklin Jones'] first book *The Knee of Listening* (1972), to Wilber's later book *The Eye of Spirit* (1997) whose last chapter is "Always Already: The Brilliant Clarity of Ever-Present Awareness," one of the most brilliant essays the integral pandit has ever written.

94. Ken Wilber, *Sex, Ecology, Spirituality* (1995), p. 326.

95. Adi Da Samraj [Da Free John], *Nirvanasara* (1982), pp. 145-146.

96. Lex Hixon, *Mother of the Buddhas: Meditation on the Prajnaparamita Sutras* (1993), p. 234.

97. Robert Thurman interviewed by Tami Simon (of Sounds True) on *Insights On The Edge*, 2015.

98. Adi Da Samraj [Da Free John], *Nirvanasara* (1982), p. 148 ["Stages of Life" capped].

99. Ken Wilber, *The Religion of Tomorrow* (2017), p. 21.

100. Ken Wilber, *Sex, Ecology, Spirituality* (1995), p. 327.

101. Adi Da Samraj [Da Free John], *Nirvanasara* (1982), p. 157 ["Stages of Life" capped].

102. Georg Feuerstein, *The Yoga Tradition* (1998), p. 210.

103. Adi Da Samraj [Da Free John], *Nirvanasara* (1982), p. 155 ["Stages of Life" capped].

104. Ibid., p. 243 ["Stages of Life" capped].

105. Ibid., p. 111 ["Stages of Life" capped].

106. Cyrus Stearns, *The Buddha from Dolpo* (1999), p. 83.

107. Adi Da Samraj [Da Free John], *Nirvanasara* (1982), p. 106.

108. Ibid., p. 107.

109. Ibid., pp. 107-108, 113 ["Stages of Life" capped].

110. Keith Dowman, "Introduction," *Masters of Mahamudra* (1985), pp. 13-14.

111. Dalai Lama, Tenzin Gyatso, *The Union of Bliss and Emptiness: A Commentary on the Lama Choepa Guru Yoga* (1988), p. 15.

112. Dilgo Khyentse, *The Wish-Fulfilling Jewel: The Practice of Guru Yoga According to The Longchen Nyingthig Tradition* (1988) translated by Konchog Tenzin, p. 3.

113. See: *In God's Company: Guru-Adepts As Agents for Enlightenment in the Integral Age* (2022) by Brad Reynolds.

114. Jigme Lingpa, *The Dzogchen Innermost Essence Preliminary Practice* (1982), p. 64, quoted in John Powers, *Introduction to Tibetan Buddhism* (1995, 2007), p. 311.

115. Jonathan Landaw and Andy Weber, *Images of Enlightenment* (1993), p. 172.

116. John Powers, *Introduction to Tibetan Buddhism* (1995, 2007), pp. 310-311 [caps added].

117. See: *Last Days of the Buddha: Maha Parinibbana Sutta* (1998, Sri Lanka: Buddhist Publication Society) translated by Francis Story and Sister Vajira, where the Buddha (from the Pali) purportedly said: "Behold, O monks, this is my advice to you. All component things in the world are changeable. They are not lasting. Work hard to gain your own salvation."

118. John Powers, *Introduction to Tibetan Buddhism* (1995, 2007), p. 310 [caps added].

119. See: *Gurus In America* (2005) edited by Thomas Forsthoefel and Cynthia Ann Humes; *American Guru: From Transcendentalism to New Age Religion* (2014) by Arthur Versluis; *The Guru Drinks Bourbon?* (2016) by Dzongsar Jamyang Khyentse; *Spiritual Transmission: Paradoxes and Dilemmas on the Spiritual Path* (2018) by Amir Freimann, afterword by Ken Wilber.

120. See: Adi Da Samraj, *My "Bright" Word* (2005), *My "Bright" Sight* (2014); *My "Bright" Form* (2016); *The Aletheon* (2009).

121. Ken Wilber, *Sex, Ecology, Spirituality* (1995), p. 703, 1n.

122. Jamgon Kongtrul, *The Torch of Certainty* (1977), translated by Judith Hanson, p. 11.

123. Adi Da Samraj [Da Free John], *The Bodily Location of Happiness* (1982), p. 70.

124. See: *In God's Company: Guru-Adepts As Agents for Enlightenment in the Integral Age* (2022) by Brad Reynolds.

125. Chögyal Namkhai Norbu, *Dzogchen: The Self-Perfect State* (1989), p. 61 [title caps added].

126. Ibid., p. 62 [title caps added].

127. Gautama Buddha, *The Diamond Sutra* (1969) translated by A.F. Price and Wong Mou-Lam, pp. 33, 53.

128. See: John Powers, *Introduction to Tibetan Buddhism* (1995, 2007), p. 22.

129. Ibid., pp. 23-24 [caps added].

NINETEEN

SIXTH STAGE & SEVENTH STAGE ENLIGHTENMENT

All of the Great Siddha-Gurus (of whatever Real degree of Real-God-Realization)—Who have Taught and Transmitted the Inherently Divine Truth of Reality to living beings—have given their devotees the Graceful Gift of Satsang [Guru Yoga]. Satsang has always been the essential activity of the Great Siddha-Gurus. The Great Siddha-Gurus have never come merely to give a conceptual Teaching—to fabricate a myth, a belief-structure for the mind, a patterning of ego-mentality. The Great Siddha-Gurus have always brought and given themselves. They have always entered into relationship with their devotees, and (altogether) with the conditionally manifested "worlds".

— **Adi Da Samraj**, *My "Bright" Word*[1]

Avatar Adi Da Samraj is a fully Enlightened "Buddha" according to most available evidence. What this means exactly cannot be said by those of us outside of Enlightenment or yet unenlightened. Divine Enlightenment lies outside of logic or reasoning (or the mind)—it's *trans-logical*, one of its defining qualities. Indeed, it even transcends the sense of being a separate self—thus it's *trans-egoic* or *trans-personal* (yet still deeply personal for it is seen with the heart as much as the mind). It's paradoxical, without a doubt. A koan. The sound of one hand clapping. What can be ascertained about "it" if one studies the Great Enlightenment Tradition carefully is that there are different "stages" or degrees or phases of Enlightenment. Once a person awakens where self is *totally* transcended—even beyond "I" being aware there's a "God" or feeling connected with the cosmos (a state itself called "Cosmic Consciousness")—there is a transformation that occurs where the Enlightened *state* is made more permanent by becoming a *stage* of human possibility [see chart below]. This is what a "Buddha" is. Awake 24/7.

Higher Stages of Life 4 – 7

t r a n s p e r s o n a l		A t m a n		Real God ☆
4th STAGE LOWER to HIGHER MENTAL	**5th STAGE** YOGIC ASCENT	**6th STAGE** TRANSCENDENTAL AWAKENING		**7th STAGE** WHOLE BODY ENLIGHTENMENT
SPIRITUALIZATION	HIGHER YOGIC EVOLUTION	AWAKENING *TO* ATMAN		AWAKENING *AS* ATMAN
• heart awakening • growth of devotion to the Divine or God	• mysticism/esoteric anatomy • visions, raptures, OBEs, other Yogic phenomena	• Self-Realization of True Self • meditation on Consciousness prior to all forms (*nirvikalpa*) • Void (*sunyata*)		• Brahman-Atman • Nirvana-samsara • "open-eyes" (*sahaj*) • Buddhanature

ARROW OF EVOLUTION → ego death *satori* **Witness** ☆ Divine Transformation "Out Shining"

→ —— SUBTLE —————— /\ —— CAUSAL —/ \— NONDUAL —→
Translation

→ — frontal personality purification — —→ EVOLUTION TRANSCENDED *Jivamukti* Liberated Human Being

└———————— deeper personality purification — — — —→ KARMIC PURIFICATION CONTINUES

© chart by Brad Reynolds

In other words, *after* Enlightenment the body-mind-soul of the individual seems to go through a process of purifying previous self-generated and karmic patterns. It's almost like the dross remainders of our current incarnation have to be burnt off or purified before our Enlightenment is completely full and totally Free. Some rare few seem to zip right into that purified state thus probably not incarnating with much residual karma in the first place, such as our most famous Saints and Sages like Ramana Maharshi (or Jesus Christ and the Buddha). But scholars like myself really can't say. We only know them through written records, often not even given from their own hand, or from their historical influence. They are the advanced-tip few, while we're just the average-mode masses—yet we are *all* God, equal in essence if not form. Enlightenment sees Only God, God Only; Consciousness Only, Only Consciousness.

In Hinduism there is what is known as **prarabdha karma** or the left-over karma after Enlightenment where the Enlightened being is not making any more personal karma but is letting the left-over patterning of the body-mind-soul run its course for the rest of his or her lifetime. This might account for some of the eccentricities of certain God-Realized Adepts, but then again, it's next to impossible for karmic beings like us to know. But this process only begins with authentic God-Realization (or Divine Enlightenment), not with subtle visionary or yogic experiences. What is important to know about Adi Da, therefore, is that the Reality-Way of Adidam transcends egoity "from the beginning" (as he says) through an Awakening initiated by his Heart-Transmission of the Seventh Stage Fully-Enlightened Consciousness (in Satsang):

> What there Is to Realize is (potentially) limited only by the disposition of the devotee, and by the characteristics, the disposition, and the mode, or stage, of Realization of the Realizer. Therefore, My Gift to My devotees is the Gift of Most Perfect Realization, seventh stage Realization, through My Divine Avataric Work with them. That is part of the Unique Characteristic of My Divine Avataric Transcendental Spiritual Gift here. Yet, the process of devotion to the Realizer is most ancient, and it is the great secret—and, of course, it has been most fruitfully entered into only by a relative few.[2]

The Buddhists, perhaps the world's greatest Enlightenment tradition producing the most Enlightened beings in history, followed by Advaita Vedanta as a close second, have accounted for this disparity by pointing to an in original or "sudden" Enlightenment and then by recognizing a Final or Complete Enlightenment. As the Zen Master and scholar Garma C. C. Chang points out: "Zen only *begins* at the moment when one first attains *Satori* [*Wu*, in Chinese]; before that one merely stands outside and looks at Zen intellectually. In a deeper sense, *Satori is only the beginning, but it is not the end of Zen.*"[3]

This is why the Chinese Ch'an ("Zen" in Japanese) Buddhists distinguished between *chien* or "to see" and "the view" (or being Enlightened) and *hsing* or "the practice," "the action," and "the work" (or the disciplined practices under a competent Master) [see Chapter 17]. Master Chang continues:

> *Chien* in its broader sense implies the overall understanding of the Buddhist teaching; but in Zen it not only denotes the understanding of Zen principles and truth, but often implies also the awakened view that springs from the "Wu" (*Satori*) experience. *Chien*, in this sense, can be understood as "seeing reality" or "a view of reality." But while it signifies the seeing of reality, it does not imply the "possession," or "mastery" of reality... In other words, after one has attained *Satori*, [one] should cultivate it until it reaches its full maturity.[4]

This full maturity in the Enlightened State is called **Samyaksambodhi** by the Buddhists or the final and perfect Enlightenment of Buddhahood. In some sense, this indicates the difference between "sudden" and "gradual" Enlightenment, a topic too involved to be discussed much here. Thus, one Zen proverb states: "The truth should be understood through sudden Enlightenment [*satori*], but the fact [complete realization] must be cultivated step by step."[5] This means *sadhana* (or spiritual disciplines) and a devoted seriousness are necessary even though paradoxically Enlightenment cannot be *caused*. Here sadhana is not a means of *seeking* for God but of *living* in the body and the world, happily and at peace in a perpetual state of Divine Communion. Thus, even after initial Enlightenment—usually verified by a competent Master—there still is the response (and personal responsibility) of living in Guru Yoga-Satsang, of living "Right Life" (as Buddha and Adi Da maintain). Before and after Enlightenment the Adept-Guru is honored and served for they have a unique function for humanity (as well as for their devotees). Not every Enlightened person, however, becomes a Master; perhaps most don't. Rinpoche Tenzin Wangyal masterfully explains why:

> The Master in Guru Yoga is not just one individual, but the essence of Enlightenment, the primordial awareness that is your true nature.

The Master is also the Teacher from whom you receive the Teaching. In the Tibetan tradition, we say the Master is more important than the Buddha. Why? Because the Master is the immediate messenger of the Teachings, the one who brings the Buddha's wisdom to the student. Without the Master we could not find our way to the Buddha. So we should feel as much devotion to the Master as we would to the Buddha as if the Buddha suddenly appeared in front of us.[6]

Avatar Adi Da seems to have accounted for these extremely subtle differences about the Enlightened State when he distinguishes between the Sixth and Seventh Stages of Life. Again, I cannot discourse on the degree necessary to make a fully accurate account of what he actually intends and means. Indeed, I have probably made some errors in this book in describing these differences accurately since I only read and study the material myself (balanced by my own "sudden" Realization); I am not a Guru, only a pandit. One of the reasons for this difficulty is that it seems Adi Da himself has somewhat shifted his own perspective or Teaching on the Sixth and Seventh Stages of Life. Initially he conceded there were other Seventh Stage Realizers in the Great Tradition; later, that only Adidam truly reflects the Seventh Stage Way, yet it's with good reason he makes this distinction [see Adi Da's own writings, such as *The Aletheon*, for further clarification].[7] Thus I am in no position to know for sure since I have never had a conversation with him about these matters (and now will never be able to). Yet both the Sixth and Seventh Stages of Life, in Adi Da's model, are known traditionally as "Enlightenment" (or God-Realization), yet the Avatar makes a distinction.

Adi Da's "**Seven Stages of Life**" model, therefore, becomes the ideal vehicle for designating these distinctions in developmental growth. As I continue to point out, they overlap with Ken Wilber's AQAL or "**Spectrum of Consciousness**" model [see Appendix I]. The chart below is a brief summary of these models based on the evolution of consciousness incorporating the "Seven Stages" as arising within the "Spectrum" aligned with the seven chakras of traditional Yoga [see next page].

Seven Stages + 7 Chakras in the Spectrum of Consciousness

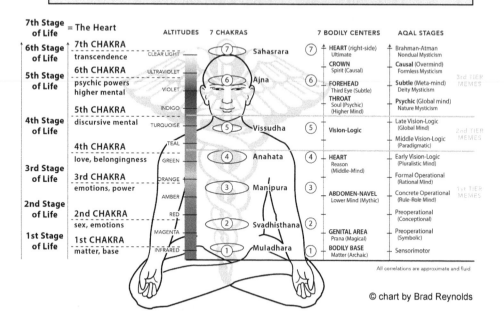

© chart by Brad Reynolds

Heart Conductivity (after Adi Da Samraj)

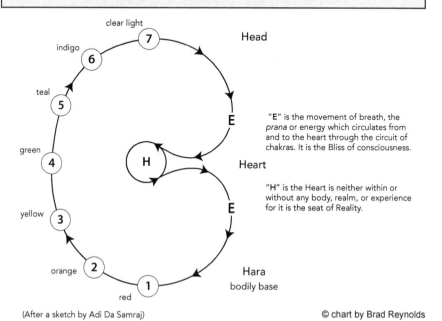

"E" is the movement of breath, the *prana* or energy which circulates from and to the heart through the circuit of chakras. It is the Bliss of consciousness.

"H" is the Heart is neither within or without any body, realm, or experience for it is the seat of Reality.

(After a sketch by Adi Da Samraj)

© chart by Brad Reynolds

MEDITATION (SIXTH STAGE) IN THE MARKETPLACE (SEVENTH STAGE)

In the 1970s and 1980s, Adi Da subdivided the subtle phases of Enlightenment into what seems to gravitate around the traditional differences made between (in Vedanta terms) *Nirvikalpa Samadhi* and *Jnana Samadhi* (Sixth Stage) and then *Sahaj Samadhi* and *Bhava Samadhi* (Seventh Stage). **Nirvikalpa Samadhi**—experienced as the Sixth Stage of Life (or upper terminal of the Fifth Stage)—is formless or causal awareness, as it's usually defined, a realization of the "formlessness" and "emptiness" and "voidness" of self and universe, like the Buddhists generally maintain. While **Jnana Samadhi** is Self-Realization or realizing that Atman (the "inner God")—the "Witness" of all phenomena (and self)—is one with Brahman (the "outer God"), and thus is usually defined in positive terms such as with *Sat-Chit-Ananda* ("Being-Consciousness-Bliss"). Yet, truly, is ineffable. In the Sixth Stage of Life, with Nirvikalpa and Jnana Samadhi—or **"Nirvana"** (in strict Hinayana Buddhist terms)—this awakened state usually involves the interior inversion of awareness so that it becomes dissociated (or turned away) from the outside physical realm often absorbed in deep meditation—the classic Yogi meditating in a cave or at a retreat center seemingly oblivious to what surrounds him or her (which is an extremely useful practice and high state-stage of development). Let's refer to this definition given by Adi Da (published in 1982):

> In the Sixth Stage of Life, the body-mind is simply relaxed into the
> Life-Current, and attention (the root or base of the mind) is inverted

away from gross and subtle states and objects of the body-mind, and toward its own Root, the ultimate Root of the ego-self, which is the "**Witness**" Consciousness (when attention is active) and also simple Consciousness (prior to objects and self-definition). The final result of this conditional Self-Realization or the intuition of Radiant Transcendental Being via the exclusive self-essence (inverted away from all objects).[8]

Sahaj Samadhi—experienced as the Seventh Stage of Life—on the other hand, is "open eyes" or living in the natural state of the *jivanmukta* (or the "liberated being") who has realized the True Self (Atman) as "Void" or "Empty" (*sunyata*) yet is still associated with all arising phenomena (Brahman) seeing them as "One Taste" (as the Buddhist say) or a "Prior Unity" (in Adi Da's words). The entire Kosmos is experienced as having no interior and exterior but just Being the One buzz of God, so to speak (to inadequately put it in words). There is "no self" (*anatma*) that experiences an "inside" and "outside," so its nondual prior unity transcends all possibility of being described with words or ideas. It is simply a tacit understanding of Reality as It IS. Beloved Adi Da clarifies (as published in 1982):

> In the Seventh Stage of Life there is native or radical intuitive identification with the Radiant Transcendental Being, the Identity of all beings (or subjects) and the Condition of all conditions (or objects). This intuitive identification (or radical Self-Abiding) is directly Realized, entirely apart from any dissociative act of inversion. And, while so Abiding, if any conditions arise, or if any states of body-mind arise, they are simply recognized in the Radiant Transcendental Being (as transparent or unnecessary and non-binding modifications of Itself. Such is **Sahaj Samadhi**, and it's inherently free of any apparent implications, limitations, or binding power of phenomenal conditions.[9]

Bhava Samadhi is the "One Taste" of God experienced to such a degree there is no arising of any objectification but simply effortless abiding in the Radiance of Real God.[10] In Bhava the eyes can be open or closed yet there is no differentiation of forms just the endless formlessness prior to all qualification, modification, or objectification—pure Divine luminous Love-Bliss. What Buddhists call "**Clear Light Bliss**," what Vedantists call "*Sat-Chit-Ananda*," what Adi Da names the "**Bright**" or "**Conscious Light**" (or "**Radiant Transcendental Being**"), yet, truly, ineffable beyond words or names. "The Tao that can be named is not the eternal Tao; the name that can be named is not the Eternal Name," etc. In Bhava the entire Kosmos (and self-sense) is totally "**Outshined**" in the utter Bliss of our Divine Condition which manifests as "**Translation**" after death (in Adi Da's terms), or perhaps the "**Rainbow Body**" (in Buddhist terms) (though I am making no exact correspondences). Bhava is totally beyond description but is only absolutely realized. Again, let's refer to Adi Da (published in 1982):

> If no conditions arise to the notice, there is simply Radiant Transcendental Being. Such is **Bhava Samadhi**, about Which nothing sufficient can be said, and there is not Anyone, Anything, or Anywhere beyond It to be Realized.[11]

Both the Sixth and Seventh Stage samadhis see and know Godhead, per se, but Sixth Stage *Nirvikalpa-Jnana* is more inner-directed whereas Seventh Stage *Sahaj-Bhava* is Awake beyond interiors-exteriors whether the eyes are open or closed, whether the mind is active or not. Adi Da suggests (again, from 1982): "The Seventh Stage Realization tends to occur spontaneously in the case of Sixth Stage Sages of the highest type, particularly those who are less grounded in the conflict with Nature, who have entered into the Sixth Stage of Life on the basis of the Wisdom of the Seventh Stage, and who exercise the free intuitional capacity to make the subtle transition between the Sixth and the Seventh Stage points of view."[12] Truly, only the Adepts and Buddhas know!

Ultimately, there is Only Conscious Light; Only God. See: impossible to describe! Zen, for example, tries to account for this slight shift in view [as we saw in Chapter 17], with the Ten Ox-Herding paintings: *Jnana* Samadhi is pure Emptiness (the circle) while *Sahaj* Samadhi is "entering the marketplace" or living in the human community. The householder—or business person (or whomever)—can live the fully Enlightened life, the Good Life (or Right Life), without losing Enlightenment (or God-Awareness) in the world of conditional forms.[13] This is what the Reality-Way of Adidam Ruchiradam offers all people: a daily practice of living Real Religion moment-to-moment with every breath. The chart below crudely outlines these samadhi subdivisions:

STAGE OF LIFE	SAMADHI	CHARACTERISTICS
Sixth Stage of Life	*Nirvikalpa*	Emptiness / Void Nirvana Witness / *Turiya*
	Jnana	True Self / Atman *Sat-Chit-Ananda* "I Am"
Seventh Stage of Life	*Sahaj*	Atman-Brahman "Open Eyes"
	Bhava	*Turiyatita* "Radical Enjoyment"
Reality-Way of Adidam	Radical Understanding	self-transcendence
	Atma-Nadi	"Searchlessly Beholding"
	Translation	"Outshining"

Ken Wilber first began writing and studying Adi Da (in the mid-1970s) when these distinctions, only truly recognizable by a Fully-Enlightened Adept, were first published so the pandit used them to his (and our) advantage. Indeed, I propose this is part of the breakthrough power that Wilber's "**spectrum of consciousness**" model had when he originally published [outlined in the chart to the right]. This is particularity evident with the addition of the "**spectrum of mysticism**" or "**hierarchy of religious experience**"[14] now called "**Waking Up**"—because Wilber had essentially added Adi Da's higher Stages of Life to modern psychology's early developmental stages of "**Growing Up**" (i.e., from infancy to adulthood studied by researchers such as Piaget, Kohlberg, Loevinger, Erikson, et al.). This generates a "**full spectrum**" of consciousness evolution from babies to Buddhas. Currently, of course, Wilber has overlaid the "spectrum" of "levels" (or stages) with the "four quadrants" to create his "**all quadrants, all levels**" model of AQAL [see Appendix I].

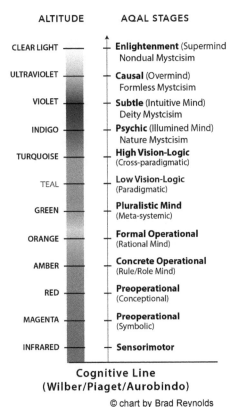

ALTITUDE	AQAL STAGES
CLEAR LIGHT	**Enlightenment** (Supermind) Nondual Mystcisim
ULTRAVIOLET	**Causal** (Overmind) Formless Mystcisim
VIOLET	**Subtle** (Intuitive Mind) Deity Mystcisim
INDIGO	**Psychic** (Illumined Mind) Nature Mystcisim
TURQUOISE	**High Vision-Logic** (Cross-paradigmatic)
TEAL	**Low Vision-Logic** (Paradigmatic)
GREEN	**Pluralistic Mind** (Meta-systemic)
ORANGE	**Formal Operational** (Rational Mind)
AMBER	**Concrete Operational** (Rule/Role Mind)
RED	**Preoperational** (Conceptional)
MAGENTA	**Preoperational** (Symbolic)
INFRARED	**Sensorimotor**

Cognitive Line
(Wilber/Piaget/Aurobindo)
© chart by Brad Reynolds

Wilber's integral model was made even more powerful since his intellectual views were also grounded in his own experiential practices and awakenings (including *satori*), thus he was able to communicate them in unprecedented ways to humanity's great benefit.[15] Wilber went on to subdivide the Sixth Stage of Life into what he called Casual or "**Formless Mysticism**" (*nirvikalpa*) while the Seventh Stage is "**Nondual Mysticism**" (*sahaja*), the "One Taste" of God "always already" Realized.[16] These quotes from *The Atman Project: A Transpersonal View of Human Development* (1980) wonderfully (and accurately) describe these most subtle distinctions in the highest state-stages of conscious awareness that are available to all human beings (written while he was studying under Adi Da's influence). These articulations, for one, put Wilber squarely on the map in the field of transpersonal psychology and brought him his worldwide fame (for his gifted writing skills explained these views so clearly and simply, to his great credit). Wilber begins by identifying the "**Causal**" or "**Formless**" structure-state (or Sixth Stage of Life):

[In the **Sixth Stage** of Life or "High-Causal" Mysticism] all manifest forms are so radically transcended that they no longer need even appear or arise in Consciousness. This is total and utter transcendence and release into Formless Consciousness, Boundless Radiance. There is no self, no God, no final-God, no subjects, and no thingness, apart from or other than Consciousness as Such.... Known as **Nirvikalpa Samadhi** (in Hinduism), **nirodh** (Hinayana Buddhism), **Jnana Samadhi** (Vedanta)—and it is the eighth of the ten Zen ox-herding pictures [the circle] which depict the stages to supreme Enlightenment.... unknowing or perfectly divine ignorance in cessation, boundless Consciousness, primal or formless Radiance, perfectly Ecstatic... Formless Self-Realization, the transcendent Witness.[17]

Then he masterfully goes on to describe the "**Nondual**" and Ultimate structure-state of consciousness development (or the Seventh Stage of Life):

[In the **Seventh Stage** of Life or "Nondual" Mysticism] passing through nirvikalpa samadhi, Consciousness totally awakens as its Original Condition and Suchness (*tathata*), which is, at the same time, the condition and suchness of all that is, gross, subtle, or causal. That which witnesses, and that which is witnessed, are only one and the same. The entire World Process that arises, moment to moment, as one's own Being, outside of which, and prior to which nothing exists.... This is **Sahaja Samadhi**, the Turiya state, the Svabhavikakaya—the ultimate Unity, wherein all things and events, while remaining perfectly separate and discrete, are only One [the tenth Zen ox-herding picture of being in the marketplace]. Therefore, this is not itself a state apart from other states; it is not an altered state; it is not a special state—it is rather the suchness of all states. This is the final differentiation of Consciousness from all forms in Consciousness, whereupon Consciousness as Such is released in Perfect Transcendence which is not a transcendence from the world but a final transcendence as the world.[18]

Adi Da began to speak about these distinctions (i.e., "inner" Sixth Stage and "outer" Seventh Stage Enlightenment) at least since 1977 with *The Paradox of Instruction* (which Wilber devoured) when he began publishing (and talking about) his Teaching regarding the Seven Stages of Life. However, as an Avatar, a genuine Guru (not merely a pandit), Adi Da was concerned about differentiating his Teaching—"**The Way of Radical Understanding**"—from what he called "**The Great Path of Return**" which is the yogic attempt to traditionally *seek for* Enlightenment as a "Goal" to be achieved.[19] This is the crux of what makes Avatar Adi Da Samraj's Reality-Way of Adidam different, and a completion of, all the teachings of traditional Enlightenment. The Way of Adidam Ruchiradam, through the sacred relationship with the Siddha-Guru (in Satsang), *begins* with sudden Enlightenment (or "Sighting"), not as a path to seek or gain Enlightenment as is traditionally taught.

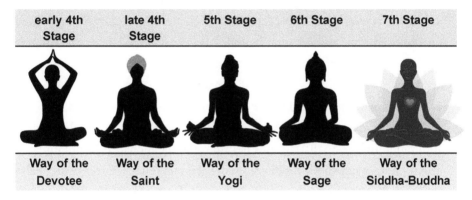

early 4th Stage	late 4th Stage	5th Stage	6th Stage	7th Stage
Way of the Devotee	Way of the Saint	Way of the Yogi	Way of the Sage	Way of the Siddha-Buddha

The Avatar pointed out that the ancient religious-yogic "Path of Return" begins by first involving the *gross* (or body-based) "descending" path or the "**Way of the Yogis**," and with the *subtle* (or inner mind) "ascending" path or "**Way of the Saints**," which are the Fourth and Fifth Stages of Life, respectively. (Of course, a reasonable argument can be made that the Fourth Stage of Life is more about the devotional "Way of the Saints" while the Fifth Stage of Life is more about kundalini ascension practiced by the "Way of the Yogis," which is why Adi Da often exchanges the terms.[20]) Beloved Adi Da then delineated the "**Way of the Sages**" as the *causal* (or root) path to represent the Sixth Stage of Life, and reserved the "**Way of the Siddhas**" as the Seventh Stage of Life, also called the "**Way of the Heart**" (and the "**Way of Radical Understanding**"). However, very importantly, the Avatar never intended to indicate a strictly linear progression from the Sixth to Seventh Stage of Life (which is how the ego often interprets this process). Wilber brilliantly absorbed then integrated these fine distinctions of the Avatar's into his own work (from 1979 onwards).

Only a fully God-Realized Siddha could make these extremely subtle (and enlightened) distinctions with any degree of accuracy. Highly sensitive (and awakened) scholars like Wilber (and Georg Feuerstein, for example) capitalized on these profound distinctions. Indeed, I believe it helped empower Wilber's work with a depth of insight that propelled him far beyond his contemporaries. Importantly, Adi Da points to the **Jnanis** of the causal path (Sixth Stage) as sometimes being oriented to the Heart on the right (as spoken about in the *Upanishads* and with Ramana Maharshi). This distinguishes the formless Causal Realization (of the Sixth Stage of Life) from the traditional yogas of kundalini ascension involving subtle realm visions of lights and sounds, such as with Shabd and Nada Yoga, etc. (which represents the Fifth Stage of Life). As Heart-Master Da pointed out: "The general traditions of spiritual practice in the gross and subtle paths do not carry a stream of teaching which acknowledges the Heart, the causal path, and the primacy of that Realization."[21] By doing so, Adi Da makes clear the distinction between the traditional yogic Paths of Return or seeking for God versus his most radical (or "at the root") Way of Radical Understanding:

> The Way of Radical Understanding, which I am Here to demonstrate and Teach, is founded in awareness of all the possibilities, and their limitations, discovered in the experiments of the traditions. It agrees with the principal evidence of the Jnanis, or Sages, but sees that their way is, commonly, a search generated from the same sense of dilemma which motivates the searches of Yogis of the gross path and Saints or Yogis of the subtle path [Fourth and Fifth Stages]. And it also sees that the realization of the Heart awakened when it is pursued as a Goal is an exclusive realization [Sixth Stage]...
>
> Therefore, the Way of Radical Understanding involves no search

for the Heart as Goal, no reductive, ascetic, world-denying strategy of return, and thus no exclusive or conditional realization.... The Man of Understanding [Seventh Stage Realizer] realizes all the manifest functional or conventional dimensions to be not other than the Heart, and thus he may retain all his [or her] dimensional "bodies" [gross, subtle, causal], or planes of manifest being, in the Play of Conscious Light that is Life....

The Man [or Woman] of Understanding does not *turn* to the Heart, but instantly and *from the beginning* stands Present *as* the Heart, without strategically excluding or binding any dimension of his being or the arising worlds.[22]

Adi Da is able to bring clarity to this important distinction between the Sixth Stage and the Seventh Stages of Life. It boggles the mind, since, paradoxically, "you" cannot *become* Enlightened; you can only *be* Enlightened.

If you study Adi Da's Teaching-Word closely you will find this principle active and evident from the very beginning of his Teaching-Revelation (first given in 1972) to his very last book (in 2008). The Avatar has been consistent even if some of his technical definitions have shifted slightly. However, after the "Divine Emergence" Event of 1986, and then by the early 1990s, Adi Da began to revise these more straightforward definitions as he continued to review the Great Tradition. This confuses many casual readers—and critics—of his Teaching, even confounding his students, like myself (at times), since as I say we tend to fall short of his fully Enlightened Realization. And yet when you are in the Field of His Heart-Transmission it make *perfect* sense.

For example, I learned first in the early 1980s by studying and accepting these original definitions of the Sixth and Seventh Stages of Life (as did Wilber), so I feel comfortable with them since they are also intellectually satisfying and explanatory in distinguishing between Nirvikalpa-Jnana and Sahaj-Bhava Samadhi. Therefore, I feel I can easily recognize several Adepts in history as exhibiting Nondual "Seventh Stage" Enlightenment living in full identity with the Divine Condition with "open eyes," in the natural state of Divine Samadhi (whatever the name). I marvel at their wisdom, compassion, and humor as they *always* express the same Realization of the One regardless of culture or century; or so it seems to me. Adi Da, however, now calls them "premonitory" Seventh Stage Adepts, not as a diminishment of their Nondual Mystical

Realization, but more because their Teaching Methods tend to reflect Sixth Stage formlessness (and "Emptiness") mysticism, either that or they're focused on yogic Fifth Stage goals, or Fourth Stage devotional practices. I can see and understand that view too. Besides, ranking people is *not* the point: acknowledging their authenticity is the point. The Awakened Adepts *are* humanity's bequeathed inheritance from God's Great Tradition of Global Wisdom—they are here for all of us to celebrate and embrace as God's universal Gift given to "everybody-all-at-once" (as this book has tried to show).

Lao Tzu   **Buddha**   **Jesus**   **Shankara**   **Rumi**

Ultimately, of course, the Way is only about Divine Enlightenment or God-Realization which is miraculously (and paradoxically) only a "tacit understanding," nothing more (since it transcends mind altogether). It's not about being omniscient or knowing about every little thing. It's not even an "experience," per se, for the knower is gone ("blown out" in Nirvana) thus it transcends all experiences, including mystical visions and yogic blisses. Yet It IS Absolute Clear Light Bliss! This Truth, therefore, can only be *realized*, not published. Only Enlightenment reveals Truth and Eternal Happiness and Peace and Liberated Humor, not intellectual understanding, such as, for example, knowing about how chemistry works or how stars are born, etc. As the Avatar humorously but accurately explains:

> Most Perfect Realization of Reality Itself utterly destroys your ego-ic life—so watch out! The "trouble" with seventh stage Divine Self-Realization is that there is no "one" left over to enjoy "It"! … because the one who is seeking is the "price" that must be paid in order to Realize "It". You imagine that "you" will enjoy the satisfaction of having achieved Realization, or of having Realization Given to you—but all of that is nonsense. Realization is not something "you" will achieve or enjoy—because the ego is the "price".[23]

As all true Enlightenment traditions have taught, it is in the surrender of self and the transcendence of all thoughts in no-mind (or "ego-death") that truly Awakens us to our Divine Condition, our Buddha-Nature, the "One without a second" as Atman-Brahman, to know God via Divine Ignorance (or "not-knowing"). This "Real God" has nothing to do with "God the Creator," or even "God the Good," but is "God as the Real" (as one of Adi Da's essays refers to "It"[24]). I cannot, of course, begin to cover the depth and profundity of the Avatar's considerations on these serious and scholarly, yet mostly *spiritual*, matters (as generations henceforth will continue to study and realize). It is up to each individual to explore them further for himself or herself, preferably under the guidance of an authentic Guru-Adept, and see for yourself that God is Real.[25]

Avatar Adi Da's Seventh Stage Way

Adi Da, of course, is having none of this confusion professed by scholars, intellectuals, and religionists! His Enlightenment and Teaching-Revelation demands right understanding. And indeed, this is one of the reasons I so heartily support his Views. Therefore, in the early 1990s Adi Da came out and declared that his Way of the Heart, the Reality-Way of Adidam Ruchiradam, as being the only true "**Seventh Stage Way.**" This is because even the revered Enlightenment traditions of Buddhism and Vedanta tend to suggest a method of seeking or proposing a problem to overcome. One, Hinduism, suggests we need to discover (or re-discover) the Atman or our inner awareness as being God (the True Self) which has been lost by our ignorance; the other, Buddhism, suggests we need to eliminate our suffering by discovering Nirvana (or our innate Buddha-Nature). Both paths of Wisdom recommend we do certain exercises and disciplines (especially meditation), to find your Master-Guru (or Lama), and then act as if we could *cause* Enlightenment. Yes, we should (and must) do those practices, but still, "you" can't get there from here. Nor can you just be an ordinary ego and be Enlightened. It is a Divine Paradox worth realizing, for only the Truth will set you Free. All Adepts of the Great Tradition of Global Wisdom challenge you to *find out!* not simply read books or ponder philosophically.

Adi Da insists that the seeking for Enlightenment is an illusion. This is why the Seventh-Stage Realized Avatar suggests that *only* a genuine sacred *relationship* with a Realized-Master (in Satsang) is capable of initiating true Enlightenment via the *transmission* of the Enlightened State (and even then, nothing is guaranteed). But if you don't make yourself available it's certain nothing will happen (other than an ordinary life of suffering and ignorance… and death). Guru Yoga-Satsang is the best and quickest way as the Great Tradition unanimously declares. This, and this alone, is the true "secret" in God's Great Tradition of Global Wisdom. Guru Yoga and Satsang with an authentic Adept-Realizer *is* The Way. Then life is lived *as* Enlightenment seeing God everywhere whatever arises (with no avoidance). This is the Seventh Stage Way.

Study the Great Tradition and find out for yourself! The Way of Adidam, therefore, does not truly *begin* until Awakening has already occurred. Until you *see* and *hear* Adi Da's Teaching-Argument you will not understand; so you must "listen" (to the Guru's Teaching-Word).[26] Then the devotee responds to what has been revealed. The search is over. The practice of Adidam *begins* by recognizing the Divine as always already present, not as the result of doing practices or even being devotionally disposed. It begins by recognizing the Avatar's Enlightened State which is *your* enlightened state as well. Sadhana is then a process of recognition in response to knowing God (through the Guru) as your Divine Condition and ever-present Reality. When you are Enlightened: all there is God Only, Only God; Thou Art That. No problem. Live Life in Happiness always already Free.

Therefore, Buddhism and Vedanta overall, and for all practical purposes, are Sixth Stage methods and paths of Enlightenment that *seek* Enlightenment, according to Adi Da, although they do foreshadow Seventh Stage Enlightenment (and in certain cases realize it). Adidam, on the other hand, via the Guru's Transmission *initiates* Enlightenment *first*, from the beginning, based on understanding the search (and dilemma) of the separate self-activity and then transcending this contraction by being ever-present to "**searchlessly Behold**" Reality as It IS, which is "Me" (as Adi Da says). Of course, Adi Da also emphasizes that we cannot pigeon-hole any of the world's great esoteric religious traditions into being one stage or the other because there is such a wide variance in the various practitioners and Realizers within any certain historical period. Hence, it's easy to see how this entire discussion becomes circular and just an exercise of the mind, of the "Talking School." Therefore, I will not make any definitive statements but recommend that each person, if interested, take up their own course of study on these topics. Nothing is more enjoyable.

Go read and seriously study the texts of Enlightenment from the "Divine Library" of humankind as your religious occupation and duty [see Chapter 2]. Study the Sages and Siddhas. Find an authentic Guru. Read *The Collected Works of Ramana Maharshi*, for example, or the *Upanishads*, some of my favorites; read Shankara and Lao Tzu and Nagarjuna, other excellent examples, but mostly (when ready) read and study Avatar Adi Da Samraj, particularly his last great volumes addressing the Great Tradition and its most famous Realizers, including *The Pneumaton* (2011), *The Gnosticon* (2010), and of course, his ultimate magnum opus, *The Aletheon* (2009). Then, perhaps, *The Dawn Horse Testament* (2005), but this esoteric thousand-some page manual is beyond the reach of most (especially at the start). But it's best when you are ready, when you already *understand* (the ego-self as an activity of contraction). Read his incomparable autobiography *The Knee of Listening* (1972, 2007); a great place to start. Then *My "Bright" Word* (originally *The Method of the Siddhas*), the first year of Talks given to his devotees about "Understanding," "Money, Food, and Sex," "Meditation and Satsang," and "Guru As Prophet," for example. The precision that the Global Avatar or Jagad Guru Adi Da Samraj brings to these subjects and thoroughly *spiritual* matters is unprecedented!

But for most of us, the subtle distinctions between Sixth and Seventh Stage

Enlightenment are practically worthless until the Divinely Enlightened State informs our awareness about Real God (beyond the mythic stories of "God" you've been told about). Mind games and intellectual battles are *not* Enlightenment. I prefer to exalt over ALL the great Enlightened beings of history, discovering each scattered throughout the Great Tradition of Global Wisdom from every culture and country, and then use their inherited wisdom to support and penetrate my own understanding, deepen my awareness, inspire and enliven my heart. After all, it is only the "Practicing School" that produces real results. In other words, it works best when *chien* ("the view") arises before *hsing* ("the practice"), as our Ch'an Masters say. And no approach, it appears, is more effective in initiating the Enlightened State than Guru Yoga-Satsang under a genuine Guru-Adept, as this book has tried to emphasize. Re-discover for yourself what is real (and what is fake). It is our life's true purpose: to know God *for real!* Grow Up and Wake Up (then Clean Up and Show Up) and discover the spiritual power and reality of the real Guru-Adept and God's true existence.

Atma Nadi Shakti Yoga: Translation As "Outshining"

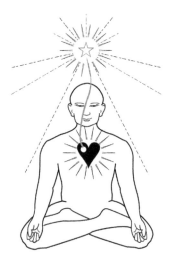

Satsang is, really, all about God-Realization; nothing more, nothing less. That is the only Wisdom that is true Happiness and Love-Bliss. This is the only real way to be free of ego and the self-contraction (or unlove), as all the Masters have explained, endlessly. Only the Truth will set you Free, no Guru alone can do it for you since you must respond (for It IS "always already the case"). But the Guru is our greatest benefit as an Agent of God's Grace. The problem, however, comes from the error that's consistently enacted even among the sincere practitioners of Eastern Wisdom and Western Religion, and that is *to search* for Truth or God (or Enlightenment). Adi Da calls this the "**search for solution**," which is why he sets his Reality-Way of Adidam apart from the Great Tradition's search for God and Enlightenment:

> The "great tradition" is the "search for solution", or the "search for The Divine"—based on the problematic pattern generated by the self-contraction (or egoity, or "point of view"). The Way of Adidam is not merely another form of practice based on the "great tradition" paradigm of the search. The Way of Adidam is not, in any sense, a development of the "great tradition", nor is The Way of Adidam the "end-stage" of the "great tradition". Rather, The Way of Adidam Is The Way That Inherently Transcends egoity. Therefore, The Way of Adidam Inherently Transcends the entire "great tradition" (or "great path of return").[27]

Adi Da offers at least two major breaks from the Great Tradition's spiritual search:

(1) first, is that the **Way of Radical Understanding** "does not assume the reactive principle of the search in dilemma... Therefore, Truth or Reality becomes not the Goal but the very Principle of life";

(2) second, it involves the "**regeneration of Amrita Nadi**" (or *Atma Nadi* the "current of Enlightened Love-Bliss") which is the "non-exclusive realization of the Heart... and thus, also of the descending and ascending circle of subtle and gross life, which is generated via the causal dimension from the prior [nondual] or Absolute Light that is the Heart, or Very Consciousness Itself."[28]

This is the unique advantage of Avatar Adi Da Samraj's appearance in our world at this time. Adi Da brilliantly and perfectly summarized this uniqueness from the beginning of his Teaching-Revelation, as this quote from *The Paradox of Instruction* (1977) shows:

> The "**Great Path of Return**," wherein the dimensions of the world

are experienced, should be utterly separated from the **Path of Radical Understanding**, wherein the dilemma of self is undone. The paths of return, pictured in the Great Traditions, are the key to the perennial [esoteric] science of the world to which every age has been devoted. The study of the phenomena of that great experiment can surely serve to clarify the childishness of our present sciences, limited as they are to the assumption of the gross dimension and the gross world. And the wisest of men [and women] may then do science in a more expansive milieu than we have recently assumed. Such men [and women] will make good use of the reports and even some of the methods of the Great Path of Return. But mankind should no longer engage the path of return as a search or a necessary way toward God, Reality, Self, or Truth.

All the Divine Teachers of the past have served the realization and communication of this perfect "Yoga" of understanding. All paths may be understood when examined relative to the various descriptions of the Way of Radical Understanding given in [My] literature. But the precise, full, and radical formulation of the Way of [Adidam] and its independence from the traditional paths of return has not been given among [humankind] before this time. You may prove this to your own satisfaction by examining the teachings of all traditions [the Great Tradition of Global Wisdom] in the light of this Way of Radical Understanding. Then you may test it in your own case by the enjoyment of this specific practice or Way of Life [in Adidam Ruchiradam].[29]

The search (of ego) is undone because our Divine Condition is *always already the case*, and thus is "seen" when Avatar Adi Da is "recognized" to be an authentic Agency of the "Divine Person" (or Consciousness Itself). This Reality-Way of Adidam Ruchiradam culminates in "**Atma Nadi Shakti Yoga**," Adi Da's unique offering to humankind that goes beyond anything offered in the Great Tradition of Global Wisdom. Specifically, it involves ***Ruchira Shaktipat*** or Avatar Adi Da's unique Heart-Transmission of *Atma Nadi* (or *Amrita Nadi*, literally, the "Divine Current of Love-Bliss"), the greatest yoga that transcends-and-includes all previous yogas. I truly believe this is the case, so let's allow the Avatar to affirm in His Words:

Atma Nadi Shakti Yoga Is a Process "radically" (or always "at the root") apart from (or intrinsically prior to) all psycho-physical ego-patterning.

This must be tacitly understood—at the "root" of the body-mind-complex.

Thus, Atma Nadi Shakti Yoga is not any kind of seeking "method".

Atma Nadi Shakti Yoga Is a Unique Process.

The Process of Atma Nadi Shakti Yoga is not identical to any process that can be found in the first-six-stages-of-life context of the Great Tradition of humankind....

Atma Nadi Shakti Yoga is not merely about some kind of "evolving" of the patterns of the ego.

Atma Nadi Shakti Yoga is not the "great path of return".

Atma Nadi Shakti Yoga is not a process of developing the potentials of the gross, subtle, and causal patterning of the conditional persona....

The entire process of Atma Nadi Shakti Yoga Is the Divine Transcendental Spiritual Process of "Brightening".

Most Ultimately, Atma Nadi Shakti Yoga Demonstrates Itself As Divine Translation—in Which all conditionality Is Perfectly Outshined.

Thus, Atma Nadi Shakti Yoga Is the Intrinsically egoless Process of Divine Self-Magnification....

I am Calling for everyone to surrender into the Process of Divine Translation.

That is what the devotional relationship to Me is about—the Outshining of conditional existence altogether, in all planes of "possibilities", here and elsewhere and everywhere....

Outshining Is Atma Nadi Shakti Yoga.

Outshining Is the "Radical" (or Always "At-the-Root") Reality-Way of Adidam Ruchiradam.[30]

Avatar Adi Da has always emphasized that it is the Heart on the right (where Consciousness causes the body-mind-soul to live from the heartbeat, to breathe the Spirit-Current of conductivity, the root of the causal domain) that then extends in an S-shaped curve (like a "seahorse") via the current of

Atma Nadi descending and arising to and from the Infinite Divine Conscious Light Above (and Beyond). The Avatar calls this terminal point Above (and Beyond) with the term the "**Midnight Sun**" (known most fully in Bhava Samadhi). Ultimately, this transformation and transfiguration results in what the Avatar calls "**Translation**" or "**Outshining**" of all conditional existences and possibilities in the "Bright" of Real God (beyond all descriptions or qualifications). These words here fail miserably. It must be *directly* experienced and known (and felt). The culmination and profundity of His Teaching-Revelation is *unique* in contrast to the Great Wisdom Tradition of humankind, though foreshadowed or hinted at with its greatest Adept-Realizers.[31]

This is, it seems to me, why Adi Da Samraj claims his **Reality-Way of Adidam** as being the Completion and Fulfillment of the Great Tradition and why he uses such phrases as "The Only-By-Me Revealed and Given Seventh Stage of Life" (which often confuses less-than-fully enlightened scholars, pandits and others) [see Chapter 10]. This Revelation is beyond words and ideas (or books, even those written by Adi Da), so I can only point you to the "**Threshold Personality**" of Avatar Adi Da Samraj himself who is drawing you to Outshine the conditional universe(s) in the Midnight Sun or Divine Light of Real God. This suggestion is so far from "ego-inflation" or conceit, as some critics blindly say about Adi Da, because He only confesses Absolute Nondual Truth (beyond all ego or self or conditional worlds). Avatar Adi Da is God's Great Gift to humanity (and all beings) *if* one sees and uses this relationship of Satsang with Him rightly.

This grand sacred ineffable process of Divine Realization or "always already" Enlightenment is what generates a genuine devotional response to Guru as God, not as a cultic reaction to an authority figure. The embodiment of Adi Da Samraj offers a direct portal to the Godhead via the Heart. This approach is fully in harmony with the ancient way of devotion to the Adept-Realizer, the essence of Guru Yoga-Satsang known (and practiced) throughout the millennia. Adi Da is not pulling your leg but opening your Heart to God Itself! The Avatar once more perfectly explains this totally "Radical" Reality-Way of Adidam as being the fulfillment and completion of the Ancient Walk-About Way of all Awakened Adepts, the Way of Real Religion practiced (and lived) without seeking but seeing (and knowing) and serving God as Conscious Light:

> The disposition of the ancient Walk-About Way is simply to turn to the Realizer in the very moment of sighting the Realizer. Just so, My true devotees simply turn to Me on sight. They turn to Me [the "Bright"] with everything "inside" and everything "outside"—such that the entire body-mind is turned to Me, rather than turned on itself and wandering in its patterning. Such devotional turning to Me [as "Real God"] is a simple matter....
>
> My Sitting before you, without speaking, is Sufficient.
> That mere Sitting, without speaking, is My Essential Teaching.
> There is nothing more fundamental than That.
> Simply Behold Me [as Conscious Light].[32]

This means, quite simply and plainly, there is *no seeking* for God in the Reality-Way Adidam but the eternal enjoyment of ever-present Divine Communion *now* with every breath and heartbeat. Instead of turning to ego and the world, turn to the Divine embodied in the Adept-Realizer as Avatar Adi Da Samraj—who is your modern-day incarnated Guru-Buddha-Christ in the Third Millennium. This means to *commune with* the Divine Condition as Reality *in the present* since It IS "always already the case" (even right now!), just as It IS. Real God is Great! DA is all and All! Truly, all the great traditions of Guru Yoga, practiced for millennia in India, Tibet, and the East (and even in the West with devotion to Jesus Christ) *is* The Way: "Follow Me!" God Only! Only God! DA Only! Only DA! We are *always already* Free—*Aham Da Asmi*: "I Am Da!"—as the Divine Avatar has always said:

> In the Way of Adidam, there are no actions that are purposed <u>toward</u>

Divine Self-Realization. Rather, for My true devotee, all actions are expressions of a <u>Prior State</u> of heart-Communion with Me [as Conscious Light]. That <u>Prior</u> heart-Communion with Me [as Real God] is what makes your actions true demonstrations of devotion to Me [as Guru]. That <u>Prior</u> heart-Communion with Me—rather than any strategy of "good intentions"—is what makes any right action true evidence of the Way of Adidam.[33]

But, truly, don't believe *me*, as a pandit-scholar and author; listen to Him as your Guru-Adept; then only the heart knows for sure… There really is nothing else to say.

DA! DA! DA!

Chapter 19 Endnotes

1. Adi Da Samraj, from the Talk "One-Pointedness" in *The Method of the Siddhas* (1972, Los Angeles, Revised and re-Named as My "Bright" Word, 2007).

2. Adi Da Samraj, *The Gnosticon* (2010), p. 328 [Adi Da does not capitalize the "Stages of Life" as I do].

3. Garma C. C. Chang, *The Practice of Zen* (1959), p. 51 [italics in original]; one of the best books I know of about Zen and the Buddhist Enlightenment tradition; highly recommended!

4. Ibid., pp. 51-52.

5. Ibid., p. 163.

6. Tenzin Wangyal Rinpoche, *The Tibetan Yogas of Dream and Sleep* (1998), p. 101.

7. See: "Adi Da as First, Last, and Only Seventh Stage Adept" by Chris Tong, Ph.D. at AdiDa UpClose.org.

8. Adi Da Samraj, "The Seventh School of God-Talk" (essay) in "Preface" to *The Song of the Self Supreme: Astavakra Gita* (1982), p. 18 ["Stages of Life" capped].

9. Ibid., p. 18 ["Stages of Life" capped].

10. See: Adi Da Samraj [Bubba Free John], *The Paradox of Instruction* (1977), pp. 208-209.

11. Adi Da Samraj, "The Seventh School of God-Talk" (essay) in "Preface" to *The Song of the Self Supreme: Astavakra Gita* (1982), p. 18 ["Stages of Life" capped].

12. Ibid., p. 18 ["Stages of Life" capped].

13. See, for example: *The Holy Teaching of Vimalakirti* (1992) translated by Robert A. F. Thurman, and *Ordinary Enlightenment: A Translation of the Vimalakirti Nirdesa Sutra* (1972, 2002) translated by Charles Luk; *The Vimalakirti Sutra* is a classic Mahayana scripture that emphasizes spiritual practice in the midst of secular life since Vimalakirti was a married householder as well as an Enlightened Buddha.

14. See: Ken Wilber, *The Atman Project* (1980, 1996), *A Sociable God* (1982, 2005).

15. See: "Introduction: Ken Wilber's Personal Odyssey" in *Embracing Reality: The Integral Vision of Ken Wilber* (2004, 2012) by Brad Reynolds.

16. See: Ken Wilber, *The Religion of Tomorrow* (2017) where he basically calls the Sixth Stage as "Ultraviolet Overmind" (Fulcrum-11) and the Seventh Stage as "White Supermind" (beyond fulcrums) now using Aurobindo's terms. However, for me, Wilber has currently become overly intellectual in his descriptions acting as a pandit, therefore not exhibiting the force of Enlightened Realization as does Adi Da Samraj as a Fully-Realized Adept-Guru.

17. Ken Wilber, *The Atman Project* (1980), p. 73 [bold and caps added].

18. Ibid., p. 74 [bold and caps added].

19. See: Adi Da Samraj [Bubba Free John], *The Paradox of Instruction* (1977), Chapter 3: "The Great Path of Return vs. the Radical Path of Understanding"; also see: "God-Talk, Real-God-Realization, Most Perfect Divine Self-Awakening, and "The Seven Possible Stages of Life" in *The Aletheon* (2009), *The Gnosticon* (2010), and *The Pneumaton* (2011).

20. See: *Growing In God: Seven Stages of Life from Birth to Enlightenment—An Integral Interpretation* (forthcoming) by Brad Reynolds.

21. Adi Da Samraj [Bubba Free John], *The Paradox of Instruction* (1977, 2nd edition), p. 151.

22. Ibid., pp. 154-156 [some title caps added].

23 Adi Da Samraj, The Seventh Way (2009), p. 17.

24. See: Adi Da Samraj [Da Free John], *Nirvanasara* (1982), "God as the Creator, the Good, and the Real."

25. See: Adi Da Samraj, *The Gnosticon* (2010), and *The Pneumaton* (2011), fulfilled in *The Aletheon* (2009).

26. See: *Meeting Adi Da: A Mandala of Approach to Avatar Adi Da Samraj* (forthcoming) by Brad Reynolds.

27. Adi Da Samraj, *The Ancient Walk-About Way* (2006), p. 95 (note Adi Da here does not title cap the "great tradition" unlike in most instances).

28. Adi Da Samraj [Bubba Free John], *The Paradox of Instruction* (1977), pp. 153-154, 156.

29. Ibid., pp. 164-165 [some title caps added].

30. Adi Da Samraj, from the Essay "Atman Nadi Shakti Yoga" in *The Gnosticon* (2011), p. 208, 211, 213, 218.

31. See, for example: "The Unique Sixth Stage Foreshadowings of The Only-By-Me Revealed and Given Seventh Stage of Life" in *The Gnosticon* (2010).

32. Adi Da Samraj, *The Ancient Walk-About Way* (2006), pp. 67-68.

33. Ibid., p. 74.

TWENTY

GURU SATSANG
IN ADIDAM RUCHIRADAM

There is a clear sympathy between the... Reality-Way of Adidam (or Adidam Ruchiradam) and the traditional Non-dualist Teachings [of Buddhism and Advaita Vedanta, etc.]. Nevertheless, the Reality-Way of Adidam is not merely a re-statement or a re-presentation of the traditional Non-dualist Teachings. The Reality-Way of Adidam is a new Revelation That Completes the Great Tradition as a whole.

— **Adi Da Samraj**, *The Gnosticon*[1]

ADVAITAYANA BUDDHISM:
THE REALITY-WAY OF ADIDAM

hen set within the context of the Great Tradition of Global Wisdom of humankind, Buddhism and its wisdom teachings can serve our understanding about the proper relationship with today's modern-day Gurus [see Chapters 17-18]. A truly integrated form of Vedanta and Buddhism, grounded in Nondual Enlight-

enment (or Self-Realization), in addition to a deeper understanding of the
esoteric traditions of the West, shows how Guru-Adepts or Wisdom Masters are
essential for the emerging Integral Age. This is particularly true with Avatar Adi
Da Samraj who has simply titled his Teaching "The Way of the Heart" or "The
Way of Radical Understanding," but he also identifies the "**Reality-Way of
Adidam Ruchiradam**" as being a hybrid called "**Advaitayana Buddhism**"—a
new modern-day *yana* or "vehicle" combining the best of Buddhism (with its
"realism") with Advaita Vedanta (with its "idealism").[2]

The benefit that traditional Buddhism and Hinduism offers to modern
people by emphasizing the relationship to a genuine Guru-Adept becomes
monumental when a *Jagad Guru* or World-Teacher and Global Avatar such
as Adi Da Samraj appears. These traditions affirm that the Enlightened
State in one person can profoundly influence others, even millions, via the
sacred transformative method of Guru Yoga-Satsang enacted when the Adept's
Heart-Transmission or Spirit-Baptism is active. Yet, as premodern, modern,
and postmodern individuals, we must be schooled in the Great Wisdom Tradition to fully understand the larger context within which such a rare person
appears. This is not cultism but the potential for inducing God-Realization
in other human beings, that is, *if* their recognition-response to a genuine
Guru-Adept is adequate and open to such possibilities.

Tibetan Buddhists, for example, honor their Lamas and Rinpoches above
all others, as true devotees of Hinduism and Advaita Vedanta, Jainism, Sikhism, Siddha Yoga, Sant Mat, etc., deeply honor their Holy Gurus. All world
religions have a Founding Adept-Realizer at their root, a "divine person"
considered most holy among all others, to which their faith and allegiance is
aligned and awakened. The Great Enlightenment Tradition itself continues to

thrive around the world generating a universal Perennial Philosophy grounded in *Sophia* or a divine esoteric knowledge [see Chapters 7-8], even though it does so with halting difficulty in this emerging post-postmodern global era—the rising Integral Age. Indeed, Guru Yoga may be questioned and feared now more than any other time in history due to scientific materialism and atheism.

The actions and Teachings exhibited by someone like Adi Da, including the power of his *siddhis* (or paranormal abilities) and even his "Crazy Wisdom" teaching methods, are clarified under the wise guidance and historical precedence of Buddhism (especially the Tibetan-Vajrayana variety). By adding the best of Hinduism and Advaita Vedanta, plus all other universal esoteric forms of mysticism exhibited by genuine Adept-Realizers, we have a template to distinguish the true Gurus from the false. We can learn through the Great Tradition how to better recognize and access the Global Avatar born for all humankind.

Although Adi Da was trained mostly in the Siddha Yoga tradition of India (under the discipleship of Swami Rudrananda, Swami Muktananda, and Bhagavan Nityananda, et al), he has time and time again affirmed that the essential Realization—or Awakening to the Transcendental Truth (of Real God)—is the *same* (or equivalent) in both Hinduism and Buddhism, as in all major esoteric religions. It is in and as Consciousness Itself that Enlightenment is realized, not in books, traditions, philosophy or the rituals of religion. Therefore, the renowned American-born Awakened Adept adamantly affirms: "The Way That I Teach effectively Realizes the Buddhist ideal of the transcendence of conditional existence as well as the Advaitic ideal of Identification with the Transcendental Reality... [Yet] this Way of Advaitayana Buddhism is inherently free of the exclusiveness that tends to be associated with the classical Buddhist and Advaitic goals."[3] This is because, as the twentieth-century born Avatar goes on to clarify:

> There is an inherent Sympathy (and necessary equation to be made) between the Buddhist proposition of the "Nirvanic" Condition and the Advaitic proposition of the Brahmanic Atman ["True Self"]. This Sympathy (and this equation) is obvious to all actual Realizers (whatever their tradition may be) of That Which Intrinsically Transcends conditional existence.[4]

The point is that the name or tradition itself is not most important but it is the actual Realization of our innate divinity and knowing that we are "God" (in Western terms) or the "True Self" (in Eastern terms) that determines its authenticity. It is the same Universal Truth for all human beings, regardless of race, religion, culture, or ethnicity (or sexual orientation, etc.). In this case, the nondual enlightened perspectives of Buddhism and Vedanta, these great esoteric lineages from the East, instruct us and confirm similarities with the "Radical" Teaching-Transmission of Avatar Adi Da Samraj. Study them and see for yourself.

As some examples, both describe "Buddha-Nature" and the "True Self" (in their terms) as being the "Prior Unity" of "Real God" or the "Radiant Transcendental Being" (in Adi Da's terms); each reveals an empty-luminosity, a "Clear Light Void," as the Buddhists say, affirmed by Adi Da as "The 'Bright'" and "Conscious Light" or "Reality Itself." Both views recognize "Consciousness Itself" as our "naked awareness" or "Mind-Only" as being the fundamental One Divine Reality.[5] Avatar Adi Da, as previously reviewed, has discussed these topics in great detail [see Chapter 10], especially in his recent volumes *The Gnosticon* (2010) and *The Pneumaton* (2011), and epitomized in *The Aletheon* (2009), the Avatar's summary text.

GOD IS NOT WITHIN—WE ARE IN GOD

Chere are also strong parallels between the Buddha's Teaching of *anatma* or *anatta* (or "no-self") and Adi Da's Teaching of Radical Understanding that sees or *understands* the ego-I (or self) as *an activity* of interdependent co-arising processes or "pattern patterning"(in Adi

Da's words) not an actual entity or self that is eternal. According to Buddhism and Adi Da, there is no real separate self in reality—it is an illusion that is temporary (and relative) thus obscures the true nature of Reality. We, as the self-contracting activity, identify with our body and its perspectives generated by the inner mind; this makes us afraid and thus we turn away (or contract) from love, our true condition. As Nagarjuna explained in *The Diamond Sutra* (ca. 2nd century CE): "Buddha Teaches that all things are devoid of selfhood, devoid of personality, devoid of entity, and devoid of separate personality.... Though the common people accept egoity as real, the Tathagata declares the ego is not different from non-ego."[6] In this case, the activities of the self, our incarnated body-mind, must be disciplined in Right View, Right Living, Right Meditation, and Radical Devotion in order to function in the best possible way. Most modern consumers fail at these disciplines miserably, being fully self-centered and self-indulgent. We need guidance to break and see through this psycho-physical patterning of egoity. We need true Gurus like we need air.

Consequently, if the True Self is not really an eternal "soul" within the body but only *appears* to be within (from the ego's perspective), then in truth the ego-soul arises within the True Self (i.e., within Atman-Brahman or Buddha-Nature). Only the *essence* or "root" of the soul and all things, including the so-called ego-I, are eternal and infinite (beyond time and space). Adi Da Samraj, therefore, like the Buddha, counters the message contained in Jesus's famous saying: "The Kingdom of God is within you" (Luke 17:21) with a more fully Enlightened View. While true enough at certain Stages of Life—God is found within, since God is brightest in the heart—yet the appearance of our body-mind and self-soul is only relative, not Absolute (except in essence), according to these Great Sages.

To question this common wisdom of being human—for we do in fact *feel separate*—is a *radical* (or "at the root") message, therefore it is offensive to many ears including most "New Age" (or spiritual) sentiments in our current postmodern times. This is because these Adepts are saying that in truth there is no eternal soul (*atman*); or rather, the "soul" as a reincarnating sense of being a separate self arises *within* Eternity, not the other way around. It seems paradoxical to the logical mind for attention or awareness does feel "it" is *within* the body-mind, which is why the self-sense is only perfectly transcended in the Enlightened Heart. Otherwise, the ego-self would be the fundamental reality; but ultimately, it is not (in truth). Only God IS. Paradoxically, this fact is what is *realized* in Enlightenment: there is NO self, Only Consciousness, the "Divine Person" of "I Am," not a separate soul or self or "I"—thus we are absolutely Free in truth. Only an Enlightened Adept, such as Avatar Adi Da, can openly confess: "God is outside us. God is not within us. We are in God. What we perceive or conceive within are only reflections or indications of God—but we take all of that to be ourselves. God is not *other* than ourselves, because we inhere in God."[7] Such subtle distinctions are vastly important as the modern-day Avatar explains to further enlighten us:

> The "Kingdom of God" is not within. There is nothing within us but mechanical facts and illusions, just as the whole world before us. The [real] "Kingdom of God" is a matter of the literal Translation of the whole bodily being of the individual into the unqualified and All-Pervading Light of the World.[8]

Even the "soul" does not survive death endlessly (although it does often journey from lifetime to lifetime, according to the Masters), thus it becomes "immortal" only by "**Outshining**" itself in its "**Translation**" into the Divine Domain of Bright Conscious Light. This can happen either today (in this moment)—even *as* the body—or after death. It is only by the *sacrifice of self* or surrendering the ego-I into the All-Pervading Divine Presence that is true God-Realization... or Nirvana... or Atman awareness... or *Gnosis*, et al. Buddhism, for example, calls it the "Great Transference into the Body of Light."[9] Such Translation in (and as) the "Bright" is not a place to go, therefore, it is also a State of consciousness to *realize* (in "ego-death") in the here and now. As only one example (among countless), the *Lankavatara Sutra*, one of Buddhism's greatest wisdom scriptures, declares where and what is Nirvana:

> Nirvana is... the manifestation of Noble Wisdom, which is Buddhahood, [which] expresses itself in Perfect Love for all; it is where the manifestation of Perfect Love that is Tathagatahood expresses itself in Noble Wisdom for the enlightenment of all—there, indeed, is Nirvana! ... if [the people] only realized it, they are already in Tathagata's Nirvana, for, in Noble Wisdom, all things are in Nirvana from the beginning.[10]

Once more, we see the Buddha expresses and affirms that Enlightenment is "**always already the case**" (as Adi Da's words have made popular, for example, in Ken Wilber's writings). Therefore, what the global Avatar from the third millennium America CE (of the Common Era) and Gautama Buddha from the first millennium India BCE (five hundred years before Christ), in addition to the successive lineages of Buddhist Adepts and Hindu Siddhas, are *all* clearly and unanimously saying is there is *no one* (self or atman or soul) *within*. This is a paradox nearly beyond belief, especially for modern ears.

We seem certain our interior is real. But it's only *relatively* real, not absolutely real, as the Sages explain. Seeing an "inside" or interior is part of the illusion that the separate self generates by living in the body and thus seeing (with our eyeballs) an "outside" or exterior world from our individuated "point of view" or perspective. Such a decidedly radical message that there is no self (in Ultimate Reality) seems to nullify the beliefs of many religions about the soul and an afterlife. However, there is only the True Self, the Witness Consciousness or Consciousness Itself (or God Only)—what Adi Da calls the "Divine Person," what Buddha called "Buddha-Nature" (*Tathāgatagarbha* and *Buddhadhātu*). This divine paradox literally goes beyond logical comprehension; thus this awareness can only *be realized* by the heart, not figured out by the mind. Since God *is* Love and Light (as *The Bible* says), then "everything" is always already perfect, a sentiment generally not understood by most. Samsara *is* Nirvana, and vice versa! God Only, Only God!

But do not misunderstand. This Nondual View is not saying that our sense of ego-I isn't *relatively* real, for it is. We are here *now* so we must surrender to life to be full of life. There is hatred (or unlove) and evil in the world, without a doubt. Enlightenment only awakens us to the fact that the feeling of being a separate self is not *absolutely* real. Nevertheless, the self creates real problems too, obviously. The self, since birth, experiences traumas and maladaptations distorting our view of Reality. But only Real God (or Transcendental Consciousness), our innate Buddha-Nature, is *truly* real. Only *this* Realization or insight allows the soul to rest beyond the wounds and hurt, disappointments and failures, and to surrender itself totally and fully into our Divine Condition and to actively *be* Love and Happiness *now* (and even in death) regardless of conditions or circumstances. Adi Da affirms this view absolutely, is what I have learned from him.

Since each person does in fact *experience* a sense of self arising from the body's five senses and the mind's countless thoughts, then we need to realize and understand that sense stimuli and brain processes are only "**patterns of**

patterning" (in Adi Da's words). Our sense of self is really just electromagnetic molecular patterns in the brain creating a false sense of self-identity. Let's allow the Enlightened Avatar to wisely reveal what is true:

> The old saying that Truth is within is not true. The Truth is absolutely not within. Within is "me". Within is the inside of "me". Conventional mysticism and conventional religion are addressed to our inwardness, because the psyche, the inner being and mind, can feel itself to be separate from the body and the physical environment and all the conditions of mortal existence of which we are afraid, all the conditions that can die.... Mystical experience is promoted as a solution to suffering, as an answer to doubt and fear, just as saviors and popular religious concepts are offered for the same purpose.
>
> But the Realization of God or Truth appears, and spontaneously, only in the instant of self-transcendence or ecstatic annihilation of mind, of inwardness, of self-consciousness or the reflection of oneself in experience. Ego-death, self-transcendence, or the transcendence of mind, then, is the "narrow gate," the necessary doorway to the realization of Truth.... God-Realization, or liberation in Truth, is most fundamentally a matter of ego-death, or the death of the illusion of the inner consciousness, the separate "I", the mind of self-centered presumptions and experiential limits.[11]

This is why Buddhism (and Adidam) says "Right View" is radically understanding that the sense of self actually arises from the processes of "**Interdependent Origination**" (a fundamental Buddhist teaching). In Enlightenment, the self is seen to be "Empty" (*sunya*) of any substantial essence since it only arises as an *activity* of conditional phenomena. We can each *realize* this truth, as the Adepts always say, and thus feel free of self. Adi Da claims that this *activity* of the conditional self-contraction (or Narcissus) is exactly what must be *consciously* understood and transcended to know God for real. In Buddha's case, he teaches us about **anatma** or "no atman," no self, Only Nirvana, Mind-Only; Adi Da teaches about the "Bright," Real God, the Prior Unity of Conscious Light (Consciousness Only), which is the simple "Feeling of Being" or Love-Bliss and Happiness, "Reality Itself" that is "always already the case" (in Adi Da's words). We are *within* God—see?

Adi Da, thousands of years after Gautama, affirms a view similar to the Buddha's by teaching about Radical Understanding: there is no self, just the *activity of self-contraction* or "**avoiding relationship**"—identified as "**Narcissus**" (in Adi Da's terms). This activity is what gives us the feeling-sense that "I" is a separate self inside an outside world (but that's only an illusion). What is different from the Buddha is that Adi Da teaches us not to seek for Nirvana (or release) or for God (to be saved) but to simply *understand* we are creating the activity of self. It is not happening *to us*; it's as if we are pinching ourselves. The activity of self-contraction is like a clenched fist, a common mudra or symbol used by Adi Da, whereas God-Realization is an open hand, free in relationship to Reality. Simply understand and surrender the ego-activity to *realize* God.

Adi Da, 1972
clenched fist of Narcissus

Adi Da, 1972
open hand of Relationship

Henceforth, the Avatar summarizes this understanding (or insight) in a simple but profound formula: "**The ego is an activity, not an entity.**"[12] Such "**Radical Understanding**" is a fundamental tenet of Avatar Adi Da's Teaching-Work, similar to the Buddha's first two Noble Truths (on suffering), but perhaps even more penetrating because it outlines the basic requirement for self-transcendence that allows or aligns us to open and receive and surrender to the Guru-Adept's Heart-Transmission: simply understand and "turn to Me" (turn to Real God). Such self-understanding and open receptivity initiates our Enlightenment by receiving the Guru's Spirit-Baptism [see below]. In this case, the Awakened Buddha of the Axial Age in the premodern East is not the only Guru-Adept with whom Avatar Adi Da appears in the likeness of, or has a continuity with, for there was an Adept from the premodern West too (as we'll see next).

BIRTHDAY MESSAGE FROM JESUS CHRIST
& AVATAR ADI DA

The hour cometh, and now is, when the true worshipers shall worship the Father in Spirit and in Truth: for the Father seeketh such to worship Him. God is Spirit: and they that worship Him must worship in Spirit and in Truth.

— **John 4: 23-24**

To epitomize (and summarize) the amazing year of 1982—what I have called Adi Da's "Miracle Year" (*annus mirabilis*) due to his prolific publication of books and discourses[13]—the modern Avatar of America gave us a special "Birthday Message" encapsulating not only his own but also the Divine Teaching from the Adept of Nazareth, Jesus Christ. This gracious message, delivered first as a recited essay, then followed by a longer talk, was a special form of Spirit-Blessing bequeathed to all generations on that miraculous day of November 3, 1982, the incarnated Divine Person's forty-third birthday. On that commemorable day, Avatar Adi Da compared his Heart-Transmission (*Hridaya Shaktipat*) to that of the Spirit Baptism given all those years ago by Jesus of Nazareth. At the same time, those personally gathered around the American Adept's radiant Company felt its authenticity permeate their bodies and hearts, not just their listening minds.[14] The Guru's Spirit-Baptism was bodily palpable, not just a figment of imagination. Importantly, Adi Da pointed out that both Adepts first require a person be "born again" or converted—a conversion or *metanoia*—from a conventional life to one based on God-Realization and acting as love in all relations.

Around two thousand years ago, Jesus was asked what is the greatest commandment of all, to which the Guru of Galilee replied: "To love God with all your heart, and with all your soul, and with all your mind. This is the first and greatest commandment. And the second is like it, to love your neighbor as yourself [similar to the Golden Rule: 'Do unto others as you would have others do unto you']." (Mark 12: 30-31) In this case, as Adi Da pointed out, the *New Testament* teaches there is only one unpardonable sin: "Truly I tell you, all sins and blasphemes will be forgiven for the sons of men. But whoever blasphemes against the Holy Spirit will never be forgiven, but is guilty of an eternal sin," as Jesus once told them. (Mark 3:28-29)

The word "**sin**," as Adi Da explained (who was himself a student of Biblical Greek when he attended a Lutheran seminary in the mid-1960s), comes from the ancient Greek word ***hamartia***, which means, "to miss the mark" (from an archery term). Therefore, the act of sin, as Jesus and Adi Da emphasize, is to dissociate from God, to deny the living Divine or Holy Spirit altogether and so to be divorced from forgiveness and mercy. Avatar Adi Da, therefore, affirms Jesus's essential message: "To deny the Divine is to be in a perpetual state of dissociation from the Divine, and, therefore, dissociation from forgiveness. Only once we have ceased to deny the Divine is forgiveness possible. Therefore, sin is simply the denial of the Holy Spirit or denial of the Spiritual Divine."[15] We can clearly see that both Adepts, from the ancient one to the modern one, are urging us to *turn to God*—"Turn to Me" and "Come unto Me," as they both teach—in order to intimately *know* the Divine Reality of Real God as Love-Bliss and thus be forgiven. Sin no more. Meet the mark! Only then may we repent our sin of "missing the mark" and thus be converted to actual God-Communion, here and *now*, in the *present* (not at a later date or in another world or heaven realm).

Earlier that evening to celebrate his day of birth, the American-born World-Teacher's devotees performed music and skits as one of their birthday gifts for their Beloved Guru, showering him with many presents that night. Everyone was entertained with joy and humor and laughter as the Guru-Adept saturated the room with his Spirit-Blessing and radiant Transmission. As it got late, after the children had been put to bed, the Maha-Siddha announced to those present: "I have a gift for you too."[16] It was a short essay about two pages long called "**A Birthday Message from Jesus and Me**," which was then followed with an explanatory discourse (both later published in *The Fire Gospel: Essays and Talks on Spirit Baptism*). It was a potent message about being converted or "**born again**" by Spirit Baptism (or the Transmission) given by a Realized Guru-Adept, and then how to practice love for all others (and all of Nature) as you *feel* your love for God. Service and love to others comes easiest when love of God reigns supreme in your heart. It was an enlivening and intimate message since most people listening had a Christian upbringing (being Westerners). At the same time, the verbal Teaching was simultaneously being accentuated by the Guru's powerful Heart-Transmission—the real Spirit Baptism spoken about in the Christian scriptures. The communication was a delightful offering that only an Awakened Adept could impart, thus its import will always ring true across the generations. Adi Da then paraphrased Jesus's sacred message for all to hear anew:

> You must be born again. You must be born in the Spirit, you must receive the Spirit, you must enter into Communion with the Spirit. God is Spirit. Man is Spirit, every individual is a spirit, and all of the spirits, including the entire world, are arising in God, in intimate, eternal Communion with the Spirit of God. Religion is to repent or be converted from an unspiritual point of view, the whole life of self-possession and the mortal mind, and to enter fully into Communion with the Divine as the Living Spirit.[17]

Avatar Adi Da on that special day was confirming the importance of being "reborn," which is a phrase that comes from Jesus answering questions from the Pharisee **Nicodemus**, who had come to see the Nazarene Master at night, away from his official public priesthood, since he had personally seen "God be with him [Jesus]." (John 3: 2) Upon coming into the Company of the Great Adept Jesus, Nicodemus asked for the Guru's most sacred Teaching, unto which Jesus said: "Unless a man be born again, he cannot see the Kingdom of God." (John 3: 3) Rabbi Nicodemus, a learned scholar of the Jewish tradition and *Old Testament* (the *Tanakh*, or Hebrew Bible, including the *Torah*), was puzzled: "How can a man be born when he is old? Can he enter the second time into his mother's womb?" (John 3: 4) Yet Jesus was not speaking about physical birth but a psychic or *spiritual* birth. He was referring to a *re-birth* or "conversion" (*metanoia*, in Greek) to turn away from the self-centered ways of the ego-I to the way of Divine Communion with the living God (Who is Love). In modern English, and with clarifying force to be heard anew by today's New Age of spiritual listeners, Adi Da explained exactly the same message in his well-articulated essay:

> Those who love God totally (as self-transcending spirits, surrendered as the total body-mind, feeling as and in the Self-Radiant Energy or Spirit of Being) also inevitably love others, Communicate or Magnify God in the worlds, and always transcend themselves in all relations, under all conditions, and in every state. Therefore, be **"born again"**—be reborn or re-Lived now—by the discovery and affirmation that you and all beings and things are Spirit, or an eternal

process of Energy (rather than unconscious and mortal matter)....
Awaken and Be in the Spirit and *then* fulfill the double Law of the
Spirit—which is to love God, or the Transcendental Spirit-Being,
until you become Love, and so love all others.[18]

I mean, really, what could be a greater message than this? It was true during
the days of Jesus as it is true today during the days of Adi Da who has been
incarnated here into our global culture. Spirit Baptism is eternal and unconditional, not dependent on eras of time or history but only dependent on your
own conversion to seeing and realizing God.

"Born Again" via Spirit-Baptism

Verily, verily, I say unto thee, except a man be born again,
he cannot see the Kingdom of God.

— **John 3: 3**

Heart-Master Adi Da continued to explain the import of his enlightening essay: "Being born again in the Spirit... is in some sense a
message about everybody's 're-birthday' or spiritual birth,"[19] as the
modern Adept paraphrased the ancient Teaching of Jesus. It truly was a birthday message from Jesus and "Him" (Adi Da as the Divine Person). This is not
unusual, for often the Adept-Realizers of the Great Tradition bring the same
message of Enlightenment to the common people, regardless of century or
culture, often clarifying a previous Adept's Teaching in today's terms.

During his talk, Adi Da pointed to similarities (or a likeness) of his Teaching with some of the world's great religious traditions, such as Advaita Vedanta

and Buddhism, but also with Christianity, as he explains: "I also Teach, as Jesus Taught, the radical religion of the Spirit…. Jesus likewise taught esoteric means of living in Communion with the Spiritual Divine, but those means have been lost within the tradition…. The story of Jesus reports a person Transfigured and Transformed by intimacy with the Spiritual Divine."[20] In this sense, the American-born Avatar is correct to claim: "I am an individual of the same type as Jesus and other Adepts who have Taught and Demonstrated the radical religion of the Spirit and who have Baptized individuals in the Spirit."[21] **Spirit-Baptism**, in other words, is the real "secret Teaching" taught by Adept-Realizers the world over, yet it is a message only a few truly understand while the rest of us remain unaware and ignorant.

Consequently, Nicodemus was still perplexed so he questioned the Master again: "How can these things be?" (John 3: 9). This is when Jesus answered by teaching one of the most esoteric passages in *The Bible*, yet today most Christians tend to reinterpret his words in exoteric or literal ways and thus miss the point (or "miss the mark," i.e., they sin). For example, when Jesus spoke: "For God so loved the world that he gave his only begotten Son, that whosoever believeth in Him should not perish, but have everlasting life" (John 3:16), he was actually talking about recognizing the Guru as an Agent or vehicle of God's Grace via the agency of Spirit-Transmission. Such baptizing the soul with the descent of Spirit can potentially initiate a Spiritual Awakening to God-Realization for a disciple or devotee. This is a genuine function of a true Guru, if you use them properly: "whosoever believeth in Him."

Jesus was explaining it is the Spirit-Baptism given by an Awakened Adept that is most important for true spiritual life—"that Light is come into the world"—not preaching metaphorical stories about the "washed-by-the-blood-of-Jesus mythology" or the "salvation-through-the-death-of Christ mythology," as Adi Da pointed out during his birthday talk. By activating the process of Satsang or Guru-Yoga both Adepts are revealing the "esoteric process of being God-born and ultimately Translated into the Divine Condition,"[22] as Adi Da explained, that is, to *truly* enter the Kingdom of God. The descent of the "**Dove**" represents the decent of Holy Spirit infilling the two hemispheres (or "wings") of the inner brain in a bath of Eternal Ecstasy. Jesus was disclosing to Nicodemus, who was now listening attentively to the Message of Christ or one who is a "son" of God, the "Anointed One" (or Messiah), that is, a genuine Guru-Adept, on how to truly love God:

> The hour cometh, and now is, when the true worshippers shall worship the Father in Spirit and Truth: for the Father seeketh such to worship Him. God *is* Spirit: and they that worship him must worship him in Spirit and in Truth. (John 4: 23-24)

This is the true yogic or *esoteric* (or "inner-directed") Teaching about the reality of Spirit (or God) existing right here and now (for it is "always already the case," in Adi Da's words). The real spiritual process is not simply about believing in certain myths or stories about Jesus or using him as a "substitute sacrifice," but rather to turn your attention to "the Father" or Real God Itself as Formless Spirit, which is Truth. This is how we are converted from the self-contraction of the ego-I and the mythic limits of exoteric religion—to be "reborn" in Spirit via Divine Communion. Avatar Adi Da continues to paraphrase and explain the real esoteric Teaching of Jesus Christ:

> Jesus preached a radically simplified form of religion. He preached what I call basic religion. Only one affair is religion: the conversion from self, and all views based on self-possession and mortal self-consciousness, to Communion with the Living Spirit-Being or Radiant Transcendental Being, the recognition that all of Nature is made of that One, that every being is a spirit and one with the Transcendental Spirit. That which is born of the Spirit, he said, is Spirit, *is* of the same nature, and, therefore, can Realize a state of perfect Identification with that Great Spirit or Transcendental Being, and by that perfect Divinity be drawn into the Domain of unqualified spiritual existence.[23]

In this case, Adi Da, like Jesus Christ, "preached a Way of life that involved stepping outside the bondage to tradition and institutionalized religiosity"[24] in order to find or *realize* God directly, *presently*. Yet both Adepts are here not just to criticize the conventional religion of their day, which they both do adamantly, but are primarily here to baptize people, their responding devotees, with the *Shaktipat*-Energy of the Holy Spirit. **Shaktipat** is a Sanskrit term indicating a "descent' ("to fall," *pata*) of "psychic energy" (*shakti*) given from an advanced Yogi or Guru to another person [see Chapter 3]. Hinduism considers this an act of God's Grace as part of a genuine Guru's sacred function since it can have an awakening (and transforming) effect on the person receiving the Shaktipat transmission or Spirit-Blessing. Once the descending Spirit goes down the frontal line of the body opening the heart and reaching to the "vital center" down to the bodily base (as Adi Da explains), then the "serpent" (or Life-Energy) turns to ascend or rise up the spinal line into the inner brain core with an Awakening force into higher states of consciousness and mysticism. This potentially initiates subtle and divine-like experiences far beyond ordinary daily experience. Yet, these experiences are not Enlightenment itself (which ultimately transcends all conditional energies and visions, even subtle ones).

This process is what traditional Kundalini Yoga addresses by focusing on the ascension of Life-Energy up the spinal line (via the chakras) where some traditions teach this is actually the way to Enlightenment. The Fifth Stage of Life ascent of kundalini up the spine awakens and activates subtle and higher states of consciousness, without a doubt, but it is not Divine Enlightenment (Sixth or Seventh Stage of Life), according to the fully Awakened Siddha-

Gurus.[25] The "descent" of Spirit-Force generally involves Fourth Stage of Life phenomena while "ascent" is mostly Fifth Stage phenomena (in Adi Da's model). Adi Da (and other Adepts), however, teach that Enlightenment (or Self-Realization) is not merely about kundalini or subtle state experiences and mystical visions but is a Heart-Awakening to the Transcendental Divine Presence of Real God. Kundalini is an esoteric part of the mystical process that stabilizes higher states of awareness thus is a higher-order Stage of Life but it is not Enlightenment fully realized. The circulation of Spirit-Energy in the body-mind complex is part of the responsibility and practices of the esoteric Yogas and Higher Stages of Life. This is another principal reason why we need an authentic Guru-Yogi to guide us and serve our spiritual growth.

Avatar Adi Da, who was initiated into Kundalini Yoga first by Swami Rudrananda ("Rudi") in New York City, and later by Swami Muktananda in India (during the late 1960s), verifies that the descent of Spirit-Baptism (or Holy Spirit) involves an actual transmission or exchange of Spiritual Energy. Often it is felt as the descent of the sensual feminine or Goddess-Power, known as *Shakti*, while *Shiva* is the ascending formless Transcendental aspect of the One Divine. It is an ecstatic force that presses down in the body to turnabout and rise up, sometimes as tingles, other times as violent spasms (known as *kriyas*). The Enlightened Spiritual Master continued explaining during his sacred birthday talk:

> [My] Shaktipat is Spirit-Baptism… or true Shaktipat (without certain of the peculiar philosophic and psychic limitations of the Hindu tradition). Shaktipat is popularly associated with the orientation of the Fifth Stage realization, which has been superimposed on the process that is true Shaktipat…. It is the same process that occurs in My Company [via Adi Da's Heart-Transmission], but to which you are freely oriented, without Fifth Stage limitations [via Adi Da's Satsang]. In this Way [of Adidam], you are called to enter into a process of perfect unification with the Living Spirit to the point of Enlightenment, transcending all conditional realizations at the [subtle or even causal] level of experience or presumed knowledge."[26]

What Adi Da is talking about is *real* religion, not downtown religion, but the true religion that awakens and purifies the esoteric anatomy of the human being, from toe to crown, from the first chakra to the seventh chakra (and above) then down again into the heart (on the right) to radiate to Infinity. This process serves the bodily surrender of self into the living Current of Spirit coordinated and conducted with the breath—the "**Circle of Conductivity**" (in Adi Da's terms). The *conversion* from self-centered egoic habits and tendencies to circulating and breathing the Living Spirit of God is the real practice of a spiritual life dedicated to Divine Communion. This is how we are turned to Love, to real spiritual life, to the Divine Life by the "fire" of Spirit-Baptism. Such Baptism is best served by cultivating a loving relationship with a qualified Adept-Transmitter in Satsang, as Adi Da has constantly emphasized. This is what Nicodemus was having trouble comprehending, as we all tend to do, but it is precisely the process that Jesus, and later Adi Da, are teaching.

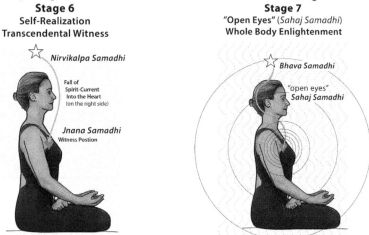

Adi Da, like Jesus, would go on to clarify: "You are called first to the Spiritual Divine, and you must enter into this conversion physically, emotionally, psychically.... To accommodate the Spiritual Divine in every feature of your existence, to be devoted to It wholly and entirely, not merely in the mind with a kind of subjective acknowledgment, but very practically, physically, emotionally, mentally, psychically, is the practice."[27] Such "**spiritual conversion**," as Adi Da goes on to say, comes from being "converted from self" to seeing God as a Living Spiritual Reality of Energy (or as the Holy Spirit). The incarnated Avatar explained further: "This restoration of intimacy with the Living Divine is likewise a restoration of intimacy with all other conditions of existence and all other beings. When love of God returns, then love of others also returns."[28]

True religion, Adi Da claims, is not to not turn away from life but to open fully to Life. The Guru-Adept personally (and bodily) demonstrates this very truth to everyone who will listen to him and hear him, whether in the room with him on that blissful birthday evening or to those millions who will be approaching him now and into the future. This is not just philosophy, but the gift of *Sophia-Gnosis* or Divine Awakening. As the Master-Adept explained at the essay's end, the great gift of real religion is offered only with genuine Guru Yoga-Satsang:

> Only this is true and useful religion. Religion is self-transcending Spirituality. It is to be restored to inherently Free Spirit-living, and not merely to submit to the myths and rituals and dogmatic beliefs and the lifeless or Spirit-less disciplines of the concerned social ego.
>
> Accept the Spirit-Blessing of the Adept Spiritual Master. Even the body-mind is only Energy. Realize the Spirit-Being is the Reality in which self and world are arising as spontaneous but unnecessary and non-binding modifications of Itself. Be the Spirit-Being only. See all things and beings in and as Spirit. And always Magnify the Spirit-Force, which is Love, Blessing, Tolerance, Forgiveness, Help, Healing, Nurture, Delight, Joy, Bliss, Peace, and total Happiness.[29]

SPIRIT-FIRE BAPTISM

The Spirit-Baptism that flows or radiates from a genuine Adept—their **"Spiritual Transmission"**—is a real, bodily-felt, heart-awakening *transmission* of Spirit or Energy (not just the energy of, say, electrical currents though it is still a form of the same Light). Spirit-Energy is one full of emotion, feeling, love, and pure participatory awareness. Hence, the modern Avatar affirms the ancient Message of the Messiah: "From Jesus's point of view, the whole process of repentance, forgiveness, and restoration to God is a matter of *spiritual conversion* or the realization that God is the Living Spiritual Reality, always Present, All-Pervading, the Source and Substance of Existence."[30] This is why it takes more than just being purified by the "**Water Baptism**" (as John the Baptist gave to the people), which is a genuine purification and repentance of egoic and negative habit patterns, but also involves being touched by the "**Fire Baptism**" of Spirit-Transmission (*Ruchira Shaktipat*), the baptism that *transforms* consciousness to actual God-Realization. Only an authentic Adept-Realizer or genuine Guru gives this Gift through the Grace of God. Only the heart knows for sure.

When John the Baptist initiated Jesus of Galilee with the ritual of water baptism in the River Jordan (when the "dove" of Shaktipat descended on Jesus) the Baptist declared: "I indeed baptize you with water unto repentance [i.e., forgiveness of sin]; but He that cometh after me is mightier than I, whose shoes I am not worthy to bear; He shall baptize you with the Holy Ghost [Spirit], and *with* fire." (Matthew 4: 11) Adi Da graciously explains this passage's true significance in relation to his own presence on Earth: "Whenever you are in My Company, whenever you give Me your attention, then you are as good as sitting in the room with Me where this Baptism is being given. I do not stand in a river to perform the water ritual. I stand in the fire to perform the Spirit ritual, which purifies, enlivens, and grants Enlightenment. It is the perfect Baptism."[31] It is the "fire" or transmission of Conscious Light, the "Bright" (in Adi Da's words), or the radiance of the Awakened Heart, which is actually our own innate Divine Consciousness magnified to the infinite degree. This is the whole purpose for the Avatar's (and other Guru-Adepts') appearance here on Earth as the Great Tradition of humankind testifies throughout the millennia. Adi Da, as he has done on many occasions, explains the psycho-physics of Spiritual Transmission, the great Gift given from the genuine Guru-Adept to others:

> The Guru manifests as Light. It is not a light you can visualize, but it is the Presence that you know in understanding. When I come to My devotee, I work between the top of the head and that place in the midbrain, because I am always working to move down into the

life of My devotee.... Your meditation is to surrender to Me and draw
this Light into the body....

God does the yoga.... When you sit for meditation, conduct the
Light in the Way I have described to you. Do this always. Always be
surrendered to Me. Always breathe the Light. Always conduct My
Light in this Circle. Do it naturally, not as a rigid yogic process, but
as a devotee, as a lover.[32]

Fortunately, Avatar Adi Da is much clearer about explaining and demonstrating the truth of this spiritual process of Spirit-Baptism than the historical
records or Gospels indicate Jesus had shared with his disciples. Yet, to be fair,
we don't know exactly what Jesus taught for he wrote nothing down, whereas
Adi Da's Teaching-Word has been recorded with precision in numerous publications and on tape. All of his "yellow pages" (legal pads) first written out
by his own hand have been archived for posterity, as have the audio and vid-
eotape and film recordings, so the extant record is extensive. There never will
be confusion about what he said, though there's bound to be some confusion
exactly what he meant (due to our egoic perspectives). Hence the modern-day
World Avatar explains the significance of the Spirit-Transmission received in
His Company as devotees cultivate a relationship to an Enlightened Adept
(which remains true to this very day and beyond):

> The import of My Presence here is that I [Am] a Baptizer, an Agent
> of Transmission. Part of the import of My Presence here is that I
> consider the Argument of the Way and consider the right culture of
> devotees and develop the practices in your company, but the ultimate

import of My Presence here is simply that I be Present, not merely to exist but to Baptize, to Transmit the Spirit-Awakening.[33]

This is precisely what people coming into Adi Da's Company, back then and even today (through the Agencies he left behind), feel and *realize* as they witness and experience the Holy Spirit-Transmission of God's Divine Presence via Guru Yoga-Satsang. God, in other words, is magnified and transmitted by the genuine Guru, such as with Adi Da Samraj, as the sacred Great Tradition of Global Wisdom has long proclaimed. As Jesus himself announced: "I that speak unto thee am *He*," in response to a woman who saw his Divine Presence and proclaimed him the Messiah, the Christ, the Anointed One. (John 4: 25-26) Adi Da Samraj, as an authentic Avatar or Divine Incarnation, speaks with the same enlightening force calling us all into Divine Recognition of God as Spirit alive here and now animating the whole Kosmos and our very sense of self. The American Adept once more artfully explained by echoing the sentiments of Christ:

> I do not call you merely to believe in God, but I Baptize you in this Spiritual Force and call you to act differently, to submit to it physically, to breathe it, relax into it, animate it, manifest it through service and love in all relations. I call you to worship God in Spirit, as Spirit, worship God spiritually, through spiritual means, through living, through meditation, not through conventional prayer. I call you to realize that you are one with this Spirit, not merely experiencing It but identical to It, so that you may, by overcoming every fraction of the self-contraction, Realize a state of perfect and uncaused Identification with It, Realize a perfect equation with the Divine Being and Condition.[34]

Yet, first, in order to receive this Divine Gift of Spirit-Baptism a person must give the gift of his or her own life with heartfelt devotion; to surrender their ego-I (and self-contraction) in order to receive the Adept's Spirit-Baptism of Divine Transmission. Otherwise, the sacred processes of genuine spiritual life (or sadhana) will not be activated or sustained, in which case it becomes the greatest of sins or "to miss the mark." This fact becomes the Avatar's profound recommendation to everyone: "The first thing to Realize is that God gives the Gift of Grace and that God gives the Gift of Grace through the Siddha, the Adept who is your Master. You must find such a Master."[35] Indeed, it is for our own good… and for the world's.

Obviously, the Adept from Galilee was such a Master too. And though he lived over two thousand years ago his Spiritual-Transmission can still be felt today (at least in some ways) by devoted practitioners who turn to him as Savior and the Light of the world (as many Christians will testify). Yet the actual lineage of Transmission from generation to generation, especially in the West, has generally been corrupted by the surrounding religious institutions and mythic interpretations, as was the case with Jesus brought about by the failures of the Christian Church. Consequently, a modern-day Adept born in America has appeared to righten what has gone astray, as they always do (via God's Grace). *Now* in our current emerging Integral Age there was born (on November 3, 1939) such a one appearing in a likeness similar to all previous Enlightened Adept-Gurus. This time he has appeared in our modern times, as a Westerner, born in the United States (not in the East), yet given to the whole world as World-Teacher or *Jagad Guru*. It is time we wake up and realize and honor the Divine Presence of Avatar Adi Da Samraj as an authentic Spirit-Baptizing Guru-Adept.

Avatar Adi Da would continue explaining (and baptizing) on that ecstatic evening celebrating his birth and incarnation, nearly a month shy from Jesus's globally celebrated birthday on Christmas Day. As he graciously delivered this sacred **"Birthday Message from Jesus and Me,"** he told his congregating and attentive devotees: "In spite of all the mythology laid upon Jesus [by the Christian Church] in the *New Testament*, what comes through is still a Spirit-born [or re-born] personality who was Transfigured, Transformed, magnified, made effective as a Siddha [or "Completed One"] by virtue of God-Communion, Spiritual Communion."[36] If understood properly, as Adi Da instructs: "The Teaching of Jesus need not be criticized. It stands in the great tradition of Siddhas."[37] This is because Christ preached about an "essentially esoteric process of being God-born and ultimately Translated into the Divine Condition [in what *The Bible* calls Jesus's 'Transfiguration']."[38] We too are called *to practice* with our own sadhana and to live true Divine Communion with God as Spirit and Truth, with all our heart, with all our mind, with all our might, turning to (and following) the Company of a genuine Guru-Adept in Satsang. "Follow Me" is the command both Jesus and Adi Da proclaim to everyone in order to see and know God as your Divine Condition. Such is the offering given by the Reality-Way of Adidam Ruchiradam now available to everyone. Hence, I heartily suggest you "turn to Him!"

The Great Adepts of East and West, the true Siddhas, Avatars, and Divine Incarnations have come to Liberate or "Save" us all by awakening our awareness to living a life of Love by seeing God as Spirit and practicing Divine Communion in Truth, each and every day, with each and every breath. Thus, I, too, can only recommend: "You must find such a Master." Truly, what could be a greater Message than this?

OM! MA! DA!

☆

Chapter 20 Endnotes

1. Adi Da Samraj, *The Gnosticon* (2010), p. 438.

2. See: Adi Da Samraj, *Nirvanasara: Radical Transcendentalism and the Introduction of Advaitayana Buddhism* (1982) with an Introduction by Georg Feuerstein; also see: *The Gnosticon* (2010), Part Sixteen: "Advaitasara / Nirvanasara: The Root-Essence of The Truth and The Way and The Means and the Realization of Indivisible Transcendence"; and *The Pneumaton* (2011) by Adi Da Samraj.

3. Adi Da Samraj [Da Free John], *Nirvanasara* (1982), p. 99; also see: *The Gnosticon* (2010) and *The Pneumaton* (2011).

4. Adi Da Samraj, from the essay "To Realize Nirvana Is To Realize The True Self" in *The Gnosticon* (2010), pp. 340-341.

5. See, for example: *Void and Fullness in the Buddhist, Hindu and Christian Traditions: Sunya–Purna–Pleroma* (2005) edited by Bettina Bäumer and John R. Dupuche; *Clear Light of Bliss: The Practice of Mahamudra in Vajrayana Buddhism* (1982, 1995) by Geshe Kelsang Gyatso; *The Record of Transmitting the Light: Zen Master Keizan's* Denkoroku (2003) translated by Francis Dojun Cook; *The Buddha from Dolpo* (1999) by Cyrus Stearns.

6. Nagarjuna, *The Diamond Sutra in The Diamond Sutra and The Sutra of Hui Neng* (1969, Boulder, CO: Shambhala Publications), p. 53, 64.

7. Adi Da Samraj, "The Lion Sutra" in *Come Into the Presence That Is God* (1981), p. 27; also listen to "This I Have Noticed" on the CD *The Truth Is The Only Profound* (1998) by Ray Lynch.

8. Adi Da Samraj, *The Enlightenment of the Whole Body* (1978), p. 460.

9. See: Chögyal Namkhai Norbu, *Dzogchen: The Self-Perfected State* (1989), p. 61.

10. *Lankavatara Sutra* in *A Buddhist Bible* (1938, 1970), edited by Dwight Goddard, p. 356 (last page).

11. Adi Da Samraj [Da Free John], from the Talk "Ego-Death and the Chaos of Experience" given on January 1, 1979, published *Scientific Proof of the Existence of God Will Soon Be Announced by the White House* (1980), p. 162, 164.

12. Adi Da Samraj [Franklin Jones], *The Method of the Siddha* (1973, 1978), p. 16.

13. See: *Meeting Adi Da: A Mandala of Approach To Avatar Adi Da Samraj* (forthcoming) by Brad Reynolds.

14. For example, a woman devotee present at Adi Da's forty-third birthday celebration, Denise Marrero, wrote: "The Master gave a beautiful discourse on a new essay that had just been read to the gathering.... I was simultaneously Awakened into the realm of Spirit or Conscious Being in the Master's Company. It was the Gift of Spirit-Baptism, about which He was speaking that night.... Tears came to my eyes, my heart melted, and the Master's face became the center of the sun. The circuit of conductivity was constant, full, and blissful, and it was immediately tacitly obvious that everything is Da. I saw what a potent and perfect Source of Awakening He is." *The Fire Gospel* (1982), pp. 92-93.

15. Adi Da Samraj, from the Talk (given on November 3, 1982) titled "A Birthday Message from Jesus and Me" in *The Fire Gospel: Essays and Talks on Spirit Baptism* (December 1982), p. 68.

16. See: Frank Marrero, *A Monkey's Tale for the Divine Person: Leelas in Praise of Beloved Adi Da Samraj* (2017).

17. Adi Da Samraj, from the Talk (given on November 3, 1982) titled "A Birthday Message from Jesus and Me" in *The Fire Gospel* (1982), p. 69.

18. Ibid., p. 65.

19. Ibid., p. 67.

20. Ibid., p. 80.

21. Ibid., p. 81.

22. Ibid., p. 81.

23. Ibid., p. 71.

24. Ibid., p. 67.

25. See: Gopi Krishna, *Kundalini: The Evolutionary Energy in Man* (1971, 1997, Shambhala Publications); Lee Sannella, The Kundalini Experience (1976, 1987, Integral Publishing); John White, Kundalini, Evolution and Enlightenment (1998, Paragon House).

26. Adi Da Samraj, from the Talk (given on November 3, 1982) titled "A Birthday Message from Jesus and Me" in *The Fire Gospel* (1982, Middletown, CA: The Dawn Horse Press), p. 83 ["Stages of Life" capped].

27. Ibid., pp. 81-82.

28. Ibid., p. 73.

29. Ibid., p. 66.

30. Ibid., p. 69 [italics added].

31. Ibid., p. 76.

32. Adi Da Samraj [Da Free John], from the Talk: "Guru Enters Devotee" (January 3, 1974) in *The Bodily Location of Happiness* (1982, Middletown, CA: The Dawn Horse Press), pp. 42, 45-46.

33. Adi Da Samraj, from the Talk (given on November 3, 1982) titled "A Birthday Message from Jesus and Me" in *The Fire Gospel* (1982, Middletown, CA: The Dawn Horse Press), p. 77.

34. Ibid., p. 82.

35. Adi Da Samraj, from the Talk (given on December 25, 1982) titled "The Feast of God in Every Body" in *The Dreaded Gom-Boo* (1983), p. 311.

36. Adi Da Samraj, from the Talk (given on November 3, 1982) titled "A Birthday Message from Jesus and Me" in *The Fire Gospel* (1982, Middletown, CA: The Dawn Horse Press), p. 81.

37. Ibid., p. 81.

38. Ibid., p. 79; p. 81: "The story of Jesus reports a person Transfigured and Transformed by intimacy with the Spiritual Divine. It suggests also that he was Translated."

PART III

GURU YOGA-SATSANG IS GLOBAL WISDOM

TWENTY ONE

GURU YOGA-SATSANG:
EAST AND WEST

God and the Guru will only show the way to release;
they will not by themselves take the soul to the state of release.
In truth, God and the Guru are not different....
Those who have come within the ambit of the Guru's gracious look will be saved
by the Guru and will not get lost; yet, each one should, by his [or her] own effort
pursue the path shown by God or Guru and gain release.

— **Ramana Maharshi**, 20th century[1]

METHOD OF GURU-ADEPTS:
SATSANG IS GURU YOGA

The word "**guru**" has several meanings even in India, where it originated. As previously explained, the syllable "*gu*" means "shadows" or "darkness," while "*ru*" is someone who disperses the dark. "**Guru**" (in Sanskrit) literally means "one who dispels darkness," or symbolically, "one who reveals the light." This is the esoteric definition offered by several sacred texts, including some *Upanishads*. There is also another one used by the Brahmin or priestly class of ancient India calling *guru* the "weighty one," from the "preceptor" who performs the ceremonies as a "senior instructor" or even "royal teacher."[2] Therefore, the word "guru" (with a small "g") also means simply "a teacher," as it's used in today's common parlance, for example, where a master musician is the "guru" to his practicing student, or there are "marketing gurus" or "sports gurus," etc. This is perhaps the most common usage in the West since someone's "guru" is bringing some "light" or insight and understanding to the subject being studied.

Nonetheless, in its ultimate meaning, the title "**Guru**" (with a capital "G") refers to someone who teaches another person about ultimate or esoteric and inner spiritual matters concerning life, death, and God. These are the "**Sat-Gu-rus**" or "teachers of the Real," for they alone are capable of initiating a spiritual seeker into the supreme "knowledge of the Absolute" (*brahma-avidya*). Yet, don't be fooled: most gurus are not Gurus! Some will steal your wealth, abuse their position, or lead you astray. As the *Kula-Arnava-Tantra* explained:

> There are many *gurus* on Earth who give what is other than the Self, but hard to find in all the worlds, O Devi, is the *Guru* who reveals the Self. (13.106)
>
> Many are the *gurus* who rob the disciple of his wealth, but rare is the *Guru* who removes the afflictions of the disciple. (13.108)
>
> He or she is a [true] *Guru* by whose very contact there flows the supreme Bliss (*ananda*). The intelligent man or woman should choose such a one as his [or her] *Guru* and none other. (13.110)[3]

The real Gurus—what I'm calling "genuine Gurus" or "**Guru-Adepts**"—teach us about the Divine Light Itself, the Ultimate Reality—En-Light-en-ment, the Self-Realization of our Divine Condition.

In Tibetan Buddhism the title *Lama* is similar to the Sanskrit word *Guru*, historically used for a venerated Spiritual Adept or head of a monastery, while today it designates a degree of spiritual attainment and certified authority to instruct others on the sacred teachings of Buddhism [see Chapter 18]. A real Guru—specifically a "**Sat-Guru**" or *Sadguru*, a "Truth Guru"—can be one of the most important persons you will ever meet in this lifetime. Such a person is a "**Siddha-Guru**," or "Completed One" (*Siddha*) who is authentically *teaching* and *transmitting* Spirit-Baptism (*shaktipat*). This comes from their Realized State of attainment from the higher Stages of Life thus replicating *your* highest State-Stage potential [see Chapter 22]. Ultimately, this Divine Realization given by the Guru simply reveals (or magnifies) your innate Buddha-Nature or Atman (True Self); therefore these genuine Gurus are supremely attractive if we see or understand them in the right light. The most unique Gurus, those who often profoundly affect human history, are often called "**Maha-Siddhas**" (or "Great Gurus," where *maha* in Sanskrit means "great") since these Awakened Adepts of the Great Tradition reflect and radiate the *Siddhi* (or "Spirit-Power") of Reality most intensely (and fully) given from Heart to heart.

Nonetheless, this notion of a *Guru* (especially with a capital "G") scares Westerners silly; or they simply scoff it off as being irrelevant to modern times, a relic from the mythic worldview, or worse, an object of blind cultic veneration. Yet this is a fractured fallacy, an egoic error, for when used correctly and with a mature mind there's no justifiable reason why a spiritual relationship with a genuine Guru should scare anyone away. Nor should we be afraid when we discover how attractive a Guru can be without succumbing to cultic numbness or lack of rational judgment. When seen as an Agent of God, the Guru becomes spiritually alive and even intensely physically attractive, like opening the heart to a lover. Then it's easier to develop a devotional love relationship which can be cultivated on many levels but primarily as a *spiritual* one, one full of Spirit Baptism and authentic Spiritual Revelation [see Chapter 23]. Once a person "falls in love," with either a Guru or intimate partner, the heart (and mind) will follow its natural course. We know when we are *in love*. We can't be argued into falling in love with someone; we simply *love* them.

In this case, such "**Divine Distraction**" deepens your spiritual understanding, both in mind and heart, especially once the Supreme Reality or seeing Real God is revealed in the Company of the Guru.[4] **Guru Yoga** is, therefore, a *sacred* relationship built on the desire to know God (or the nondual Godhead). Such Satsang with an Awakened Adept-Realizer is thus a very *sacred* matter, one that has been honored since most ancient times by the world's wisest people. It has been recorded in some of the world's oldest and most profound books, from the *Rig Veda* to the *New Testament*, from the *Bhagavad Gita* to the *Guru Gita*, from the *Upanishads* to *The Dawn Horse Testament* (of Adi Da Samraj), to countless other texts in the "Divine Library" of universal Global Wisdom Tradition and its attending Perennial Philosophy [see Part I]. Thus, genuine Guru-attraction (and devotion) is no joke nor mere cultism. It is an esoteric ("inner-directed") process.

Now consider this: since ancient times the relationship with a Guru—a Spiritual Teacher, a God-Realized Master or Awakened Adept—has been universally revered to be *the most important relationship* in a person's life. It is the primary focal point of most of the world's religions, such as with Jesus Christ or Gautama Buddha (the most obvious examples), but also with Krishna, Mahavira, Zoroaster, Lao Tzu, Confucius, Nagarjuna, Bodhidharma, Padmasambhava, Muhammad, Nanak, and so on. Since primordial times, even before humankind was "civilized" (that is, before writing), the Spiritual Master, the Adept-Realizer or genuine Guru has always been *the source* of true religion and authentic spirituality. Sitting in their company, down by their feet (before Westerners sat in chairs), they teach and transmit Divine Wisdom; you often swoon in their Presence where the nectar of sacred bliss fills your being and awareness. They reveal the Light behind (and in) the darkness of the world.

As we saw, Adi Da has called this lineage of history the "**Ancient Walk-About Way**," the secret heart of Spirituality that has existed since primordial times [see Chapter 11]. This Ancient Way of recognizing the Realized Adept, as one scholar explained, is "the root essence of even the most ancient forms of human Spirituality—the natural, nonverbal response to the mere sight of an Illumined being."[5] These "Masters" in the highest Stages of Life are the ones who have realized, and then taught, the real purpose of religion: *how to know God* (as your Divine Condition). This cannot be denied if you study the evidence. This is what they do. Indeed, all of the world's major religions can trace their origins to a highly evolved (or enlightened) Spiritual Master and Founding Teacher, whether East or West, North or South. This is a fact of profound significance, one that most modern people fail to recognize and embrace as being an effective method for awakening and guidance on your spiritual journey. But now we need to turnabout and receive what our wisest ancestors have given to us... and dismiss what corporate consumerism is offering in their place. The choice is ours; the choice is *yours!*

We need to move beyond this "sin" of dismissing the true Guru and "hit the mark" (i.e., practice Satsang). These "**Adept-Realizers**" (as Adi Da calls them) are not ordinary folks (as you may have heard). They are beacons of Divine Light leading us out of the darkness of spiritual ignorance to receive the ecstasy of Love-Bliss-Happiness that is Real God. But if you overlook their Light or shut them off you will miss the brightness of God awakened as your true condition. It's an opportunity not to be missed. Yet, only with the "**Seven Stages of Life Model**," given to us by Avatar Adi Da Samraj (and supported by such modern theorists as Ken Wilber and Sri Aurobindo), are we capable of clearly recognizing each Guru's level of development and degree of attainment in the higher Stages of Mysticism (the "hierarchy of religious experience," in Wilber's terms) [see Appendix I].

In this case, it is critical to understand that the most important Guru-Adepts, especially the Avatars, are not simply another highly-evolved human being such as a Yogi or Saint, which in itself is a very rare occurrence (and still to be valued). But, rarer still, are the advanced-tip few who seem to have been born with the specific *function* to teach, instruct, guide, and reveal the path and way of Nondual Divine Enlightenment (or Self-Realization) to others. Miraculously, the most highly evolved Adepts **transmit** psychic or spiritual energy (*shaktipat*) to stimulate Enlightened Awakening, not just evoke higher states of consciousness [see Chapter 3]. They are the "**Adept-Transmitters**," the Spirit-Baptizers, the most highly evolved Gifts from God.

Not only do such people teach us about the Sacred Way but they also instruct and demand disciplines (*sadhana*) from their devotee-students on right living (or "Right Life"), on how to love and be a good person in the community of human beings while traveling the sacred path of Awakening. This is because the spiritual path requires ego-transcending practices of equanimity, health, and service, as well as meditation (and other esoteric practices). In other words, sadhana (or true spiritual living) demands both "Growing Up" *and* "Waking Up" (in Wilber's terms), a complete and integral lifestyle exercising (and accelerating) all human potentials.

Amazingly, such profound Guru-Adepts are not just awake to God themselves, whether male or female, but they have been naturally (or spontaneously) gifted with special abilities, traditionally known as *siddhis* (or "powers"). These siddhis are advanced psychic capacities that assist in their function to be a Guru to others. Even rarer still, historically, are certain individuals—known as **Avatars** or **Divine Incarnations**—who have tremendous talent to serve others in this sacred manner. Not only do they have psychic and extraordinary abilities, as mentioned, but they can also exchange or transmit their enlightened condition or State of Awakening to other living beings (human and otherwise), at least temporarily, when a person is in their physical company or near their Holy Sites. This can also be done by simply giving them your attention even if separated by many miles or eras—the real secret of Guru Yoga-Satsang: give the Guru your attention.

| Paramahansa Yogananda | Anandamayi Ma | Meher Baba | Amma | Neem Karoli Baba |

Such Adept-Realizers are a Great Help to humankind as a Spiritual Servant, a Divine Agent, which is why they have been revered and venerated so highly in the world's religious and wisdom traditions. Adi Da Samraj is such a one (as this book argues), and so he has said this about the sacred function of an authentic Guru-Adept:

> The Adept Spiritual Master is not merely an independent Realizer of the Truth. The true Adept is a "**Siddha**", or a Living Agent of Help and Awakening [to others]. Thus, beyond the Work of Communicating the Arguments of the Way, the Adept is Present to Transmit the Power of Awakening.
>
> On this basis, the practice of devotees is made fruitful by self-transcending or self-surrendered association with the Divine Help and Awakening Power. The Way is not fulfilled by the efforts of the ego, but by the ego's transcending itself in Communion with its Ultimate Help.[6]

Such "*Siddhi*" (with a capital "S"[7]) or Divine Awakening Power has a profound effect on the person or devotee on the receiving end of such Spiritual Agency and Transmission. The Guru's Transmission purifies, balances, and ultimately serves the individual in seeing and knowing God or the Divine Domain as Reality. Usually the purification occurs in a progressive or evolutionary manner following the Seven Stages of Life [see Appendix I] but also in spontaneous moments of Grace revealing a "taste" of Enlightenment. In the Reality-Way of Adidam (and, for example, in Zen and Dzogchen), the Avatar insists that practice only truly begins *after* such a moment of heart-awakening (or "Seeing"). Then seeking for God (or the "divine experience") is no longer the motivation for doing spiritual practices but sadhana-Satsang becomes a recognition-response to seeing God for real, from the heart, always already. Yet, its effectiveness still depends on the seriousness of the devotee [see Chapter 23].

This function of Spirit-Baptism (via the Guru's Transmission) begins to purify or relieve a person of their accumulated *karma* (Sanskrit for "action") thus helping to release personal limitations or habit patterns. According to the Perennial Philosophy only a fully-enlightened being transcends the universal law of karma, thus he or she has the spiritual ability to help purify and release the karma of other beings. As our yoga scholar Georg Feuerstein explains: "There is no trace of egoity in the truly enlightened being, for the ego has been replaced by the Self."[8] Nonetheless, taking on such karma for the sake of others can still have a negative effect on the body of the Adept for it is a real psycho-physical process in Nature. Purification brings up toxins in the body and the mind of the devotee that must be released and processed (including shadow work). Yet, the true Guru's compassion and love for all beings, and their born function, compels them to serve and help people unceasingly. The Guru is, truly, our greatest friend.

| Sri Ramana Maharshi | Bhagavan Nityananda | Baba Muktananda | Swami Rudrananda | Adi Da Love-Ananda |

The Divine Siddhi of such a genuine Guru-Adept is a Gift of Grace beyond compare in the occupation of humankind. Incredibly, the unenlightened person, in other words, can become (at least momentarily) Enlightened through the Guru's Grace—i.e., to know God for real, in your heart—by simply giving the Guru your attention and thus opening to their Shaktipat-Transmission. What an incomparable and precious gift. As only one example, a modern-day Dzogchen Master of Buddhism clearly explains:

> The value of Transmission is not only that of introducing the [enlightened] state of knowledge, but lies in its function of bringing about the maturing of the Transmission, right up until one reaches [Divine] Realization. For this reason the relationship that links the Master and disciple is a very close one. The Master, in Dzogchen, is not just like a friend who helps and collaborates with the disciple; rather the Master is himself or herself the path. This is because the practice of contemplation develops through the unification of the state of the disciple with that of the Master.[9]

As always, the power to practice a spiritual lifestyle for permanent adaption and stabilization in the higher (and highest) states of consciousness rests *only with you* and your relationship to your Guru-Adept. *You* must do the practice; make the effort; walk the talk; turn to Guru (as God) and engage the yoga to receive the Spirit-Transmission. This is the essence of authentic Satsang and why it's so highly valued in all esoteric religions. Such processes or ideas may seem ludicrous and far beyond the scope of the Western mind, especially for our modern scientifically and materialistically-oriented populous enamored with a consumer culture replete with political battles, religious fundamentalism, scientific atheism, and general confusion. Have you not noticed? Nevertheless, the validity of the Guru-Adept is reaffirmed by methodological investigation based on engaging in authentic spiritual practices and real meditation. This is done best, therefore, in Satsang, the sacred relationship with an authentic Adept-Guru… and the rest is up to God… and Grace. But it starts with you… and the Guru.

JESUS CHRIST:
LOSING SATSANG IN THE WEST

Unfortunately, the ultimate and true significance and potency of the Guru-devotee relationship is mostly unknown and not taught in the West. The reason is simple, because according to the traditional Western worldview there has only been *one* "Guru," only one person who can lead people to God-Light, and that was Jesus Christ. Yet if you truly look at the relationship with Christ that is suggested by Christianity and the Church (whether Catholic or Protestant) you will find it reflects the required relationship with a genuine Guru. Truly, if you want to know about the essence of the Guru-devotee relationship, then study Jesus Christ and his relationship with his twelve disciples, those who were his devoted devotees in life and after death.

Jesus made serious demands on his disciples by commanding them: "Whoever wants to be My disciple must deny themselves and take up their cross and Follow Me!" (Matthew 16:24) And he wasn't joking; this was a serious commitment. He expected his devotees to drop their livelihoods, their careers, their families, to follow Him and His Teaching. What does this mean? It means the Guru-devotee relationship, such as with Christ, becomes the Way by which a person learns to live in Spirit or the Holy Spirit of God (John 3:5). By "following Christ" as Guru-Adept and believing he is the "Son of God," is how a divine life is lived. This is the deepest message of Christianity; not simply to have a "personal relationship" with Christ as if he were merely a friend or companion for the ego-self to feel comforted or reassured. Spiritual life is more difficult than that and applies to all people regardless of their provincial religious inheritance, to women as well as to men, even to children. Indeed, as Jesus (and all Adepts) insisted, we must be "born again" in Spirit and Truth to really know God as the Divine Reality [see Chapter 20].

Such a conversion or *metanoia* founded on ethical disciplined practices and meditation was (and is) a serious matter according to Jesus, back then and today as well. A relationship with an authentic Adept-Guru is a profound acknowledgment, for Jesus (as any genuine Guru) is calling us to an authentic spiritual life demanding an ego-transcending lifestyle based in compassionate love and knowledge of the Divine Reality of the Kosmos. Jesus, in other words, can be best understood as a true Guru or Avatar (a descended incarnation of God), a Great Siddha, for he acted like one.[10] Like Jesus, a Guru-Adept expects us to act like true devotees or disciples, not mere believers of myth and fantasy salvation techniques [see Chapter 24]. A true Guru (or Sat-Guru) expects from his or her devotees their self-sacrifice, self-surrender, and service in the transcendence of the ego-I's limits and boundaries. This is freely expressed as devotion and love given in order to Awaken us as a radiant presence and happy human being living a Divine Life on Earth.

For the West, the problem of dismissing the appearance of a genuine Guru in any generation, especially in today's modern world, started when Jesus and his Teachings (and Presence) were proclaimed by the Christian Church (and St. Paul) to be the "Only One," the *only* "Son of God." They claim that "**The Greatest Story Ever Told**" means no one else can achieve Jesus's status or degree of God-Realization, therefore, we must turn to him as our "Savior" instead of replicating his state of enlightened consciousness. Nonetheless, as an authentic

Adept, Jesus still offers transforming power by opening people's hearts to God thus helping them to convert to more positive living and moral ethics (if not actual sadhana).

The Christian Church did not want other Gurus—such as **Apollonius** of Tyana (fl. 50 CE) or **Plotinus** (205–270 CE) or **Iamblichus** (245–325 CE)— to teach or enlighten the populace since it would undermine their authority and "ownership" of the loving Adept from Galilee. This fact alone has helped create the unenlightened disaster of Western civilization; a tragedy we're still desperately struggling to overcome. In this case, we must turn to other Awakened Adepts in history to find brighter lights leading us out of our dark ignorance. And that includes those from the most recent past too, such as Sri Ramana Maharshi and Avatar Adi Da Samraj, among others.

It is now time to listen more attentively to our Awakened Masters about living a life that expresses the compassion and love and wisdom of God-Realization or Divine Enlightenment. We need to transcend our parochial limitations and culture-bound (or tribal) identities. We need to transcend our views of religious provincialism and scientific materialism and to live the life of a Yogi and Saint, even as an "ordinary" person. This is what Jesus wants us to do (as well as Adi Da). The *New Testament* "**Gospels**" (Mark, Matthew, Luke, John), for example, combined with the recently discovered "**Lost Gospels**" or "**Gnostic Gospels**" (of the *Nag Hammadi* library), review the life and teachings of Jesus of Nazareth in an expanded manner pointing us beyond the traditional Church's doctrinal limitations. Taken together they are very instructive about the relationship expected between Master and devotee (or disciple) and so must be seriously studied with an open heart to awaken the mind to higher (and deeper) understandings.

To follow the Guru or God-Realized Adept is how God brings us, the masses of ordinary unenlightened people, closer to knowing "Him" as Divine Spirit; that is, through God's Agents, God's Incarnations, via God's Avatars, East or West, male or female. Even the West has known about this sacred relationship, mostly through Jesus Christ, but sometimes through its Saints and wisest Philosophers, yet science definitely has no clue. Governments and economics have even less wisdom about these sacred and profound matters of human existence so they deny them altogether (except in mythic fables). Our globe is mired in wars and generational hatreds that only the enlightened heart (and mind) can release and transform. We must learn how to transcend our inherited tribalisms and establish a new global order based on our Prior Unity as the human race and our Divine Condition—a real Integral Age! We *must* heal the planet of our industrial toxins and restore Nature to Her pristine beauty and health. We must… or we die (or become horribly crippled). We have to choose to survive: We must Wake Up!

It is *our responsibility*, therefore, to be schooled again by God's Great Tradition of Global Wisdom, to study the past Adept-Realizers and their lives and Teachings, and adjust our lives accordingly. We must Grow Up so we can Wake Up (and Clean Up and Show Up). We do know better; don't you? We are thereby called to enact genuine devotional commitments when we actually find a Real Guru in our midst who may serve us directly and intimately during our precious human lifetime. Such a sacred relationship awakens us to our highest potentials and ultimate purpose here on Earth. It is no longer a matter of East or West, ancient or modern, religious or scientific; the time is *now* and the space is *global*. It is a matter of *relationship* and love, just like the Masters said.

Chapter 21 Endnotes

1. Sri Ramana Maharshi, "Who Am I" in *The Collected Works of Sri Ramana Maharshi* (2015, 13th edition), pp. 43-44.

2. Georg Feuerstein, *The Yoga Tradition* (1998), p. 14.

3. Kula-Arnava-Tantra recited in *The Yoga Tradition* (1998) by Georg Feuerstein, p. 15.

4. See: *In God's Company: Guru-Adepts As Agents for Enlightenment in the Integral Age* (2022) by Brad Reynolds.

5. RSO (Naitauba Ruchira Sannyasin Order of Adidam Ruchiradam), *The Reality-Way of Adidam* (2010), p. 44.

6. Adi Da Samraj, *What Is the Conscious Process?* (1983), pp. 19-20.

7. The traditional Sanskrit term siddhi (with an uncapitalized "s"), in Adi Da's terminology, refers to various yogic processes and psychic powers that are less than the Siddhi (capital "S") denoting the Divine Awakening Power or Spirit-Transmission. The Siddhi of Enlightenment comes through the unobstructed Agency of the fully-enlightened Sat-Guru or Siddha (or Maha-Siddha), one whose Enlightenment is perfected and pure and who is graced with the spontaneous capacity to Awaken others to transpersonal insights and ultimately to God-Realization.

8. Georg Feuerstein, *The Yoga Tradition* (1998), p. 14.

9. Chögyal Namkhai Norbu, *Dzogchen: The Self-Perfected State* (1989), p. 64.

10. See: *The Second Coming of Christ: The Resurrection of the Christ Within You* (2004, 2008) by Paramahansa Yogananda. The author of *Autobiography of a Yogi* (1946) takes the reader on a profoundly enriching journey through the four Gospels, verse by verse, as Yogananda illumines the universal path to oneness with God taught by Jesus to his immediate disciples but now obscured through centuries of misinterpretation by Westerners; highly recommended reading.

TWENTY TWO

GURU YOGA-SATSANG:
GURU-DEVOTEE RELATIONSHIP

*The humanely incarnate Spiritual Master is Divine Help
to the advantage of those in like form.
When My devotee enters into right relationship with Me,
changes happen in the literal physics of one's existence.
I am not just talking about ideas. I am Talking about literal transformations
at the level of energy, at the level of esoteric super-physics
(beyond physical limitations you characteristically presume),
at the level of the Unlimited Condition of the Divine Conscious Light.*

— **Adi Da Samraj**, 1978[1]

e in the West, living in a modern scientific-minded consumer culture, have tried (unsuccessfully) to dispense with religion altogether. Perhaps we need to revise our views on religion and update our understanding of authentic spirituality. In this case, we need to reverse our anti-spiritual attitudes and honestly look at, study, and honor the genuine Adept-Gurus by understanding how they serve our spiritual growth… and God-Realization. Not only does this approach—the method of

Guru Yoga-Satsang—transcend the closed-mindedness of religious provincialism, its truth goes far beyond anything science can provide or will ever be able to prove. It is, after all, the past Wisdom of the Ages and for all Ages to come. Even then, we must transcend mere intellectual appreciation and admiration of a Guru's functional and psychic powers and actually *cultivate* or practice a real *relationship* with such a highly-evolved God-Realized person.

Guru Yoga, when practiced correctly, is *not* cultic mind games (or "brainwashing") but is a living sacred relationship revealing Real God. I do mean that literally. Satsang not only helps us to Wake Up (to the higher Stages of Life) but to Grow Up (and mature the earlier Stages of Life). In most cases, a serious degree of human maturity is required before Enlightenment can awaken in us which is why practical life disciplines and meditative practice (*sadhana*) are needed. Guru Yoga-Satsang, according to God's Great Tradition of Global Wisdom, is the best and most efficient (and time-honored) way to transcend the self and realize our Divine Condition. Even the person who has had profound spiritual experiences and intuitions of God-Realizing awareness can still be deeply served by a relationship with an authentic Adept-Guru.

Nonetheless, anyone claiming to be a Guru must be authenticated through demonstration and evidence as indicated within the Great Tradition of Enlightenment that preceded them[2] [see Part I]. This is because *every* Spiritual Adept has had his or her own Master-Guru as well but, in the end, Only God (or the Supreme Reality) is the ultimate Guru to everyone. Then we realize that not only is our own personal Guru an embodiment of God but so is everyone (and everything) else arising within God. The difference is, of course, the Guru has a specific function to teach and lead others out of the darkness of ignorance into the light of wisdom (as the title *gu-ru* indicates).

This process of instruction creates *lineages* of Enlightened Masters, as we have seen, descending down through human history to keep their spiritual traditions and transmission alive during every generation [see Part II]. They also spring up at any time or place when needed by humanity and spiritual aspirants. A genuine Guru, therefore, can establish his or her own lineage of Enlightened Masters, if all goes well. Ultimately, it is a matter of God's Grace coupled with our ability to recognize this sacred process of Satsang and serve it. Only through testing and intellectual discrimination do we discover if a person is born to serve our Enlightenment. It's up to each of us to choose which Spiritual Master we prefer to listen to, and then take up the Way of sadhana in Satsang that they offer. Then we are doing the yoga of the Practicing School, not just the Talking School of punditry [see Chapter 4].

SUPREME ATTRACTION:
BECOMING WHAT YOU MEDITATE ON

This sacred relationship between devotee (or student) and the Guru—Satsang—is fundamentally served by a single universal truth: "*You become what you meditate (or put your attention) on.*" In other words, if you meditate on money, then wealth becomes your obsession; if sports, you become a sports junkie; if it's your iPhone, then Facebook becomes potentially addictive, and so on. Hence, to meditate on the Guru as God (or God as Guru) you become God-like (or God-aware). Avatar Adi Da, therefore, recommends: "The best thing you can do is to associate with the greatest possible Transmission. Since everything is transmission, spend time in the Company of the One Who spontaneously Transmits That Which Is Inherently Perfect and Ultimate."[3] This is what Adi Da calls the "**Principle of Supreme Attraction**," where he clearly explains:

> You become (or Realize) What (or Who) you meditate on—the ancient Essence of the Spiritual Way is to meditate on (and otherwise to grant feeling-attention to) the Adept-Guru, and (thereby) to be Attracted (or Grown) beyond the "self"-contraction (or egoity).[4]

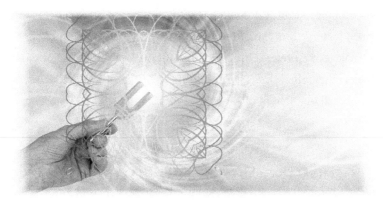

In the case of Guru Yoga, what is meditated upon is the *samadhi* or ecstatic "State" (or state-stage) of God-Communion that is experienced and lived by the Awakened Adept. Since existence is all One Consciousness (or God), then we can replicate the Guru's samadhi by becoming resonant with it. It is like two tuning forks: when one is struck and begins to vibrate, the other tuning fork close to it will sympathetically vibrate at the same rate or frequency. This is because, in depth, both Guru and devotee are "always already" the same Consciousness (or Conscious Light); one of them (the Guru) has simply mastered this state while the other (the devotee) has not. Avatar Adi Da succinctly outlines the resonant attraction:

> The entire Spiritual Way is a process based on the understanding (and transcending) of attention, or the understanding (and the transcending) of the inevitable and specific results of attachment to, or reaction to, or identification with every kind of conditional object, other, or state. This Spiritual understanding is expressed in a simple traditional formula (and prescription for practice): *You become (or duplicate the qualities of) whatever you meditate on* (or whatever you identify with via the "surrender" that is attention itself).
>
> Since the most ancient days, this understanding has informed and inspired the practice of real practitioners of the Spiritual Way. Likewise (since the most ancient days), and on the basis of this very understanding, Spiritual practitioners have affirmed that the Great Principle of Spiritual practice is **Satsang**, or the practice of life as

self-surrender to the bodily Person, the Transmitted Spiritual Presence, and the Realized State of a Spiritually Realized Adept (or true Guru, or Sat-Guru) of whatever degree or stage [of life].[5]

"*Satsang*" in Sanskrit (from ancient India) means "contact with the Real," thus it's commonly used to describe time spent in the company of holy or wise people (male or female), specifically with Awakened Adepts or Enlightened Siddhas, the Gurus and Sat-Gurus of humankind. This is done by either being in their physical company or coming to their Holy Sites, studying or listening to their Teaching, or simply giving them your attention and devotion, wherever you are, whatever you are doing. Traditionally, Satsang is seen as the true or right relationship with Spiritual Energy itself.

These practices include focusing on your Guru-Adept via their *murti* (or venerated image and photograph), visiting the burial shrine of such a Saint or Siddha, visualizing an archetypal deity, singing songs of praise and chants, doing *puja* (sacred ceremonies), study and listening to their Teaching-Word, participating in the community of their devotees, etc., but mostly by being in contact in some way with your chosen human Guru (living or dead). Satsang also occurs via contemplative meditation or real prayer as a recollection of love and feeling, not just with mental thoughts (though using thought as well). It is ultimately Divine Communion established as awakened devotion and awareness of Real God, aligned with bodily equanimity and steady breathing, as the heart opens to resonate with the Enlightened State of the Guru-Adept.

In Tibetan Buddhism this approach is called "**Guru Yoga**," for, as one scholar points out: "In Vajrayana Buddhism reliance on the Guru is of utmost importance and devotion to the Guru is held to be the very root of the path…. It depends upon the continuous transmission of enlightening insight from one mind to another through the medium of the Guru-disciple relationship."[6] In India, Hindus use the term "**Satsang**" (*satsanga*) to indicate the

sacred relationship with the human Guru. Consequently, this book has used the phrase "**Guru Yoga-Satsang**" since they both involve the same sacred process where one term is from Tibet, the other from India, respectively. Even

though their precise practices may vary in form, they do not vary in intention or result. Any authentic and *spiritual* relationship between a Spiritual Master and a student-devotee, i.e., a person who wants to learn about spiritual truths, qualifies for this special, sacred engagement. Such a time-honored human connection should not be lost simply because of scientific materialism and the ad-

vantages (and disadvantages) of modern technology or a consumerist lifestyle. It is *our* responsibility to cultivate this sacred relationship lying at the heart of all religions, even in the modern world. We must participate with a clear mind, not cultic blindness; be wise, not a fool; be enlightened, not egoic.

Transcending Doubt:
Fear of Guru-Cults

In this book I have not focused much on the fear of cults in reaction to the idea (or possibility) of there being real Gurus as Agents of God-Realization since I have examined this subject in detail elsewhere: see my book *In God's Company: Guru-Adepts As Agents for Enlightenment In The Integral Age* (Bright Alliance). In other words, I do not overlook the modern mind's reaction to and doubt about the incredible potency and power of the Guru's Spirit-Transmission that I am claiming is possible. It is very important to address the fear of Guru-cults directly and honestly. This is why in this book I have suggested that studying the Great Tradition of Global Wisdom is one crucial step to helping us differentiate true Gurus from the false and fake ones.

Nonetheless, the mood of fear about Gurus is based on the fact that there are actual cults run by incompetent spiritual teachers and outright charlatans and frauds, some even quite dangerous. I am not minimizing this. In fact, there are more fake gurus than authentic ones. However, our fear of cults also comes from the mood of doubt we have about any type of divine "super-physics" being true or real at all, let alone being necessary for spiritual growth. Most people simply doubt that a Guru as an Agent of God is even possible because we have science today and don't need such archaic techniques of religion. Again, this is exactly why we need to study the world's Great Wisdom Tradition of human spirituality to authentically appreciate what is being offered.

Only by understanding the content of the world's wisdom texts as a whole—our "Divine Library" [see Chapter 2]—and then to experience the tangible spiritual presence of a genuine Guru (not just an intellectual comprehension), will our doubts ever be eased. Yet, doubt is the mood of the ego altogether supported by its arrogance, so even after Satsang is engaged, even after you find your true Guru, your doubts will not be entirely erased... until the instant of Divine Enlightenment itself. In Satsang, there are often mood swings and phases of doubting which is normal, and why spiritual practice (or sadhana) takes sincere devotion and commitment, like any worthwhile enterprise. There will be difficulties, questions, frustrations, and even anger, which is why one must be persistent. Use your heart and real intelligence to lead the way.

Think about it: the entire mood of our modern society is one of doubt. Science, for one, doubts everything, every theory, every idea it has, even its own discoveries, for this is what perpetuates its forward progress. That is fine because science is a method of investigation and inquiry, therefore questioning doubt is the key to its future discoveries. But as a life philosophy, this approach can be crippling. Such constant doubt weakens our perception and understanding of Reality as a whole and the actual Truth of our born existence. It is a sign of the ego-mind, not the heart. Indeed, this is why spiritual life is an evolutionary or developmental process in consciousness: we must transition into Waking Up after we first Grow Up! If it was easy, everyone would be Enlightened. This is precisely why the Guru-Adepts are here: to help us grow to God knows where. This is why we must use our heart, not just our mind and bodily senses. Thus, if we're not careful our doubt will ruin our chances of becoming wise as we turn our back on what is most real. Just because modern science is amazing (and entertaining), this is no reason to shut the doors to our inherited Ancient Wisdom. Avatar Adi Da explains:

In this age of scientific materialism, doubt is the only certainty and the only substance of mind. Therefore, the people in this age are profoundly crippled in their ability to grasp matters of higher certainty or to relate to subtler mental and physical processes. Likewise, they have been wounded in the root wherein we are naturally moved toward Truth (rather than what is merely and temporarily factual or true). Therefore, this is an age in which people demonstrate little ability to understand and practice real religion or spirituality. Transcendental Awakening or Divine Realization has been reduced in the popular mind to the status of mere literary mythology. Because of all of this, My Teaching Work suffers a vague reception, and what I have made plain is commonly regarded to be unreal.[7]

Such doubt and uncertainty of the authentic spiritual process (in many cases, if not most) also pervades the modern mind's study of sacred texts since university scholars tend to be scientifically-based and researched-oriented. As we saw, scholars often advocate the Talking School of ideas, not the Practicing School of real Yoga and disciplines [see Chapter 4]. In addition to scientific materialism, our born religious provincialism also skews our entire approach to the world's Great Wisdom Tradition [see Chapter 1]. We are usually biased to what we already know. We tend to accept what we have been taught as children without much questioning as adults (often because we're busy making a living and raising a family, etc.). Once again, this is another major reason why we *need* an Enlightened Guru and awareness of our Global Wisdom inheritance to guide us through the maze of religious teachings and potential spiritual-mystical experiences. This is what Avatar Adi Da can do for us, as this book has tried to show. Let's allow the Heart-Master once more to clarify:

> The Great Tradition suffers the same situation [of being doubted]. The modern interpreters of the traditions generally do not approach their subject as practitioners and wise advocates. Rather, they approach their subject with this "scientific mind," empty of everything but doubt and doubt's opinion. The usual interpreters of religion and spirituality are not themselves really religious or spiritually motivated.... And it is this same disability that makes popular interest, understanding, practice, and ultimate conversion to the Way of Truth so unlikely in this age.[8]

This mood of doubt, however, can be overcome and transcended through understanding and investigation of the full spectrum of human potentials and possibilities. We must be schooled by the spiritually Awakened Adepts and not simply rely on our own insights or those of our parents, friends, teachers, and the popular media, or even of science alone. Fortunately, this spiritual Help is evident as the Grace of God takes on many forms and is embedded in many life lessons, therefore, it's up to us to listen closely! And then it is up to us to set our course to one of compassion, love, and spiritual understanding enacted as a living relationship to what is Real (and Divine).

GURU YOGA-SATSANG:
RELATIONSHIP, NOT TECHNIQUE

*A*vatar Adi Da uses the word *Satsang* in its fullest sense to signify a *living* and *spiritual relationship* between a genuine Guru with his or her devotees—"contact with the Real." This living, personal and sacred relationship affects every level of life and consciousness, and thus provides the all-inclusive condition within which *sadhana* (or spiritual practice) is done and accomplished. Literally, Satsang enacted is being "in the Company" of the "Divine Person," i.e., the heart-radiance of Consciousness Itself which is Real God. As long recognized in India, the pinnacle of the world's ancient wisdom, Satsang is the "**Method of the Siddhas**"[9]—where a *Siddha* is a "Completed One" or a God-Realized Enlightened being, male or female. Importantly, Adi Da as Siddha-Guru has always offered a living *relationship* of love and instruction to his devotees, not simply *methods*, such as yogic or visualization techniques, for there is no need *to seek* for God but *to live with* God *now* in Divine Communion (always already *realized*).

This sacred process of Satsang—the relationship between Guru and devotee or the Siddha and student—has been the essence of all religions since the beginning of humankind, as this book has emphasized. Who truly knows how far back this sacred tradition goes? It occurred long before written records, lost in oral teachings, hidden in our collective unconscious memory. This is why, as we've seen [in Chapter 11], Adi Da uses the phrase "**The Ancient Walk-About Way**" to indicate the wandering of early human beings in a global diaspora spreading out over the Earth over 50,000 years ago BP (Before Present).[10] Even back then, he suggests, "people were being 'religious' and Spiritual,"[11] thus recognizing those most gifted—the "advanced-tip few" (in Ken Wilber terms)—who would explore and demonstrate the potentials for consciousness transformation inherent in us all. This relationship is amplified by the lineage of descendant disciples evident in many of the world's greatest religions and esoteric yogas. Within the historical record, it is possible to trace the lineages from Masters to their devotees if one knows what to look for: Wisdom-Transmission.

For example, in Judaism (not necessarily based on a blood lineage but a spiritual heritage) there was Abraham (2000 BCE) and his sons (and their descendants) leading to Jacob to Moses to David and Solomon to Jesus, and so on; in Christianity there's Jesus (30 CE) and his twelve disciples plus St. Paul and early Church Fathers; in Taoism there is Lao Tzu and Chuang Tzu (6th c. BCE) and the Chinese temple-monasteries of priests and martial artists; in Buddhism, from Siddhartha Gautama (500 BCE), the "Buddha," to his surviving disciples reaching down the generations for millennia; in Zoroastrianism, there's Zoroaster (1500 BCE or 600 BCE) and his attending priesthoods; in Hinduism there's Rama and Krishna (2nd millennium BCE) and their brahmins and gopis to Shankara and the Sages of Advaita Vedanta; in ancient Greece there's Orpheus (7th c. BCE), Pythagoras (7th c. BCE), and Parmenides (6th c. BCE) and their long line of Pre-Socratic philosophers or "lovers of wisdom" up through Sokrates to Plato to Aristotle (and all those who followed afterwards in Western history); in ancient Egypt their tradition reaches from Imhotep (27th c. BCE) to Hermes Trismegistus (2nd c. BCE or CE) to countless others schooled in their Mystery Schools; or later in India there's the Nath Siddha Yoga lineage founded by Gorakshanath (in the 11th to 12th c. CE) and the following generations of incarnated Siddha-Gurus, plus many,

many more, all the way into our current century [see Part II]. Although this list was mostly men, there are many women too; plus, most are unknown or barely known, while a mere handful have become world renowned. Yoga scholar Georg Feuerstein explains in introductory comments to an essay by Adi Da:

> Turning to the Great Tradition of religion and spirituality, we find innumerable accounts of individuals who approached Spiritual Teachers and had to endure a dramatic trial of self-purification and humility. If spiritual maturity is to develop, we must enter the gate of self-understanding and behold the ego and our God-denying actions directly. The vision is sobering, but it is required of all who would be Awakened to the spiritual way.[12]

Today, if we diligently study these Adepts, we can still learn from these great historical advanced-tip individuals about the contours of religious and spiritual life. This is what the world's religious traditions have attempted to do in every generation. Everyone inherits the wisdom from their forebears; no one can do it alone. For example, the Buddha's Dharma or Teaching of Truth has been kept alive and relevant by a lineage of Enlightened Adepts from India to South Asia to China to Japan to Tibet, and even now into the West. For more than twenty-five centuries this Teaching-Transmission of Nirvana awakens anew in each generation. It too awakens with us in the modern world when we consciously practice and study the Buddha's principles and precepts of loving compassion and mindfulness, of Guru Yoga and meditation. The Wisdom Masters are always ready to teach us about our innate wisdom, love, and awakened consciousness, whether they live today or hundreds (or thousands) of years ago. It is, after all, *our* Great Tradition of Global Wisdom! Use it wisely! But use it!

This sacred relationship between Adept and student-devotee takes place on several levels in the spectrum of transpersonal consciousness as embodied with the advanced-tip Prophets, Shamans, Saints, Yogis, Sages, and Siddhas, each reflecting different Stages of Life (or degrees) of God-Realization[13] [see Appendix I]. They, women and men of all races and classes, are our sacred inheritance to whom we should be most grateful [see Part I]. Avatar Adi Da adroitly explains the purpose of the authentic Adept's Agency to God-Realization:

> The Adept is simply the Agency of That which is to be Realized. He or she is a useful and remarkable Agency, a unique mechanism in nature, a hole in the universe through which the Transcendental Influence moves through to the world. Therefore, this remarkable Agency, when it occurs, should be used. It should be acknowledged and understood as it is. People should know how to relate to it, how to use it as a unique instrument of the Divine. Adepts appear to serve your Realization.[14]

Since Satsang or the relationship with a genuine Guru-Adept is a true function in Nature and has always been, then it is a reality inherent in the human condition. Hence it is critical to our future evolution—and world peace—to become better equipped to rightly honor and engage in this sacred activity of Guru Yoga. Truly, Satsang as a relationship with a Spiritual Master is a Blessing and Joy beyond compare! It is not a burden nor is it a cult. Only direct knowledge of God—i.e., Enlightenment—is our true Salvation no matter who you are or where you come from. Let us learn to open our hearts and minds to this sacred (and timeless) Truth and not shun it due to some bad examples and rotten apples (i.e., fake gurus) or by listening to misleading myths about previous Master-Siddhas. Rather, let's turn our attention to those Bright Lights who are genuine Gurus acting as God's Gift and Grace given to us all. Such a relationship initiates the "super-physics" or subtle-energies lying *in potentia* within our embodied esoteric anatomy encapsulating our evolutionary inheritance as enfolded and unfolded through the Seven Stages of Life (as we'll see next).

GURU-FUNCTION:
SUPER-PHYSICS OF ENLIGHTENMENT

The essential function of the Guru-Adept is to get devotees involved in the psycho-physical processes of bodily and mental and soulful *transformation* to Whole Body Enlightenment.[15] This "super-physics" involves an actual energy-exchange of *spiritual transmission—**Shaktipat*** or Spirit Baptism—that responds to the radiation (and intensification) of Conscious Light given from the Guru. It goes from Heart to heart. This is the fundamental Light of Real God being magnified in the Guru's Company (whether physically or spiritually), therefore, Adi Da points out:

> True Spiritual life is not just a change in your mind…. Divine Enlightenment is a literal change of the *whole body*…. Those changes are as literal as the "evolutionary change" from a dinosaur to a human being—and they are as dramatic as that, but they principally occur at more subtle levels of the physics of the conditional being. There are literal changes in the nervous system, literal changes in the chemistry of the body, literal changes in the structural functioning of the brain.[16]

These subtle-energy processes of higher consciousness evolution, grounded in the heart and inner brain core, often invoke kundalini currents and subtle energies which have been universally acknowledged by the most highly-evolved beings practicing esoteric transpersonal spirituality (such as with Yogis and Saints). It often involves the alchemy of vertical kundalini ascension and mystical visions. It stimulates our glandular biochemistry and influences the health of the body-mind on interior and exterior levels (in an AQAL or "four-quadrant" tetra-interactive manner). Yet, ultimately, Enlightenment is more than energies and experiences of the inner self or soul (no matter how subtle, or even, causal). Enlightenment is about awakening the heart to God-Realization, a silent, tacit understanding of utter self-transcendence beyond words and description.

Awakening Enlightenment in others, therefore, is a special function in human evolutionary potential—one only offered by the most-advanced Guru-Adept or Spiritual Master (in the Sixth or Seventh Stage of Life). It is they who can best serve this process to completion for they have already fulfilled it themselves, in person. This is why coming into such Wise and Enlightened Company is such a profound and sacred occasion; one to be celebrated and honored not dismissed or doubted. Avatar Adi Da affirms this sacred task:

> The Spiritual Master has many functions: to exemplify the Way, to Argue the Way, to Bless devotees, to Interfere with them, to Transmit the Spiritual Influence tangibly to them so that they will then, having understood themselves, be capable of spiritual growth. The function of the Adept does not come to an end. The Adept is the continuous resource and resort of devotees....
>
> My Purpose is not only to Teach and be of use to you during My lifetime, but to establish you in such a relationship to Me that after My lifetime an Agency will continue to exist sufficient for this practice.[17]

A Guru must appear in human form in order to serve as a real function for other living people to realize the epitome or ultimate potential of human development. The first and foremost function of a Guru is to help his or her devotees come to realize the ultimate nature of Reality, which in the West has been called "God" (or "Godhead"), and in the East, the Supreme Self (*Atman*) and Buddha-Nature (*Buddha-dhātu*). Known as Divine Enlightenment or Self-Realization this ultimate state-stage of consciousness is signified by a wide variety of traditional names: *satori* (Zen), *prajna* (Hinduism), *bodhi* (Buddhism), *rigpa* (Tibetan), *wu* (Taoism), or *gnosis* (Greek), among others. But it is not a name to be named but a State to be realized.

The Realized Guru or Awakened Spiritual Master is here to help *enlighten* you to your true condition and nature, what the Sufis call our "Supreme Identity," what a Zen Master calls your "Original Face" (even "before the Big Bang," as Wilber noted). Only in Satsang, or a profound relationship with God as Guru, is the confused suffering of self truly healed of its fear and feeling of separative existence. This Liberation is felt as a profound depth in the heart. Adi Da affirms: "The living Spiritual Master is the ultimate Healer, and the mere Presence of such a one is the most benign healing Influence. Without obstruction or limitation of any kind, the Spiritual Master incarnates the All-Pervading Radiance and Transcendental Consciousness of God. Those who enter in His Company enter the very Presence of God."[18] This is, therefore, the most sacred of all concerns. Only this process is the *real* function or *true* purpose of the genuine Guru: here to help you *see* and *realize* the Love-Bliss of Consciousness Itself, to *recognize* the Divine Person and Ultimate Reality of Everything... the Divine Mystery of existence. Thus, the Avatar continues to reveal in a spontaneous talk:

> Guru is a function. It is a specific and special activity. In fact, there is only one Guru. God is the Guru, and the function of Guru is eternal. It does not simply come into the world when some knowable human Guru appears, nor does it leave at the end of a lifetime of such a one. The function of Guru is always present, always active, always available....

> The entire purpose of such a one is to reveal God, to reveal the functions of God, so that devotees who find God also in such a human Guru may always live in God, enjoy the great Siddhis, true Siddhis, that are the Divine itself, while they live, and even beyond the lifetime of that human Guru.
>
> Such a Guru does not appear in the world in order to create a cult in which he [or she] is forever afterwards the object, the fetish, of mere belief and acknowledgment. There is an appropriate form of relationship to the human Guru, and it is not the cultic form.
>
> Truly, the devotee must understand in the Company of his human Guru, and he must discover that the One who is his human Guru, and the specific function that is always lived to him through his human Guru, are the Divine activity. The Divine must be free to do its work.[19]

To initiate or help reveal such sacred and paradoxical Enlightenment, the Guru will resort to a variety of functions and skillful means to try to bring this Awakening about for it always involves ego-transcendence. Therefore, the devotee or approaching student must be receptive and open, not a mere curiosity seeker, in order to make right use of the Guru's full function and transforming powers to reveal God. This process at times includes the notorious paradox of the so-called "**Crazy Wisdom**" and "**Holy Madness**" teaching methods [see Chapter 11]. The Guru, in this case, is here to initiate "ego death," to assist us in transcending our limited self-identity and social-egoity as "I", "me", and "mine", involving our clinging attachments to the incarnated body-mind and its functions and relations. At times the Guru may appear "crazy" by violating apparent (and reasonable) social norms but they are not insane. In fact, they are the most sane of us all. The actions of the genuine Guru are truly borne of love. It is our task to respond appropriately.

The Guru often actively undermines the devotee's search by starting with the demand for spiritual disciplines, such as a controlled diet, regulated sexuality, maintaining work and family obligations, study and meditation, and so on. These disciplines then interfere with (and righten) a person's failed (or weak) behavior patterns and addictive attachments. Most people don't want this regulation or commitment, don't want to be disciplined; thus, most of us resist the Guru's Demand and Spiritual Teachings in general. But not everyone. Just like a professional athlete will take on strict disciplines to achieve specialized results, so too can the common person take on certain practices (or sadhana) to serve his or her spiritual growth. Living authentic Satsang takes a strong will and a true degree of real human maturity, which is why such evolution in consciousness needs to be motivated by love and God-Realization, not egoic power quests.

When this disciplined way of life is done as a spiritual practice grounded in the Enlightened Love-Bliss of the Heart, then you realize your greatest potential and utmost Happiness. But it is not merely a *method* of self-improvement, for it involves the *relationship* of self-surrender in Divine Communion from the Heart. Deep down inside everybody simply wants just this, for it's based on our natural, most holistic human condition, whether we know it or not. Understanding and accepting the true function of the Guru-Adept will initiate you on a sacred journey, direct you on a path of deepening your spiritual awareness. Adi Da once again explains the evolutionary advantage of Satsang: "To enter into the Process that the Sat-Guru represents is like moving out of the slime and ultimately standing up as a human being, growing from the state of an amoeba to manhood."[20] Not a small evolutionary "step" for a man or a woman but a "giant leap" for Enlightenment.

This is why the Guru-devotee relationship is the ancient *esoteric* way, the hidden "secret" behind all the world's religions, lying within our incarnated human anatomy waiting for us to realize the fullest expression of humankind as a consciously-aware species. Its validity has been verified by countless generations, at least by a few in every generation. Thus, it would be foolish to dispense with it or ridicule it with doubt and mockery, since such sacred Satsang is an initiation of "fire" or real Spirit-Baptism given to us by our beloved Gurus, our true Spiritual Masters. Indeed, the Awakened Adepts have only come to demonstrate and offer us their Wise Company as a transparent human Agency to Real God. They are here for us to see and know this truth for ourselves, in person, by opening our hearts to where Only God knows. And, no doubt, God Knows (and Loves) for God is Consciousness and the Heart.

Chapter 22 Endnotes

1. As only one example among countless, see: Jeffrey J. Kripal, T*he Flip: Epiphanies of Mind and the Future of Knowledge* (2019, NYC: Bellevue Literary Press).

2. See: *In God's Company: Guru-Adepts As Agents for Enlightenment in the Integral Age* (2022) by Brad Reynolds.

3. Adi Da Samraj, from the Essay "Adept-Realizers Are The Root of All Esoteric Traditions" in *The Pneumaton* (2011), p. 191.

4. Adi Da Samraj, from the Essay "The Great Esoteric Tradition of Devotion To The Adept-Realizer" in *The Pneumaton* (2011), p. 202.

5. Adi Da Samraj, from the Essay: "The Great Esoteric Tradition of Devotion To The Adept-Realizer" in *The Pneumaton* (2011), p. 199 [emphasis added].

6. Jonathan Landaw and Andy Weber, *Images of Enlightenment* (1993), p. 153.

7. Adi Da Samraj [Da Free John], *Nirvanasara* (1982), p. 57.

8. Ibid., pp. 57-58.

9. See: Adi Da Samraj [Franklin Jones], *The Method of the Siddhas* (1973, 1978, 1992), his second published book of his first Talks to devotees (given in 1972) describing the sacred relationship, not a method, he is offering as Siddha-Guru in Satsang (or "The Method of the Siddhas"), now published as an updated (and final) version called *My "Bright" Word* (2005).

10. See: "The Ancient Walk-Abut Way" in *The Gnosticon* (2010), pp. 736ff.

11. Adi Da Samraj, September 8, 2004 quoted in *The Reality-Way of Adidam* (2010), p. 45.

12. Georg Feuerstein, as editor, Chapter 5: "Salvation and Liberation" in *The Fire Gospel* (1982) by Adi Da Samraj [Da Free John], pp. 131-132.

13. See: Adi Da Samraj, *The Seven Stages of Life* (2000); and also see: *Growing In God: Seven Stages of Life from Birth to Enlightenment—An Integral Interpretation* (forthcoming) by Brad Reynolds.

14. Adi Da Samraj [Da Free John], *The Fire Gospel* (1982), p. 165.

15. See: Adi Da Samraj, the essay "The Super-Physics of Divine Enlightenment" in *The Pneumaton* (2011), pp. 209ff; also see: the essay "The Divine Physics of Evolution" in *The Enlightenment of the Whole Body* (1978), pp. 245ff.

16. Adi Da Samraj, from the essay "The Super-Physics of Divine Enlightenment" in *The Pneumaton* (2011), pp. 211-212.

17. Adi Da Samraj [Da Free John], *The Fire Gospel* (1982), p. 165.

18. Adi Da Samraj. *The Eating Gorilla Comes in Peace* (1978), p. 461.

19. Adi Da Samraj, *No Remedy* (1975/1976), pp. 8-9.

20. Adi Da Samraj, "Unpublished Talk," January 28, 1978 in *Spiritual-Transmission and Self-Surrender* (1984), p. 14.

TWENTY THREE

GURU-ADEPTS:
AGENCY FOR ENLIGHTENMENT

*Spiritually Realized Adepts (or Transmission-Masters, or True Gurus) are
the principal Sources, Resources, and Means of the esoteric (or Spiritual) Way.
This fact is not (and never has been) a matter of controversy among real Spiritual
practitioners.... The traditional term "Guru" (spelled with a capital "G") means
"One Who Reveals the Light and thereby Liberates beings from Darkness".*

— **Adi Da Samraj**, 2000[1]

GURU-ADEPTS:
AGENCY OF GOD

The Guru-Adept is not a golden calf, an idol for cultic worship and egoic fascination, or one of gleeful childish dependence as if he (or she) were a parental force or image, a projection of unconscious fantasies.[2] Overall, a strong ego or sense of personal selfhood, supplemented by disciplined practices (including meditation) and self-understanding, is a prerequisite for Guru Yoga-Satsang to be most effective. This is because such maturity allows us to more easily resonant with the Enlightened State of the authentic Guru as being our own Divine Consciousness since they too have lived a disciplined yogic lifestyle. The Master can sit still with no problem (otherwise they are no Master). The world needs as many genuine spiritual practitioners as possible, men and women *from all* cultures and nations, for the times ahead are going to be difficult as we struggle to grow beyond today's immature religious fundamentalism and scientific materialism. We are not to use the Master Guru as a cultic crutch but as an Agent transparent to Real God, our own Divine Nature (or Buddha-Nature).

We must take up and *exercise* the esoteric qualifications for the evolution of consciousness by learning through education and practice about the actual Guru-devotee relationship. Then we can rightly integrate the developmental processes of "Growing Up" *and* "Waking Up." The Guru is God's demand for us to transform our egoic selfishness into enlightened compassion and be active as love in all relations. Our wisest ancestors told us this too for they have provided a "Divine Library" creating a Great Tradition of Global Wisdom for all humankind to access. By studying under a true Spiritual Master—a genuine Guru-Adept, an awakened Avatar, a Divine Incarnation—it becomes necessary to serve the Enlightenment of *all* beings in order to realize world peace and universal Happiness. Only God-Realization grounded in our Prior Unity will create global peace among the world's diverse populations and this *is* possible because it's our inherent (and most real) condition.

The Way to overcome the unenlightened life in the modern/postmodern world—to bring depth into a global civilization living on consumerism and superficiality—is to **cultivate** *Satsang* or a living relationship with a genuine Guru, a true Spiritual Master, an Adept of Spiritual Knowledge and Divine Wisdom. Adi Da Samraj offers such a sacred process, the Way of the Heart—the Reality-Way of Adidam—to those who sincerely approach him as Guru-Adept. Satsang is the path to Enlightenment or Self-Realization that has been practiced for millennia, so there is no reason to think that we as a global culture have moved beyond this time-honored path. It is innate in our very own anatomy and just awaits to be awakened. Our technology and democracy does not eliminate the need to develop and evolve our consciousness and inner awareness of our inherent Divine Nature.

A relationship of devotion and commitment to Guru Yoga-Satsang, the revered path of India and Tibet, is a fundamental tenet of the universal Perennial Philosophy living at the core of all esoteric religions. As is often said in Buddhism: "If you want to receive the blessings of a Buddha, you must see your Guru as a Buddha."[3] *Fifty Verses of Guru-Devotion* (Verse 22), a popular Buddhist text, outright proclaims: "A disciple with the good qualities of compassion, generosity, moral self-control and patience, should never regard as different his Guru and the Buddha."[4] There's a saying in India that sees the Guru as being even greater than God since the Guru helps awaken us to knowledge of Real God. Such admonitions do not make the Guru more than human but presents him or her as being a *human agent* of the Divine, transparent to the Real. Thus, they should be accorded the proper respect and devotional attitude, which at the beginning and in the end (and along the way) serves *your* Enlightenment. It is as simple (and difficult) as that.

When we realize that they teach and serve us as we serve them then God-Realization dawns and peace and love becomes real for us, not just theory. Yet it takes disciplined practice and meditation to recognize the Guru's true function. This *conversion* includes properly handling the "business" of "money, food, and sex" (in Adi Da's words)—what Wilber calls "Growing Up"—as well as exercising proper esoteric practices of meditation in Divine Communion or "Waking Up" (in Wilber's terms). Avatar Adi Da, as always, teaches us about the spiritual functions of the True Guru and Spiritual Adept and how they should not be abused as a cultic idol:

> The Spiritual Master is a Transparent Reminder of the Divine Reality, a Guide to the ecstatic Realization of the One Reality in Which all conditions arise and change and pass away. The Spiritual Master is not to be made into the merely "objectified" idol of a cult, as if the Divine Being were exclusively contained in the objective person and subjective beliefs of a particular sect. Rather, right relationship to the Spiritual Master takes the form of free devotional response to the Spiritual Master's Radiant State.[5]

Such a "free devotional response" is a natural outcome of transcending cultic bias and understanding the proper function and true purpose or Agency of the genuine Guru-Adept, the truly authentic Adept-Avatar. This embodies the essence of true human maturity and religion at its best and most complete. It is a life of awakened equanimity grounded in the ecstatic love-bliss of life seen arising as radiant Spirit, nothing less than that.

Why Choose a Guru?

What's the point in having a Guru anyway? Isn't the "inner Guru" the True Guru? Isn't it just a weakness to need somebody else to tell you how to live? If God is everything then why honor somebody else as being "closer to God"?

The main reason a person has a Guru is *to see* (or know) God Itself; not just to see the Guru as a "God-Man"—though he or she is God too—but to see each and every thing as God or Buddha-Nature, one and all. This is to know God with certainty (in the heart) and without doubt (in the mind). Do you know the Godhead or the Ultimate Nondual Truth of Reality without any doubt? Do you *really* know "what" or "who" God—Brahman, Tao, Allah, et al—is, *in truth*? Maybe you don't care, being a modern/postmodern person using science as your path of knowledge but at times I bet you do—or at least it makes you wonder. If you do care about God or the Reality of the Divine then a genuine Guru, a true Spiritual Master, would be good for you to better know God or the Divine Reality (whatever "That" IS). For that's why Gurus are here; that's their "job": to help *you see* God as Consciousness in truth, in person, as the Truth of Reality, as the simple Feeling of Being. That event (or view) will transform your consciousness and personality in ways impossible to achieve when living from the perspective of the ego or the common culture.

Soon after his Teaching-Work began, Adi Da pointed out that Satsang is *not seeking* for God but being able *to live* God-Realization *in the present* under all conditions, in all relations, as the Avatar clarifies:

> To be a devotee, to live in Satsang, is to live God as your present Condition. It has nothing to do with seeking God, nothing to do with Narcissus [or the ego-I].... So the foundation of our work is Satsang, Divine Communion, not the need to discover the Self, not the need to discover the Divine, but Satsang itself, present existence in the Condition of the Divine.... The Guru's command to meditate on Him is not the command to meditate on the human figure, the cultic Guru. It is the command to meditate upon the Divine Person [Real God].[6]

Only the person, woman or man, who *truly* wants to know about God will make good and proper use of a genuine Guru. The false use of the Guru is nothing but cultism, just another object or fetish of the ego, a strategy of the seeker (Narcissus). This is true whether you're afraid of them or devoted. If you're only interested in yourself and the world of things, in all your possessions (whether as inner or outer experiences), or in increasing self-power, then an authentic spiritual life of self-transcendence, let alone one involving a Guru, won't be attractive to you. Only a person who deeply desires to know about the Truth of life and death (and beyond) will use the Guru rightly. It is a divine opportunity for *everyone!*

We thus need these living examples who embody our future evolutionary potentials to show us the Way of Truth, the Way of the Heart. Learning from the Heart-Master is the ancient Way, the sacred Way long recognized by all religions and mystics the world over. They are the beating heart at the core of God's Great Tradition of Global Wisdom. Nonetheless, the expressions or Teachings about this divine process have also been *evolving* or growing in depth as the evolution of consciousness and culture unfolds on planet Earth [see Chapter 10].[7] Now, with worldwide communications it is possible for the relationship of Guru Yoga-Satsang to reach millions (or billions) of people, especially with an authentic World-Teacher or *Jagad Guru*, such as with Adi Da Samraj.

Therefore, it is crucial to distinguish between genuine Gurus and false or fake Gurus (as this book hopes to help clarify).[8] I am suggesting that to resort to an authentic Enlightened Master is okay, it's safe; for it's one of the most powerful (and direct) "Ways" to *realize* God (or Ultimate Reality) for real. At a minimum, you will at least get to know the Divine (and yourself) better, as verified by centuries of spiritual practitioners. Yet you will be tested; your mind will have to confront itself and learn to surrender its habits, its negative tendencies and sacrifice its attachments. Honestly, there are no definitive guarantees; it's a mysterious process of Divine Grace (thus indeterminate). Fortunately, the formless Mystery of God descends or appears from the Divine Light to manifest in human form in order to teach all beings about the Truth of Real God (and will continue to do so in the future). The universe is actually geared toward revealing the Divine Light to you since the Real Guru *is you* (as God) *serving you* (and all of us)! Nevertheless, today many people angrily ask:

"How could a Guru be a worthy function in modern democratic societies?"

"How can the Guru be more Awake than all the rest of us?"

But these are misunderstandings because the Guru is not to be made into the "Big Man" in the middle of things; not meant to be the "Queen Bee" of the hive, the "King" of the mountain. They may be a "Spiritual Hero" but they are actually more like an anti-hero. Their function is to awaken us beyond the ego-self to the Nothing that IS Everything, the egoless Divine Person; a wonderful yet notorious paradox. This is a Great Mystery, one even beyond belief. God is to be experienced directly, to be *realized spiritually* (as Spirit). Avatar Adi Da explains in a talk given within the first year of opening the doors to his Siddha-Ashram (in 1972):

> Guru is a function. It is not a form of "status." It is not something to be achieved. It is not a big guy who appears among a lot of little guys. It is not a form of superiority or narcissism. Guru is a function of the very Self or Reality, appearing in human terms. The relationship between Guru and disciple is not loaded with any of the things that are involved in the relationship between superior men and weak men. That relationship has nothing to do with the ordinary drama of conflict. The human Guru may seem to be like other men to the usual man and the seeker, but when a man truly lives with his Guru, knows him as Guru, then Satsang has begun.[9]

Either this makes some sense to you or not, but sooner or later it will (or could). For the Guru as a function for God-Realization is the essence of the world's mystical tradition of spirituality; it is our universal inheritance as the human race: God's Great Tradition of Global Wisdom—read the texts of the Divine Library to see for yourself [see Chapters 1-3]. The Great Tradition of humankind and its Perennial Philosophy teaches us that such Divine Awakening is our natural birthright so we can learn about this sacred relationship and bring it into the sphere of our understanding. May all beings be blessed to Awaken to the Unspeakable Divine… please go to find your true Guru with intelligence and heartfelt recognition… and shine on!

FUNCTION OF THE GURU-ADEPT: PRACTICAL *AND* SPIRITUAL GIFTS

When it comes to the ego-I, the self-contraction of Narcissus, one of the most important functions of the Guru is to "kick ass,"[10] so to speak, i.e., to challenge the ego as well as to Bless and Awaken the individual person—they go hand in hand, balancing and integrating one another. Sadhana is a "fire" (*tapas*) or purification that burns away the dross of the ego before the Divine Light can clearly be seen. Adi Da calls this apparent dichotomy (or paradox) of the Guru function as being his "**Power Foot**"— the Guru's fiery and purifying "Father Force" that challenges the ego—plus his "**Beauty Foot**"—the gentle, nurturing "Mother Force" of Divine Blessing. One "kicks ass" through demanding proper discipline and equanimity while the other offers a "Big Kiss" of sweetness and love-blessing. Transcending the ego allows love to flow forth as a blessing, if understood (and enacted) properly. This is what Satsang with the Siddha-Guru offers every individual who takes up the practice (in the Reality-Way of Adidam).

Thus, the only reason to submit or tolerate such an undertaking is that sadhana-Satsang offers genuine Awakening-power for the transformation of consciousness. Such ego-transcendence serves and teaches a human to be love in all relations, to awaken to Reality as It IS and be Happy under all conditions by *seeing* (and *feeling*) God everywhere. Ego must be both transcended and integrated to become transparent to God. The process of development is learning to live as love and compassion balanced by wisdom and skillful means, all grounded in the prior unity of Divine Realization. Your awakened heart becomes the confirmation that such Satsang is real and beneficial. Satsang is the "**Method of the Siddhas**" or the Way of the "Completed Ones" (which is what *siddha* means in Sanskrit). Once more, Beloved Adi Da clearly explains:

> [Satsang] involves the Real Physics of the Absolute Universe. And there is a real Agency for it…. If you establish yourself in right relationship to it, it begins to duplicate itself in your case. It is not as if you are a robot being transformed by some computer. Rather, it is a living and human relationship. But it is not like the "doctor-patient" or "mommy-daddy-baby" relationship either. Irresponsible people cannot enter into it. You must be responsible for yourself.[11]

The Guru function of Satsang can essentially be reduced to two principal activities: (1) the *practical* (or exoteric) Teachings (of "Growing Up"), and (2) those that involve the *spiritual* (or esoteric) Teachings of human spirituality (of "Waking Up"). Let's briefly review both the *practical* and *spiritual* aspects of the <u>**Guru-Adept's Teaching-Functions**</u>:

(1) **Practical**—*exoteric* or "outer" functions—the Teachings on what Adi Da calls "money, food, and sex,"[12] and social relations, including bodily health, diet, breath (*prana*) or the "conscious exercise" of conductivity, responsibility to other beings (human and nonhuman) and the eco-environment of Nature, emotional-sexual development, familial relations, childhood and college education, work and good livelihood, intelligent discrimination and study, living in cooperative community, social services, universal tolerance, enlightened politics, creative work and the arts, the practice of love and compassion for all beings in all relations, and so on.

(2) **Spiritual**—*esoteric* or "inner" functions—the Teachings on Prior Unity and "always already" Happiness (beyond all seeking) and "Radical Understanding" of the self-activity thus transcending the contraction of the ego-I known as "Narcissus" (in Adi Da's terms); an active devotional life, including chanting, *puja* (sacramental rituals) or bodily worship of the Living God, prayer, contemplation, conductivity of the descending-ascending currents in the frontal and spinal lines (with *pranayama* or breathing exercises), yogic techniques of inversion, such as meditation, subtle consciousness exploration, dream yoga, lucid dreaming, death and dying, including "pointing-out instructions," the Witness Consciousness, Divine Communion, Guru-devotion; Divine Heart-Transmission (*Hridaya Shaktipat*) via the exchange of the Guru's State of Divine Enlightenment *transmitted* to the receptive devotee (at least temporarily), Conscious Light Translation (after death), and so forth.

Such profound functions of any authentic Guru are what guides a person in the growth of their inherent spiritual potential for that is what *authentic transformation* in the evolution of consciousness is about. Adi Da makes it clear throughout his Teaching that not only does Satsang provide practical and spiritual disciplines but its main function is to awaken awareness of God in the heart beyond the search. From this "always already" Happiness the disciplines arise. The practices do not seek for God, as the traditional yogas tend to teach, but are a response to the Guru's primary function, as Beloved Da explains:

All that occurs for any man or woman is the process I have been describing. The search winds down. The individual falls somehow into his [or her] ordinariness, his [or her] suffering. Then [the devotee] becomes available to Satsang. When [a devotee] begins to live Satsang as his [or her] real condition, associated with it may be feelings that he [or she] has chosen one Guru among others. But such "choices" are purely secondary. In fact, there is no choice. There is only the sudden availability of one who truly functions as Guru. In the life of every true disciple, there has only been the sudden communication of the Heart.[13]

Nothing short of Whole Body or Complete Enlightenment (*samyaksam-bodhi*) is truly sufficient for true human happiness, beyond even temporary awakenings or mystical experiences. To be *always already* Happy (and at peace), to understand and transcend the contraction that is ego-I, to be love, and not to react and create more suffering, is the practical result of real Satsang and God-Communion. Such "practices" are the true Way and foundation for a happy, blissful, awakened human life. According to the Great Wisdom Traditions of humankind these processes of growth and maturity (in the higher Stages of Life) are the very reason we have been born on planet Earth. It is *our responsibility* as an individual and global culture to actively engage this sacred process of Guru Yoga-Satsang (when done rightly, not cultically). Thus we truly need the service and Gift of Grace provided by a genuine Guru-Adept, or an authentic Avatar, whomever that may be in your particular case. The point being: Find *your* Guru; then serve them as they serve you!

NINE GIFTS OF THE GURU-ADEPT

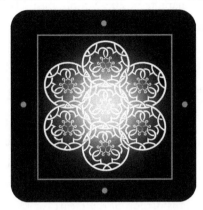

ext let's review the "**Nine Functions of the Siddha-Guru**"[14] that amplify these two basic principal activities involving the *practical* and *spiritual* functions of the genuine Spiritual Master [see above]. Theses nine gifts were compiled by author and scholar of the Great Tradition (and devotee of Adi Da Samraj), James Steinberg, as presented in his well-researched book *Love of the God-Man* (1990), summarized (and paraphrased) as follows:

(1) **Guru-Adept as the Giver of Divine Transmission-Blessing to devotees**—this energy exchange or transmission involves the direct Heart-Transmission (*Hridaya Shaktipat*, or, in Adi Da's case, *Ruchira Shaktipat*) given from Guru to devotee that is the core essence of *Satsang* or the Way of the Heart; ultimately this Spirit-Transmission (or Spirit-Baptism) is the Supreme Divine Blessing present in all the worlds (and throughout all universes) for it is the Radiance or "Holy Spirit" of God Itself given by the God-Realized Guru. Nonetheless, in essence, it is "always already" available and never absent since it is eternal; it is only the ego-self that contracts away from its pure Presence in moments of illusion and unlove. This power or energy of Conscious Light is magnified and transmitted via the presence of an authentic Adept-Realizer or at their empowered Holy Sites; this Shaktipat-Transmission involves the "super-physics" of God-Light (operating in the gross, subtle, and causal domains of existence),

yet ultimately, it's a Divine Mystery only activated by an authentic Guru-Adept [see Chapters 9, 20]. Simply put: "Transmission of the Divine Condition to the devotee is the Guru-Principle"[15] in its fullness because this Heart-Transmission or Spirit-Baptism accelerates one's spiritual practice (*sadhana*) in the evolution of consciousness from birth to Enlightenment. We should all resort to its Grace as a gift of Divine Intervention.

(2) **Guru-Adept as the Object of Contemplation for devotees**—the Adept-Guru as Spirit-Transmitter becomes an "object" of meditation, a common practice of **Guru Yoga** the world over as devotees resort to this Ever-Present Transmission of the Heart (or Divine Person) in the bodily (human) form of the Guru. This becomes the means for their Remembrance and meditation on the Divine Condition revealed to them by the Grace of their Guru's Enlightened State (and Transmission); this *is* **Satsang** as Adi Da instructs: "The moment to moment feeling-Contemplation of My bodily (human) Form, My Spiritual (and Always Blessing) Presence, and My Very (and Inherently Perfect) State" is the Way of the Heart; in this case, the Guru's Enlightened State is potentially replicated in any devotee's consciousness in order to awaken us to our "always already" Divine Consciousness, which is the unique advantage of Guru Yoga-Satsang [see Chapter 22].

Guru-Adept as Demand and Guide to establish a culture of expectation and inspiration for devotees—the Adept-Guru becomes an inspiration for practice (or *sadhana*) since they themselves have already accomplished the process of Divine Enlightenment; since the event of Enlightenment is such an arduous and complex process of self-understanding and self-transcendence then a devotee cannot go through it without a competent Guide or Guru (as history has shown); this includes obedience to the practical and spiritual discipline which are the Guru's demand for self-transcending practice culminating in God-Realization and Divine Communion. "**Cooperative community**" (in Adi Da's words), or "The 'Bright'-House Adidam," is to move out of the domain of the social ego or the consumer culture of the common world "to demonstrate the principle of <u>cooperation</u> in the field of daily relations" with other devotees such that, as Adi Da explains, "[everyone is] called to embrace the principle of <u>simplicity</u> in the field of daily activity (such that all matters of desiring, acquiring, and having are rightly and appropriately moderated,"[16] similar to traditional ashrams and monasteries, proving that sadhana-Satsang is a Practicing School (not a Talking School).

(3) **Guru-Adept as Clarifier and Purifier of the Great Tradition of Human Spirituality**—the Enlightened Guru knows about and clarifies the entire religious history of humankind (as this book has shown) since *they are* in fact the primary subject of religion and its highest goals (as evident, for example, by Buddha and Christ); the Great Tradition of Spiritual Texts and Teachings (or the "Divine Library") has never been available for so many people as today (since esoteric texts throughout human history have always been rare and hidden, seldom seen and heard by most people); therefore this "wilderness of doctrines" (in Adi Da's words) needs to be clarified, classified and rightly honored since they *all* contribute to our overall understanding about the process of living in Divine Communion; only a true Adept-Guru can put this plethora of religious and spiritual teachings into proper perspective from the point of view of Full Enlightenment; in the opinion of many (regardless of the complaints of a few) no one Adept in human history has had such a *global* (or non-provincial) perspective of religion, both East and West, than has the World-Teacher Adi Da Samraj; thus we would do well to listen to and study the Great Tradition in conjunction with his Teaching-Word in order to see (or not) for ourselves.

(4) **Guru-Adept as Prophet: One who Instructs the entire world by His criticism**—includes critical reviews of the conventional world, ordinary politics, today's religions, religious, secular, and scientific philosophies and competing worldviews because the true Adept-Guru "speaks as the Voice of the Divine"[17]— "**The Heart's Shout**"[18]—for the Guru as Prophet not only criticizes but calls everyone with urgency to genuine spiritual practice (*sadhana*), thus calling us to what is greater than the common worldly destiny; examples of this prophetic

voice abound throughout the Great Wisdom Tradition of human-kind, as well as being forcefully given in the Teaching-Word of Adi Da Samraj. This includes what Adi Da has called his "Power Foot" which demands discipline and the rightening of one's life to principles of Divine Communion (which are, in turn, a gift of his "Beauty Foot" or Divine Blessings) [see above].

(5) **Guru-Adept as Giver of the Written and Spoken Teaching, whose Word is a Unique Transmission of Blessing Grace**—the Written and Spoken Teaching-Word is how Adept-Realizers and Siddha-Gurus instruct their students and inform devotees over the generations; in the modern/postmodern era, Avatar Adi Da Samraj is an unprecedented event in human history since he has appeared when nearly everything he has said or done has been recorded or written down (including countless hours of recorded Talks on tape); the Dharma or Teaching of Truth has usually been recorded throughout human history by the written word, if recorded at all, yet usually it has been done a generation or more after the Adept has passed away and then usually only fragments have been preserved, or worse, the originals have been lost altogether (there are, of course, important exceptions); Source-Books and Source-Literature (and now Source-Audio and Image-Recordings) are the methods of engaging the mind of the student by the Guru so the heart may open to surrendering the self to the Spirit-Current of the Divine Reality magnified by the Spiritual Radiance of a genuine Guru and authentic Avatar.

(6) **Guru-Adept as Demonstrator of the Teaching in life's activities and conditions, whose Teaching Leelas (or stories) clarify every aspect of human existence**—the recorded and oral stories (*leelas*) surrounding the Guru are actual and real-life demonstrations of the Teaching of Enlightenment given *in person*; beyond the gift of the "Word" alone these life lessons demonstrate the intellectual teaching in concrete terms; the stories or *leelas* (or "play") of the world's Great Gurus instruct the soul in both practice and Revelation since they show their Guru to be an Agency of the Divine Presence, not the actions of an ordinary ego at all; the Guru's life stories verify the sacred process and

practices that his (or her) devotees are engaged in; the leelas of the Guru-Adepts recorded throughout the history of the Great Tradition are a principal subject of all the world's Holy Scriptures, from East and West, North and South, embodied as the sacred inheritance of humankind—precisely why we should engage in their serious study [see Part I]. Interestingly, we discover that even though Gurus are human, for they can still get angry or have bodily desires, they are also able to let go of negative emotions more quickly than most of us. Hence the human Guru demonstrates that the Divine is also fully *human*, susceptible to errors and mistakes (regardless of what cultic idol worship may prefer), yet fundamentally they are full of boundless (unconditional) love and divine grace.

(7) **Guru-Adept as Creator of the Means or Agencies by which Blessing-Transmission may forever be made available**—these include Holy Sites and Sanctuaries established by (and for) the Adept-Guru, especially their burial site (or Mahasamadhi Site), sacred places on Earth established for future generations; these Holy Sites and relics are forms of Agency and Instrumentality that are radiating the Master-Guru's Blessing Power that is passed on through the generations; this includes, importantly, the lineage of mature devotees who can carry on the Blessing Work of an Enlightened Adept-Guru in the best possible circumstances; however, historically the lineage is usually broken or corrupted (or dies out) within a generation or so after the Guru's lifetime—an excellent example of trans-generational Enlightened lineages that survived and thrived are found in the history of Buddhism; in modern times, Adi Da Samraj has left behind one of the most comprehensive set of circumstances created for the continuity of his Blessing-Transmission, including the "Three Jewels" (recognized by Buddhism): (1) Complete Teaching-Word (the "Dharma"), (2) a full account of the Leelas or stories of the Adept's life (the "Buddha"), (3) a serving Institution, Culture, and Community (the "Sangha")—called the Reality-Way of Adidam Ruchiradam—plus (4) Spiritually-Empowered Sanctuaries, and (5) Mature Devotees (the esoteric renunciate order).

(8) **Guru-Adept as Giver of Transcendental Blessing to the world**—the authentic Adept-Guru Works on every level of existence from the gross to the subtle to the causal domains yet their Work is mostly Transcendental or inherently Spiritual and Nondual in nature; their Work is a Divine Mystery (beyond scientific explanation) since it arises out of the Heart of God (as the blissful current of *Amrita Nadi*), the Divine Domain of Consciousness Itself, thus it affects the "super-physics" of the Kosmos (and Cosmic Mandala) and every living being; in whatever way appropriate the Adept-Guru brings Blessing-Power, Love, and Light into the world (on levels most people cannot fully comprehend), including the all-important Divine Heart-Transmission (*Hridaya Shaktipat*), the awakening agency of Real God or Conscious Light (*Ruchira Shaktipat*) that aligns and purifies the body-mind of all human beings who are awakening their hearts to Real God-Realization and Divine Communion.

May all beings be blessed to know (and realize) the authenticity of these truths and Guru-functions.

A New Integral Age: Global Cooperation

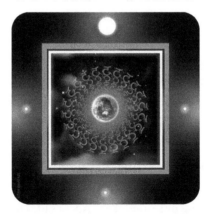

These primary nine functions of the genuine Guru-Adept are best practiced and received as an individual living within a larger cooperative community (such as in an ashram, sangha, or monastery), yet their influence also needs to be activated within the larger conventional society or world-culture as well. In fact, in the Integral Age the Wisdom and Compassion of the world's wisest Adept-Realizers needs to pervade and influence the larger society as a whole from the local to the national to the international levels. Obviously, such an influence has been lacking throughout much of world history and look where it's gotten us: a world in constant conflict with only small packets of fleeting peace!

The evolutionary potential of the human race is better than this, therefore, we must more effectively enact and exercise our Divine Destiny. Consciousness must evolve from dangerous strategies of survival to acts of cooperation and tolerance. In his simple formula for world peace, Avatar Adi Da has stated: "**Cooperation + Tolerance = Peace**,"[19] so "the answer" (or solution) has been given. In his book *Not-Two Is Peace: The Ordinary People's Way of Global Cooperative Order* (2009, 2019), the Global Guru emphasizes that it is only by discovering our Prior Unity ("Not-Two")—both *physically* as the human race and also *spiritually* (as One God)—will the world's diversity of people ever find true tolerance and world peace.

This enlightened approach is truly a guiding light but *we must* cultivate it *within* ourselves first and then bring it *without* into the world and to others and our communities around the globe. All lives matter in the end (and at all times), but past injustices must be righted, justice restituted, and truly, only the Way of the Heart, the Way of self-understanding and self-transcending spiritual practice and meditation will serve to improve the conditions of the world, our natural environment, and everyone's lives altogether—"**everybody-all-at-once**" (exactly as Adi Da says).

To consciously cooperate by following and accessing these primary functions of the genuine Guru-Adept are the best actions any person can do in their lifetime, according to God's Great Tradition of Global Wisdom (as we've seen). These Great Adepts have been given to us by Divine Grace for our own advantage in order to become Enlightened and Self-Realized. It is ultimately *up to us* to access and use them properly (not cultically). Yet, it seems, the conventional world has no idea (or clue)… but they should! Avatar Adi Da Samraj, in harmony with the world's Perennial Philosophers, explains: "The Hindu traditions state that the best thing a man or woman can do is spend time in Satsang, in the company or the condition of relationship and discipleship to the realized Sage…. Satsang is understanding. Satsang is the obviation of a [devotee's] dilemma. Satsang is the activity and communication of Truth."[20] Truly, this admonition applies to us all, regardless of our country of origin, since it is a Transcendental Divine process.

According to the Great Tradition of humankind, from the primordial days of the Ancient Walk-About Way, it has always been the living, active *relationship* between the Enlightened Master and his or her sincere devotees (or students) that helps to generate the most sacred relationship possible for any human being, woman or man, child or adult, regardless of race, creed, religion, sexual-preference, and ethnicity (or even level of intelligence). Real Satsang frees you from the fear of death to awaken you to the Beauty and Love of Life and Light beginning *right now* in the present (not merely as a future possibility). Read the world's scriptures, learn to know your birthright inheritance as presented in the world's Divine Library; go see for yourself and discover this argument's validity and veracity. It is our sacred (and ultimate) calling, even our duty to ourselves and humanity, to access and use this sacred Satsang—this *living relationship* with a genuine Guru-Adept and Awakened Avatar. Please, do so to whatever degree you can muster to proactively participate in the global evolution of spiritual consciousness.

May it be so!

DA! DA! DA!

Chapter 23 Endnotes

1. Adi Da Samraj, from the Essay "The Great Esoteric Tradition of Devotion To The Adept-Realizer" in *The Aletheon* (2009), p. 161.

2. See: *In God's Company: Guru-Adepts As Agents for Enlightenment in the Integral Age* (2022) by Brad Reynolds.

3. Jonathan Landaw and Andy Weber, *Images of Enlightenment* (1993), p. 109.

4. Asvaghosa, *Fifty Verses of Guru-Devotion by Asvaghosa* (1976), p. 18.

5. Adi Da Samraj, from the essay: "Adept-Realizers Are the Root of All Esoteric Traditions" in *The Pneumaton* (2011), p. 191.

6. Adi Da Samraj [Bubba Free John], *Garbage and the Goddess* (1974), p. 91, 175.

7. See: Ken Wilber, Up from Eden (1981, 2007); *The Eye of Spirit* (1997, 2001); *The Religion of Tomorrow* (2017).

8. See: *In God's Company: Guru-Adepts As Agents for Enlightenment in the Integral Age* (2022) by Brad Reynolds.

9. Adi Da Samraj [Franklin Jones], *The Method of the Siddhas* (1973, 1978), p. 308, from the Talk "No One Survives Beyond the Moment" (given in 1972).

10. A well-known saying from Adi Da's first years of Teaching was "dead Gurus can't kick ass!" (*The Method of the Siddhas*, p. 225), which was fully appropriate when he was alive instructing people in sadhana-Satsang as they entered his ashram; yet, truly, if a current devotee sincerely engages sadhana (in Satsang) in His Company, even today after his death (or Mahasamadhi), the ego will be frustrated (as well as blessed). Through the Agency of Adi Da's Teaching-Word and the Good Company of his community of devotees in Adidam the ego will (and can) feel it is getting an "ass kicking" with the demand of discipline, without a doubt. Yet, it is not about this alone, of course, since Satsang will mostly feel like a "Big Kiss" or heart opening showing why the disciplines of Right Life and Right View are needed (and warranted).

11. Adi Da Samraj, original talk "The Divine Physics of Evolution" in *The Enlightenment of the Whole Body* (1978), p. 249; now see: "The Super-Physics of Divine Enlightenment" in *The Pneumaton* (2011), p. 213.

12. See: Adi Da Samraj, *My "Bright" Word* (2005), originally Chapter 3 in *The Method of the Siddhas* (1973).

13. Adi Da Samraj [Franklin Jones], *The Method of the Siddhas* (1973, 1978), p. 308, from the Talk "No One Survives Beyond the Moment" (given in 1972).

14. See: James Steinberg, *Love of the God-Man: A Comprehensive Guide to the Traditional Guru-Devotee Relationship* (1990), pp. 160-188: "The Nine Principal Functions of the Sat-Guru"; and a condensed version, *Divine Distraction: A Guide to the Guru-Devotee Relationship* (1991) [new edition forthcoming].

15. James Steinberg, *Love of the God-Man* (1990), p. 162.

16. Adi Da Samraj, *The Aletheon* (2009), pp. 664-665.

17. James Steinberg, *Love of the God-Man* (1990), p. 178.

18. See: *The Heart's Shout: The Liberating Wisdom of Da Avabhasa* (1993) by Adi Da Samraj [Da Avabhasa].

19. See: Adi Da Samraj, *Not-Two Is Peace: The Ordinary People's Way of Global Cooperative Order* (2009 3rd edition, 2019 4th edition) by The World-Friend Adi Da.

20. Adi Da Samraj, *The Method of Siddhas* (1973, 1978), p. 308; now in *My "Bright" Word* (2007).

TWENTY FOUR

DEVOTEE'S RESPONSE: ENLIGHTENMENT NOW

The specific Guru-Function is associated with the Great Principle of devotional Communion with the Adept-Guru (and with the unique Spiritual understanding of attention). Therefore, since the most ancient days, all truly established (or real) Spiritual practitioners have understood that devotional Communion with the Adept-Guru is, Itself, the Great Means for Realizing Real (Acausal) God, or Truth Itself, or Reality Itself".

— **Adi Da Samraj**, 2008[1]

GIFT OF THE DEVOTEE: GURU DEVOTION

Satsang or Guru Yoga is a two-way street: not only does the Guru-Adept provide sacred functions to serve his or her devotee but we too must serve the Guru. The "function" or responsibility of the devotee (or student) of any genuine Guru or Adept-Realizer is *to practice* their instructions, to "**engage the injunctions**" (as Ken Wilber likes to say)—to *do the Yoga*, to live the "Practicing School" (not merely the "Talking School")—to do spiritual disciplines or *sadhana* as a condition of Guru Yoga-Satsang. This process *transforms* the development of consciousness from infancy to the emergence of a personal ego-"I" into adulthood to potentially catapult us into the transpersonal and mystical Stages of Life via self-transcendence and dedicated meditation. In other words, each one of us may become a Shaman, Yogi, Saint, Sage, or Siddha, or simply a beautiful person awakened to God Consciousness. In Ken Wilber's AQAL terms, this process is about transforming "**states into traits**" which means converting *temporary* experiences of altered and awakened *states* of consciousness into the *permanent traits* that accompany the highest (and most complete) *stages* (or *structures*) in the evolution of Enlightened Awareness (i.e., growing or evolving from the first Three Stages into the Fourth Stage then to the Seventh Stage of Life).[1]

In Avatar Adi Da's developmental model of the Seven Stages of Life most spiritual consciousness growth in the Great Tradition involves the first Six Stages of Life (specifically with the Fourth to Sixth Stages) while the Seventh Stage is reserved for complete Whole Body Nondual Enlightenment, a rare occasion [see Appendix I].[2] A devotee's responsibility, therefore, is to transform his or her temporary experiences of Darshan-Transmission and various intuitive mystical insights into permanent Awakened God-Realization actively being love in all relations. The devotee must function through disciplined conscious exercises and practices (*sadhana*) to fulfill the Guru-Adept's Way of *Satsang* by going beyond the contracting compromises of our Narcissistic ego-activity.

Satsang is the time-honored path of the world's Great Siddhas and wisest Spiritual Adepts regardless of culture or century, from Krishna to Buddha to

Christ to Ramana to Adi Da, et al [see Part II]. Every one of them demands we live *right life* and *right devotion* (as they did in relation to their own Gurus) to achieve their degree of Awakened Realization (and Stage of Life). From a Guru-Adept's point of view (especially Avatar Adi Da's) the result of sadhana-Satsang is to live a life-positive existence full of love and creativity involving the whole bodily being. Our life's purpose is to *live in* God, not *seek for* God. The Avatar emphasizes that his Way of the Heart is life-positive, not world-denying:

> The Reality-Way of Adidam is "world"-positive, life-positive, body-positive, sex-positive, happiness-positive, and in every sense positive. My devotees have learned this through the trial of their own "experiment" and "foolishness". Therefore, they highly value and cherish that "experiment" and that "foolishness". They are even more "foolish" now in their freedom, since they no longer suffer the doubt, "self"-division, and "self"-hatred that are the essence of conventional minds and the common suffering of humankind.[3]

The main function of the devotee is to naturally follow his or her Guru's instructions, to take up the recommended practices and disciplines, and hence replicate the Guru's Realization (or state-stage of development). This has been a principal purpose of Satsang cultivated by devotees and Gurus in the past and inevitably into the future. It has been universally proclaimed throughout the world's sacred scriptures and spiritual texts. Nevertheless, the primary purpose is to become Enlightened or God-Realized, knowing Truth or Reality as It IS, to be a force of love and wisdom in the world. Ultimately, the Guru-devotee relationship is a reciprocal one since each serves one another. Yet, the Guru gives the greatest gift of God-Realization so we must give back. This is why the famous Tibetan Buddhist sutra *Fifty Verses of Guru-Devotion*, attributed to Asvaghosa (80–150 CE), clearly suggests:

> Giving to your Guru is the same as making continual offerings to all the Buddhas [Enlightened Adepts]. From such giving much merit is gathered. From such collection comes the supreme powerful attainment of Buddhahood [or Enlightenment].[4]

This admonition is true whether we're speaking about any of the world's greatest Spiritual Masters. Every culture has had its own special Master-

Adept, but now it's time for a World-Adept to emerge in order to unite the religious aspirations of humankind like never before. Adi Da Samraj is potentially this Maha-Siddha if our response to his Satsang is genuine. The need for our emerging global culture to spiritually align with the authentic self-transcending and *spiritual* methods of the Guru-Adepts has become a vital necessity. A true Integral Age must go beyond the limits of both the Eastern (Alpha) and the Western (Omega) mind. We must move past premodern mysticism and religious myths while transcending (yet including) modern science. Adi Da provides this spiritual capacity and authentic relationship (and leadership) that humanity needs and requires. This is true even after his Mahasamadhi (or bodily death) since his Heart-Transmission is still profoundly active, especially if a person goes to his spiritual Agencies maintained at his Sacred Sanctuaries in Fiji, California, Europe, Australia, India, and elsewhere. Adi Da frequently addressed the importance of his Agencies, as he does here:

> The appearance of the Adept is a very rare event. When it occurs and a Great Teaching arises, a great opportunity also appears.... My purpose is not only to Teach and be of use to you during my lifetime, but to establish you in such a relationship to Me that after my lifetime an Agency will continue to exist sufficient for this practice.
>
> I expect you to use the Divine Influence Transmitted in My Company, not just while I am alive, but after I am gone, so that the process will continue.... I have already established means that will continue beyond my lifetime, such as the Sanctuaries... [they are] a place of Transmission and always will be. Even the Teaching is a direct Transcendental Agency.
>
> Among all the Agencies that will continue and that are already secured... there must be a living community of people who have practiced in all the stages [of life]. Thus, there must be a community of people practicing in the advanced stages.... because I am not coming back![5]

A living *transformative* relationship with a genuine Guru is the esoteric secret behind the world's religious teachings, as this book has tried to show. It's best we don't deny this sacred process and corrupt the Transmission of God-

Light under the complaint of cultism, as many Westerners do. The Satsang-relationship is not simply philosophy or theology, nor even an integral philosophy, or any one of the many mental ramblings of the inquisitive mind and egoic self. It far transcends even the practical knowledge gained by scientific investigation into the material processes of Nature. It even transcends the limits of yogic mysticism or extraterrestrial possibilities. It is the natural outcome of heartfelt realization of Divine Existence because it reflects the Truth of Reality. This process of spiritual *transformation* of consciousness in Satsang leads to Whole Body Enlightenment, the ultimate potential of all human beings. It is to everyone's advantage, not just for any individual, nation, or tribe but for the whole world. Satsang awakens the heart to Real God thus confirming that the true function of the Adept-Guru is to reveal the Divine Truth to every individual (whether a devotee or not).

But we cannot forget that Guru Yoga-Satsang is also a "**fire**"—called *tapas* or "heat"—since ego-transcendence frustrates the self-sense of the ego (and its conventional addictions). Satsang is difficult and demanding as well as blissful. Satsang is not a practice of egoic glory or self-fulfillment but one of self-surrender and service to others. Thus, Satsang is not easy to fulfill under the various conditions and demands of modern life. Consequently, many modern people become discouraged for their lives are already busy and complicated. Who's going to take the time to meditate and study the sacred Dharma?

Nonetheless, this is no reason to shun the special relationship to a Guru altogether. Learn at least to study them and honor them. To live Satsang is to live a life of delicious delight in Divine Communion, when lived correctly. It is a sign of real human maturity, not childish cultism. It empowers people to awaken to their innate higher potentials unlocking the best of their born existence. Your life and love relations become brighter. Your creativity increases, your happiness deepens, and your mind finds true peace. According to the Masters, Satsang also serves our journey after death and into possible future lifetimes. What, then, could be a greater Message and practice than this?

In his essay titled "Adept-Realizers Are The Esoteric Root of All Esoteric Traditions" published in *The Pneumaton* (2011), Avatar Adi Da reviews the functions of the God-Realized Adept operating as Siddha-Guru for others:

> The Adept-Realizer, or Spiritual Master, has many functions—to exemplify the Way, to argue the Way, to Bless devotees, and (thus) to interfere with the usual attitude and disposition of devotees, and to Transmit Spiritual Influence tangibly to devotees so that they will then, having understood themselves, be capable of Spiritual growth. The function of the Spiritually Realized Adept, therefore, does not come to an end with the arising of any particular result. The Adept-Realizer (or Guru) is the continuous and unending resource and resort of his or her devotees.[6]

When you feel God and Love-Bliss awaken in the heart as a direct result from your relationship in Satsang with someone like Adi Da Samraj, then you will feel boundlessly grateful and thankful. Your joy may be so profound that your knees bend and you bow down in gratitude and love. Since the Adept-Realizer ultimately gives the gift of God-Realization, then the student or devotee is naturally moved to give back in a sacred cycle of gift-giving called *prasad* (in Sanskrit).

PRASAD—RETURN THE GIFT TO THE GIVER

In exoteric or ceremonial terms the relationship of Satsang between a devotee and his or her Guru is performed via a simple ritual, one that Adi Da has emphasized as being archetypal of the entire process. He calls it the "**Sacrament of Universal Sacrifice**" since it enacts the law or principle of *mutual sacrifice* involving surrender of self between both devotee (or student) and the Guru-Adept. Not only does the devotee surrender (or turn attention) to the Guru, but the Guru is *always* surrendering to devotees (and all beings) by instructing and serving their spiritual development. This mutual exchange process is ***Prasad*** (in Sanskrit) which means "return the gift to the giver."

The devotee first offers the gift of self by transcending the ego's flow of thoughts or the separative act that is the "avoiding of relationship" (in Adi Da's terms). Then the Guru returns the gift of Prasad after it has been infused with his (or her) Spiritual Heart-Transmission. By these means the devotee is initiated into a deeper intuition of our Divine Condition. Yet, like many reciprocal relationships, the gift of seeing God as your own consciousness depends upon one's ability to receive it—ultimately, it's a gift of Divine Grace. But when it works, there's nothing like it. No one has made this process of Satsang clearer and more evident than Avatar Adi Da Samraj. Read his literature, turn to Him as Siddha-Guru, and practice his Way of the Heart—the Reality-Way of Adidam Ruchiradam—and discover for yourself.

The *exoteric* or bodily enacted ritual of Prasad usually involves small objects as symbolic gifts of exchange. This ceremony becomes an esoteric process between Guru and devotee performed as the simple act of gift giving. The devotee brings a gift, generally a flower, fruit, or leaf (or any appropriate object, even money) and offers it at "the Feet" (i.e., the body or photograph) of the Guru as a symbol of his or her self-sacrifice to the Divine Reality embodied in the Guru. Prasad consecrated this way is a bodily and mental *symbol* of self-surrender. A similar process also occurs in meditation when one's mind-thoughts are surrendered into Spirit, the Heart-Transmission of the Adept, as breathing is steadied and attention is set free for heartfelt Divine Communion.

Gestures of this symbolic ritual, such as respectfully bowing (including full-body prostrations), are done to gratefully acknowledge the Guru's Divine Transmission and Gift of Instruction for the spiritual transformation of consciousness. This process is further acknowledged by the Guru by returning to the devotee a piece of fruit or a sweet (or small gift) as a symbol of the *Shaktipat* Heart-Transmission which the Guru gives freely to all beings. A traditional example of this ritual in Christianity is the sacrament of Holy Communion or the Eucharist (in Catholicism), which is when Jesus (as God's Agency) offers his "body" (bread) and "blood" (wine) so the disciple may be aligned with the Holy Spirit of the Father (God).

In Adidam (during Adi Da's years in the body), this sacrament of universal sacrifice of Prasad was most often performed during occasions of **Darshan** (or the "Sighting" of the Guru) when Adi Da would sit in silent meditation with his devotees. Many of the ceremonial photos of Adi Da and devotees seen by the public are enacting this practice or **puja** (Sanskrit for "worship") as the "bodily worship of the Living God" (in Adi Da's words). For example, when Adi Da places his open hands over a dish of fruits or cookies he empowers them with his Siddhi-Transmission or Spirit-Blessing; then they are given out to attending devotees who gratefully receive the Guru's blessing. During meditation this process is replicated inwardly: surrender (of self) and reception (of Spirit). Even now (after his bodily death) these puja ceremonies of Prasad, when done in the Adidam community of devotees (or alone), can evoke devotional feelings and reception of Adi Da's Heart-Transmission. I also liked to envision Adi Da's hands as blessing humankind as a whole, not merely empowering a bowl of fruit.

Prasad, therefore, represents the gift of surrendering the emotional habits and thought-patterns of the ego in order to open the self to receive the Avatar's *Ruchira Shaktipat*, the Spirit-Baptism that descends from the Bright Divine Domain into the heart of the devotee. When done in a devotional manner there is a heart opening revealing the Divine Reality more clearly. Such Prasad, in other words, is a form of Holy Communion, not cultism. My experience during these occasions always felt them to be a sincere and tender gesture of gratitude, not a cultic ritual of artifice. It is a simple occasion, not one of exaggerated emotionalism. Beyond mental *theology* this is **theurgy** (or "God work") when bodily enacted rites are used to support the spiritual practices that actually produce real inner transformation. It is a time-honored tradition, in both East and West. At best, it is Enlightenment *now*, in real life, in real time: the bodily and heartfelt worship of the Living God.

This process of self-surrender is also remembered and practiced in daily life since this puja is the essence of Divine Communion. The Way of Adidam does not turn devotees away from the world through inward inversion (such as with meditation) but embraces the world—while transcending the point of view of the ego-self—as being the "body" (or Spirit) of God. Avatar Adi Da explains:

> The Way that I Teach does not involve the strategic negation of either the functional self or the Realm of Nature. The self-contraction is simply to be observed, understood, and transcended, so that the Divine Self-Identity is Revealed. The Divine Self-Identity is not *within* the self. It is not an interior subjective essence. The Divine Self-Identity is the Radiant Consciousness from and in which the egoic self-consciousness is contracting.[7]

The sacrificial surrender and opening of the self-contracted ego-I allows Spirit-reception to synch up with every breath in the here and now. This mutual sacrifice (and gift) is ultimately about heart-feeling, not mind and thoughts. However, it's not emotionalism either or hyping up the body-mind to feel better; it is about ecstatic self-transcendence in moment-to-moment Divine Communion. When done properly the radiant form of the Avatar (or Divine Incarnation), who has already "sacrificed" his ego (in the Seventh Stage of Life), shares with the devotee an intuition of the Divine Heart by radiating his Enlightened State. In my experience, *this* is precsiely what happens in the Reality-Way of Adidam Ruchiradam, nothing less. This is the genuine process of Guru Yoga-Satsang available to all.

Many stories (or *leelas*) about Avatar Adi Da are based on people's direct experiences in His Company that confirm this *spiritual* reception of Spirit Awakening, as thousands have confessed. Scholar James Steinberg points out: "The mutually sacrificial relationship between the Realizer and the aspirant is the centerpole of the entire Spiritual Process."[8] When the devotee opens his or her heart to surrender self by moving beyond the limitations of the contracted ego-I, then the Guru's Transmission offers the Gift of Divine Revelation to the devotee. It is as simple (and profound) as that. This is Grace-in-action.

Yet don't be fooled: nothing is guaranteed since this esoteric process is ultimately an act of Grace (or a mysterious process). The ego must surrender so the devotee is open to receive the Guru's Spirit-Baptism. What is certain is that the ego can shut down its own Divine Help, thus spiritual practice and devotion becomes essential. The gesture of sadhana practiced in Satsang is the response running the *esoteric* relationship between the authentic Spiritual Master and student, between the Guru-Adept and devotee, as is evident throughout human history in the Great Tradition of Global Wisdom… as is evident even today [see Part I]. True Satsang, in Adi Da's words, is a "**recognition-response**" to seeing and *realizing* God's living Presence, not a rote ritual of mind or ego or done for the self's glory. May all beings be blessed to receive this Divine Gift of Grace and then give back the gift of love and service in return for awakening to Real God.

THE LESSON OF LIFE: *BE* ALWAY ALREADY HAPPY

In the Way of Radical Understanding as taught by Adi Da Samraj, one of the most important responsibilities of the devotee is to become accountable and responsible for the self-contraction or the unloving activity of the ego. Since he first began teaching, Adi Da points out that the ego-I (or our sense of being a separate self) is best *understood* not as an entity inside but as an *activity* of contraction upon the innate bliss (and happiness) of Consciousness Itself. In his words, the contracted ego is an activity of "avoiding relationship"[9] or turning away from love. We are all doing this activity of self-contraction, often felt as a knot or tension in the body (usually in the heart or the vital center of the navel) or simply as the dilemmas and problems in life. The ego is constantly thinking or trying to pleasurize itself to avoid the pain and suffering of feeling alone, separate, and afraid. To *understand* that *it is us* who is generating this activity helps us to *consciously* release it and be love in all relations; no need to blame others. Love-Bliss and Happiness are our natural condition, our primordial state, teaches Adi Da, so it's best (and possible) to *be happy* and loving without attaining anything. The American-born Avatar directly reveals:

> The Spiritual Divine Incarnates or becomes Obvious in the Living body-mind and the world when attention is released from the self-contraction into the Divine or Transcendental Self-Identity—and when the body is released from the self-contraction and from the egoic mind into the Free Condition that is the Matrix of Nature and the Current of Life and Light that pervades the total world.
>
> If we [establish] ourselves in the conscious process of always present understanding—or the present transcendence of the self-contraction that is sin itself ["missing the mark"]—then we will also and naturally be moved to Live in the Spiritual Divine. Our sins will begin to be purified and fall away once we begin actively to transcend the act and presumption that is sin itself.[10]

During the early years of his own sadhana (in the 1960s), Adi Da recognized that the ideal myth typifying this egoic activity is "**Narcissus**," the handsome young man of Greek mythology. Narcissus became so fascinated with his own reflection in the pond by contemplating his self-image he avoided all other activities and relationships. Fascinated only with himself, Narcissus even avoided the beautiful Echo calling his name (again and again and again), the young lady who was deeply in love with him. The ego is not just the outer personality or unconscious motivations studied by modern psychology (yet includes that as well) but it is mostly the *felt-sense* of being a separate "I" or entity. This feeling of separateness and self-concern goes beyond mere survival needs for it exists at the root of all suffering, the core of our psychological turmoil and dilemma. If you would only radically *understand* that you are generating this activity, this reactivity, then only *you* can release it and feel the Divine or God as Love.

The *Brihad-Aranyaka Upanishad* long ago in the forests of India noted: "It is from the other that fear arises."[11] Adi Da continues: "Where there is the slightest sense of an 'other'—wherever there is the presumption of separateness, wherever there is 'self'-contraction—there is fear. And fear motivates seeking, the entire life of illusion, the entire conditional display. All this drama of separateness and seeking is merely an illusion (or a disturbance) of natural cosmic Energy—and <u>you</u> (as the act of 'self'-contraction) are 'causing' it. The entire drama is totally unnecessary".[12] Ken Wilber too recognized this primary psychological error of the ego-self as he explains (with some help from Kierkegaard):

> Wherever there is self, there is trembling; wherever there is other, there is fear. However—and this is where the [spiritual] traditions transcend mere existentialism—these [spiritual] psychologies maintain that one can go beyond fear and trembling by going beyond self and other; that is, by transcending subject and object in *satori, moksha*, the Supreme Identity. But those traditions also maintain that the great liberation finally takes place only at the sagely level of causal/ultimate adaptation. All lesser stages, no matter how occasionally ecstatic or visionary, are still beset with the primal mood of ego, which is sickness unto death.[13]

This sensation of a separative ego-I is an *activity* of contraction away from love, away from the natural relatedness of life, away from the Happiness that is "always already the case" (as Adi Da says). By pointing out that our ego is an *activity* and that *we* (or every ego-I) are creating this for ourselves, then we can release it and simply *be happy*. No need for desire or to *seek* for happiness: just be happy! In his early Teaching-Years, Avatar Adi Da summarized this formula of understanding in what he called **The Lesson of Life:**

> **"You cannot <u>become</u> Happy. You can only <u>be</u> Happy."** Happiness is not a matter of subsequent action (or seeking) but of prior being. Happiness is Being Itself. Therefore, Happiness must be presently Realized, since It cannot ever be attained on the basis of Its prior non-realization.[14]

Once this self-activity is *understood*, the ego-contraction can be *transcended*. As Adi Da explained: "The Way that I Teach is based upon the serious observation and understanding of the entire process and mechanism of un-Happiness. It is only when the mechanism and full extent of un-Happiness is appreciated that the Way of Happiness Itself can be Realized."[15] Hence this is the "**Way of Radical Understanding**" taught by Avatar Adi Da Samraj (etymologically "radical" means "forming the root" or "at the root"). By *understanding* "I" create the self-contraction—like creating a fist—then "I" can release it (like an open hand).

The responsibility, therefore, for a person (or devotee) who has "heard" this argument, that is, realized the truth of this message—having tested its validity by observing one's life and activities—is to counter the self-contraction (or activity of Narcissus) by surrendering self and "expanding" to Infinity as the all-pervading Spirit of God. This means to *practice being love* in all relations; in other words, to simply *be Happy*. Happiness and Love-Bliss is our "always already" Enlightened Condition, according to Adi Da and all the world's Great Gurus. We don't have to generate it through method or technique or wait for special circumstances, those "million-dollar moments." We need only *understand* our contraction away from the truth of love, transcend it in awareness and then simply *be present* as Happiness Itself, our natural condition (or Buddha-Nature). As Adi Da noted: "Devotees of Real God ask for nothing but God."[16] This is the Adept-Guru's practical and spiritual message to everyone: turn to God and be Happy! This is the truth of Avatar Adi Da's Way of the Heart. How will *you* respond?

Avatar Adi Da is a living demonstration of this very Divine Realization of Happiness and the Enlightened State (even after his Mahasamadhi or bodily death). As he had always taught his devotees, the World Avatar instructs each of us: **"You always know how (or what it would be) to look, feel, be and act completely Happy"**[17]—so just *do that* by surrendering self and being God-Realized *now!* This is the Guru-Adept's great admonition to all beings (for all time).

"You always know how (or what it would be) to look, feel, be and act completely Happy" — Avatar Adi Da

This is the "**secret of change**," as Adi Da long ago explained: "You should look and feel and be and act completely happy under all conditions. Change your way of action and the subjective dimension itself will change naturally."[18] Instead of contracting as the self in the mood of fear, sorrow, and anger, *be love* in all relations, under all conditions, around the globe, to all beings (human and nonhuman), now and forever into the future. Love one another as if they are yourself (for they are); love the planet; love Nature; love all beings; love yourself. *This* is the practice Avatar Adi Da teaches; this is the import of genuine Guru Yoga-Satsang. *This* is the fruit (or gains) from living in *relationship* with him as Adept-Guru and God as Living Spirit. Let's listen again to the Avatar ask what you will do:

> Will you surrender to the Reality in which you are arising, or will you defend yourself for the rest of your life? Will you contract, will you withdraw, withhold, dissociate, separate, turn upon yourself? Will you avoid all relations, contract from them? Will you react, or will you simply remain in the natural position prior to the recoil?

Will you be present? Will you not avoid relationship? Will you shine as love to Infinity? Will you enter into complete Fullness of feeling relative to that Condition in which you are arising? Will you do that as a principle of existence, rather than what you are tending to do, which is to contract upon yourself and become afraid?

The recoil is the action that you perform, and it contains all suffering. But if you persistently remain present in relationship, then you begin to develop a different mind, you create a different form of life, and you become subject to a new understanding, a new Revelation. You begin to recognize the mere Presence of God. You begin to enjoy transformation of your conventional state by Divine Grace.[19]

A relationship with the Enlightened Guru in Satsang, who is always already Happy and Free, allows a person to observe (and understand) more deeply *their own activity* of unlove, of unhappiness (instead of blaming others or conditions). Instead of getting upset with the Guru over their perceived activities or behaviors (or Crazy Wisdom) it's better to look closer at your own unhappiness and transcend *your* reactivity. The call and demand is to always *be love* (under all conditions); to live love; to live right relationship with God, with the Guru, and with all other beings and relations in the Kosmos, at all times *now!* Enlightenment is the "ordinary mind" (as Zen says) *not* contracting or turning away from love. God-Realization is not hyped-up supernatural powers but simply the wisdom of being natural in the body, breathing and being happy. Satsang is not a childish cult but the maturity of an Awakened human being recognizing God as ever-present *now!* The liberated person (or devotee) is not elsewhere but is simply present and happy here and *now!* Adi Da has made this extremely clear in His Teaching and Heart-Transmission. Let me quote the Avatar at length as he asks us to sin ("miss the mark") no more:

> The Realm of Nature, or the total world of beings, is a multidimensional psycho-physical cosmos. The Transcendental Divine is the Ultimate Identity of all beings and the Truth or Real Condition of the entire Realm of Nature.
>
> While yet remaining utterly Transcendental, the Divine Being is unqualifiedly Radiant as the Identity and Condition of the total world and all beings. Therefore, the Divine Being pervades the total

world and all beings as "Spirit," the Radiant Life-Current, or the literal Sea of Light, of which all beings and things are but temporary and finite modifications made of the various constituents or elements into which this Sea of Light is fractioned in the Mystery of Nature....

The Transcendental Divine is the Truth of the world and every being. The Life of devotional Unity with the Spirit of the Transcendental Divine is the inevitable evidence of the Realization of Truth. Spiritual Life is that practice which is founded on the understanding of self and Realization of Truth. Apart from such understanding and Realization, the self is the effective obstruction to self-understanding, Transcendental Realization, and Spiritual Life.

Until there is profound self-observation, self-understanding, and Transcendental Realization, the self is the active forgetting of the Spirit and the prior or eternal Oneness of the self, the world, and the Radiant Transcendental Being. Such forgetting of the Divine Truth, Reality, and Identity, and Condition is "sin." Sin is the self-contraction, the presumption of a concretely independent, separate, and separative self. It is the act in which the Transcendental Spiritual Divine is simultaneously denied and forgotten....

Spiritual Life requires the abandonment of sin, or else there is no Enlightenment and no end to sinning [and suffering]. What must we do? We must understand sin itself ["missing the mark"]. We must constantly observe and understand Narcissus, the machine of self-contraction, and always presently Awaken to that Disposition which is prior to the self-contraction and its consequences. We must Awaken to the Divine Self-Condition. We must cease to sin or suffer sin by Realizing the Divine Condition, Identity, Reality, Truth, Happiness, and Spiritual Substance. Only in that case do we transcend sin itself and live the Truth in the world.[20]

Only this type of *radical understanding* of self, one that initiates real ego transcendence as awakening awareness of Real God can ever end all conflicts, evaporate all wars, bring justice and equality to the human race, save the planet, realize always already Happiness. It is the principal message of Adi Da Samraj as Guru-Adept and World-Teacher, as Avatar and Jagad Guru, echoing throughout the centuries radiating from the heart of all enlightened beings.

Yet, fortunately, it seems never to have been clarified better than in the Wise Company of Avatar Adi Da Love-Ananda, the Ruchira ("Bright") Buddha.[21]

The admonition to *be love* instead of reacting to unlove and projecting unhappiness (in its multitude of forms) is true *spiritual life* in its essence. We do not need our ancient traditions to be a spiritual person but only to live in Spirit and Truth *presently* (like Jesus said). Thus it is our ever-present responsibility as a person, as a devotee of God, to positively project love and compassion to all beings and to protect and honor our Spiritual Master-Adepts who all bring light into a world (or cave) of darkness and ignorance (as Sokrates said).

Avatar Adi Da has made this Lesson of Life most obvious; it is the crux and core of His Teaching (outside of Satsang itself); it *is* the Reality-Way of Adidam Ruchiradam. Seeing (and knowing) God in Adi Da's Divine Company is the devotee's response to realizing Enlightenment *now!* He is the "Bright" Light or our Beloved Guru literally leading us out of the cave of shadowy illusions and evil, freeing us from samsara and maya. As any reasonable, open-hearted intelligent person must acknowledge, this wisdom is also the core morality and ethics found in all the world's religious teachings taught by all spiritual Sages throughout human history as God's Great Tradition of Global Wisdom.

The Teachings and Transmission of Divine Enlightenment is our universal inheritance bequeathed to us from God's Great Guru-Adepts. It is the Gift of Grace given to humanity by humankind's greatest Gurus and wisest women and men. *To be love*, to act as love, to give love, to know God *as* Love—what greater act and responsibility could be enacted for ourselves, for others, for our community, our nation, our Earth, our Kosmos? Let's give Avatar Adi Da Samraj himself the last (but not final) word:

So be Free.

Love God.

Be absolute Love.

Be free in your feeling and attention.

Give yourself up to Infinity.

Do not worry about having to be the beloved on your own account.

Sin no more. Do not miss the mark.

Do not contract upon yourself.

Love Me, live, and purify the Earth.

Not a single circumstance of experience is the Truth.

Love is the Truth, Love is Happiness,

and it turns you toward the destiny of God.[22]

Chapter 24 Endnotes

1. See: Ken Wilber, *The Religion of Tomorrow* (2017).

2. See: *Growing In God: Seven Stages of Life from Birth to Enlightenment—An Integral Interpretation* (forthcoming) by Brad Reynolds.

3. Adi Da Samraj [Da Free John], "Our Defense of the Body in God" Talk from February 1982 in *The Way of Divine Grace: A New Revelation of Spiritual Practice for Modern Men and Women: An Introductory Course on the Wisdom-Teaching of Master Da Free John* (Prepared by the Education Department of The Johannine Daist Communion. Only edition: 1984, Middletown, CA: The Dawn Horse Press)

4. Asvaghosa, *Fifty Verses of Guru-Devotion by Asvaghosa* (1976), p. 17.

5 Adi Da Samraj [Da Free John], *The Fire Gospel* (1982), p. 166.

6. Adi Da Samraj, "Adept-Realizers Are The Esoteric Root of All Esoteric Traditions" in *The Pneumaton* (2011), p. 190.

7. Adi Da Samraj [Da Free John], *The Fire Gospel* (1982), p. 195.

8. James Steinberg, *Love of the God-Man* (1990), p. 245.

9. See: Adi Da Samraj [Franklin Jones], *The Knee of Listening* (1972, 2004), *The Method of the Siddhas* (1973), which is now updated to *My "Bright" Word* (2005).

10. Adi Da Samraj [Da Free John], *The Fire Gospel* (1982), p. 194.

11. *Brihad-Aranyaka* Upanishad, I.IV.2.

12. Adi Da Samraj, *The Pneumaton* (2011), p. 534.

13. Ken Wilber, *A Sociable God* (1983), p. 50.

14. Adi Da Samraj [Da Free John], *The Bodily Location of Happiness* (1982), p. 97.

15. Ibid., p. 97.

16. Adi Da Samraj, *The Pneumaton* (2011), p. 534.

17. Adi Da Samraj [Da Free John], "Happiness Is Satsang" in *The Bodily Location of Happiness* (1982). p. 178.

18. Adi Da Samraj [Bubba Free John], *The Paradox of Instruction* (1977), p. 268.

19. Adi Da Samraj, "Will You Surrender, or Will You Contract?" in *Compulsory Dancing* (1980), p. 83.

20. Adi Da Samraj [Da Free John], from "The Incarnate Spirit of the Transcendental Divine" in *The Fire Gospel* (1982), p. 187, 188, 191.

21. See: I*n God's Company: Guru-Adepts As Agents for Enlightenment in the Integral Age* (2022) and *Meeting Adi Da: A Mandala of Approach to Avatar Adi Da Samraj* (forthcoming) by Brad Reynolds.

22. Adi Da Samraj [Da Free John], "The Golden Great Bright-Foreheaded Warrior" in *"I" Is The Body of Life* (1981), p. xxii.

Appendix I

Observe Me Standing Free Forever In The Center Of The Great Tradition
and "World" Circumstance Of all-and-All.
Observe Me Standing Free everywhere In The Great Tradition,
In Every Historical Period Observe My Likeness
In all times and places and cultures—but Know That
My Avatarically Self-Revealed Divine Word,
and All My Avatarically Self-Manifested
Divine Transcendental Spiritual Work, Is My Own.

— **Adi Da Samraj**
The Dawn Horse Testament

APPENDIX I

SEVEN STAGES OF LIFE:
MAPPING CONSCIOUSNESS EVOLUTION

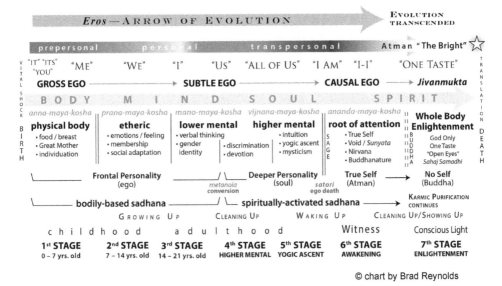

© chart by Brad Reynolds

o set the stage, so to speak, let's take a brief tour through Avatar Adi Da Samraj's "**Seven Stages of Life**" developmental model to better orient you to this book's basic perspective in appreciating Guru Yoga-Satsang in the Integral Age. The Seven Stages of Life is one of Adi Da's greatest gifts to humankind since it clarifies the bewildering subtleties of the world's spiritual teachings, from faith and belief to the highest yogas and stages of mysticism, the growth from a baby to a Buddha, from birth to Enlightenment [see chart above].[1] Only from the Fully Enlightened perspective, i.e., from the Seventh Stage of Life, do all of the partial truths of humanity, including those of the various Gurus and Adepts, become clarified so we may see everything inclusively as *one spectrum* of Clear Bright Divine Light revealing Real God as Consciousness-Cosmos. Significantly, the Seven Stages of Life framework parallels Ken Wilber's "**Spectrum of Consciousness**" developmental model—including all "four quadrants" of "**AQAL**" or the *exteriors* and *interiors* of *individuals* and *collectives*—since both models are following and outlining the universal "**basic structures**" or "**stages**" of human growth and "**states**" of human consciousness.

Since every person is born "at square one" (in Wilber's words), beginning with "vital shock" (in Adi Da's words), the lowest level of development, we are able to witness the fundamental developmental processes active in our unfolding evolution through a human lifetime, from conception to childgood to adolescence to adulthood to death, and even beyond; in other words, from the womb to the tomb. In these models there is a progressive arc of evolving complexity (complexification) where consciousness is best seen from the perspective of God Consciousness, our ultimate developmental potential. This is what the Seven Stages of Life / Spectrum of Consciousness models provide, which is why they are so useful for humanity. The graphic below depicts the "**Complete Human Life Cycle**" by overlaying Adi Da's "**Seven Stages**" on Wilber's "**Spectrum**" to picture the potential developmental arc (or spiral) growing from the *prepersonal* to the *personal* to the *transpersonal* stages of life, from babies to Buddhas, from infants to Sages:

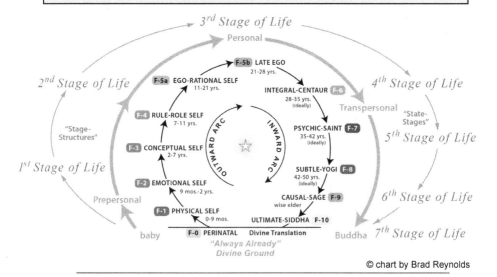

Complete Human Life Cycle

© chart by Brad Reynolds

Overall, the first Three Stages of Life (1–3) cover the development and coordination of the body-mind complex growing from infancy to childhood to adolescence to early adulthood in developing our physical and emotional and mental "bodies," i.e., evolving from the *prepersonal* to *personal* **stages** (thus preparing us to stand "on the brink of the transpersonal," as Wilber says, or the Fourth Stage of Life). The first Three Stages of Life, in this case, represent what Integral Psychology now calls "**Growing Up**"—from "me" to "we" to "I"—thus it involves the "**Frontal Personality**" or ego-I, our sense of being a separate self, also known as the "**self-system**"[2] that is navigating all the streams and waves, the levels and lines, the structures, stages, and various states (from *waking, dreaming, deep sleep,* to *altered* states). **States** of consciousness, which Wilber's Integral Psychology emphasizes more than Adi Da's model, can have important transformative effects on our level or stage of development.

Adaptation to and *horizontal* integration of a particular stage is called *translation*, while the *vertical* shift to a higher stage is *transformation* (in Wilber's terms). The higher *transpersonal* states, for example, such as psychic and subtle experiences, causal and nondual awakenings, can act as "**attractors**" that encourage the ego-I or sense of self-identity to expand conscious awareness into further growth or "**Waking Up**" (in Wilber's words). Such awareness of the entire progressive developmental arc allows us to avoid the "**pre/trans fallacy**" or confusing the prepersonal and transpersonal simply because neither is solely personal, one of Wilber's fundamental contributions to modern psychology. It is the self-system that is the balancing act of the psyche, involving the domains of *unconscious, subconscious,* and *conscious* elements of awareness (including subpersonalities, shadows, projections, etc.). The development of the **compound individual** person optimally reaches maturity and equanimity by early adulthood (21 years of age), ready for the creative adventure of life in the larger world culture and Kosmos, including further spiritual growth.

With adulthood maturity, the later Stages of Life (4–7) involve the *transpersonal* (or "personal-plus") stages, again, what's called "**Waking Up**"—as we grow from "all of us" to "I Am" to "One Taste"—awakening the "**Deeper-Psychic Personality**," traditionally known as the "**soul**" (which supposedly transmigrates from lifetime to lifetime). These transpersonal stages have produced "**advanced-tip**" individuals known as Shamans, Saints, Yogis, Sages,

Siddhas, and Buddhas, and so on. The levels or stages currently used by Wilber
in the Spectrum of Consciousness correlate closely to Adi Da's Seven Stages of
Life model as pictured in the two rainbow spectrum graphics below:

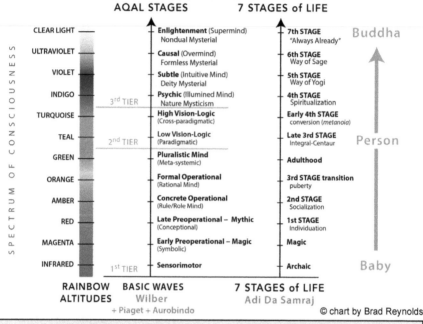

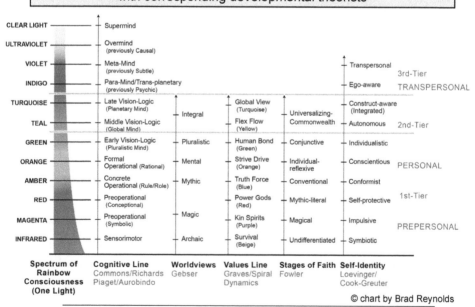

In all cases (thus potentially for *every* human being), Whole Body Divine Enlightenment is available for everyone, since it *transcends-yet-includes* the soul (*atman*) or any sense of being a separate self by happily dissolving into the Prior Unity and Love-Bliss of the True Self (Atman), which is Consciousness Itself (the "Divine Person" or Real God), the true Source-Condition (or Creator) of the cosmos-Kosmos (Brahman)—a condition known as God-Realization (*gnosis, satori, prajna, rigpa,* plus other traditional terms). Ultimately, this evolutionary process involves "**Divine Translation**" (in Adi Da's words), an "**Outshining**" of all conditional forms and relative realities merging the self-soul into the "**Brightness**" of the Transcendental Divine (the final transformative phase in the Seventh Stage of Life), the pinnacle of all evolution (and ultimate purpose of our birth).[3]

AQAL ANALYSIS:
"ALL-QUADRANTS, ALL-LEVELS"

The "**Four Quadrants**"—Ken Wilber's term for the evolution of (1) *interiors* and (2) *exteriors* of (3) *individual* and (4) *collective* holons (or whole/parts)—can be mapped alongside Adi Da's Seven Stages of Life Model since they're both reflecting natural human developmental patterns, from birth to Enlightenment. The "*quadrants*" include the basic "stages" or "structures" or "waves" or "levels" of consciousness and bodily development (which are generally permanent yet are "transcended-and-included" as growth proceeds), as well as including the various "lines" or "streams" of development (which are more temporary and transitional) as the "**self-system**" navigates growth (or evolution) through a "morphogenetic developmental space" (in Wilber's terms). All of these "four conditions" of evolving holons (i.e., interiors-exteriors in individuals and collectives), as Wilber emphasizes, *tetra-interact* with corresponding *correlates* in the inner and outer domains of human experience (thus solving or erasing the dualistic body-mind "problem"). Human and social holons exist and operate as wholes within the larger holism of the expanding Kosmos (proceeding, generally, in a "transcend-and-include" manner).

This developmental process generates Integral Theory's so-called "**AQAL**" Matrix—"**A**-ll **Q**-uadrants, **A**-ll **L**-evels"—the "morphogenetic developmental space or field" that includes "all quadrants, all levels, all lines, all states, all types, etc.," which exist as the compound human holon. Wilber explains: "What the Great Nest represents, in my opinion, is most basically a great mor-phogenetic field or developmental space—stretching from matter to mind to spirit—in which various potentials unfold into actuality."[4] The graphic below outlines the corresponding characteristics of the "Four Quadrants" found in their respective developmental spaces or fields (where the self-system is repre-sented by Leonardo da Vinci's "Vitruvian Man") [see chart below]:

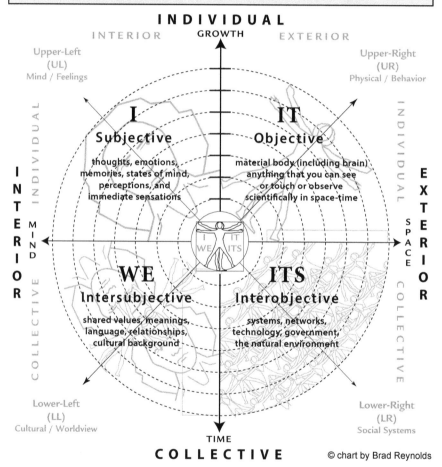

AQAL Analysis: Four Quadrants + All Levels

INDIVIDUAL

GROWTH

INTERIOR   EXTERIOR

Upper-Left (UL)
Mind / Feelings

Upper-Right (UR)
Physical / Behavior

I
Subjective
thoughts, emotions, memories, states of mind, perceptions, and immediate sensations

IT
Objective
material body (including brain) anything that you can see or touch or observe scientifically in space-time

INTERIOR INDIVIDUAL MIND   SPACE INDIVIDUAL EXTERIOR

I IT WE ITS

WE
Intersubjective
shared values, meanings, language, relationships, cultural background

ITS
Interobjective
systems, networks, technology, government, the natural environment

COLLECTIVE   COLLECTIVE

Lower-Left (LL)
Cultural / Worldview

Lower-Right (LR)
Social Systems

TIME

COLLECTIVE   © chart by Brad Reynolds

    Importantly, every one of the Seven Stages of Life can be subjected to an "**AQAL Analysis**," which Wilber claims is necessary to be truly *integral* (or all-inclusive). This is the case since, after all, everything is One Divine Reality: Only God, God Only!

AVATAR ANALYSIS:
"ALWAYS ALREADY"

I n harmonious appreciation of both the Seven Stages and AQAL Spectrum models, I maintain that Adi Da's "**Seven Stages of Life**" model is fully AQAL-compliant, for it includes all quadrants, all levels, all stages, all states, all lines, all types, et al, as interiors and exteriors operating or "tetrameshing" as the "Stages of Life."[5] That is, the Seven Stages of Life includes (and transcends) the full spectrum of interiors and exteriors in the evolutionary growth of individual human holons, as well as being evident in collective worldviews, therefore, the Seven Stages include all "four quadrants" ("all the way up, all the way down," as Heraclitus and Wilber say).

Most important, although both models emphasize interior psychological development, they embrace all forms of evolution, from the cosmic to biological to spiritual, as all arising within (and as) Divine Spirit-in-action in an unspeakable display of wonder and awe. This is Reality as it IS, since, as Avatar Adi Da Teaches, Reality is "always already the case," a phrase Wilber has often used throughout his career.[6] "Always Already" is the both the Divine "**Ground**" and "**Goal**," the *immanent* and *transcendent* aspects of existence altogether, thus there is no need to seek for God because God is "always already the case." Simply Awaken and *realize* God IS the case as It IS.

It is true, Wilber's model of "**Spirit-in-action**" is more specific, filling in the details provided by modern psychology (including Spiral Dynamics), as well as science as a whole, thus further subdividing the unified spectrum by coloring in the rainbow, so to speak, thus making sure all "four quadrants" of interiors and exteriors in individuals and collectives, "all the way up, all the way down," are included. Hence, Wilber's Integral Psychology is proficient at identifying healthy psychological development through the unfolding stages, as well as suggesting treatment modalities and psychotherapies for the various forms of dysfunctional psychopathologies arising within each level (or structure).

Adi Da's model, on the other hand, is more general in outlining the basic features and growth patterns in human development since he is most concerned with your Enlightenment, not just psychological health (which is also included). This is why Avatar Adi Da offers Satsang or Guru Yoga, a spiritual *relationship* with an Enlightened Guru-Adept involving *transformative* spiritual practices (or sadhana), whereas the integral pandit provides a more intellectual and philosophical map of psychology for better *translating* (or interpreting) the various levels and stages of life. As Wilber often claimed: "I am a pandit [or philosopher], not a Guru." In this case, I maintain Adi Da's presentation is the most true and valid since it is the most enlightened, simple and direct.

Adi Da Samraj
(1939–2008)

Ken Wilber
(b. 1949)

For us, as humanity, both models effectively work together in a grand and gracious harmony creating an illuminating "map," which is not the territory of Reality but is describing our overall evolutionary development from infancy to Atman consciousness, from becoming babies to being buddhas (i.e., if all goes well). Both explain, for example, that gross-physical brain chemistry and subtle-energy chakras have their place; that atomic molecules and visions of gods and goddesses (as archetypes) address their unique levels of existence; that biology involves etheric and subtle energies (not yet uncovered by science); that the mind is embraced by soul, which is ultimately transcended-yet-included by causal spirit and nondual awakening (in the Heart).

In addition, collective socio-cultural evolution is recognized to mirror the development of the human compound individual—as "**onto-phylo parallels**" — among other revealing insights. It is a breakthrough understanding worthy of everyone's diligent study. Science, overall, does not contradict these views but supports them, although its language and mindset (or materialistic philosophy) cannot fully confirm or comprehend them either. Hence, the perspectives of science and spirituality, each opening or using different "eyes" or modes of knowing, each offering their own forms of valid knowledge acquisition, are able to share and give to us a more-embracing overall vision of reality.

SEVEN STAGES OF AQAL:
CHARTS & TABLES

*A*vatar Adi Da's model follows, yet expands upon, the traditional division of the number seven, such as with the seven chakras (reflected in our esoteric anatomy), to describe the seven *potential* **stage-structures** of human life (with a period of overlap between stages and ages); Wilber's version includes ten (often more) **"fulcrums"** ("F-#"), each with early and late phases, the major "turning points" in human development as he integrates the complex interplay of "**state-stages**" in our unfolding developmental growth.

The charts below briefly yet fairly comprehensively summarize the "**Seven Stages**" of our developmental potential using terminology from both the Avatar's and integral pandit's models. The first two tables outline the popular and widely-used developmental "**spectrum of consciousness**" based on Ken Wilber's version of Don Beck's "**Spiral Dynamics**"[7] (founded on Clare Grave's research), including correspondences to Wilber's collective worldviews (founded on Jean Gebser's work[8]) lined up with Adi Da's Seven Stages of Life model.

The second two tables are a "condensed outline" summary of the unfolding "**Seven Stages of Life**" (with their corresponding animal-symbols[9]), as outlined by Adi Da Samraj; which is followed by a table using Ken Wilber's "**integral psychology**"[10] terminology to depict the unfolding *state-stages* with their corresponding *worldviews* pictured as a rainbow of colors (roughly based on the color memes of Spiral Dynamics).

These tables are then followed by more detailed, expanded tables and charts (two for each stage) showing each Stage of Life with its corresponding AQAL Map in all Four Quadrants—the Upper-Left "I" of the *individual interior* holon; the Lower-Left "We" of *collective interior* holons; the Upper-Right "It" of *individual exterior* holons; and the Lower-Right "**Its**" of *collective exterior* holons—thus combining both models of development into one harmonious unity. The Avatar and integral pandit provide us with a brief overview of our human evolutionary story as the unfolding Stages of Life. This is the principal perspective used in this book (and my other books) to better appreciate the developmental potential being offered by genuine Guru Yoga-Satsang when guided by an authentic Enlightened Adept-Guru [see the following pages]:

Spectrum of Consciousness Evolution

Developmental Correlates

	Basic Structure	Age	FULCRUM	General Characteristics	Worldview	Relational Exchanges	Stages of Life
ONTOGENY					**PHYLOGENY**		
phantasmic-sensorimotor / emotional	-subatomic -atomic **MATTER** -molecular -polymer -cellular	Divine Ground *Bardos* peri-natal BPM:	**F-0** BIRTH	•undifferentiated, pleromatic	PRIMORDIAL INHERITANCE	material exchange	
	SENSATION	0	**F-1**	•self-enclosed, uroboric	ARCHAIC-	-food	
	PERCEPTION	-	PHYSICAL		UROBOROS	-labor	
	exocept	5/9 mos.	**SELF** infant	•hallucinatory wish fulfillment subject-object fusions	archaic- magical	emotional exchange	
	"hatching"						
	IMPULSE	9 mo.	**F-2**	"selfobject"			
	IMAGE		**EMOTIONAL**	•egocentric, word magic, narcissistic;	MAGICAL-	sex	
	SYMBOL	2 yrs.	**SELF**	locus of magic power = ego	TYPHON	-safety,	
rep-mind	**endocept**	2 - 4 yrs.	**F-3** self-concept	•ego omnipotence challenged; security; ego omnipotence transferred to gods	magic-mythic MYTHIC-	power -belonging	
	CONCEPT					mental exchange	
	transition		early childhood	•concrete-literal myths	MEMBERSHIP		
conop	**RULE/ROLE**	7 - 11 yrs.	**F-4**	locus of magic power = deified Other	(mythic literal)	-membership	
	late		**ROLE SELF**	•rationalization of mythic structures	mythic-	discourse	
	transition		education	demythologizing, formalizing	rational	-self-reflective exchange	
formop	**FORMAL** early	11-21 yrs.	**F-5**	•static universal formalism	RATIONAL		
	late		adult **MATURE**	•static systems/contexts	formalism		
	transition	21 yr. onwd.	**EGO** conversion	•pluralistic systems, dynamic- multiple contexts/histories	PLURALISTIC relativism	-autonomous exchange	
postformal	**VISION-** early						
	LOGIC middle		**F-6**	•integrates multiple contexts	HOLISTIC	- vision-logic	
	late	ca. 28 yr.	**CENTAUR** sadhana	•cross-paradigmatic; dialectical	integralism	- global exchange	
			psychic	developmentalism as World Process	PSYCHIC-	soul	
transpersonal	**PSYCHIC** early		**F-7**	•union with World Process; nature	SAINT	exchange	
	(vision) late		**SAINT**	mysticism; gross realm unity	shamanic,	-psychic vision	
		ca. 35 yr.	**YOGI**		yogic	-God communion	
	SUBTLE early		**F-8**	•union with creatrix of gross realm;	SUBTLE-YOGI		
	(archetypal)		high subtle	deity mysticism; subtle realm unity	archetypal,	-God union	
	late	ca. 42 yr.	satori		deity	spiritual exchange	
	CAUSAL early		**F-9**	•union with source of manifest realms;	CAUSAL-SAGE		
	(formless)		**SAGE**	formless mysticism; causal unity	formless	-Godhead identity	
Enlightenment	late	ca. 50 yr.	Enlightenment				
	NONDUAL early		**F-10** nondual	•union of form and formless;	NONDUAL	-sahaja samadhi	
	middle		**SIDDHA**	nondual mysticism; One Taste unity	Enlightened	-bhava samadhi	
	late	Divine Goal		•Divine Translation	*jivamukta*		

Based on Ken Wilber, *Up From Eden* (1981), *Integral Psychology* (2000)

AQAL Altitudes + Stages of Life

SPIRAL DYNAMICS COLORS

STAGES of LIFE   FULCRUMS/WORLDVIEWS   ALTITUDES of DEVELOPMENT

Color	Altitude	Description
3rd Tier		
CORAL	ULTRA VIOLET POST INTEGRAL (TRANS-PERSONAL)	Realizes Oneness. Exhibits wisdom, joy & love. Seen in saints and sages throughout history; Great Tradition.
2nd Tier		
TURQUOISE	TURQUOISE INTEGRAL (INTEGRAL-PLURAL)	Sees the World as alive and evolving. Holistic & Kosmos-centric. Lives from both individual self and trans-personal Self. Emerging now.
YELLOW	TEAL INTEGRAL (INTEGRAL-PLURAL)	Sees natural hierarchy and systems of systems. Holds multiple perspectives. Flexible, creative and effective. Online 50 years (1970 CE).
1st Tier		
GREEN	GREEN POSTMODERN (MENTAL-PLURAL) — Ecology, BLM	World-centric. Values pluralism & equality. Relativistic & sensitive. Civil rights & environmentalism. Online 200 years (1800 CE).
ORANGE	ORANGE MODERN (MENTAL-RATIONAL) — Science, Economics, Law	Values rationality & science. Individualism & democracy. Capitalism & materialism. Risk-taking & self reliance. Online 400 years (1600 CE).
BLUE	AMBER TRADITIONAL (MYTHIC-MEMBER) — Rural, USA Myth	Ethno- or nation-centric. Values rules, roles & discipline. Faith in a transcendent God or Order. Socially conservative. Online 5,000 years BP.
RED	RED WARRIOR (MYTHIC-MAGIC) — underground militias, gangs	Ego-centric, vigilant & aggressive. Impulsive and ruthless. Courageous determined and powerful. Online 15,000 years BP.
PURPLE	MAGENTA TRIBAL (MAGIC-TYPHON)	Sees the world as enchanted. Values ritual & deep community. Individual subordinate to group. Online 50,000 years BP.
BEIGE	INFRARED ARCHAIC (ARCHAIC-UROBOROS)	Dawning self-awareness. Survives through instinct, intuition and banding with others. Online 250,00 years BP.

COLLECTIVE — INDIVIDUAL

WILBER–GRAVES

STAGES of LIFE (ADI DA SAMRAJ) — FULCRUMS/WORLDVIEWS (WILBER-GEBSER)

- Seventh Stage of Life — Siddha — F-10 — Nondual Mysticism
- Sixth Stage of Life — Sage — F-9 — Causal Mysticism
- Fifth Stage of Life — Yogi — F-8 — Subtle Mysticism
- Fourth Stage of Life — Saint — Nature Mysticism — Shaman

Transpersonal
- early — Initiation — Integral-Centaur
- Late Vision-Logic — F-7
- Fourth Stage of Life — Spiritualization — Psychic exchange
- Early Vision-Logic

Conversion

Personal
- F-6 (adulthood) — Postmodern-"We" — pluralism
- Third Stage of Life — Integration — Mutual exchange
- F-5 (14–21 y.o.) — Modern-Ego — formop — Symbolic exchange
- F-4 (7–14 y.o.) — Mythic-Membership — conop
- Second Stage of Life — Socialization

Prepersonal
- F-3 (4–7 y.o.) — Verbal-Membership — late preop
- Magic-Mythic
- F-2 (2–4 y.o.) — Emotional exchange — early preop
- First Stage of Life — Individuation — Magic-Typhon
- F-1 (0–2 y.o.) — Physical exchange — sensorimotor
- Archaic-Uroboric

ADI DA SAMRAJ   WILBER–GEBSER

© chart by Brad Reynolds

Seven Stages of Life
Condensed Outline
Adi Da Samraj

ANIMAL SYMBOL	STAGE OF LIFE	CHARACTERISTICS	
	1ST STAGE OF LIFE Individuation	Conception to birth ("vital shock") to infancy to early childhood, from archaic (body-mind fusion) to magic and magic-mythic (primary process) worldviews; preop to conop.	
	2ND STAGE OF LIFE Socialization	Childhood to early adolescence involving etheric to emotional-sexual (differentiation) to socio-cultural development and integration.	
	3RD STAGE OF LIFE Integration	Adolescence and the emergence of will-power and rational reasoning (form-op) coupled with maturing sexual identity.	
	4TH STAGE OF LIFE Spiritualization	Spiritualization involves a "conversion" (*metanoia*) to the Divine or spiritually-based life expressing devotion and increased spiritual sadhana and meditation; bhakti-yoga, mantras, prayer, etc.	
	5TH STAGE OF LIFE Yogic Ascent	Yogic ascent of kundalini Life-Energy from the gross-physical to subtle-mind domains of attention; traditional Yogas and Yogis, including devotional Saints often displaying psychic-siddhis (or paranormal powers).	
	6TH STAGE OF LIFE Witness	Advanced Sages and Siddhas (*Jnanis*) who totally transcend self or ego-I (known traditionally as "ego-death") to discover the inner Witness-Consciousness (*Turiya*) or True Self-Realization; the Void or *sunyata*.	
	7TH STAGE OF LIFE Divine Enlightenment	Complete Divine Enlightenment where everything and every possible relative reality is tacitly realized to be the Absolute Reality or knowing God/Godhead to be "Always Already the Case."	

Ten Fulcrums
Ken Wilber's Integral Psychology
(+Spiral Dynamics)

		FULCRUM	CHARACTERISTICS
FIRST TIER			
Infrared	F-1	ARCHAIC-UROBOROS	Dawning self-awareness; survives through instinct, intuition, and banding with others. Online: 250,000 yrs. BP
Magenta	F-2	TRIBAL-ANIMISTIC	Sees the world as enchanted; values ritual and deep community; individual subordinate to group. Online: 50,000 yrs. BP
Red	F-3	MAGIC-MYTHIC WARRIOR	Ego-centric, vigilant and aggressive, impulsive and ruthless; courageous, determined, powerful. Online: 15,000 yrs. BP
Amber	F-4	MYTHIC-MEMBERSHIP TRADITIONALISM MYTHIC-RATIONAL	Ethno- or nation-centric; values rules, roles, discipline; Faith in transcendent God or Order; political-religious hierarchy; socially conservative. Online: 5000 yrs. BP
Orange	F-5	MODERN-RATIONAL	Values rationality, science, individualism, democracy, capitalism, materialism; risk-taking, self-reliant. Online: 500 yrs
Green	F-6	POSTMODERN-PLURALISM	Values pluralism, equality; relativistic and sensitive; civil rights, environmentalism; world-centric. Online: 150 yrs/
SECOND TIER			
Teal	F-7	HOLISTIC SELF	Sees natural hierarchy and systems of systems; holds multiple perspectives; flexible, creative, effective. Online: 50 yrs.
Turquoise		INTEGRAL-CENTAUR PSYCHIC-NATURE MYSTIC	Sees the world-kosmos as alive and evolving; holistic, kosmo-centric; lives as individual self + transpersonal Self
THIRD TIER			
Indigo / Violet	F-8	SUBTLE MYSTIC PARA-MIND	Yogic ascent of kundalini Life-Energy from the gross-physical to subtle-mind domains of attention; traditional Yogas and Yogis, including devotional Saints often displaying psychic-siddhis.
Ultraviolet	F-9	CAUSAL MYSTIC META-MIND	Advanced Sages and Siddhas (*Jnanis*) who transcend self (known traditionally as "ego-death") discovering the inner Witness-Consciousness (*Turiya*) or True Self-Realization; the Void or *sunyata*.
Clear Light	F-10	NONDUAL MYSTIC OVERMIND	Complete Divine Enlightenment where everything and every possible relative reality is tacitly realized to be the Absolute Reality or knowing God/Godhead to be "Always Already the Case".

© chart by Brad Reynolds

1st Tier
"Growing Up" — Frontal Personality

1ST STAGE OF LIFE

Infancy to Childhood	0–7 years olds [infrared-red]

INDIVIDUAL

First Stager
Physical Self
Emotional Self
Conceptual Self
"me"

Individuation

COLLECTIVE

Archaic-
Uroboros

Magic-
Typhon

STRUCTURES

Sensorimotor—Preoperational (birth–7 yrs.)

INFRARED

F-1 **Archaic** to **Archaic-Magic** (0–2 yrs.)—**Infant**
• Vital shock (birth) • "hatching" (9 mo.)
MAGENTA • First chakra: survival • **Sensorimotor**

F-2 **Magic-Animisn / early Preop** (2–4 yrs.)—**Toddler**
• Early Mind • language • Eye of Flesh
RED • Second chakra: emotion-etheric

F-3 **Magic-Mythic / late Preop** (4–7 yrs.)—**Child**
• kindergarten • losing teeth (6–7 yrs.)
• elementary school

STATES

"peak" child states: **causal to dreaming to waking state**
• **physical-sensory**: matter, sensation, perception, object perm
• **phantasmic-emotional**: bioenergy, libido, *élan vital*, *prana*
• **"image mind"**: mental "picturing" using images
• **Rep-mind** or **Preop** thinking: **symbols** (2–4 yrs.): talking
• **concepts** (4–7 yrs.) • **"will-mind"** • first-third chakra

CHARACTERISTICS

The **First Stage of Life** is when individuation takes place beginning with an emphasis on growing the gross-physical body and developing a sense of being a separate self, which is why modern psychology calls it **"ego-centric"** (or centered around the self's safety and survival needs) as the early mind emerges from **sensorimotor** to **preoperational** cognition with language differentiating mind from body. This is the "archaic" [crimson] and "magic" [magenta] worldviews leading from uroboric immersion in Nature to individualized separation as infants grow into toddlers into early childhood ideally set within the nurturing environment of family and spiritualized social culture.

1ˢᵀ STAGE OF LIFE — AQAL "All-Quadrants, All-Levels"

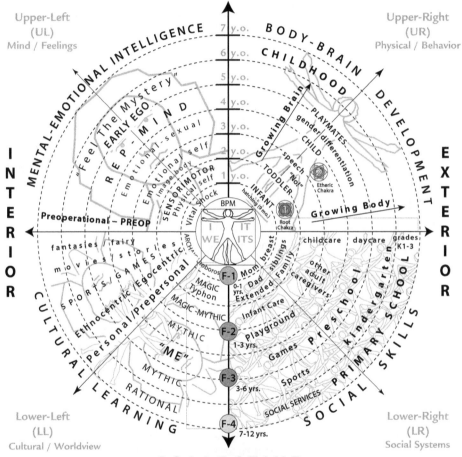

INDIVIDUAL

Upper-Left
(UL)
Mind / Feelings

Upper-Right
(UR)
Physical / Behavior

INTERIOR

EXTERIOR

MENTAL-EMOTIONAL INTELLIGENCE

BODY-BRAIN DEVELOPMENT

CHILDHOOD

7 y.o.
6 y.o.
5 y.o.
4 y.o.
3 y.o.
2 y.o.
1 y.o.

"Feel The Mystery"
EARLY EGO
REP-MIND
Emotional-sexual
emotional self
image-body self
SENSORIMOTOR
Physical self
Vital shock
Preoperational – PREOP

Growing Brain
PLAYMATES
gender differentiation
CHILD
speech
"No!"
TODDLER
INFANT
hatching (9 mo.)
Etheric Chakra ②
Root Chakra ①
Growing Body

childcare   daycare   grades K1-3

BPM
I   IT
WE   ITS

fantasies   fairy
movies   stories
SPORTS / GAMES
Ethnocentric / Egocentric
Personal / Prepersonal
CULTURAL LEARNING
ARCH?
Ouroboros
MAGIC Typhon
MAGIC-MYTHIC
MYTHIC
"ME"
MYTHIC
RATIONAL

Mom   breast
Dad   siblings
Extended Family
Infant Care
Playground
Games
Sports
SOCIAL SERVICES
other adult caregivers

Preschool
kindergarten
PRIMARY SCHOOL
SOCIAL SKILLS
PRIMARY SKILLS
SOCIAL

F-1   0-1 yrs.
F-2   1-3 yrs.
F-3   3-6 yrs.
F-4   7-12 yrs.

Lower-Left
(LL)
Cultural / Worldview

Lower-Right
(LR)
Social Systems

COLLECTIVE

INDIVIDUATION
"Growing Up"
1ˢᵗ Tier

© chart by Brad Reynolds

1ˢᵗ Tier
"Growing Up" — Frontal Personality

SECOND STAGE OF LIFE	
Childhood to Puberty	**7–14 years olds** [amber]

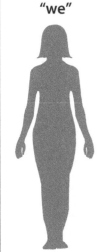

INDIVIDUAL		STRUCTURES
Second Stager Rule-Role Self **"we"**	**Concrete Operational** (7–11 yrs.) **AMBER** **F-4** **Mythic / Conop** (7–12 yrs.)—**child to preteen** • early mental • mythic-membership • etheric-emotional • ethnocentric **Mythic-Rational / Formop** (11–14 yrs.)—**puberty** • school • sports • service	

		STATES
	"peak" childhood states: imagination, role-playing • **Rule/Role mind**: take the *role* of others • **"sense mind"** • perform *rule* operations: multiplication, division, class inclusion • operates on sensory-concrete objects	

		CHARACTERISTICS
Socialization group identity **COLLECTIVE** Mythic- Membership	The **Second Stage of Life** is when **socialization** takes place with an emphasis on developing the **emotional-sexual** functions (and differentiations) involving the **etheric** energies of Nature, which are actively coordinated with the growing physical body; when the **"magic-mythic"** [red] evolves into **"mythic"** [amber] worldviews of **concrete operational** cognition the dominate mental characteristics that involve **"we-centered"** or **"ethnocentric"** morality (and self-identity) culminating in the **"mythic-rational"** [amber-orange] or **"traditional"** worldview. This is the stage when we develop emotional sensitivity with etheric Nature and other beings (animals and humans) while learning how to engage **"membership"** in the family while expanding awareness to the culture-society (with friends) as the gross-physical body and brain continues to grow.	

2ND STAGE OF LIFE — AQAL "All-Quadrants, All-Levels"

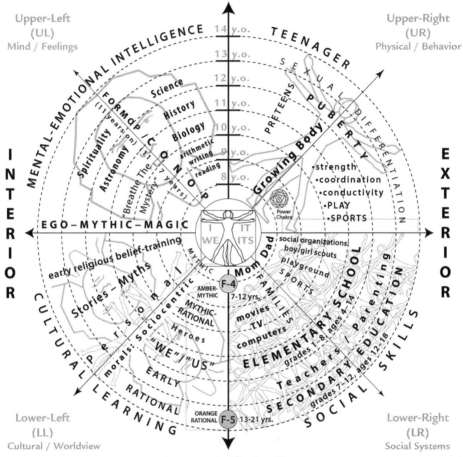

INDIVIDUAL

Upper-Left
(UL)
Mind / Feelings

Upper-Right
(UR)
Physical / Behavior

INTERIOR

EXTERIOR

MENTAL-EMOTIONAL INTELLIGENCE

TEENAGER

14 y.o.
13 y.o.
12 y.o.
11 y.o.
10 y.o.
9 y.o.
8 y.o.

SEXUAL DIFFERENTIATION

FORMOP (11 years)

CONOP ("concrete" 7 years)

Science
History
Biology
arithmetic
writing
reading

Spirituality
Astronomy
"Breathe The ___"
Mystery

PRETEENS
PUBERTY

Growing Body

Power Chakra

• strength
• coordination
• conductivity
• PLAY
• SPORTS

EGO–MYTHIC–MAGIC

I IT
WE ITS

early religious belief-training

Stories – Myths

personal

morals: sociocentric

Heroes

"WE"/"US"

EARLY RATIONAL

MYTHIC

AMBER-MYTHIC
7-12 yrs.

MYTHIC-RATIONAL

F-4

Mom Dad

FAMILIES

movies
TV
computers

social organizations:
boy/girl scouts
playground
SPORTS

ELEMENTARY SCHOOL
grades 1-8, ages 4-14

Teachers / parenting

SECONDARY EDUCATION
grades 7-12, ages 12-18

SOCIAL SKILLS

ORANGE RATIONAL F-5 13-21 yrs.

CULTURAL LEARNING

Lower-Left
(LL)
Cultural / Worldview

Lower-Right
(LR)
Social Systems

COLLECTIVE

SOCIALIZATION
"Growing Up"
1st Tier

© chart by Brad Reynolds

1ˢᵗ Tier
"Growing Up" — Frontal Personality

THIRD STAGE OF LIFE	

Adolescent to Adult	7–14 years olds [amber]

INDIVIDUAL		
Third Stager Mature Ego Sensitive Self "I"  **Integration**	**Formal Operational** (11 yrs. onward) **ORANGE** **Mental-Ego** / Formop (14–18 yrs.)—**teen** **F-5** • will power • sexual differentiation • independence / rebellion • Eye of Mind **Mental-Rational** / Pluralism (18–21 yrs.)—**adult** **GREEN** • rationality / science • discriminative mind **F-6** **Early Integral-Centaur**—adulthood • whole body-mind integration • holism • world-centric • transition to Fourth Stage	**STRUCTURES**
	"peak" formal-reflexive states: "think about thinking" • **formop**: self-reflexive • hypothetico-deductive • **vision-logic**: integrative, dialectical, creative synthetic • networks of relationships, "operates on" formop • **panoramic logic**: higher-order synthesizing, **"higher mind"**	**STATES**
	The **Third Stage of Life** is when integration takes place with the further development of mental functions (formal operations), including rational deductive reasoning [**orange**], a stronger sense of self, coupled with the increased function of will-power and self-directed intention to integrate with the maturing of the emotional-sexual character and physical body all being coordinated by the **"self-system"** ideally grounded in a holistic and balanced psycho-spiritual lifestyle, so that a healthy functioning ego or sense of "I" emerges [**green-teal/early vision-logic**], otherwise there's often dysfunctional behavior patterns and **psychopathologies**. True health and maturity is the purpose for "bodily-based sadhana" or psychological development supported by transpersonal psycho-spiritual practices all set within a cooperative community of family, friends, and the larger social order, ideally guided by a genuine Guru-Adept.	**CHARACTERISTICS**
COLLECTIVE Mental-Ego "the Hero" 		

© chart by Brad Reynolds

3RD STAGE OF LIFE — AQAL "All-Quadrants, All-Levels"

INDIVIDUAL

Upper-Left
(UL)
Mind / Feelings

Upper-Right
(UR)
Physical / Behavior

INTERIOR

EXTERIOR

Lower-Left
(LL)
Cultural / Worldview

Lower-Right
(LR)
Social Systems

COLLECTIVE

INTEGRATION
"Growing Up"
1st Tier

© chart by Brad Reynolds

2ⁿᵈ Tier

"Cleaning Up" — Deeper-Psychic Personality

FOURTH STAGE OF LIFE

"Servant" (devotee)	21 years onward [teal-turquoise]

INDIVIDUAL	STRUCTURES

INDIVIDUAL

Priest/ess
Shaman
devotional Saint
early Yogi

"all of us"

Conductivity

Divine
Communion

COLLECTIVE

Integral-Centaur

STRUCTURES

Vision-Logic to **Nature Mysticism**

Teal

F-6 **Integral-Centaur**—mid-to-late adulthood
• conversion "peak" experience (*metanoia*)
• Eye of Spirit • service to others
• kosmos-centric • Web of Life

Turquoise

F-7 **Psychic-Centaur**—Nature Mysticism
• spiritual practices / devotion to Divine-Spirit
• Cosmic Consciousness / one with Nature

STATES

"peak" psychic states: "Third Eye" (*ajna chakra*)
• preliminary meditation stages • heart opening
• **"illumined mind"** • culminates in **"Cosmic Consciousness"**

CHARACTERISTICS

The **Fourth Stage of Life** (21 years–onward) is the phase of **spiritualization** as the compound human individual adult (as a psycho-physical complex) [**green-teal-turquoise**] begins to surrender "beyond itself" into the Divine Source-Condition of the Kosmos, or (as Wilber says) when "a soul is on the brink of the transpersonal," thus stimulating devotional openness to God. This is when **exoteric** ("outer-directed") religion transforms—by **"Cleaning Up"**—into **esoteric** ("inner-directed") spirituality with **"conductivity"** of the Spirit-Current (via the breath)—initiating **"Waking Up"** (in Wilber's terms)—by breathing as/in **"Divine Communion"**, so we feel, as Adi Da explains: "a conditional union with the Spiritual Presence (or Spiritual Current) of That Divine Source." This **"Nature Mysticism"** culminates with **"Cosmic Consciousness"** opening the heart chakra (the middle station of the heart) to the **"Third Eye"** (*ajna chakra*) awakening transpersonal thinking and self-transcending love of God, the Source-Condition of the Kosmos, from atoms to Atman. Since adaptation is usually unstable, awareness must be cultivated (via "spiritually-based sadhana"), or else the **"Fourth Stage Error"** fails to transcend the state-stages of mysticism and spiritual seeking.

© chart by Brad Reynolds

4ᵀᴴ STAGE OF LIFE — AQAL "All-Quadrants, All-Levels"

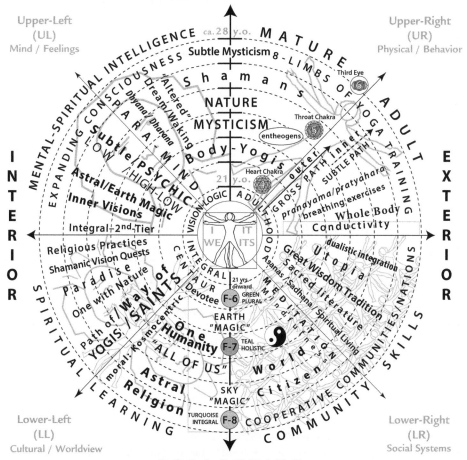

SPIRITUALIZATION
"Cleaning Up"
2ⁿᵈ Tier

© chart by Brad Reynolds

3rd Tier

"Waking Up" — Deeper-Psychic Personality

FIFTH STAGE OF LIFE

"Soul" (jiva/atman)	middle adulthood [indigo-violet]

INDIVIDUAL		

STRUCTURES

advanced Yogi ascended Saint

"I Am"

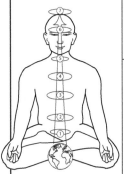

Subtle (Deity) Mysticism (yogic practitioner)

Violet

F-8

Yogi-devotee—kundalini ascent / inner brain
• Savikalpa samadhi: "ecstasy with forms"
• "Third Eye" (*ajna*) to Crown chakra (*sahasrara*)
• renunciation-celibacy • Tantra • theism

STATES

"peak" subtle states: *savikalpa samadhi, yidam*
• seat of archetypes, "Platonic Forms", personal deity forms
• subtle audible illuminations (*nada, shabd*) • **"intuitive mind"**
• culminates in **"God Consciousness"** ("I Am")

Arrow Kundalini Ascent

Ascent of Consciousness

CHARACTERISTICS

The **Fifth Stage of Life** (middle adulthood) involves the yogic ascent of subtle energies (*kundalini*) up the spinal line into the inner brain core to awaken states of **"Subtle (Deity) Mysticism"** [**indigo**]. These inward meditative states stimulate the kundalini **Life-Energy** (*shakti*)—or **"Circle of Conductivity"** and **"Arrow"** (in Adi Da's terms)—to activate the esoteric anatomy (chakras and channels) rising up the spine into the brain and beyond (from the bodily base to the "third eye" to the crown chakra), such as in *Savikalpa Samadhi* ("ecstasy with form"). Adi Da explains: "The plane of conditional 'self'-awareness ascends, to become dominantly subtle (or psychic)…and the Realization of conditional union with…the Divine Source [God-consciousness] …involves the ascent of attention, that eventually goes beyond physical [gross] references, and (at last) even beyond mental [subtle] references [**violet**]." However, identification with these conditional-temporary mystical state experiences, which are very blissful, slips into the **"Fifth Stage Error"** since a yogi often confuses "the garbage and the Goddess" (as Adi Da Teaches), therefore, "spiritually-based sadhana," under guidance of the Guru-Adept, must continue until Whole Body Enlightenment.

COLLECTIVE	
Shaman	Yogi

© chart by Brad Reynolds

5ᵀᴴ STAGE OF LIFE — AQAL "All-Quadrants, All-Levels"

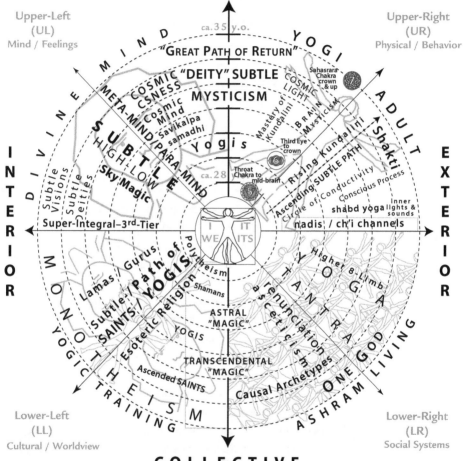

PATH of YOGIS / SAINTS
"Waking Up"
3ʳᵈ Tier

© chart by Brad Reynolds

3rd Tier
"Waking Up" — Witness-Emptiness

SIXTH STAGE OF LIFE

Witness "True Self" (Atman)	elder adulthood [ultraviolet]

INDIVIDUAL		
Arhat **Jnani Sage** **Siddha-Sage** "I-I" 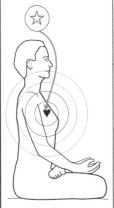 **Sahasrara to Heart on the right**	**Causal-Formless Mysticism**	**STRUCTURES**

STRUCTURES

Ultra-Violet **F-9**

Jnani / Sage—Witness Consciousness
- Jnana samadhi: "formless ecstasy"
- Heart-root (right-side) • *Turiya* state
- Emptiness-Bliss (*sunyata*) • Atman

STATES

"peak" causal states: *nirvakalpa samadhi, jnana samadhi*
- unmanifest transcendental ground • **"Overmind"**
- the Void (Mahayana), the Formless (Vedanta), the Abyss
- *Nirvana* (Theravada) • formless "True Self" (Atman)

CHARACTERISTICS

The **Sixth Stage of Life** (elder adulthood, or spontaneously at any age) is when the root of attention, or the "causal base" of the mind, is totally surrendered—traditionally known as "ego-death" (*satori*) so that "the Ultimate 'root' of the ego-'self'" is known to be the **Witness Consciousness** (*Turiya*), the True Self, prior to all objects and any sense of being a separate entity (correlated at root in the heart on the right). Known as *Nirvakalpa Samadhi* ("formless ecstasy")—or **"Formless Mysticism"** [ultraviolet]—it is felt as **The Void** or **Emptiness** (beyond self and all objects) or "Being Beyond Being" (Plotinus) and "God Beyond God" (Eckhart), thus is often expressed **"Abide As That"** (the True Self). However, this introverted and meditative state is often dissociated from the objects of the world-Kosmos, the archetype of the renunciate-ascetic Sage. Adi Da calls this tendency of dissociation, even when realizing Atman, the **"Sixth Stage Error"** (or **"Arhat's disease,"** in Wilber's terms), which is only fully transcended (and integrated) in the Nondual Mysticism of the Seventh Stage of Life.

COLLECTIVE

Saviors   Buddhas

6ᵀᴴ STAGE OF LIFE — AQAL "All-Quadrants, All-Levels"

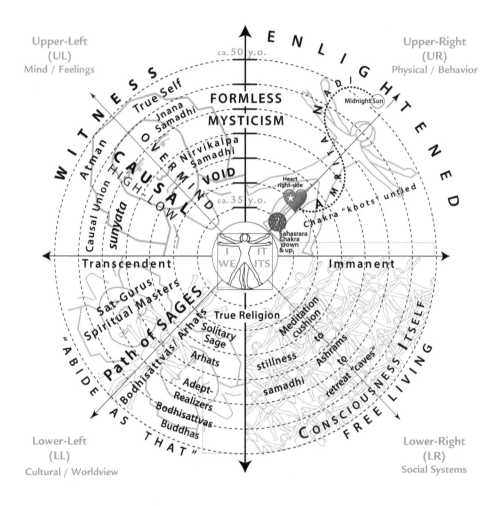

PATH of SAGES
"Witness"
3ʳᵈ Tier

© chart by Brad Reynolds

"Always Already"
Enlightenment — God-Realization

SEVENTH STAGE OF LIFE

Divine Enlightenment	any age [clear conscious light]

INDIVIDUAL		
Jivanmukti **Siddha-Guru** **Bodhisattva** "One Taste"	Ultra-Violet **F-9**	**Nondual Mysticism** **Siddha-Buddha**—Ultimate Consciousness • *Sahaj samadhi*: "Open-Eyes" • One Taste • Godhead / Absolute Spirit • *Atma-nadi / Amrita Nadi* • *Turiyatita* state	**STRUCTURES**

"peak" nondual states: *sahaj samadhi, bhava samadhi*
• "always already" • Ground-Goal • **"Supermind"**
• Suchness (Mahayana) • Atman-Brahman (Vedanta)
• The One & the Many • "nirvana is samsara" (Heart sutra)

STATES

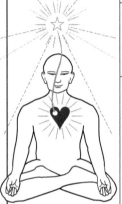

Amrita Nadi
Christ
Buddha
Avatar

The **Seventh Stage of Life**, the apex of consciousness evolution (and all existence), known as **Divine Enlightenment** or Real God-Realization—or **"Nondual Mysticism"** [**clear light**]—which is when "there Is Prior and Non-conditional (or Inherent, and Inherently Most Perfect) Self-Identification with Self-Existing and Self-Radiant Transcendental (and Self-Evidently Divine) Being, or the Divine Conscious Light" (in Adi Da's words), whether conditions arise or not arise—thus is often expressed **"I Am That"** or **"I Am"** (Consciousness Itself). In traditional terms, **"Whole Body Enlightenment"** is known as *Sahaj Samadhi* ("open eyes") or the integration of forms with the formless, yet also includes the complete transcendence of all forms in Radiant Formlessness known as *Bhava Samadhi* or when *Amrita Nadi* is "regenerated" from the heart on the right rising to the Conscious Light above and beyond the head (the **"Midnight Sun"** or "Divine Domain") leading to **"Divine Translation"** or **"Outshining"** (after death). This state-stage is our highest potential of existence, the farthest reaches of human nature, extending even beyond death.

CHARACTERISTICS

COLLECTIVE
Avatars / Siddhas

© chart by Brad Reynolds

7ᵀᴴ STAGE OF LIFE — AQAL "All-Quadrants, All-Levels"

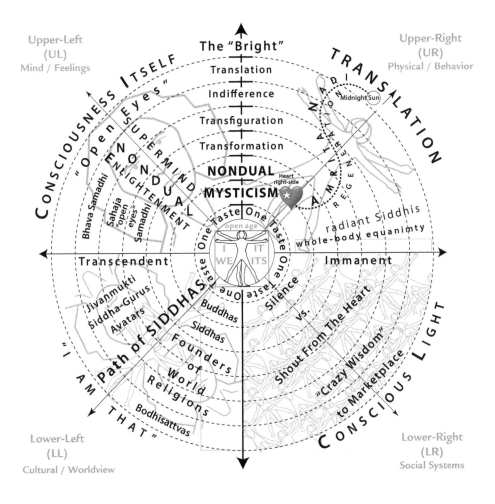

Upper-Left (UL) — Mind / Feelings
Upper-Right (UR) — Physical / Behavior
Lower-Left (LL) — Cultural / Worldview
Lower-Right (LR) — Social Systems

The "Bright"
Translation
Indifference
Transfiguration
Transformation
NONDUAL MYSTICISM
One Taste

CONSCIOUSNESS ITSELF
"Open Eyes"
SUPERMIND
NONDUAL ENLIGHTENMENT
Bhava Samadhi
Sahaja "open eyes" Samadhi
TRANSLATION
NADI
AMRITA NADI
REGENERATION
Midnight Sun
Heart right-side
radiant Siddhis
whole-body equanimty

Transcendent — I IT WE ITS — Immanent
open age

Path of SIDDHAS
Jivanmukti
Siddha-Gurus
Avatars
Buddhas
Siddhas
Founders of World Religions
Bodhisattvas
"I AM THAT"

Silence vs. Shout From The Heart
"Crazy Wisdom"
to Marketplace
CONSCIOUS LIGHT

PATH of SIDDHAS
"The Heart"
"Always Already"

© chart by Brad Reynolds

Appendix Endnotes

1. See: *Growing In God: Seven Stages of Life from Birth to Enlightenment—An Integral Interpretation* (forthcoming) by Brad Reynolds

2. See: Ken Wilber, *The Eye of Spirit* (1997), p. 227; *Integral Psychology* (2000); *Transformations of Consciousness* (1986).

3. This short review of the "Seven Stages of Life" is primarily based on Adi Da Samraj seminal essay "God-Talk. Real-God-Realization, Most Perfect Divine Self-Awakening, and The Seven Possible Stages of Life" in *The Pneumaton* (2011); also see: Ken Wilber, *Integral Psychology* (2000); *The Atman Project* (1980, 1996); *Transformations of Consciousness* (1986).

4. See: Ken Wilber, *Integral Psychology* (2000), p. 12; also see: p. 27: "The Great Nest is simply a great morphogenetic field that provides a developmental space in which human potentials can unfold. The basic levels of the Great Nest are the basic waves of that unfolding: matter to body to mind to soul to spirit.... Through these general waves in the great River, some two dozen different developmental streams will flow, all navigated by the self on its extraordinary journey from dust to Deity ['dirt to Divinity' was in original manuscript]."

5. See: books emphasizing the Seven Stages of Life by Adi Da Samraj, *The Seven Stages of Life* (2000), *Real God Is The Indivisible Oneness of Unbroken Light* (2002), *The Truly Human New-World Culture Of Unbroken Real God-Man* (2001), *The Only Complete Way To Realize The Unbroken Light of Real God* (2000), *My "Bright" Word: The Divine Siddha-Method Of The Ruchira Avatar* (2007).

6. See, for example: Ken Wilber, *The Spectrum of Consciousness* (1977): "'It is always already the case' is a phrase used extensively by Franklin Jones [Adi Da Samraj]," where the last chapter in Wilber's first book was titled "That Which Is Always Already"; also see, twenty years later, the last chapter to *The Eye of Spirit* (1997) titled "Always Already: The Brilliant Clarity of Ever-Present Awareness," one of his most profound and brilliant chapters ever penned.

7. See: Don Beck and Christopher C. Cowan, *Spiral Dynamics: Mastering Values, Leadership and Change* (1996, 2005); Don Beck, plus others, *Spiral Dynamics in Action: Humanity's Master Code* (2018).

8. See: Ken Wilber, *Up from Eden* (1982, 2007); Gebser, Jean, *The Ever-Present Origin* (1949, 1985).

9. Animal images for the Seven Stages of Life, as conceived by Adi Da Samraj, originally published in *The Laughing Man* magazine.

10. See: Ken Wilber, *Integral Psychology: Consciousness, Spirit, Psychology, Therapy* (2000).

Acknowledgments

I need to thank and acknowledge so many people and dear friends and supporters I am bound to leave some out. First and foremost, this book would not be possible without the Divine Presence of Avatar Adi Da Samraj. Secondly, my thanks and gratitude goes to my principal integral "guru" Kenneth Earl Wilber II. Next, unending thanks and gratitude goes to my publisher and integral brother Dustin DiPerna (of Bright Alliance) without whose support this book would not exist, as well as my literary agent the generous John White (an angel in my life). Artistically, divine thanks goes to Judith Parkinson, Adi Da's principal artist whose gorgeous creations graced this book to lift it into another realm. Editorially, sincere thanks for my other "set of eyes," Brad Brown and William Kopoecki who read and re-read my endless revisions. Loving thanks to those from Adidam who have always supported my work and writings, particularly James Steinberg, Carolyn Lee, and most importantly, Megan Anderson, without whose guidance and support this book would never have seen the light of day.

I also would like to thank those friends and women who gave me time and love and served my spiritual growth in becoming a better man, you know who you are; thank you. And to my men friends who supported me intellectually and spiritually, a list too long to include everyone, but particularly, Frank Marrero, Terry Patten, Brad Brown, John Burton, Dave Puccini, and Steven Elliot. A special thanks to those mystic music musicians whose divine music and lyrics inspired me for decades and have constantly led me forward and upward, especially Jimi Hendrix, The Beatles, George Harrison, John Lennon, Jon Anderson, Neil Young, Bob Dylan, and hundreds more. A special nod to all my brothers and sisters in the Integral Community, whose friendship and books teach and enrich me constantly. To all my fellow devotees in Adidam, thank you for seeing and recognizing His Divine Presence and for your integrity and friendship through thick and thin. To my family, my dear mother, Barbara Jean and my father, Corbin Dexter (who's death on my birthday allowed me to begin my writing career), to my brothers Mark David and Curt Andrew. To my future wife, I am still waiting. To Real God, you are the Only One for me. God is Gracious.

Bibliography

Abbott, Edwin A. *Flatland: A Romance of Many Dimensions* (1884, 1984, Harmondsworth, Middlesex, England).

Adi Da Samraj [Franklin Jones], *The Knee of Listening: The Early Life and Radical Spiritual Teachings of Franklin Jones* (1972, 2004, Middletown, CA: The Dawn Horse Press).

Adi Da Samraj [Franklin Jones], *The Method of the Siddhas: Talks with Bubba Free John on the Spiritual Technique of the Saviors of Mankind* (1973, 1978, Middletown, CA: The Dawn Horse Press).

Adi Da Samraj [Bubba Free John], *The Paradox of Instruction: An Introduction to the Esoteric Spiritual Teaching of Bubba Free John* (1977, Middletown, CA: The Dawn Horse Press).

Adi Da Samraj [Bubba Free John], *Scientific Proof of the Existence of God Will Soon Be Announced by the White House* (Middletown, CA: The Dawn Horse Press, 1980).

Adi Da Samraj [Bubba Free John], *Enlightenment of the Whole Body: A Radical and New Prophetic Revelation of the Truth of Religion, Esoteric Spirituality, and the Divine Destiny of Man* (1978, Middletown, CA: The Dawn Horse Press).

Adi Da Samraj [Da Free John], *Eleutherios: The Only Truth That Sets The Heart Free* (1982, 1998, 2001, Middletown, CA: The Dawn Horse Press).

Adi Da Samraj [Da Free John], *Nirvanasara: Radical Transcendentalism and the Introduction of Advaitayana Buddhism* (1982, Clearlake, CA: The Dawn Horse Press).

Adi Da Samraj [Da Free John], Preface to *The Song of the Self Supreme: Astavakra Gita* (1982, Clearlake, CA: The Dawn Horse Press) translated by Radhakamal Mukerjee.

Adi Da Samraj [Da Free John], Talk "The Great Tradition," January 22, 1983 (unpublished; cassette only).

Adi Da Samraj [Da Free John], *The Dawn Horse Testament* (1985, Middletown, CA: The Dawn Horse Press).Adi Da Samraj,

Adi Da Samraj [Da Free John], *Nirvanasara: Radical Transcendentalism and the introduction of Advaitayana Buddhism* (Middletown, CA: The Dawn Horse Press, 1982).

Adi Da Samraj, "Preface" to *The Song of the Supreme Self: Astavakra Gita* (1982) translated by Radhakamal Mukerjee.

Adi Da Samraj [Franklin Jones], *The Knee of Listening* (1972, LA: The Dawn Horse Press; 2004, Standard edition, enlarged and updated, Middletown, CA: The Dawn Horse Press).

Adi Da Samraj [Franklin Jones], *The Method of the Siddhas* (1973, LA, The Dawn Horse Press).

Adi Da Samraj [Da Free John], *The Fire Gospel: Essays and Talks on Spiritual Baptism* (1982, Clearlake, CA: The Dawn Horse Press).

Adi Da Samraj, *The Basket of Tolerance* (prepublication edition, 1988).

Adi Da Samraj, *Real God Is The Indivisible Oneness of Unbroken Light* (1999, Middletown, CA: The Dawn Horse Press).

Adi Da Samraj, *The Seven Stages of Life* (2000, Middletown, CA: The Dawn Horse Press).

Adi Da Samraj, "The Realization of the Beautiful" Talk given on March 30, 2001, [unpublished].

Adi Da Samraj, *Science and the Myth of Materialism* (2003 CD).

Adi Da Samraj, *The Ancient Walk-About Way* (2006, Middletown, CA: The Dawn Horse Press).

Adi Da Samraj, *Reality Is All The God There Is: The Single Transcendental Truth Taught by the Great Sages and the Revelation of Reality Itself* (2008, Rochester, VT: Inner Traditions).

Adi Da Samraj, *Atma Nadi Shakti Yoga* (2008, Middletown, CA: The Dawn Horse Press).

Adi Da Samraj, *My "Bright" Word* (1973, 2005, Standard edition, enlarged and updated, Middletown, CA: The Dawn Horse Press).

Adi Da Samraj, *Science Is a Method, Not a Philosophy* (2010, 2-CD set).

Adi Da Samraj, *Not-Two Is Peace: The Ordinary People's Way of Global Co-operative Order* (2009, 3rd edition)

Adi Da Samraj, *The Aletheon* (Middletown, CA: The Dawn Horse Press, 2009).

Adi Da Samraj, *The Gnosticon* (Middletown, CA: The Dawn Horse Press, 2010).

Adi Da Samraj, *The Pneumaton* (Middletown, CA: The Dawn Horse Press, 2011).

Adi Da Samraj, *My "Bright" Sight* (2014, Middletown, CA: The Dawn Horse Press).

Adi Da Samraj, *My "Bright" Form* (2016, Middletown, CA: The Dawn Horse Press)

Arieti, Silvano, *The Intrapsychic Self: Feeling, Cognition, and Creativity in Health and Mental Illness* (1967, NY: Basic Books).

Armstrong, Karen, *A History of God: The 4,000-Year Quest of Judaism, Christianity and Islam* (1993. Ballantine Books)

Armstrong, Karen, *A Short History of Myth* (2005, Edinburgh, Scotland: Canongate Books, Ltd.)

Armstrong, Karen, *The Great Transformation: The Beginnings of Our Religious Traditions* (2006, NYC: Alfred A. Knopf).

Aurobindo, Sri, *The Life Divine* (1939, 1990, Wilmot, WI: Lotus Light Publications).

Aurobindo, Sri, *The Essential Aurobindo* (1987, Great Barrington, MA: The Lindisfarne Press), edited by Robert McDermott.

Aurobindo, Sri, *The Integral Yoga* (1993, Twin Lakes, WI: Lotus Light Publications)

Aurobindo, Sri, *A Greater Psychology: An Introduction to the Psychological Thought of Sri Aurobindo* (2001, NYC: Tarcher/Putnam) edited by A. S, Dalal, foreword by Ken Wilber.

Atisha, *The Great Path of Awakening* (1987, Boston: Shambhala Publications) translated by Ken McLeod.

Atisha, *Atisha's Lamp for the Path To Enlightenment* (1997, Ithaca, NY: Snow Lion Publications), commentary by Geshe Sonam Rinchen, translated and edited by Ruth Sonam.

Asvaghosa, *Fifty Verses of Guru-Devotion* (1976, Library of Tibetan Works and Archives).

Bardach, A. L., "What Did J.D. Salinger, Leo Tolstoy, and Sarah Bernhardt Have in Common?" in *The Wall Street Journal Magazine*, WSJ.com.

Batchelor, Stephen, *Verses From the Center: A Buddhist Vision of the Sublime* (2000, NY: Riverhead Books).

Batchelor, Stephen, *The Tibet Guide: Central and Western Tibet* (1998, Boston: Wisdom Publications), Foreword by the Dalai Lama.

Bäumer, Bettina and Dupuche, John R., editors, *Void and Fullness in the Buddhist, Hindu and Christian Traditions: Sunya–Purna–Pleroma* (2005, New Delhi: D.K. Printworld).

Beck, Don Edward, and Cowan, Christopher C., *Spiral Dynamics: Mastering Values, Leadership, and Change* (1996, Malden, MA: Blackwell Publishers; 2005, Wiley-Blackwell).

Beck, Don Edward, with Teddy Hebo Larsen, Sergey Solonin, Dr. Rica Viljoen, Thomas Q. Johns, *Spiral Dynamics in Action: Humanity's Master Code* (2018, Wiley).

Bellah, Robert N., *Beyond Belief: Essays on Religion in a Post-Traditionalist World* (1970, Berkeley, LA, Oxford: University of California Press).

Bellah, Robert N., *Religion in Human Evolution: From the Paleolithic to the Axial Age* (2011, Cambridge, MA: The Belknap Press of Harvard University Press).

Benoit, Hubert, *[The Supreme Doctrine] Zen and the Psychology of Transformation* (1955, 1990, Rochester, VT: Inner Traditions)

Boorstein, Seymour, M.D., *Clinical Studies in Transpersonal Psychotherapy* (1997, NY: SUNY), foreword by Ken Wilber.

Beauregard, Mario, and O'Leary, Denyse, *The Spiritual Brain A Neuroscientist's Case for the Existence of the Soul* (2007, SF: HarperOne).

Burkert, Walter, *The Orientalizing Revolution: Near Eastern Influences on Greek Culture in the Early Archaic Age* (1992, 1998 Harvard University Press).

Brunnholzl, Karl, translator, *In Praise of Dharmadhatu by Nagarjuna* (2007, Ithaca, NY: Snow Lion Publications).

Campbell, Joseph, *The Hero With a Thousand Faces* (1949, 1968, Bollingen Series, Princeton University Press).

Campbell, Joseph, *Occidental Mythology: The Masks of God, Volume 1–4* (1959, 1962, 1964, 1968; 1991, NY: Arkana Press).

Campbell, Joseph, *The Flight of the Wild Gander* (1969, 1990, Harper Perennial; 2018, Novato: CA: New World Library).

Camphausen, Rufus C., *The Divine Library: A Comprehensive Reference Guide to the Sacred Texts and Spiritual Literature of the World* (Rochester, VT: Inner Traditions, 1992).

Capra, Fritjof, *The Tao of Physics: An Exploration of the Parallels Between Modern Physics and Eastern Mysticism* (1975, Boulder: Shambhala Publications).

Capra, Fritjof, *The Turning Point: Science, Society, and the Rising Culture* (1982, Simon & Schuster).

Chang, Garma C. C., *The Buddhist Teaching of Totality: The Philosophy of Hwa Yen Buddhism* (1994, Pennsylvania State University Press).

Chang, Garma C. C., translated and annotated by, *The Hundred Thousand Songs of Milarepa, Volume One* (1962, Boston: Shambhala Publications).

Chang, Garma C. C., *The Six Yogas of Naropa and Teachings on Mahamudra* (1963, 1977, Ithaca, NY: Snow Lion Publications).

Chaudhuri, Haridas, *The Evolution of Integral Consciousness* (1977, Wheaton, IL: Quest Books).

Chetanananda, Swami, *Vivekananda: East Meets West (A Pictorial Biography)* (1995, Vedanta Society of St. Louis), Preface by Huston Smith.

Chomsky, Noam, and Edward S. Herman, *Manufacturing Consent* (1988, Pantheon.)

Chomsky, Noam, *Media Control: The Spectacular Achievements of Propaganda* (2002, Seven Stories Press; 2nd ed.).

Christian, David, *Origin Story: A Big History of Everything* (2018, Little Brown).

Christian, David, *Maps of Time: An Introduction to Big History* (2004, 2011, University of California).

Coleman, Barks, translator, *The Essential Rumi, New Expanded Edition* (2004, SF: HarperOne).

Cohen, Andrew, *Evolutionary Enlightenment: A New Path to Spiritual Awakening* (2011, NYC: SelectBooks, Inc.)

Cohen, Andrew, *Living Enlightenment: A Call for Evolution Beyond Ego* (2002, Lenox: MA: Moksha Press), foreword by Ken Wilber.

Combs, Allan, *The Radiance of Being: Complexity, Chaos and the Evolution of Consciousness* (1995, St. Paul, MN: Paragon Books).

Combs, Allan *The Radiance of Being: Understanding the Grand Integral Vision; Living the Integral Life* (2002, St. Paul, MN: Paragon Books), foreword by Ken Wilber.

Cook, Francis Dojun, translator, *The Record of Transmitting the Light: Zen Master Keizan's* Denkoroku (2003, Boston: Wisdom Publications).

Cornford, F. M., *From Religion to Philosophy: A Study in the Origins of Western Speculation* (1912, 1991, Princeton University Press).

Cornford, F. M., translator, *The Republic* (1945, New York & London: Oxford university Press).

Connelly, Ben, *Inside Vasubandhu's Yogacara: A Practitioner's Guide* (2016, Somerville, MA: Wisdom Publications)

Cozort, Daniel, *Highest Tantra Yoga: An Introduction to the Esoteric Buddhism of Tibet* (1986, Ithaca, NY: Snow Lion Publications).

Crittenden, Jack, "What Is the Meaning of 'Integral'?" foreword in *The Eye of Spirit* (1997, Boston: Shambhala Publications) by Ken Wilber.

Dalai Lama, Tenzin Gyatso, *The Union of Bliss and Emptiness: A Commentary on the Lama Choepa Guru Yoga* (1988, Ithaca, NY: Snow Lion).

Deida, David, *Finding God Through Sex: A Spiritual Guide to Ecstatic Loving and Deep Passion for Men and Women* (2002, Austin, TX: Plexus), foreword by Ken Wilber.

DiPerna, Dustin, *Purpose Rising: A Global Movement of Transformation and Meaning* (2017, Bright Alliance Publishing), ed. by Emanuel Kuntzelman and Dustoin DiPerna.

Dowman, Keith, translator, *The Divine Madman: The Sublime and Songs of Drukpa Kunley* (1980, London: Rider).

Eisler, Riane, *The Chalice and the Blade: Our History, Our Future* (1987, SF: Harper & Row).

Elgin, Duane, *Awakening Earth: Exploring the Evolution of Human Culture and Consciousness* (1993, NY: William Morrow and Company, Inc.).

Eliade, Mircea, *From Primitives to Zen: A Thematic Sourcebook of the History of Religions* (1967, 1977, Harper & Row, Publishers).

Eliade, Mircea, *A History of Religious Idea, Volumes 1–3* (1978, 1982, 1985, The University of Chicago Press).

Encyclopedia of Eastern Philosophy and Religion, The (1989, 1994, Boston: Shambhala Publications).

Feuerstein, Georg, *Yoga: The Technology of Ecstasy* (Los Angeles: Jeremy P. Tarcher, 1989), foreword by Ken Wilber.

Feuerstein, Georg, *Structures of Consciousness: The Genius of Jean Gebser: An Introduction and Critique* (1987, Lower Lake, CA: Integral Publishing).

Feuerstein, Georg, *The Shambhala Encyclopedia of Yoga* (1990, NYC: Paragon House).

Feuerstein, Georg, *Holy Madness: The Shock Tactics and Radical Teachings of Crazy-Wise Adepts, Holy Fools, and Rascal Gurus* (1991, NY: Paragon House).

Feuerstein, Georg, *Holy Madness: Spirituality, Crazy-Wise Teachers, and Enlightenment* (1990, 2006 revised and expanded edition, Prescott, AZ: Hohm Press).

Feuerstein, Georg, *Whole or Transcendence? Ancient Lessons for the Emerging Global Civilization* (1974, 1992, NY: Larson Publications).

Feuerstein, Georg, *The Yoga Tradition: Its History, Literature, Philosophy and Practice* (1998, Prescott, AZ: Hohm Press), foreword by Ken Wilber.

Ferguson, Marilyn, *The Aquarian Conspiracy: Personal and Social Transformation In the 1980s* (1980, LA: Jeremy P. Tarcher).

Fields, Rick, *How the Swans Came to the Lake: A Narrative History of Buddhism in America* (1992, Boston: Shambhala Publications).

Fields, Rick, with Peggy Taylor, Rex Weyler, and Rick Ingrasci, *Chop Wood, Carry Water: A Guide to Finding Spiritual Fulfillment* (1984, Los Angeles: Jeremy P. Tarcher, Inc).

Fieser, James, and Powers, John, *Scriptures of the World's Religions* (2018, Sixth Edition, NYC: McGraw-Hill Education).

Forsthoefel, Thomas and Hume, Cynthia Ann, editors, *Gurus In America* (2005, Albany, NY: SUNY).

Freimann, Amir, *Spiritual Transmission: Paradoxes and Dilemmas on the Spiritual Path* (2018, Rhinebeck, NY: Monkfish Book Publishing), Afterword by Ken Wilber.

Freke, Timothy and Gandy, Peter, *The Hermetica: The Lost Wisdom of the Pharaohs* (1997, NYC: Tarcher/Penguin).

Garfield, Jay, translator, *The Fundamental Wisdom of the Middle Way: Nagarjuna's Mulamadhyamakakarika* (1995, Oxford University Press).

Gautama Buddha, *Last Days of the Buddha: Maha Parinibbana Sutta* (1998, Sri Lanka: Buddhist Publication Society) translated by Francis Story and Sister Vajira.

Gebser, Jean, *The Ever-Present Origin [Ursprung Und Gegenwart]*, (1949, 1953, 1985, Athens, OH: Ohio University Press).

Gebser, Jean, "The Foundations of the Aperspectival World," *Main Currents of Modern Thought*, Vol. 29, No. 2, 1972, pp. 80-88.

Gebser, Jean, "The Integral Consciousness," *Main Currents of Modern Thought*, Vol. 30, No. 3, 1974, pp. 107-109.

Gilligan, Carol, *In A Different Voice: Psychological Theory and Women's Development* (1982, 1993, Cambridge: Harvard University Press).

Goleman, Daniel, *The Meditative Mind: The Varieties of Meditative Experience* (1988, NY: Tarcher/Putnam).

Gregorius, Paulos, *Neoplatonism and Indian Philosophy* (2002, SUNY Press).

Philip Goldberg, *American Veda: From Emerson and The Beatles to Yoga and Meditation: How Indian Spirituality Changed the World* (2010, NY: Harmony Books).

Goddard, Dwight, editor, *A Buddhist Bible: The Favorite Scriptures of the Zen Sect* (1938, 1966, 1970, Boston: Beacon Press).

Gomez, Luis O., *The Land of Bliss: The Paradise of the Buddha of Measureless Light: Sanskrit and Chinese Versions of the Sukhavativyuha Sutras* (1996, Honolulu: University of Hawaii).

Grey, Alex, *Sacred Mirrors: The Visionary Art of Alex Grey* (1990, Rochester, VT: Inner Traditions), introductory essay by Ken Wilber.

Grey, Alex, *The Mission of Art* (1998, Boston: Shambhala), foreword by Ken Wilber.

Grey, Alex, *Transfigurations* (2001, Rochester, VT: Inner Traditions), contribution by Ken Wilber.

Grof, Stanislav, *The Cosmic Game: Explorations of the Frontiers of Human Consciousness* (1998, SUNY Press).

Grof, Stanislav, *Psychology of the Future: Lessons From Modern Consciousness Research* (2000, SUNY press).

René Guénon, *The Symbolism of the Cross* (2001, 2004, 4th edition, Sophia Perennis).

Gyatso, Geshe Kelsang, *Clear Light of Bliss: The Practice of Mahamudra in Vajrayana Buddhism* (1982, 1995, London: Tharpa Publications).

Hall, Manly P., *The Secret Teachings of All Ages: An Encyclopedic Outline of Masonic, Hermetic, Qabbalistic and Rosicrucian Symbolical Philosophy* (1928, 2007, A & D Publishing).

Andrew Harvey, *The Way of Passion: A Celebration of Rumi* (2000, Tarcher-Perigee).

Andrew Harvey, *Turn Me to Gold: 108 Poems of Kabir* (2018, Unity Press).

Heidegger, Martin, *Introduction to Metaphysics* (1959, New Haven and London: Yale University Press).

Heisenberg, Werner, *Physics and Philosophy: A Revolution in Modern Science* (1958, NYC: Harper Torchbooks).

Herman, Arthur, *The Cave and the Light: Plato Versus Aristotle, and the Struggle for the Soul of Western Civilization* (2020, NY, Random House).

Hirsch, Emil, *The Dawn of Religious Pluralism* (1993, Open Court Publishing Company, La Salle, IL).

Hixon, Lex, *Coming Home: The Experience of Enlightenment in Sacred Traditions* (1978, 1989, LA: Jeremy P. Tarcher), foreword by Ken Wilber, 1989.

Hixon, Lex, *Great Swan: Meetings with Ramakrishna* (1992, Boston: Shambhala Publications).

Hixon, Lex, *Mother of the Buddhas: Meditation on the Prajnaparamita Sutra* (1993, Wheaton, IL: Quest Books), foreword by Robert A. F. Thurman.

Huxley, Aldous, *The Perennial Philosophy* (1944, 1970, NY: Harper & Row).

Huxley, Aldous, *The Doors of Perception* (1954, 2009, Harper Perennial Modern Classics).

Huxley, Aldous, "Introduction" in *Bhagavad Gita: The Song of God* (1944, 1987, Hollywood, CA: Vedanta Press).

Jackson, Carl T., *Vedanta for the West: The Ramakrishna Movement in the United States* (1994, Indianapolis, Indiana: Indiana University Press).

Johnsen, Linda, *Lost Masters: Sages of Ancient Greece* (2006, Honesdale, PA: Himalayan Institute Press; 2016, Novato, CA: New World Library).

Kapur, Kamla K., *The Singing Guru: Legends and Adventures of Guru Nanak, the First Sikh* (Mandala Publishing, 2015).

Kegan, Robert, *The Evolving Self: Problem and Process in Human Development* (1982, Cambridge: Harvard University Press).

Kegan, Robert; Lahey, Lisa Laskow, *An Everyone Culture: Becoming a Deliberately Developmental Organization* (2016, Harvard Business Review Press).

Kerényi, Karl, *Dionysus: Archetype; Image of Indestructible Life* (Princeton University Press, 1976).

Kerényi, Karl, *Eleusis: Archetypal Image of Mother and Daughter* (1967, 1991, Princeton University Press).

Khenpo, Nyoshul, *Natural Great Perfection: Dzogchen Teachings and Vajra Songs* (1995, Ithaca, NY: Snow Lion Publications).

Khenpo Tsultrim Gyamtso Rinpoche (author), Lama Shenpen Hookham, translator, *Progressive Stages of Meditation on Emptiness* (1986, Oxford: Longchen Foundation).

Khyentse, Dilgo, *The Wish-Fulfilling Jewel: The Practice of Guru Yoga According to The Longchen Nyingthig Tradition* (1988, Boston: Shambhala Publications) translated by Konchog Tenzin.

Khyentse, Dzongsar Jamyang, *The Guru Drinks Bourbon?* (2016, Boulder, CO: Shambhala).

Kilty, Gavin, trans., *The Splendor of an Autumn Moon: The Devotional Verse of Tsongkhapa* (2001, Boston: Wisdom Publications).

King, Martin Luther, Jr., *A Testament of Hope: The Essential Writings of Martin Luther King, Jr.* (1986, SF: Harper & Row), James Washington, ed.

Kirk, G.S., Raven, J.E., Schofield, M., *The Presocratic Philosophers* (1957, 1983, Second Edition, Cambridge University Press).

Kitagawa, Joseph Mitsuo, *The Quest for Human Unity: A Religious History* (1990, Minneapolis MN: Fortress Press).

King, Martin Luther, Jr., A Testament of Hope: The Essential Writings of Martin Luther King, Jr. (1986, SF: Harper & Row), James Washington, editor.

Kingsley, Peter, *In the Dark Places of Wisdom* (1999, Golden Sufi Center).

Kingsley, Peter, *A Story Waiting to Pierce You: Mongolia, Tibet, and the Destiny of the Western World* (2010, Point Reyes, CA: The Golden Sufi Center).

Koestler, Arthur, *The Ghost in the Machine* (1967, NY: Viking Penguin).

Koestler, Arthur, *Janus: A Summing Up* (1978, NY: Vintage Books).

Kongtrul, Jamgon. *The Torch of Certainty* (1977, Boulder, CO: Shambhala Publications) translated by Judith Hanson.

Kripal, Jeffrey J., *Comparing Religions* (2014, West Sussex, UK: Wiley Blackwell).

Kripal, Jeffrey J., *Esalen: America and the Religion of No Religion* (2007, Chicago: The University of Chicago Press).

Krishna, Gopi. Kundalini: *The Evolutionary Energy in Man* (1971, 1997, Shambhala Publications).

Landaw, Jonathan and Weber, Andy, *Images of Enlightenment: Tibetan Art in Practice* (1993, Ithaca, NY: Snow Lion Publications).

Lee, Carolyn, *The Promised God-Man Is Here* (1993, Middletown, CA: The Dawn Horse Press).

Lee, Carolyn, *Adi Da: The Promised God-Man Is Here* (2003, Middletown, CA: The Dawn Horse Press).

Lee, Carolyn, *The Avatar Of What Is: The Divine Life and Work of His Divine Presence* (2007, 2017, Middletown, CA: The Dawn Horse Press).

Lingpa, Jigme. *The Dzogchen Innermost Essence Preliminary Practice* (1982, Dharamshala: Library of Tibetan Works and Archives).

Lovejoy, Arthur O., *The Great Chain of Being* (1936, 1965, Cambridge: Harvard University Press).

Luk, Charles, translator, *Ordinary Enlightenment: A Translation of the Vimalakirti Nirdesa Sutra* (1972, 2002, Boston: Shambhala Publications).

Maslow, Abraham, *The Farther Reaches of Human Nature* (1971, NYC: Viking Press).

McEvilley, Thomas, *The Shape of Ancient Thought: Comparative Studies in Greek and Indian Philosophies* (2002, NYC: Allworth Press).

McGilchrist, Iain, *The Master and His Emissary: The Divided Brain and the Making of the Western World* (2009, New Haven: Yale University Press).

McIntosh, Steve, *Evolution's Purpose: An Integral Interpretation of the Scientific Story of Our Origins* (2012, NY: SelectBooks).

McMullen, Michael D., *The Baha'i: The Religious Construction of a Global Identity* (2000, Atlanta, GA: Rutgers University Press).

Miller, Barbara Stoler, translator, *The Bhagavad-Gita: Krishna's Counsel in Time of War* (1986, NYC: Bantam Books).

Mitchell, Stephen, ed., *The Enlightened Mind: An Anthology of Sacred Prose* (1991, NY: HarperCollins).

Mitchell, Stephen,ed., The Enlightened Heart (1989, NYC: HarperCollins).

Moller, Violet, *The Map of Knowledge: A Thousand-year History of How Classical Ideas Were Lost and Found* (NYC: Anchor Books. 2019).

Moore, Meido, *Hidden Zen : Practices for Sudden Awakening & Embodied Realization* (2020, Boston: Shambhala Publications).

Mullin, Glenn H., *Readings on the Six Yogas of Naropa* (1997, Ithaca, NY: Snow Lion Publications).

Murphy, Michael, *The Future of the Body: Explorations Into the Further Evolution of Human Nature* (1992, LA: Jeremy P. Tarcher).

Murti, T. R. V., *The Central Philosophy of Buddhism: A Study of the Madhyamika System* (1955, New Delhi: HarperCollins Publishers India).

Nagarjuna, *The Diamond Sutra* (1969, Boulder: Shambhala Publications) translated by A.F. Price and Wong Mou-Lam.

Narayananda, Swami, translator, *The Guru Gita* (1972, Bombay, India: India Book House)

Nasr, Seyyed Hossein Nasr, *Knowledge of the Sacred* (1989, Albany, NY: SUNY).

Needleman, Jacob, *The Sword of Gnosis: Metaphysics, Cosmology, Tradition, Symbolism* (1974, 1986, Boston: Arkana).

Nelson, John E, M.D., *Healing The Split: Integrating Spirit Into Our Understanding of the Mentally Ill* (1994, SUNY), foreword by Ken Wilber, preface by Michael Washburn.

Nietzsche, Friedrich, *The Birth of Tragedy* (1872, NYC: Barnes & noble, 2006).

Nietzsche, Friedrich, *Philosophy in the Tragic Age of the Greek* (1873, NYC: Regnery Publishing, Inc.,).

Nietzsche, Friedrich, The Birth of Tragedy (1872)

Nisker, Wes, *Crazy Wisdom* (1990, Berkeley" Ten Speed Press).

Nisker, Wes, *Buddha's Nature: Evolution as a Practical Guide to Enlightenment* (1998, NY: Bantam Books).

Norbu, Chögyal Namkhai, *Dzogchen: The Self-Perfect State* (1989, Ithaca, NY: Snow Lion Publications).

Novak, Philip, *The World's Wisdom: Sacred Texts of the World's Religions* (1994, San Francisco: HarperOne).

Oxford Dictionary of World Religions, The (1997, Oxford University Press), John Bowker, editor.

Odier, Daniel, *Crazy Wisdom of the Yogini: Teachings of the Kashmiri Mahamudra Tradition* (2021, Rochester, VT: Inner Traditions).

Ogilvy, James, editor., *Revisioning Philosophy* (1992, SUNY Press).

Plato, *Symposium of Plato* (1989, Berkeley: University of California Press) translated by Tom Griffith.

Perennial Dictionary of World Religions, The (1981, SF: Harper & Row), Keith Crim, general editor.

Perry, Whitall N., *A Treasury of Traditional Wisdom* (Fons Vitae; 1971, 2000 2nd edition).

Phipps, Carter, *Evolutionaries: Unlocking the Spiritual and Cultural Potential of Science's Greatest Ideas* (NYC: Harper Perennial, 2012).

Plotinus, *The Enneads* (Burdett, NY: Larson Publications, 1992) translated by Stephen McKenna.

Plotinus, *Plotinus* (1953, NYC: Collier Books) translated by A. H. Armstrong.

Powers, John, *Introduction to Tibetan Buddhism* (2007 revised edition, Boulder: Snow Lion).

Price, A. F. and Wong Mou-Lam, translators, *The Diamond Sutra and The Sutra of Hui Neng* (1969, Boulder: Shambhala Publications).

Ramana Maharshi, Sri, *The Spiritual Teachings of Ramana Maharishi* (1972, 1988, Boston: Shambhala Publication s, Inc.), foreword by C. G. Jung.

Ramana Maharshi, Sri, *Talks with Ramana Maharshi: On Realizing Abiing Peace and Happiness* (2001, Carlsbad, CA: Inner Directions Publishing,), foreword by Ken Wilber.

Ramana Maharshi, Sri, *The Collected Works of Sri Ramana Maharshi* (2006, San Rafael, CA: Sophia Perennis).

Ramana Maharshi, Sri, *The Collected Works of Sri Ramana Maharshi* (2015, 13th edition, Tiruvannamalai, India: Sri Ramanasramam).

Ram Dass, *Be Love Now: The Path of the Heart* (2010, NYC: HarperCollins Publishers).

Ray, Paul, and Anderson, Sherry Ruth, *The Cultural Creatives: How 50 Million People Are Changing the World* (2000, NY: Three Rivers Press).

Reich, Charles, *The Greening of America* (1983, LA: Jeremy P. Tarcher).

Rothberg, Donald and Kelly, Sean, *Ken Wilber In Dialogue: Conversation with Leading Transpersonal Thinkers* (1998, Wheaton, IL: Quest Books).

Rowan, John, *The Transpersonal: Psychotherapy and Counseling* (1993, 1998, London & NY: Routledge).

Russell, Peter, *The Global Brain: Speculations on the Evolutionary Leap to Planetary Consciousness* (1983, LA: Jeremy P. Tarcher).

Ryan, M. J., ed., *The Fabric of the Future: Women Visionaries of Today Illuminate the Path to Tomorrow* (1998, Berkeley: Conari Press), foreword by Ken Wilber.

Reynolds, Brad, *Embracing Reality: The Integral Vision of Ken Wilber* (NY: Tarcher/Putnam, 2004).

Reynolds, Brad, *Where's Wilber At? The Vision of Ken Wilber in the Third Millennium* (Paragon House, 2006).

Reynolds, Brad, "The Pandit: Standing on the Shoulders of the Sat-Guru—The Influence of Adi Da Samraj on the First Books of Ken Wilber" (January 2016) at IntegralWorld.net.

Reynolds, Brad, "Defending Adi Da Samraj: Transcending the Cult of Guru-Haters" (February 2016) at IntegralWorld.net.

Reynolds, Brad, "Standing Up for Adi Da: Devotees Have a Divine and Different View" (March 2016) at IntegralWorld.net.

Reynolds, Brad, *God's Great Tradition of Global Wisdom—Guru Yoga-Satsang in the Integral Age* (Occidental, CA: Bright Alliance, 2021).

Reynolds, Brad, *In God's Company: Guru-Adepts As Agents for Enlightenment in the Integral Age* (Occidental, CA: Bright Alliance, 2022).

Reynolds, Brad, *Growing In God: Seven Stages of Life from Birth to Enlightenment—An Integral Interpretation* (forthcoming, Paragon House).

Sannella, Lee, *The Kundalini Experience* (1976, 1987, Integral Publishing).

Scotton, Bruce, Allan B. Chinen, John R. Battista, eds., *Textbook of Transpersonal Psychiatry and Psychology* (1996, NY: BasicBooks), foreword by Ken Wilber.

Scholem, Gershom G., Major Trends of Jewish Mysticism (NY: Schocken Books, 1954).

Schuon, Frithjof, *The Transcendent Unity of Religions* (1959, Wheaton, IL: Quest Books, 1984), Introduction by Huston Smith.

Schuon, Frithjof, *The Essential Writings of Frithjof Schuon* (Element Books, 1991), edited by Seyyed Hossein Nasr.

Schwartz, Tony, *What Really Matters: Searching For Wisdom in America* (NY: Bantam Books, 1995).

Seager, Richard, *The Dawn of Religious Pluralism: Voices from the World's Parliament of Religions, 1893* (1993, Open Court Publishing Company, La Salle, IL).

Shankara, *The Crest Jewel of Discrimination* (1947, 1975, Hollywood, CA: Vedanta Press) translated by Swami Prabhavananda and Christopher Isherwood.

Shantideva, *The Way of the Bodhisattva* (1997, Boston: Shambhala Publications) translated by the Padmakara Translation Group.

Shambhala Publications Inc., *The Encyclopedia of Eastern Philosophy and Religion* (1994, Boston: Shambhala Publications).

Shapiro, Eddie and Debbie, ed., *The Way Ahead: A Visionary Perspective for the New Millennium* (1992, Rockport, MA: Element Books), essay by Ken Wilber.

Sharma, Jyotirmaya, *A Restatement of Religion: Swami Vivekananda and the Making of Hindu Nationalism* (2013, Yale University Press).

Shaw, Miranda. *Passionate Enlightenment: Women in Tantric Buddhism* (1994, Princeton University Press).

Simmer-Brown, Judith, *Dakini's Warm Breath: The Feminine Principle in Tibetan Buddhism* (2002, Boston: Shambhala Publications).

Smith, Huston, *Forgotten Truth: The Common Vision of the World's Religions* (1976, HarperSanFrancisco).

Smith, Huston, *Beyond the Post-Modern Mind* (1982, 1989, Wheaton, IL: Quest Books).

Smith, Huston, *The World's Religions: Our Great Wisdom Traditions* (1991, NYC: HarperCollins).

Smith, Huston; Griffin, David Ray, *Primordial Truth and Postmodern Theology* (1989, SUNY Press).

Smith, Huston, *Cleansing the Doors of Perception: The Religious Significance of Entheogenic Plants and Chemicals* (2000, NYC: Tarcher/Putnam).

Smith, Huston, *Why Religion Matters: The Fate of the Human Spirit in an Age of Disbelief* (2001, SF: HarperSanFrancisco).

Smith, Huston and Novak, Philip, *Buddhism: A Concise Introduction* (2003, SF: HarperSanFrancisco).

Smuts, Jan *Holism and Evolution* (1926, London: Macmillan; 1973, Wesrport, CN: Greenwood Press).

Snellgrove, David, *Religion as History, Religion as Myth* (2006Bangkok, Thailand: Orchid Press).

Sotillos, Samuel Bendeck, editor, *Psychology and the Perennial Philosophy : Studies in Comparative Religion* (2013, Bloomington, IN: World Wisdom).

Soyan, Shaku, *The Dawn of Religious Pluralism* (1993, Open Court Publishing Company, La Salle, IL).

Stace, Walter T., *The Teachings of the Mystics; Selections From the Great Mystics and Mystical Writings of the World* (1961, New American Library).

Stearns, Cyrus, *The Buddha from Dolpo: A Study of the Line and Thought of the Tibetan Master Dolpopa Sherab Gyaltsen* (1999, Albany, NY: SUNY).

Steinberg, James, *Love of the God-Man: A Comprehensive Guide to the Traditional and Time-Honored Guru-Devotee Relationship, the Supreme Means of God-Realization* (1990, Clearlake, CA: The Dawn Horse Press).

Steinberg, James, *Divine Distraction: A Guide to the Guru-Devotee Relationship* (1991, Clearlake, CA: The Dawn Horse Press).

Steinberg, James, "Pure From the Beginning: Beloved Adi Da's Call for the Universal Acceptance of the Great Tradition As the Common Inheritance of Humankind" in *Adi Da Samrajashram*, Vol. 1, No. 4, 2015.

Stewart, Jampa Mackenzie, compiled and edited by, *The Life of Longchenpa: The Omniscient Dharma King of the Vast Expanse* (2013, Snow Lion).

Strong, John S., *The Experience of Buddhism: Sources and Interpretations* (1994, Wadsworth Publishing).

Surya Das, Lama, *Awakening the Buddha Within: Eight Steps to Enlightenment: Tibetan Wisdom for the Western World* (NY: Broadway Books, 1997).

Surya Das, Lama, *Awakening the Buddhist Heart: Integrating Love, Meaning, and Connection into Every Part of Your Life* (2000, Broadway Books).

Swimme, Brian, *The Universe Story: From the Primordial Flaring Forth to the Ecozoic Era—A Celebration of the Unfolding of the Cosmos* (1994, San Francisco: HarperOne).

Tagore, Rabindranath, translator, *Songs of Kabir* (1915, 1977, NY: Samuel Weiser).

Tarthang Tulku, *Ancient Tibet: Research Materials* (1986, Berkeley, CA: Dharma Publishing).

Teilhard de Chardin, Pierre, *The Phenomenon of Man [Le Phenomene Humain]*, (NY: Harper & Row, 1955, 1959, 1965).

Thompson, William Irwin, *Coming Into Being: Artifacts and Texts in the Evolution of Consciousness* (NY; St. Martin's Press, 1996).

Thurman, Robert A. F., T*he Holy Teaching of Vimalakirti: A Mahayana Scripture* (Pennsylvania State University Press, 1976, 1992).

Thurman, Robert A. F., *The Central Philosophy of Tibet: A Study and Translation of Jey Tsong Khapa's Essence of True Eloquence* (Princeton, NJ: Princeton University Press, 1984), foreword by the Dalai Lama.

Thurman, Robert A. F., *The Tibetan Book of the Dead: Liberation Through Understanding in the Between* (NY: Bantam Books, 1994).

Thurman, Robert A. F., *Essential Tibetan Buddhism* (Edison, NJ: Castle Books, 1995).

Thurman, Robert A. F., *Inner Revolution: Life, Liberty, and the Pursuit of Real Happiness* (NY: Riverhead Books, 1998).

Thurman, Robert A. F., and Wise, Tad. *Circling the Sacred Mountain: A Spiritual Journey Through the Himalayas* (NY: Bantam Books, 1999).

Tsongkhapa, *The Splendor of an Autumn Moon: The Devotional Verse of Tsongkhapa* (2011, Boston: Wisdom Publications) translated and edited by Gavin Kilty;

Tsongkhapa, *The Great Exposition of Secret Mantra: Yoga Tantra, Volumes 1-3* (2016, 2017) by Tsongkhapa with a Commentary by the Dalai Lama, translation, editing, and explanatory material by Jeffrey Hopkins;

Tsongkhapa, *The Great Treatise on the Stages of the Path to Enlightenment: Lam Rim Chen Mo: Volumes 1-3* (2000-2002, 2014-2015, Ithaca, NY: Snow Lion Publications) by Tsong-khapa, translated by The Lamrim Chenmo Translation Committee, Joshua W. C. Cutler, Editor-in-Chief.

Trout, Stan (Swami Abhayananda), *History of Mysticism: The Unchanging Testament* (1987, Fallsburg, NY: Atma Books).

Tulku Urgyen Rinpoche, *The Dzogchen Primer: Embracing the Spiritual Path According to the Great Perfection* (2002, Boston: Shambhala Publications), Compiled and edited by Marcia Binder Schmidt.

Uzdavinys, Algis, *Orpheus and the Roots of Platonism* (2011, The Matheson Trust)/

Vaughan, Frances, *The Inward Arc: Healing In Psychotherapy and Spirituality* (1985, 1995, Nevada City, CA: Blue Dolphin Publishing, Inc.)

Vaughan, Frances, *Shadows of the Sacred: Seeing Through Spiritual Illusions* (1995, Quest Books), foreword by Ken Wilber.

Versluis, Arthur, *American Guru: From Transcendentalism to New Age Religion* (2014, Oxford University Press).

Vivekananda, Swami, *The Life of Swami Vivekananda, Volume 1* (1979, Calcutta: Advaita Ashram, revised and enlarged edition) by his Eastern and Western disciples.

Walsh, Roger, *The Spirit of Shamanism* (1990, LA: J. P. Tarcher).

Walsh, Roger; Vaughan, Frances, "The Worldview of Ken Wilber" (Chapter 7) in *Textbook of Transpersonal Psychiatry and Psychology* (1996, NY: Basic-Books), with Scotton, et al.

Walsh, Roger, *Essential Spirituality: Exercises from the World's Religions to Cultivate Kindness, Love, Joy, Peace, Vision, Wisdom, and Generosity* (1999, NY: John Wiley & Sons, Inc.), foreword by Dalai Lama.

Ward, Keith, *Images of Eternity: Concepts of God in Five Religious Traditions* (1987, 1993, Oxford, England: Oneworld Publications).

Wangyal Rinpoche, Tenzin, *Wonders of the Natural Mind* (2000, Snow Lion; new edition) Foreword by His Holiness the XIV Dalai Lama.

Wangyal Rinpoche, Tenzin, The Tibetan Yogas of Dream and Sleep (1998, Ithaca, NY: Snow Lion).

Wasson, R. Gordon, Albert Hoffman, Carl Ruck, The Road to Eleusis (1998, 2008, North Atlantic Books).

Whitmont, Edward C., *Return of the Goddess* (1992, NY: Crossroad).

White, John, ed., *The Highest State of Consciousness* (1972, NY: Doubleday & Company, Inc.).

White, John, *What Is Enlightenment? Exploring the Goal of the Spiritual Path* (1985, 1995, NY: Paragon House).

White, John, *A Practical Guide to Death and Dying* (Wheaton, IL: 1980, 1988).

White, John, *The Meeting of Science and Spirit: Guidelines for a New Age: The Next Dynamic Stage of Human Evolution, and How We Will Attain It* (1990, NY: Paragon House).

White, John, *Kundalini, Evolution and Enlightenment* (1998, Paragon House).

White, John, "Foreword" to the second edition of *The Spectrum of Consciousness* (1977, 1993, Wheaton, IL: Quest Books) by Ken Wilber.

Whyte, Lancelot Law, The Next Development In Man (1948, 1950, NY: Mentor Books).

Wiesel, Elie, *Souls on Fire: Portraits and Legends of Hasidic Masters* (1972, MYC: Random House).

Wilber, Ken, "The Spectrum of Consciousness," *Main Currents in Modern Though*t, November/December 1974, Vol. 1, No. 2.

Wilber, Ken, "The Perennial Psychology and the Spectrum of Consciousness," *Human Dimensions*, Summer 1974, Vol. 4, No. 2 {guest editor John White].

Wilber, Ken, "Psychologia Perennis: The Spectrum of Consciousness," *The Journal of Transpersonal Psychology*, Vol. 7, No. 2, pp. 105-132.

Wilber, Ken, *The Spectrum of Consciousness* (1977, Wheaton, IL: A Quest Book, Theosophical Publishing House).

Wilber, Ken, *The Spectrum of Consciousness* (1977, 1993, Wheaton, IL: Quest Books), 20th Anniversary edition (foreword by John White).

Wilber, Ken, *No Boundary: Eastern and Western Approaches to Personal Growth* (1979, Los Angeles: Center Publications).

Wilber, Ken, "Are the Chakras Real?" in *Kundalini, Evolution, and Enlightenment* (1979, NYC: Anchor Press/Doubleday), edited by John White.

Wilber, Ken, *The Atman Project: A Transpersonal View of Human Development* (1980, Wheaton, IL: A Quest Book, Theosophical Publishing House; 1996, Quest Books).

Wilber, Ken *Up from Eden: A Transpersonal View of Human Evolution* (1981, NY: Anchor Press/Doubleday Books; 2007, Quest Books).

Wilber, Ken, editor, *The Holographic Paradigm and Other Paradoxes: Exploring the Leading Edge of Science*, (1982, Boulder: Shambhala Publications).

Wilber, Ken, *A Sociable God: A Brief Introduction to a Transcendental Sociology* (1983, NY: Anchor Press/Doubleday Books; 2005, Shambhala Publications).

Wilber, Ken, *Eye to Eye: The Quest for the New Paradigm* (1983, NY: Anchor Press/Doubleday Books).

Wilber, Ken, editor, *Quantum Questions: Mystical Writings of the World's Great Physicists* (1984, Boulder: Shambhala Publications).

Wilber, Ken, "On Heroes and Cults," *The Laughing Man*, Vol. 6, No. 1 [reprint of 1979 Foreword].

Wilber, Ken, with Jack Engler and Daniel P. Brown, *Transformations of Consciousness: Conventional and Contemplative Perspectives on Development* (1986, NY: Paragon House).

Wilber, Ken, edited with Dick Anthony and Bruce Ecker, *Spiritual Choices: The Problem of Recognizing Authentic Paths to Inner Transformation* (1987, NY: Paragon House).

Wilber, Ken, *Eye to Eye: The Quest for the New Paradigm* (1990. 2nd edition, Boston: Shambhala Publications).

Wilber, Ken, *Grace and Grit: Spirituality and Healing in the Life of Trey Killam Wilber* (1991, Boston: Shambhala Publications).

Wilber, Ken, *Sex, Ecology, Spirituality: The Spirit of Evolution* (1995, Boston: Shambhala Publications).

Wilber, Ken, *A Brief History of Everything* (1996, Boston: Shambhala Publications).

Wilber, Ken, *The Eye of Spirit: An Integral Vision for a World Gone Slightly Mad* (1997, Boston: Shambhala Publications).

Wilber, Ken, *The Marriage of Sense and Soul: Integrating Science and Religion* (1998, NY: Random House).

Wilber, Ken, *One Taste: The Journals of Ken Wilber* (1999, Boston: Shambhala Publications).

Wilber, Ken, *A Theory of Everything: An Integral Vision for Business, Politics, Sciences, and Spirituality* (1999, Boston: Shambhala Publications).

Wilber, Ken, *The Collected Works of Ken Wilber, Volumes 1-4* (1999, Boston: Shambhala Publications).

Wilber, Ken, *The Collected Works of Ken Wilber, Volumes 5-8* (2000, Boston: Shambhala Publications).

Wilber, Ken, *Integral Psychology: Consciousness, Spirit, Psychology, Therapy* (2000, Boston: Shambhala Publications).

Wilber, Ken, *Boomeritis: A Novel That Will Set You Free* (2002, Boston: Shambhala Publications).

Wilber, Ken, *The Simple Feeling of Being: Embracing Your True Nature* (2004, Boston: Shambhala Publications) compiled and edited by Mark Palmer, Sean Hargens, Vipassana Esbjörn, and Adam Leonard.

Wilber, Ken, *Integral Spirituality: A Startling New Role for Religion in the Modern and Postmodern World* (2006, Boston: Shambhala Publications).

Wilber, Ken, *The Fourth Turning: Imagining the Evolution of an Integral Buddhism* (2004, Kindle only);

Wilber, Ken, *Integral Buddhism and the Future of Spirituality* (2018, Boston: Shambhala Publications).

Wilber, Ken, *The Religion of Tomorrow: A Vision for the Future of the Great Traditions* (2017, Boston: Shambhala Publications).

Wilkinson, Philip, *Religions: Belief, Ceremonies, Festivals, Sects, Sacred Texts* (NY: Metro Books, Visual Reference Guides, 2016).

Woodhouse, Mark B., *Paradigm Wars: Worldviews for a New Age* (1996, Berkeley: Frog, Ltd.).

Yogananda, Paramahansa, *Autobiography of a Yogi* (1946, 1979, Self-Realization Fellowship).

Yogananda, Paramahansa, *The Second Coming of Christ: The Resurrection of the Christ Within You* (2004, Self-Realization Fellowship).

Integral Art & Studies
IntegralArtandStudies.com

Books by Brad Reynolds
on Ken Wilber's Integral Vision

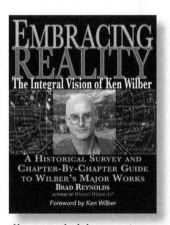

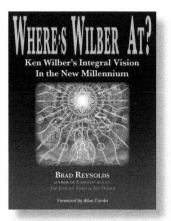

Aguide to a deeper understanding of Guru Yoga-Satsang as practiced for millennia in the world's Great Tradition of Global Wisdom of Humankind. These Guru-Adepts have founded all of the world's the major religions plus they teach and *transmit* to everyone the truth of our own inherent divinity — that we are God — and how we too may become Enlightened or God-Realized and evolve through the Stages of Life happily and with wisdom. In particular, this book introduces you to the modern-day Guru-Adept Avatar Adi Da Samraj and why he is so valuable to us as spiritual practitioners in today's emerging Integral Age.

Coming in 2022 at Amazon.com

Brad Reynolds

author-philosopher
graphic design / artist / book layouts

web: **IntegralArtandStudies.com**

ढ़

CPSIA information can be obtained
at www.ICGtesting.com
Printed in the USA
BVHW041341190122
626621BV00004B/199